Networking Explained

Networking Explained

MICHAEL A. GALLO, PH.D.
Florida Institute of Technology

WILLIAM M. HANCOCK, PH.D.
Network-1 Security Solutions, Inc.

**Digital
Press**

Boston · Oxford · Auckland · Johannesburg · Melbourne · New Delhi

Digital Press™ is an imprint of Butterworth–Heinemann.

 A member of the Reed Elsevier group

 Recognizing the importance of preserving what has been written, Butterworth–Heinemann prints its books on acid-free paper whenever possible.

 Butterworth–Heinemann supports the efforts of American Forests and the Global ReLeaf program in its campaign for the betterment of trees, forests, and our environment.

Library of Congress Cataloging-in-Publication Data

Gallo, Michael A.
    Networking explained / Michael A. Gallo, William M. Hancock.
      p.   cm.
    Includes bibliographical references and index.
    ISBN 1-55558-214-1 (alk. paper)
    1. Computer networks. I. Hancock, Bill. II. Title.
  TK5105.5.G35 1999
  004.6—dc21   99-19218
                                   CIP

British Library Cataloguing-in-Publication Data
A catalogue record for this book is available from the British Library.

The publisher offers special discounts on bulk orders of this book.
For information, please contact:
    Manager of Special Sales
    Butterworth–Heinemann
    225 Wildwood Avenue
    Woburn, MA 01801-2041
    Tel: 781-904-2500
    Fax: 781-904-2620

For information on all Butterworth–Heinemann publications available, contact our World Wide Web home page at: http://www.bh.com

10 9 8 7 6 5 4 3

Printed in the United States of America

To Dee Dee Pannell

a superb computer and network systems director, and a remarkable lady

Contents

Preface

This book is about networking. We wrote this book to provide a comprehensive overview of the scope and dynamics of computer networks and networking. The book is aimed at computer professionals who are interested in furthering their knowledge of the fundamental principles of computer networks, enhancing their capabilities in networking, or considering changing their professions to the field of networking.

The book employs an easy to follow question-and-answer format that was modeled after a terrific book on statistics by James Brewer: *Everything You Always Wanted To Know about Statistics But Didn't Know How to Ask*. We structured the question-answer format to emulate a conversation between a networking professional and the reader. The questions are representative of those asked by individuals who are interested in computer networks and who wish to gain additional understanding of the subject. The answers are intended to give the reader a broad foundation in networking concepts. It is our hope that you will find the conversational tone engaging, informative, and entertaining.

Given its format and level of coverage, the book can be equated to a snorkeling adventure. We primarily stay at the surface to examine the features, attributes, technical issues, and concepts of networks. Occasionally, we will hold our breath and dive under to explore a particular concept in more detail. We do not, however, discuss any particular topic in too much depth. Such an undertaking is better left for more technical books, which are analogous to a scuba diving expedition.

Organizational Structure

We have organized the material in this book around four major parts. The first part represents the basic foundations of networking and comprises the first three chapters: Elements of Computer Networking (Chapter 1), Network Topologies, Architectures, and the OSI Model (Chapter 2), and The Internet and TCP/IP (Chapter 3). The second part provides detailed coverage of various concepts related to the first three layers of the OSI model and comprises the next four chapters: Physical Layer Concepts (Chapter 4), Data Link Layer Concepts and IEEE Standards (Chapter 5), Network Hardware Components—Layers 1 and 2 (Chapter 6), and WANs, Internetworking, and Network Layer Concepts and Components (Chapter 7). The third part of the book examines specific LAN or WAN protocols, technologies, and services. These include: Ethernet (Chapter 8), Token Ring (Chapter 9), FDDI (Chapter 10), ISDN (Chapter 11), Frame Relay (Chapter 12), SMDS (Chapter 13), and ATM (Chapter 14). The last part of the book provides information about two related topics of networking, namely Dialup and Home Networking (Chapter 15) and Network Security Issues (Chapter 16). Although the chapters are structured logically to follow each other and build on previous learned knowledge, this does not preclude the chapters from being read in any order. This is because we wrote the chapters to also be independent of each other. Throughout every chapter, key terms or concepts that were either presented in an earlier chapter or discussed in a later chapter, are explained in the current context with a note to the reader to reference the appropriate chapter where the term or concept is discussed more completely.

All chapters are also formatted consistently. Each chapter begins with an introduction that includes a bullet list of the major topics discussed. Topics also contain corresponding question numbers, thereby making it easy to quickly locate information about a particular topic. Questions are categorized hierarchically by subject so that busy readers who seek answers to specific questions can find them easily. End-of-chapter commentaries are also provided. These commentaries consist of transitional material that identifies other chapters in the book containing additional information related to the current discussion.

Throughout the book, illustrations, tables, and special boxed text are included to help develop further understanding. At the end of the book you will find several appendixes that embellish some of the concepts presented in the chapters, a glossary of terms, a bibliography, and an index.

What This Book Is and Isn't About

This book serves as an excellent foundation on which current and future network managers and administrators can build a solid knowledge base of data communications standards and present and emerging network technologies. After reading this book, you will accrue a greater understanding of and appreciation for networks and networking. This book will help you understand basic networking terminology, components, applications, protocols, architectures, standards, and implementation strategies. The reader is cautioned that this is *not* a "how-to" book. We do not provide specific information relative to network management or configurations. Thus, the material contained here will not help you perform such tasks as setting up a domain name server, configuring a network printer, or installing or managing an office network. However, your knowledge, appreciation, comprehension, and awareness of the concepts involved in such activities will be more acute after reading this book. To quote a former student who was taught using earlier drafts of this material in a data communications and networking course: "The material cleared a lot of things up for me. It tied together a lot of loose ends I had for ten years as a network administrator."

Secondary Audiences

In addition to its primary audience, this book lends itself to three secondary audiences. First, the book is appropriate for computer-networking hobbyists or nonprofessionals who desire to gain a working knowledge of the vocabulary, concepts, and current technologies related to networking. Second, the book is suitable for individuals who have a working knowledge of networks, but lack an understanding of the fundamental concepts and theoretical underpinnings of networks. Finally, the book can be used as a companion resource in an academic setting. Over the past three years various forms of this material have been incorporated in a course on data communications and networking for undergraduate and graduate students. Given its present form and idiom, students will benefit more from this book if it is used in conjunction with textbooks such as Tanenbaum's *Computer Networks* or Stallings' *Data and Computer Communications*.

Web Page Information

A web page that corresponds to this book has been set up at http://www.network-1.com. This site, which is being hosted as a courtesy by Network-1 Security Solutions, Incorporated, includes hypertext links to all of the web sites referenced in the book and transparency masters of the figures in the book. The transparency masters are available in either PostScript form or Adobe Acrobat PDF. An errata list containing additional information or corrections (once errors are discovered) will also be provided at this site.

Acknowledgments

As is so often the case in any writing endeavor, this book involved more than just the work of the authors. Networking projects dating back to the late 1980s/early 1990s served as the genesis of much of the material contained in this book. Key individuals who were involved in these early projects deserve recognition: Kevin Barry, Notre Dame University; Joel Blatt, Florida Institute of Technology; Joe Boyle, Brevard County (FL) Schools; Tony Carroll, SCT/Florida Tech; Steve Dagley, Netscape Communications; Terry Dickerson; Dick Enstice, Florida Institute of Technology; Muslim Gadiwalla, St. Petersburg (FL) City Government; Ben Goldfarb; Sue Gruskin, U.S. Department of Education; Jack Hahn and the staff of the former SURAnet; Bill Huttig; Don Klein, Sebastian (FL) River High School; Saul Klein, Brevard County (FL) Schools; Don (Truck) Lewis; Judy Lipofsky, SCT/Florida Tech; Dale Means, Florida Institute of Technology; Karin Nicholson; Ann Owen, SCT/Florida Tech; Michael Pennick, University Park Elementary School (FL); Marshal Perlman, Digi International; Pat Pinchera, Sun Microsystems; Dave Pokorney, University of Florida; Jim Rishebarger, Palm Bay (FL) High School; Phil Rose, Brevard County (FL) Schools; Bob Russo, Network-1 Security Solutions, Inc.; Bill Schmid, Florida Information Resource Network (FIRN); Martin Schnipper, Vero Beach (FL) High School; Carolyn Simmons, Rockledge (FL) High School; Bill Shoaff, Florida Institute of Technology; and Stephen Wee, Modus Operandi, Inc.

In addition to our early networking projects, this book benefited from the contributions of former students at Rollins College (FL) and Florida Institute of Technology, as well as from participants of seminars and workshops we conducted at various regional and national conferences. These individuals helped us identify the topics and manner in which to present the material, and contributed many of the questions given in the book.

We are also grateful to the authors of the articles, books, RFCs, and other reference material listed in the Bibliography. These publications served as invaluable resources for confirming that our illustrations and responses to the questions posed were accurate, complete, and up-to-date. (*Note:* Given the dynamic nature of the networking field, keeping current requires reading journals such as *Communications of the ACM, Data Communications, IEEE Communications Magazine, IEEE Network, Network Computing, Network Magazine,* and *Network World*. Consequently, we strongly encourage the reader to, at worst, regularly review articles from these and other similar publications, and at best, subscribe to them.)

Three people who are exemplars in their field also deserve special recognition: Dan Stack of Harris Corporation, a former colleague whose ability to accurately assess the source of network failures or related problems is unparalleled, was instrumental in the success of several of our networking ventures; Steve Lindsey of Sun Microsystems, another former colleague who was responsible for getting one of us involved in this profession, always provided assistance whenever needed despite his busy schedule; and Dee Dee Pannell of SCT/Florida Tech, a former supervisor and colleague—who has experienced much in her role as director of computer and networking services—was unfailing in her support of us and our projects. We are truly appreciative of all she has endured over the past few years.

We are also indebted to the reviewers of this book, particularly Phil Miller, Director, Technical Services EMEA Worldwide Training, Xyplex Networks, whose suggestions and constructive, thought-provoking comments were well appreciated and incorporated throughout. It is with pleasure that we also acknowledge and thank the editorial staff of Digital Press for their contributions to the project, specifically: Liz McCarthy, former Digital Press Acquisitions Editor, who initially signed this project; Pam Chester, Assistant Editor, who was on the firing line throughout the project and served as a source of inspiration and guidance; Jodie Allen, Production Editor, whose eye for detail and formatting suggestions improved the overall appearance and presentation of the material; and Phil Sutherland, Publisher, who inherited this project and guided it to completion.

Personal gratitude is also extended to Dr. Ralph Alberg for understanding our need to "work on the book," and to Carole Finnie of the Area Center for Educational Enhancement at Florida Institute of Technology for tolerating our extended periods of grumpiness and insensitivities. Finally, a very special note of appreciation and thankfulness is given to Jane Edgar. Without her support, patience, understanding, and love, this project would never have been completed. We love you, Janie!

Chapter 1

Elements of Computer Networking

In this chapter we present the basic definitions of several terms related to computer networks. Understanding these definitions is critical because they serve as the foundation of our study of networks and will be used and expanded upon in subsequent chapters. An outline of the terms and concepts defined and discussed follows:

- Computer Networks (Questions 1–12)
- Applications vs. Application Protocols (Questions 13–17)
- Interoperability (Questions 18–19)
- Internet, internet (Internetwork), Intranet, Extranet (Questions 20–22)
- LAN, MAN, WAN, PAN, GAN, SAN (Questions 23–24)
- Decentralized vs. Centralized vs. Distributed Systems (Questions 25–27)
- Network Computers (NC) (Questions 28–29)
- Network Operating Systems (NOS) (Question 30)
- Client/Server vs. Peer-to-Peer (Questions 31–36)
- Serial vs. Parallel Communications (Questions 37–40)
- Synchronous vs. Asynchronous Communications (Questions 41–44)
- Simplex vs. Half-Duplex vs. Full-Duplex Communications (Questions 45–46)
- Network Standards (Questions 47–54)

1. What is a computer network?

A computer network is a collection of computers and other devices that use a common network protocol to share resources with each other over a network medium.

2. That's a mouthful. Can you break this down for me, please? There are several terms I do not understand.

Sure. Where do you want to start?

3. First of all, you say a computer network is a collection of computers and other devices. What other devices?

In our definition we use the term *device* to represent any entity that is connected to a network. Such entities may be terminals, printers, computers, or special network-related hardware units such as communication servers, repeaters, bridges, switches, routers, and various other devices, most of which will be discussed in detail in later chapters. Devices can be either local or remote. The device originating communication across a network is called the *local device* or *sending device*, and any device within the network that is accessed from this local device is called the *remote device* or *receiving device*. In a telephone network, the telephone handsets we all use are devices. So is the interconnecting hardware at the phone company that allows handsets to talk to each other. A network requires many diverse types of devices in order to work.

4. So *device* is a generic term.

Correct.

5. What about *node*? I see this term used frequently.

The word *node* is commonly used interchangeably with device; both terms refer to any equipment that can access a network. You also frequently see the term *station* used in the literature. *Station* is synonymous with *device* and *node*.

6. If *device* and *node* are generic terms that refer to any entity connected to a network, then why do you use the term *computers* in your definition?

We prefer to distinguish between devices and computers. As network devices, computers are called *hosts* (or *servers*) or *workstations* (also called *desktops* or *clients*). This terminology refers to computer systems that have their own operating systems (such as Windows). Thus, a workstation might be a personal computer such as an Apple Macintosh or any of the many Intel-based machines (commonly called IBM-PCs or compatibles); a graphic workstation such as those manufactured by Sun Microsystems, Silicon Graphics, IBM, Hewlett Packard, Digital Equipment Corporation (DEC); a super-minicomputer such as DEC's VAX or an IBM AS/400 system; a super-microcomputer like DEC's Alpha; or perhaps a mainframe such as an IBM ES-9000.

7. With so many different types of nodes connected to a network, what mechanism do they use to find each other?

You are referring to the concept of "addressing," which is discussed in Chapter 2. For now, suffice it to say that a network node is assigned a unique address that allows other systems or devices to locate them. It is similar to a house's street address—knowing the street helps to find where you want to go, but having the house number means you will eventually find the exact location of your destination. Another analogy is the phone system you use all the time. Each phone (a node) has an area code and a number (an address). The area code provides information about the node's location within the global telephone network, and the telephone number is the devices specific identification number within that locale. Systems and call "routers" at the phone company are programmed to provide information to other network devices to get the call from your phone handset to the proper destination (the phone number you are calling).

8. OK. Next is *network protocol*. What does this mean?

Let's take this in two parts, starting with the term *protocol*. From a general perspective, a *protocol* is an accepted or established set of procedures, rules, or formal specifications governing specific behavior or language. For example, when eating in a fancy, expensive restaurant, patrons are usually required to observe a specific dress protocol (e.g., men typically have to wear a jacket and tie). Other restaurants, such as the ones frequented by the authors, may have different dress protocols: no shoes, no shirt, no service. If you were to meet the Queen of England, once again you would need to observe a certain protocol. When applied to networking and data communications, a *network protocol* is a formal specification that defines how nodes are to "behave" or communicate with each other. Among other things, network protocols define how data are to be formatted, how data integrity is to be maintained, and how data are transmitted and received between nodes. In short, a network protocol specifies the vocabulary and rules of data communication.

9. Can you give me some examples of a network protocol?

A good example consists of the individual protocols that are part of the TCP/IP suite. TCP/IP stands for "Transmission Control Protocol/Internet Protocol," which serves as the basis of the Internet. (See Chapters 2 and 3 for more information about TCP/IP and the Internet.) Although TCP/IP specifies two particular protocols (TCP and IP), it is also used to name the set of protocols that includes not only TCP and IP, but also many others. This set of protocols is called the TCP/IP *suite*. (When a bunch of related and interoperating protocols are put together in a package on a system, we call it a suite.) Another protocol that is part of the TCP/IP suite is FTP, or "File Transfer Protocol," which specifies how to do file transfers. HTTP, the Hypertext Transport Protocol, is used for the World Wide Web (WWW), and defines how servers need to transfer documents (Web pages) to clients (Web browsers). Three protocols used for electronic mail (e-mail) with which you might already be familiar are the Post Office Protocol (POP), the Simple Mail Transfer Protocol (SMTP), and the Internet Mail Access Protocol (IMAP). All of the foregoing are network protocols that are also part of the TCP/IP suite. Today's networks employ a great multitude of protocols, ranging from very simple to quite complex. Protocols are the glue that binds together computer networks because they define how specific operations are to be performed.

10. Are there other sets (or suites, as you called them) of network protocols?

Yes. One you might be familiar with is *AppleTalk*, which is a network protocol suite used by Apple Computer, Inc., originally in its line of Macintosh computers and now available in many other operating systems. Another example is the set of protocols that are part of Microsoft Corporation's Windows NT operating systems. Sometimes, computer networks are named by their protocols. For example, a network that consists of devices supporting AppleTalk is referred to as an AppleTalk network. Similarly, a TCP/IP network implies a set of devices linked together that uses the TCP/IP suite as its set of rules for communication.

11. OK. Getting back to your definition of computer networks, I now understand what you mean by devices and network protocol. One last thing you mentioned that I am unclear about is "network medium."

In addition to protocols, nodes have to be connected to each other in some manner in order to share resources or receive services via a network. The physical environment used to connect members of a network is referred to as a *medium* (the plural of which is *media*). Network media come in two broad categories: cable and wireless. Examples of cable include twisted-pair, coaxial, and fiber-optic cable. Examples of wireless include radio waves (including microwave and satellite communication) and infrared radiation. Network media will be discussed in more detail in Chapter 4.

12. So, computer networks require media and protocols because without a link, resources cannot be shared, and without protocols, communication cannot be understood even if a link exists. Is this correct?

Right. Network media provide an environment in which communication can take place, while protocols are necessary to ensure that communications are understood. This is similar to a telephone conversation between one person who speaks only Italian and another who speaks only Russian. If a telephone circuit (i.e., network link) for this conversation is not available, then these two individuals cannot speak to each other (i.e., they cannot share resources). Given a circuit, the two individuals can now speak and hear each other's voices (i.e., transmission), but communication cannot take place because neither individual is capable of understanding the other's message—they speak different languages. Networking happens when a common wiring infrastructure connects nodes that share a common protocol infrastructure—just like human communication.

13. Regardless of the protocol used, don't most computer networks support similar network-related applications like e-mail?

Yes they do. Although the function of these applications across different networks is similar, the manner in which they are implemented is protocol-dependent. For example, e-mail messages can be exchanged between hosts connected to a TCP/IP network because they speak the same language. Similarly, e-mail messages can be exchanged between hosts of a Windows NT network because, once again, they speak the same language. However, e-mail messages cannot be exchanged directly between a host connected to a TCP/IP network and a host connected to a Windows NT network because they may use different application protocols for electronic mail. Consequently, although different networks might be functionally equivalent in that they support similar applications (e.g., TCP/IP and NT networks both support electronic mail), the manner in which these functions are implemented is not the same. As an example, UNIX systems support the e-mail protocol we previously mentioned, called SMTP, which is a component of the TCP/IP suite of protocols.

NT systems support a different e-mail system called Exchange. By default, they cannot interoperate directly even though they are both connected to same network. However, Exchange can be configured to communicate not only "native" with its own protocols, but also to simultaneously support TCP/IP and SMTP so that UNIX and NT users can exchange e-mail.

A network may have many protocols and many applications. Not all of them necessarily talk directly with each other. Software functions called *gateways* (explained later) allow conversion (like a linguistic translation) between some application protocols. In other areas the problems are solved simply by supporting more than one application protocol at the same time. While this sounds complex, usually a little care in the planning cycle makes everything work well when activated for use.

14. So what you are saying then is that there is a difference between an application like e-mail and the protocol that defines it.

Exactly! To help understand this better, consider the hierarchy in Figure 1-1. At the root layer we have a network protocol suite (TCP/IP). The next layer shows three network applications that are part of this suite (e-mail, file transfer, and virtual terminal). The third layer contains the protocols that define these applications (SMTP and POP for e-mail, FTP for file transfer, and Telnet for virtual terminal). The last layer identifies a specific program that users can use for these applications. A similar tree diagram can be drawn for NT, or any other protocol suite. In short: A network protocol suite provides the specifications for network applications such as e-mail. These applications have specific protocols that define how the application is to be implemented on the network. The application protocols also include specific user programs that we use to interact with the application.

15. Can you give me an example to make this a little more concrete?

Sure. Let's use e-mail as our example. E-mail is a network application that involves creating, sending, receiving, and storing messages electronically. These activities are per-

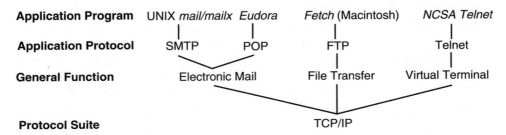

Figure 1-1. A protocol suite contains specific network applications (e.g., e-mail), which in turn are defined by specific application protocols (e.g., SMTP). These application protocols are part of specific application programs (e.g., UNIX mail) that provide a user with an interface to interact with an applications. The application protocol also defines the manner in which an application is to be implemented between two hosts connected to a network.

formed by using a "mail program," which provides a utility for users to (among others) compose, read, save, delete, and forward e-mail messages. This mail program is an application program that resides on a host. A mail program is also concerned with issues such as how a host accepts or rejects mail, how mail is stored on a system, how a user is notified of the arrival of new mail messages, and so forth. A mail program does not, however, manage the network exchange of e-mail messages between two hosts. Rather, the method by which e-mail is transferred from one host to another is handled by an electronic mail protocol like SMTP, IMAP, or POP, which are e-mail application protocols that are part of the TCP/IP protocol suite.

Other network applications are similar to e-mail. They consist of an application program that provides the user with an interface to interact with the application, and they contain a related application protocol that defines the manner in which an application communicates over a network. Thus, file transfer programs provide users with an interface for copying files to or from a remote host, and virtual terminal programs provide users with an interface for establishing a login on a remote host. These applications also have corresponding protocols (FTP and Telnet, respectively) that define the rules local and remote hosts must follow to run the application across the network.

16. Is there a one-to-one correspondence between an application program and network application?

No. Some network applications support more than one application protocol. For example, the public domain package NCSA Telnet, supports both the virtual terminal protocol (Telnet) and the file transfer protocol (FTP). As another example, consider the software product from Netscape Communications, Netscape Navigator. This product supports several protocols including those for network news (NNTP), e-mail (SMTP, POP, and IMAP4), the World Wide Web (HTTP), and file transfers (FTP).

17. I can understand why nodes have to use the same protocol, but do users also have to use the same program in order to communicate with one another? For example, if I use Eudora as my e-mail application, does that mean that anyone to whom I want to send e-mail must also use Eudora?

No, not at all. Remember, an application program simply provides the user with an interface to interact with the application. Behind this application is an associated protocol, which is transparent to the user. As long as the application's corresponding protocol understands another application's protocol everything should work out. Thus, you might use Eudora as your e-mail package, but someone else might choose to use the e-mail program that is part of Netscape Navigator, and still a third person might use the e-mail application that is part of Microsoft's Internet Explorer. It doesn't matter—all these applications support protocols that understand each other. It's similar to a superhighway. Not all vehicles are the same, but they all have rules on what they can do in the lanes, how fast they can go, and how they get on and off the road. We all know what happens when someone violates the rules on a road—it's messy. The concern you have is a valid one. It also is part of a much larger network-related issue known as *interoperability*.

18. Interoperability? What's that?

Interoperability refers to the degree in which products (software and hardware) developed by different vendors are able to communicate successfully with each other over a network. During the heyday of proprietary (private, vendor-specific, or in-house) networks, interoperability really wasn't an issue as long as one stuck with a specific vendor's products and protocols. Occasionally a third-party vendor would set up shop and develop an application that had more bells and whistles (called *valued-added features*) than your vendor was offering. In order to do so, though, this third-party vendor had to receive permission from the primary vendor; which usually implied paying a licensing fee. Today, however, with TCP/IP being an "open" standard, and with the Internet's extremely rapid growth, vendors who want to write and sell TCP/IP-based applications are free to do so without fear of violating any proprietary copyrights. Although the protocol specifications for the TCP/IP suite of applications are freely available, the interpretation of these protocols by different vendors is not always the same. This, coupled with the fact that there is no governing body to oversee the development of TCP/IP-based products, sometimes leads to incompatible products.

19. Thanks for the tip. Is this something I really need to be concerned about?

You should be cognizant of it, particularly if you are a network manager responsible for the applications that run across your network, at whom fingers will point when things go wrong. Most computer vendors strive for interoperability with other vendors' products. In fact, one of the largest networking trade shows in the world is called Networld+Interop (for interoperability). Each year at Networld+Interop competing vendors convene to display their products and to demonstrate how they can interoperate with other vendors' products. Still, the issue of interoperability is paramount, and you should exercise care when considering using network products from different vendors.

20. Is the Internet a computer network?

Although it might appear that way, the Internet is not a computer network. Back in our answer to Question 1, we said that a computer network "is a collection of computers and other devices." The Internet does not consist of a collection of computers and other devices. Instead, it consists of a collection of computer networks.

Just as computers can be connected to one another to form a network, computer networks can be connected to one another creating what is known as a network of networks, or an *internet*. For example, a network located in an office on one floor of a building can be connected to another network located on a different floor of the same building. Collectively, these two interconnected networks represent an internet.

21. Why did you write "internet" and not "Internet?" Is there a difference between the two?

The term *internet* is an abbreviation for *internetwork*, which refers to a collection of interconnected networks that functions as a single network. When used as a proper noun and spelled with a capital *I*, the Internet refers to the world's largest internetwork, which

consists of hundreds of thousands of interconnected networks worldwide, and has associated with it a certain culture. The Internet also implies a set of networks that support the
same network protocol, namely, TCP/IP. Thus, the Internet is a collection of computer networks based on a specific set of network standards (TCP/IP), which describe how the
computers of each individual network are to communicate with each other. The Internet
allows individual, autonomous networks to function and appear as a single, large network.
The Internet and TCP/IP are discussed in more detail in Chapter 3.

22. OK, I'm really confused now. I've heard of something called an intranet. How is that different from an internet?

It's easy to get confused with all the network buzzwords. An *intranet* is the internal
network implementation of traditional Internet applications within a company or an institution. Examples of applications that run on corporate or institutional internets are Web
servers, e-mail, newsgroups. There are many others. It is, in the strictest sense, still an
internet (notice the lack of a capital *I*), but it is easier to understand that the speaker is
referring to the internal corporate network by calling it an intranet. To make things even
more confusing, a popular networking term for an interconnection from the internal intranet to a customer or noncompany network that is not the Internet connection is called an
extranet connection. This may involve a leased-line connection or some other network
type of connection; it may also involve the use of a secure protocol to "tunnel" through the
Internet.

In summary, an *intranet* is an internal company network that implements traditional
Internet services; an *extranet* is a network connection to noncompany entities that are not
being accessed via an Internet connection; and *the Internet* is a series of worldwide network services available from an Internet Service Provider (ISP), which is discussed in
more detail in Chapter 3.

23. Are the networks connected to the Internet called *local area networks* or *LANs*?

Some are and some are not. Computer networks frequently are classified by the geographical area they encompass. One classification is *local area network* (LAN). Another is
wide area network (WAN). A LAN generally interconnects computing resources within a
moderately sized geographical area. This can include a room, several rooms within a
building, or several buildings of a campus. Since the term "moderately sized" is not well
defined, some people quantify a LAN's range by restricting it from a few feet to several
miles or kilometers (the IEEE usually relates this to 10 km or less in radius). In contrast to
a LAN, a WAN interconnects computing resources that are widely separated geographically (usually over 100 km). This includes towns, cities, states, and countries. Following
the quantification of a LAN's range, a WAN would span an area greater than five miles
(eight kilometers). A WAN can be thought of as consisting of a collection of LANs.

24. So the Internet consists of a collection of WANs and LANs?

That's correct. You should note, though, that some people make further distinctions
between LANs and WANs. One such distinction is *metropolitan area network* (MAN),
which interconnects computing resources that span a metropolitan area. For example, con-

sider a large business organization with buildings located throughout a local county or city. If each building has its own independent LAN, and if these LANs were interconnected to one another (thus forming an internet), the resulting network could be considered a MAN since all of the buildings are located within the same metropolitan area, namely, the local county. MANs generally refer to networks that span a larger geographical area than LANs but a smaller geographical area than WANs.

Another classification is *personal area network* (PAN), which refers to the small computer networks that are found in private homes. The relatively low cost of computers and the resulting growing number of multicomputer homes is driving the need for PANs as home computer users begin to realize the convenience of interconnecting their computers. For example, PANs can interconnect multiple home computers to the same printer, thereby eliminating the need to purchase separate printers for each computer. PANs can also enable home-based computer users to use a file server on which application software and user data can reside but are accessible from any machine connected to the home network. PANs also provide all members of a household with convenient access to home-based shared computing resources from their private rooms (e.g., a child's bedroom, home office, or kitchen).

As an interesting note, IBM has created a device that is worn like a pager by humans and is connected to the wearer's skin via small sensors. Using the conductivity of the skin of the wearer as the network medium, the device can communicate with another wearer of a comparable device to exchange information between the personal devices. IBM calls this type of network a personal area network as well, although it is somewhat different than the above definition of a PAN.

Still another classification is *global area network* (GAN), which refers to a collection of WANs that span the globe. For example, many businesses such as McDonald's Restaurants have operations in many different countries throughout the world. The interconnection of these individual business locations makes up a GAN. Finally, there is *storage area network* (SAN), which is a network dedicated exclusively for storing data.

25. Sometimes when I hear people talk about computer networks, they often use terms like *decentralized*, *centralized*, and *distributed*. For example, I overheard one network manager say that as networking becomes more distributed there is a greater need for centralized control. What do these terms mean?

The terms *centralized*, *decentralized*, and *distributed* are part of the old MIS (management information systems) vocabulary, and are more applicable to the use of computing, not networking, resources. To understand the differences among them, consider an organization's typical computing needs: accounting, inventory, and maintenance of personnel records. Computers can handle these functions in several ways: (1) offices or departments have their own systems, independent of each other, and maintain separate databases germane to their specific activities (decentralized system); (2) a single computer provides all the computing resources for all offices and departments (centralized system); or (3) computers are linked together to provide, in a transparent manner, the required computing resources and information processing needs of the entire organization (distributed system). Distributed systems bear the greatest resemblance to computer networks.

26. In what way are distributed systems similar to networks?

A distributed system consists of independent computers interconnected to one another. The primary difference between the two is that in a distributed environment resources are made available to the user in a transparent manner. What this means is that users are unaware that the computers are interconnected. From a user's perspective, a distributed system appears as if it were a single system. Using specially designed software, all functions of a distributed system are handled without users ever having to explicitly request a specific service. In a networked environment, though, users must explicitly identify what it is they want done.

27. Can you give me an example of how a distributed system differs from a computer network?

Sure. Consider the task of editing a file that resides on a remote system. In a distributed environment a user would simply "call up" the file to be edited and the system would make the file available. In a computer network, however, the user must first know on what remote host the file resides, and then either (a) transfer the file to the local host (which involves running a file transfer program), or (b) establish a login to the remote host on which the file is located (which involves running a virtual terminal program to log into the remote host). Thus, in a distributed system the file appears local to the user regardless of where the file actually resides within the system, whereas in a computer network the user must be cognizant of the file's residence and then explicitly perform some function to gain access to the file. Although not exactly a computer network, there is considerable overlap between distributed systems and computer networks. Suffice it to say that a distributed system represents a special case of a network, with the major distinction being the software as opposed to the hardware.

28. Where do network computers fit into all of this?

A *network computer* (NC) is an inexpensive ($500 or less) network access device with functionality that allows some applications to be run, but not as complete as what would typically be found on a PC or a workstation of some sort. Notice that we use the term "device" here. Although the term "computer" is part of their name, NCs are not computers; they have a specialized, proprietary (and highly restricted) operating system and are usually diskless (i.e., most have no hard disk drives for local storage). NCs are stripped-down systems that use the network to access their applications dynamically. For example, if you need a word processor, a copy of a word processing application is downloaded from a network server to your NC and stored in its memory (RAM) for you to use. Any documents you create are uploaded to and saved on the server. The idea behind NCs is to offer businesses a tremendous reduction in cost-of-ownership for each desktop location where a more expensive traditional terminal or PC would otherwise be used. By incorporating a massive server, or server "farm," with user NCs, companies can save money compared with purchasing fully-loaded PCs for each user and dealing with their management and maintenance.

29. This sounds like centralized computing to me.

In a sense it is—what goes around comes around. What do you call a computing device that relies on the network for its application? A terminal. The NC concept is very reminiscent of the era when terminals (dumb or otherwise) were connected to a mainframe. (The MIS people called this a network; we know better now.) It also is similar in concept to diskless UNIX workstations and X-terminals.

30. Speaking of network computers, what is a network operating system?

It depends on one's perspective. The term *network operating system* (NOS) can refer to software that is installed on a system to make it network-capable. Examples include IBM's LAN Server, Banyan's VINES, and Novell's NetWare (also known as Intranet-Ware). In each of these cases, the NOS is independent of a computer's native operating system—it is loaded "on top" of the computer's operating system and provides the computer with networking capability based on a particular protocol. If, on the other hand, a computer's native operating system includes built-in network support, then a NOS refers to that particular OS. Examples include Sun Microsystems' Solaris Operating System, Hewlett-Packard's HP-UX Operating System, and Microsoft's NT Server 5.0. You can think of the NOS in this case meaning *networkable* operating system.

31. Another term I frequently encounter is *client/server.* What does this mean?

Most network communications and applications today are based on a paradigm called the *client/server model.* This model describes network services (e.g., file transfers, terminal connections, electronic mail, and printing) and the programs used by end users to access these services. The client/server model can be thought of as dividing a network transaction into two parts: The client side (or front end) provides a user with an interface for requesting services from the network, and the server side (or back end) is responsible for accepting user requests for services and providing these services transparent to the user. Both terms—client and server—can be applied to either application programs or actual computing devices.

32. I need an example.

Let's assume you are using Microsoft Word on a networked PC to write a document. Let's further assume that the printer you will use to print this document is a networked device accessible by your PC. Thus, we have a common scenario in which an end user using an application program (Word) needs to access a specific network service (printing). In this context, the application program becomes a client when it relays the print request to the printer, while the printer is the server, which accepts and services this request. It's similar to being served in a restaurant. You are the client who issues a request (you order a Caesar salad), and your waiter or waitress is the server who services your request (brings you the Caesar salad).

33. I understand the concept. What I was hoping for was a little more detail. For example, would you walk me through a TCP/IP client/server example?

OK. A typical TCP/IP client/server interaction works as follows:

- A server process is started on a host. This process notifies the host that it is ready to accept client requests. The server process then waits for a client process to contact it to request a specific network application service.

- Independent of the server process, a client process is started. This process can be invoked either on the same system that is hosting the server process, or on another computer that is connected to the same network to which the computer supporting the server process is connected. Regardless of which system is involved, a client process is usually initiated by a user through an application program. A request for service is sent by the client process to the host that is providing the requested service and the server program running on that host responds to the request.

- When the server process has fully honored the client's request, the server returns to a "wait" state and waits for another client request from the same or another client.

In TCP/IP, server processes on some systems (such as UNIX) are commonly referred to as *daemons* and are designated by the letter *d* at the end of a program's name. (*Note:* On operating systems such as Windows NT, OpenVMS, and OS/400, different nomenclature is used.) For example, the virtual terminal program *telnet* represents the client side and its companion *telnetd* (pronounced "telnet dee") is the server side. Similarly, the file transfer program has both a client and a server side, *ftp* and *ftpd*. An example of a TCP/IP-based client/server interaction is shown in Figure 1-2. Host A is running an http server process (*httpd*), and a user on B is requesting a specific document from this server using a Web browser such as Microsoft's Internet Explorer or Netscape's Navigator. The Web browser is the application that supports the http client protocol. When the server receives the request, it processes it by transferring the requested Web page or document to the client.

Computer systems that run specific server programs are commonly referred to by the application service they provide. For instance, a host that accepts and provides mail service is known as a *mail server*; a computer that provides users access to files remotely is

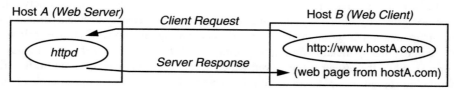

Figure 1-2. Example of an http client/server process. Host A is running a web server process, and host B is running a web client process (i.e., a web browser). When a user on host B opens a location (i.e., a web address or URL), a connection is established to the machine at that address. The server accepts this address and services it by transferring the requested document to the client machine that made the request.

known as a *file server*; a computer running httpd is known as a *Web server*; and a computer that runs a network news protocol (e.g., NNTP) is known as a *news server*.

34. Thanks. That was helpful. Along this same line, what does *peer-to-peer* mean?

Peer-to-peer is another model on which some network communications and applications are based. In a peer-to-peer environment, each networked host runs both the client and server parts of an application. (Contrast this to a client/server environment in which a host is capable of running only client-based applications, only server applications, or both client and server applications, thereby acting as a server for one application but a client for another application.) This is accomplished by installing the same NOS on all hosts within the network, enabling them to provide resources and services to all other networked hosts. For example, each networked host in a peer-to-peer environment can allow any other connected host to access its files or print documents on its printer while it is being used as a workstation. Once again, the key distinction between peer-to-peer computing and client/server computing is the former requires each networked host to run both client and server parts of all applications. Examples of peer-to-peer networks include Microsoft's Windows NT and Windows 95/98, Apple's AppleTalk, Artisoft's LANtastic, and Novell's Personal NetWare. Peer-to-peer networks are relatively inexpensive to purchase and operate, and are fairly easy and straightforward to configure. They represent a cost-effective model for small organizations or departments that want to enjoy some of the benefits of networking but do not have the requisite resources (financial, human, or equipment). However, peer-to-peer networks can be less reliable than client/server based networks. They usually also require the use of more powerful workstations for certain activities (e.g., sharing a database) than a client/server based network.

35. So if my PC is running Windows 98 and is connected to a network, then any other PC running Windows 98 that is connected to the same network can access files on my machine because of this peer-to-peer thing. Is that correct?

Yes, provided your machine has been configured for this access. It's just like Apple Macintoshes, which support AppleTalk. If you go into the Control Panel and invoke "file sharing," you can make your Macintosh accessible to any other machine connected to the same network that also is running AppleTalk. In Windows, you select My Computer, followed by the disk you are interested in sharing, and then right-click the mouse. If your network Control Panel applet has been configured for file sharing, you will see the word "Sharing" in the menu and you simply select it and then set up the parameters for sharing that will be allowed. (If sharing is already enabled on a Windows 95/98 or NT system, you will see a picture of a hand holding the device icon.) This is the concept of peer-to-peer networking—it enables users to easily share resources on a network.

Network printing is implemented in a similar manner. For example, a locally connected printer in Windows NT 4.*x* can be configured as a network device. During the initial configuration process, the "Add Printer Wizard" provides two radio buttons—Shared and Not Shared. Selecting "Shared" makes the printer accessible network-wide. (You also have to give it a name and identify the operating systems that will print to this printer so the proper device drivers are installed.) Now, assuming users have the proper access permissions, this printer appears as an available resource whenever users browse network resources in Windows NT Explorer.

36. Is this also true for client/server? Can other machines access my machine if they are running the same NOS?

No. In the client/server model, it is important to note that a network service can only be provided if a server program responsible for servicing a request is running on a particular host. For example, look back at Figure 1-2. If host A was not running the httpd process, then the request from host B would not be honored. This is why PCs used to access Internet services such as e-mail or the World Wide Web are relatively secure from being compromised by "outside" users. These machines usually run client versions of Internet-related applications. For example, Eudora is an Internet-based mail client program that requests mail service from a mail server. It makes a connection to another machine running the server process to retrieve mail for a user. If you are running Eudora on your PC, Eudora users on other machines cannot connect to your machine just because you are running Eudora as well; your machine is not running an appropriate mail *server* program (Eudora is a client, not a server). Although some PC- or Macintosh-based Internet applications can be configured as servers (e.g., there are mail, ftp, gopher, and WWW server applications available for PCs and Macintoshes), most users only run the client side of these applications. As a result, without a server process running on a system, a network connection to that system cannot be made by another machine.

37. OK. I now understand the differences between client/server and peer-to-peer networking. What's next?

We're going to change directions now and get down to the bits. Let's talk about *serial* and *parallel communication*.

38. I am pretty familiar with these two terms already. Serial communication means sending data one bit at a time; parallel communication means sending data in parallel, like eight bits at a time. Is this right?

Yes. Should we skip these terms then?

39. No. Go ahead and review them for me. It can't hurt.

As you said, *serial* communication (also referred to as *serial transmission*) is a data transmission method in which the bits representing a character of data are transmitted in sequence, one bit at a time, over a single communications channel. Serial transmission is limited to the speed of the line. *Parallel* communication (also called *parallel transmission*) refers to the simultaneous transmission, each on a separate channel, of all the bits representing a character. In contrast to serial communications, a parallel link transmits a group of bits at one time. The number of bits varies from device to device. Consequently, assuming the line speeds were the same, in the same amount of time required to transmit one bit

Serial Communication

$1 \rightarrow 0 \rightarrow 0 \rightarrow 0 \rightarrow 1 \rightarrow 0 \rightarrow 1 \rightarrow$

(1 channel transmits 1 bit at a time)

Parallel Communication

$1 \rightarrow$
$0 \rightarrow$
$0 \rightarrow$
$0 \rightarrow$
$1 \rightarrow$
$0 \rightarrow$
$1 \rightarrow$

(8 parallel channels transmit 1 bit)

Figure 1-3. Illustration of serial and parallel communications. Here, the character E, which is 1000101 in binary, is transmitted one bit at a time (serial communication) and 8 bits at once in parallel.

of information to a remote node over a serial line we can transmit eight bits (or more) of data over a parallel line. (See Figure 1-3.)

40. If parallel communication is so much faster than serial communication, why are most network links serial-based?

Although parallel communication is capable of transmitting data more quickly than serial communication, it does have its limitations. For instance, parallel communication requires a relatively complex communication link, which is achieved through the use of large, multiwire cables. Also, the longer the parallel link, the worse the degradation of the electrical signal from the most distant nodes. Consequently, in most networking applications, parallel communication is limited to peripherals directly connected to a system and for communication between systems that are relatively close to each other (in many cases, within a few yards or meters of each other). Serial communication, on the other hand, with its simpler data path, is slower but enables data transmission to occur over existing communications systems that were not originally designed for such transmission. As a result, serial communications are seen nearly everywhere, including in terminal-to-systems connections, via leased phone lines for data transfers, dialup lines, and satellite links.

41. Wait a minute. How does the receiver of a serial transmission know when a complete unit of data has been received? For example, in Figure 1-3, a single character, E, was transferred. What happens if a second character (say, X) is transferred immediately after the first? How does the receiving node identify the beginning (or ending) of a character when all it is seeing is a stream of bits (0s and 1s)?

That's a good question. Obviously, without some way of identifying the beginning (or ending) of a character, the transmitted data would be indecipherable, resulting in some sort of communication breakdown. Two methods can be employed to resolve this problem: We can either synchronize the sending and receiving nodes so that the receiving node always knows when a new character is being sent, or we can insert within the bit stream special "start" and "stop" bits that signify the beginning and end of a character. The former technique is called *synchronous* communication and the latter is called *asynchronous* communication. Synchronous communication is also tied to the clocking inherent on the link.

42. Oh yes. I recall these two terms, but I always have trouble remembering which is which. Can you help?

You bet. *Synchronous* communication implies that communication between two nodes is monitored by each node. That is, all actions resulting in data transmission (and general link conditions) are closely synchronized between the nodes. If data are to be transmitted or received, then the nodes are aware of this transmission almost immediately and prepare for the exchange based on ordered data rates and sizes. Thus, the sending and receiving nodes are "in sync" with each other. *Asynchronous* communication (commonly referred to as *async*) is characterized by the encapsulation of data within special *start* and *stop bits*. Hence, asynchronous communication is sometimes called *start-stop transmission*. A direct consequence of the inclusion of these start-stop bits in the bit stream is that data can be transferred at any time by the sending node without the receiving node having any advance notification of the transfer. Thus, a receiving node does not necessarily know when data are being sent or the length of the message. An example of async communications is a computer terminal (sender) connected to a system (receiver). The system does not know when someone will begin entering data on a terminal. As a result the system must always be in a "ready" state. Async communication lines remain in an idle state until the hardware on the line is ready to transmit data. Since the line is idle, a series of bits have to be sent to the receiving node to notify it that there are data coming. At the conclusion of a transmission, the node has to be notified that the transmission is complete so that it can return to an idle state, hence the stop bits. This pattern continues for the duration of the time the link is operative. We like to view the difference between these two terms from the perspective of a mugging. Are you interested?

43. In getting mugged, no. In hearing how they can be related to a mugging, yes.

In an asynchronous mugging, you know you are going to be attacked, you are ready for it, but you do not know when it will occur. In a synchronous mugging, you not only know you are going to be mugged, but you also know when, so again, you are ready.

44. Where is each type of communication found with respect to networks?

A variety of both types of communications is found on most computer networks. Most terminals, dialup modems, and local links are asynchronous in nature. Synchronous communication tends to be more expensive than asynchronous because of the need for sophisticated clocking mechanisms in the hardware. However, synchronous communication can eliminate up to 20 percent of associated overhead inherent in asynchronous communication. (This overhead percentage is easy to compute. If we need two bits—one start and one stop bit—for each eight bit character transmitted on a serial link, then two out of every ten bits are "wasted" on overhead functions.) This allows for greater data throughput (i.e., the amount of real data that can be transferred in a given period) and better error detection. Synchronous communications are typically seen in higher speed connections.

45. All this talk about serial, parallel, synchronous, and asynchronous communications reminded me to ask about simplex and duplex communications.

Serial, parallel, synchronous, and asynchronous communications represent different techniques for transferring data. Associated with the techniques are three different modes of data transmission used for communication purposes; each corresponds to a specific type of circuit—simplex, half-duplex, and full-duplex. These modes specify the protocols sending and receiving nodes follow when transferring data. Figure 1-4 contains a summary of these three transmission modes.

46. Would you please review these for me?

Simplex communications imply a simple method of communicating. In a simplex communications mode, data may flow in only one direction; one device assumes the role of sender and the other assumes the role of receiver. Furthermore, these roles may not be reversed. An example of a simplex communication is a television transmission—the main transmitter sends out a signal (broadcast), but it does not expect a reply since the receiving devices cannot issue a reply back to the transmitter. It's like a very boring person telling you his or her life story and you can neither interrupt it nor get away from it. . . . Sigh.

In *half-duplex* transmission, data may travel in either direction, but only one unit can send at *any one time*. While one node is in send mode, the other is in receive mode. Half-duplex communication is analogous to a conversation between two polite people—while one talks, the other listens, but neither talks at the same time. An example of a half-duplex communication is a citizens band (CB) transceiver. Users of a CB transceiver can either be

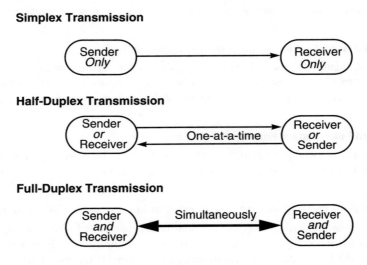

Figure 1-4. Illustration of three different transmission modes.
Simplex is a "fixed" one-way transmission; half-duplex is a two-way
transmission, but only one way at a time; full-duplex is a
simultaneous two-way transmission.

senders or receivers but not both at the same time. Another example of half-duplex communication is like a very polite game of tag between two people. Only two can play, only one can be "it" at a time, and you know who is going to be "it" next, don't you?

A *full-duplex* transmission involves a link that allows simultaneous sending and receiving of data in both directions. Imagine, if you can, two people talking at the same time and each one understanding the other one perfectly. Compound this idea with the added benefit of not having to talk about the same thing. This is the realization of full-duplex communications—two separate but parallel transmissions occurring simultaneously. A full-duplex line can be thought of as the combination of two simplex lines, one in each direction.

47. OK. Let's move on to the last topic of the chapter, namely, network standards.

A veritable plethora of network standards has been developed defining such things as hardware interfaces, communication protocols, and network architectures. Network standards establish specific rules or regulations to be followed. Standards also promote interoperability among different hardware and software vendors' products.

48. How are network standards created and by whom?

Standards are developed in several ways. First, they can be developed through formal standards organizations. These organizations can be classified into four major categories: (1) National, (2) Regional, (3) International, and (4) Industry, Trade, and Professional. A list of some of the influential organizations within these categories is given in Table 1-1. Standards organizations are composed of delegates from the government, academia, and from vendors who will be developing products based on the proposed standards.

49. How long does it take to get a standard approved?

The formal standards process, which is designed to ensure that a consensus is reached, is often lengthy and sometimes can take years before a proposed standard is approved. The process also is politically charged. A summary of this process is given in Table 1-2.

50. What kind of standards are there?

Standards can be viewed from four different perspectives. There are *de jure* standards, *de facto* standards, *proprietary* standards, and *consortia* standards.

51. Wow. I didn't realize there were so many. Could you summarize them for me?

Sure. *De jure* standards are approved by a formal, accredited standards organization. ("De jure" is Latin for "by right, according to law.") Examples include modem protocols developed by the International Telecommunications Union (ITU), the EIA/TIA-568 Standard for Commercial Building Telecommunications Wiring developed by the Electronic Industries Association (EIA) and Telecommunications Industries Association (TIA), and standards for local area networks developed by the Institute for Electrical and Electronic Engineers (IEEE). (*Note*: These standards are discussed in subsequent chapters.)

Table 1-1. Network Standards Organizations

National Standards Organizations
(Generally responsible for standards within a nation and usually participate in that nation's international activity)
- American National Standards Institute (ANSI)
- British Standards Institute (BSI)
- French Association for Normalization (AFNOR)
- German Institute for Normalization (DIN)

Regional Standards Organizations
(Restrict their activity to a specific geographical region but generally influence standards outside their regions)
- Committee of European Posts and Telegraph (CEPT)
- European Committee for Standardization (CEN)
- European Computer Manufacturers' Association (ECMA)

International Standards Organizations
(Promote standards for worldwide use)
- International Standards Organization (ISO)
- International Telecommunications Union (ITU)—consists of ITU-T, which is responsible for communications, interfaces, and other standards related to telecommunications; and ITU-R, which is responsible for allocating frequency bands in the electromagnetic spectrum for telecommunications, and for making recommendations relating to radio communications. (*Note:* ITU-T is the former CCITT—Consultative Committee for International Telephony and Telegraphy.)

Industry, Trade, and Professional Standards Organizations
(Restrict their activity to member interest areas but generally influence other areas)
- Electronic Industries Association (EIA)
- Telecommunications Industries Association (TIA)
- Institute for Electrical and Electronics Engineers (IEEE)

(Adapted from Conrad, 1988.)

Table 1-2. The Network Standardization Process

Planning Phase
- Proposals submitted by vendors or organizations are examined.
- A determination is made whether there is a need to establish a standard.
- If a need is found, the development of a project is authorized and assigned to a technical committee.

Development Phase
- Committee prepares a working paper describing the scope of the proposed work.
- Liaisons with other standards groups are established.
- A draft proposal of the standard is produced.
- Draft is voted on and all negative comments are addressed.
- Draft is submitted to parent organization for discussion and approval.

Approval Phase
- All members of the organization vote on draft.
- Draft is made available to the public for review.
- Draft is ultimately approved as a standard.

Publication Phase
- The new standard is published.

(Adapted from Conrad, 1988.)

De facto standards are those that have come into existence without any formal plan by any of the standards organizations. Rather, they are developed through the industry's acceptance of a specific vendor's standard, which is placed in the public domain. ("De facto" is Latin for "from the fact.") One example is Network File System, (NFS), a de facto file-sharing protocol standard developed by Sun Microsystems. Sun placed the specifications of this protocol in the public domain so that other vendors could implement it. This resulted in widespread use of NFS and established NFS as a de facto standard. NFS is now implemented on a variety of UNIX systems (including those from Sun, IBM, Silicon Graphics, DEC, and HP), as well as Macintosh and Intel-based systems. Another potential de facto standard is Java.

Proprietary standards are those developed in a manufacturer-specific manner. This implies that their specifications are not in the public domain and are only used and accepted by a specific vendor. In the early days of networking, proprietary standards were the rule of the day. Although such standards are now frowned upon, many still exist. Some of the most well-known are from IBM (e.g., IBM's Systems Network Architecture, or SNA). Novell's IPX protocol, which is based on Xerox's XNS protocol, is also proprietary in nature. Proprietary standards lock a customer into a vendor-specific solution and make it difficult for customers to use products (software or hardware) from other vendors.

Consortia standards are similar to de jure standards in that they too are the product of a formal planning process. The difference is the planning process and development of such standards are not conducted under the auspices of a formal standards organization. Instead, specifications for standards are designed and agreed upon by a group of vendors who have formed a consortium for the express purpose of achieving a common goal. These vendors pledge their support for the standards being developed by the consortium and also develop and market products based on these mutually agreed upon set of standards. An example of consortium-based standards include Fast Ethernet, the early efforts for Asynchronous Transfer Mode (ATM Forum), and Gigabit Ethernet, all of which are discussed in later chapters of this book.

52. As a network manager, how do I know which standard to accept?

Obviously, you want to try to avoid proprietary standards and adopt de jure standards. Unfortunately, this is not so easy to do because standards are starting to fall victim to the relatively short life cycle of a technology. Even worse, the standards organizations (especially the big ones like ISO, ITU, ANSI, IEEE and others) must reaffirm, remove, or change a standard within five years of its creation. This can result in multiple versions of a standard, depending upon which year is being addressed. Further, a standard developed today for directory services (which is known in the business as X.500) may be completely rewritten and different four years hence when the next meeting of the ITU comes around to discuss the standard. A concept for a standard exists for a long time; however, the actual technical detail may last a short time, depending upon the standard.

53. What do you mean by this?

Consider the changes in modem technology. Within a 36-month period in the 1990s, data transmission rates for modems increased from 9600 bits per second (bps) to 14,400 bps to 28,800 bps to 33,600 bps to 56,000 bps. The standards on which each new modem technology was based were originally proprietary. Although users (in most cases) were given vendor assurances that their modems would be compliant with the forthcoming de jure standard, users still faced a purchasing dilemma: Should I invest in the newer technology now, even though it is proprietary, or should I wait for the technology to be approved by a formal standards organization before I commit my resources?

54. That's a good question. What's the answer?

Unfortunately, there is no easy answer to this question. You should be cognizant of the relatively short life cycle of technology and understand that technology will always experience different stages of maturity as it evolves. This situation, coupled with the lengthy process of formal standardization, means we cannot rely solely on de jure standards to achieve interoperability. The realistic approach to achieving interoperability will most likely involve a combination of de jure, de facto, proprietary, and consortia standards.

End-of-Chapter Commentary

The terms discussed and defined in this chapter serve as the basis for understanding many of the concepts presented in the remaining chapters of the book. These terms will be further expanded, and additional terms will be defined as new concepts are introduced. In the event that you need a quick review of these or any other terms, see the glossary. We now turn our attention to Chapter 2, which addresses the subjects of network topologies, architectures, and the infamous OSI and TCP/IP models.

Chapter 2

Network Topologies, Architectures, and the OSI Model

In this chapter we present several fundamental networking concepts. We begin with an overview of network topologies, giving examples of the two most general designs on which most topologies are based: point-to-point and broadcast. Next, we examine the concept of network architecture. As part of this discussion we introduce the idea of "layering" and present the Open Systems Interconnect (OSI) networking model as an example of layered architecture. We conclude the chapter with an introduction to TCP/IP and show how it relates to the OSI model. An outline of this material discussed follows:

- Network Topologies (Questions 1–31)
- Network Architectures (Questions 32–33)
- The OSI Model (Questions 34–41)
- Introduction to the TCP/IP Model (Questions 42–48)

1. What is a network topology?

A *network topology* is the basic design of a computer network. It is very much like a map of a road. It details how key network components such as nodes and links are interconnected. A network's topology is comparable to the blueprints of a new home in which components such as the electrical system, heating and air conditioning system, and plumbing are integrated into the overall design.

2. In which ways can nodes and links be interconnected?

There are three general interconnection schemes: *point-to-point*, *broadcast*, and *multidrop*.

3. Start with point-to-point. What's that?

A *point-to-point network* consists of nodes that can only communicate with *adjacent nodes*. It's like looking into a telescope and seeing only one planet out the eyepiece.

4. What do you mean by adjacent nodes?

Adjacent nodes are nodes that are next to each other. Adjacency is typically expressed by stating the number of *hops* required for data to travel from the source node to the destination node. A *hop* is a connection to or from an intermediate node on the path from the source to the destination. Adjacent nodes are always one hop from each other. Thus, one hop implies two directly connected (*line-of-sight*) nodes. In a more complex form, a point-to-point network might consist of thousands of nodes connected to adjacent nodes, with these adjacent nodes connected to other adjacent nodes, and so on.

5. What happens if a node needs to communicate with a nonadjacent node?

It does so indirectly via other adjacent nodes. The source node first transmits a message to its adjacent node. This message is passed serially through each intervening node until it finally reaches the destination node. Passing data through an adjacent node to another node is typically called *bridging* or *routing*, depending on the passing technique used to transfer the information.

6. Which network topologies are based on the point-to-point design?

There are several. Three very common ones are *star*, *loop*, and *tree*.

7. What does a star topology look like?

A *simple star* configuration is shown in Figure 2-1(A). A key characteristic of a star is the presence of a central processing hub, which serves as a wire center for connecting nodes. In order for nodes to communicate with each other, all data must pass through the hub. Consequently, a hub represents a single source of failure. A typical star configuration is shown in Figure 2-1(B). This is a 10BASE-T network (a type of Ethernet) consisting of nodes connected to an "Ethernet switch" via unshielded twisted-pair cable (UTP). (10BASE-T networks, Ethernet switches, and UTP cable are discussed in detail in subsequent chapters.)

8. What does a loop look like?

A *loop* is a modified version of a star. In a loop, nodes are connected via dedicated wiring instead of through a centralized hub. An example of a simple loop is shown in Figure 2-2(A). This involves only one connection between any two nodes. Note that a single link failure does not cause the entire network to fail. Thus, loops are more reliable than stars. A highly reliable and more expensive loop design involves each node being connected to every other node. This is called a *complete loop* and is shown in Figure 2-2(B). Note that in a complete loop every node is adjacent to every other node. (*Note*: A complete loop is also referred to as a *fully-meshed* design.)

9. What about a tree?

A *tree* topology is a hierarchical configuration. It consists of a root node or hub that is connected to second level nodes or hubs. These "level 2" devices are connected to "level

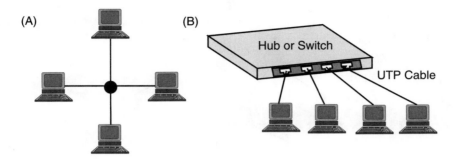

Figure 2-1. A simple star configuration (A) involves a wiring center (or hub) to which all nodes are connected and through which all data must pass. The hub represents a single source of failure because if it fails then all connected nodes will not be able to communicate. A typical hub configuration is shown in (B).

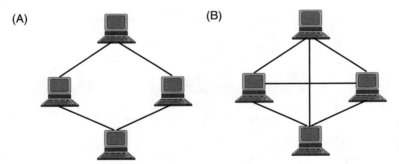

Figure 2-2. A loop design (A) is a modified star configuration. Instead of using a wiring hub, nodes are connected directly by dedicated wiring. If every node has a link to every other node, then we have a complete loop (B). (A complete loop is also called fully-meshed.) Note that in a complete loop the number of links each node has is one less than the number of nodes in the network. Loops are more reliable than stars because the potential for a single source of network failure is removed.

3" devices, which in turn are connected to level 4 devices, and so forth. A simple tree topology is shown in Figure 2-3. One application of a tree topology is IEEE 802.12, known as 100VG-AnyLAN (see Chapter 8), in which hubs are cascaded to form a hierarchical topology. An example of this network is shown in Figure 2-4.

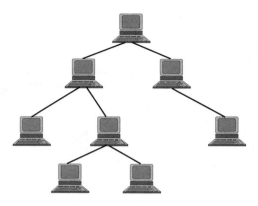

Figure 2-3. A simple tree topology consists of nodes interconnected in a hierarchical configuration.

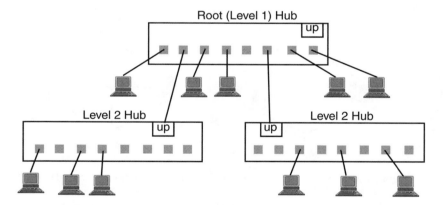

Figure 2-4. An example of a two-level hierarchical topology in a 100VG-AnyLAN network. Each hub has at least one uplink port, which connects to a higher-level hub; every port can be used as a downlink port to connect to an end node or a lower-level hub.

10. Let's move on to broadcast. What is it and what distinguishes it from point-to-point?

A *broadcast* design consists of nodes that share a single communications channel. In a point-to-point design nodes do not share a common channel but instead are directly connected to each other.

11. Is this like a telephone party line?

Yes it is, and you are dating yourself. In contrast to point-to-point design, data sent by one machine are received by all other nodes connected to the shared channel. Hosts receiving a transmission check the destination address of the message to determine if it is intended for them. If not, they discard the message. Thus only the destination node responds. As an illustration, consider a classroom setting with a teacher and 23 students. If the teacher asks one student a question, all 23 students hear the question but only the chosen student responds. This is analogous to a broadcast network.

Compare this to point-to-point communication. Let us now assume that one student, Carole, wants to tell her friend, Grace, who is sitting two rows over and three seats behind Carole, to wait for her after class. To get this message to Grace, Carole turns to Tom and says, "Tell Grace to wait for me after class." Tom turns to the person next to him, Pocahontas, and says, "Tell Grace to wait for Carole after class." This message continues being passed from one person to the next until it finally reaches Grace. This is an example of a point-to-point design.

12. Since all nodes hear a transmission in a broadcast design, is it possible for a node to send the same data to more than one node during the same transmission?

Yes. In fact, there are three different types of messages. The first is a *unicast* message, which is destined to only one recipient. The second is a *multicast* message, which is destined to a group of recipients. It is important to note that a node "knows" that it is in a multicast group by its networking software "telling" it to listen to the multicast messages for the group. In many cases, the sending system to the multicast group does not know which nodes are actually members of the group. The third is a *broadcast* message, which is destined to all hosts connected to the network. A broadcast message is a special multicast message. (*Note*: In IPv6, discussed in Chapter 3, there is also the concept of *anycast*.)

13. How is one type of broadcast message distinguished from another?

This is protocol-dependent. Some protocol suites do not use broadcast and only use multicast. Others do not use multicast and use broadcast for group addressing needs. Would you like an example?

14. Yes. Tell me how it is done in Ethernet/802.3 networks.

An Ethernet/IEEE 802.3 address consists of 48 bits (eight bytes) that are represented as 12 hexadecimal digits (0-9, A-F) and partitioned into six groups of two. For example, 08:00:20:01:D6:2A is a valid Ethernet/802.3 address. If the second hexadecimal digit (from the left) of a destination address is 0 or an even digit (2, 4, 6, 8, A, C, E), then the message is unicast. Thus, 08:00:20:01:D6:2A is a unicast address because its second digit is 8, which is even. If this second hexadecimal digit is odd (1, 3, 5, 7, 9, B, D, F), then the message is multicast. Ethernet broadcast messages, which are special multicast messages, use the address FF:FF:FF:FF:FF:FF. (See Box 5-2 in Chapter 5, and Appendix A for additional information about Ethernet/802.3 addresses.)

15. Since it is possible for a node to send the same data to more than one node during the same transmission, is it also possible for more than one node to send data at the same time?

Well, they can try but they are not going to be successful. Since all nodes share the same communication channel, they must contend for the channel when they transmit. Consequently, broadcast-based networks require some sort of method for governing those cases when two or more nodes attempt to transmit data at the same time.

16. What sorts of protocols are there for resolving such squabbles among nodes?

There are many. We provide an overview of some of the more popular ones in Chapter 5 and describe them in more detail in subsequent chapters.

17. OK. Now that I know a little bit about broadcast designs, which topologies are based on this design?

Broadcast networks employ several topologies. They are *bus*, *ring*, and *satellite*.

18. Could you give an illustration of each of these broadcast-based designs?

Yes. A typical bus configuration is shown in Figure 2-5, a ring is shown in Figure 2-6, and a satellite is shown in Figure 2-7.

Figure 2-5. Typical bus configuration, an example of a topology based on a broadcast design.

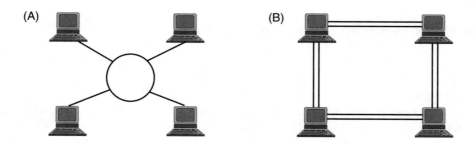

Figure 2-6. Typical ring configuration, an example of a topology based on a broadcast design. In (A), a logical ring topology is shown; in (B) a physical ring topology is shown.

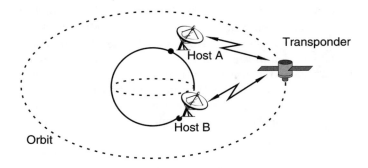

Figure 2-7. Typical satellite configuration. Nodes use antenna to send and receive data.

19. It's quite apparent from Figure 2-5 how a bus is a broadcast topology. It clearly shows all the nodes connected to the same channel. What about the ring and satellite configurations? How are they broadcast-based?

If you look closely at Figure 2-6 you will notice that all nodes are connected to the same ring, which serves as the shared medium. Remember, a broadcast design means all nodes share a single communications channel, and that messages sent by one node are received by all others connected to this channel.

20. How is a ring different from a loop, which is shown in Figure 2-2, and which is point-to-point? They almost look the same.

You are right. They look similar. The subtle difference is mired in our definitions. In a broadcast system, nodes share a single communications channel. In a point-to-point system, we have the concept of adjacency—nodes can only communicate with the node next to them. If you examine the loop topology in Figure 2-2, you will notice that the nodes do not share a single channel. There is a specific, dedicated link between any two nodes.

21. I hate to belabor this ring thing, but could you give me an idea of how a ring works?

Sure. In a classic ring topology, messages are passed from node to node around the ring. The direction of rotation can either be clockwise or counterclockwise (or both), depending on the technology. As is the case for the bus topology and for all broadcast systems, some method must govern simultaneous ring access. Note that although data are passed from node to node, this is not a point-to-point topology because all the nodes share the same communications channel. Thus, logically, the topology of a ring involves all nodes sharing the same communications channel. Physically, though, the communications are point-to-point.

22. OK. Now what about satellite networks? What makes them broadcast systems?

In a satellite communication system, data transmissions from a land-based antenna to the satellite are generally point-to-point. However, all nodes that are part of the network can receive the satellite's *downlink* transmissions. (A downlink is the communication link from the orbiting satellite to one or more ground stations.) This classifies them as broadcast systems. For example, many schools in the United States have satellite downlink capabilities. Whenever an educational program is broadcast via a satellite system, school sites wishing to receive this transmission simply tune their receivers to the proper frequency.

23. Can all networks be classified as either point-to-point or broadcast?

Mostly. However, sometimes networks are classified by the manner in which they transmit data, instead of their topology.

24. How so?

Well, consider a point-to-point system, in which data are transferred from one adjacent node to the next. Networks of this type are called *store-and-forward* networks because data are stored on one node and forwarded to the next node repeatedly en route to the destination node. Store-and-forward requires that the entire content of the transmitted message be received before it is forwarded. (*Note*: Store-and-forward is only one method of data transmission. Others include cut-through and hybrid switching. Both are discussed in Chapter 6.)

25. What's a multidrop network design?

In some types of networks, especially factory networks and those used to control real-time activities like power company networks, a particular design concept called a *multidrop* network is frequently used. In a multidrop network, each system is connected to a common cable plant and assigned a specific number that will be used to communicate with the system and also to establish priority of when a system will be communicated with from a master control system. This allows total control over the prioritization of traffic on the network as well as total control over the use of the network.

26. Why are multidrop networks popular only in factories?

They are not terribly fast networks and would not work well in offices where users may want to share large disk drives and applications. They are typically used for command-and-control operations and some light data transfer of material information or tracking information (like bar codes).

27. Are there any other designations?

Yes. Networks are classified as *circuit-switched* or *packet-switched*.

28. What are they?

In a *circuit-switched* network, a dedicated physical circuit must be established between the source and destination nodes before any data transmission can take place. Furthermore, this circuit must remain in place for the duration of a transmission. The public telephone system, known formally as the Public Switched Telephone Network (PSTN), is a good example of a circuit-switched network.

In a *packet-switched* network, instead of using a dedicated physical circuit for every node-to-node communication, nodes share a communications channel via a *virtual circuit*. A virtual circuit is a nondedicated connection through a shared medium that gives the high-level user the appearance of a dedicated, direct connection from the source node to the destination node. Messages are partitioned into smaller messages called *packets*, which may contain only a few hundred bytes of data, accompanied by addressing information. Packets are sent to the destination node one at a time, at any time, and not necessarily in a specific order. The network hardware delivers the packets through the virtual circuit to the specified destination node, which is responsible for reassembling them in the correct order. Most computer networks are packet-switched. A packet is the smallest unit of data that can be transferred via such a network.

29. Could you please explain the concept of virtual circuits in a little more detail?

A virtual circuit is created by multiplexing (Chapter 4) a physical link so that the physical link can be shared by multiple network programs or data transmissions. This concept is extremely valuable for providing low-cost communications capabilities, because it is very expensive to provide dedicated links for every data transmission, as in circuit-switched networks. A definition of *virtual* has been memorably coined in this way: "If you can see it and touch it, it's *physical*; if you can see it but can't touch it, it's *virtual*; if you can't see it and can't touch it, it's *gone*."

30. Is the main difference between circuit-switched and packet-switched the type of link or circuit that is used—namely, one is dedicated and the other is virtual?

Not quite, virtual reader. The main difference between circuit and packet switched networks is the use of *bandwidth*. Bandwidth is the maximum capacity of a communications channel (see Chapter 4). In a circuit-switched network, a circuit's performance is predetermined and fixed. This means that bandwidth is allocated in advance and guaranteed for the entire transmission. Once a circuit is established, the full capacity of the circuit is available and the capacity of the circuit will never be reduced due to other network activity. This advantage of circuit-switched networks also gives rise to a disadvantage. Specifically, circuit costs are independent of the amount of data being transmitted; therefore, any unused bandwidth is wasted.

On the other hand, packet-switched networks acquire and release bandwidth dynamically as needed. One major advantage is that several communications can occur between nodes concurrently using the same channel. Again, this advantage becomes a disadvantage when, as packet-switched networks become overloaded with more traffic, delays and congestion are introduced. Nevertheless, packet-switched networks are cheaper and offer better performance than circuit-switched networks. Furthermore, given recent developments in high-speed switching hardware, the channel capacity issue has eased a bit. Table 2-1 provides a summary of the differences between circuit- and packet-switching.

31. Given the advantages and disadvantages of circuit and packet-switched networks, why not combine the two so you could have the best of both worlds?

You are referring to *hybrid switching*, which combines the principles of both circuit and packet-switching. This technique first partitions a message into packets (packet-switching) and transmits each packet via a dedicated circuit (circuit-switching). As soon as a packet is ready for transmission, a circuit meeting appropriate bandwidth requirements is established between the sending and receiving nodes. When the packet reaches its destination, the circuit is broken down so that it can be used again. This scenario has many advantages but it requires extremely fast circuit-switching equipment.

32. Let's move on to network architecture. What is it?

Network architecture is a formal, logical structure that defines how network devices and software interact and function. Thus, the architecture defines communication protocols, message formats, and standards required for interoperability. New hardware or software products created within a specific architecture are generally compatible with other products created within the same architecture.

33. Who creates or designs network architectures?

Network architectures are designed by standards organizations and manufacturers. For example, IBM designed the Systems Network Architecture (SNA), Digital Equipment designed the Digital Network Architecture (DNA), and the International Organization for Standardization (IS0) designed the Open Systems Interconnect (OSI) architecture.

Table 2-1. Circuit-Switching vs. Packet-Switching

Circuit-Switched	Packet-Switched
1. Bandwidth is allocated in advance and is guaranteed for the entire transmission.	1. Bandwidth is acquired and released dynamically on an as-needed basis.
2. Once circuit is established, the full capacity of the circuit is available for use, and the capacity of the circuit will never be reduced due to other network activity.	2. Several communications can occur between nodes concurrently using the virtual links over the same physical channel.
3. Circuit costs are independent of the amount of data being transmitted and hence any unused bandwidth is wasted.	3. As packet-switched networks become overloaded with more traffic, delays and congestion are introduced.
	4. Packet-switched networks are more cost-effective and offer better performance than circuit-switched networks.

34. I'm familiar with all three. In fact, I've even heard SNA called some disparaging things as a joke by some people. Tell me, what's the big deal with OSI?

Well, once upon a time—a long, long time ago—there was no such thing as a network architecture. Companies designed rather rude, crude, and socially unacceptable proprietary software and hardware communications products without any consideration to the implementation of a coherent architecture—the long-term technical effect of decisions made when something is constructed. Eventually, issues of interoperability and design began to emerge as new networks were being developed. To address these issues, and to accommodate interconnection of the various proprietary and heterogeneous networks, ISO developed in 1974 an architecture and reference model intended to serve as the foundation for future standards activities. The resulting model was OSI, or more formally, the *reference model for open systems interconnection*. The OSI model provides a detailed set of standards for describing a network; it is a framework for the development of network protocol standards.

35. What's so special about the OSI model?

It formally defines and codifies the concept of *layered* network architecture. It uses well-defined operationally descriptive layers that describe what happens at each stage in the processing of data for transmission.

36. What's so great about layers?

Networks are nontrivial systems. Given a network's complex nature, it is extremely difficult to design an architecture that (1) has a high degree of connectivity, (2) is reliable, and (3) is easy to implement, use, and modify. Layers help reduce this complexity. By organizing a network's functions into a series of hierarchical layers, the design of a network is greatly simplified. For example, a layered approach enables the functions and services of one layer to be completely independent of and isolated from other layers. This allows us to change a layer's capabilities without significantly modifying the entire architecture. So as new technologies become available for one layer, they can be implemented without affecting the other layers. In theory, a layer can be completely removed, dramatically changed, and reinserted without affecting the other layers above or below it.

37. Is this like modular programming?

You bet it is. Just as large computer programs are partitioned into separate, independent program modules, layers partition a network architecture into separate, independent components. Each layer is responsible for performing a specific set of functions and for providing a specific set of services. Specific protocols define both the services and the manner in which these services are provided.

38. What are the layers of the OSI model?

The layers of the OSI model are (from top to bottom): Application, Presentation, Session, Transport, Network, Data Link, and Physical. These layers are numbered in descending order from seven to one. Each layer consists of two parts: a *service definition*, which defines the type of service a layer provides, and a *protocol specification* that details the rules governing the implementation of a particular service. Lower layers provide services to upper layers. Collectively, these layers define the communication capabilities needed to effect communication between any two devices. Figures 2-8, 2-9, and 2-10 provide additional information about OSI layers.

39. What kind of services do layers provide to each other?

There are two different types of services: *connection-oriented* and *connectionless*. Some layers have an additional type of service called *multiplexing*, but this does not necessarily transcend all layers of the architecture. Services are available at *service access points (SAPs)*, with each SAP having a corresponding address. (*Note:* In UNIX, a SAP is called a *socket*, and a SAP address is a *socket number*.)

40. Define *connection-oriented* service.

Connection-oriented means that prior to the transfer of data a physical (and virtual) link is established between the sending and receiving nodes. This link remains in effect for the duration of the session. After the session is completed, the link is removed. Characteristics of a connection-oriented service include: wasted bandwidth, because the link must remain established even during idle periods of a transmission; a high potential for a hung network, since there is always a possibility that a link will not be terminated; and (on the bright side) guaranteed sequential arrival of packets at the destination node.

The telephone system is an example of connection-oriented service. You establish a connection (you dial a number); you transfer data over this circuit when the connection is made (you begin talking when the receiver is picked up); communication occurs in the proper sequence (words and sentences are received in the correct order); and you release the connection at the conclusion of the transfer (you hang up the phone, which frees the circuit). Note also the issues of wasted bandwidth and a hung network. If a telephone connection has been made but no one is talking, bandwidth is wasted because the circuit is established but not being used. Anyone trying to contact your house during this period of silence would be greeted by a busy signal—a "hung" connection.

41. What about connectionless service?

Connectionless service differs from connection-oriented service in that no physical link is established between sending and receiving nodes prior to data transmission. Instead, a message is partitioned into packets and routed through the network. Each packet is independent of the other packets that carry parts of the message and hence must carry a destination address. (*Note:* Addressing is not necessary for connection-oriented service because a physical, dedicated link is established between sending and receiving nodes before transmitting data.) Packets can arrive out of order. Think of the post office as providing connectionless service. If you send someone five separate letters numbered one through five, you must place the recipient's address on each letter. Once mailed, the letters do not necessarily follow exactly the same delivery route, and it is possible for the recipient to receive the letters out of sequence (e.g., letter three is received before letter two).

STAPLES
Unbeatable Every Day
945 NORTH POINT DRIVE
ALPHARETTA,GA 30004
(678)366-0245

| STANDARD | 385882/ 1 00003 20630 |
| SALE | 0560 12/06/00 07:08 PM |

QTY	SKU	PRICE
1	#5 1/2 INVITATION	
	074319193944	2.83
1	#5 1/2 INVITATION	
	074319193944	2.83
	SUB TOTAL	5.66
7.00%	TAX	0.40

TOTAL   **$6.06**

| CASH | 10.00 |
| CHANGE | 3.94 |

****

STAPLES WILL
NOT BE UNDERSOLD!

****

YOUR UPS SHIP & PACK HEADQUARTERS

STANDARD   25682 4 00003 20630
SALE   05&0 12/03/00 07:08 PM

QTY SKU   PRICE

1 #5 1/2 INVITATION
   074319179944   2.83
1 #5 1/2 INVITATION
   074319179944   2.83
   SUB TOTAL   5.66
   7.00% TAX   0.40
   TOTAL $6.06
   CASH   10.00
   CHANGE   3.94

****

STAPLES WILL
NOT BE UNDERSOLD!

****

YOUR UPS SHIP & PACK HEADQUARTERS

Application (7)
• Consists of protocols that define specific user-oriented applications such as e-mail, file transfers, and virtual terminal. • Examples include FTAM (File Transfer, Access, and Management) for remote file handling, X.400 (for e-mail), and CMIP (Common Management Information Protocol) for network management.
Presentation (6)
• Provides for data formats, translations, and code conversions. • Concerned with syntax and semantics of data being transmitted. • Encodes messages in a format that is suitable for electronic transmission. • Data compression and encryption done at this layer. • Receives message from Application layer, formats it, and passes it to the Session layer. • In practice, this layer is usually incorporated within the Application layer.
Session (5)
• Provides for coordination between communicating processes between nodes. • Responsible for enforcing the rules of dialogue (e.g., does a connection permit half duplex or full duplex communication), synchronizing the flow of data, and reestablishing a connection in the event a failure occurs. • Examples include AppleTalk Data Stream Protocol for reliable data transfer between two nodes, NetBEUI (an extension of NetBIOS), and Printer Access Protocol for accessing a PostScript printer in an AppleTalk network. • Uses the Presentation layer above it and the Transport layer below it.
Transport (4)
• Provides for error-free delivery of data. • Accepts data from the Session layer, partitions data into smaller packets if necessary, passes these packets to the Network layer, and ensures that packets arrive completely and correctly at their destination. • Examples involve varying classes of the OSI *Transfer Protocol*—TPx, where $x = \{0, 1, 2, 3, 4\}$. Each class describes a specific level of service quality such as whether a transmission provides for error detection or correction, or if the service is "connection-oriented" or "connectionless."
Network (3)
• Responsible for the end-to-end routing or switching of data to establish a connection for the transparent delivery of data. • Addresses and resolves all inherent problems related to the transmission of data between heterogeneous networks. • Uses the Transport layer above it and the Data Link layer below it. • Formatted messages are referred to as packets.
Data Link (2)
• Responsible for the transfer of data between the ends of a physical link. • Provides for error detection, "framing," and flow control. • Resolves problems due to damaged, lost, or duplicate frames. • Formatted messages are referred to as frames rather than packets.
Physical (1)
• Responsible for transmitting raw bits over a link; it moves energy. • Accepts frames from the Data Link layer and translates the bit stream into signals on the physical medium, which lies below it. • Concerned with issues such as the type of wire being used, the type of connector (i.e., interface) used to connect a device to the medium, and signaling scheme.

Figure 2-8. Summary of the OSI layers and functions.

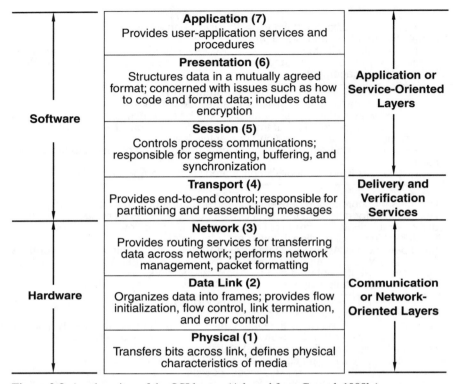

Figure 2-9. Another view of the OSI layers. (Adapted from Conrad, 1988b.)

Connectionless service is either *reliable* or *unreliable*. Unreliable service requires no acknowledgment of receipt of data from the receiving node to the sending node. This is called a *datagram service*. Reliable service requires an acknowledgment. This is called an *acknowledged datagram service*. Using our post office metaphor, these services compare with mailing a "regular" letter versus mailing a registered letter with a return receipt request.

42. Can you sum all this up with an example?

We could, although the best and most practical example—the Internet—requires additional information that has not yet been presented. For example, the Internet is based on the TCP/IP protocol suite, part of which is discussed in Chapter 3. Also, we have not yet presented detailed discussions of some of the OSI layers, such as the data link and network layers, which are presented in Chapters 5 and 7, respectively. Since you asked, we will give you an example but without a lot of elaboration.

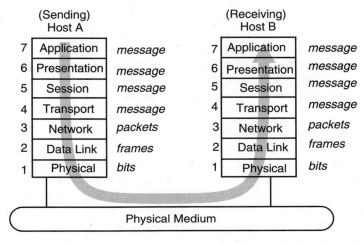

Figure 2-10. The OSI layering process begins at the application layer of the source machine where a message is created by an application program. This message moves down through the layers until it reaches layer 1. Underlying layer 1 is the actual physical medium. Data are then transmitted across this medium to the receiving host where the information works its way up through the layers. As messages move down the layers, they are encapsulated with headers that are germane to a specific layer. These headers are removed as the data are passed upward through corresponding layers at the receiving host.

43. Go for it. I promise not to ask for additional information.

OK. We will send a message across the Internet. First, however, we need to give you a little addressing methodology. Three different addresses are needed to send a message from one node to another. The first address is the *hardware address*, which uniquely identifies each node. Hardware addresses are provided by the data link layer. The second address is the *network address*, which identifies the network to which a node is connected. In TCP/IP, this is called an *Internet address* or an *IP* (for Internet Protocol) *address*. Network addresses operate at the network layer. Each network node that is part of the Internet has a unique IP address. (*Note*: IP addresses do more than simply identify the network. See Chapter 3 for additional information about IP.) The third address is called the *port address*, which uniquely identifies a specific user application such as e-mail. All network applications have corresponding identifiers called *port numbers*. To send a message from one node to another, a message is first created at the application layer. It undergoes whatever formatting is required as it works its way down through the layers. When the message reaches the network layer, a network address is assigned to the message. This network address identifies the specific network to which the destination host is connected. Depending on the protocol, this service is either connectionless or connection-oriented. For example, Telnet and SMTP are connection-oriented services. The network layer determines the path the message must follow to reach the destination node. It also encapsulates packets into IP datagrams and passes them to the data link layer. At the data link layer, the destination node's hardware address is added to the packet. This address uniquely identifies the location of the destination node within the destination network. The data link layer, among other tasks, also formats the packet into *frames*, which are like packets but exist at a lower level and checks, the integrity of each frame (see Chapter 5). Frames are then passed to the physical layer, which places them on the medium for transmission.

44. How does TCP/IP compare to OSI?

TCP/IP's development preceded the OSI model by several years. Both had similar design goals, however, to fill a need for interoperability among heterogeneous computer systems. Unlike OSI, TCP/IP was never intended to be an international standard. It was developed to satisfy the need to interconnect various United States Department of Defense projects, including computer networks, and to allow for the addition of dissimilar machines to the networks in a systematic, standardized manner.

45. Does TCP/IP also have seven layers like OSI?

No. As a pre-OSI protocol architecture, it was not designed specifically with layers the way the OSI model was designed and it does not fit neatly into the seven layers of the OSI model. However, we can envision TCP/IP's layers as similar to the OSI layers since many of TCP/IP's functions are similar to those of the OSI model.

46. So what are the layers?

There is no universal agreement on the description of TCP/IP as a layered model. It has been described as having anywhere from three to five layers—depending on an author's perspective. For our purposes, we elect to describe TCP/IP as a four-layered architecture, as shown in Figure 2-11.

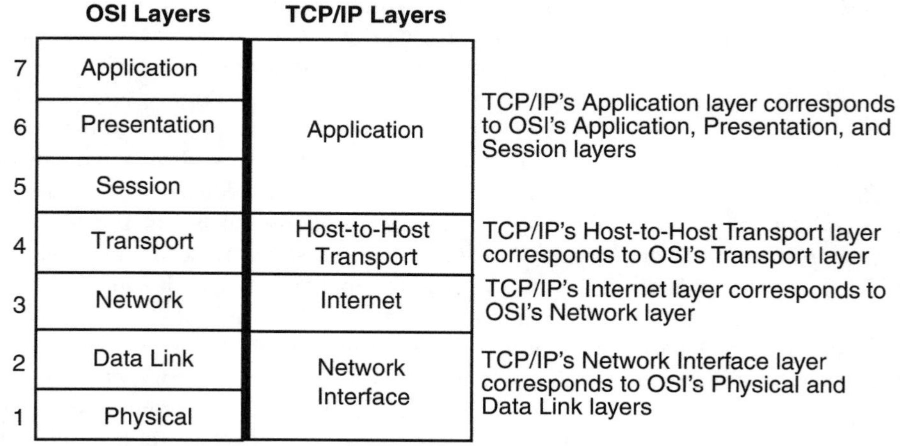

	OSI Layers	TCP/IP Layers	
7	Application	Application	TCP/IP's Application layer corresponds to OSI's Application, Presentation, and Session layers
6	Presentation		
5	Session		
4	Transport	Host-to-Host Transport	TCP/IP's Host-to-Host Transport layer corresponds to OSI's Transport layer
3	Network	Internet	TCP/IP's Internet layer corresponds to OSI's Network layer
2	Data Link	Network Interface	TCP/IP's Network Interface layer corresponds to OSI's Physical and Data Link layers
1	Physical		

Figure 2-11. A comparison of the OSI and TCP/IP Layers.

47. Are the layers similar in terms of the functions and services they provide?

Yes. The TCP/IP *application layer* serves as the communication interface for users by providing specific application services to the user such as remote terminal login (i.e., virtual terminal), file transfer, and e-mail. Corresponding application protocols include Telnet, FTP, and SMTP. The TCP/IP *host-to-host transport layer* (known simply as the *transport layer*) is responsible for end-to-end data delivery. This layer is defined by two protocols: the *Transmission Control Protocol* (TCP) and *User Datagram Protocol* (UDP). A brief description of each follows.

- **TCP.** This is the TCP of TCP/IP. It is a connection-oriented protocol that performs several functions including: providing for reliable transmission of data by furnishing end-to-end error detection and correction; guaranteeing that data are transferred across a network accurately and in the proper sequence; retransmitting any data not received by the destination node; and guaranteeing against data duplication between sending and receiving nodes. Application protocols using TCP include Telnet, File Transfer Protocol (FTP), Simple Mail Transport Protocol (SMTP), and Post Office Protocol (POP).

- **UDP.** This is a connectionless protocol providing an unreliable datagram service. It does not furnish any end-to-end error detection or correction, and it does not retransmit any data it did not receive. UDP requires very little overhead since it does not provide any protection against datagram loss or duplication. Application protocols based on UDP include the Trivial File Transfer Protocol (TFTP), Network File System (NFS), the Simple Network Management Protocol (SNMP), the Bootstrap Protocol (BOOTP), and Domain Name Service (DNS).

The TCP/IP *Internet layer* (also called the *network layer*) transfers user messages from a source host to a destination host. The heart and soul of this layer is the *Internet Protocol*, which is the IP of TCP/IP. IP is a connectionless datagram service responsible for routing packets between nodes. In short, IP receives data bits from the lower layer, assembles the bits into packets (IP datagrams), and selects the "best" route based on some *metric*. (A metric is a description of the "cost" of a route used by routing hardware and software to select the best possible route.)

The TCP/IP *network interface layer* connects a host to the local network hardware. Its functions include making a connection to the physical medium, using a specific protocol for accessing the medium, and segmenting data into frames. It effectively performs all of the functions of the first two layers of the OSI model.

A summary description of the TCP/IP model is given in Figures 2-12 and 2-13.

48. What is OSI's role given that the Internet is based on TCP/IP?

At one point during the early 1990s, it was believed by many that the OSI protocols were going to become "the" network standard for everyone. Even the U.S. Government got into the act by establishing GOSIP (Government OSI Profile), which mandated all government organizations purchase OSI-compliant networking products beginning in 1992. In 1995, however, GOSIP was modified to include TCP/IP as an acceptable protocol

Application (4)
• Similar to OSI Application Layer. • Serves as communication interface by providing specific application services • Examples include email, virtual terminal, file transfer, WWW.

Transport (3)
• Defined by two protocols: **Transmission Control Protocol (TCP)** • This is the TCP of TCP/IP. • Is a connection-oriented protocol. • Provides reliable data transmission data via end-to-end error detection and correction. • Guarantees data are transferred across a network accurately and in proper order. • Retransmits any data not received by destination node. • Guarantees against data duplication between sending and receiving nodes • Application protocols include Telnet, FTP, SMTP, and POP **User Datagram Protocol (UDP)** • Is a connectionless protocol. • Provides unreliable datagram service (no end-to-end error detection or correction. • Does not retransmit any unreceived data. • Requires little overhead. • Application protocols include Trivial File Transfer Protocol (TFTP), NFS, Simple Network Management Protocol (SNMP), Bootstrap Protocol (BOOTP), and Domain Name Service (DNS).

Internet (2)
• Heart and soul is Internet Protocol (IP)—the IP of TCP/IP. • Transfers user messages from source host to destination host. • Is a connectionless datagram service. • Route selection is based on some metric. • Uses Internet or IP addresses as a road map to locate a host within the Internet. • Relies on routers or switches (dedicated nodes that connect two or more dissimilar networks). • Integral part is Internet Control Message Protocol (ICMP), which uses an IP datagram to carry messages about state of communications environment.

Network Interface (1)
• Connects a host to the local network hardware. • Makes a connection to the physical medium. • Uses a specific protocol for accessing the medium. • Places data into frames. • Effectively performs all functions of the first two layers of the OSI model.

Figure 2-12. Summary of the TCP/IP layers and functions.

suite for GOSIP compliance. Today, OSI protocols are in use, but their presence pales in comparison to that of their TCP/IP counterparts. Nonetheless, the OSI model has had a lasting impact on networks, including TCP/IP. The model continues to provide a detailed standard for describing a network. It is from this perspective that the network design community continues to regard the OSI model as a theoretical framework for the development of networks and their architecture.

	OSI Layers	Included Protocols		TCP/IP Layers
7	Application	FTP Telnet	SNMP TFTP	Application
6	Presentation	Finger SMTP	NFS DNS	
5	Session	POP	BOOTP	
4	Transport	TCP	UDP	Host-to-Host Transport
3	Network	IP		Internet
2	Data Link	Network Interface Cards		Network Interface
1	Physical	Transmission Media		

Figure 2-13. A third comparison of the OSI and TCP/IP layers. (Adapted from Miller, 1992.)

End-of-Chapter Commentary

On this note we conclude our discussion of network topologies, architectures, and the OSI and TCP/IP models. We will expand upon this material in subsequent chapters. For example, in Chapter 3, we give a detailed presentation about the Internet and TCP/IP protocols, and we expand the concept of the OSI layers in later chapters. Chapter 4 is dedicated to the physical layer; Chapter 5 presents a discussion on the data link layer; network hardware components that operate at either layer 1 or 2 are presented in Chapter 6; and Chapter 7 addresses concepts relating to the network layer. Other chapters also expand on specific layer 2 and layer 3 protocols.

Chapter 3

The Internet and TCP/IP

Various information about the Internet and TCP/IP was presented in Chapters 1 and 2. We examined the general concept of an internet, contrasted it with the Internet, and introduced Internet-related terms such as intranet and extranet. We also introduced several TCP/IP-based application protocols such as the Simple Mail Transfer Protocol (SMTP) and the Post Office Protocol (POP) for e-mail, the File Transfer Protocol (FTP) for file transfers, and the Hypertext Transfer Protocol (http) for web applications. In this chapter, we expand our discussion of the Internet and TCP/IP from a networking perspective. The topics discussed include:

- History of the Internet (Questions 1–11)
- vBNS, Internet2, and Next Generation Internet (Questions 12–14)
- Internet Administration and Governance (Questions 15–17)
- History of TCP/IP (Questions 18–20)
- Overview of TCP and IP (Questions 21–23)
- IPv4 Addresses and Subnetting (Questions 24–25)
- IP Address Assignments (Questions 26–27)
- IP Name Resolution (Questions 28–30)
- IPv6 (Questions 31–36)
- Internet Services, Resources, and Security (Questions 37–38)

1. Could you start things off by defining the Internet?

Certainly. Defining the Internet today is a bit more problematic than it was several years ago. Its definition varies from person to person. For example, in Chapter 1, we defined the Internet as a collection of computer networks based on a specific set of network standards—TCP/IP. Other users, whose focus might be on the information they have acquired or the people with whom they have communicated, might define the Internet as a global collection of diverse resources, or as an electronic community of people. Still others, whose only experience with the Internet is using the World Wide Web, might say the Internet and World Wide Web are synonymous and hence the Internet is the World Wide Web.

Consequently, defining the Internet is a function of perspective. Regardless of the definition or perspective, the Internet interconnects individual, autonomous computer networks and enables them to function and appear as a single, global network.

2. How did the Internet get started?

The Internet's roots can be traced back to 1957 when the United States formed the Advanced Research Projects Agency (ARPA) within the Department of Defense (DoD). The formation of ARPA was the United States' response to the USSR's launch of Sputnik, the first artificial Earth satellite. ARPA's mission was to establish the United States as the world's leading country in defense and military applicable science and technology. ARPA, which later became known as Defense ARPA (DARPA), established in 1969 an early internetwork called ARPANET. The builder of ARPANET was Bolt, Baranek, and Newman, now known as BBN Communications. Originally, the Internet meant ARPANET and access to ARPANET was restricted to the military, defense contractors, and university personnel involved in defense research. ARPANET technology was based on packet switching, and in 1969, with the connection of its first four nodes—Stanford Research Institute (SRI), University of California at Santa Barbara (UCSB), University of California at Los Angeles (UCLA), and University of Utah—ARPANET heralded the era of packet switching networking.

3. I recall that the university I attended had a BITNET connection. Was this similar to ARPANET?

Not quite. BITNET, which stands for "Because It's Time Network," was a low-speed and inexpensive academic network consisting of interconnected IBM mainframes. BITNET was one of several cooperative, decentralized computer networks that formed in the late 1970s and early 1980s on college and university campuses to serve the academic community. Using a proprietary IBM-based network protocol, BITNET connectivity was via 9600 bps leased circuits and was based on the store-and-forward principle. Networking services available via BITNET included file transfer, e-mail, and an IBM application called *remote job entry* (RJE). In an RJE environment, small processors located at remote sites were used to transfer "jobs" to and from a main computer that served as the "master" to these smaller processors. This scheme is based on a paradigm known as *master/slave*. BITNET eventually merged with another early academic network called the Computer Science Network (CSNET) to form the Corporation for Research and Educational Networking (CREN).

4. Was CSNET like the ARPANET?

CSNET was similar to the ARPANET. It was a large internetwork developed to provide connectivity to the nation's computer science community. The development of CSNET was grounded in the restricted use of the ARPANET. Owned by the Department of Defense, ARPANET's use was prohibited by anyone outside the defense community. In an effort to increase collaboration among the nation's computer scientists, the National Science Foundation (NSF) funded CSNET. Recognizing that the most popular ARPANET service was e-mail, the developers of CSNET initially thought an e-mail-only based network could be developed to connect academic and research institutions that did not have access to ARPANET. CSNET eventually evolved into a *metanetwork*—it consisted of several different physical networks logically designed to serve one community. Connectivity to CSNET was via a centralized machine called CSNET-RELAY, and connectivity to CSNET-RELAY was via other networks. These included a public packet switching network called X.25NET, a dialup network called Phonenet, and the ARPANET. CSNET provided its users with Internet-type services such as e-mail, member registry, and domain name service (DNS). Other services such as file transfer and remote logins were also available on some parts of CSNET. CSNET, BITNET, and CREN have since disbanded now that Internet access is easily attainable.

5. Friends of mine talk about a network called UUCP. What was this network like?

They probably also had a FidoNet connection. The UUCP network is a global network of interconnected UNIX machines. Standard telephone lines serve as the medium for connectivity, and the network is based on the store-and-forward principle. (See Figure 3-1.) Using a suite of programs known as UUCP (UNIX-to-UNIX Copy), users can exchange e-mail and network news (also called Usenet news). Given its minimal requirements (UNIX machine, modem, and telephone connection) and relatively inexpensive nature, the UUCP network grew quickly throughout the world and is still in existence today.

6. OK. So what happened next? How did ARPANET become the Internet?

Around 1983, the academic and research science community convinced Congress that the United States had to meet the Japanese supercomputing challenge.

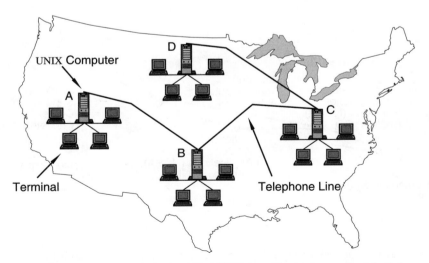

Figure 3-1. An example of a nationwide UUCP network. A message from host A to host D would first be transferred to host B, then to host C, and finally to host D.

7. Time out. What was the Japanese supercomputing challenge?

The Japanese government committed itself to a national goal of developing a computer capable of displaying common sense, possessing a general knowledge about how the world works, having insight into human nature, having a vocabulary of 10,000 words, and speaking and understanding English and Japanese, all by the end of the 1980s. In the United States, Japan's national goal was perceived as analogous to the United States' national goal of the 1960s of putting a man on the moon and returning him safely to Earth by the end of that decade. Suffice it to say the Japanese supercomputing challenge was taken very seriously in the United States.

8. I see. OK. Continue with what you were saying before I interrupted you.

In responding to the Japanese challenge, Congress authorized the National Science Foundation (NSF) to fund the construction and operation of U.S. supercomputer centers. By the end of 1985, six such centers were established throughout the country. These centers also were connected to the ARPANET, which had by then (1984) split into two separate networks—ARPANET, for nonmilitary and research purposes, and MILNET, an unclassified military network. The supercomputer center network and the ARPANET were interconnected at Carnegie Mellon University (CMU) in Pittsburgh, Pennsylvania. Thus, network traffic originating at any of the supercomputer centers and destined for the ARPANET (or vice versa) was first sent to CMU and then transferred to the local ARPANET node. (See Figure 3-2.)

With a supercomputer center network in place, the next issue to address was to provide researchers with direct and convenient electronic access to these centers from researchers' home institutions. To meet this challenge, NSF began funding in 1986 the development of a national "backbone" network. Eventually, a three-level or tiered network evolved con-

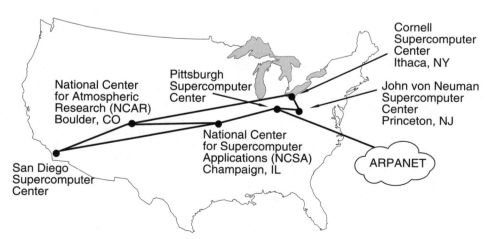

Figure 3-2. The National Science Foundation's supercomputer network. This network interconnected the six NSF funded supercomputer centers. The network also was interconnected to the ARPANET through a node at Carnegie Mellon University in Pittsburgh.

sisting of a backbone network, several regional or mid-level networks, and local area networks of colleges and universities. (See Figure 3-3.) The regional networks were organized geographically either by state (e.g., NYSERnet—New York State Educational Research Network—serviced New York State) or region (e.g., SURAnet—Southeastern Universities Research Association Network—serviced the southeastern part of the country). Thus, the backbone provided connectivity to the regional networks, which in turn provided connectivity to campus LANs. (See Figure 3-4.) The first two levels of this network (the national backbone and the regional networks) became known as NSFNET and was a model for interconnecting independent and autonomous networks. Initially, the

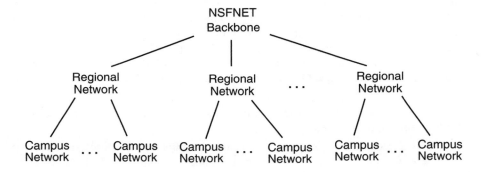

Figure 3-3. The NSFNET Hierarchy.

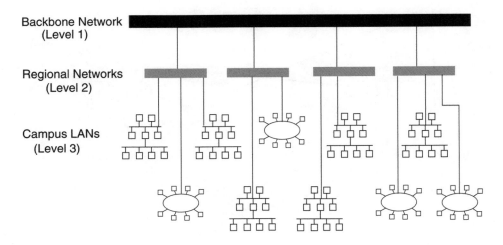

Figure 3-4. Example of the three levels of networks that evolved from the National Science Foundation's networking initiative. The first two levels made up NSFNET.

NSFNET backbone was based on 56 kbps leased circuits. From 1989 to 1992, the backbone was reconfigured twice to handle increasing traffic loads. This reconfiguration included adding new circuits, deleting others, and increasing the backbone's bandwidth—first to T1 (1.5 Mbps) and then to T3 (45 Mbps). The T3 backbone is shown in Figure 3-5.

During the 1980s, other government organizations such as the Department of Energy (DOE) and the National Aeronautics and Space Administration (NASA) also began developing their own private networks. These networks interconnected the NSFNET. Eventually, all of these government-sponsored networks, including NSFNET, ARPANET, MILNET, and SPAN (the Space Physics Analysis Network), became known as the Internet. Although the Internet was comprised of many different networks, the NSFNET was perceived as *the* Internet by many people. This perception was grounded in the NSFNET's national presence and by its open door policy to any research or educational organization. In fact, through its networking infrastructure program, the NSF provided funding to any college or university that wanted to connect its LAN to the NSFNET. (A modified version of this program exists today and extends to K–12 schools.) Funds were used to purchase hardware and pay for high-speed line charges related to a school's NSFNET connection.

9. How did the Internet evolve from a research and academic network to one that is available to the general population?

As NSFNET became more popular, the business community quickly took notice and realized there was money to be made from it. Connectivity to the NSFNET backbone, however, was governed by NSF's Acceptable Use Policy, which—although usually

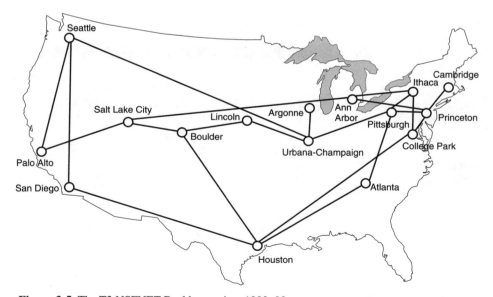

Figure 3-5. The T3 NSFNET Backbone, circa 1992–93.

ignored and often broadly interpreted—restricted the use of the NSFNET backbone to educational or research activities. This meant that the NSFNET could not be used for commercial purposes. In response to this policy the Commercial Internet Exchange (CIX) was born in the early 1990s to meet the emerging connectivity needs of the commercial market. CIX was a subscription organization that consisted of a consortium of commercial and nonprofit regional network providers that started offering Internet service independent of the NSFNET backbone and without NSF's restriction on traffic type. It established a national backbone comprised of different telephone carriers (e.g., Sprint, MCI) and interconnected the NSFNET backbone at selected points. Thus, commercial Internet traffic might start at a local organization, travel through various regional providers, get routed to a CIX node, and then get transferred to another CIX provider without ever crossing the NSFNET backbone.

During the early to mid-1990s, a commercial Internet began to take shape, consisting of "20 percent bottom line" people instead of research or educational visionaries. During this period private Internet service provider (ISP) businesses were started by entrepreneurs who recognized the growing demand for Internet access by both the general public and the business community. ISPs ranged from small "mom and pop" operations that provided connectivity to a specific locale, to regional or state providers, to national and international providers. The source of connectivity for these ISPs was the backbones developed by the major long distance telephone carriers—Sprint, AT&T, and MCI—all of whom operated their own private national networks independent of NSF access restrictions.

10. What happened to ARPANET and NSFNET?

ARPANET was decommissioned in 1990, and the level of commercialization of the Internet led the National Science Foundation to remove the NSFNET backbone from active service on April 30, 1995. This latter action, however, did not occur without considerable forethought. For example, in May 1993, two years prior to NSFNET's retirement, NSF solicited proposals to design a new infrastructure capable of serving the needs of not only government, research, and educational organizations, but also those of the commercial user and general public. Furthermore, NSF maintained its commitment to the educational and research communities that comprised NSFNET by subsidizing the regional network providers' connections to a commercial network service provider. This support ends in 1999. Most of the regional providers selected MCI as their primary carrier; the remaining few chose Sprint or ANS, which was purchased by America Online in 1995. Today, network traffic such as e-mail, web browsing, and file transfers is carried by commercial providers; the former NSFNET regional networks now receive connectivity through commercial network service providers; and NSFNET's three-tiered hierarchical national backbone has been supplanted with several independent backbones that interconnect at specially designated exchange points (more on this later) where ISPs meet and distribute traffic. (See Figure 3-6.)

Summarizing its history, over the past 30 years the Internet has evolved from a United States Department of Defense network research project (ARPANET), to an NSF subsidized educational and research data communications medium for university, government, and research personnel (NSFNET), to a commercial, global network linking tens of mil-

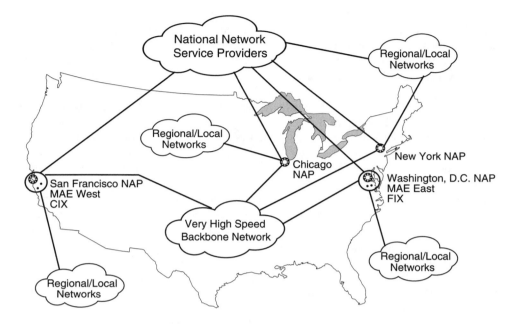

Figure 3-6. The new national network infrastructure consists of a "private" very high speed backbone network service funded by NSF, several independent commercial backbones operated by network service providers such as Sprint, MCIWorldCom, and AT&T, and various interconnection centers where traffic from network providers is exchanged. Network service providers also interconnect the former NSFNET regional networks and thousands of smaller networks operated by independent Internet Service Providers (ISPs) which provide businesses, schools, and individual users access to the Internet.

lions of consumers, businesses, schools, and other organizations. Today, nearly every country in the world has some form of Internet connection. Initially, the ARPANET was the Internet. NSF then entered the picture and the Internet was perceived as a collection of various networks anchored by NSFNET. Today, both ARPANET and NSFNET have given way to a commercially flavored Internet that is transforming the Internet from its roots as a collection of networks to a global network of communities. (*Note:* Various network connectivity maps are available from ftp://ftp.cs.wisc.edu/connectivity_table/.)

11. What is the current design of the Internet?

The current Internet—the one that is available to the common people—consists of several high-speed backbones owned by the major telecommunications organizations such as Sprint, AT&T, and MCI WorldCom. The Internet also relies on Network Access Points (NAPs), a Routing Arbiter (RA), and interregional connectivity. Network Access Points (NAPs) are Internet traffic exchange points that provide centralized Internet access to

Internet service providers. NSF funds four NAPs in the United States, one each in New York, Chicago, Washington, D.C., and San Francisco. These NAPs are operated respectively by Sprint, Ameritech Advanced Data Services (AADS), Metropolitan Fiber Systems (MFS), and Pacific Bell. NAPs serve as critical, regional "switching stations" where all different network backbone providers meet and exchange traffic on each other's backbone. For example, if you have an Internet account from AT&T and your next-door neighbor receives Internet service from Sprint, then an e-mail message sent from you to your neighbor (or vice versa) is exchanged at one of the regional NAPs. In addition to NAPs, several other non-NSF interconnect sites have been established. These include two metropolitan-area exchange (MAE) points, one each on the east and west coasts of the United States and known as MAE East and MAE West, and federal and commercial exchanges (FIXs and CIXs). (See Figure 3-6.) The Routing Arbiter (RA) project facilitates the exchange of network traffic among the various independent backbones. Special servers that contain routing information databases of network routes (i.e., electronic roadmaps) are maintained so that the transfer of traffic among the various backbone providers meeting at a NAP is facilitated. (The concept of routes and routing is discussed in Chapter 7.) NSF awarded the RA project to two organizations—Merit and the Information Sciences Institute (ISI) of the University of Southern California.

12. What do you mean by "the one that is available to the common people"? Is there another Internet?

Yes there is; it is the very high speed Backbone Network Service (vBNS), which is another NSF-funded research and educational network. The contract to develop and operate this network was awarded by NSF to MCI in 1995. The vBNS is a nationwide backbone network that currently operates at 622 Mbps (OC-12) and has a strict usage policy—only those involved in high-bandwidth research activities are permitted to use it. The high bandwidth is achieved by running ATM (see Chapter 14) over SONET (see Chapter 7). This backbone is expected to be upgraded to OC-48 in 1999. See http://www.vbns.net for additional information about vBNS.

13. What's this network used for?

The vBNS is a medium for the deployment and evaluation of new high-speed internetworking technologies. When control of NSFNET was passed to the private sector for commercial purposes, academic researchers lost their ability to develop and test new network technologies on a national scale because of frequent congestion and other inherent problems. The vBNS restores to researchers an appropriate testbed-research environment. Access to the vBNS is restricted to only those organizations that receive NSF awards under NSF's high performance connection program. Less than 100 organizations are currently connected to the vBNS. The science and research advanced via vBNS will eventually improve the design and performance of the current Internet. (*Note:* MCI WorldCom maintains a vBNS website that contains various information, including vBNS network maps, press kit materials, presentations, papers, articles, and a frequently asked questions (FAQs) document. See http://www.vbns.net.)

14. Are there any other Internet-related initiatives beside vBNS?

Yes. There is Internet2, the Next Generation Internet (NGI) initiative, and the National Information Infrastructure (NII) initiative. Internet2 is a collaborative project of the University Corporation for Advanced Internet Development (UCAID). It comprises over 100 U.S. universities, government organizations, and private sector firms. Internet2's mission is to develop advanced Internet technologies and applications that support the research endeavors of colleges and universities. Internet2 members use the vBNS to test and advance their research. Additional information about Internet2 can be found at http://www.internet2.edu.

The NGI initiative, announced by President Bill Clinton in 1996, is a research and development (R&D) program for (guess what?) designing and testing advanced network technologies and applications. This initiative's mission is also to forge collaborative partnerships between the private and public sectors. It is anticipated that the vBNS will serve as the medium for NGI. Although President Clinton pledged $100 million per year for three years, funding for NGI has not been approved as of this writing. Additional information about NGI can be found at http://www.ngi.gov.

Finally, there is the granddadday of them all—the National Information Infrastructure (NII)—a Federal policy initiative to facilitate and accelerate the development and utilization of the nation's information infrastructure. The perception of the NII is one of a "seamless web" of telecommunications networks consisting of computers, specialized databases, radios, telephones, televisions, and satellites. The NII is expected to provide consumers with convenient and instantaneous access to nearly any kind of information ranging from research results, to medical and educational material, to entertainment.

15. Who administers the Internet?

The governance and administration of the Internet is overseen by various organizations composed mostly of volunteers from the global Internet community. These organizations consist of the Internet Society (ISOC), the Internet Architecture Board (IAB), the Internet Engineering Task Force (IETF), and the Internet Research Task Force (IRTF). The administrative organizational structure of the Internet is shown in Figure 3-7.

The Internet Architecture Board (IAB), formerly known as the Internet Activities Board, is responsible for the overall planning and designing of the Internet. Some of its responsibilities include setting Internet standards, managing the publication of RFC documents (see below), and resolving technical issues. Assigned to the IAB are the Internet Engineering Task Force (IETF) and the Internet Research Task Force (IRTF). IETF is primarily concerned with addressing short- or medium-term Internet engineering issues. For example, IETF was responsible for examining the design and implementation of a new Internet Protocol, IPv6 (discussed later), the Open Shortest Path First (OSPF) routing scheme (see Chapter 7), and other initiatives such as enabling TCP/IP to more efficiently support multimedia. IRTF works on long-term research projects. An example of its work is the e-mail privacy issue. Both task forces also have steering committees that prioritize and coordinate their respective activities. IETF's steering committee is called the Internet Engineering Steering Group (IESG), and IRTF's steering committee is called the Internet Research Steering Group (IRSG).

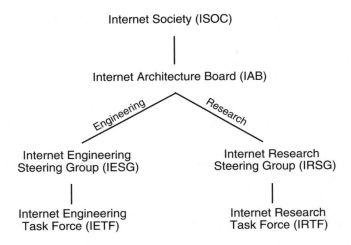

Figure 3-7. The administrative organizational structure of the Internet.

The ultimate authority of the Internet is the Internet Society (ISOC)—an international organization comprised of volunteers who promote the Internet as a medium for global communication and collaboration. ISOC publishes a newsletter called *Internet Society News*, which provides its readers with information surrounding the administration and evolution of the Internet. More information about ISOC, IAB, IETF, and IRTF can be obtained from their respective web sites: ISOC (http://www.isoc.org); IAB (http://www.iab.org/iab); IETF (http://www.ietf.org); and IRTF (www.irtf.org);

16. How are Internet standards developed?

Internet standards are initially developed by IETF, reviewed by IESG, and ultimately approved by the IAB. Throughout the standards development process, Request for Comments (RFCs), which address various aspects of a particular protocol under consideration, are prepared by the RFC editor. These RFCs usually contain technical information about a protocol, but they can also provide nontechnical information as well. Approved standards are promoted internationally by ISOC. However, corresponding RFCs never become international standards, although the ISO may take information from them.

17. What are RFCs?

Nearly all of the information about the Internet's history and its protocols are contained in documents known as Request for Comments. RFCs are the working notes of the Internet research and development community. They provide network researchers and designers a medium for documenting and sharing new ideas, network protocol concepts, and other technically-related information. They contain meeting notes from Internet organizations, describe various Internet protocols and experiments, and detail standards specifications. As we mentioned above, all Internet standards are published as RFCs (however, not all RFCs are Internet standards). In addition to RFCs are FYIs (For Your Information), which also cover Internet-related topics but in a less technical manner. There are presently over 2,400 RFCs ranging from the serious to the not so serious. Two less serious RFCs written during Christmas are RFC 968, *'Twas the Night Before Start-up*, written by Vint Cerf in 1985 (Cerf is widely known as the father of the Internet) and RFC 1882, *The 12 Days of Technology Before Christmas*, written in 1995 by Bill Hancock, one of the authors of this book. To facilitate the dissemination process, and to maintain a spirit of openness, RFCs and FYIs are available online at http://www.rfc-editor.org.

18. What is TCP/IP's history? For example, how did it become the network protocol of the Internet?

TCP/IP, which stands for *Transmission Control Protocol/Internet Protocol*, is a formal protocol suite that is primarily based on two sub-protocols—TCP, an OSI Layer 4 protocol, and IP, an OSI Layer 3 protocol. TCP/IP's history is tied to the development of the ARPANET, which initially was based on a protocol called the *Network Control Protocol* (NCP). The ARPANET's original design was grounded in two fundamental principles: The physical network was assumed not to be completely reliable, and network protocols could not be dependent on any proprietary hardware or software. The presumption of a completely unreliable network might seem a little odd at first. However, the ARPANET was a Department of Defense project, and as such, accepted the reality that the physical network could be disrupted by a catastrophic event. This spurred TCP/IP's development. The nonproprietary principle, coupled with the success of the early ARPANET, led to TCP/IP becoming available on a wide variety of hardware and software platforms.

Helping in the development of TCP/IP were Vint Cerf and Robert Kahn. In the early 1970s, both Cerf and Kahn, as part of an ARPA internetworking research program, developed the idea of gateways and wrote the first specification for the basic TCP/IP protocols now used in the Internet. The idea behind the development of TCP/IP was to enable different packet networks to be interconnected so the host computers did not have to know anything about the intermediate networks linking them together. By 1982, ARPA established TCP/IP as the protocol suite for ARPANET, and the Department of Defense declared them standards for military use. This led to one of the first definitions of an internet as a connected set of networks, specifically those using TCP/IP, and "Internet" as connected TCP/IP internets. The idea behind the Internet was the seamless linking of many different kinds of packet switched networks. This was facilitated by the robustness of TCP/IP, which enabled data communications across analog lines, packet radios, satellite links, Ethernet networks, and others.

As the ARPANET grew in the 1980s, so did computer networking. The popularity of computer networks was helped in part by the proliferation of individual computers and workstations—users wanted to interconnect their systems together. Recognizing the potential of a large marketplace, networking's popularity quickly led to the development of several proprietary networking protocols. This, in turn, also led to problems of interoperability. Within a closed, homogeneous networking environment (e.g., DECnet or SNA), interoperability was not an issue because all networked devices spoke the same language. This was not the case, however, in a heterogeneous or mixed-vendor environment.

Around this same time, the University of California at Berkeley's Computer Science department was enhancing the original version of the UNIX operating system. Called BSD UNIX, one of its new features was the incorporation of the TCP/IP protocol suite. This software was freely available and soon became quite popular at universities throughout the country. Given that TCP/IP was bundled with UNIX, and that TCP/IP was being used successfully in a real-time network (ARPANET), the National Science Foundation mandated that all NSF-funded supercomputer centers and computer networks that comprised NSF-NET use TCP/IP as their network communications protocol. NSF's mandate essentially established TCP/IP as a *de facto* standard.

19. How did TCP/IP become so dominant? Wasn't OSI supposed to be "the" network protocol?

Yes. In the early to mid-1990s, the networking literature was replete with articles that extolled various advantages and virtues of OSI compared to TCP/IP. Many network administrators, in fact, developed strategies to eventually migrate their TCP/IP-based networks to OSI. Some even professed that everyone's network should only support a single protocol: OSI. In spite of all the hoopla and hyperbole, OSI never emerged as "the" network protocol, particularly in the United States. Several reasons (all speculative, of course) why this happened include the following:

- *Standards Development:* TCP/IP and OSI differ in the way their standards are developed and tested. As a formal international standards organization, ISO possesses considerable inertia. The process of developing standards is painstaking. From the initial development of OSI, ISO has tried to do everything at once, and from the top down. In stark contrast to this approach, TCP/IP supports an open process for standards-making participation by its end users. The development of new or modification of existing TCP/IP protocols is also done on an as-needed basis. Furthermore, research, development, and testing of new or modified protocols can be performed on a production network, the procedure is in the open via RFC documents, and distribution of TCP/IP standards is free. (OSI protocols are copyrighted and carry a nominal purchasing fee.)

- *Snob Factor:* The underlying policy of TCP/IP was directed at connecting hosts primarily within the United States—specifically academic, research, government, and military organizations. OSI, on the other hand, was the product of an international standards body (ISO). Consequently, many European users perceived TCP/IP as a parochial *de facto* standard specific to the United States and wanted to embrace OSI. In the United States, though, users did not want to accept anything "different" and stayed true to TCP/IP.

- *Versatility and Robustness:* Compared to OSI, TCP/IP is simple and dependable, it has a proven track history (more than 25 years), it is nonproprietary, its developers have a pragmatic approach to its enhancement, and it meets the networking needs of a diverse population including researchers, educators, and business personnel. Some people—including Vint Cerf, who professes "IP over everything"—think of TCP/IP as the universal language of networking.

- *The Internet:* TCP/IP is inextricably linked to the Internet.

20. How does TCP/IP compare to the OSI layers?

See Chapter 2, specifically, Figures 2-11, 2-12, and 2-13.

21. In reviewing these figures, I have a question about the transport layer. How do you decide whether to use TCP or UDP?

You don't. This determination is made by the application program. For example, in Figure 2-13, examples of programs that use TCP include FTP, Telnet, Finger, SMTP, and POP. Similarly, examples of programs that use UDP include SNMP, TFTP, NFS, DNS, and BOOTP. What is important to understand here is that TCP/IP has two different transport layer protocols—TCP and UDP. TCP is connection-oriented and provides for reliable network transmission. UDP is connectionless and provides unreliable network transmission. This implies that UDP cannot recover from lost packets. Thus, the application must detect lost data and retransmit them. UDP also has no ability to perform error or flow control. This makes UDP faster than TCP in performance when the network is not congested because it carries less overhead than TCP. However, when the network is congested, UDP-based applications will most likely result in session timeouts and poor performance.

22. OK. Let's focus on TCP/IP's network layer. What else can you tell me about it besides what is already presented in Chapter 2?

(*Note:* Most of the information presented here is linked to Chapter 7, which deals specifically with network layer issues. The reader is encouraged to reference the appropriate figures and tables of this chapter.)

The network layer transfers user messages from a source host to a destination host. In TCP/IP, the heart and soul of this layer is the Internet Protocol, which is the IP of TCP/IP. IP receives data bits from the lower layer, assembles the bits into packets (called IP datagrams), and selects the "best" route based on some metric to route the packets between nodes. (*Note:* A metric is a description of the "cost" of a route used by routing hardware and software to select the best possible route. See Chapter 7 for more information.)

IP is connectionless, which implies that every datagram must contain the address of the destination node. This address, called an Internet or IP address (see Box 3-1), is assigned to a node's network interface as part of the node's initial network configuration. An IP address uniquely identifies a host similar to the way a social security number uniquely identifies a person. It is used by the network layer as a road map to locate a host within the Internet by determining what path a datagram is to follow en route to its final destination.

Datagrams destined for a host connected to the same local network as the sending host are delivered directly by the sending host. To transfer datagrams destined for a host connected to a remote network, however, IP relies on routers or switches (see Chapter 7), which connect two (or more) dissimilar networks to each other. In the context of the network layer, routers and switches are frequently referred to as gateways. Thus, an IP gateway routes packets between the networks to which it is connected. (An illustration of this concept is given in Figure 7-4.) As datagrams are routed through the Internet, each intermediate gateway maintains a routing table that contains entries of the location of the next gateway a datagram should be transferred to based on the destination address of the datagram. A UNIX and Microsoft NT command line utility that displays IP routing information for a local host is *netstat*. An example of this command's output is shown in Table 7-4.

When a datagram passes through an intermediate gateway en route to another network, it is called a hop. IP routing is usually accomplished via a simple hop-by-hop algorithm. If a packet doesn't incur a route through a router, then it hasn't incurred a hop. If, on the other hand, a packet transverses through two gateways in reaching its final destination, then we say the destination is two hops away. For example, in Figure 7-5, packets from H1 to H2 that follow the R1-R2 path require two hops since packets pass through two routers en route from source to destination. However, packets from H1 to H2 that follow the R1-R4-R5-R3-R2 path, require five hops. A UNIX program that depicts the gateways a packet transverses is called *traceroute*. (The corresponding Microsoft NT command is called *tracert*.) The output of a specific trace made from one web server to another is shown in Figure 7-6.

An important concept in routing a packet is that of "cost." Each link to another gateway has a pseudo-cost assigned to it by the network manager of the link. This pseudo-cost is used to compute the maximum cost allowed by a system to reach another system. Most routing algorithms used for IP routing use a least-cost/least-hops methodology. This means that the primary path a datagram takes is determined by the least-cost to transfer the packet from source to destination. If something on that path fails, then the next least-cost is used. If there are two or more paths with the same cost, then the least-hops is computed and the shortest hop path with the least-cost is taken. A side-effect of this type of routing is used by the routing algorithm to determine that a system is not reachable. What happens in a gateway is the destination node's cost goes to infinity. Thus, by definition, the node is simply too expensive to reach and hence is unavailable to the network.

Although gateways are used to deliver packets from one network to another, IP does not guarantee that a packet will indeed be delivered to its destination. If an intermediate gateway, for example, contains incorrect or stale routing information, packets might get lost. IP does not take any action to retransmit undelivered packets. This is done by higher-level protocols, specifically TCP. Additionally, IP fragments and reassembles datagrams when necessary so they do not exceed the maximum packet length (called the maximum transmission unit, or MTU) a physical network is capable of supporting. If a packet's size is greater than a network's MTU, the packet is broken into smaller units (called fragmenting) and sent to the destination in the form of several separate datagrams. The complete packet is then reassembled at the destination node before it is passed to the higher levels. Reassembly of an IP datagram can only occur at the destination node and not at any of the intermediary nodes the datagrams transverses. This is because IP is a connectionless datagram service—datagrams can take different paths en route to their destination and hence an intermediary node might not receive all of the fragmented datagrams.

23. OK. In Figure 2-12, I see that IP includes something called ICMP. What is this?

An integral part of IP is the Internet Control Message Protocol, ICMP, which uses an IP datagram to carry messages about the communications environment of the Internet. Although ICMP is layered above IP, it is generally discussed and shown with IP (as it is in

Figure 2-12) because of its relationship to IP. ICMP allows interconnected nodes to exchange messages to report flow control problems, to report that a destination node is unreachable, to notify a host to use a different gateway to route packets, and to test the status of a link to a remote host. For example, if a gateway receives a datagram destined for a host that is unreachable, the gateway will send an ICMP "host unreachable" message to the originator. This message is triggered when the local router sends an Address Resolution Protocol (ARP) request to the target node requesting the node's MAC sublayer address. On an Ethernet network, the MAC address is the node's Ethernet address. (See Chapter 5.) The ARP request is a network broadcast that announces the target node's IP address and requests the node to return its MAC address. If the node does not reply within a specified period of time, then a "host unreachable" message is sent by the router to the source node. A "host unreachable" message signifies that the target host is not connected to the local network, the target host is a valid local node but is currently offline, or the local network is congested and the router's ARP request is timing out before it reaches the target host. Another example of an ICMP message is "network unreachable." This message is sent by a router when it cannot reach the target network. This can be due to a downed link (e.g., a cable cut or disconnected port), an incorrectly configured network address mask (see Box 7-3), or an incorrectly entered network address.

An example of an ICMP-based application is the UNIX and Microsoft NT command *ping*, which allows one node to test the communication path between it and a destination node. The output of this command in verbose mode is shown in Figure 3-8. Normally ping simply reports whether a destination node is "alive." In verbose mode, ping reports the roundtrip time of a packet between source and destination. Note how ping gives specific information about the condition of the network environment. For example, lengthy roundtrip times would indicate some sort of problem between the source and destination nodes, and the percent of packet loss is also beneficial in assessing the condition of a link.

24. What about IP address schemes? I hear people talk about different types of address classes like Class B and Class C. What is this all about?

Internet addresses (called IP addresses for short) are node addresses that identify their location within the Internet. IP addresses play an important role in the successful delivery

```
gallo@bb> ping -s zeno.fit.edu
PING zeno.fit.edu: 56 data bytes
64 bytes from zeno.fit.edu (163.118.5.4): icmp_seq=0. time=128. ms
64 bytes from zeno.fit.edu (163.118.5.4): icmp_seq=1. time=127. ms
64 bytes from zeno.fit.edu (163.118.5.4): icmp_seq=2. time=128. ms
64 bytes from zeno.fit.edu (163.118.5.4): icmp_seq=3. time=120. ms
64 bytes from zeno.fit.edu (163.118.5.4): icmp_seq=4. time=130. ms
^C
----4.5.118.163.in-addr.arpa PING Statistics----
5 packets transmitted, 5 packets received, 0% packet loss
round-trip (ms) min/avg/max = 120/126/130
```

Figure 3-8. Output of the *ping* program using the *s* option.

of data across the Internet. If a node cannot be located, then data cannot be delivered to it. Currently, two versions of IP addresses are available: Version 4 (IPv4) and version 6 (IPv6). Information about IP version 4 (IPv4) addresses is given in Box 3-1; information about IPv6 is given later in the chapter.

25. I also hear people use the term "subnetting." What does this mean?

Subnetting refers to the partitioning of a network address space into separate, autonomous subnetworks. For example, a "flat" (no subnetting) class C address consists of 256 host IDs (2^8). As indicated in Box 3-1, IP reserves two of these IDs for special purposes. These are always the first and last host IDs. The first ID is used to identify the network itself (although historically this is the "all zeroes" broadcast address); it represents the overall network address. The last ID specifies the network's broadcast address. Thus, given the class C network identifier of 198.42.239: the address 198.42.239.0 is reserved for network identification; the address, 198.42.239.255, is reserved for broadcasting; and the remaining 254 addresses, from 198.42.239.1 to 198.42.239.254, are used as host IDs. As a result, a "flat" class C address consists of one network address, one broadcast address, and 254 unique host IDs.

Through subnetting, this same class C network can be partitioned into multiple network addresses, each with its own set of unique host IDs. For example, one subnetting scheme that involves using the high-order bit of the host ID as part of the network address results in two subnetworks. Each subnet has its own network and broadcast addresses and supports a maximum of 126 host IDs. Another subnetting scheme that uses the two higher-order bits of the host ID as part of the network address results in four subnetworks. Once again, each subnetwork has its own network and broadcast addresses. In this case, though, each of the four subnetworks can only support a maximum of 62 host IDs. Key to subnetting is a network's subnet mask. The concept of subnetting and subnet mask is detailed in Box 3-2. Subnetting is an efficient way of using the limited IPv4 address space.

26. Who controls the allocation of Internet addresses?

Control of IP addresses has been governed by the Internet Assigned Numbers Authority (IANA). The IANA service has authority over all number spaces used in the Internet, including Internet addresses. IANA has long been a part of the University of Southern California's Information Science Institute, and until his death on October 16, 1998, under the direction of Internet pioneer Jon Postel.

A new IANA is forthcoming. The Internet Corporation for Assigned Names and Numbers (ICANN), a private, nonprofit corporation with international representation, was expressly formed to assume the responsibilities currently being performed by IANA and other government organizations that provide domain name service. The transition from a U.S. government–controlled service to a private organization governed by an international board of directors is expected to take place over the next year or so. Additional information about IANA is available at http://www.iana.org.

BOX 3-1: IPv4 Addresses

Every node connected to a TCP/IP network has an Internet, or IP, address. IP version 4 addresses (IPv4) consist of 32 bits (0 through 31) partitioned into four groups of 8 bits each (called *octets*). Since it is difficult for us to read addresses in binary notation, IP addresses are expressed in decimal form; a decimal point (read as "dot") separates the octets. An example of an Internet address is 204.163.25.37. Each octet of an IP address is treated as an independent unit. Since octets comprise eight bits, decimal equivalents range from $2^0 = 1$ to $2^7 = 128$ per octet. This is illustrated below using x to represent bits.

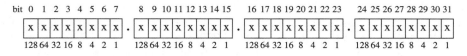

Thus, the bit pattern for the address 204.163.25.37 is as follows:

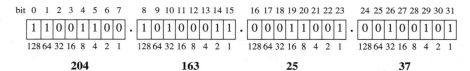

IPv4 addresses are organized into one of five classes—A, B, C, D, or E. Classification is determined by the value of the first four bits (bits 0 through 3).

Class A. If bit 0 is 0, then the address is a Class A address and begins with a decimal number ranging from 0 to 127. (*Note:* 0 and 127 are reserved.) Thus, the bit pattern of the first octet ranges from 00000000 to 011111111. An example of a Class A address is 13.123.17.8.

Class B. If the first two bits are 10, then the address is a Class B address and begins with a decimal number ranging from 128 to 191. Thus, the bit pattern of the first octet ranges from 10000000 to 10111111. An example of a Class B address is 163.118.5.4.

Class C. If the first three bits are 110, then the address is a Class C address and begins with a decimal number ranging from 192 to 223. Thus, the bit pattern of the first octet ranges from 11000000 to 11011111. An example of a Class C address is 198.42.239.17.

Class D. If the first four bits are 1110, then the address is a Class D address and begins with a decimal number ranging from 224 to 254. Thus, the bit pattern of the first octet ranges from 11100000 to 11101111. Class D addresses are used for multicast addresses.

Class E. If the first four bits are 1111, then the address is a Class E address. All Class E addresses are reserved for future use.

Continued on next page

BOX 3-1: IPv4 Addresses (Continued)

In addition to address classes, IPv4 addresses also distinguish between the address of a network (called the *network identifier*) and the address of a host (called the *host identifier*) connected to a specific network. This is similar to a telephone number—an area code identifies the region, and the phone number identifies a specific location in that region. Class A addresses use bits 1 through 7 for the network ID, and bits 8 through 31 for the host ID; Class B addresses use bits 2 through 15 for the network ID, and bits 16 through 31 for the host ID; and Class C addresses use bits 3 through 23 for the network ID, and bits 24 through 31 for the host ID. This is illustrated below. (*Note:* Class D and Class E addresses are not shown but follow a similar pattern.)

bit 0 1 2 3 4 5 6 7 8 9 10 11 12 13 14 15 16 17 18 19 20 21 22 23 24 25 26 27 28 29 30 31

0	Network ID	Host ID

└─ Designates Class A Address

bit 0 1 2 3 4 5 6 7 8 9 10 11 12 13 14 15 16 17 18 19 20 21 22 23 24 25 26 27 28 29 30 31

1 0	Network ID	Host ID

└─ Designates Class B Address

bit 0 1 2 3 4 5 6 7 8 9 10 11 12 13 14 15 16 17 18 19 20 21 22 23 24 25 26 27 28 29 30 31

1 1 0	Network ID	Host ID

└─ Designates Class C Address

Finally, each address class allows a different maximum number of possible networks and hosts. These upper limits are based on the number of bits used for the network and host identifiers. For example, since Class A addresses use seven bits (bits 1 through 7) for the network identifier and 24 bits (bits 8 through 31) for the host identifier, there are a maximum of $2^7 = 128$ Class A networks, each capable of supporting $2^{24} = 16,777,216$ hosts. Similarly, Class B addresses have a maximum of $2^{14} = 16,384$ networks and $2^{16} = 65,534$ hosts; and Class C addresses support $2^{21} = 2,097,152$ networks, each capable of supporting $2^8 = 256$ hosts. (*Note:* IPv4 reserves the use of all 0s or all 1s for special addresses. As a result, each of the above calculations should be reduced by two to yield the true number of unique networks and hosts allowable for each network class.)

(See Box 3-2 for information about subnetting IPv4 addresses, and Figure 3-13 for the format and structure of IPv6 addresses.)

BOX 3-2: Subnet Masking

A subnet mask partitions an IPv4 address into two parts: the network ID and host IDs. The concept of subnet masking is as follows:

If a bit in an IPv4 address is used as part of the network ID, then the corresponding mask bit is set to 1. If a bit in an IP address is used as part of the host ID, then the corresponding mask is set to 0.

For example, the Class C IPv4 address, 192.203.97.0, with subnet mask 255.255.255.0 implies that the network address is 192.203.97, the host ID addresses corresponding to this network range from 192.203.97.1 to 192.203.97.254, and the network broadcast address is 192.203.97.255. (See Box 3-1 for more information about IPv4 addresses.)

To conserve the IPv4 address space, network addresses are subnetted by borrowing bits from the host ID portion of the network address. To illustrate this concept, consider the following Class C address, which has its last octet (the part that represents the host ID) expanded into its 8-bit equivalent with corresponding decimal values.

192.203.97.
Network Address
| 128 | 64 | 32 | 16 | 8 | 4 | 2 | 1 |
Host ID Portion

If we "steal" the highest-order bit of the host ID portion of this address (i.e., 128) to use as part of the network address, then the subnet mask becomes 255.255.255.128.

192.203.97.
| 1 |
| 128 | 64 | 32 | 16 | 8 | 4 | 2 | 1 |
Network Address   Host ID Portion

Thus, one bit is for subnetting and seven bits are for host IDs. This yields $2^1 = 2$ subnets and $2^7 = 128$ host IDs. Since each network requires one address to name the network and one for broadcasting, the actual number of host IDs per subnet is $2^7 - 2 = 126$.

	Subnet 1	Subnet 2
Network Address:	192.203.97.0	192.203.97.128
Host IDs:	192.203.97.1 to 192.203.97.126	192.203.97.129 to 192.203.97.254
Broadcast Address:	192.203.97.127	192.203.97.255

(*Note:* It should be observed that the "all ones" subnet is not recommended in the RFCs and hence, should be avoided. As a result, having a mask 1-bit wide would allow only one subnet to be defined, subnet 0; subnet 128 would be illegal.)

Continued on next page

BOX 3-2: Subnet Masking (Continued)

Similarly, if the two left-most bits of the host ID are used (128 + 64), the subnet mask is 255.255.255.192. This implies $2^2 = 4$ subnets, each with $2^6 - 2 = 62$ host IDs.

	Subnet 1	Subnet 2	Subnet 3	Subnet 4
Network Address:	192.203.97.0	192.203.97.64	192.203.97.128	192.203.97.192
Host IDs:	192.203.97.1 to 192.203.97.62	192.203.97.65 to 192.203.97.126	192.203.97.129 to 192.203.97.190	192.203.97.193 to 192.203.97.254
Broadcast Address:	192.203.97.63	192.203.97.127	192.203.97.191	192.203.97.255

Routing protocols need to support subnet masking in order to determine correct routing information. For example, consider the destination address 192.203.97.143 with the subnet mask 255.255.255.192. Let's examine an expanded view of these addresses.

Mask: 255.255.255.

1	1	0	0	0	0	0	0
128	64	32	16	8	4	2	1

Host ID: 192.203.97.

1	0	0	0	1	1	1	1
128	64	32	16	8	4	2	1

The correct subnet is determined by "masking" the bits in the host field from the 1-bits in the mask. This is done by combining these bits via a logical AND.

$$\begin{array}{rl} \textbf{Mask:} & 1\ 1\ 0\ 0\ 0\ 0\ 0\ 0 \\ \textbf{Host ID:} & 1\ 0\ 0\ 0\ 1\ 1\ 1\ 1 \\ \hline \textbf{Result of logical AND:} & 1\ 0\ 0\ 0\ 0\ 0\ 0\ 0 \end{array}$$

Since $10000000_2 = 128_{10}$, the correct subnet is 128. That is, the host with address 192.203.97.143 is attached to the subnetwork whose address is 192.203.97.128. Furthermore, when the six bits of the host ID (001111) are added to the corresponding bits of the mask, the result is 001111_2, which is equal to 15_{10}. Thus, the destination address, 192.203.97.143 is correctly identified as host 15 on subnet 128 of network 192.203.97. If the routing protocol does not support subnet masking, then the destination address corresponds to host ID 143 on network 192.203.97.0, which is incorrect.

27. How are IP addresses assigned?

The assignment of IP addresses is handled in a distributed fashion via an Internet Registry (IR) system, which is hierarchical in structure involving several organizations. Starting at the top, this hierarchy consists of IANA (see preceding paragraph), Regional Internet Registries (RIR), and Local Internet Registries (LIR). RIRs are established under the authority of IANA and include the American Registry for Internet Numbers (ARIN), the Asian-Pacific Network Information Center (APNIC), and Réseaux IP Européens Network Coordination Centre (RIPE NCC). ARIN, which assumed registry responsibilities from InterNIC, is the RIR for North America, South America, the Caribbean, and sub-Saharan Africa; APNIC is the RIR for countries in the Asian Pacific region (e.g., Japan, China, Thailand); and RIPE NCC is the RIR for Europe and surrounding areas. LIRs are established by IANA and RIRs. In some cases, LIRs are also Internet Service Providers (ISPs). The way IP address assignments work is as follows: The IANA allocates blocks of IP address space to Regional Internet Registries. The RIRs allocate blocks of IP address space to their Local Internet Registries. LIRs then assign addresses to either end users or ISPs. The assignment of IP addresses using this structure enables routing information for end users to be aggregated once it leaves a provider's routing domain. This reduces the number of route announcements and state changes throughout the Internet. (See Chapter 7 for more information about routing.) There has been some discussion of establishing two more RIRs, one for South America and one for Africa.

28. Whenever I use the Internet I never deal with IP addresses. I always use real names like www.att.com. Is there some sort of translation that takes place that's transparent to me?

Yes. Every host (well, almost every host) that is connected to the Internet has both an IP address and corresponding logical name. This logical name, which is generically referred to as a domain name, is another type of addressing construct used for identifying Internet nodes. For example, the IP address that corresponds to www.att.com is 135.145.9.134. The translation from logical name to IP address, called name resolution, makes it easier for us to deal with Internet addresses. After all, we are mere humans and, as such, have a limited capacity for memorizing long strings of numbers, particularly when they are formatted as IP addresses, and especially if they are IPv6 addresses, which are 128 bits long. Without name resolution, web site addresses or e-mail addresses (Remember: You are nobody unless you are somebody@somewhere.com) could not employ names of organizations, descriptive titles, acronyms, and the like. They would all be numerically based.

29. Could you explain this translation process?

Yes we can. Before we do, though, it might be helpful to first understand the concept of domain names. Domain names are organized in a hierarchical tree-like fashion. At the top of the tree are top-level domains. There are currently seven three-letter descriptive top-level domains that represent general entities, plus two-letter country codes assigned to different countries throughout the world. The top-level domains include *com* for commercial organizations (e.g., for-profit companies); *edu* for educational organizations (currently restricted to only four-year colleges and universities; all other schools are part of the us country domain); *gov* for government organizations or agencies (currently restricted to U.S. federal government agencies); *int* for international treaty organizations; *mil* for U.S. military organizations; *net* for Internet service providers; and *org* for any miscellaneous organization including not-for-profit organizations. The two-letter country codes are those specified in the ISO-3166 document. Examples include *us* for United States, *ca* for Canada, and *au* for Australia. Under each top-level domain are sublevels, and each lower level is considered a subdomain of its immediately preceding higher level. There has been considerable discussion to create additional top-level domains to be more reflective of today's Internet, but this is unlikely to happen within the next couple of years.

When expressed as a logical Internet address, the domain name hierarchy is structured from right-to-left—the top level is at the right and the bottom level at the left—and consists of multiple levels separated by dots. For example, www.att.com is a three-level structure. Its top-level domain is com, att is a subdomain within com, and www is the name of a host within att. (*Note:* If the lowest level is the name of a host, then the entire structure is called a fully-qualified domain name—FQDN). As another illustration, consider the six-level domain name, pirate.pbhs.brevard.k12.fl.us. Its top-level domain is us; fl is a subdomain in us (it's for the state of Florida); k12 is a subdomain within fl (it represents public schools from kindergarten through twelfth grade); brevard is a subdomain of k12 (it's the name of a county school district), pbhs is a subdomain of brevard (its the name of a specific school); and pirate is the name of a host within pbhs. This is another fully-qualified domain name. (See Figure 3-9.)

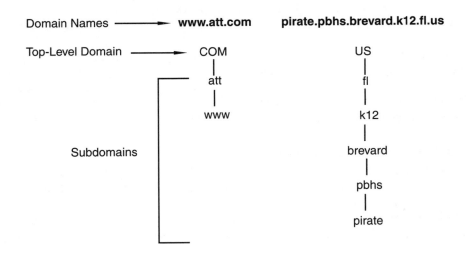

Figure 3-9. Domain names are structured in a right-to-left hierarchy. The top-level domain is the rightmost part of an address. All sublevels are subdomains of their immediately preceding higher-level domain. If a domain name includes the hostname as its lowest level, then the structure is called a fully-qualified domain named.

To translate domain names to IP addresses, a domain name service is used. The translation process involves configuring host machines as domain name system (DNS) servers. DNS servers store specific address information about a particular domain or subdomain. DNS servers are located at each top-level domain and at various subdomains within a top-level domain. Special root servers are also used to process inter-domain DNS requests. Each subdomain has at least one DNS server that is authoritative for that domain. This means that it contains accurate and complete domain name-IP address resolution records for all the connected hosts within that domain. For example, in Figure 3-10, let's assume that a user on host pirate wants to connect to the web server raider, which is in the rhs.brevard.k12.fl.us domain. The web browser on pirate places a DNS query to the DNS server for brevard.k12.fl.us, which is authoritative for the brevard.k12.fl.us domain. This DNS server looks up the information in its database and returns the address 204.128.70.3. Now suppose this same user wants to connect to the web server, www.att.com. A similar query is made to the brevard.k12.fl.us DNS server. This time, though, it does not have any information about the att.com domain and hence cannot resolve the name. This DNS server then initiates a process of trying to get the name resolved. Each DNS server has the address of other name servers, including at least one root server. If a DNS server cannot resolve a name, it replies by specifying the name server that should be contacted next. Eventually, a root server gets involved. Root servers maintain information about all the authoritative name servers for each top-level domain. Thus, if the brevard name server cannot get www.att.com resolved by the higher-level name servers within its domain, a root server will eventually provide it with the att.com DNS server's address. The brevard name server then contacts the att.com name server, which will return the address 135.145.9.134. The brevard name server then sends this information to the client process on pirate. The brevard server will also store this address locally in its cache along with other names it has resolved recently. This helps reduce the number of DNS lookups and makes the DNS process more efficient.

A UNIX and Microsoft NT program that is used to acquire the IP address of a domain name is *nslookup*. To find the IP address of a domain name, simply enter nslookup followed by the domain name. For example, "nslookup www.att.com" returns the address 135.145.9.134. This command can also be used for IP address resolution, which translates numerical IP addresses to corresponding domain names.

30. Is DNS the only method of name resolution?

No. A simple, but inefficient alternative is to maintain on every local machine a host file that contains the fully-qualified domain names and their respective IP addresses of all the hosts you need to contact. Some operating systems enable you to use both DNS and host files. For example, a host might be configured to use host table lookup first and DNS second. This way if a host cannot resolve a hostname via its local host file it can then place a DNS query.

31. OK. Let's move on to IPv6. Why was it developed?

IPv6 was developed for the same reason other new Internet protocols have been developed or existing ones modified: growth. Due to the tremendous growth of the Internet, the number of available IPv4 addresses is shrinking. Furthermore, with the deployment of

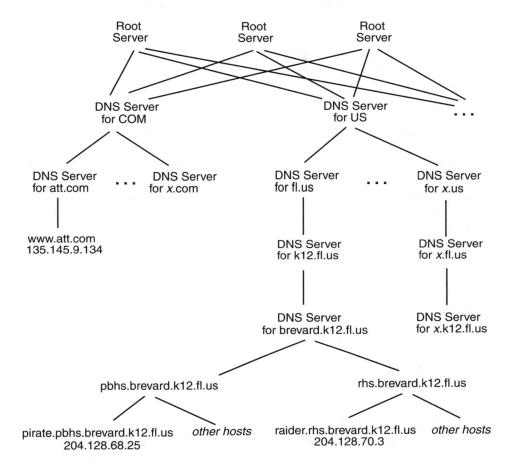

Figure 3-10. DNS servers provide name resolution service. Each subdomain has at least one name server that is authoritative for that domain. That is, it maintains complete and accurate information about all the hosts within its subdomain. Name servers also have the address of other servers they can contact in the event they cannot resolve a name locally. Name servers also have the address of at least one root server, which provide inter-domain name resolution capability.

more networks, routing tables are overflowing and unable to handle the demand of maintaining information about every network. This depletion of IP addresses and routing table overflow is analogous to the telephone company running out of area codes and old telephone switches unable to place calls to certain numbers. This is why we now have area codes with middle digits other than 0 or 1, a new toll free 888 exchange in addition to the traditional 800 exchange, and multiple area codes serving the same area. Although the original developers of TCP/IP in the early 1980s accounted admirably for the future growth of TCP/IP, no one could have predicted the exponential growth that is occurring within the Internet today.

Although the driving force behind this phenomenal growth can be linked to the computer market, this probably will not be the case in the near future. Indeed the computer market will continue growing; there are still many schools and small businesses not yet connected to the Internet. However, the future growth of the Internet will probably be fueled by several new markets including the following:

Personal Communication Devices. Fax machines, personal digital assistants (PDAs), telephones, and nomadic units that rely on wireless communications are very popular. Eventually, these devices will be network-addressable and hence require a unique IP address. Furthermore, some of these devices must be capable of automatically configuring (and reconfiguring) themselves with correct addressing information when moved from one remote location to another.

Networked Entertainment. Video-on-demand, stereos, CDs, and interactive television will one day be network-addressable. For example, in a world of networked television sets, every TV will effectively become an Internet host and require a unique IP address.

Networked Controlled Devices. A wide range of devices from simple appliances such as lights and electronic security devices, to heavy motors such as heating and air conditioning units, or any other equipment currently controlled by analog switches, will be controlled via networked communications.

Each of these markets is huge, and they all have a common attendant characteristic—they all bring to the table a new set of requirements that IPv4 does not support. For example, there will be a need for (among others) large-scale routing, automatic configuration and reconfiguration of host addresses, and built-in authentication and encryption for security purposes. In addition to providing such functionality, it also is imperative that the new IP continues to support existing applications.

32. OK. What does IPv6 bring to the table?

IPv6, which is sometimes called IPng (for next generation), provides a solution that resolves current addressing problems and is capable of delivering the necessary functionality for emerging markets. Designed as an evolutionary replacement, IPv6 maintains most IPv4 functions, relegates certain functions that either were not working or were rarely used in IPv4 as optional, and adds new functionality that is missing from IPv4.

Some of the specific differences between IPv4 and IPv6 are readily apparent when you examine the format and content of their headers, shown in Figures 3-11 and 3-12, respectively. Three obvious differences are (1) size—the IPv4 header length is of variable length because of its Options and Padding fields, but IPv6 is a fixed 320 bits; (2) the number of fields—IPv4 has 14 fields, but IPv6 has only eight; and (3) address field size—source and destination addresses are 32 bits each in IPv4, but 128 bits each in IPv6. The address fields make up 80 percent of the IPv6 header (256 bits). Without these two fields, the IPv6 header is only 64 bits in length, which makes it much smaller than the corresponding IPv4 header. (*Note:* Although the IPv4 header has 14 fields, it is unusual to see more than 12 in use. The Options field is rarely used and hence the Padding field, which is only used for alignment when options are used, is also rarely required.)

Although IPv6 embodies a "less is more" philosophy-structure, it still supports a wide variety of options. Consider, for example, the Next Header (NH) field, which specifies the

4	4	8	16	16	3	13	8	8	16	32	32	Variable	
V	HL	ST	TL	ID	F	FO	TTL	P	HC	SA	DA	OPT	PAD

V   This 4-bit field specifies the protocol *Version* number. For IPv4, it is 0100.

HL   This 4-bit field specifies the *Header Length* in 32-bit words. It is needed because the OPT and PAD fields do not have fixed lengths. (*Note:* The header length does not include the length of the user data field, which immediately follows the PAD field. The data field is not shown here because it is not part of the header.)

ST   This 8-bit *Service Type* field specifies the manner in which a packet (i.e., datagram) is routed. It contains three subfields as show below:

Precedence (3 bits)	Type of Service (4 bits)	MBZ (1 bit)

- The *Precedence* subfield specifies the priority of the datagram (from 000 = normal to 111 = network control).
- The *Type of Service* (TOS) field specifies transport control information relative to delay, throughput, reliability, and cost. For example, 1000 = minimize delay; 0100 = maximize throughput; 0010 = maximize reliability; 0001 = minimize monetary cost; and 0000 = normal service (default). (See RFC 1349 for more information about TOS.)
- The *MBZ* ("must be zero") field is currently unused.

TL   This 16-bit field specifies the *Total Length* of the packet. Given the field's 16-bits, the maximum size of an IPv4 packet is 2^{16} = 65,535 bytes.

ID   This 16-bit field specifies the unique *Identification* number that was assigned to the packet. This number is used to reassemble fragmented packets.

F   This 3-bit *Flag* field is used to control fragmentation.

FO   This 13-bit *Fragment Offset* field provides reassembly information for fragmented packets.

TTL   This 8-bit *Time To Live* field is a counter (often called a *hop count*) that specifies the number of seconds a packet is permitted to remain alive (i.e., active) on the Internet. This field gets decremented whenever it is processed by a router. When TTL = 0, the packet is discarded and an error message is sent to the source node that sent the packet.

P   This 8-bit field specifies the Layer 4 *Protocol* used to create user data.

HC   This 16-bit field contains *Header Checksum* information, which is used for maintaining packet integrity.

SA   This is the 32-bit IP *Source Address*. (See Box 3-1.)

DA   This is the 32-bit IP *Destination Address*. (See Box 3-1.)

OPT This variable-bit field is reserved mostly for control *Options* (e.g., network testing or debugging). Eight options are available, and the length of this field varies depending on the option used.

PAD This variable-length *Padding* field is used in conjunction with the Option field. It pads the option field with enough zero bits to ensure that the header length is a multiple of 32 bits.

Figure 3-11. Format and contents of an IPv4 header. The length of each field is given in bits. (Adapted from RFC 791, RFC 1702, and RFC 1349.)

4	4	24	16	8	8	128	128
V	P	FL	PL	NH	HL	SA	DA

V   This 4-bit field specifies the protocol Version number. For IPv6, it is 0110. This is the only field that has exactly the same meaning and position in both IPv4 and IPv6 headers.

P   This 4-bit field specifies the Priority of the packet data. This field is new to the IP header; it was not part of IPv4. There are $2^4 = 16$ different priority levels, which are divided into two groups. The first group, which is specified by priority levels 0 through 7, designates packets that can respond to congestion control. For example, in an IP-based frame relay network, in the presence of congestion, the destination node can reset its transmission window value to 0, which effectively informs the sender to stop transmitting data to the receiver until a non-zero window size is received from the receiver. (See Chapter 12.) The second priority group is specified by priority levels 8 through 15 and designates packets that cannot respond to congestion control. This second priority group is used for critical data such as voice and video. These packets will not backoff in response to congestion control.

FL   This 24-bit Flow Label field designates packets that require special handling. One use of this field is to provide Quality of Service (QoS) via RSVP. This field is new to the IP header; it was not part of IPv4.

PL   This 16-bit field specifies the Payload Length of the user data that follows the header. IPv6's PL replaces IPv4's Total Length field, which specifies the length of the header and data.

NH   This 8-bit Next Header field replaces IPv4's Protocol field. NH specifies the type of header that immediately follows the IPv6 header. NH enables extension headers to be inserted between the IP header and the TCP or UDP headers that precede user data. An example of this field is the use of IPSec's authentication and encryption headers for security. This field also effectively replaces IPv4's Header Length and Option fields.

HL   This 8-bit Hop Limit field is used to specify the number of seconds a packet can remain active on the Internet. The value of this field is decremented by 1 second each time it passes through a router. HL replaces IPv4's TTL field.

SA   This field carries the 128-bit IP Source Address. Except for its length, SA has exactly the same meaning as IPv4's SA field. Its location within the packet is different, though.

DA   This field carries the 128-bit IP Destination Address. Except for its length, DA has exactly the same meaning as IPv4's DA field. Its location within the packet is different, though.

Figure 3-12. Format and contents of an IPv6 header. The length of each field is given in bits. (Adapted from RFC 1752, RFC 1883, and RFC 2373.)

type of header that immediately follows the IPv6 header. NH enables extension headers for optional layer 3 data to be inserted between the IP header and the upper layer headers (e.g., TCP or UDP) that precede user data. An example of this field is the use of IPSec's authentication and encryption headers for security. (See Chapter 16.) NH effectively combines the functions of IPv4's Protocol, Header Length and Option fields. IPv6 also provides support for prioritizing traffic via its 4-bit Priority (P) field, and for assigning special handling designations (e.g., QoS) to packets through its 24-bit Flow Label (FL) field. Both of these features were not available in IPv4. Additional information about IPv6 can be found in RFC 1883, which contains a complete set of specifications for the new protocol. The Internet-Draft, "The Case for IPv6," also contains information about IPv6. (*Note:* Internet-Drafts are working documents of IETF. Drafts are valid for at most six months and are subject to change at any time. See http://www.ietf.org for more information.)

33. What's the scoop on IPv6 addresses?

As stated above, one of the most significant differences between IPv4 and IPv6 is IP address size, which was increased from 32 bits in IPv4 to 128 bits in IPv6. (See Box 3-1 for information about IPv4 addresses.) Thus, IPv6 addresses have four times as many bits as IPv4 addresses (128 vs. 32). This means there are 2^{128} IPv6 addresses versus 2^{32} IPv4 addresses. Evaluating 2^{128} with our outdated calculator, the result is displayed in scientific notation as $3.402823665 \times 10^{38}$. Hinden (1996), however, was able to calculate this value exactly: 340,282,366,920,938,463,463,374,607,431,768,211,456. When compared to IPv4's 4 billion addresses (i.e., 4,294,967,295), you start to get some feel for the size of IPv6's address space. Hinden also reported that there are enough 128-bit IPv6 addresses to, at worst, provide each square meter of the Earth's surface with 1,564 addresses, and at best, 3,911,873,538,269,506,102 addresses. The new address space also allows for more levels of addressing hierarchy, simpler autoconfiguration of addresses, and will support other network protocol addresses. Other notable features include:

- Support for three types of addresses—unicast, anycast, and multicast. Unicast addresses identify a single interface. Anycast addresses are assigned to a set of interfaces and routed to the nearest one assigned to that address. The determination of which node is nearest is based on the metric used by the routing protocol. (See Chapter 7.) Multicast addresses are assigned to a group of interfaces and delivered to all of the interfaces in the assigned group. (*Note:* IPv6 addresses are assigned to physical interfaces, not nodes.)

- Support for auto-readdressing, which allows a packet to be automatically routed to a new address.

- Support for autoconfiguration of network addresses. IPv6 hosts can acquire their network address dynamically. This is done via a "plug and play" method or through full support for the Dynamic Host Configuration Protocol (DHCP).

- Support for data authentication, privacy, and confidentiality. (See Chapter 16.)

- Support for priority routing. This enables a source node to assign a delivery priority level to its outgoing packets. This enables "real-time" packets (e.g., packets carrying full-motion video data) to be sent at a constant rate without interruption of delivery.

34. What's an IPv6 address look like?

An IPv6 address is quite different in appearance than an IPv4 address. IPv6 addresses, like IPv4 addresses, are still grouped into classes (see Box 3-1). The delimiter, however, is no longer the familiar "dot" notation. IPv6 addresses are written as eight 16-bit integers, which are expressed in hexadecimal form and separated by colons. For example, 2A01:0000:0000:0000:12FB:071C:04DE:689E is a sample IPv6 address. To reduce the complexity in writing an IPv6 address, leading zeros in a hex group can be eliminated. Thus, the sample address can be expressed as 2A01:0:0:0:12FB:71C:4DE:689E. Frequently, many IPv6 addresses also contain contiguous strings of 0 bits. For example, IPv6 support of IPv4 address formats involves placing zeros in either the higher-order 80 or 96 bits of an IPv6 address. (More on this later.) In such cases, a double colon can be used to designate multiple zero groupings. Thus, the sample IPv6 address given above can be expressed in a reduced form as 2A01::12FB:71C:4DE:689E. In this example, the double colon denotes three hex groupings of 0000. The double colon notation can only be used once in an address. It also can be used to designate leading or trailing zeros of an address.

As noted in the preceding paragraph, IPv6 provides support for IPv4 address formats. Such addresses are referred to as "IPv6 addresses with embedded IPv4 addresses." Two different formats are available. The first consists of 96 higher-order 0 bits followed by the 32-bit IPv4 address. A convenient format for expressing this is to mix the colon and dot delimiters. For example, the IPv4 address, 206.43.152.78, is expressed in IPv6 form as 0:0:0:0:0:0:206.43.152.78. This address can be further reduced by using the double colon delimiter to represent the leading zeros of the address. Thus, an equivalent form is ::206.43.152.78. This address is formally called an IPv4-compatible IPv6 address and is used to represent nodes that support IPv6 but must route IPv4 packets over an IPv6 network. A second format consists of 80 higher-order 0 bits, followed by one hex grouping of Fs, followed by the IPv4 address. Thus, our sample IPv4 address is expressed in this form as ::FFFF:206.43.152.78. This address type is called an IPv4-mapped IPv6 address and is used to represent IPv4 nodes that do not support IPv6.

The first field of an IPv6 address is a variable-length Format Prefix, which specifies the various categories of addresses. Examples of some prefixes and their meanings follow:

- **010** designates an IPv6 Provider-Based Unicast address, which is assigned to nodes connected directly to the Internet. The general structure of an IPv6 provider-based unicast address is shown in Figure 3-13.

- **1111 1110 10** designates a Link-Local address, which is assigned to isolated network sites. An isolated site is one in which nodes are connected to a network, but the network does not have a router and is not connected to the Internet.

- **1111 1110 11** designates a Site-Local address, which is assigned to sites that have a router connection but are not connected to the Internet.

- **1111 1111** designates a Multicast address.

- **0000 0000 0000 0000 0000 0000** designates an embedded IPv4-compatible IPv6 address.

Additional information about the IPv6 addressing architecture can be found in RFC 1884, RFC 2073, RFC 2373, and RFC 2374.

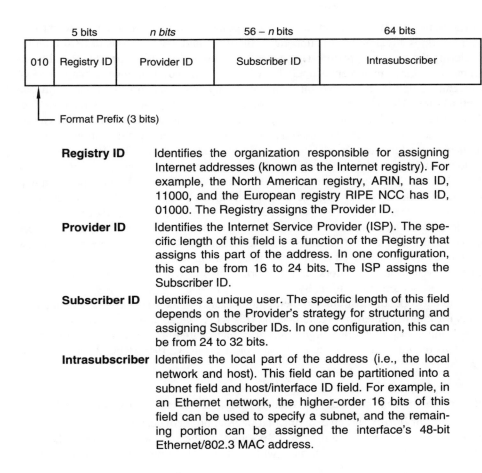

5 bits	*n bits*	56 – *n* bits	64 bits
010	Registry ID	Provider ID	Subscriber ID	Intrasubscriber

Format Prefix (3 bits)

Registry ID   Identifies the organization responsible for assigning Internet addresses (known as the Internet registry). For example, the North American registry, ARIN, has ID, 11000, and the European registry RIPE NCC has ID, 01000. The Registry assigns the Provider ID.

Provider ID   Identifies the Internet Service Provider (ISP). The specific length of this field is a function of the Registry that assigns this part of the address. In one configuration, this can be from 16 to 24 bits. The ISP assigns the Subscriber ID.

Subscriber ID   Identifies a unique user. The specific length of this field depends on the Provider's strategy for structuring and assigning Subscriber IDs. In one configuration, this can be from 24 to 32 bits.

Intrasubscriber Identifies the local part of the address (i.e., the local network and host). This field can be partitioned into a subnet field and host/interface ID field. For example, in an Ethernet network, the higher-order 16 bits of this field can be used to specify a subnet, and the remaining portion can be assigned the interface's 48-bit Ethernet/802.3 MAC address.

Figure 3-13. General structure of an IPv6 provider-based unicast address. (Adapted from RFC 2050, RFC 2073, and RFC 2374.)

35. How will the Internet convert from IPv4 addressing to IPv6? It sounds like this is much more than a simple upgrade. Surely, this cannot occur overnight.

You're right. IPv6 is more than an IPv4 upgrade; it's a completely new version of the Internet Protocol. Its addressing is different, its headers are more specialized, it provides for more options including flow control and security, and it supports host mobility autoconfiguration along with some other new features. You are also correct in your observation that the conversion cannot occur overnight. It is unlikely that every Internet user will switch to IPv6 on a predetermined date and time. Can you image the entire Internet world being in synch and pressing the Return key at the same time? Hardly. Instead, the Internet must slowly and methodically migrate from IPv4 to IPv6 over several years.

Migrating to an IPv6 Internet, without disrupting the current operation of the existing IPv4 network, is a real issue. It is imperative that IPv6 and key functions of IPv4 interoperate during the transition period. The current IPv6 migration plan supports several types of transitions. First, incremental upgrades will be permitted. This means that any IPv4 device can be upgraded to IPv6 independent of any other networked device, with one exception—the DNS server must first be upgraded to handle IPv6 address records. Second, incremental deployment will be supported. This means that new IPv6 nodes can be installed at any time without any modifications necessary. Third, the transition must support current IP addresses. Thus, if an existing IPv4 node is upgraded to IPv6, it does not have to be assigned a new IPv6 address. Rather, it can continue using its existing IPv4 address. Finally, there should be little or no preparation work needed on the part of a network administrator to either upgrade a device from IPv4 to IPv6 or deploy a new IPv6 device. Overall, this transition is to be processed in two phases. At the end of Phase 1 both IPv4 and IPv6 devices will coexist on the Internet; at the end of Phase 2 only IPv6 devices will exist. During Phase 1 it is believed that IPv6 and IPv4 nodes will interoperate, new IPv6 devices will be deployed in an incremental fashion with few interdependencies, and end-users, system administrators, and network operators will be capable of making the transition without too much difficulty.

To aid network administrators in their renumbering efforts, an organization called Procedures for Internet Enterprise Renumbering (PIER) is available. Information about PIER can be found at http://www.ietf.org/html.charter/pier-charter.html. Additional information about IPv6 renumbering issues is also available from RFC 1916, RFC 2071, and RFC 2072.

36. I have one more innocuous question relative to IPv6. What happened to IPv5?

Version 5 of IP (IPv5) is an experimental Internet protocol designed for real-time, parallel data transmissions. So, although it appears that the Internet Engineering Steering Group (IESG) skipped a version number when it assigned the number 6 to the new protocol, in reality this was not the case.

37. What type of services or resources does the Internet provide?

One of the main attractions of the Internet is the services and resources that are available from it. Some of the services include e-mail, remote logins, file transfers, network news—an electronic forum that consists of special interest groups and discussions (there are currently over 14,000 network news groups that cover a very wide and diverse number of topics), search tools or "engines" that allow a user to locate specific information based on user input, communication resources such as Talk and Internet Relay Chat (IRC), interactive games, and web browsers that enable you to view resources that have been formatted as hypertext files. There is streaming audio and video, which enable users to listen to audio recordings or view videos in real-time. There are also programs that enable two-way interactive videoconferencing to take place via the Internet. Through these services users can acquire information about nearly anything.

There are also several high-profile Internet services or resources available. These include electronic commerce (e-commerce), Voice Over IP (VOIP), and Virtual Private Networks (VPNs). E-commerce involves using the Internet for credit card purchases of items such as automobiles, airline tickets, computer-related products, and books; VOIP enables users to place telephone calls across the Internet; and VPNs enable organizations to establish private interconnected corporate LANs using the Internet (see Chapter 7).

38. With all of these different services and resources available over the Internet, the issue of security emerges. How secure is the Internet?

(*Note:* The subject of network security, including types of attacks, hardware strategies for dealing with these attacks, and security-related protocols such as IP Security (IPSec), is discussed in Chapter 16.)

Internet security is undoubtedly of paramount concern for users. Unfortunately, the TCP/IP protocol suite was not initially designed with security in mind. This was not an oversight on the part of the original designers of TCP/IP. Remember: TCP/IP was initially developed to serve the research and academic communities to facilitate the exchange of research and scholarly activities. Inherent in this academic endeavor was a presumption of trust and honesty. Also, many of the compromises of TCP/IP protocols today were not anticipated by the TCP/IP designers 20 years ago.

The first major security breach of the Internet occurred on November 2–3, 1988, when a student exploited a security "hole" in the Simple Mail Transfer Protocol (SMTP). Now known as the "Worm incident," many of the computers connected to NSFNET at that time were affected and rendered useless. Since then, there have been many attempts (some successful, some not) to exploit known weaknesses in other TCP/IP protocols. There also is no shortage to the number of individuals who have nothing better to do than search for creative ways to compromise a system.

In response to these attacks, several approaches are available. The easiest thing to do is not connect a system or network containing critical data to the Internet. A second strategy is to encrypt sensitive data prior to transmission across the network. A third approach is to install filters on routers that either deny or permit certain traffic to enter your network. Alternatively, special-purpose firewall devices that serve as buffers can also be installed between your network and the outside world. On the protocol front, there is secure http for protecting web transactions, e-mail security is available via Secure MIME (S/MIME) and Pretty Good Privacy (PGP), and several protocols have been developed to help secure VPNs, including the Point-to-Point Tunneling Protocol (PPTP), Layer 2 Forwarding (L2F), Layer 2 Tunneling Protocol (L2TP), and IP Security (IPSec). All are discussed in Chapter 16. It should also be noted that all the hardware based or protocol-software based protection in the world can easily be undermined by irresponsible users. As a result, it is important that organizations establish and enforce network security and acceptable use policies, educate users about network security issues, and employ common sense practices such as don't give unauthorized people your password. See Box 16-3 for additional suggestions. Finally, several resources are available online that are specifically geared to Internet security. The best place to begin is the Computer Emergency Response Team (CERT), located at http://www.cert.org.

End-of-Chapter Commentary

In this chapter, we discussed various aspects of the Internet, including its history, current and planned backbones, governance structure, resources and services, and security. We also presented an overview and brief history of TCP/IP and its relationship to the Internet, and we examined several concepts of the Internet Protocol (IP). These included IPv4 and IPv6 addressing schemes, subnetting, and name resolution. Some of the information in this chapter is linked to earlier and later chapters. Many of the examples used throughout the book are presented from an Internet perspective. These include Chapters 1, 2, 7, 11, 12, 15, and 16. Chapter 2 also examines the TCP/IP model and compares it to the OSI reference model. Chapter 7 contains a discussion of subnetting, routing, and virtual private networks that use the Internet. Finally, the security issues, including IPSec, are presented in Chapter 16. You are encouraged to review these chapters to gain additional information about the Internet and its related protocols.

Chapter 4

Physical Layer Concepts

In this chapter we present an overview of the first layer of the OSI model, namely, the physical layer. This is the "touch-and-feel" layer. It provides for the physical transmission of data. As part of our presentation we discuss various transmission media, including twisted pair, coaxial, and fiber-optic cables. We also examine various forms of wireless and satellite communications. An outline of the major topics discussed follows:

- Physical Layer Issues (Questions 1–8)
- Analog vs. Digital Communications (Questions 9–23)
- Bandwidth (Questions 24–29)
- Multiplexers and Multiplexing Strategies (Questions 30–35)
- Noise (Questions 36–39)
- Shannon's Limit (Questions 40–47)
- Physical and Electrical Characteristics of Wire (Questions 48–58)
- Transmission Media—UTP, STP, Coaxial, Fiber-Optic (Questions 59–97)
- Wireless Communications (Questions 98–108)
- Satellite Communications (Questions 109–121)

1. What is the physical layer?

The physical layer is the lowest layer (layer 1) of the OSI Reference Model. The OSI model was discussed in Chapter 2.

2. What does the physical layer do?

Before sending data on the network, the physical layer on the local node must process the data stream, translating *frames* received from the data link layer (layer 2) into electrical, optical, or electromagnetic signals representing 0 and 1 values, or bits. A frame is a specially formatted sequence of bits that incorporates both data and control information. (Frames are discussed in more detail in Chapter 5.) The local physical layer is responsible for transmitting these sequences of bits through the network medium to the physical layer of the remote node, where frames are reconstructed and passed to the data link layer there.

3. If you were to use one word to describe the physical layer what would it be?

Wire. Or, if you are from the state of Texas (U.S.A.), it's called "wharr."

4. Wire?

Yup. Actually, it's a little more than just wire, but wire gives you an idea of what we are dealing with when we speak about the physical layer. You see, all aspects related to a transmission medium used for data communications, including both wired and wireless environments, are defined by physical layer protocols and specifications. These include the type of cable and connectors used, the electrical signals associated with each pin and connector—called *pinouts* or *pin assignments*—and the manner in which bit values are converted into physical signals.

5. Can you give me an example?

Sure. In fact, we'll give you two. For the first example, consider an Ethernet or an IEEE 802.3 local area network. (See Chapter 5 for the distinction between Ethernet and IEEE 802.3.) The physical layer of this network (abbreviated PHY in the documentation) defines, among other things, the type of cable permitted (e.g., unshielded twisted pair—UTP, coaxial, or fiber), the connectors we can use (e.g., 8-pin modular, BNC), maximum length of the wire (e.g., 100 meters, 185 meters), and the type and level of termination (e.g., 50 Ω impedance for Ethernet/802.3 coaxial cable and 100 Ω for UTP). A second example of a physical layer specification is the EIA RS-232C standard, which defines the electrical and physical characteristics used in serial communications. RS-232C specifies a 25-pin data bus (DB) connector that serves as an interface between a computer, referred to as the data terminal equipment or DTE, and a peripheral device such as a modem or printer, referred to as the data communications equipment or DCE. A later version of the RS-232C standard is RS-423, which defines a 9-pin DB connector. DB-9 connectors implement some of the signals from DB-25 and are used on IBM-PC or compatible micro-computers as a rear panel space-savings measure. The pinouts for the DB-25 and DB-9 connectors are shown in Figure 4-1.

6. Does the physical layer have anything to do with physics?

Why, yes it does. What gave it away?

7. Because the word "physical" has as its root the word "physic." I think I know where we're going with this, but before we get there let me just say that it's been a while since I studied physics, so please be gentle.

We will. We'll avoid quarks, photons, and the Theory of Relativity. However, you need to know a little bit about one simple, physical concept.

8. What is it?

Harmonic motion—and it has nothing to do with Nostradamus.

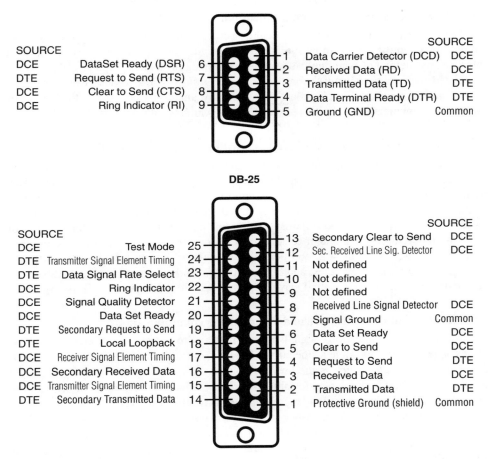

Figure 4-1. Pinouts of connectors used in RS-232-C serial communications. The DB-9 connector (top) is frequently used for the low-speed serial port(s) on personal computers. The DB-25 connector (bottom) is frequently encountered in modems. The numbers correspond to the pins of the connector; the accompanying text describes the signals associated with each pin. The column labeled "Source" refers to the signal source, either the Data Terminal Equipment (DTE) unit (i.e., the computer) or the Data Communications Equipment (DCE) unit (i.e., a peripheral device such as a modem).

9. What's harmonic motion and why do I have to learn about it?

We'll answer the second part of this question first. Don't worry. It's also called *simple harmonic motion* because it is a very simple concept. You need to be familiar with the concept of harmonic motion because it will help explain *analog communication*. Analog communication is used in phones (both landline and cellular), modems, fax machines, cable television, and lots of other devices and network services.

10. Tell me more about analog communication.

The term *analog* refers to any physical device or signal that can continuously vary in strength or quantity, for example, voltage in a circuit. The term *analog communication* refers to any method of communication based on analog principles. Typically, this term is associated with voice transmission rather than data transmission because voice transmission facilities, such as the telephone, were initially analog-based. The "other" type of physical communication is *digital communication*, which we'll talk about later.

11. What does harmonic motion have to do with analog communication?

To answer this question, consider an object attached to a spring that is suspended from a ceiling (Figure 4-2). If you pull on the attached weight and release it, the spring begins oscillating up and down. In a frictionless environment, this up and down motion would continue forever. This idealized motion is called simple harmonic motion, which is the basic model for vibratory or oscillatory motion and can occur in many different types of wave motion. Examples include mechanical oscillators such as mass-spring systems similar to that shown in Figure 4-2, and pendulums; periodic motion found in the earth sciences such as water waves, tides, and climatic cycles; and electromagnetic waves such as alternating electric currents, sound waves, light waves, radio waves, and television waves.

12. OK, but what does this have to do with analog communication?

In analog communications, signals flow across a wire in the form of electromagnetic waves. These waves resemble a sine curve (Figure 4-3) and have the following three characteristics: *amplitude*, which is the level of voltage on a wire (or the intensity of a light beam when dealing with fiber-optic cable); *frequency*, which is the number of oscillations, or cycles, of a wave in a specified length of time; and *phase*, which is the point a wave has advanced within its cycle. A frequency rate of one cycle per second is defined as one Hertz (abbreviated Hz) in honor of Heinrich Rudolf Hertz (1857-1894), a German physicist who in the late 1880s was the first to produce radio waves artificially. Thus, hertz is a measure of frequency in cycles per second. The reciprocal of the frequency is called the *period*, which is the amount of time it take to complete a single cycle, that is, seconds per cycle.

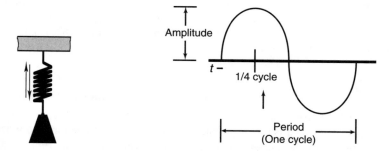

Figures 4-2 (left) and 4-3 (right). In Figure 4-2, an object is attached to a spring that is suspended from a ceiling. When pulled and released, the spring oscillates up and down. This oscillation is called simple harmonic motion. In Figure 4-3, one cycle of a sine curve is shown.

13. Can you bring this down to earth for me?

Sure. Consider the act of speaking over the telephone. If you speak softly or whisper, the amplitude (volume) decreases. If you speak loudly or scream, the amplitude increases. If you speak in a high-pitched voice, the frequency changes to more cycles per second than if you speak in a low-pitched voice, which requires fewer cycles per second. AM/FM radio, television speakers, public address systems, and most important of all, traditional telephones, are all examples of analog devices (although there is a fast-growing trend toward a full-digital telephone system both in business and wireless networks).

14. How does this relate to data communications?

In data communications, data are represented in analog form by varying the voltage of the wave (called amplitude modulation, abbreviated AM), by varying the frequency (called frequency modulation, abbreviated FM), or by varying the phase (called phase modulation or phase shifting) of a wave. Phase modulation is often used for modems. (*Note:* Modems are discussed in Chapter 15.)

15. How does the term "wavelength" relate to this discussion?

Wavelength, as the name implies, is a measure of the length of a wave. It is the distance an electrical or light signal travels in one complete cycle. Radio signals are often described and classified according to their wavelength. For example, "the 40-meter ham band" is an explicit reference to radio waves that are approximately 40 m long. In the RF spectrum (discussed later in this chapter), "short-wave radio" and "microwave radar" are relative references to different wavelengths.

For light signals, which are used in fiber-optic transmissions, wavelength and frequency are inversely related. That is, as one increases, the other decreases. This relationship is expressed using the formula, $\lambda = \dfrac{c}{f}$, where λ is the wavelength in meters, c is the speed of light, 3×10^8 meters per-second, and f is the frequency in Hertz. The concept of wavelength will be elaborated on later in the chapter

16. If analog communication is more often associated with voice transmission, then digital communication must be used for data transmission, right?

Right! Digital communication refers to any type of communication in which data are represented in the form of binary digits. Digital communication is more difficult to implement over airwaves (wireless), but it provides a much more reliable communications environment with much less noise and distortion than an analog connection method.

17. I need more information. Keep going.

OK. In digital communications, signals are called *discrete*. That means that they are binary in nature—off or on, one or zero. What makes a signal discrete is that there is no in-between. This is similar to a light bulb—either it is off or it is on—there is no "sort of on" or "sort of off" (although you could put a dimmer in the circuit, making the light bulb an

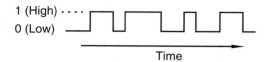

Figure 4-4. Example of a digital signal waveform.

analog device!). Therefore, we can conclude that a digital signal consists of two (and only two) states: electrical current applied, or no current at all. On most systems, if power is applied, it is considered "on" and is usually interpreted as "1" by a computer. If there is no power, then we have an "off" state and this is interpreted as "0." This is called *binary interpretation*, and the "on" and "off" states are interpreted as bits 1 and 0, respectively. Figure 4-4 shows a typical digital waveform as measured over some time interval.

18. So, I create a digital signal by merely applying a current or turning it off? Is it that simple? Does the voltage matter?

Yes, voltage matters, but life in the real world is not that simple. Each type of digital circuit has a particular specification for which a *range of voltages* represents a zero and another represents a one. This is necessary because of real-world factors such as electrical noise, cable resistance, and differences in ground potential between the transmitter and the receiver. We'll get deeper into some of these factors later, but for now, consider an example involving RS-232C. In RS-232C, a zero is represented by any voltage between −5 and −15 volts and a one is represented by any voltage between +5 and +15 volts. Let's say that the transmitter sends a one, for which it uses 12 volts. By the time it gets to the receiver, however, the potential might be reduced to 10 volts because of the electrical resistance of the wire. Nevertheless, the receiver interprets the signal as a one because it falls between +5 and +15 volts. A less technically-oriented example is a game of darts. You get credit for a bulls-eye if your dart hits anywhere within the appropriate circle. If it were required to hit a single point for a bulls-eye, there would be far fewer bulls-eyes. Thus, the "engineers" who designed the game of darts took into account some real-world factors.

19. In your RS-232C example, there is a big "hole" from −5 to +5 volts. Why is this?

For one thing, random electrical signals, called *noise*, can create false signals in this range. Therefore, when engineers design communication circuits, they must take into account the possibility of noise interfering with communications. In the real world of communication signaling, things are not quite as simple as "on" and "off."

20. What happens if the receiver detects, say, +3 volts.

Nothing.

21. Nothing?

Nothing. *Nada, rien, bupkas,* zip, zilch. The receiver "sees" neither a zero nor a one.

22. What happens if the receiver gets more than 15 volts?

This is worse, because both the transmitter and receiver will probably fail completely. At this point, all is lost and ones and zeros don't matter anymore. Such destructively high voltages might be the result of a nearby lightning strike, a component failure at either end, or a high-voltage power line short-circuiting to the communication cable.

23. What else do I need to know about analog vs. digital communications?

For one thing, there is often some confusion about the "speed" or capacity of a communications channel and the terms used to describe it.

24. Such as?

Well, for starters, how about bandwidth?

25. OK. What is bandwidth?

In analog communications, *bandwidth* refers to the total capacity of a communications channel. It is the difference between the highest and lowest frequencies capable of being carried over a channel. The greater the bandwidth, the more signals that can be carried over a given frequency range. For example, typical voice-grade lines transmit frequencies from 300 Hz to 3300 Hz. Thus, the bandwidth is 3300 Hz − 300 Hz = 3000 Hz, or 3 kilohertz (kHz).

In digital communications and networking, bandwidth refers to data rate—the amount of data that can be transferred over a communications medium in a given period. Data rate is measured in bits per second ("bps") and can vary considerably from one type of channel to another. For example, LANs have data rates ranging from 4 million bits per second (referred to as megabits per second and abbreviated as Mbps) to 1,000 Mbps; the bandwidth of dialup connections using modems ranges from 300 bps to 33,600 kilobits per second (33.6 kbps) or 56 kbps; and WANs that use high-speed circuits can range anywhere from 1.5 Mbps to 45 Mbps to 622 Mbps and higher.

26. You say we measure data rate in bits per second. Isn't this the same as baud rate?

No. There is a difference. A *baud* is a unit of signaling speed, named after the French engineer Jean Maurice Emile Baudot (1845-1903). It is another term used to express the capacity of a channel, but it is, indeed, different from bits per second. The speed in baud is equal to the number of times the line condition (i.e., frequency, amplitude, voltage, or phase) changes each second. At low speeds (under 300 bps) data rate (measured in bps) and baud rate are the same because signaling methods are relatively simple. As speed increases, signaling methods become more complex. Baud rate then differs from data rate because several bits are typically encoded per baud. That is, each signal can represent more than one bit of information.

27. I need an example.

OK. Consider a communications channel transmitting at 2400 baud. This means that the signaling rate of the channel is changing 2400 times per second. If each signal is used to represent one bit, then the baud rate is equal to the data rate—the data rate is 2400 bps. However, if each signal represents four bits, then the baud rate remains at 2400, but now the data rate is $4 \times 2400 = 9600$ bps. Thus, the channel's bandwidth is 9600 bps.

28. So you are saying that a baud rate of *x* does not always equal *x* bps.

Right you are! If each signal event represents exactly one bit, then baud rate is equal to data rate. However, since this is rarely the case in data communications, you should not consider baud rate and data rate synonymous. Unless otherwise noted, we will always express bandwidth in terms of bps or bits per second (or as a multiple of bps, namely, kbps, Mbps, Gbps).

29. While we're at it, is there a difference between bandwidth and throughput? I often hear these two terms used interchangeably.

So do we, and there is, indeed, a difference. When applied to data communications, bandwidth represents the theoretical capacity of a communications channel expressed in bits per second. To understand the difference between bandwidth and throughput, let's assume the network we use is a Fast Ethernet LAN. This type of network has a maximum transfer rate of 100 Mbps. (*Note:* We discuss Fast Ethernet in Chapter 8.) Does this mean we can expect all data transfer rates to be at 100 Mbps? No. Extraneous factors such as a node's processing capability, input/output processor speed, operating system overhead, communications software overhead, and amount of traffic on the network at a given time all serve to reduce the actual data rate. Consequently, there is a difference between the maximum theoretical capacity of a communications channel and the actual rate of data transmission realized. This "reality rate" is known as *throughput*. Throughput refers to the amount of data transmitted between two nodes in a given period. It is a function of hardware/software speed, CPU power, overhead, and many other items. Thus, bandwidth is what is theoretically possible in a channel; throughput is what the channel really achieves. Just because a LAN architecture is specified to operate at a certain data rate, it is not valid to assume that this rate will be the actual throughput achieved on any given node or group of nodes.

30. What else do I need to know about what happens at the physical layer?

Have you heard of multiplexing?

31. Does this have anything to do with a mux?

Yes it does. *Mux* is a casual abbreviation standing for *multiplexer*. What do you know about a mux?

32. We have them at work. I think they have something to do with being able to split a single communications channel into multiple channels. Is this right?

Pretty much so. A mux (acronym for multiplexer) is a device that does multiplexing, which is a technique used to place multiple signals on a single communications channel.

Multiplexing partitions a channel into many separate channels, each capable of transmitting its own independent signal. Consequently, many different transmissions are possible using a single medium. (See Figure 4-5.) For example, through multiplexing, a communication medium is divided into separate channels with one channel transmitting data, another transmitting voice, and a third transmitting video. Each of these separate, independent transmissions can occur simultaneously.

33. I seem to recall there are different ways to do multiplexing. For example, something called *time domain multiplexing* comes to mind.

Right you are! Multiplexing can indeed be performed in several ways, including time domain multiplexing (TDM), frequency division multiplexing (FDM), demand access multiplexing (DAM), statistical multiplexing, wavelength division multiplexing (WDM), code access multiple access (CAMA), code demand multiple access (CDMA), inverse multiplexing and other techniques. (In case you haven't yet figured it out, we had alphabet soup for lunch today.)

34. Can you give me a quick overview of the more popular multiplexing methods? I don't think it's necessary to spend a lot of time discussing them, but I do want to have some familiarity with them. So just give me the *Reader's Digest* version, please.

Let's take these methods one at a time:

Frequency Division Multiplexing (FDM). This technique partitions the available transmission frequency range into narrower bands, each of which is a separate channel. The idea behind FDM is to divide the main frequency into appropriate subfrequencies with each subfrequency customized to the bandwidth of data that it must carry. This makes FDM very efficient and cost-effective. An example of FDM is the broadcast method used by television stations. The FCC allocates a range of frequencies called a channel for a station to use and the station subdivides this band into various subchannels. One subchannel carries engineering information for the station's technical staff, a second carries the analog signal for audio reception at the television set, and a third subchannel carries the video signal. What a remote unit can receive depends on the frequency for which the unit has been configured. FDM-based transmissions are parallel in nature. (See Figure 4-6.)

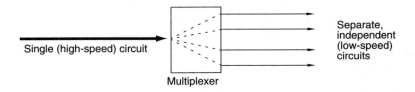

Figure 4-5. Multiplexing entails conversion of a single communications channel into several separate and independent channels. The device that accomplishes this feat is called a multiplexer, or mux, for short.

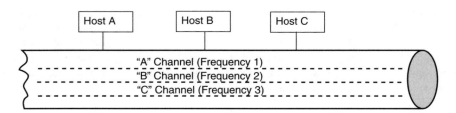

Figure 4-6. In frequency-division multiplexing the frequency of a communications medium is divided into subfrequencies, which are assigned to connected nodes, resulting in parallel transmissions.

Time Division Multiplexing (TDM). Time division multiplexing (TDM) assigns to each node connected to a channel an identification number and a small amount of time (i.e., a time slot) in which to transmit. Unlike FDM-based transmissions, which are parallel in nature, TDM-based transmissions are serially sequenced. Thus, nodes take turns transmitting over the channel, with each time slot permanently assigned to a specific channel. The amount of time a node gets for data transmission is a function of the number of nodes competing for the channel, the order in which nodes are requested for information (called the polling order), and the *clocking interval* of the TDM device.

Demand Access Multiplexing (DAM). In demand access multiplexing, a pool of frequencies is managed by a "traffic cop." The traffic cop assigns pairs of communications frequencies to a requesting station—one pair for transmission, a second pair for reception. This is the "demand" part—you "demand" a pair of frequencies and if available, the traffic cop assigns them to you. The traffic cop then connects the two pairs of frequencies to another set of frequencies. This is the "access" part. When one or both stations are finished communicating, the allocated frequencies are deallocated and returned to the frequency pool, where they are made available for other incoming requests. This is the multiplexing part. DAM is similar to virtual memory allocation on computers. A "pool" of memory exists for all running processes. When a new process is started, memory is allocated from the pool. When the process is completed, the associated memory returns to the pool for use by another process. A major use of DAM exists in cellular communications.

Statistical Multiplexing. This method of multiplexing allocates part of a channel's capacity only to those nodes that require it (i.e., have data to transmit). This strategy permits a greater number of devices to be connected to a channel because not all devices necessarily require a portion of the channel at exactly the same time. A statistical multiplexer "senses" which input channels are active and then dynamically allocates bandwidth to these channels.

Wavelength Division Multiplexing (WDM). Wavelength division multiplexing is used with fiber-optic cables. In fiber-optic technology, electrical signals originating from a sending computer are converted into optical signals using a light source such as an LED or laser. (Fiber-optic issues are discussed later in this chapter.) WDM involves the simultaneous transmission of these light sources over a single fiber-optic channel. The light sources, which are of different wavelengths, are combined by a WDM multiplexer and transmitted over a single line. En route to their destination, the wavelengths are amplified simultaneously by optical amplifiers. When the signals arrive, a WDM demultiplexer separates them and transmits them to their respective destination receivers. We give an illustration of WDM in Figure 4-7. WDM can be beneficial from both cost and performance perspectives. On the cost side, WDM saves money because it increases bandwidth without requiring the installation of additional fiber. The idea of minimizing or completely eliminating new fiber installations is attractive because installing new fiber can be expensive. On the performance side, WDM consolidates data from separate channels onto a single line. WDM also can reduce the number of optical-to-electrical conversions—required by today's fiber-optic networks—by implementing a strictly optical transmission method.

Inverse Multiplexing. Inverse multiplexing is the reverse of multiplexing. Instead of partitioning a single communication medium into several channels, an inverse multiplexer combines several "smaller" channels (i.e., low-speed circuits) into a single high-speed circuit. For example, through inverse multiplexing, two T1 circuits (1.544 Mbps) can be combined to form a 3 Mbps channel. Several Internet service providers use this strategy to offer their customers a larger "pipe" to the Internet. This technique is also sometimes generically called *line aggregation.*

35. That was great. Thanks. May I pause for a minute or two to let it sink in?

You're welcome! Pauses are essential to learning. Go ahead and take a break. We'll be here when you return. At that time we'll talk some more about the physical layer.

36. OK. I'm back. Let's dive right back into those physical layer issues.

Certainly! We promised a while back that we would address the issue of noise. Now is the time.

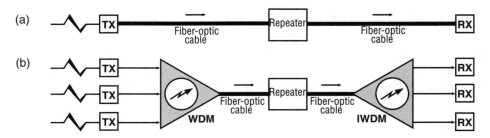

Figure 4-7. In a typical fiber-optic installation (a), a fiber-optic transmitter converts an electronic signal into light, which is sent through the fiber-optic cable to its destination. Repeaters, which are optical amplifiers, regenerate the light signal at appropriate points along the way. With wavelength division multiplexing (b), electronic signals originating from multiple data sources, each operating at different wavelengths, are combined into a wavelength multiplexer (WDM) and output onto a single fiber-optic cable. A demultiplexer (IWDM) is employed at the receiving end to split the signals. (Adapted from Clark, 1997.)

37. Noise? You mean like loud, senseless shouting, or a crying baby in a restaurant?

OK, we'll be precise. We mean *electrical* noise. (You're not that far off, though.) In the context of data communications, noise is any undesirable, extraneous signal in a transmission medium. It occurs in two forms—*ambient noise* and *impulse noise*. Ambient noise, also called *thermal noise*, is always present and is generated primarily by transmission equipment like transmitters, receivers, and repeaters. Ambient noise also can be induced by external sources such as fluorescent light transformers, electrical facilities, heat, and, in fact, the background radiation from the Big Bang. If ambient noise is present, receiving equipment can have problems in distinguishing between incoming signals. Impulse noise consists of intermittent, undesirable signals induced by external sources such as lightning, switching equipment, and heavy electrically operated machinery such as elevator motors and copying machines. Impulse noise increases or decreases a circuit's signal level; this causes the receiving equipment to misinterpret the signal. Whichever the type or source, noise degrades the quality and performance of a communications channel and is one of the most common causes of transmission errors in computer networks. Although some noise is always present, much of it can be avoided through proper cable installation. (See Appendix C for guidelines on installing UTP cable.)

38. That was interesting. Are you going to make noise about anything else?

Yes, there's one more type of noise we'll touch on briefly: *intermodulation noise*. Recall our discussion of frequency division multiplexing and that we can mix multiple frequencies of data transmission on a single transmission medium. Intermodulation noise occurs when two of the frequencies interact to produce a phantom signal at a different frequency, which can be either the sum or the difference of the two original frequencies. For example, let us assume for simplicity that, in a frequency division multiplexing environment, a coaxial cable carries three different signals, at frequencies f_1, f_2, and f_3. Intermodulation noise can occur if f_3 is equal to the sum or difference of f_1 and f_2. Either way, the spurious signal at frequency f_3 can interfere with the transmission of valid data at that frequency.

39. That was a little esoteric, but I'm glad you touched on it. Are we done with noise?

Why, yes. Yes we are. We're going to discuss one subject that is related to noise, though, before we move on to a discussion of transmission media.

40. What noise-related subject might that be?

Shannon's Limit.

41. You caught my interest—I used to have a cat named Shannon. So what's Shannon's Limit?

We like cats, too, but the only relationship between felines and noise involves wailing related to their hunger and sex drives, not networking. Shannon's Limit is a mathematical theorem, named for the mathematician who derived it, Claude Shannon, that describes a model for determining the maximum data rate of a noisy, analog communications channel. (*Note:* A second theorem, Nyquist's Theorem, serves to determine the maximum data rate of a channel for noiseless environments. We will not discuss Nyquist's theorem.) Shannon's Limit is given by the following formula:

$$\text{Maximum Data Rate } (MDR) = H \log_2(1 + \left(\frac{S}{N}\right))$$

- *MDR* is given in bits per second (bps)
- *H* = bandwidth in Hertz (Hz)
- $\left(\frac{S}{N}\right)$ = a measure of the signal-to-noise ratio in decibels (dB)

42. Forget about it. You just lost me.

Hold on now. We think you'll find Shannon's Limit fascinating once we do an example.

43. OK, but before you give me an example, tell me what this signal-to-noise ratio thing is.

The signal-to-noise ratio (abbreviated SNR) is a measure of signal quality expressed in decibels (dB). It is the ratio of signal strength to background noise on a cable. More specifically, SNR is the ratio between the desired signal and the unwanted noise in a communications medium. In plain, late twentieth century English, it's how badly a line sucks.

44. All right. I'm ready for an example.

A good example of an application of Shannon's Limit is modem speeds. A recent standard for modem speeds specifies a data rate of 28,800 bps (28.8 kbps). Some modems are capable of achieving speeds of 33,600 bps (33.6 kbps). Modem speeds, however, peak at 33.6 kbps or 38.4 kbps. The reason for this can be explained by Shannon's Limit.

45. Wait a minute now. What about 56K modems that are supposedly capable of 56,000 bits per second?

Shannon's Limit does not apply to 56K modems. You see, Shannon's Limit is based on analog channels only. The communication channels used for 56K modems include a mix of both digital and analog channels. More specifically, 56K modems require a digital link between an Internet service provider (ISP) and the telephone company; the link between a customer and the provider is analog. We explain this in Chapter 15.

46. So what you are saying is if my ISP does not have a digital link to the telephone company and I maintain my standard analog telephone link in my home, the best connection speed I will ever realize with my modem is 33.6 kbps?

That's correct. However, even with a top speed of 33.6 kbps or 38.4 kbps, many users very rarely achieve this speed. If there is any degradation of the line they are using, the modem cycles down (this is called *link negotiation*) to a lower, more reliable speed. For example, how many times have you actually made a consistent connection at 28.8 kbps or 33.6 kbps? Once again, we discuss this in much greater detail in Chapter 15.

47. Can you give me an example of how to use Shannon's Limit to do a calculation?

Yes. See Box 4-1. You might need to review some college algebra concepts (e.g., logarithmic functions) to fully understand and appreciate this example.

48. Now that I have some understanding of the physical layer, what should we discuss next?

How about discussing cables?

49. Good subject: wire. Let's talk about wire.

OK. We'll begin with a general overview of cable.

50. What did you have in mind?

We thought we would describe some attributes of cable that are common among all network media except, of course, wireless media.

51. OK. What are some common attributes of wire?

All physical media, regardless of their type, share three common elements. First, a *conductor* serves as a medium for the physical signal. This conductor is composed of either copper wire (e.g., twisted-pair and coaxial cable) or glass or plastic fiber (e.g., fiber-optic cable). In the case of copper, the wire can be stranded (composed of several thin wires) or solid (a single, "thick" strand). Stranded wire is usually stronger and more flexible. Furthermore, the thickness of a wire is given in terms of gauge, which represents the conductor's diameter. The lower the gauge, the thicker the wire. Thus, 22-gauge wire is thicker than 24-gauge. Most often, wire gauges are expressed in terms of AWG—American Wire Gauge—which is a classification system for copper wire based on a wire's cross-section diameter. For example, AWG 24 means that the conductor's diameter is 0.51 mm. The smaller the AWG number, the larger the diameter.

Second, there is usually some sort of *insulation* material surrounding the conductor. The insulation serves as a protective "barrier" to the conductor by preventing the signal from "escaping" and preventing electrical interference from "entering."

Box 4-1: Example of Shannon's Limit

Given $10\left[\log_{10}\left(\dfrac{s}{n}\right)\right]$:

- If $\left(\dfrac{s}{n}\right) = 10$, then $10\left[\log_{10}\left(\dfrac{s}{n}\right)\right] = 10[\log_{10}(10)] = 10(1) = 10$. Thus, SNR = 10 dB.

- If $\left(\dfrac{s}{n}\right) = 100$, then $10\left[\log_{10}\left(\dfrac{s}{n}\right)\right] = 10[\log_{10}(100)] = 10(2) = 20$. Thus, SNR = 20 dB.

- If $\left(\dfrac{s}{n}\right) = 1000$, then $10\left[\log_{10}\left(\dfrac{s}{n}\right)\right] = 10[\log_{10}(1000)] = 10(3) = 30$. Thus, SNR = 30 dB.

and so on.

Example: If $H = 3000$ Hz and the signal-to-noise ratio (SNR) is 30 dB, what is the MDR?

Solution: Note from above that 30 dB implies $\left(\dfrac{s}{n}\right) = 1000$. Using Shannon's Limit we have

$$\begin{aligned} MDR &= (H)\left[\log_2\left(1 + \frac{s}{n}\right)\right] \\ &= (3000)[\log_2(1 + 1000)] \\ &= (3000)[\log_2(1001)] \end{aligned}$$

At this stage we must now solve for $\log_2(1001)$. There are several ways in which this can be done. We can use a calculator that is capable of solving logarithms in base 2, we can use natural logarithms, or we can estimate the value. We will demonstrate the last two methods since we do not have a calculator capable of solving log functions in base 2.

Using Natural Logarithms

$$\begin{aligned} \log_2 1001 &= x \\ 2^x &= 1001 \\ \ln 2^x &= \ln 1001 \\ x \ln 2 &= \ln 1001 \\ x &= \frac{\ln 1001}{\ln 2} \\ x &\approx \frac{6.909}{0.6931} \\ x &\approx 9.967 \end{aligned}$$

Substituting 9.967 into the equation:

$MDR = (3000)(9.967) = 29{,}902$ bps

Using Estimation

$$\log_2 1001 = x$$
$$2^x = 1001$$

$2^1 = 2$	$2^6 = 64$
$2^2 = 4$	$2^7 = 128$
$2^3 = 8$	$2^8 = 256$
$2^4 = 16$	$2^9 = 512$
$2^5 = 32$	$2^{10} = 1024$

Note that $\log_2(1001)$ must be between 9 and 10 since the logarithm's argument (1001) is between $2^9 = 512$ and $2^{10} = 1024$. Since it is closer to 10 we estimate it to be 9.9. Substituting 9.9 into the equation:

$MDR = (3000)(9.9) = 29{,}700$ bps

As a result, the maximum data rate of a communications channel with these parameters is approximately 30,000 bps (30 kbps). Note that this is the upper limit and in practice will rarely be achieved on a consistent basis.

Finally, the conductor and insulation are encased in an outer sheath or "jacket." This jacket is composed of any of a number of materials, such as polyvinyl chloride (PVC) for non-plenum cable, or Teflon for plenum cable. Plenum cable is used for cable "runs" through a return air system. The Teflon coating provides a low-flame spread and does not release toxic fumes as quickly as PVC does in the case the cable burns during a fire. Both PVC and Teflon give off nasty toxic gases when burning. Teflon, however, is fire retardant (which is not the same as "fire *resistant*," where fire would not start) and takes much longer to get to a burning point. This decreases the chance of toxic fumes to affect people in a burning structure at the beginning of the fire.

52. You've described physical attributes. What about electrical characteristics?

Good question. The performance of a "wired" network is greatly dependent upon the electrical characteristics of the cable used. Since bits ultimately become physical signals at the physical layer, signal quality is an important consideration when selecting a specific medium. Three very important electrical characteristics directly associated with signal quality are *capacitance, impedance,* and *attenuation.*

53. What is capacitance?

Capacitance is the property of a circuit that permits it to store an electrical charge.

54. How does capacitance relate to signal quality?

The *capacitance* of a cable determines its ability to carry a signal without distortion, which is the "rounding" of a waveform (see Figure 4-8) due to a stored charge between the conductors of the cable. The more distorted a signal becomes, the more likely a receiving node will be unable to distinguish between zeros and ones. High quality cable has low capacitance—the lower the capacitance, the longer the distance a signal can travel before signal distortion becomes unacceptable.

We must make an important point about capacitance and network data cabling. While network cable can have low characteristic capacitance per meter, the overall capacitance of the cable increases as the cable gets longer. Because of noise and other problems in transmission, a maximum cable length of about 100 meters exists for unshielded twisted-pair (UTP) network cable. This is true for even low capacitance, high quality UTP cable, which is used in a great preponderance of LANs. If the UTP cable is replaced with

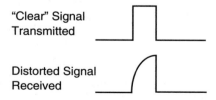

Figure 4-8. Capacitance eventually will distort a transmitted signal. (Adapted from Leeds & Chorey, 1991.)

shielded twisted pair (STP)—which is very popular in token ring networks—there is still a maximum limitation under perfect conditions of about 100 meters. The reason for this limitation, however, is completely different than that for UTP cable. As STP cable gets longer, the capacitance builds up. This results in enough signal degradation to require some sort of signal amplification or re-generation for a signal to travel a greater distance.

55. So that's why there's a 100 meter length restriction on the UTP cable we use for our Ethernet LAN.

That's part of the reason. There are other reasons as well, which we will address in our discussion on Ethernet/802.3 LANs in Chapter 8.

56. What is impedance?

Impedance is a measure of the opposition to the flow of electric current in an alternating current circuit. Measured in ohms (abbreviated by the Greek symbol, omega, Ω), impedance is a function of capacitance, resistance, and inductance. *Impedance mismatches*, caused by mixing cables of different types with different characteristic impedances, can result in signal distortion. Cable manufacturers always list a cable's impedance so you should pay close attention to these measurements. Also, different network hardware types may require different impedance values and may not work with values that are out of the range of performance for the hardware. For instance, most token ring equipment require 150 Ω of impedance. On the other hand, Ethernet/802.3 twisted-pair networks want 85-111 Ω and don't appreciate 150 Ω at all.

57. What is attenuation?

Attenuation is the decrease in signal strength, which occurs as the signal travels through a circuit or along a cable. The longer the cable, the greater the attenuation. Also, the higher the frequency of the signal, the greater the attenuation. Different types of cables are also subject to different amounts of attenuation. For example, in twisted-pair cable, the attenuation rises sharply as the signal frequency increases, whereas with coaxial cable, it rises less sharply as frequency increases. Fiber-optic cable, which is tuned for a specific wavelength, exhibits very low attenuation per unit of distance *at that wavelength*. Attenuation is measured in decibels (dB) of signal loss. When selecting cable, you should choose a type that has a low measure of attenuation for the network speeds and distances involved. Signal quality is affected most by the combination of attenuation and capacitance. (See Figure 4-9.)

58. So these electrical characteristics are common among all types of copper wire?

Yes.

59. What types of cable can you use for networks?

Many different types of cable can be used for networks. Of all the different types, though, you can really classify them into two general categories—copper and fiber-optic. These two categories can then be partitioned into more specific types. For example, copper

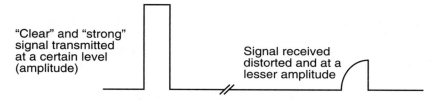

Figure 4-9. The combined effects of capacitance and attenuation result in a signal that is received distorted and weaker than what it was when it was transmitted. This can severely impact the performance of a network. (Adapted from Leeds & Chorey, 1991.)

cable includes unshielded twisted-pair (UTP), shielded twisted-pair (STP), IBM cable, and coaxial cable. Fiber-optic cable includes both glass and plastic fiber. There also is single mode fiber and multimode fiber.

60. What's the most popular type of cable used in networks today?

That would probably be UTP—unshielded twisted-pair. It works with many different types of networks.

61. Why is it called "twisted-pair?"

The name comes from how it is constructed. Twisted-pair cable consists of at least two insulated copper wires that have been twisted together. Data transmission requires four wires (two pairs): one pair to transmit data, and one pair to receive data. UTP used in data networks has a twist in the cable about every six inches (approximately 15 cm).

62. Is this true for both unshielded and shielded twisted-pair cable?

Yes.

63. Do both types also have the same physical attributes we discussed earlier, namely, conductor, insulation material, and outer sheath?

Yes. Both UTP and STP consist of an inner core called a *conductor wire*, which is made of copper (or is comprised of copper and other metals such as tin or silver). The conductor wire is insulated by a *dielectric* material such as polyethylene. In UTP cable, this ensemble is housed within an outer jacket. In STP cable, though, each conductor wire-pair is wrapped in a foil *shield*, and all such cable pairs are encased within a copper or tinned copper braid shield. The foil and braid shields make the wires less susceptible to electrical interference and noise. Figure 4-10 contains a sketch of both types of cables.

64. I've heard the expression "Cat 5" used instead of UTP What does this mean?

Cat 5 is short for "Category 5" as defined by EIA/TIA-568 standard.

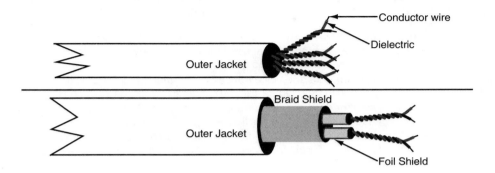

Figure 4-10. Sketch of a UTP cable (top) and an STP cable (bottom). Pairs of wires are twisted around each other. One pair is used to transmit data; a second pair is used to receive data. Note the extra shielding in the STP cable.

65. What's an EIA/TIA-568 standard?

EIA stands for Electronic Industries Association and TIA stands for Telecommunications Industry Association. These organizations jointly developed the EIA/TIA-568 standard, which is a North American standard that is used world-wide. It specifies the type of cable that is permitted for a given speed, the type of connectors that can be used for a given cable, and the network topology that is permitted when installing cables. The standard also defines the performance specifications cables and connectors must meet. In short, EIA/TIA-568 represents a comprehensive standard for premises wiring that addresses network design and performance characteristics for physical media. Within the EIA/TIA-568 standard, there is an A version (568A) and B version (568B) that are used for industrial and nonindustrial networks, respectively. (For more information about TIA, check out its web site at http://www.tiaonline.org.)

66. Are there any other categories other than Category 5?

Yes there are. The EIA/TIA-568 standard for UTP cable classifies the cable into the following five categories: Categories 1, 2, 3, 4, and 5. Several other categories also exist, but they have not been standardized by EIA/TIA. They include Enhanced Category 5, Category 6, Category 7, Category 6/Class E, and Category 7/Class F. There's also a category for STP. Table 4-1 contains a summary of these categories.

67. What's the most popular category and why?

Of the various UTP cable types, Categories 3 and 5 receive the most attention in LAN circles today. However, with higher-speed LANs such as 100 Mbps and 1 Gbps Ethernet/802.3 becoming more commonplace, nonstandard Enhanced Cat 5, Cat 6 and Cat 7 are

Table 4-1. Descriptions of Twisted Pair Cable Categories

Category	Description
Category 1*	Used for voice transmission; not suitable for data transmission
Category 2*	Low performance cable; used for voice and low-speed data transmission; has capacity of up to 4 Mbps
Category 3*	Used for data and voice transmission; rated at 10 MHz; voice-grade; can be used for Ethernet, Fast Ethernet, and Token Ring
Category 4*	Used for data and voice transmission; rated at 20 MHz; can be used for Ethernet, Fast Ethernet, and Token Ring
Category 5*	Used for data and voice transmission; rated at 100 MHz; suitable for Ethernet, Fast Ethernet, Gigabit Ethernet, Token Ring, and 155 Mbps ATM
Enhanced Category 5	Same as Cat 5 but manufacturing process is refined; higher grade cable than Cat 5; rated at 200 MHz; suitable for Ethernet, Fast Ethernet, Gigabit Ethernet, Token Ring, and 155 Mbps ATM (not yet formalized as of this writing)
Category 6	Rated at 200 MHz; suitable for Ethernet, Fast Ethernet, Gigabit Ethernet, Token Ring, and 155 Mbps ATM (not yet formalized as of this writing)
Category 6 (Class E)	Similar to Category 6 but is a proposed international standard to be included in ISO/IEC 11801
Category 6 (STP)	Shielded twisted pair cable; rated at 600 MHz; used for data transmission; suitable for Ethernet, Fast Ethernet, Gigabit Ethernet, Token Ring, and 155 Mbps ATM
Category 7	Rated at 600 MHz; suitable for Ethernet, Fast Ethernet, Gigabit Ethernet, Token Ring, and 155 Mbps ATM (not yet formalized as of this writing)
Category 7 (Class F)	Similar to Category 7 but is a proposed international standard to be included in ISO/IEC 11801

* EIA/TIA-568 Standard

receiving considerable attention. Category 3 is popular because it is the most common wire used for voice transmission in telephone systems. Furthermore, recent IEEE LAN protocols include a specification for Category 3 cable as a LAN medium for 100 Mbps networking. By using its existing cabling plant for local area networking, an organization does not have to modify its wiring infrastructure, thus saving a considerable amount of money. Category 5 and the other higher category copper UTP cable are popular because they are "data-grade" (not voice-grade, as is Category 3 cable). Category 5 is quite plentiful and has emerged as the cable of choice for 100 Mbps LANs. Organizations retrofitting their wiring infrastructure, or those engaged in new installations, are typically installing either Category 5 or Enhanced Category 5 cable. Data grade cable is usable for voice or data. Voice-grade cable is usable for voice and for some types of data connections, depending on the transmission speed and technique used.

68. Sounds good. So there's no reason why I shouldn't use UTP for all my network cabling, right?

Although UTP cable is a popular LAN medium, at the higher frequencies required by higher-speed networks, these cables pose problems in data transmission. Two major factors are attenuation, which we discussed earlier, and crosstalk.

69. I recall the discussion of attenuation. Attenuation occurs when the strength of a signal degrades as it travels along the cable. What's *crosstalk*?

Crosstalk is electrical interference—it's another example of noise, which we discussed earlier in the chapter. Crosstalk occurs when energy radiated from one wire-pair "spills over" into another pair. In one type of crosstalk, called *near-end crosstalk* (abbreviated NEXT), a signal on the transmit pair is so strong that it radiates to the receive pair. A direct consequence of this spilled-over radiation is that the receiving device cannot decipher the real signal. The combined effects of distortion and crosstalk result in an irregular variation in the shape or timing of a signal. This irregular variation is called *jitter* (kind of like a nervous person). Jitter is primarily caused by mixing unshielded and shielded cable.

70. What causes crosstalk?

Several factors, including the closeness of the wire pairs, the quality of the wire, and the number of twists per feet, cause crosstalk. Twisting wire pairs reduces crosstalk between a specific signaling pair. NEXT increases significantly for the first 60 feet (approximately 18 m). Higher quality cable (read: more expensive) contains higher quality wire compositions, better insulation, and improved twist per foot ratios between cable pairs, all of which will reduce NEXT.

71. I can understand how UTP cable is conducive to crosstalk, but what about STP cable? Is it also susceptible to crosstalk?

In contrast to UTP, STP cable can dramatically reduce the hazards of crosstalk and noise because individual wire pairs are shielded. STP is still susceptible to the same kinds of interference that can wreak havoc over UTP, however. The difference is that STP can withstand more noise abuse than UTP and therefore can provide a more reliable transmission medium. STP cable, however, typically has a much higher impedance, which can cause signal reflections on transmission systems which require a lower impedance cable—and that means data errors.

72. In your list of different cable types you mentioned IBM cable. What is this?

IBM has its own classification of cable—the IBM Cable System (ICS)—which specifies nine types of cable. Of the nine "types" defined, specifications are available for only seven; types 4 and 7 are not defined. Table 4-2 contains a summary of ICS. Be very careful not to confuse ICS cable types with the Categories of cable specified by EIA/TIA-568. A "type" is a grouping of categories and fiber-optic cables in a bundle based upon which "type" is being selected. A "category" is an EIA specification for a cable's construction.

Table 4-2. IBM Cable System

Type	Description
Type 1	2-pair STP, 22-gauge solid wire; used for Token Ring networks.
Type 2	Contains UTP and STP; 4-pair UTP, 22-gauge solid wire used for voice.
Type 3	2-pair UTP, 22-gauge solid wire used for data; 2-, 3-, or 4-pair UTP cable with 22- or 24-gauge solid wire; pairs must have a minimum of 2 twists/foot; voice-grade only.
Type 4	Not defined.
Type 5	Fiber-optic; 2 glass fiber cores at 100/140 micron; 62.5/125 micron fiber also allowed and is recommended by IBM; used as main ring of a Token Ring network.
Type 6	2-pair STP, 26-gauge stranded wire; used mostly as a patch cable to connect a node to a network.
Type 7	Not defined.
Type 8	2-pair STP, 26-gauge flat solid wire; designed for under-carpet installations.
Type 9	2-pair STP, 26-gauge solid or stranded wire; contains a plenum outer jacket; used for between-floor runs.

73. Why does IBM have its own classification?

The twisted-pair IBM cable is similar to non-IBM twisted-pair cable with one exception—the IBM version has more stringent specifications. This is why IBM adopted its own classification; it wanted to make certain that cable used in proprietary IBM environments satisfied IBM's high standards. IBM is not the only company to develop its own standards. Lucent Technologies (which used to be a major component of AT&T) and Anixter both have their own versions of cable bundles and specifications for installation.

74. What is the alternative to twisted-pair cable?

There are two alternatives: coaxial cable (or simply, coax), and fiber-optic cable.

75. Start with coax. How different is it from twisted-pair in terms of its construction?

Coax, pronounced CO-axe, consists of a single-wire conductor, surrounded by a dielectric material and two types of shielding, a foil shield and a braided shield, arranged concentrically and encased in a PVC or Teflon outer jacket. (See Figure 4-11.) This design heavily resists interference, and has a high bandwidth. It is not totally impervious to noise, but it offers much more protection against the hazards that afflict UTP. The internal single-wire conductor can be stranded or solid; the former is preferred for hostile environments.

76. I have heard the terms "thin" and "thick" used when describing coax." What do these terms mean?

Technically, coaxial cables exist in many, many cross-sectional diameters, ranging from several millimeters to several centimeters. In computer networking, coax is described

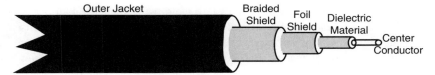

Figure 4-11. Sketch of a coaxial cable typical of the types used in computer networks. Two layers of shielding provide protection against external noise and interference. The outer jacket protects the cable from the elements and may either be polyvinyl chloride (PVC) or Teflon; the latter is appropriate for cable runs in air plenums. (Adapted from Leeds & Chorey, 1991.)

as either thick or thin. Thick coax is used as the medium for "thick Ethernet," which is known as IEEE 802.3 10BASE5. Depending on the manufacturer, the cable's outer diameter ranges from 0.375-inch to 0.405-inch (0.96 cm to 1.04 cm). Thick coax resembles a garden hose and is known as "Etherhose" in slang terms in the industry. It has a designation of RG-8 with 50 Ω impedance. This medium is expensive and outdated; networks based on it today are usually inherited, not installed. Thin coax is used as the medium for "thin Ethernet," which is known as IEEE 802.3 10BASE2. Its outer diameter ranges from 0.175-inch to 0.195-inch (0.448 cm to 0.5 cm). Thin coax is designated RG-58 and it, too has 50 Ω impedance.

In analog coaxial networks, such as cable television networks in a residential community, cable such as RG-9 may be used which typically has a greater impedance factor (62 Ω to 76 Ω) and differing electrical characteristics from those of RG-8. Similarly, RG-59 with an impedance of 75 Ω, is used for home TV cable, but it looks almost the same as RG-58. It is easy to become confused, because the cables within each genre look practically the same. In fact, use of the wrong type of cable is one of the most frequent causes of insidious network failure. Therefore, because not all coaxial cables are electrically the same, you must be careful to select the right one for the types of network equipment being considered for use.

77. I'm still a bit confused. Can you go over this again for me?

OK, no problem. We'll go over it again, because the distinction is very important. Although the cable used for cable TV outwardly resembles thin or thick coax, they are not the same electrically. Thin cable used for cable television is designated RG-59 and has 75 Ω impedance. This is quite different from thin network coax, which has a 50 Ω impedance. As discussed earlier, impedance mismatches—caused by mixing cables with different impedances—can result in signal distortion.

78. Besides impedance differences, are these two coax cables functionally equivalent?

Not really. Coaxial cable can function in two different ways—baseband and broadband. Baseband uses the entire bandwidth of the coaxial cable to carry a single signal, whereas broadband shares the bandwidth of the coaxial cable among multiple signals. Baseband is primarily used in LANs; broadband is primarily used in cable TV applications and high-performance, shared telephone network systems. Comparing the two, baseband is relatively simple and inexpensive to install, requires inexpensive interfaces, and is ideally suited for digital transmission. Broadband equipment is much more expensive, is based on analog signaling, requires expensive amplifiers to strengthen its signal, and personnel to maintain it. Broadband transmission can achieve higher bandwidth than baseband transmission, however.

79. So, I guess there aren't any more types of copper cable, right?

We'll mention one more type of copper cable for completeness, because it exists in some computer networks, albeit proprietary ones that are a vestige of the mainframe days. It's called *twinaxial* cable (twinax, for short). It is much like coaxial cable except that there are *two* inner conductors instead of one. Because it is not used in the networks we discuss in this book, we'll stop right here.

80. OK. What about fiber-optic cable? What can you tell me about it?

Fiber-optic cable is used in LANs as an alternative to copper cable. It carries data signals in the form of modulated light beams. The electrical signals from the sending computer are converted into optical signals by a light source—a light-emitting diode (LED) or a laser. With an LED source, the presence of light represents a 1, and the absence of light (i.e., no light pulse) represents a 0; with the laser source, which emits a continuous low level of light, a 0 is represented by the low level and a 1 is represented by a high intensity pulse. This modulation technique is called *intensity modulation*. The light pulses enter one end of the fiber, travel through the fiber, and exit at the other end of the fiber. The received light pulse is then converted back to electrical signals via a photo detector, which is a tiny solar cell.

81. What does fiber-optic cable look like physically?

Fiber-optic cable consists of a glass fiber covered by a plastic buffer coating and surrounded by Kevlar fibers. The Kevlar fibers give the cable its strength. It is the same material used to make bulletproof vests and combat helmets. The Kevlar fibers are surrounded by a protective outer sheath. (See Figure 4-12.) Notice once again the three primary physical attributes of cable: conductor, insulation, and outer sheath.

82. Whenever my colleagues talk about fiber, they inevitably use numbers like 62.5 and 125. What do these numbers mean?

The numbers refer to the size of the glass fiber, which consists of two parts: An inner glass cylindrical *core* and an outer concentric glass *cladding* that has different optical characteristics than the core. The core diameter and overall outside diameter are measured in microns (a micron is one micrometer, which is one millionth of a meter) and abbreviated by the symbol μm. A standard size is 62.5/125 μm. The 62.5 means 62.5 μm and specifies to the diameter of the inner glass core; the 125 means 125 μm and specifies the diameter of the outer concentric glass cladding. In Europe, 80/100 μm fiber is common.

Figure 4-12. Sketch of a fiber-optic cable. (Adapted from Codenoll Technology Corporation, 1993.)

83. What's the purpose of having an inner glass core and an outer glass cladding?

These are the key elements of fiber-optic cable. The outer cladding of the glass is reflective; the inner core of the glass is transparent. Light goes through the transparent core, but remains in the core by bouncing off the reflective cladding, which is like a cylindrical mirror that is around the core. Thus, light stays in the fiber core as if it were a "light pipe" the same way water stays in the hollow core of a metal clad pipe.

84. I would think that with light bouncing all around inside the cable you would lose some of it at the other end of the cable?

There obviously will be some loss, but not all fiber-optic cable permits light to bounce around.

85. Are you saying there are different types of optical fiber?

Yes.

86. What are they?

The two general types are known as *multimode* and *single mode* fiber-optic cable.

87. What is the difference between them?

The difference between single and multimode fiber is based on the diameter of the core and the manner in which light rays travel through the medium.

88. Start with multimode fiber. What is its core diameter and how does light travel through it?

In multimode fiber, the core diameter ranges from 50 μm to 100 μm (i.e., from about 1/500th of an inch to about 1/250th of an inch). Also, in multimode fiber, different rays of light bounce along the fiber at different angles as they travel through the core (see Figure 4-13). Therefore, the light rays actually travel different total distances as they go from one end of a long fiber-optic cable to the other end. Since some light rays travel longer distances and some travel shorter distances, while the speed of light is a constant; therefore, some of the rays will arrive at the other end of the cable later than others. A consequence of this is that a pulse of light that enters one end of the cable might exit the other end with a little more spread (or dispersion) since some of the light rays get to the other end sooner

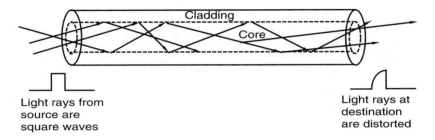

Figure 4-13. In multimode fiber, the distance light rays travel through a cable varies. Some rays travel longer distances from sending and receiving nodes; others travel shorter distances. The cladding layer reflects any stray light waves, causing signal distortion at the receiving end. (Adapted from Codenoll Technology Corporation, 1993.)

while others get there later. Thus, there is some amount of signal distortion at the receiving end of a transmission.

89. How does single mode fiber differ from multimode fiber?

In single mode fiber, the core diameter is 7 μm to 9 μm, which is about one 3000th of an inch. Therefore, it is considerably thinner. When the diameter of the core is reduced to the order of a wavelength, the light cannot bounce off the walls of the core, allowing only a single ray of light, called the *axial ray*, to pass. (Single mode implies a single-ray on a given frequency of light.) In single mode systems, a light wave entering the fiber exits with very little distortion, even at very long distances and high data rates. (See Figure 4-14.) In advanced systems (like synchronous optical network, or SONET, which is discussed in Chapter 7), single mode fiber transmission systems may allow multiple light sources in different light spectrums to interoperate over the same fiber (very similar in concept to multiple channels of TV on a cable system in a neighborhood). In this manner, the same fiber can increase its carrying capacity by changing out the electronics on both ends of a fiber link as additional speed is required through the fiber medium.

90. What about applications? When is one favored over another?

In a typical building or campus network, you usually do not have to worry about single mode vs. multimode. Either can be used for almost any application. However, if you are connecting cities across a country (such as telephone and cable companies are currently doing), then single mode fiber is used for these long distances. If either will do, it boils down to cost. Multimode fiber cable is much cheaper than single mode fiber cable.

91. Earlier you mentioned that the outer sheath of fiber-optic cable is made of Kevlar. Could you expand on this please?

Sure. The outer sheath (or *jacket*) keeps the fiber safe and must meet any local electrical and cabling codes. Typically, fiber is enclosed in a fiber jacket called a *buffer* that is

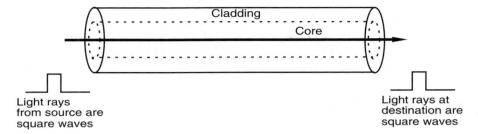

Figure 4-14. In single mode fiber, all light rays travel the same distance from sending to receiving node. A direct consequence of this is no signal distortion at the receiving end, which results in higher bandwidth than multimode fiber, and lower attenuation per kilometer than multimode fiber. Single mode fiber is the ultimate medium for long distance connectivity. (Adapted from Codenoll Technology Corporation, 1993.)

used to separate the fiber itself from any external contact and to protect the fiber from damage. Buffers range from standard dielectric, foam, or, in the case of fibers that may be submerged in water or other liquids, gel-packed fiber. In such environments, gel-pack is useful, as when water invades a cable it can expand or contract (based upon pressure and temperature) and damage the fiber(s). *Tight buffered* cables allow maximum protection for the fiber; *loose buffered* cables are useful in locations where the fiber (or *tube*) around the fiber will expand and contract (usually outdoors). A loose buffer (tube) around the fiber allows the buffer to expand and contract independently of the fiber itself.

Cables are jacketed with a variety of materials ranging from aluminum and Kevlar, to PVC. Which jacket is used depends upon local fire codes and electrical codes as well as where the cable is to be placed in the structure. As mentioned earlier, some materials such as PVC give off noxious fumes when burned and are therefore not allowed in areas where there is a return air plenum. Each jacket type has a variety of cable "stiffeners" inserted between the fibers to give the cable some rigidity and to afford the cable some strength when pulled or suspended. How many stiffeners and the type of stiffeners used (for example, aluminum rods inserted in the jacket) vary from vendor to vendor.

92. How durable are the fibers?

Fibers, after a time, can develop micro-fractures (cracks) or strain fractures in suspended fibers. Fiber that has been physically pulled may have stress fractures. Many other nasty things can happen to perfectly good fiber. Glass fiber has very high tensile strength. The problem is that if a crack develops on the surface of the fiber it may cause the fiber, eventually, to break or will cause optical dispersion problems in the meantime. This structural problem is similar to that of a pane of glass. Glass is fairly strong, but when scribed, the glass is easily broken. Further, when the pane is scribed and placed under strain, the scribed line will lengthen and weaken the pane, eventually causing breakage. Fiber cable can succumb to this problem.

Another problem is *bend radius*. While fiber is much more flexible than copper cable and can be bent in much smaller radii than equivalent copper, microbends may appear in fiber that has been bent too tightly or "kinked." Microbends can cause light path disruption and increase the loss of the cable. Areas subject to chemical exposure, radical temperature changes, nuclear radiation, and other disruptive effects require special consideration in cable jacketing and type of fiber used. Check with the local installation specialist to find out which fiber type is best for your environment.

93. What advantages does fiber-optic cable have over copper cable?

Fiber-optic cable is *the* ideal network medium when cable is involved. It is immune to electromagnetic interference (EMI) and other types of externally induced noise, including lightning. It is unaffected by most physical factors such as vibration. Its size is smaller and its weight lighter than copper. It has much lower attenuation per unit of length than copper. It can support very high bandwidth. With copper cable, we speak of bandwidth on the order of Mbps or Gbps, with Gigabit Ethernet. With fiber-optic cable, we can speak of bandwidth in terms of Mbps, Gbps, terabits per-second (Tbps), and beyond. In short, fiber is the most effective medium available in terms of bandwidth and reliability.

94. So, given all that good stuff, why do we even bother with copper?

First of all, glass fiber (the most common type of fiber) is more expensive than copper. Second, the signal strength of fiber degrades when there is any light loss. Third, if used as the medium for a LAN, it is limited to either a point-to-point or star configuration.

95. Earlier you mentioned plastic fiber. What is this?

Plastic fiber is an alternative to glass fiber. Constructed of plastic rather than glass, plastic fiber is more flexible than glass fiber. It also can be used in areas where it might be subjected to pressure that would crush a glass fiber. For example, if an office chair rolls over plastic fiber, the fiber springs back to its originally cast shape; glass fiber, on the other hand, breaks and hence, must be cut and spliced. Plastic fiber, although available today, is not yet as popular as glass fiber. There are several reasons, including vendor availability, vendor expertise, manufacturing-related problems, and a very young set of standards for plastic fiber (it is known in IEEE circles as GRINPOF-graded index plastic optical fiber).

Plastic fiber is also very easy to terminate and install. Glass fiber requires cutting and painstakingly careful polishing to ensure that signal loss is minimal at a splice or connection point. Plastic fiber is cut with a knife and heated in a special hand-held device that looks like a hair dryer. Through heat, the fiber is terminated and automatically polished, and is available for use about 60 seconds later. Over time, plastic fiber will become the medium of choice for high-speed to-the-desktop connections due to its bandwidth, ease of installation, relative cheapness, and flexibility. At this writing, however, it is still pretty new in the industry and will require time to become popular.

96. Is there anything else I should know about fiber?

Yes. One more thing. If you are planning a fiber optic installation today, then you should keep in mind the following: multimode, graded-index, dual window fiber with a median frequency of 1300 nanometers.

97. What does all this mean?

We already explained the multimode part. *Graded-index* refers to a specific method in which light pulses are guided along the cable from source to destination. If you look at Figure 4-13, you will note that the light pulses are reflected off the cladding—this is what guides them from source to destination. This is an example of multimode *step-index*. In multimode graded-index, variations in the density of the core medium change its *index of refraction* such that light is refracted (i.e., bends) toward the center of the fiber. So instead of showing light as a "V" and inverted "V" pattern as shown in Figure 4-13, we have more of a "rounded" pattern ⁀⁀⁀⁀. The last part, *dual window, 1300 nm*, refers to the fiber's ability to operate at more than one frequency. Specifically, dual window 1300 nm means that data can be transmitted at a wavelength of 1300 nanometers (a nanometer, abbreviated nm, is 1/1,000,000,000 of a meter) with a corresponding frequency of 625 Mbps, one standard frequency step higher at 1550 nm (corresponding frequency of 2.4 Gbps), or one standard frequency step lower at 850 nm (155 Mbps). This is important if you want to use fiber for existing networks such as Ethernet/802.3 (which is perfectly happy with 850 nm) and later upgrade to ATM (which requires 1300 nm and 1550 nm for higher speed connections).

98. OK. We've covered twisted-pair, coaxial, and fiber-optic cable. These are "wired" or cable-based media. What about wireless communication?

In wireless communication, signals travel through the atmosphere instead of through a physical cable.

99. Through the atmosphere? What about satellite broadcasts? There is no atmosphere in space.

Oops, you got us. You're right, reminding us of that old joke about someone giving a review of a restaurant on the moon: Great view but no atmosphere. We stand corrected. Let's substitute *atmosphere* with *space*. So, in wireless communication, signals travel through space.

100. What types of wireless communications are there?

There are two general types of wireless communication: *radio transmission* and *infrared transmission*.

101. What's radio transmission?

Radio transmission refers to any wireless technique that uses radio frequencies (RF) to transmit information. RF transmissions are very popular today for wireless data services. RF frequencies typically used for data communications are in the 800 MHz to 900 MHz range of the electromagnetic spectrum. (See Figure 4-15.) In the United States, the Federal Communications Commission (FCC) has approved additional frequencies for wireless data services to operate in the 1.85 GHz to 2.20 GHz range. This slice of the RF

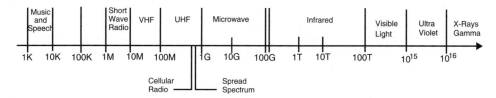

Figure 4-15. The electromagnetic spectrum (in Hz). Higher frequencies support greater bandwidth. (Adapted from Breidenbach, 1990.)

spectrum is used for, among others, pagers, Personal Digital Assistants (PDAs), laptops with PC cards (formerly known as PCMCIA cards), and cellular telephones. In a data communications network, signals from laptop wireless machines are transmitted via built-in antennas to the nearest wireless access point, which serves as a wireless repeater. These access points are connected to a backbone cable system. (See Figure 4-16.) Radio waves typically are used to enhance existing cable systems rather than replace them. They are still susceptible to electromagnetic interference (EMI), however, and cannot penetrate interior drywalls or concrete bearing walls, particularly walls in buildings with steel frameworks, unless at a high enough frequency, which shortens range of effective signal reach.

102. How does microwave communication fit into the wireless arena?

Microwave is another RF transmission method. It uses high frequency waves and operates at a higher frequency in the electromagnetic spectrum. (See Figure 4-15.) The microwave spectrum encompasses frequencies between 2 and 40 GHz. Access to these frequencies is strictly controlled by the FCC in the United States; therefore, users of microwave transmitters must be licensed. The FCC also monitors these frequencies for compliance.

Microwave transmissions are considered a *line-of-sight* medium. Since microwave signals travel in a straight line, the transmitter and receiver must be in each other's line-of-sight. If not, because of their very short wavelength, microwave signals degrade once they encounter an obstruction. Even water droplets in the atmosphere attenuate microwave signals. Consequently, it is necessary to "spec out" the environment to ensure that a microwave transmitter and receiver will have a clear line of sight, sufficient power to offset attenuation, and a small enough distance between stations before installing them. A microwave medium uses parabolic antennas mounted on towers up to 30 miles apart. Because of the impact of the curvature of the earth on the line of sight, the higher the tower, the greater the range. (Sharpen your pencil and try to calculate how tall the towers would have to be to transmit a line-of-sight signal from, for example, Miami to Lisbon, a distance of about 6700 km.)

103. What kind of data rates are microwave transmissions capable of?

Rates typically range up to 45 Mbps.

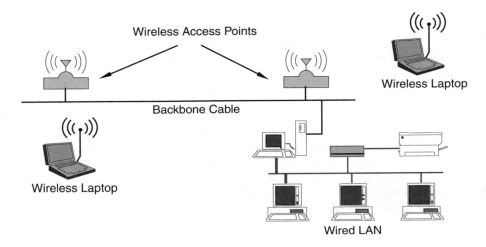

Figure 4-16. One example of a hybrid wireless environment. The "wireless access points" are directly connected to a backbone cable and serve as wireless repeaters for the wireless laptop computers. Completely wireless LANs also are possible. (Adapted from Karvé, 1997a.)

104. What are the advantages and disadvantages of microwave communication?

Line-of-sight media such as microwave are less expensive to install than cable for moderate distances in most situations. Microwave also offers a relatively high data rate (for a wireless medium). It also requires little or no maintenance, is fairly easy to implement, and has no recurring monthly or yearly costs as is the case with leased circuits. On the other hand, line-of-sight transmissions are subject to environmental and atmospheric conditions (rain, fog, high humidity), as well as electromagnetic interference from many sources including solar flares and sunspots. Furthermore, if units are placed too close to each other, overloading and signal interference can result. Because of these environmental and atmospheric drawbacks, you should not rely upon microwave communication completely for mission critical operations. However, if an application can endure an occasional failure, then such media are acceptable.

105. Looking at Figure 4-15, I was wondering if you could give me some of the more common frequencies and their applications?

OK. Let's see. Cellular communications generally operate in the 824-849 MHz range and the 869-894 MHz range; cordless phones and unlicensed wireless LANs (WLANs) operate in the 902-928 MHz range; pagers and beepers operate in the 931-932 MHz range; and general, unlicensed commercial use operates in the 2.4-2.5 GHz range or 5.8-5.9 GHz range. Frequencies in the 902-928 MHz range are quite popular for data communications equipment. The 902-928 MHz band is also known as the Industrial, Scientific, Medical (ISM) band, and it is not regulated by the FCC in the United States. The airwaves at these frequencies, however, are crowded. Higher frequencies in the GHz range are less crowded, but access is controlled by the FCC. If licensing is to be avoided, then one must accept the attendant consequence, namely low power, which cannot penetrate obstructions such as walls. This greatly reduces the range of a wireless network.

106. While we're at it, could you also try to explain "spread spectrum" to me? I bought my Mom a cordless phone that said it was "spread spectrum," which I told her made it better, even though I didn't understand the technology.

Did she ask you if it would make you call her more often? Go ahead—take a break and call her. She'll appreciate it and we'll still be here when you get back.

Spread spectrum is a radio technology that has been around since World War II. It refers to a security technique and not a specific frequency, although it typically is employed in devices that operate within the 902-928 MHz range. Spread spectrum transmission camouflages data by mixing signals with a pseudonoise (PN) pattern and transmitting the real signal with the PN pattern. The transmission signal is spread over a range of the frequencies in radio spectrum.

107. What about infrared technology? I noticed that my laptop computer has an infrared port.

Infrared (IR) transmission is another line-of-sight medium. It uses electromagnetic radiation of wavelengths between radio waves and visible light, operating between 100 GHz and 100 THz (Terahertz). IR is generally restricted to LANs within or between buildings. IR transmission can occur in one of two ways: directed and diffused. Directed IR requires an unobstructed line-of-sight connection between transmitter and receiver. It is basically a "point and beam" medium. In a diffused IR environment, a transmitter "floods" a specific area with a strong infrared signal. The light emitted from the transmitter is spread over a wide angle. The IR signal is transmitted by reflecting off of ceilings, walls, and other surfaces. This is how a TV remote control device works. Thus, diffused IR can be thought of as a broadcast medium, whereas directed IR is point-to-point. Note that as a line-of-sight medium, IR is susceptible to some of the same kinds of problems as microwave, although it is less susceptible to electromagnetic interference than microwave.

108. OK, this is fine, but I have heard of something called "lightwave wireless." What is that?

In countries without a wire-based network infrastructure, it is much easier to implement a wireless connection topology than a wire-based topology. *Lightwave* connectivity refers to the use of line-of-sight laser-based connection facilities that allow long-distance light-based wireless networking without the need to install cable. Through the use of lightwave, a highly sophisticated transmission network is installed much more quickly than running fiber and yet provides a high bandwidth solution for the installer. Lightwave is an ideal solution for many African countries and even for China, where cable infrastructure is almost nonexistent.

109. Where does satellite communication fit into this?

Satellite communications are based on RF transmissions. Satellite communication systems consist of ground-based (also called terrestrial) stations made up of a parabolic antenna (transmitter/receiver) and orbiting transponders. The transponder receives a microwave signal from the ground unit (this transmission is called an *uplink*), amplifies it, and then transmits it back to Earth (the return signal is called a *downlink*). The higher the altitude of a transponder, the longer it takes to traverse its orbit around the earth. An object located approximately 22,000 miles (36,000 kilometers) above the equator is said to be in a *geosynchronous* orbit or a *geostationary Earth orbit* (*GEO*). A satellite placed at this altitude (called a GEO satellite) traverses its orbit at approximately the same rate as the Earth rotates. Thus, the satellite appears stationary with respect to the Earth's rotation. (See Figure 4-17.) (*Note:* A geostationary earth orbit is also known as the *Clarke orbit*, named after author Arthur C. Clarke.)

110. Doesn't it take time for a signal to travel 22,000 miles up and 22,000 miles down?

Yes it does. Although signals travel at the speed of light, GEO satellite systems have high latency. Consider, for example, a typical satellite transmission involving two remote nodes. The sending node transmits a message to the satellite (sender-satellite uplink), the satellite transmits this message to the destination node (satellite-destination downlink), the destination node sends an acknowledgment to the satellite (destination-satellite uplink), and the satellite transmits the acknowledgment to the sender (satellite-sender downlink). The total distance involved in this transmission is four times 22,000 miles or 88,000 miles. Dividing by the speed of light (186,000 miles per second), this transmission incurs a total *propagation delay* of nearly one-half second (470 milliseconds). GEO satellites can incur propagation delay anywhere from 274 milliseconds to as much as 1,050 milliseconds. If you happen to have a home-based satellite system and cable TV, with each system connected to a different television, you probably know what we mean by propagation delay. If

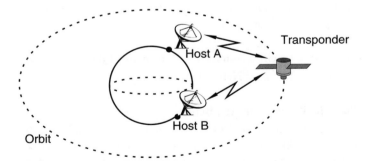

Figure 4-17. Illustration of a satellite communication system. The transponder, a type of repeater, listens to some part of the spectrum. When it hears an incoming signal, it amplifies the signal and then rebroadcasts it at a different frequency. The downward signals can cover a large or narrow area.

both televisions are set to receive the same program, the cable TV will receive its broadcast slightly ahead of the satellite-based TV. A direct consequence of this latency is that the longer it is, the less bandwidth the system can support. In contrast, microwave transmissions have a 3 ms/km delay, and coax has a 5 ms/km delay.

111. How many satellites can be placed in a GEO orbit?

Not many. Satellites can operate at different frequencies. To prevent frequency interference, satellites cannot be placed any closer than four degrees apart at the same altitude. A quick calculation reveals that only 90 satellites can be placed at the same altitude. A constellation of only eight, however, is needed to provide worldwide coverage.

112. Besides propagation delay and the limited number of GEO satellites, what other disadvantages of satellite communications are there?

First, satellite communications are expensive. It costs a lot of money to build and then deliver a satellite to its correct orbit. For example, you would probably not want to contract with NASA to launch a satellite into geosynchronous orbit to network two geographically dispersed sites. Well, you might want to, but your chief financial officer or budget manager might blow a gasket. Second, satellites have a limited operating life, and required maintenance or service can get very expensive. Again, please check with your boss before launching one. Signals from satellite communications can also be interfered with or blocked by buildings, foliage, or various atmospheric conditions. Finally, satellite transmissions are easily susceptible to eavesdropping (that is, they can be monitored by unauthorized personnel). Thus, implementing appropriate security precautions is important.

113. What advantages do satellite communications offer over land-based links?

Probably the biggest advantage of satellite communication is they can reach geographically remote areas. This includes countries that have no or little communications or wiring infrastructures. Another advantage if you own the satellite system (e.g., NASA) is there are no recurring leased line charges. If you do not own your own satellite, then there are recurring transponder fees or charges for leasing satellite time.

114. I've heard about a satellite communications project involving Bill Gates.

You must mean the Teledesic Network project.

115. Right. That's it. What is this all about?

The Teledesic project comprises 840 interlinked *low-Earth orbit* (*LEO*) satellites that are to provide global access to voice, data, and video communications beginning in the year 2002. It is supposed to support one million full-duplex E1 (2.048 Mbps) connections and have a capacity that will support millions of simultaneous users.

116. Besides cost, what are the major differences between LEO and GEO satellites?

As noted earlier, GEO satellites orbit at approximately 22,000 miles at a rate that approximates that of the Earth's orbit making them appear stationary in their relationship to the Earth. LEO satellites orbit anywhere from 300 miles to 1,200 miles, and their velocities are greater than that of GEOs. Also, only eight GEO satellites are needed to provide global communications. Depending on their orbit, a constellation of up to 48 LEOs are needed for global coverage. Because GEO satellites' orbit matches the Earth's, they are always in communication with an Earth-based antenna. LEO satellites are only in sight of a terrestrial antenna for at most 15 minutes. Consequently, a LEO-based satellite communication must be transferred from one satellite to another within the constellation. LEO satellite systems also do not suffer from the type of propagation delay found with GEO satellite systems. The propagation delay of LEO satellites ranges from 40 milliseconds to 450 milliseconds making them better candidates to support interactive applications such as video-conferencing. There are also *medium-Earth orbit* (*MEO*) satellite systems, which usually orbit from 6,000 miles to 12,000 miles and have a latency of approximately 250 milliseconds; MEOs need a constellation of 20 satellites for global coverage.

117. What kind of bandwidth are satellite communications capable of?

The bandwidth capability of satellite systems varies and is a function of the frequency at which the satellites transmit. Four common frequencies are *C-band, Ka-band, Ku-band,* and *V-band*. C-band is 6 GHz uplink and 4 GHz downlink. Ka-band is 28 GHz uplink and 18 GHz downlink. Ku-band is 14 GHz uplink and 12 GHz downlink. V-band is above 30 GHz and is still being researched and developed.

118. Are there any other projects along this line?

Yes. There are several. One of them, called Iridium, is sponsored by Motorola, Lockheed Martin, Raytheon, and Sprint. It consists of 66 LEO satellites, all of which have been deployed. Iridium began providing global wireless voice, paging, fax, and other data services during the last quarter of 1998. The service is, as expected, expensive. The cost of an Iridium telephone starts at $3,000, and a satellite call costs $3 per minute. Nevertheless, Iridium users can place and receive calls anywhere in the world.

A second one, Globalstar, is an international telecommunications partnership. This system involves 48 LEO satellites, of which four have been launched as of this writing. Globalstar is planning to launch all 48 satellites by mid-1999. These satellites will bring cellular telephone service to some of the world's remotest areas. Some companies such as Motorola are also considering GEO-LEO hybrid systems that permit the user to determine which method (GEO or LEO) an application should be sent.

A third project by Angel Technologies, consists of telecommunications-equipped airplanes, dubbed "metro-area satellites," which fly 50,000 feet above cities. Although still in the design stage, the project proposes that planes fly in eight-hour shifts, 24 hours a day to provide constant coverage. It is speculated that anyone within a 75-mile radius of the coverage area will be able to use these planes for fast satellite-based network connections. The project is expected to be launched sometime in 2000 with the Los Angeles area slated as the initial implementation site.

119. What's the future for wireless communication?

The future of wireless looks promising. After eight years of existence, a standard was finally developed for wireless LANs (WLANs). It is called IEEE 802.11, and it was approved in 1997. This standard defines both the physical and data link layers for wireless communication. (We discuss the IEEE 802.11 data link layer in Chapter 5.) The standard defines three different physical layers. Two are RF-based; the third is infrared. Also, in January, 1997, the FCC opened up three new segments of the spectrum for wireless LANs: 5.15 GHz–5.25 GHz, 5.25 GHz–5.35 GHz, and 5.75 GHz–5.85 GHz. These bands have nearly no wireless congestion, and the higher frequencies are conducive to the development of products that operate at Ethernet speeds.

120. Please give me a little more detail about the three physical layers of 802.11.

OK. The two RF-based physical layers are called Direct Sequence Spread Spectrum (DSSS), and Frequency Hopping Spread Spectrum (FHSS). Both operate at the 2.4 GHz to 2.4835 GHz ISM band. (See question 105 for more information about the ISM band.) Data transmission rates for DSSS and FHSS initially were defined at either 1 Mbps or 2 Mbps. However, in mid-1998, the IEEE passed a new standard jointly developed by Lucent Technologies and Harris Semiconductor that supports data rates of 5 Mbps and 11 Mbps. These new rates rely on the same 2.4 GHz ISM band.

DSSS operates by spreading a signal over a wide range of the 2.4 GHz band. FHSS operates by transmitting short bursts of data on different frequencies. One burst is transmitted on one frequency, a second burst is transmitted on a second and different frequency, and so forth. Since each uses a different transmission method, the two RF physical layers cannot interoperate. The third physical layer defined in 802.11 is diffused infrared. It has the backing of IBM. As of the late 1990s, most wireless media products are based on the RF physical layers.

121. Given a WLAN standard, will WLANs be the next wave in networking?

It's tough to predict in this business. We think that WLANs will eventually carve out a niche market for themselves. There are several barriers to the success of WLANs, however. For example, equipment remains expensive. WLAN data rates also are relatively slow in comparison with their wired counterparts, Fast Ethernet and Gigabit Ethernet. Finally, in recent years many companies have spent millions of dollars upgrading their wire plants with either fiber, Category 5, or Enhanced Category 5 cable so they can support Fast Ethernet, Gigabit Ethernet, or ATM. Why would they now want to scrap their cable plants and invest in WLANs?

End-of-Chapter Commentary

You should now have a good understanding of the fundamental concepts and terms related to the physical layer and the different types of transmission media (both wired and wireless) used at the physical layer. Many of these concepts are discussed in later chapters in specific contexts. In Chapters 7, 8, 9, 10, and 14, the various copper and fiber-optic cables presented here are discussed from the perspective of their specific LAN applications; in Chapter 6, key physical layer concepts are applied to specific physical layer hardware components; and Appendix C contains guidelines for installing UTP cable. Our next order of business is the data link layer, which is the subject of Chapter 5.

Chapter 5

Data Link Layer Concepts and IEEE Standards

In this chapter we discuss the second layer of the OSI model, namely, the data link layer. This layer handles the transfer of data between the ends of a physical link—it is responsible for transferring data from the network layer on the source machine to the network layer on the destination machine. We discuss this layer from the perspective of the IEEE LAN architecture rather than the OSI model. As part of this perspective, we introduce the various IEEE LAN standards and the two general IEEE algorithms that serve as the basis for LAN protocols. An outline of the terms and concepts defined and discussed follows:

- IEEE (Questions 1–3)
- IEEE's Perspective of the Data Link Layer (Questions 4–6)
- Framing (Questions 7–11)
- Ethernet/802.3 Frames (Questions 12–15, 33–34)
- Flow Control (Questions 16–17)
- Error Control (Questions 18–32)
- MAC Sublayer (Questions 35–44)
- Random Access Protocols (Questions 36–44)
- Token Passing Protocols (Questions 45–47)

1. What is the IEEE?

IEEE (pronounced "eye triple E") stands for the Institute of Electrical and Electronics Engineers, a professional society founded in 1963. IEEE members include engineers, scientists, and students. One of its many activities is to act as a coordinating body for computing and communication standards. Many international standards from the International Organization for Standardization (ISO) and the International Electrotechnical Commission (IEC) are based on IEEE networking standards. For additional information about these organizations, see http://www.ieee.org; http://www.iso.ch; and http://www.iec.ch.

2. What does IEEE have to do with local area networks?

In the early days of local area network development, there were no standards for LANs. Chaos and instability were the order of the day. Proprietary vendor standards ruled, customers became customers-for-life, and companies got fat. The dearth of industry-wide standards effectively prevented customers from using "outside" products for fear of incompatibility. In February 1980, the IEEE assumed responsibility for setting LAN standards, primarily for the physical and data link layers, following the OSI model. IEEE conducted its standards development under the auspices of the IEEE Computer Society. We provide a list of these standards in Table 5-1. (Corresponding ISO/IEC standards are given in parentheses.)

3. Looking at Table 5-1, I notice that all of the IEEE standards start with 802. Why?

IEEE's development of LAN standards was assigned the project number 802, for February 1980 (get it? 2/80 or 802), and the committee's collective body of work has become known as Project 802. The standards that have resulted are identified as IEEE 802.*x*.

Table 5-1. Summary of IEEE Project 802 LAN Standards

IEEE 802.1 Defines an architectural overview of LANs.

IEEE 802.2 Defines the Logical Link Control, which describes services for the transmission of data between two nodes. (ISO/IEC 8802-2)

IEEE 802.3 Defines the Carrier Sense Multiple Access/Collision Detection (CSMA/CD) access method commonly referred to as Ethernet. Supplements include 802.3c (10 Mbps Ethernet); 802.3u (100 Mbps Ethernet known as *Fast Ethernet*), and 802.3z and 802.3ab (1000 Mbps Ethernet known as *Gigabit Ethernet*). (ISO/IEC 8802-3)

IEEE 802.4 Defines the token bus network access method.

IEEE 802.5 Defines the logical ring LAN that uses a token-passing access method; known also as Token Ring. (ISO/IEC 8802-5)

IEEE 802.6 Defines metropolitan area networks (MANs).

IEEE 802.7 Defines broadband LANs (capable of delivering video, data, and voice traffic).

IEEE 802.9 Defines integrated digital and video networking—Integrated Services LANs (ISLANs). (ISO/IEC 8802-9)

IEEE 802.10 Defines standards for interoperable LAN/MAN security services.

IEEE 802.11 Defines standards for wireless media access control and physical layer specifications.

IEEE 802.12 Defines the "demand priority" access method for 100Mbps LANs; known also as 100 Base-VG or 100VG-AnyLAN.

IEEE 802.13 (Defines nothing—IEEE was concerned about the superstitious overtones associated with "13.")

IEEE 802.14 Defines a standard for Cable-TV based broadband communication.

4. Enough of the history lesson. What does this have to do with the data link layer?

IEEE initiated its development of LAN standards with an architectural model, defined in IEEE 802.1. This architectural model corresponds to the two lowest layers of the OSI Model. The difference between the IEEE and OSI models, though, is that the IEEE divides OSI's data link layer into two parts—the *logical link control sublayer* (LLC) and the *media access control sublayer* (MAC). (See Figure 5-1.) Note that MAC has nothing to do with Apple Computer's Macintosh.

5. This is all well and good and enlightening. However, what, exactly, is the data link layer?

In network architecture, the purpose of the data link layer is to regulate and format transmission of information from software on a node to the network cabling facilities. The data link layer is typically implemented on a node as a *device driver.* A device driver is a software component that is specific to both a piece of hardware, such as an Ethernet/802.3 network interface controller card (NIC), and the operating system of the computer in which it is installed. For instance, the data link layer of Ethernet/802.3 could be a card you purchased from a network vendor such as SMC, 3Com, or Intel. The vendor includes a device driver with the card to enable the operating system on your computer (such as Windows, MacOS, NT, or UNIX) to recognize the card and allow the software protocol(s) to "talk" to the card when they are accessed.

More simply, the data link layer is the "glue" between the wire and the software on a node. Without it, the particular network connection will not operate at all. The data link layer creates the network environment for the wire and dictates data formats, timing, bit sequencing, and many other activities for each particular type of network.

6. So what do the sublayers within the data link layer do?

The LLC sublayer, defined in IEEE 802.2, is the upper half of the data link layer. It encompasses several functions, including framing, flow control, and error control. The MAC sublayer is the lower half of the data link layer. It provides media access management protocols for accessing a shared medium.

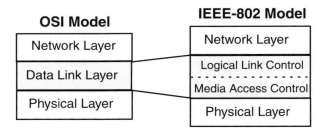

Figure 5-1. The IEEE's perspective of the data link layer.

7. Huh? Could you please give me a little more detail? Why don't you start with the LLC sublayer and framing. What is framing?

Framing refers to the process of partitioning a bit stream into discrete units or blocks of data called *frames*. Thus, it is the manner in which a specific network type formats the bits sent to the cable. Specific formats and timing sequences exist for each LAN type.

8. Why is it necessary to partition a bit stream into frames?

Framing enables sending and receiving machines to synchronize the transmission and reception of data because frames have detectable boundaries. Framing also facilitates error detection and correction. Once a bit stream has been partitioned into frames, specific information about the contents a frame is computed and transmitted within the frame. Using this information, a receiving node can determine the integrity of a received frame.

9. How is framing accomplished?

A common procedure involves inserting start and stop bits before and after the transmitted data message. For example, if we use the bit pattern 01111110 (six consecutive 1-bits) as our start-stop flag, and if the data set (i.e., the message being transmitted) consists of 11101111, then the frame is 0111111011101111101111110. (The framing protocol associated with each type of network specifies the actual bit pattern used for these start-stop flags.) Thus, the data set has been "framed" by distinct boundaries consisting of start-stop flags.

10. What happens if a data message has the same pattern as the start-stop bits? How do we distinguish real user data from the start-stop bits?

Aha! Good thinking! Because the start-stop flags must be distinguishable from user data, they must be unique. If a data message contains a sequence of bits identical to the start-stop flag, then we must alter the data set to guarantee the uniqueness of the start-stop bit patterns. One way to do this employs a process known as *bit stuffing*. For example, suppose a data set consists of the bit string 0111111001111101, and our start-stop flag is 01111110. Note that the data message includes one instance of our start-stop flag. We implement bit stuffing by "stuffing" a 0-bit immediately after every fifth consecutive 1-bit in the data stream. The receiving node "unstuffs" these 0-bits by deleting every 0-bit that follows five consecutive 1-bits. We illustrate bit stuffing in Figure 5-2.

11. Can you give me an example of a "real" frame?

Sure thing. How about an Ethernet frame?

12. Good. Show me an Ethernet frame.

Before showing an Ethernet frame, we need to make a distinction between Ethernet and IEEE 802.3, which many people call Ethernet. This distinction is necessary because Ethernet and IEEE 802.3 frame formats are different. Instead of getting into a detailed dis-

Data set to be transmitted: 1 1 1 1 1 1 0 0 1 1 1 1 1 0 1 1

Data set after bit stuffing: 1 1 1 1 1 **0** 1 0 0 1 1 1 1 1 0 **0** 1 1

Data set after bit stuffing and
start-stop bits have been inserted: **0 1 1 1 1 1 1 0** 1 1 1 1 1 **0** 1 0 0 1 1 1 1 1 **0** 0 1 1 **0 1 1 1 1 1 1 0**

Thus, the frame to be transmitted is:

0 1 1 1 1 1 1 0   1 1 1 1 1 0 1 0 0 1 1 1 1 1 0 0 1 1   0 1 1 1 1 1 1 0

Start of Frame   User Data with bit stuffing   End of Frame

The data link layer on the receiving machine removes the start and stop bits and unstuffs the data set by removing the 0-bits that follow each set of five consecutive 1-bits.

Figure 5-2. An example of bit stuffing, which is used for framing when the data set contains the start-stop bits pattern.

cussion about these differences (we save that for Chapter 8), just be aware that Ethernet and IEEE 802.3 are not really the same. IEEE 802.3 is broadly deployed but old habits die hard and people continue to call it Ethernet. To avoid confusion, or to create more if you're so inclined, we use the nomenclature Ethernet/802.3 in this book when we want to refer to what people commonly call Ethernet.

13. There you go again, throwing a monkey wrench into the works. So show me the IEEE 802.3 frame, already.

Let's look at the general format of an IEEE 802.3 frame, shown in Figure 5-3. Note that an IEEE 802.3 frame consists of eight fields: preamble, start frame delimiter, destination address, source address, length count, data, pad, and CRC checksum (see below). The preamble, used for synchronization, consists of seven identical bytes (56 bits). Each byte (8 bits or octet) has the bit pattern 10101010. The start frame delimiter (S), which indicates the start of a frame of data, consists of the bit pattern 10101011. This is the start-stop flag used in IEEE 802.3. The destination address is the hardware address of the receiving station—normally 48 bits (the standard provides for a 16-bit value, but no one uses it). The source address is the hardware address of the sending station, also 48 bits in length. Both of these addresses are MAC sublayer addresses, which we will discuss shortly. (Also see Appendix A.) The length count (L) is a two-byte field that indicates the length of the data field that follows. The data field contains the actual user data (i.e., the transmitted message). The data field is subject to minimum and maximum sizes, which are 46 and 1500 bytes, respectively. The pad field (P) contains dummy data that "pads" the data field up to its minimum length of 46 bytes, if necessary. Its size ranges from 0 to n bytes, where n is the number of bytes needed. Finally, the checksum field (CRC) contains the information needed for error detection, which is yet another task performed by the data link layer in the LLC sublayer. It is also called the Frame Check Sequence (FCS) and it is four bytes long. (*Note:* CRC stands for Cyclic Redundancy Check and is discussed later in the chapter.)

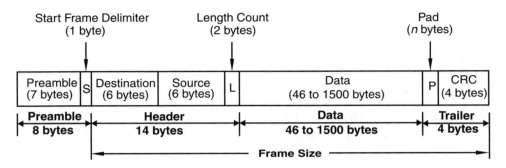

Figure 5-3. The contents and structure of an IEEE 802.3 frame.

14. Now I know what an IEEE 802.3 frame is all about. I have another question, though. I have seen a protocol analyzer display frames with only four fields instead of eight, and you also show four fields in Figure 5-3. Why is that?

Obviously, you bought a cheap protocol analyzer. Seriously, though, it's because the eight individual fields of an IEEE 802.3 frame can be grouped into four main fields: *preamble* (preamble plus start frame delimiter), *header* (source and destination addresses plus length count), *data* (user data plus padding), and *trailer* (the CRC checksum). If we ignore the preamble, the aggregate of the header, data, and trailer fields ranges from a minimum of 64 bytes to a maximum of 1518 bytes. These represent the minimum and maximum sizes of an IEEE 802.3 frame.

15. In your answer to Question 13, you stated that the source and destination addresses of an IEEE 802.3 frame are "MAC sublayer addresses." You also called them "hardware addresses." Please elaborate.

Certainly. (See Box 5-1.) As you read this box, it is important to note that a MAC sublayer address is not the same as an Internet address. The *MAC sublayer address* is nothing more than the hardware address of a particular node. If the node is connected to an Ethernet/802.3 network, then we refer to the hardware address as the Ethernet/802.3 address. If the node is connected to a Token Ring network, then the hardware address is called the *Token Ring address*. It all depends on the MAC sublayer protocol. You also should not confuse a MAC address as the address of a Macintosh computer. A list of Ethernet/IEEE 802.3 vendor prefixes is given in Appendix A.

16. Yes! It's starting to making sense. I've seen this terminology before and I think I'm starting to understand it. Can we move on to the concept of flow control?

Sure. *Flow control*, which is another function of the LLC sublayer, refers to a process that controls the rate at which data are exchanged between two nodes. Flow control involves a feedback mechanism that informs the source machine of the destination machine's ability to keep up with the current flow of data transmission. Usually, a source node may not transmit frames until it receives permission from the destination machine.

Box 5-1: IEEE 802.3 MAC Sublayer Addresses

Ethernet addresses, also known as hardware or MAC addresses, are installed in ROM by the manufacturers of Ethernet controllers (i.e., the Ethernet network cards). The custodian of these addresses is the IEEE, which assigns addresses on a group basis to vendors who manufacture Ethernet hardware devices used in a heterogeneous network environment.

Ethernet addresses consist of 48 bits, represented as 12 hexadecimal digits (0–9, A–F), and partitioned into six groups of two. An example of an Ethernet address is 08:00:20:01:D6:2A. (*Note:* Dashes are sometimes used in place of colons, and sometimes no delimiter is used to separate the byte-pairs. Also, the letters A–F are used to represent the numbers 10–15, respectively. These letters are usually written in uppercase.) The higher-order three bytes (i.e., the leftmost six hexadecimal digits) correspond to the manufacturer of the Ethernet device, and the lower-order three bytes correspond to the serial number of the device. For example, the address 08:00:20:01:D6:2A corresponds to an Ethernet controller manufactured by Sun Microsystems because the leftmost three bytes, 08:00:20, have been assigned to Sun; the remaining three bytes specify a unique serial number assigned by Sun to the device. Other examples of vendor prefixes include 00:00:0c (Cisco), 00:00:1D (Cabletron), and 08:00:07 (Apple). (See Appendix A for more information about Ethernet vendor prefixes.)

There are three different types of destination addresses. The first is called a *unicast* address, which essentially means that data are being transmitted to only a single network interface (i.e., device). Unicast destination addresses are denoted by either a 0 or an even number (2, 4, 6, 8, A, C, E) in the second hexadecimal digit of the vendor prefix. A *multicast* or *broadcast* address enable data to be transmitted to more than one destination node at the same time. A multicast address specifies a vendor-specific group of nodes. For example, the multicast address, 09-00-87-90-FF-FF, is for Xyplex terminal servers. Ethernet frames that have their destination fields set to this address will be received by all Xyplex terminal servers connected to the network. If a node wants to send data to *all* network connected devices, then a broadcast address is used. This address is given as FF:FF:FF:FF:FF:FF. Multicast and broadcast Ethernet addresses are denoted by using an odd number (1, 3, 5, 7, 9, B, D, F) as the second hexadecimal digit.

Ethernet addresses should not be confused with Internet addresses. The former are six-byte addresses that have been "burned" into the controller card; the latter are logical addresses that correspond to a specific network protocol and are assigned by a network administrator and configured through software. If a device is connected to an Ethernet network, which in turn is connected to the Internet, then the device will have both Ethernet and IP addresses assigned to it. The Address Resolution Protocol (ARP), which is part of the TCP/IP protocol suite (see Chapters 2 and 3), is used to resolve IP addresses to Ethernet addresses. An ARP request is a network broadcast that announces the target node's IP address and requests the node to return its MAC address. On UNIX and Windows NT systems, this protocol can be invoked on the command line by the *arp* application program. Using the "a" extension (*arp -a*) displays the contents of the current ARP table maintained by the local host.

17. Why is flow control important?

Flow control is necessary because it is possible for a sending node to transmit frames at a rate faster than the destination node can receive and process them. This can happen if the source node is lightly loaded and the destination node is heavily loaded, or if the source node has a faster processor than that of the destination node. Thus, flow control provides a mechanism to ensure that a sending node does not overwhelm a receiving node during data transmission. For example, consider a network that consists of several 80486 PC clients and a Pentium PC file server. Clearly, the processing speed of the server is much greater than that of the clients. In this scenario, the server is able to transmit frames to a client faster than the client can process them. Without flow control, the client's buffers will eventually fill with "backlogged" frames sent by the server. With its buffers full, the client will discard any subsequent data it receives. This can result in retransmissions by the sending node, which can exacerbate network congestion.

18. How about error control? You mentioned error detection in the description of the IEEE 802.3 frame. Is this part of error control?

Yes it is. The term *error control* refers to the process of guaranteeing reliable delivery of data. That is, the data received are identical to the data transmitted. Two basic strategies exist for dealing with errors. One method is to provide enough information in the data stream to enable the destination node to detect an error. We call this *error detection*. Once a destination node has detected an error it can do one of two things: it can either request a retransmission from the sending node, or it can determine what the correct data should be and change them accordingly. Both methods are forms of *error correction*. We call the first *error correction through retransmission*, and the second, *autonomous error correction*.

19. How does the sending node know if it has to retransmit a frame?

Error control involves the use of acknowledgments—the receiving node provides the sending node with feedback about the frames it has received. A positive acknowledgment means a frame was received correctly; a negative acknowledgment (or no acknowledgment) implies a frame was not received correctly. Negative acknowledgments imply that the sending node needs to retransmit the frame.

20. What kinds of safeguards does error control employ?

To guard against the possibility of lost or destroyed frames (due to hardware failure) the data link layer supports timers. If a frame or acknowledgment is lost, the sending node's time limit eventually expires, alerting it to retransmit the frame. To guard against a destination node accepting duplicate frames, outgoing frames are assigned sequence numbers, which enable a destination node to distinguish between a frame that has been retransmitted from an original one. The management of timers and sequence numbers is an important function of the data link layer because it ensures that each frame is received by the network layer exactly once and in the correct order.

It is important to note that not all LAN types implement sequence numbering at the frame level. In fact, very few do. In most LANs, the software above the data link layer must determine that something is missing and negotiate retransmission of the information. Just because the feature might exist in a specification does not mean that it is necessarily implemented in practice.

21. How is error correction actually accomplished?

As we stated above, error correction can be performed in one of two ways. The first strategy, error correction through retransmission, is straightforward. If a destination node detects that a frame of data it received is not identical to the frame sent, then it requests the sending node to retransmit the original frame. The second strategy, autonomous error correction, is a little more complex, and does not rely on retransmissions. Instead, the destination node, upon detecting a bad data frame, corrects the error(s) itself. Autonomous error correction requires that a transmitted frame contains enough information to enable the destination node to correct any detected errors without requesting a retransmission. Note that error correction implies error detection.

22. I'm curious. I understand the need for error control, but what causes network errors in the first place?

Networks are fallible, complex systems, and errors occurring during data transmission are an inherent part of these systems. Network errors are caused by a wide variety of conditions. For example, errors can be caused by interference on the wire, hardware problems, software bugs, protocol-related problems (such as incompatible protocols at either end), and buffer overflow. Some errors are intermittent—they come and go. These are the most difficult to detect. Others are hard errors that are easily identified. In a properly functioning network, however, errors usually are a function of line synchronization failures, cross talk, defective hardware, and protocol-related errors (e.g., "collisions" in Ethernet/802.3).

23. Can you give a concrete example of error control in action?

Yes we can. We'll illustrate error control with an example of single-bit error correction. This involves using parity. Are you familiar with the concept of parity?

24. Yes, but it's been a while. So why don't you review it for me.

OK. *Parity* refers to the use of an extra bit (called a *parity bit* or a *redundant bit*) to detect single-bit errors in data transmissions. Parity can be specified as even, odd, or none. Even parity means that there must be an even number of 1-bits in each bit string; odd parity means that there must be an odd number of 1-bits in each bit string; and no parity means that parity is ignored. The extra bit (i.e., the parity bit) is forced to either 0 or 1 to make the total number of bits either even or odd. For example, consider the character *A*. Its ASCII representation is 1000001. Note this has two 1-bits, and two is an even number. If we require even parity then we must append a 0 to this bit string because we need to maintain an even number of 1s. If we require odd parity, then we need to append a 1 because we need an odd number of 1s. (See Figure 5-4.) When a single-bit error occurs, the receiver interprets the bit string as a different character than the one sent. Parity checking with one

- Bit string of "A":   1 0 0 0 0 0 1
- For even parity, parity bit is 0:   1 0 0 0 0 0 1 **0**
  (even number of 1-bits)
- For odd parity, parity bit is 1:   1 0 0 0 0 0 1 **1**
  (odd number of 1-bits)

Figure 5-4. Example of parity bits.

additional parity bit can *detect* this type of error. Unfortunately, however, a single parity bit does not provide enough information to *correct* the error.

25. I thought you said that parity can be used for both detection and correction of errors. How can parity be used for error correction?

As we stated earlier, to effect autonomous error correction sufficient information must be included in a transmitted frame to enable the receiving node to correct any detected errors on its own, avoiding the need for retransmission. Redundancy bits (also called *check bits*) provide this information. A data set composed of both user data and redundancy bits is called a *codeword*. Using parity, we can construct codewords to correct single-bit errors only. We illustrate how this works in Appendix B.

26. I just reviewed Appendix B. That's a lot of work just to correct a single-bit error.

You bet it is. Autonomous error correction is expensive to implement. Several extra bits are required to convey redundant information so that the receiving node can locate an error. In the example given in Appendix B, we needed four extra bits just to be able to detect the location of a single-bit error. Once the position of such an error is located, though, correction is easy—simply complement the bit at that position. Consequently, autonomous error correction is usually implemented in simplex channels, where retransmissions cannot be requested, or in those instances where retransmission is more costly than implementing an autonomous error correction scheme. For most situations, though, using retransmissions is the preferred method of error correction.

27. What about correcting multibit errors?

Unfortunately, the price goes up. What we mean by this is we must increase the codeword's size to enable us to correct additional bits, adding a significant amount of overhead to the transmission. If the physical layer is screwing up so badly that we expect many multi-bit errors, we probably ought to consider re-engineering or replacing the equipment.

28. What error control strategy does Ethernet/802.3 use?

Ethernet/IEEE 802.3 uses error detection with retransmission. If you look back at Figure 5-3, you will see that the last field in the frame is the *checksum*, used to detect errors. The checksum technique employed by Ethernet/802.3 is called *CRC-32*.

29. What's a CRC-32 checksum?

We're glad you asked. Are you ready for a little bit of mathematics?

30. OK. Just a little bit. Promise?

Sure. CRC stands for *cyclic redundancy check*, which is an extremely powerful and robust error detection method. To check a series of bits, CRC first constructs a polynomial whose terms' coefficients are the values of each of the bits. Thus, a data set with n bits corresponds to an $n-1$ degree polynomial; the leftmost bit is the coefficient of the x^{n-1} term. For example, the eight-bit data set, 10111101, is equal to the seventh-degree polynomial, $1x^7 + 0x^6 + 1x^5 + 1x^4 + 1x^3 + 1x^2 + 0x^1 + 1$, or equivalently, $x^7 + x^5 + x^4 + x^3 + x^2 + 1$. In the next step, the polynomial, is divided by a predetermined *generator polynomial*. (Thus, the data set is the dividend and the generator polynomial is the divisor.) The remainder of this division is the CRC checksum, which is included with the frame. In an Ethernet/IEEE 802.3 frame, for example, the CRC checksum is the last field. The receiving node performs an analogous procedure on a received frame, using the same generator polynomial. If the CRC checksum calculated by the receiving node is equal to what was sent, then the frame is interpreted as correct. If the two CRC checksums do not match, then the sending node is notified of this and the entire frame is retransmitted.

Three standard generator polynomials are:

- **CRC-16,** a 16-bit checksum used for various file transfer protocols. Its generator polynomial is $x^{16} + x^{15} + x^2 + 1$.

- **CRC-CCITT,** a 16-bit checksum that serves as an international standard. Its generator polynomial is $x^{16} + x^{12} + x^5 + 1$.

- **CRC-32,** a 32-bit checksum used in most LAN protocols. Its generator polynomial is $x^{32} + x^{26} + x^{23} + x^{22} + x^{16} + x^{12} + x^{11} + x^{10} + x^8 + x^7 + x^5 + x^4 + x^2 + x$. (CRC-32 is used in Ethernet/802.3 and Token Ring.)

31. How efficient is CRC in detecting errors?

The efficiency of CRC is a function of the generator polynomial used. CRC-16 and CRC-CCITT will detect 100 percent of all single and double errors, all errors with an odd number of bits, all bursts of 16 bits or less, 99.997 percent of 17-bit error bursts, and 99.998 percent of 18-bit and longer error bursts. With CRC-32, however, the chances of bad data being received and not detected are approximately one in 4.3 billion (2^{32-1}).

32. Wow! So although errors are inevitable in networks, thanks to CRC-32 there is little chance that they will go undetected, right?

That's right. However, this does not mean that you should be negligent in your responsibility as a network manager or administrator. You should always strive to minimize network errors by replacing *IS Class* media and equipment. OK. Enough of the LLC sublayer. We need to move on to the MAC sublayer.

33. Before we proceed to the MAC sublayer, could you give me some examples of bad Ethernet/802.3 frames?

Sure, but before doing so we suggest you first review Figure 5-3. For instance, it will be helpful to know that the length of an IEEE 802.3 frame ranges from a minimum of 64 bytes to a maximum of 1,518 bytes. Go ahead. We'll wait. We have lots of time.

34. OK. I've finished my review. Now give me some examples of bad Ethernet/802.3 frames.

Ethernet/802.3 errors manifest themselves as bad or invalid frames. We will discuss causes of these errors in Chapter 8, but for now, we give a summary of them:

Oversized Frames. Oversized frame have more than 1,518 bytes but also have a valid CRC checksum. Oversized frames usually indicate a software problem such as a faulty network driver. The industry slang term for this condition is a "long" frame.

Runt Frames. Runt frames are short frames. They are at least 8 bytes but less than 64 bytes long and have a valid CRC checksum. Runts usually indicate a software problem such as a faulty network driver.

Jabbers. Jabbers are oversized frames that have an invalid CRC checksum. Jabbering is caused when a station has transmitted for too long. This normally causes an invalid CRC. Jabbers usually indicate a hardware problem, typically a faulty transceiver.

Alignment or Frame Errors. These are frames that do not end on a "byte-boundary." A frame error is detected when the total number of bits is not a multiple of eight (i.e., they cannot be grouped into an exact number of eight-bit bytes).

CRC Errors. Frames with CRC errors are of the proper size and alignment but have an invalid CRC checksum. CRC errors are caused by noise, bad connections, and faulty network hardware.

35. Alright—on to the MAC sublayer! Why is it necessary and what does it do?

LANs employ a broadcast topology, meaning the nodes of a LAN share a single communications channel, and must all contend for the same medium in order to transmit data. This is analogous to a large group of college students contending for the only working telephone in a dormitory lobby—it can be a long wait when things are busy. Because of the potential chaos associated with such contention, LANs must employ protocols that define the *who*, the *how*, the *when*, and the *for how long* of channel allocation. Enter the medium access control sublayer! The MAC sublayer provides the protocols that define the manner in which nodes share the single physical transmission medium. The name says it all: Media Access Control. Two broad categories of access methods are most suitable for LANs—*random access* (sometimes called *stochastic*) and *token passing* (referred to as *deterministic*).

36. Random access—does this have anything to do with RAM?

Only indirectly, in that they both involve random access. Random access protocols define how a node can access a communications channel. These protocols employ the philosophy that a node can transmit whenever it has data to transmit. Random access protocols imply contention; in fact, sometimes we also call them *contention protocols*.

37. What do you mean by contention?

Consider a classroom in which students and teacher are engaged in an open discussion—anyone can begin speaking without needing acknowledgment. In such a setting, anyone who wants to speak must contend with others who also want to speak simultaneously. Thus, "contention" is a phenomenon in which more than one entity competes to do something at the same time.

38. Doesn't this create chaos? Not everyone will be able to hear what one person is saying?

Exactly! In order for meaningful communication to take place, speakers must follow a rule that both ensures they can speak when they have something to say, and resolves the problem when more than one person begins speaking at the same time. For example, one rule might be: "If more than one person begins speaking at the same time, everyone is to stop talking for just a split second, and then one person should take the lead and begin talking." Another rule might be to have a facilitator who calls on individuals to speak. Have you ever seen a Presidential press conference? Reporters are always shouting to get their question asked. Regardless of how many reporters attempt to ask a question, only one person at a time speaks. In some cases it is the reporter who shouts the loudest; in other cases, the President identifies the person who is permitted to speak.

39. OK. Put this in the context of a LAN for me.

Just as when more than one person attempts to talk at the same time, when two or more nodes try to communicate at approximately the same time, their transmissions "collide." In LAN terminology, we refer to this as a *collision*.

40. How does a node know when a collision has occurred?

The physical characteristics of a specific medium enable it to detect collisions. More specifically, when a collision occurs, a channel's energy level changes and nodes on the network are equipped to detect this condition. During such times, the nodes' signals become garbled.

41. What do nodes do if their signals collide?

The answer is, "It depends." It depends on a node's MAC sublayer protocol. Similar to the way people might observe different protocols when contending to speak, nodes employ various protocols to transmit data in a shared media environment. For example, to minimize the occurrence of collisions, nodes might follow a protocol that requires them to first "listen" for another node's transmission (somewhat incorrectly called a *carrier*, a term borrowed from radio terminology) before they begin transmitting data. We call these types of protocols *carrier sense* protocols. Carrier sense protocols require that before a node begins transmitting it must first listen to the wire to determine whether another node is transmitting data. Carrier sense transmission systems also employ circuitry that requires the system to "listen" to every bit transmission going out and compare that to what is actually heard on the transmission medium. If they match, wonderful. If they don't, something caused the bit to get hammered and this means the transmission is garbled. How it is handled from there depends on the transmission framing method being used.

Other protocols that do not involve collision detection involve nodes being given permission to transmit by possessing a special control frame, called a token. We call such protocols *token passing* protocols.

42. Tell me more.

OK. Let's begin with carrier sense protocols. There are four of them: (1) 1-persistent CSMA (Carrier Sense Multiple Access), (2) nonpersistent CSMA, (3) CSMA with Collision Detection (CSMA/CD), and (4) CSMA with Collision Avoidance (CSMA/CA). We'll describe these one at a time.

1-persistent CSMA. When a node has data to transmit, it first senses the channel to determine if another node is transmitting. If the channel is not busy, then the node begins transmitting. If the channel is busy, then the node continuously monitors the channel until it senses an idle channel. Once it detects an idle channel, the node seizes the channel and begins transmitting its data. With this protocol, nodes with data to transmit enter a "sense and seize" mode—they continuously listen for a clear channel, and once detected, begin transmitting data. This protocol is similar to telephones with a multiple redial feature. If it detects a busy signal when the call is first attempted, the telephone repeatedly dials the number until a connection is finally established. The "one" in 1-persistent CSMA represents the probability that a single waiting node will be able to transmit data once it detects an idle channel ($p = 1$). However, collisions can and do occur if more than a single node desires to transmit data at approximately the same time.

Nonpersistent CSMA. This protocol is similar to 1-persistent CSMA, except a node does not continuously monitor the channel when it has data to transmit. Instead, if a node detects a busy channel, it waits a random period and rechecks the channel. If the channel is idle, the node acquires the channel and begins transmitting its data. If, however, the channel is still busy, the node waits another random period before it checks the channel again. Both 1-persistent CSMA and non-persistent CSMA protocols eliminate almost all collisions except for those that occur when two nodes begin transmitting data nearly simultaneously. For example, node *A* begins transmitting data on a clear channel. A few microseconds later (which is not enough time for node *B*'s sensing circuit to detect node *A*'s transmission), node *B* erroneously declares the channel clear and begins transmitting its own data. Eventually the two transmissions collide.

1-persistent CSMA involves a significant amount of waiting and unfairness in determining which node gets the medium. It is "selfish" because nodes can grab the channel whenever they feel like it. Nonpersistent CSMA seems better because in its randomness there is fairness. In either case, though, there still remains the nagging problem of what to do about collisions. The next two CSMA protocols incorporate *collision detection* to provide a solution to the collision problem.

CSMA with Collision Detection (CSMA/CD). In this variant of either 1-persistent or nonpersistent CSMA, when a collision occurs the nodes (1) stop transmitting data, (2) send out a jamming signal, which ensures that all other nodes on the network detect the collision, (3) wait a random period of time, and then, (4) if the channel is free, attempt to retransmit their message. We illustrate the CSMA/CD algorithm in Figure 5-5.

CSMA with Collision Avoidance (CSMA/CA). This protocol is similar to CSMA/CD except that it implements *collision avoidance* instead of collision detection. As with straight CSMA, hosts that support this protocol first sense the channel to see if it is busy. If the host detects that the channel is not busy then it is free to send data. What if every host connected to a LAN is not always able to sense each other host's transmission? In such instances, collision detection will not work because collision detection is predicated on nodes being able to hear each other's transmissions. This is the case with wireless LANs (WLANs). We cannot always assume that each station connected to a WLAN will hear each other station's transmissions. One direct consequence of this is that a sending node will not be able to detect if a receiving node is busy or idle. To address this issue, we replace CD with CA and use something called *positive acknowledgment*. It works like this:

> The receiving host, upon receiving a transmission, issues an acknowledgment to the sending host. This informs the sending host that a collision did not occur. If the sending host does not receive this acknowledgment, it will assume that the receiving node did not receive the frame and it will retransmit it.

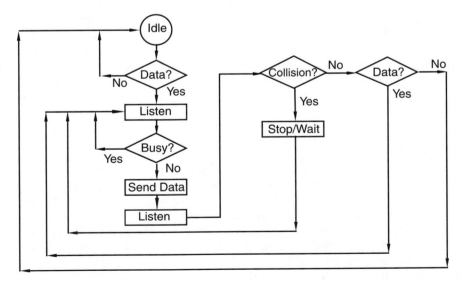

Figure 5-5. Flowchart depicting the CSMA/CD protocol.

CSMA/CA also defines special frames called *Request to Send* (RTS) and C*lear to Send* (CTS), which further help minimize collisions. A sending node issues an RTS frame to the receiving node. If the channel is free, the receiving node then issues a CTS frame to the sending node. CSMA/CA is used in IEEE 802.11 (WLANs) and with Apple Computer's LocalTalk, a low-speed, peer-to-peer network schema that remains very popular for small sites with Apple Macintoshes.

43. CSMA/CD sounds like Ethernet/802.3. Is this what Ethernet/802.3 is based on?

Right you are! One-persistent CSMA/CD is, indeed, the MAC sublayer protocol used in Ethernet and IEEE 802.3 networks. We discuss this further in Chapter 8, but because it is so broadly deployed, we will answer any other questions you might have about CSMA/CD at this time.

44. Thanks. I'll take you up on that. One question that arose when you described CSMA is just how long is "a random period?"

It can be a long time, a short time, a moderate amount of time—it's random, but it is also extremely critical. If the wait time is too short, collisions will occur repeatedly. If the wait time is too long, the medium could be in a constant idle state. Propagation delay also has an important effect on the performance of these protocols. Consider the example given in Question 41 for Nonpersistent CSMA: Node *A* senses an idle channel and begins transmitting. Shortly after node *A* has begun transmitting, node *B* is ready to transmit data and senses the channel. If node *A*'s signal has not yet reached node *B*, then node *B* will sense an idle channel and begin transmitting. This will ultimately result in a collision. Consequently, the longer the propagation delay, the worse the performance of this protocol. Even if the propagation delay is zero, it is still possible to have collisions. For example, assume both nodes *A* and *B* are ready to transmit data, but they each sense a busy channel (a third node is transmitting at the time). If the protocol is 1-persistent CSMA, then both nodes would begin transmitting at the same time resulting in a collision. The specific amount of wait time is a function of the protocol. For quick explanation purposes, though, Ethernet/802.3's "random" amount of time is between 1 and 512 *slot-times* on the cable. We will expand on this concept when we discuss Ethernet/IEEE 802.3 later (so please don't ask what a slot-time is).

45. What can you tell me about token passing protocols?

Well, unlike random access protocols, token passing protocols rely on granting nodes permission to transmit. Permission is provided in the form of a special control frame called a token. The underlying principle of token passing protocols is simple: the node that possesses the token may access the medium. Since possession of the token controls access to the medium, the possibility of contention is eliminated. The absence of contention also implies an absence of collisions. Thus, token-passing schemes are both contention-free and collision-free protocols.

The IEEE has defined two LAN protocols based on token passing. They are IEEE 802.4 (Token Bus) and IEEE 802.5 (Token Ring). While not defined by an IEEE standard,

Fiber Distributed Data Interface (FDDI) also uses a token passing technology. Token Ring and Token Bus are discussed in Chapter 9; FDDI is discussed in Chapter 10.

46. Please compare and contrast random protocols and token passing protocols.

Certainly. Random access protocols are stochastic in nature. They are predicated on the principle that the probability two computers will transmit simultaneously (i.e., within a few microseconds of each other) is near zero. Given such a low probability, these protocols permit simultaneous transmissions. They are engineered to enable nodes to both detect and resolve collisions resulting from such transmissions. Token passing protocols, in contrast, are deterministic in nature. They are predicated on the principle that no two nodes should be permitted to transmit at the same time. As such, these protocols effectively eliminate contention and are viewed as collision-free or collision-avoidance protocols. A direct consequence of determinism is that it is possible to accurately determine the worst-case performance of a LAN.

47. Which of these two protocol types is more advantageous?

Well, that depends. Each type of protocol has its own advantages and disadvantages. For example, contention protocols yield high performance for lightly loaded LANs, but when LAN traffic increases, protocol performance decreases. Performance of collision-free protocols is very predictable when a LAN is heavily loaded. However, this same feature also invokes a fixed delay even when a LAN is lightly loaded. To better understand these advantages and disadvantages, let us consider two example scenarios involving automobiles and street intersections.

In Scenario A, we have an intersection that has no traffic control device (i.e., no stop or yield signs, no flashing yellow or red lights, no traffic signal, etc.). In Scenario B, we have the same intersection, now controlled by a standard traffic signal light operated by a timer. The protocol for passing through the intersection in Scenario A is as follows: As you approach the intersection, beep your horn. If you do not hear a horn in return, you may proceed without slowing down. If you hear another horn in response to yours, slow down and proceed with caution. The protocol for Scenario B is simple: Obey the traffic signal. If it's green, you may proceed through the intersection; if it's red you must stop and wait for a green light. Clearly, in Scenario A, vehicles can pass through the intersection quite easily when traffic is light or nonexistent. On the other hand, once traffic increases, delays become more frequent and longer lasting, creating greater likelihood of collisions. Scenario A is analogous to the schemes used for contention protocols. In Scenario B, traffic is controlled via a traffic signal. Consequently, during heavy traffic loads you can predict approximately when you will be able to negotiate the intersection by counting the number of vehicles passing through while the signal is green. At the same time, however, what happens if you are stuck at this red light in very light traffic? You must still wait until the light turns green, whether the intersection is clear or not. This is a very inefficient use of time. Scenario B is analogous to collision-free protocols. Table 5-2 contains a summary of these advantages and disadvantages.

Table 5-2. Advantages and Disadvantages of Contention and Collision-free Protocols

Protocol	Advantage	Disadvantage
Contention	Faster access on lightly loaded systems	Poor performance at heavy loads
Collision-free	Very predictable at high-loads	Fixed delay required at low loads

End-of-Chapter Commentary

On this note we conclude our discussion of the data link layer. Many of the concepts we discussed here will be expanded in subsequent chapters. For example, our examination of Ethernet/802.3 LANs in Chapter 8 includes a discussion of the layer 2 differences between Ethernet and IEEE 802.3. We also examine 802.3 performance issues and address the concept of collision management, both of which are part of the data link layer. Similarly, our discussions in Chapters 9 and 10 on Token Ring and FDDI, respectively, include matters related to the data link layer. In each of these and other chapters, you will learn how the data link layer is implemented in different networks.

Chapter 6

Network Hardware Components (Layers 1 and 2)

In Chapter 4 we focused mostly on media and the physical layer (layer 1 of the OSI model), and did not include any discussion about specific network components. Similarly, Chapter 5, which examined the data link layer (layer 2 of the OSI model) did not contain any information about network devices. In this chapter we examine various network hardware devices that operate at either layer 1 or 2, specifically:

- Connectors (Questions 1–6)
- Transceivers (Questions 7–12)
- Repeaters (Questions 13–19)
- Media Converters (Question 20)
- Network Interface Cards (Questions 21–31)
- PC Cards (Questions 32–33)
- Bridges (Questions 34–45)
- Switches (Questions 46–57)

1. What are connectors?

Connectors attach components together. Several types of connectors are available, serving various purposes. For example, connectors are used to: (a) connect network interface cards, such as an Ethernet card, to a cable; (b) connect cable segments (e.g., thin coax to thin coax); and (c) terminate a segment. In this last category, connectors actually connect the cable to a terminating resistor or an array of resistors and are consequently known as *terminators*. The type of connector used is usually a function of cable type. For example, *eight-pin modular connectors* are used with UTP cable. (See Figure 6-1.)

2. Aren't these the ones that look like modular telephone connectors? I've always heard them referred to as RJ-45 connectors.

Eight-pin modular connectors do indeed resemble the standard modular telephone connectors used in the United States, and yes, they are commonly called *RJ-45 connec-*

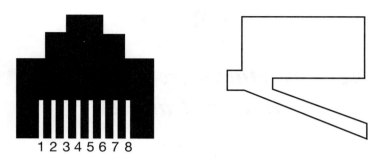

Figure 6-1. Top (left) and side (right) views of an RJ-45 connector. Formally known as 8-pin modular connectors, RJ-45s resemble standard telephone jacks and are used with UTP cable.

tors. In the strictest sense, the RJ designation refers to a specific series of connectors defined in the Universal Service Order Code (USOC) definitions of telephone circuits. "RJ" is telephone lingo for "registered jack." For example, RJ-11 refers to a four-wire connection used for standard home telephone lines in the United States. Hence, the correct term for UTP connectors used in LANs is eight-pin modular and not RJ-45. In some networking circles, though, the RJ designator has become a generic designation and implies any modular connector.

3. What is "gender," as applied to connectors? Do connectors have sex?

Watch it! Yes, connectors "mate." You can use your imagination about how the gender is derived, but a "plug" is usually "male" and a "jack" is usually "female." This universally understood terminology enables a clear specification of exactly which of a mating pair of connectors should be used in the particular application.

4. What connectors are used for coax cable?

Connectors used with thin coax are known as *BNC connectors.* (*Note:* There are several interpretations of BNC, including *Bayonet Neill-Concelman* (named after its developers), *Bayonet Nut Connector,* and *Barrel Nut Connector.* We have also seen *British National Connector.*) Several different types of BNC connectors are available and used for specific purposes. For example: *barrel connectors* are cylindrical and connect two segments of cable; *T connectors* are shaped like the letter "T" and connect a device to a cable—the horizontal part of the T connects two segments of cable (like a barrel connector) and the vertical part of the T connects the device; *end connectors* are attached to the ends of a cable segment and used to mate the cable to either a barrel or T connector; and BNC *terminators* are attached to each end of a thin coaxial trunk cable to prevent signal reflections, which can interfere with other signals. Terminators provide electrical resistance at the end of a cable and "absorb" signals to keep them from bouncing back and being heard again by the devices connected to the cable.

For the thick coaxial cable used in early Ethernet applications a *Type N* connector was employed to connect cable segments to each other (via barrel connectors) and to end terminators. N connectors are large, threaded connectors that accommodate the half-inch (12.5 mm) size of the coaxial cable. In "ThickWire" Ethernet networks, transceivers were attached to the medium either by "intrusive tap," which required the cable to be cut and female N connectors installed on both the cut ends, in turn connecting to the male N connectors on the transceiver; or by "vampire tap," which penetrated the cable. These methods are discussed in Chapter 8.

5. How about fiber-optic cable?

Several different types of fiber-optic connectors exist. Before the issuance of the EIA/TIA-568A standard, the most popular were ST connectors, which are similar to BNC connectors in that you push and turn the connectors to mate them to a device. SC connectors are those approved by the EIA/TIA-568A standard, by virtue of which they are destined to eclipse the popularity of the ST type. SC connectors, which are also called 568SC, are available in single and dual varieties, the latter designed to aid differentiation between transmit and receive fibers. SMA connectors use a threaded coupling mechanism—you attach them by screwing one end onto another. SMA connectors are designed to meet stringent military specifications. Another type of fiber-optic connector is the MIC (medium interface connector) connector used in FDDI networks.

6. What about a printer cable connector or a modem cable connector? Do they also operate at the physical layer?

You are referring to *DB* (data bus) and *DIN* (Deutsche Industrie Norm, a German industrial standard) connectors. DB connectors serve as an interface between a computer and a peripheral device such as a printer or external modem. Several types of DB connectors exist and are distinguished by the number of "pins" they contain. Common types include DB-9 (a 9-pin serial or video interface), DB-15 (a 15-pin video interface), DB-25 (a 25-pin serial interface—RS-232—or parallel printer interface), and DB-37 (a 37-pin serial interface based on RS-422). (Illustrations of DB-9 and DB-25 connectors are shown in Figure 4-1.) DIN connectors are similar, but they are circular instead of rectangular. DIN connectors are typically used to connect a keyboard to a computer.

7. OK. Enough about connectors. Let's move on to transceivers. What are they?

Transceivers are devices used in Ethernet/802.3 networks to connect nodes to the physical medium. They serve as both the physical connection and the electrical interface between a node and the physical medium, enabling the node to communicate with the medium.

8. Given the name, transceivers presumably transmit and receive signals. Right?

Precisely. Transceivers transmit and receive signals simultaneously. When a node sends data, the transmitting circuitry of the transceiver places the data bits on the medium.

Simultaneously, the transceiver's receiving circuitry listens to the transmission. If what is heard is the same as what was sent, then everything is fine. If not, the transceiver presumes that an error has occurred and notifies the node of this condition. (This error is called a "collision," which is discussed in Chapter 8.) In a nutshell, a transceiver essentially does three functions: it sends data, it receives data, and it notifies its host node if an error condition has occurred during a transmission. (*Note:* In Ethernet V2.0, a transceiver performs a fourth function: it asserts signal quality error (SQE). This is discussed in Chapter 8.)

9. Exactly where is a transceiver located in a network? Is it a separate device? Is it built into the computer? Where is it?

Today, transceivers are usually integrated into *network interface cards*, which are discussed later. This integration allows a node to be connected directly to the medium via a cable without the need for an external transceiver. A network interface card's on-board transceivers support UTP, ThinWire, and fiber-optic cable connections. Many network interface cards also can be purchased with a "universal" connector, called a 15-pin attachment unit interface (AUI), which allows a device to be connected to UTP, thick or thin coax, or fiber-optic cable via an external transceiver. (See Figure 6-2.) Ethernet/802.3 network interface cards can be purchased with any three connector types. (See Figure 6-3.)

10. Could you expand on the notion of AUI, please?

We shall, although the use of AUI connectors and cables is rapidly fading into Ethernet history. As we stated above, AUI stands for Attachment Unit Interface. It is a 15-pin D-shell type connector. (See Figure 6-4.) On the computer side, the AUI is female; on the transceiver side it is male. Many older Ethernet/802.3 devices such as bridges or switches (discussed below) could be purchased with AUI connector ports so that users could connect any of the three media types to any port using one of the external transceivers shown in Figure 6-2. As we have stated, however, the use of AUI is becoming less and less prevalent in the late 1990s.

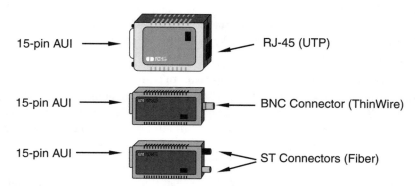

15-pin AUI ⟶   ⟵ RJ-45 (UTP)

15-pin AUI ⟶   ⟵ BNC Connector (ThinWire)

15-pin AUI ⟶   ⟶ ST Connectors (Fiber)

Figure 6-2. Three types of Ethernet/802.3 transceivers that serve as media converters. When connected to a network interface card's 15-pin AUI connector, the card is able to support twisted-pair, ThinWire, or fiber-optic cable.

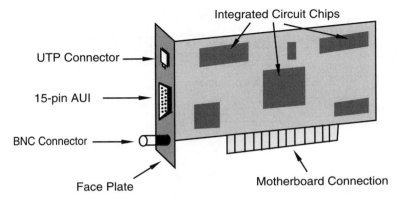

Figure 6-3. Sample Ethernet network interface card. This NIC can support any one of three media types—UTP, Transceiver Cable via an AUI, and ThinWire. NICs are installed into a node by inserting them into an expansion slot on the mother board.

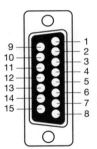

Figure 6-4.
Standard 15-pin
Attachment Unit
Interface (AUI).

ThickWire Ethernet networks also use external transceivers with AUI connectors to connect a node to the cable. In this setting, the transceiver was a bulky stand-alone device that required special transceiver cable to connect the node to the transceiver. The transceiver cable carried signals between the network cable and the node. (See Figure 6-5.) There also used to be multiport transceiver units such as the Digital Equipment Corporation DELNI, which contained eight AUI ports providing a total of eight independent transceiver cable connections. This technology is archaic, having been replaced by miniature external transceivers such as shown in Figure 6-2. There is no longer a need for transceiver cable since network cards provide a direct interface for different network media.

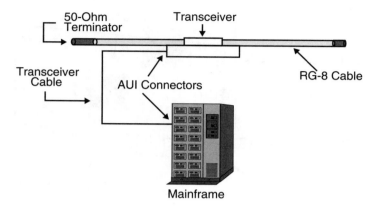

Figure 6-5. Illustration of an external transceiver used in ThickWire Ethernet LANs. Special transceiver cable is used to interconnect the node to the transceiver. The connector on the computer side is a 15-pin female AUI, and the connector on the transceiver is a 15-pin AUI male.

11. Are AUI connectors the ones that have those weird slide-lock things on them that never seem to work?

Yes, and it sounds like you have used them before. We were not able to get the slide lock to work correctly all of the time either. AUI connectors are also available with screw-in retainers.

12. OK. I now understand AUI, but what do AAUI and MAU mean?

AAUI stands for Apple Attachment Unit Interface, which was Apple's proprietary AUI. Older model Macintosh computers like the Centris 650 and Power Macintosh 7100 have built-in AAUI ports, as evidenced by yet another variety of subminiature 15-pin connector on their rear panels. In order to connect these machines to an Ethernet/802.3 LAN, you must first purchase an AAUI-to-AUI adapter to change the proprietary interface to AUI, BNC, or RJ-45. Why Apple chose to do this is anyone's guess. Later model Macintoshes have built-in standard connectors—mainly RJ45. As for *MAU*, this stands for Media Attachment Unit; it is another term for a transceiver.

13. Enough about transceivers. Let's talk about repeaters.

OK. *Repeaters*, like transceivers, provide both physical and electrical connections. Their function is to regenerate and propagate a signal.

14. Give me a little more detail. Where are they used? Why are they used?

Repeaters, which are also called concentrators, are used in Ethernet/802.3 LANs to extend the length of the LAN. You see, depending on the type of medium, the length of an Ethernet/802.3 LAN segment has specific length restrictions. For example, a 10 Mbps

Ethernet/802.3 LAN that uses UTP cable (10BASE-T), has a maximum length restriction of 100 meters, and a ThinWire (coax) Ethernet/802.3 segment (10BASE2) cannot exceed 185 meters. The reason for these restrictions is signal quality. As a segment exceeds its maximum length, the signal quality begins to deteriorate. (Recall the concept of attenuation from Chapter 4.) In many instances, these length restrictions are not always practical, so network managers have to extend their LANs by interconnecting individual segments. A repeater makes this possible. It receives signals from one cable segment, regenerates, retimes, and amplifies them, and then transmits these "revitalized" signals to another cable segment. We discuss the application of repeaters in Ethernet/802.3 LANs in more detail in Chapter 8.

15. Do repeaters introduce delay in a network?

Yes. Repeaters are a source of *propagation delay* in a network. Propagation delay is the amount of time a signal spends getting from one point in a circuit to another. It is affected by the speed and efficiency of the components between the two points.

16. Are repeaters also called hubs?

It depends on who you talk to. Some people think of a *hub* as a repeater, whereas others view a hub generically as any device that connects two or more network segments. A hub can also be a device that supports several different media. (See Figure 6-6.)

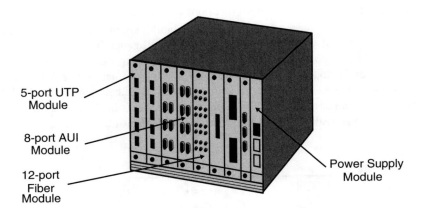

5-port UTP Module

8-port AUI Module

12-port Fiber Module

Power Supply Module

Figure 6-6. This multislot chassis-based repeater hub (also called a concentrator) can accommodate several different media types, including UTP, coax, and fiber. Since each interface module shares the same backplane as the repeater module, the Ethernet ports on each module use the same repeater. Thus repeater hubs are capable of supporting many Ethernet connections using only a single repeater. For example, if one of the modules is a 12-port ThinWire board, then this one board can support 12 separate 185-meter ThinWire segments. Since 30 devices can be connected to one ThinWire segment, this board can support $12 \times 30 = 360$ nodes.

17. What about a stackable hub? What's that?

Stackable repeater hubs consist of individual repeater units "stacked" one on top of another. Instead of a common shared backplane that is part of a chassis-based repeater, stackable hubs use a "pseudo-backplane" based on a common connector interface. An external cable interconnects the individual hubs in a daisy-chained manner. Once interconnected, the entire chain of hubs becomes a single logical unit that functions as a single repeater. Stackable hubs are less expensive than chassis-based devices. An illustration of a stackable hub is shown in Figure 6-7.

18. So what you are saying then is that when I hear the term "Ethernet hub" I shouldn't assume it is a repeater.

Correct. You need qualification. At one point, several years ago, an Ethernet hub was a repeater. Today, however, *switches* have replaced repeaters in many Ethernet/802.3 LANs and the term "hub" refers to a switch instead of a repeater. Physically, repeater and switch hubs look the same. For example, consider the illustration shown in Figure 6-8. Without any type of qualification, this 4-port device could be a repeater hub or it could be a switch. We don't know. Functionally, repeater and switch hubs are not the same. A repeater hub takes an incoming signal, amplifies it, and then repeats (i.e., broadcasts) it to all of the hub's ports regardless of the destination port. A switch, on the other hand, only transmits data between the hub's sending and receiving ports. (See Figure 6-9.) We will talk more about switches later in this chapter.

19. Is there anything else I need to know about repeaters?

There are two more pieces of information we should mention. Although repeaters are layer 1 devices, several vendors incorporate some intelligence into them. For example, many Ethernet/802.3 repeater hubs are capable of detecting Ethernet "collisions" (discussed in Chapter 8), and temporarily shutting down any segment that exhibits an excessive number of collisions. You should also know that in an Ethernet/802.3 LAN, Ethernet rules restrict the number of repeaters allowed. We discuss this in more detail in Chapter 8. For now, though, just realize that repeaters are layer 1 devices that regenerate signals.

Figure 6-7. Stackable hubs are daisy-chained together using an external cable, which enables them to function as a single hub.

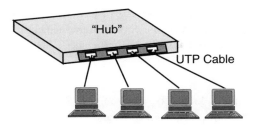

Figure 6-8. Illustration of a 4-port "hub."
Without any type of qualification, we do not
know if this is a repeater hub or a switch hub.

20. Are there any other layer 1 devices I should know about?

We'll mention just one more: *media converters*, which enable different network media
to be connected to one another. For example, using a media converter you can connect a
coaxial cable to UTP cable; coaxial cable to fiber-optic cable; a 100 Mbps Ethernet UTP
segment to 100 Mbps Ethernet fiber-optic segment; and half or full-duplex UTP segments
to 10 Mbps Ethernet fiber-optic segments. (See Chapter 8 for a discussion of 100 Mbps
Ethernet and full-duplex Ethernet.) Some people like to think of transceivers as media
converters because transceivers support various types of media via a standard AUI connection. Nevertheless, media converters operate at the physical layer and provide a simple
mechanism for extending the distance between two devices by mixing copper and fiber
cable. (*Note:* Media converters are non-standard devices and are not covered under the
IEEE 802.3 standard.)

21. What devices operate at the data link layer?

Several network devices operate at the data link layer (layer 2 of the OSI model),
including *network interface cards*, *PC cards*, *bridges*, and *switches*.

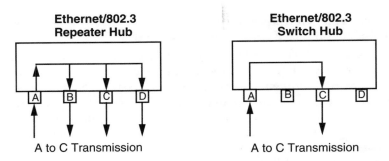

Figure 6-9. In a repeater hub, if data on port A is destined to port C, all
ports receive the data. In a switch hub, if data on port A is destined to port
C, only port C receives the data.

22. I am familiar with network interface cards. These are Ethernet cards, right?

Well, yes and no. An *Ethernet card* is a network interface card used in Ethernet/802.3 networks. Not all network interface cards are Ethernet cards, though.

23. This is confusing.

A network interface card is known by many names. Some of the more common ones are *LAN adapter, network adapter, network card,* and *network board.* Generally, we prefer to call them *NIC* (pronounced "Nick"). A NIC can support different types of networks and media. For example, an Ethernet/802.3 NIC is designed specifically for Ethernet/802.3 networks and can be purchased with connectors supporting UTP, BNC, AUI, and fiber. (See Figure 6-3.) An Ethernet NIC is often called *Ethernet card* or *Ethernet adapter.* Similarly, a Token Ring NIC is designed specifically for Token Ring networks, can support various media, and is called a *token ring card* or *token ring adapter.*

24. I see. It's a semantic thing. You have the generic name—network adapter—and the specific name—Ethernet card. But don't all NICs do the same thing?

We must equivocate yet again. In a generic sense, all NICs are functionally equivalent because they are layer 2 devices. As layer 2 devices, NICs perform typical layer 2 functions, including organizing data into frames, transferring frames between the ends of a communication channel, and managing the link by providing error control, initialization, control termination, and flow control (see Chapters 2 and 4). However, it is the network's architecture (Chapter 2) that determines the manner in which these functions are implemented.

25. Can you give me an example?

Consider the function of framing. The format of Ethernet frames is not the same as that of Token Ring frames (see Chapters 8 and 9). Hence, an Ethernet NIC does not frame data in exactly the same manner as a Token Ring NIC. A Token Ring NIC is also responsible for token-passing and includes chips for monitoring and reporting network errors.

26. Earlier you said that transceivers are usually built directly into a network interface card. Doesn't this make a NIC a layer 1 device also?

Good question. NICs do indeed have layer 1 components as part of their construction and hence perform layer 1 activities in addition to layer 2 activities. For example, on a sending node the NIC performs framing (layer 2) and converts bit values into electrical signals using an appropriate coding scheme (layer 1). At the receiving node, the NIC monitors the medium for transmissions, captures data from the medium if the frame's destination address matches the NIC's address (or if it is a broadcast or multicast), and then passes the data to the node for processing. The NIC also checks the integrity of a captured frame (error control). So, a NIC can be regarded as a combination layer 1/layer 2 device.

27. Are NICs part of a computer system, or do they have to be installed separately?

It depends. Some are built-in as an integral part of the computer's design. However, many desktop PCs, including Intel-based and Macintosh units, are not always manufactured with built-in network support. In such computers a network adapter is needed in order to connect the PC to a LAN. Add-in NICs exist for nearly all expansion slot types used in computers manufactured today.

28. What does a NIC installation involve?

Installation of a NIC is relatively straightforward—insert the card into an existing expansion slot, install special network "driver" software to enable the NIC to communicate with the networking software, reboot the machine, and test the card. On Intel-based (or compatible) machines, a NIC also must be assigned an I/O address and an interrupt request (IRQ). These assignments must be made to prevent the NIC from conflicting with other installed boards. (This is not necessary for Macintosh computers.) Many of the reputable NIC manufacturers do this via software; others require you to set DIP switches on the card. Many NICs support Plug-n-Play (PnP)—that is, they comply with the PnP specifications—which enables them to be configured automatically without user intervention.

29. What do you mean by "special network 'driver' software"?

A NIC is a network device that must communicate with its host's network operating system. This communication occurs via software called a *LAN driver*. A driver is critical to the operation of a NIC and must be written so the card supports the appropriate network protocols and operating system. Incorrect LAN drivers are invariably the source of network performance problems. Normally, a NIC requires a separate driver for each combination of network protocol and operating system. However, two specification standards— the Network Driver Interface Specification (NDIS) and the Open Data-link Interface (ODI)—provide generic interfaces that reduce the number of drivers required. Thus, a NIC that supports either NDIS or ODI only needs a single driver and can support multiple network protocols including TCP/IP, IPX/SPX, and NetBIOS. Similarly, standard driver specifications exist for MacOS's Open Transport networking.

30. Are all NICs the same? In other words, does it matter which brand I purchase?

Although most NICs, regardless of vendor, have a high degree of interoperability (e.g., an Ethernet card from one manufacturer most likely will communicate with an Ethernet card from a different manufacturer) all NICs are not the same.

31. So what do I need to consider when purchasing a NIC?

Several things. First of all, make sure the NIC's data bus is appropriate for the host system. For example, you don't want to use an 8-bit NIC in a Pentium server. At the same time you don't want to use a 32-bit NIC in a 386 workstation. Second, some NICs include an on-board processor, on-board RAM, or both. A NIC with an on-board processor is able to do more work than one without this feature and consequently relieves the host system's processor from performing certain functions. The on-board RAM provides a NIC with additional buffer space, which improves communication between the host system and the network. Assuming all things are equal and you can afford it, a 32-bit NIC with on-board processing and RAM will perform faster than a NIC without these features. Third, some NICs include on-board LEDs. For example, a UTP-based Ethernet card might contain LEDs for link status, collisions, and activity. These LEDs can provide valuable diagnostic information about the card's state or network activity. Another consideration is whether the card supports *auto-sensing* for 10/100 Mbps Ethernet/802.3 LANs, or if the card supports full-duplex networking. You should also make sure that the card you purchase is compatible with the host system's bus architecture. Thus, if your PC is an ISA bus machine or a PCI bus machine, make sure the NIC you purchase is ISA- or PCI-compatible. Finally, the drivers that come with the card must support your network and operating system. Ideally, the drivers should be either ODI- or NDIS-compliant, or both, for Intel/ Windows systems.

32. I have a laptop computer and use a PC card for network connectivity. Is this considered a NIC?

A *PC card* (Figure 6-10) serves the same purpose as a NIC, namely, to effect communication between a node and the network. So, yes, it is a type of NIC.

33. Can you tell me a little more about PC cards? Are they same as PCMCIA cards?

PCMCIA cards—PCMCIA stands for Personal Computer Memory Card International Association—were originally designed to serve as memory cards (and thus their name). They have since evolved into multipurpose plug-in devices and are today called PC cards. These devices are small (about the size of a credit card, only thicker) plug-in adapters used in portable or laptop computers. Three different "types" are available. *Type 1* cards, the earliest, are only 3.3 millimeters thick and enhance the memory capabilities of a device. Memory support includes ROM (read-only memory) and flash memory (a special form of ROM that can be reprogrammed). Some manufacturers use Type I cards for software upgrades. *Type II* cards are 5 mm thick and used for modems and network adapters for

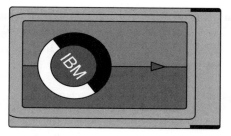

Figure 6-10. PC cards are multipurpose plug-in devices for portable computers and can be used as memory devices, modems and network adapters, or hard disk drives.

both Ethernet and token ring. These devices are similar to NICs and support various media types including RJ-11 for a modem connection and RJ-45 for UTP-based LANs. Both Ethernet/802.3 and Token Ring adapters are supported. *Type III* cards are 10.5 mm thick and are generally either miniature hard disks or wireless NICs. As of this writing, a *Type IV* card is being considered that will be approximately 16 mm thick and support hard disk drives that have a capacity greater than what is currently available from Type III cards.

PC cards are installed into an appropriate PCMCIA slot within a portable computing device. Type III slots also accept Type I or Type II cards, and Type II slots also accept Type I cards. Most laptops manufactured today contain at least one Type III or Type II slot.

34. Let's move on. From the list of layer 2 devices given earlier we still haven't talked about bridges and switches. What are they?

Bridges and switches are similar devices. We'll defer our discussion of switches until later, preferring to cover bridges first because many of the concepts and principles that apply to bridges also apply to switches. A network *bridge* interconnects two or more individual LANs or LAN segments. Unlike repeaters, which are layer 1 devices—bridges connect networks that have different physical layers. This is what makes them layer 2 devices—the physical layer is transparent to bridges. Bridges also can connect networks using either the same or different type of architectures (e.g., Ethernet-to-Ethernet, token ring-to-token ring, or Ethernet-to-token ring). (See Figure 6-11.) Two bridge standards have been defined by IEEE. The first is a *transparent bridge* and is used in IEEE 802.3 ("Ethernet") and 802.5 (token ring) networks. The second is a *source routing bridge*, which was introduced by IBM and used exclusively in token ring networks.

35. What do bridges do?

Bridges pass frames between LANs and provide filtering. They allow frames from a node on one network to be forwarded to a node on another network, but discard any frames destined for the same network from which the frames originated. Thus, bridges keep local traffic local, but forward traffic destined for a remote network. Since bridges operate at the data link layer, they check the hardware (i.e., the MAC-level) address of a particular network interface card to determine whether to forward or discard a frame.

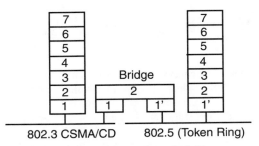

Figure 6-11. OSI representation of a bridge.
Bridges can connect networks using different
architectures such as Ethernet and Token Ring.

36. How does a transparent bridge work?

A transparent bridge is a "plug and play" unit—you connect it to your network and power it on. Operating in *promiscuous mode*, a transparent bridge captures every frame that is transmitted on all the networks to which the bridge is connected. The bridge examines every frame it receives and extracts each frame's source address, which is then added to a "learned address" table maintained by the bridge. Eventually, this table contains an entry for each unique source address and the port on which the frame was received. For example, in Figure 6-12, when node 1 (with a hardware source address of 1) transmits a frame, the bridge "learns" that node 1 is on channel A (i.e., port A) and adds a corresponding entry to its address table. The bridge also examines the destination address of the frame to determine if the frame should be forwarded or filtered. All broadcast and multicast frames always get forwarded. If the destination address is not a broadcast or multicast address, and it is not found in the bridge's address table, the frame is forwarded by default. This is what the bridge does when it is first powered on and its address table is empty. This procedure is referred to as "flooding." The only condition under which a frame does not get forwarded (i.e., it is discarded or filtered) occurs when the frame's destination address is found in the address table and corresponds to the same channel on which the frame was received. So if node 1 transmits a frame to node 3 in Figure 6-12, the bridge does not forward the frame to Channel B; the destination address (3) is a source address on the same channel on which the frame originated. On the other hand, if the destination is node 5, or if the frame is a broadcast or multicast, then the bridge forwards the frame.

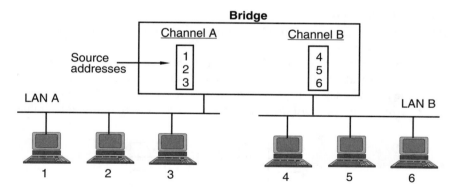

Figure 6-12. Bridges interconnect separate networks making them appear as a single network. Operating at the data link layer, a bridge builds a table of hardware addresses that identifies the address of each node and the segment to which a node is attached. Using this table, a bridge either forwards a frame from one network to the other, or discards the frame, depending if the destination node is local or remote. For example, a frame from node 3 to node 1 does not get forwarded to Channel B. Thus, none of the nodes on LAN B "sees" node 3's transmission. However, a frame from node 3 to node 5 is forwarded from Channel A to Channel B. A bridge will, however, forward any broadcast frames from LAN A to LAN B, and vice versa.

37. How does a source-routing bridge differ from a transparent bridge?

As we mentioned earlier, the source routing bridge was introduced by IBM for use in token ring networks. With source routing, the sending machine is responsible for determining whether a frame is destined for a node on the same network or on a different network. If the frame is destined for a different network, the source machine designates this by setting the high-order bit of the group address bit of the source address to one. It also includes in the frame's header the path the frame is to follow from source to destination. Source routing bridges are based on the assumption that a sending machine will provide routing information for messages destined for different networks. By making the sending machine responsible for this task, a source routing bridge can ignore frames that have not been "marked," and forward only those frames with their high-order destination bit set to one. An illustration of source routing bridges is given in Figure 6-13.

38. I have heard the term "spanning tree" used with bridges. What does this mean?

For reliability, some networks contain more than one bridge, which increases the likelihood of *networking loops*. A networking loop occurs when frames are passed from bridge to bridge in a circular manner, never reaching their destination. To prevent networking loops when multiple bridges are used, the bridges communicate with each other and establish a map of the network in order to derive what is called a *spanning tree* for all the networks. A spanning tree consists of a single path between source and destination nodes

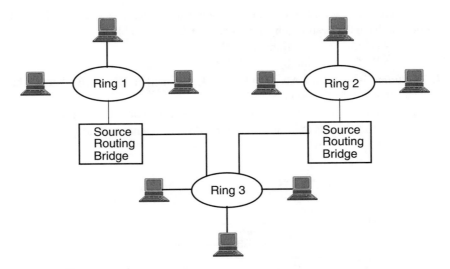

Figure 6-13. Bridges used to interconnect separate Token Ring networks are called source routing bridges. As is the case with transparent bridges used in Ethernet/802.3 networks, source routing bridges copy frames from one ring to another. They also retransmit frames to the next station on the same ring. Unlike transparent bridges, source routing bridges depend on the sending station to provide routing information for frames destined for a different network.

that does not include any loops. Thus, a spanning tree can be considered a loop-free subset of a network's topology. The spanning tree algorithm, specified in IEEE 802.1d, describes how bridges (and switches) can communicate to avoid network loops.

39. Can you give me an example of what you mean by a network loop?

Sure. Look at Figure 6-14, which has four network segments interconnected by four bridges. LAN 1 is connected to LAN 2 by B1; LAN 2 is connected to LAN 3 by B2; and LAN 3 is connected to LAN 4 by B4. Note also that LAN 1 is connected to LAN 4 by B3. Thus, multiple bridges are being used on LAN 1. Let us assume that a frame originates on LAN 1 and none of the bridges (B1-B4) has an entry for the frame's destination. Here is an example of how a network loop can develop:

1. A frame originates on LAN 1; neither B1 nor B3 has the destination address as an entry so neither know on what network the destination node resides. Hence, B1 and B3 must forward the frame to their respective LANs. That is:
   • B1 forwards the frame to LAN 2
   • B3 forwards the frame to LAN 4

2. The frame is now on LAN 2 and LAN 4. Once again, neither B2 nor B4 knows on what LAN the destination node is located since they do not have the destination address in their tables:
   • B2 forwards the frame to LAN 3
   • B4 forwards the frame to LAN 3

3. The frame is now on LAN 3, having come from different LANs, and B2 still does not have the destination address as an entry in its table:
   • B2 forwards the frame to LAN 2
   • B4 forwards the frame to LAN 4

4. The frame is now on LAN 2 and LAN 4, and neither B1 nor B3 knows the location of the destination node's LAN:
   • B1 forwards the frame to LAN'1 (We have a network loop.)
   • B3 forwards the frame to LAN 1 (We have a network loop.)

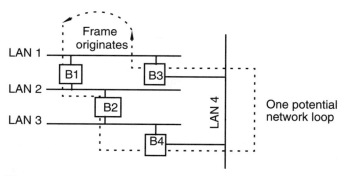

Figure 6-14. Illustration of a possible network loop.

40. So how does the spanning tree algorithm help?

The spanning tree algorithm would disable the port on B3 that connects LAN 4 with LAN 1. If B4 were to fail, the algorithm would then automatically enable the LAN 1-to-LAN 4 connection via B3.

41. Does it matter what network protocol you are using when you install a bridge?

No. Bridges are transparent to protocols operating at higher layers. This means that regardless of the network protocol being used, bridges will pass or discard frames independent of the protocol. Thus, two networks based on different protocols connected to the same bridge are viewed as a single logical network. Bridges also force the repeater count in an Ethernet/802.3 network (see Chapter 8) to return to one. Bridges, however, are highly susceptible to *broadcast storms* since they will pass broadcast frames from one network to another. A broadcast storm occurs when several broadcasts are transmitted at the same time. Broadcast storms can use up a substantial amount of network bandwidth, and in many cases, can cause a network to crash or shut down.

42. I have heard the term "store-and-forward" used when discussing bridges. What does this mean?

Bridges are indeed *store-and-forward* devices. What this means is they capture an entire frame before deciding whether to filter or forward the frame. This provides a high level of error detection because a frame's CRC checksum can be computed by the bridge and matched to that of the frame. If the CRC checksum is not correct, the frame is dropped. This prevents the propagation of corrupt frames.

43. If I had to choose between using a repeater or a bridge, which should I select?

Neither. You would want a switch (see the discussion below). In the rare instance where you do need to select between a repeater or bridge, though, the answer is, "it depends." The purpose of a repeater is to extend a network. The purpose of a bridge is to segment network traffic. In choosing between a repeater and a bridge you need to determine the manner in which the device will be used. Repeaters and bridges also provide electrical isolation. That is, if the device fails, then nodes on the same physical segment can still communicate with each other, but nodes on different segments cannot. So, if the purpose is to electrically isolate segments, then either device will do the job.

Bridges, unlike repeaters, also can connect networks in different geographical locations that require a telecommunications link for connectivity. Wireless bridges also have become available for limited-distance remote connections. Remote bridges that use radio waves can be placed up to 25-30 miles (40-48 km) apart, provided the terrain and weather allow for it, and if the bridges have directional antennas. Remote bridges using laser communication techniques can be spaced approximately 3,500 feet (1,050 m) apart.

44. Does replacing a repeater with a bridge improve Ethernet LAN performance?

Not necessarily. The performance of a bridge is measured by the number of frames per second it can forward (the *forwarding rate*) and the amount of delay that is introduced due to forwarding (the *forwarding delay*). In an ideal setting, an Ethernet/802.3 bridge forwards 14,880 64-byte frames per second. This is referred to as *wire speed*. (See Chapter 8.) Furthermore, an ideal Ethernet/802.3 bridge has a 60 ms forwarding delay for 64-byte frames. The propagation delay of a repeater is less than 3 ms. Also keep in mind that a repeater propagates errors but a bridge does not.

Before replacing a repeater with a bridge, you must design the network properly based on traffic patterns. For example, in a repeater-based LAN, it does not matter where a server is located. However, in a bridge-based LAN, if a server is placed on one physical segment, and all nodes that must communicate with the server are on a different segment, then performance will be worse than the repeater-based configuration. The concept of network segmentation and partitioning is discussed in further detail in Chapter 8.

45. What's a brouter?

A *brouter* is a combination bridge-router. That is, it is basically a bridge that has routing capabilities. We will discuss brouters in Chapter 7.

46. OK. Let's move on to switches. What are they and how different are they from bridges?

We assume you are interested in learning about Ethernet switches in particular.

47. Yes. Are there others?

Yes. Although network switches were first designed for Ethernet/802.3 LANs, the concept of switching has since been extended to other LANs including token ring, FDDI, and ATM. We'll discuss the other types in later chapters.

48. Back to Ethernet switches, please.

Ethernet switches are layer 2 devices that are essentially modified multiport bridges. Like bridges, each port on an Ethernet switch supports a separate LAN segment, and each port can accommodate different media including ThinWire, UTP, and fiber-optic cable. Furthermore, each switch port filters traffic sent over its attached segment. Thus, traffic destined for a node on the same segment does not cross the switch's port boundary; it remains local to that segment. Furthermore, if a node on one segment sends frames to a node connected to a different segment, that is, a different switch port, the frames are forwarded across the port boundary and through the switch to the appropriate destination port without any other port seeing the transmission.

49. It sounds like an Ethernet switch is the same as a bridge except for its name. What's different about switches?

What makes switches different from bridges is their architecture. Repeaters and bridges are designed for shared media LANs; the architecture of switches, however, permits multiple, simultaneous data transmission paths between ports. Each switch port is assigned a specific MAC address, with data paths between ports being hardwired and part of the switch's internal circuitry (called the *switch fabric* or *switch matrix*). When a data frame enters a switch port, the port's network adapter translates the MAC destination address of the frame to a specific switch port address and then transfers the frame to that MAC-specified destination port. Thus, the data transmission in a switch is based on a static port-to-MAC address association. Some switches support only one MAC address per port; others support more than one MAC address per port. The bottom line: Nodes connected to bridges share bandwidth; nodes connected to switches do not share bandwidth—they have "private" connections.

50. What are the various types of switches?

Ethernet switches have three basic design architectures: *store-and-forward, cut-through,* and *hybrid.*

51. Is a store-and-forward switch the same thing as a store-and-forward bridge?

Pretty much so. A switch that incorporates the store-and-forward design (sometimes referred to as a *buffering switch*) operates exactly like an Ethernet bridge—it waits until it receives an entire data frame before forwarding it. When the switch receives a frame, it first performs an integrity check to ensure that the frame does not contain any errors. As a result, data reliability is excellent in this type of switch since "bad" frames (e.g., incorrect CRC checksums) are never forwarded. After checking for errors, the switch extracts the destination address from the frame's address field, performs an address table lookup to identify the destination port to which the frame should be sent, and forwards the frame to the destination port if it is different from the port at which the frame arrived. (If the port is the same, the switch discards the frame.) An illustration of a store-and-forward switch that contains individual port buffers is given in Figure 6-15.

52. What's different about the cut-through architecture?

The cut-through architecture is what really separates switches from traditional store-and-forward bridges. A *cut-through switch* operates in the following way: If a frame arriving at one port in the switch is to be transmitted to a different port, the switch begins this transmission as soon as it reads the destination address of the frame. This technology improves Ethernet performance considerably by reducing delays.

Cut-through switches can be implemented using either a crossbar or backplane design. A *crossbar design* identifies the frame's destination address and the path within the switch the frame must follow to get to the destination port. Once these have been determined, the switch transfers the part of the frame it has already received (the preamble, start frame delimiter and destination address) to the destination port. All remaining parts of the frame (source address, length count, data, pad, and checksum) are immediately transferred as they are received by the switch via this same data path. An illustration of a crossbar switch is shown in Figure 6-16. Note that this design can introduce delay if the data path is not clear for transmission. For example, suppose a frame arrives from segment 2 destined for segment 3. If the path to segment 3 is busy (e.g., a transfer might be occurring from seg-

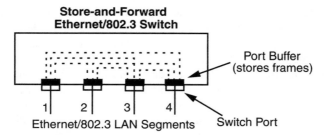

Figure 6-15. A store-and-forward Ethernet switch has buffers at each port. When a frame enters a port from a segment, the switch stores the frame in that port's buffer until the entire frame is received and checked for errors. If the frame is error-free, the destination address is identified and the frame is placed at the destination segment's port without any other port seeing the transmission. (Adapted from Majkiewicz, 1993, and Sharer, 1995.)

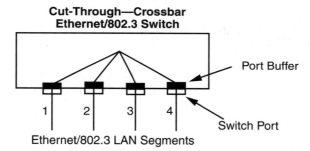

Figure 6-16. Cut-through Ethernet switches transmit frames as soon as the destination address is known. In the crossbar design, the data paths connecting the ports are all interconnected. If this path is busy with a current transmission, delays will occur. (Adapted from Majkiewicz, 1993, and Sharer, 1995.)

ment 1 to 3), then the frame must remain in segment 2's buffer until the path is clear. This can "back up" traffic on segment 2.

In contrast to the crossbar approach, the *backplane design* places frames on a high-speed backplane, which interconnects all ports. If the destination port is free, frames are immediately transferred. If the destination port is busy, frames are buffered onto the backplane until the port is clear. This eliminates the potential congestion problem of the crossbar approach. The key to this design is the switch's backplane, which requires a data rate greater than the aggregate throughput of the switch. For example, an eight-port 10 Mbps Ethernet switch has a total throughput of 80 Mbps. Given that a transmission involves at least two nodes, it is possible to have as many as four simultaneous transmissions occurring in parallel. To avoid bottlenecks, a 10 Mbps switch must be able to handle at least 40 Mbps of aggregate data flow. Typically, a cut-through switch based on the backplane design has a backplane that is at least equal to the total aggregate throughput of the segments. In our illustration, this would be 80 Mbps. Some switches have gigabit per second backplanes. Viewed from this perspective, switches do not actually increase the speed of a 10 Mbps segment. Rather, they increase the aggregate throughput capability of a network. Thus, switches simply are high throughput devices that provide the capacity for multiple segments to operate concurrently. An illustration of the backplane design is shown in Figure 6-17. Cut-through switches generally are more expensive than store-and-forward switches because of their more sophisticated circuitry. (*Note:* Ethernet cut-through switches, which are discussed in Chapter 8, neither check CRC checksum values nor minimum frame lengths. Thus, a cut-through switch will propagate "bad" frames throughout an Ethernet/802.3 network.)

53. What's a hybrid switch?

A *hybrid switch* integrates the best features of store-and-forward (reliable frame transmission) and cut-through (low latency) designs. A hybrid switch can be configured on a per-port basis to change automatically from cut-through switching to store-and-forward switching if error rates exceed a user-defined threshold. When error rates fall below this threshold, the switch reverts to cut-through switching. An additional capability is a "runt-free" mode in which the switch discards frames smaller than the mandated 64 bytes minimum size for Ethernet. This ensures the filtering of collision fragments while maintaining the low latency characteristics of cut-through switching.

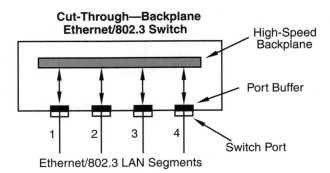

Figure 6-17. Backplane-based cut-through Ethernet switches also transmit frames as soon as the destination address is known. In the backplane design, though, data frames are placed on a high-speed backplane for transmission. The speed of this backplane is greater than the aggregate throughput of the switch. If a destination port is busy, the frame remains on the backplane; this eliminates the kind of delays inherent in the cross-bar design. (Adapted from Majkiewicz, 1993, and Sharer, 1995.)

54. How does the performance of bridges and switches compare?

Switches provide high throughput with low or fixed *latency*. Used in this context, latency is the amount of delay a network device introduces when data frames pass through it. Thus, latency is the amount of time a frame spends inside a network device such as a bridge or switch. Switch latency is usually measured from the instant the first bit of a frame enters the device to the time this bit leaves the outbound (i.e., destination) port. Depending on a switch's architecture, its latency is usually less than 100 μs. In comparison, bridge latency of 400 μs is common, and routers have latency as high as 1,500 μs (i.e., 1.5 ms). Low latency is good because the lower it is the faster a device processes a data frame. If latency is too high, then time-sensitive network protocols such as SNA or IPX can time out. Latency also is an issue for time-sensitive applications such as full-motion video.

55. How does the performance of different switch architectures compare?

Store-and-forward switches provide both traffic isolation and error immunity to any destination port. The trade-off for error immunity, though, is high latency, which can be in milliseconds rather than microseconds. Since store-and-forward switches wait until an entire frame has arrived before forwarding it, latency, which is dependent on frame size, can range from 61 μs to 1200 μs over a 10 Mbps channel. This could be a serious concern for some applications.

Cut-through switches have extremely low latency, usually on the order of 20 to 40 μs. Furthermore, since cut-through switches begin forwarding frames the moment the destination address is known, latency is independent of frame size. Thus, a maximum-size Ethernet/802.3 frame (1,518 bytes) has the same latency as a minimum-size Ethernet/802.3 frame (64 bytes). This is not the case with store-and-forward switches where latency varies directly with frame size. Considering that the total roundtrip bit propagation speed of a standard 10 Mbps Ethernet/802.3 network is approximately 51.2 microseconds, the speed of a cut-through switch approximates cable or wire speed, which is 14,880 packets per second using 64-byte packets. (See Box 8-3 in Chapter 8.) The trade-off, though, is there is no opportunity for the switch to check the integrity of a frame before it is forwarded to its destination port. Thus, if corrupt data messages are contained in the fields that follow the destination and source address fields of a data frame, the frame is still forwarded to the destination port. Errors on a specific port are propagated to other ports on the switch, or throughout the network. This reduces bandwidth and can delay forwarding error-free frames.

56. I have heard and read about "layer 3 switching" and "layer 3 switches." Frankly, I am a little confused by these concepts. Could you shed some light on this?

Sure, but not here. This is discussed in Chapter 7 when we examine the differences between routers and switches. For the moment, though, suffice it to say that Layers 2 and 3 of the OSI model are merging and it is becoming difficult to distinguish between traditional layer 2 devices such as LAN switches and layer 3 devices such as routers.

End-of-Chapter Commentary

This concludes our discussion of layer 1 and layer 2 network components. In subsequent chapters some of the concepts discussed in this chapter are extended. For example, in Chapter 7, we discuss WANs, internetworking, and network layer (layer 3) concepts and components. Two topics that are discussed in Chapter 7 that were referenced in the current chapter are routers and switches. Another topic of this chapter, Ethernet switches, is expanded on in Chapter 8. The topic of switching is also extended in later chapters. For example, token ring switching is discussed in Chapter 9, FDDI switching is discussed in Chapter 10, frame relay switching is discussed in Chapter 11, and ATM switching is discussed in Chapter 15. Finally, for a review of layer 1 or layer 2 concepts, refer to Chapters 4 and 5, respectively.

Chapter 7

WANs, Internetworking, and Network Layer Concepts and Components

In Chapters 4, 5, and 6, we introduced many of the concepts and hardware components related to layers 1 and 2 of the OSI model. Our discussion in these chapters also was relative to local area networks. In this chapter, we extend our previous discussions to wide area links. As part of this presentation we introduce the concept of internetworking from a WAN perspective and discuss the third layer of the OSI model—the network layer. An outline of the main topics we address follows:

- The Concept of Internetworking (Questions 1–2)
- WAN Circuits (Questions 3–10)
- SONET (Questions 11–13)
- Layer 3 Concepts and Issues (Questions 14–15)
- Router Protocols and Routing Algorithms (Questions 16–30)
- Switches vs. Routers vs. Layer 3/Layer 4 Switching (Questions 31–35)
- VPNs (Questions 36–38)

1. In Chapter 1, you said a WAN can be thought of as a collection of interconnected, geographically separated LANs. How are LANs interconnected to form a WAN?

Wide area networks employ a point-to-point topology. In the simplest WAN—one that interconnects two LANs—a typical scenario involves two remote bridges or routers (one at each end), interconnected via a WAN data communication circuit. (See Figure 7-1.) WANs use either circuit switching or packet switching techniques. (See Chapter 2 and Table 2-1 for more information about packet and circuit switching.) In a circuit-switched WAN, a fixed connection is established between source and destination nodes prior to transmission, each packet takes the same path, and all packets arrive in sequence. ISDN (see Chapter 11) is one example of a circuit-switched WAN. In a packet-switched WAN, connections are established during the transmission process. Thus, packets do not necessarily travel the same route and they might arrive out of sequence at the destination node. Examples of a packet switched WAN include frame relay (see Chapter 12), SMDS (see Chapter 13), and ATM (see Chapter 14). WANs represent one form of an internetwork.

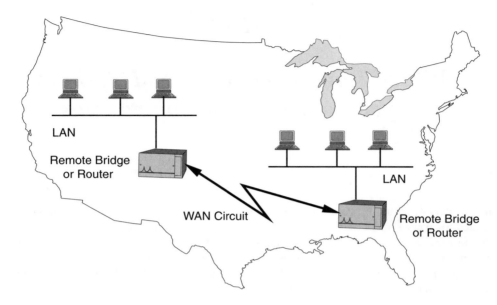

Figure 7-1. A wide are network interconnects geographically separated LANs using a point-to-point topology. A WAN transmission facility consists of remote bridges or routers and a data communication circuit.

2. What do you mean by an internetwork?

In Chapter 1, we defined an *internetwork* as a collection of interconnected networks that function as a single network. We also indicated that the Internet is the world's largest internetwork and is sometimes thought of as a *wide area internetwork* (WAI). In addition to a WAN, an internetwork can involve local networks (e.g., LAN-to-LAN or LAN-to-mainframe connections), or long-distance connections between networks requiring WAN connections (e.g., LAN-to-WAN connections). Thus, an internetwork link can connect identical (same architecture and same cabling), similar (different architecture or different cabling), or dissimilar (different hardware and software) networks. They can be located near each other or they can be far apart. While we're on the subject, you should note that internetwork links also differ in the level in which they operate. This difference affects the kinds of networks that can be linked. For example, using the OSI model:

- A repeater provides connections at the physical layer and works with only a specific LAN architecture. (See Figure 7-2(a).)

- A bridge and a layer 2 switch provide connections at the data link layer. Internetworks based on these devices support different physical layers, and can interconnect different LAN architectures (See Figure 7-2(b).) (*Note:* Different LAN architectures require different bridging techniques. For example, transparent bridging for Ethernet/802.3, source routing bridging for token ring or FDDI, and transparent/source routing bridging for mixed environments. See Chapter 6

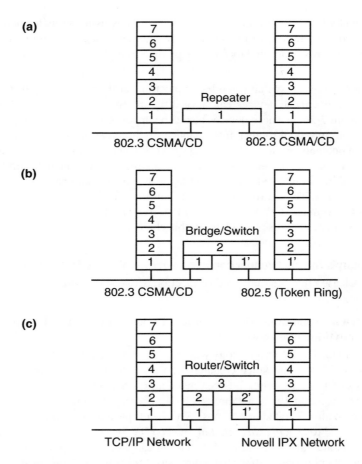

Figure 7-2. An OSI representation of internetworking. In a repeater-based internetwork (a), the LAN architecture must be the same. A bridge- or switch-based internetwork (b) has different physical layers and connect different types of LAN architectures. (*Note:* MAC-based bridges can only interconnect similar LAN architectures.) Bridges and layer 2 switches are also network protocol independent. A router- or layer 3 switch-based internetwork (c) operates at layer 3 of the OSI model and interconnects networks using different network protocols. These devices perform protocol translations.

for more information about these different bridging methods.) Bridges and layer 2 switches also are network-protocol independent, which enable them to interconnect networks using different network protocols (e.g., TCP/IP and IPX). Unlike routers, which operate at layer 3 and do protocol translations, though, bridges and layer 2 switches ignore layer 3 information. Interconnectivity is achieved by forwarding frames between networks by using hardware addresses, not network addresses. In this context, an internetwork consisting of two dissimilar networks connected by a bridge or switch can be viewed as a single, logical network.

- A router or layer 3 switch provides connections at the network layer. Internetworks that use these devices can have different physical and data link layers. (See Figure 7-2(c).) These devices also can support different network protocols (e.g., a multiprotocol router). Interconnectivity is achieved by forwarding packets from one network to another using network layer information (e.g., network addresses). In a heterogeneous networking environment in which dissimilar networks are interconnected, routers and layer 3 switches perform *network protocol translation*. Thus, a router that interconnects a TCP/IP network and an IPX network reformats TCP/IP packets into IPX packets and vice versa. Routers and layer 3 switches are discussed later in this chapter.

3. My company's Internet connection is via a leased T1 line. Is this a WAN link?

Yes it is. A leased line is a dedicated connection between two sites.

4. Can you tell me something about T1 lines? I know they are 1.544 Mbps but I don't really know anything else about them.

We'll be glad to. The T1 terminology was originally defined by AT&T and describes the multiplexing of 24 separate voice channels into a single, wideband digital signal. A T1 frame consists of 193 bits—eight bits per channel plus one bit for framing. Bits 1 through 8 are dedicated to channel 1, bits 9 through 16 are dedicated to channel 2, and so forth.

Each voice channel is rated at 64 kbps. When multiplexed into a digital signal, a voice channel is referred to as a *digital signal at level 0 (DS-0)*. Thus, DS-0 represents a single, digital voice channel rated at 64 kbps. A T1 circuit carries a DS-1 signal, which consists of 24 DS-0 channels plus one 8 kbps channel reserved for framing. This results in an aggregate bandwidth of 1.544 Mbps.

The T1 concept eventually evolved to what is known as the North American Digital Hierarchy (NADH), which consists of multiplexed T1 lines. For example, two T1 lines are combined to form a T1C circuit rated at 3.152 Mbps. (In DS terminology, T1C is known as DS-1C.) This is more than twice 1.544 Mbps because NADH uses bit-stuffing (see Chapter 5), which increases the aggregate bandwidth. A T2 circuit (DS-2) consists of four multiplexed T1 circuits and has an aggregate bandwidth of 6.312 Mbps; a T3 link (DS-3) consists of 28 multiplexed T1 circuits with an aggregate bandwidth of 44.736 Mbps; and a T4 channel (DS-4), rated at 274.176 Mbps, consists of 168 multiplexed T1 circuits. Table 7-1 provides a summary of this hierarchy.

5. What's the difference between T1 and Digital Signal terminology?

In practical terms and everyday usage, the terms T1 and DS-1 are considered synonymous.

Table 7-1. Summary of NADH Line Rates

Digital Signal	T-Carrier	Data Transmission Rate (Mbps)	Number of Multiplexed DS-0 Channels	Number of Multiplexed DS-1 Channels
DS-0	—	0.064	1	—
DS-1	T1	1.544	24	1
DS-1C	T1C	3.152	48	2
DS-2	T2	6.312	96	4
DS-3	T3	44.736	672	28
DS-4	T4	274.176	4,032	168

Table 7-2. Summary of European E-Carrier Line Rates

E-Carrier	Data Transmission Rate (Mbps)	Number of 64 kbps Channels	Number of E-1 Channels	Number of E-2 Channels	Number of E-3 Channels	Number of E-4 Channels
—	0.064	1	—	—	—	—
E-1	2.048	30	1	—	—	—
E-2	8.448	120	4	—	—	—
E-3	34.368	480	16	4	—	—
E-4	139.264	1,920	64	16	4	—
E-5	565.148	7,680	256	64	16	4

6. What terminology is used outside of North America?

T1 service has the same meaning in Australia and Japan as it does in North America (U.S. and Canada). However, in Europe, South America, Africa, parts of Asia, and Mexico, T1 is meaningless. Instead, an analogous service called E-1 (the "E" for European) is used in these locations. An E-1 carrier is normally supplied as an ISDN PRI circuit, which comprises thirty 64 kbps voice channels plus one 64 kbps channels for control ($30B + D$). The aggregate bandwidth of an E-1 carrier is 2.048 Mbps. (See Chapter 11 for more information about ISDN.) As with T1 service, E-1 links can be multiplexed into higher-capacity lines. Table 7-2 summarizes this hierarchy.

7. Why was 64 kbps selected as the basic building block of T1/DS-1 circuits?

(*Note:* Prior to reading this answer you might want to review the material in Chapter 4 that deals with analog signals.)

During the early stages of developing copper-based analog telephone networks, it was discovered that the normal range of frequencies generated by the human voice is from 300 Hz to 3,300 Hz. The difference between these frequencies, 3,000 Hz, is the amount of bandwidth telephone companies allocated to support the transmission of voice signals. In practice, though, telephone companies actually allocated 4,000 Hz channels and installed filters at 300 Hz and 3,300 Hz. Thus, voice signals that generated frequencies less than 300 Hz or greater than 3,300 Hz were discarded.

As digital technology and data applications emerged, analog technology was unable to separate voice or data from noise in a satisfactory manner. This led to the introduction of digital signaling, which requires converting analog signals to digital signals and vice versa. This analog-to-digital conversion process involves two steps: sampling and coding. Digitizing an analog signal requires regular samples of the amplitude of the signal's waveform to be taken over time so that the generated digital signal matches its corresponding analog signal. According to Nyquist's rule, analog-to-digital conversions should be done by sampling the analog signal at twice the highest frequency on the line to avoid harmonic distortion. Thus, $3300 \times 2 = 6600$ samples per second were required. However, since the telephone companies partitioned their circuits into channels of 4,000 Hz, 8,000 samples per second were actually used. The higher sampling rate also provided support for higher voice frequencies. This equates to 125 µsec per sample (1 divided by 8,000). Each sample is then converted into an eight-bit digital code: 00000000, which represents the absence of voltage, or 00000001, which represents the presence of voltage. By using eight bits, 256 (2^8) possible points can be used to partition the wave for sampling. Determining whether a sampled point gets coded 0 or 1 depends on where the along the wave the sample is taken. This coding process is called *pulse-code modulation* (PCM). Multiplying 8,000 samples per second by eight bits per sample yields 64,000 bps. Thus, the 64-kbps rate is derived from the early development of analog-to-digital conversions—the digital representation of a single analog voice call requires 64,000 bits.

It is instructive to note the construction of a T1's line rate. As stated above, each channel is sampled at a rate of 8,000 times per second. This produces an eight-bit number for each sample. Seven of these bits represent data and one bit is used for control. This yields per channel transmission rates of 56,000 bps for data and 8,000 bps for control. Since a T1 channel can support 24 simultaneous voice channels via frequency division multiplexing (FDM), we have 1,344,000 bps for data and 192,000 bps for control. Added to this is a separate 8,000 bps channel for frame synchronization. This is summarized below.

Data: 56,000 bps per channel at 24 channels = 1,344,000 bps

Control: 8,000 bps per channel at 24 channels = 192,000 bps

Framing: 8,000 bps for frame synchronization = 8,000 bps

This line rate can be further confirmed by observing that a T1 frame contains 193 bits— 168 for data, 24 for control, and 1 for synchronization; 193 bits at 8,000 samples per second yields 1.544 Mbps. A T1 service is sometimes referred to as a "bit-robbing" service because circuit control is in-band; T1 steals a proportion of the available bandwidth for control purposes. (*Note:* The European standard is based on a 256-bit frame that consists of thirty-two 8-bit time slots. Similar calculations can be done using these values. E-1 circuits are also controlled out-of-band.)

8. OK. I have also heard about fractional T1 service. Does this involve just multiplexing individual DS-0s?

Yes. Fractional T1 service (FT1), as its name implies, provides a fraction of a T1's capacity. This is achieved by combining multiple DS-0 (i.e., 64 kbps) channels. For example, 128 kbps is two DS-0 channels, 256 kbps consists of four DS-0 channels, and 512 kbps consists of eight DS-0 channels. When ordering FT1 service from a telco provider, you actually receive a full T1 channel but only pay for the number of DS-0 channels you order. (*Note:* Some U.S. carriers provide 256 kbps channels as part of their ISDN services, but these are being dropped in favor of 64 kbps channel services.)

A 64 kbps FT1 line is less efficient than a 64 kbps ISDN channel in terms of the amount of bandwidth available for data communication. This is because T1 control frames are in-band. Thus, you only get 56 kbps for data with every channel; the remaining 8 kbps are for control. ISDN, on the other hand, uses a separate channel for control and thereby provides a full 64 kbps for data. Similarly, a 128 kbps FT1 line only provides 112 kbps for data, but a 128 kbps ISDN channel provides a full 128 kbps. FT1 service is attractive to customers who do not require full T1 service but need more capacity than an ISDN 64/128 kbps line.

9. How much does T1 service cost and what kind of equipment is needed?

T1 service costs vary widely and are based on a customer's location relative to the telco provider and the type of circuit desired. Consideration also must be given to end equipment purchases and monthly service charges, which include the cost of the circuit itself and any *local loop* charges. The local loop is essentially the cable that connects the telephone central office (or exchange) with the customer's location. Local loop charges usually vary directly with the distance of the customer's location from the central office. For example, to interconnect PBXs, a *channelized* circuit is used, which requires no special equipment. (*Note:* A PBX stands for *Private Branch Exchange* and is a telephone exchange used within an organization to provide internal telephone extensions and access to the public telephone network—the modern day equivalent of what used to be called a *switchboard*.) The trade-off is that you cannot partition the T1 link. If, on the other hand, you need to partition the link, then a non-channelized circuit is needed, requiring two T1 multiplexers—one at each end of the circuit.

A T1 circuit also requires special termination equipment called a *CSU/DSU*. A *Channel Service Unit* (CSU) performs many functions. It regenerates the signal, monitors the line for electrical anomalies, provides proper electrical termination, performs framing, and provides remote loopback testing for diagnosing line problems. Some CSUs also support the Internet's Simple Network Management Protocol (SNMP). A *Data Service Unit* (DSU), which is also referred to as *Digital Service Unit*, provides the interface (usually V.35, a type of serial interface) for connecting a remote bridge, router, or switch to a T1 circuit. The DSU also provides flow control between the network and the CSU. A CSU and DSU are usually combined to form a single unit—a CSU/DSU or DSU/CSU— which is sometimes described as the digital equivalent of a modem (i.e., a "digital modem") for a T1 line. Although the functions of a CSU/DSU and modem are similar, describing a CSU/DSU as a digital modem is misleading because a CSU/DSU does not perform any type of modulation or demodulation. Instead, a CSU/DSU works exclusively with digital signals; it provides an interface between a digital computing device and a digital transmission medium. Figure 7-3 shows a typical T1-based WAN link.

Although you didn't ask the question, an E-1 circuit is terminated using a Network Termination Unit (NTU), which provides broadly similar CSU/DSU functionality. Unlike the

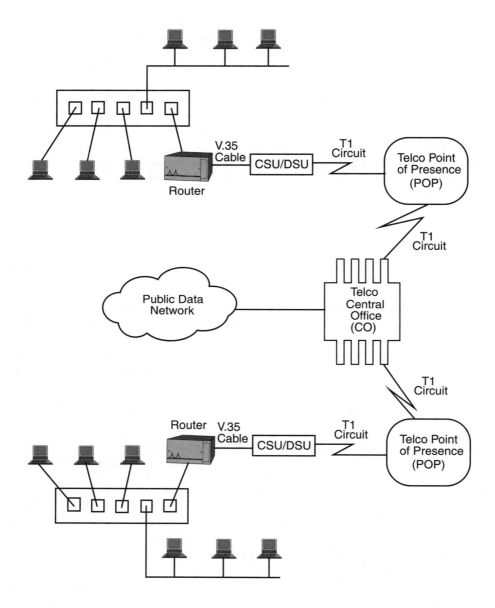

Figure 7-3. A typical configuration scheme of a leased T1 WAN connection between two sites involves a V.35 link between a router's V.35 port and a CSU/DSU. The CSU/DSU provides the interface to the T1 circuit. This circuit terminates at the telco's CO either directly or via a POP located near the customer's premises. The CO then provides connectivity to the network.

U.S. market, where the provision of a CSU/DSU is normally the responsibility of the end user, NTUs are always supplied by the telco in Europe. You should also note that line coding is different between T1 and E-1 circuits. In the United States, a technique called "bipolar with 8 zeros substitution" (B8ZS) is used; in Europe, a technique called "high density bipolar—3 zeros" (HDB-3) is used.

Prices for T1 multiplexers range from a few thousand dollars to as much as $100,000 or more depending on configuration (e.g., number of ports, bandwidth capacity). CSU/DSU units cost between $200 and $1,000. Routers are priced from around $1,000 to more than $50,000 depending on configuration needs. As we indicated earlier, circuit costs fluctuate. Factors that influence these costs include: geographical location; the telco provider (e.g., MCI WorldCom, AT&T, British Telecom, BellSouth); whether a local loop fee is required, which varies depending on the distance a customer's site is located from the telco's nearest point of presence (POP); the service contract; whether or not you commit to a short-term (one year) or long term (two to five years) subscription; the manner in which the circuit is routed; whether you will be running a WAN technology like frame relay over the link or simply using it as a dedicated leased circuit; and many others. Given the many parameters on which circuit costs are based, we opt to not provide any estimates of these costs.

10. How do T1 and E-1 compare to ISDN's Primary Rate Interface?

ISDN PRI is an ANSI and an ITU-T standard. As an ANSI standard ISDN PRI signaling consists of twenty-three 64 kbps channels for voice or data—called *B* channels—and one 64 kbps control channel—called a *D* channel. This format, known as $23B + D$, is based on the North American DS-1 service and provides 1.544 Mbps. Compared to T1 service, ISDN PRI provides more bandwidth for data because it uses a separate channel for control. Twenty-three channels at 64 kbps each yield an aggregate bandwidth of 1.472 Mbps. T1 service provides only 1.344 Mbps for data because its control is in-band. As an ITU-T standard, ISDN PRI supports a $30B + D$ format that is based on the European E-1 standard and provides 2.048 Mbps. (See Chapter 11 for more information about ISDN.)

11. I am beginning to see and hear about SONET and OC rates like OC-3. Where does this terminology fit into all of this?

Excellent question. Before we answer it, though, let's review a little history. The development and deployment of NADH led telco carriers to develop their own methods of providing T-carrier service based on NADH. This acceptance of NADH established it as a *de facto* standard. There was one problem, though. The telcos' T-carrier services were incompatible, which made it difficult for customers to exchange data between different carriers. As a result, subscribers became locked into one solution and NADH eventually became a *de facto* proprietary standard. (See Chapter 1 for additional information about standards.) In addition to proprietary inter-carrier circuits, NADH was also incompatible with the way the Europeans multiplexed their signals. In the early days of networking, when proprietary standards ruled and communications were usually restricted to within a country's own borders, these issues were not significant. In an era of open systems, standards, and global telecommunications, however, these issues are of paramount importance.

To address the difficulties inherent in inter-carrier circuits globally, two transmission technology standards were developed: *Synchronous Optical Network (SONET)* and the *Synchronous Digital Hierarchy (SDH)*. SONET is an ANSI standard; SDH is an ITU-T standard. SDH was drafted after SONET and incorporates it. SONET and SDH (frequently written as "SONET/SDH") are international physical layer standards that provide a specification for high-speed digital transmission via optical fiber. At the source interface, signals are converted from electrical to optical form. They are then converted back to electrical form at the destination interface.

In the ANSI world, SONET's terminology includes Optical Carrier level (OC-*n*) and Synchronous Transport Signal level (STS-*n*). STS rates represent electrical signals and their optical equivalents are expressed as OC rates. In the ITU-T world, the official term used is Synchronous Transport Module (STM-*n*). Table 7-3 contains a summary of OC-*n*, STS-*n*, and STM-*n* line rates. (*Note:* The designation, OC-*nc* indicates that multiple smaller circuits are concatenated to form a circuit. For example, OC-3 denotes a single 155.52 Mbps circuit, but OC-3c denotes three OC-1 circuits are concatenated to provide this bandwidth.)

12. The OC rates listed in Table 7-3 are fast. Also, isn't OC-3 what ATM uses?

You are correct in noting that OC rates are fast. The recent advances in LAN technologies (e.g., 100 Mbps and Gigabit Ethernet) rendered WAN links as the bottleneck of an internetwork. Consider, for example, a WAN that interconnects two Gigabit Ethernet LANs by a T1 circuit. Although data transmission locally is occurring at a rate of 1,000 Mbps, the transfer rate between LANs is a mere 1.544 Mbps, nearly 650 times slower. SONET resolves this bottleneck. You also are correct in noting that OC-3 is the rate used for ATM networks. In fact, 155 Mbps (OC-3) ATM and 622 Mbps (OC-12) ATM were designed specifically to use SONET as their carrier service. Also, higher rate ATM can run only over SONET.

Table 7-3. Comparison of SONET and DS Line Rates

OC-*n*	STS-*n*	STM-*n*	Data Transmission Rate (Mbps)	Number of DS-0 Channels	Number of DS-1 Channels	Number of DS-3 Channels
OC-1	STS-1	—	51.84	672	28	1
OC-3	STS-3	STM-1	155.52	2,016	84	3
OC-9	STS-9	STM-3	466.56	6,048	252	9
OC-12	STS-12	STM-4	622.08	8,064	336	12
OC-18	STS-18	STM-6	933.12	12,096	504	18
OC-24	STS-24	STM-8	1,244.16	16,128	672	24
OC-36	STS-36	STM-12	1,866.24	24,192	1,008	36
OC-48	STS-48	STM-16	2,488.32	32,256	1,344	48
OC-96	STS-96	STM-32	4,976.64	64,512	2,688	96
OC-192	STS-192	STM-64	9,953.28	129,024	5,376	192

13. Can you tell me a little more about SONET and SDH?

Sure. As we indicated earlier, SONET was developed by the telcos to address the need for a fiber-optic based standard for broadband transmissions within the telecommunications industry. Its roots are from synchronous transfer mode (STM), which is used in U.S. digital telephone networks. The basic building block of the SONET signal hierarchy is STS-1 (51.84 Mbps). This line rate is derived from the STS-1 frame, which consists of 810 eight-bit bytes transmitted at 8,000 Hz. Multiplying 810 bytes per frame, at 8 bits per byte, by 8,000 Hz yields 518,400,000 bps or 51.84 Mbps.

As a fiber-based medium, SONET offers several advantages over the copper-based T1 hierarchy. First, hundreds of thousands of simultaneous voice and data transmissions are possible using fiber. This is not feasible with copper cable. Second, fiber is immune to EMI (see Chapter 4). Third, fiber is available in either single or multimode and thus can be used for LAN connections or as the backbone of a WAN. As a synchronous transmission facility, SONET again offers several advantages over its asynchronous T1 counterpart. Bandwidth can be allocated on an as-needed basis and routes can be dynamically reconfigured. As a carrier service, SONET can serve as the transport facility for any type network technology or service, including ATM, FDDI, SMDS, and ISDN. Finally, SONET can support various topologies including point-to-point, star, and ring.

SDH has its roots in an early transport mechanism called *plesiochronous digital hierarchy (PDH)*. (*Note:* The word "plesiochronous" means "partially synchronized.") PDH is similar to STM in that both use time-division multiplexing. The difference is STM is applied to T-carrier circuits (e.g., T1 and T3), and PDH is applied to E-carrier circuits (e.g., E-1 and E-3). Aside from some minor differences, SDH is essentially the same as SONET, and at OC-3 rates and higher, the two are virtually identical.

14. Besides the physical layer, what is involved in transmitting data across a WAN?

The single, most important issue related to data transmission across WAN links is *routing*, which involves directing data packets from source to destination. Routing is a network layer function (layer 3 of the OSI model). This layer also provides services to the transport layer (layer 4) and performs congestion control.

15. Can you give me an example of how the network layer works?

Sure. We will use the TCP/IP model rather than the OSI model. (See Chapter 2 for a comparison between the TCP/IP and OSI models, and Chapter 3 for additional information about the TCP/IP protocol suite.)

The TCP/IP layer that functions similar to OSI's network layer is the Internet layer (which also is called the network layer). The heart and soul of this layer is the Internet Protocol (IP)—the IP of TCP/IP. IP is a connectionless datagram service and is responsible for routing packets between nodes. (*Note:* A datagram is an IP network layer packet. See Chapter 3 for additional information.) In short, IP receives data bits from the upper layer, assembles the bits into packets (i.e., IP datagrams), and then selects the "best" route based on some criterion, called a "metric" (e.g., distance, number of router "hops," bandwidth) the packets should take to reach their destination. Since IP is connectionless, every packet must contain the address of the destination node. This address, called an Internet or IP address, is assigned to an Internet node by a network administrator or by an automated protocol (such as Microsoft's DHCP) as part of the node's initial network configuration. An IP address uniquely identifies a host similar to the way a street address uniquely identifies a residence, or the way a social security number, driver's license number, or student ID number uniquely identifies a person. It is used by the network layer as a road map to locate a host within the Internet by determining what path a packet is to follow en route to its final destination.

Packets destined for a host connected to the same LAN as the sending host are generally delivered directly by the sending host. To transfer packets destined for a host connected to a remote network, however, dedicated routers are usually used. Routers are also referred to as *gateways*. For example, consider Figure 7-4, which contains four interconnected networks (N1 through N4), five hosts (H0 through H4), and five routers (R1 through R5). If H0 sends a packet to H1, no special router is needed to route the packet. H0 effectively serves as its own gateway for locally destined packets. However, if H0 sends a packet to H2, then at least one router is involved in the transfer. The packet could go through any of the following router paths: R1 only; R1-R2; or R1-R4-R5-R3-R2. Although routers are used to deliver packets from one network to another, IP does not guarantee that a packet will indeed be delivered to its destination. If an intermediate router, for example, contains incorrect or stale routing information, packets might get lost. IP does not take any action to retransmit undelivered packets. This is done by higher-level

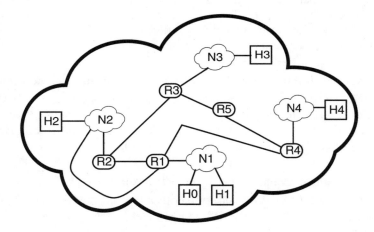

Figure 7-4. A network and associated subnetworks (subnets) are typically pictured as clouds. Shown in this figure are four interconnected subnets, N1 through N4, five hosts, H0 through H4, and five routers, R1 through R5. As an example of routing, note that data packets originating on H1 and destined for H2 can take several paths through the network. One path is through R1 only. A second path is R1-R2. Still, a third path is via R1-R4-R5-R3-R2. If the network layer is IP-based, which provides connectionless datagram service, all of these routes are possible.

protocols, specifically TCP. Additionally, IP fragments and reassembles packets when necessary so they do not exceed the maximum packet length (called the maximum transmission unit, or MTU) a physical network is capable of supporting. If a packet's size is greater than a network's MTU, the packet is broken into smaller units (called *fragmenting*) and sent to the destination in the form of several separate packets. The complete packet is then reassembled at the destination node before it is passed to the higher levels. Reassembly of an IP datagram can only occur at the destination node and not at any of the intermediary nodes the packet traverses. This is because IP is a connectionless datagram service—datagrams can take different paths en route to their destination and hence an intermediary node might not receive all of the fragmented datagrams.

When too many packets are present in a subnet, performance degrades. This situation is called *congestion*. Congestion occurs when routers are too slow, causing queues to lengthen. Additionally, if routers are too fast, queues will build up whenever input traffic is greater than the capacity of output lines (e.g., three input lines delivering packets at top speed and all need to go out on the same line). The ultimate level of congestion is known as *deadlock*, a concept with which you might be familiar if you have studied multitasking operating systems. Deadlock occurs in this context when one router cannot proceed until a second router does something, and the second router cannot proceed because it is waiting for the first router to do something. The network layer is responsible for providing congestion control, which deals with making certain that a subnet can carry the offered traffic. It is global in scope and involves all hosts, routers, and other factors. Note that congestion control is not the same as flow control, which applies to point-to-point traffic between a sender node and a receiver node.

16. How does a router determine a particular path?

The path a packet takes through a network from source to destination is a function of routing protocols. Examples include RIP (Routing Information Protocol), RIP version 2 (RIP-2), OSPF (Open Shortest Path First), and IS-IS (Intermediate System to Intermediate System). The first three are part of the TCP/IP suite and can only route IP packets. IS-IS can route both IP and OSI Connectionless Network Layer Protocol (CNLP) packets.

Routing protocols are a function of network protocols. For example, if your network protocol is TCP/IP, then several routing protocol options are available including RIP, RIP-2, and OSPF. If your network protocol is OSI's CNLP, then your routing protocol is IS-IS. Most network protocols, however, can be encapsulated in TCP/IP and routed using TCP/IP-based routing protocols. *Protocol encapsulation,* also called *tunneling*, "wraps" packets from one network protocol in a packet for another protocol. This wrapped packet can then be routed through a network using a routing protocol that is supported by the "wrapper" network protocol. AppleTalk packets, for instance, can be routed through the Internet by wrapping them into TCP/IP packets. Tunneling also is used for transporting nonroutable protocols across a WAN. For example, DEC's LAT and Microsoft's NetBEUI protocols do not provide network layer service and hence cannot be routed. These protocols can be sent across a WAN, though, by encapsulating them within a routable protocol like IP. Thus, IP tunneling is commonly used within the Internet. Tunneling effectively removes network protocol restrictions inherent in a particular network.

17. What's the difference between a *router* protocol and a routing protocol?

The term "router protocol" formally specifies three different types of router-related protocols—those that provide a service, those that greet neighbors, and those that do routing. For example, since IP provides a service to the transport layer, it is considered a network layer *service* protocol for TCP/IP. *Neighbor-greeting protocols* are those that enable nodes and routers to find each other so they know which nodes and routers are accessible. These protocols also provide address-translation capabilities. One example is the Address Resolution Protocol (ARP), which is part of the TCP/IP suite (Chapter 3). Finally, examples of routing protocols include RIP and OSPF.

18. While we are on the subject of terminology, what does IGP and BGP mean?

IGP stands for Interior Gateway Protocol. To understand IGP we need to first introduce the concept of an *autonomous system* (AS). Adjunct to the various routing protocols like RIP and OSPF is something known as *protocol areas*, which are also called *routing domains*. In the Internet, these routing domains are referred to as autonomous systems. An AS is a collection of networks controlled by a single administrative authority. The networks within an AS also share a common routing strategy. That is, the routers connecting the networks within an AS trust each other and exchange routing information using a mutually agreed upon routing protocol. The network and associated subnets shown in Figure 7-4 can be regarded as an AS if all the routers employ the same protocols.

An IGP is an Internet protocol used to exchange routing information within an AS. Examples of these *intra*domain protocols include RIP, RIP-2, OSPF, IGRP, and Enhanced IGRP. (*Note:* IGRP and Enhanced IGRP are Cisco Systems' Interior Gateway Routing Protocols.) Each AS must also support a router that can exchange routing information with other autonomous systems. Routing protocols used for this purpose are known as exterior gateway protocols. Examples of these *inter*domain protocols include EGP, the Exterior Gateway Protocol, defined in RFC 904, and BGP, the Border Gateway Protocol, defined in RFC 1105 and RFC 1771. Both EGP and BGP are part of the TCP/IP protocol suite. Of the two, however, BGP has evolved into a robust Internet routing protocol and the term "Border Gateway Protocol" is used in favor of the term "Exterior Gateway protocol."

AS, IGP, and BGP are fundamental to the way in which the Internet is designed. As a global internetwork, the Internet is partitioned into autonomous systems, which enable different areas of the Internet to be administered separately from one another. Within an AS, routers run the same interior gateway protocol. By keeping an AS administratively separate, different autonomous systems can also run different IGPs within their respective areas. For example, one AS might run RIP, another might run OSPF, and a third AS might support IGRP. These separate autonomous systems can then be interconnected via routers that run a border gateway protocol. Thus, routers within an AS communicate via an IGP, and "border" routers—those between autonomous systems—communicate via a BGP. This concept is expanded later in the chapter during our discussion of OSPF.

19. Let's get back to routing protocols. What functions do they perform?

Routing protocols perform two primary functions. They (1) determine the "best" path a packet should take when it travels through a network from source to destination, and (2) maintain routing tables that contain information about the network's topology. In the Internet world, IP is used to transport packets through the Internet based on the information contained in routing tables.

20. Could you explain how these functions work?

Certainly. Network routing protocols rely on routing algorithms to calculate the least-cost path from source to destination. A routing algorithm is that part of the network layer software responsible for deciding on which output line an incoming packet should be placed. If the subnet is packet switched, then this decision is made for every incoming packet. If the subnet is circuit switched, then routing decisions are only made when the virtual circuit is being set up.

Routing algorithms use a "least cost metric" to determine the best path. Common cost metrics include "hops" (the number of router-to-router connections a packet passes through en route to its destination), propagation delay, bandwidth, time, channel utilization, and esoteric metrics such as error rates. As an example, consider the network and associated subnets shown in Figure 7-5. The number of hops between H1 and H2 is two if the packet travels via the path R1-R2. Similarly, if the packet takes the path R1-R3-R2 or R1-R4-R5-R3-R2, then the number of hops is three and five, respectively. Given these various paths, the best or least-cost path is R1-R2 since its hop count is the smallest. Hop count metrics ignore line speeds or delays. Thus, in Figure 7-5, packets will always take the path R1-R2 (assuming the links are "up") even though it might be a "slower" path than either R1-R3-R2 or R1-R4-R5-R3-R2. A UNIX program that displays the path a packet

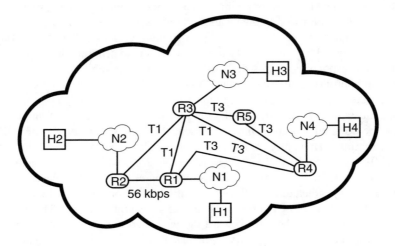

Figure 7-5. The determination of the "best" path a packet should take is based on "metrics." One metric is number of hops. Another is bandwidth. If the best path is determined by number of hops, then the route a packet takes from H1 to H2 is through routers R1-R2 because this represents the least number of hops: 2. On the other hand, if a bandwidth metric is used, then the "best" path is either R1-R3-R2, or R1-R4-R5-R3-R2.

```
traceroute -s www.fit.edu www.ucf.edu
traceroute to www.ucf.edu (132.170.240.131) from www.fit.edu, 30 hops max, 40 byte
packets
1 bsport.fit.edu (163.118.2.1)  4 ms  3 ms  2 ms
2 172.17.16.53 (172.17.16.53)  8 ms  8 ms  8 ms
3 172.17.16.30 (172.17.16.30)  86 ms  77 ms  61 ms
4 campusgw3.cc.ucf.edu (132.170.60.1)  67 ms  33 ms  16 ms
5 132.170.12.2 (132.170.12.2)  60 ms  15 ms  22 ms
6 www.ucf.edu (132.170.240.131)  13 ms * *
```

Figure 7-6. The UNIX *traceroute* program traces the route an IP packet follows from a source node to a destination node. In this figure we show the path of a packet from www.fit.edu to www.ucf.edu. The number of router hops is 5 (the last entry is the destination node, not a router). Each line shows the logical name of the router, its IP address, and the roundtrip time in milliseconds of three separate 40-byte packets (called probes) sent between intermediate routers.

traverses is called *traceroute*. (The Windows NT equivalent is called *tracert*.) The output of a trace made between two web servers—from www.fit.edu to www.ucf.edu—is shown in Figure 7-6. The numbers within parentheses are the Internet addresses of the nodes, and the numbers at the end represent the round trip time (in milliseconds) it takes a packet to reach a gateway. Three separate probes are sent between each intermediate node. Note that the source node is five hops away from the destination node. (The last address is that of the destination host, not a router.)

Routers also maintain routing tables that contain, among others, the destination address of a node or network, known router addresses, and the network interface associated with a particular router address. When a router receives a packet it looks at the packet's destination address to identify the destination network, searches its routing table for an entry corresponding to this destination, and then forwards the packet to the next router via the appropriate interface. For example, Table 7-4 shows sample routing table information generated on a UNIX system with IP address 187.96.25.2. The command used to generate this table is *netstat -r*. (Similar output can be generated on a Windows NT system using the command *route print*.) First note the table's last entry, which illustrates "local-host routing." This entry indicates that any packets destined for the local network (187.96.25.0) will be forwarded via gateway 187.96.25.2, which is the IP address of the host. In this context, the local host acts as a simple router. Now look at the second entry of the table. This entry indicates that all packets with destination address 215.103.16.227 are forwarded to the router whose address is 187.96.25.13 via interface *le0*. This router in turn will have information on where to forward the packet so that it will ultimately reach its destination. Similarly, the third entry indicates that packets with destination address 215.103.16.141 are to be forwarded to the gateway whose address is 187.96.25.35, which is accessible via interface *le1*. Finally, the second to last entry of the table references a *default route*, which is a special route that contains the address of a default router. When a router receives a packet that contains an unknown destination address (i.e., there is no entry for the address in the routing table), the router forwards the packet to the default router. As a result, if the host system receives a packet with the destination address

Table 7-4. Sample Routing Table Information

Destination	Gateway	Flags[1]	Ref[2]	Use[3]	Interface
localhost	localhost	UH	0	33106	lo0
215.103.16.227	187.96.25.13	UGHD	29	102	le0
215.103.16.141	187.96.25.35	UGHD	116	16128	le1
default	187.96.25.1	UG	0	2888304	
187.96.25.0	187.96.25.2	U	210	29024	le0

[1] U = Route is up and operational; G = Packet must pass through at least one router;
H = Route is to a specific host and not a network; D = Route was created dynamically
[2] Current number of routes that share the same link layer address
[3] Number of packets sent using this route

212.133.65.3, the host will forward the packet to the router whose destination address is 187.96.25.1 since there is no entry in the host's routing table (Table 7-4) for 212.133.65.3.

Routers exchange routing table information with neighbor routers periodically. The type of information exchanged and the frequency of routing table updates are a function of the routing protocol used.

21. I have heard the term "static route" used. What does it mean?

A *static route* is a fixed route that is entered into a router's routing table either manually or via a software configuration program. The selection of the route is determined by a network manager. Although static routes can be beneficial in some instances, they cannot be changed dynamically to compensate for changes in a network's topology.

22. What types of routing algorithms are there and how do they work?

Two general algorithms are available for computing metric information: *distance-vector* and *link-state*. The goal of both types of algorithms is to route a packet from one point in the network to another point in the network through some set of intermediate routers without "looping," a situation in which a packet is forwarded across the same link several times. The primary difference between distance-vector and link-state algorithms is the manner in which they collect and propagate routing information throughout the network. Let's examine these two algorithms separately.

Distance-vector algorithms. A *distance-vector routing algorithm* determines the distance (hence the name) between source and destination nodes by calculating the number of router hops a packet traverses en route from the source network to the destination network. An example of a distance-vector algorithm is the Bellman-Ford algorithm, which is described in Box 7-1. Two distance-vector based routing protocols are RIP and RIP-2, which exchange routing tables with their neighbors every 30 seconds. RIP and RIP-2 also support a maximum of 15 hops. Thus, if the number of router-to-router hops between

BOX 7-1: Bellman-Ford Algorithm

The Bellman-Ford routing algorithm is distance-vector based and iterates on the number of hops a source node is from a destination node. To illustrate this algorithm, consider the following undirected graph, which depicts a sample network. The vertices, *A, B, C, D, E,* and *F* may be thought of as routers, and the edges connecting the vertices are communication links. Edge labels represent an arbitrary cost. Our goal is to find the shortest path from *A* to *D* using the number of hops as the basis for our path selection.

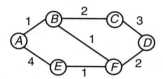

We examine the costs of all paths leading from *A* to each node on a hop-by-hop basis.

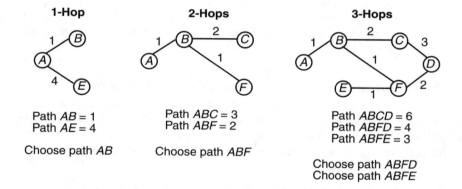

| **1-Hop** | **2-Hops** | **3-Hops** |

Path *AB* = 1
Path *AE* = 4

Choose path *AB*

Path *ABC* = 3
Path *ABF* = 2

Choose path *ABF*

Path *ABCD* = 6
Path *ABFD* = 4
Path *ABFE* = 3

Choose path *ABFD*
Choose path *ABFE*

In the last step (3 hops), two paths are selected. The first path, *ABFD,* represents the least-cost path from *A* to *D* based on the hops metric. The second path, *ABFE,* is selected because it represents the least cost path from *A* to *E*.

The final result of the Bellman-Ford algorithm yields a tree that represents the least cost incurred from the source node to every node of the network. Similar trees can be generated for every node of the network. Node *A*'s least cost tree for our example is as follows:

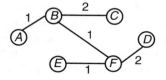

From Node *A*:
• the least cost path to *B* is *AB* = 1
• the least cost path to *C* is *ABC* = 3
• the least cost path to *D* is *ABFD* = 4
• the least cost path to *E* is *ABFE* = 3
• the least cost path to *F* is *ABF* = 2

source and destination nodes is greater than 15, then the network to which the destination node is connected is considered "unreachable." This limitation restricts the size of an internetwork to 15 consecutively connected networks.

Link-state algorithms. In a *link-state routing algorithm* every router of a network does not send every other router its routing table. Instead, routers send each other information about the links they have established to other routers. This information is sent via a link state advertisement (LSA), which contains the names and various cost-metrics of a router's neighbors. LSAs are flooded throughout an entire router's domain. (*Note:* An example of how this is done is described later in our discussion of OSPF.) Routers also store the most recent LSA they receive, and destination routes are calculated using LSA information. Thus, rather than storing actual paths (which is the case with distance-vector algorithms), link-state algorithms store the information needed to generate such paths. An example of a link-state algorithm is Dijkstra's shortest path algorithm, which iterates on length of path to determine a shortest route. Link-state based routing protocols include OSPF, OSI's IS-IS, and Netware's Link Services Protocol (NLSP). Box 7-2 illustrates Dijkstra's shortest path algorithm.

23. Please tell me more about RIP.

OK. The Routing Information Protocol Version 1 was derived from the Xerox Network System's (XNS) routing protocol, which was also called RIP. RIP was bundled with BSD UNIX in 1982 as part of the TCP/IP protocol suite and became the *de facto* standard for IP routing. As mentioned earlier, RIP uses a distance-vector algorithm that determines the best route by using a hops metric. When used in small, homogeneous networks, RIP is a very efficient protocol and its operation is fairly simple. RIP keeps all routing tables within a network updated by transmitting routing table update messages every 30 seconds. After a RIP-enabled device receives an update, it compares its current information with the information contained in the update message. Current routing table entries are replaced with updated information when the update message contains any of the following entries: (1) a route and corresponding metric to a previously unknown destination (this information is added to the existing table), (2) a new route to an existing destination with a smaller metric (the old route is replaced by the new route), and (3) a new metric for the same route to an existing destination (the old metric is replaced by the new one).

RIP uses timers to handle link or neighbor router failures. If a router does not hear from any of its neighbors within 180 seconds, the protocol assumes the node or link is dead. Once this determination is made, the router sends out a special message to its responding neighbors about this failure. Routing table entries that include routes via the dead link or node are then altered accordingly. RIP also imposes a 15-hop maximum—if a destination network is more than 15 hops away, RIP classifies the network "unreachable." In router jargon, the destination network's cost goes to infinity. Thus, the network becomes too expensive to reach and hence is unavailable.

Routers implementing RIP occasionally misinterpret old routing information as new, which can then cause routing loops. To resolve this situation, RIP employs several strategies. These include *split-horizon, split-horizon with poisoned reverse,* and *hold-down.* Let's examine these separately.

BOX 7-2: Dijkstra's Shortest Path First (SPF) Algorithm

Dijkstra's SPF routing algorithm is link-state based and iterates on the distance metric. The algorithm uses a "closest nodes" concept and is based on the following principle:

Given a source node, n, the shortest path from n to the next closest note, s, either (a) is a path that directly connects n to s, or (b) includes a path containing n and any of the previously found intermediate closest nodes plus a direct link from the last inter- mediate closest node of this path to s.

To illustrate this algorithm, consider the following undirected graph, which depicts a sam- ple network. The vertices, A, B, C, D, E, and F may be thought of as routers, and the edges connecting the vertices are communication links. Edge labels represent an arbitrary cost metric. Our goal is to find the shortest path from A to D based on distance.

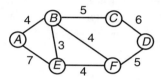

To implement this algorithm, it is helpful to maintain a running record of the successive closest nodes to the source node. We will let k represent the nth closest node. Thus, node A corresponds to $k = 0$. That is, the zero closest node to A is itself. This is the initialization step of the algorithm. We now begin our search for the successive closest nodes to A.

First Closest Node ($k = 1$)

The first closest node to A is either B or E since they are both directly connected to A. Since the AB path has a smaller cost, we select it. Thus, B is the first closest node to A.

k	Node	Path
0	A	—
1	B	AB

Second Closest Node ($k = 2$)

The second closest node to A must either be (a) a direct link from A, or (b) via a path that includes the first closest node. The possible paths and related costs are: $ABC = 9$, $ABF = 8$, $ABE = 7$, or $AE = 7$. There are two shortest paths: ABE and AE. Thus, E is the second closest node to A.

k	Node	Path
0	A	—
1	B	AB
2	E	ABE AE

Third Closest Node ($k = 3$)

The third closest node to A must be via a path that includes nodes B or E. (There are no more direct links to A.) The possible paths and related costs are: $ABC = 9$, $ABF = 8$, $ABEF = 11$, or $AEF = 11$. The shortest path is ABF. Thus, F is the third closest node to A.

k	Node	Path
0	A	—
1	B	AB
2	E	ABE AE
3	F	AEF

Fourth Closest Node ($k = 4$)

The fourth closest node to A is via a path that includes nodes B, E, or F. The possible paths and related costs are: $ABC = 9$ or $ABFD = 13$. The shortest path is ABC. Thus, C is the fourth closest node to A. Note that neither $ABEF$ nor AEF is considered at this stage of the algorithm because F was previously found to be the third closest node.

k	Node	Path
0	A	—
1	B	AB
2	E	ABE AE
3	F	AEF
4	C	ABC

Continued on next page

BOX 7-2: Dijkstra's Shortest Path First (SPF) Algorithm (Continued)

<u>Fifth Closest Node</u> ($k = 5$)

The fifth closest node to A is via a path that includes nodes B, E, F, or C. The possible paths and related costs are: $ABCD = 15$, $ABFD = 13$, $ABEFD = 16$, and $AEFD = 16$. The shortest path is $ABFD$. Thus, D is the fifth closest node to A.

k	Node	Path
0	A	—
1	B	AB
2	E	ABE
		AE
3	F	AEF
4	C	ABC
5	D	$ABFD$

Since D is the destination node, the shortest path from A to D is $ABFD$.

Split-horizon. The split-horizon strategy ensures that a router never sends routing information back in the direction from which it came. For example, let's assume router A receives a routing table update from router B. Once A receives this information, A updates its routing table to reflect the routes listed in B's routing table. Now, when A is ready to send its own routing table update to B, split-horizon prevents A from sending any updates back to B that were made based on the information B sent to A. Generalizing, with split-horizon, routing information provided by a neighbor is eliminated in any updates sent back to that neighbor.

Split-horizon with Poisoned Reverse. This strategy is similar to split-horizon with one exception: Routing information provided by a neighbor is included in any updates sent back to that neighbor. Such routes, however, are assigned a cost factor (i.e., metric) of infinity. This means that a network is unreachable. For example, consider the network shown in Figure 7-5. Note that R2 and R3 are neighbor routers, and each can claim a route to R4 through each other (e.g., R2-R3-R4, R2-R3-R5-R4, R2-R1-R3-R4, and R3-R2-R1-R4). Assume R2 receives a routing table update from R3 that includes the R3-R2-R1-R4 path. With poison reverse, R2's update to R3 indicates that R4 is unreachable (i.e., its metric is infinity). This prevents R3 from claiming that a path to R4 exists through R2. Thus, any path to R4 from R3 must either be a directly connected link (R3-R4), or through other routers (e.g., R3-R5-R4 or R3-R1-R4). The poison reverse update is also very effective in eliminating routing loops because when two routers have routes pointing at each other (as was the case in our illustration), the update will immediately make that link unreachable.

Hold-down. The hold-down strategy requires routers to not update their routing tables with any new information they receive for a prescribed period of time called the *hold-down time*. To illustrate this, let's assume that a link within a network fails. Let's further assume that two routers, A and B, exchange routing table updates, and that B has been informed of the link failure from one of its other neighbors but A has not. If A does not receive information about the failed link before it sends B a routing table update, B will receive A's update, see that the "failed" link is active, and incorrectly reinstate it. With hold-down implemented, though, *A* will receive information about the failed link before it sends an update to *B*. Thus, hold-down enables routing table updates to be propagated to all routers in a timely manner, thereby ensuring that new routes are indeed new and not old ones. By making the hold-down time longer than it takes to "count to infinity," routing loops can be avoided. (*Note:* Hold-down is not standardized and hence should be considered implementation specific.)

The format of a RIP packet is shown in Figure 7-7(a). The Command field identifies the packet as either a request (a router asks its neighbor to send its routing table), or a response (a routing table update). The Version Number field contains the version of RIP being used. The AFI field identifies the protocol family of the address contained in the Address field. Thus, if the address is an Internet address, the AFI field is coded to represent IP. (*Note:* RIP updates can be up to 520 bytes long and hence multiple entries, from the AFI, can be placed in the datagram.) The Address field is the destination address of the network being advertised. The Metric field contains the hop count to the address listed in the Address field. Using only half of its 24 bytes, RIP carries the least amount of information necessary for routers to route messages through a network. Thus, overhead is minimal. RIP is defined in RFC 1058.

24. What's the difference between RIP and RIP-2?

As originally designed, RIP does not support the concepts of autonomous systems, subnetting, or authentication. RIP also cannot interpret BGP or EGP routes. To address some of these issues, several extensions to the original protocol were incorporated to extend its usefulness. This protocol, RIP Version 2, which is shown in Figure 7-7(b), maintains RIP's Command, Version Number, AFI, IP Address, and Metric fields. RIP-2 messages that carry information in any of the unused fields from version 1 will have a 2 in the Version Number field. The content of the 2-byte unused field in both versions is ignored. Thus, a RIP-2 packet does not alter the contents of RIP.

The new features of RIP-2 include the following:

- **Authentication.** If the AFI field of the first entry in a message is FFFF, then this signifies that the message is an authentication packet. Presently, RIP-2 only supports simple passwords for authentication.

- **Interpretation of IGP and BGP Routes.** The Route Tag field enables RIP to distinguish between intradomain RIP routes and interdomain RIP routes, which are usually imported from an exterior gateway protocol like BGP or another interior gateway protocol like OSPF or IGRP.

- **Subnet Masks.** The original version of RIP assumed that all networked devices used the same subnet mask and hence did not carry subnet mask information. RIP-2 removes this assumption by supporting multiple-length subnet masks. This is an extremely important feature because today's network addresses are partitioned into subnets and routers need a subnet mask to determine routes. The Subnet Mask field contains the subnet mask, which is applied to the IP address to yield the network address. If this field is zero, then no subnet mask is included for a particular entry. (See Box 3-2 for an example of subnet masks.)

(a) RIP Packet Format

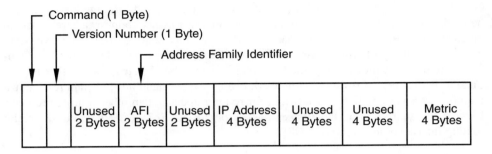

(b) RIP-2 Packet Format

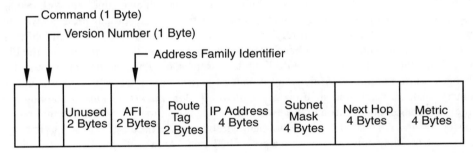

Figure 7-7. RIP version 1 packets (a) contain several unused fields. These fields are defined in RIP-2 (b), thereby extending the usefulness of the RIP protocol. RIP-2 is completely compatible with RIP. The Command, Version Number, AFI, and Metric fields have exactly the same meaning in both versions. The Version Number field for RIP-2 will have a 2 for any RIP message that carries information in any of the unused fields from version 1. The content of the 2-byte unused field in both versions is ignored. (*Note:* RIP updates can be up to 520 bytes long. Thus, multiple entries, from the AFI, can be placed in the datagram.) (Adapted from RFC 1058 and RFC 1723.)

- **Next Hop Field.** This field contains the IP address of the immediate next hop to which packets are to be forwarded based on the packet's destination address. This field eliminates packets being routed through extra hops in a system.

- **Multicasting.** Another advantage is that it instead of broadcasting updates, RIP-2 supports multicasting. This reduces the load on hosts that are not listening to RIP-2 packets.

RIP-2 is specified in RFC 1723.

25. Given it's improvements, is RIP-2 now the *de facto* Internet routing protocol?

Not really. Although RIP-2 improves RIP's capabilities, it still has several deficiencies. The biggest problem with RIP is that it was never designed for large heterogeneous networks. As a network grows, destinations that are more than 15 hops away are classified unreachable in RIP. (*Note:* RIP-2 maintains RIP's infinity count of 16 to preserve backward compatibility.) Furthermore, RIP's hops routing metric is not always the most efficient one to use. Unfortunately, the hops metric cannot be changed to any other metric. Finally, RIP is not as resistant to network changes (e.g., handling link failures), and it requires a greater amount of bandwidth for routing updates than other routing protocols because the entire routing table is sent. Many organizations still use RIP, but the major routing Internet protocol today is OSPF.

26. Tell me about OSPF. How different is it from RIP?

As noted earlier, the Open Shortest Path First protocol is an interior gateway protocol based on a link-state algorithm; RIP is distance-vector-based. Many of RIP's limitations are resolved with OSPF. For example, OSPF is specifically designed for large, heterogeneous IP networks. OSPF supports a 16-bit routing metric, which enables network managers to design least-cost routing schemes based on traffic load, propagation delays, line speed, and bandwidth, instead of relying solely on hops. Routing updates with OSPF are also very efficient and can be authenticated via passwords, digital signatures, and the like. As a link-state based protocol, OSPF updates routes only when the status of a link changes. Furthermore, OSPF does not broadcast entire routing tables to update neighbor routers. Instead, small link state packets called *link state advertisements* containing specific information about a router's network links are transmitted. OSPF also employs the concept of *areas*. Thus, updates are not bandwidth intensive because, except for area summary updates, they only occur within a prescribed area. "Area routing" also insulates intra-domain routing from external routing problems. Other features of OSPF include quick recovery after changes are made in a network's topology, resistance to routing loops, and the capability to interpret and redistribute EGP and IGP routes independently. The contents of an OSPF packet header is shown in Figure 7-8, and the protocol is specified in RFC 1583.

27. How does OSPF work?

In an OSPF environment, a collection of networks and hosts (i.e., an internetwork) is grouped together to form an area. Routers within an area, called intra-area routers, route packets among the networks of that area. Intra-area routers maintain identical topological data. OSPF areas are interconnected via area border routers, which keep separate topological data about the areas to which they are connected. These areas can then be interconnected to form an autonomous system (AS). Thus, in an OSPF environment, routers are connected together to form networks. These networks, in turn, can be connected to form areas. Autonomous systems are then formed by interconnecting areas.

To illustrate this concept, consider Figure 7-9, which shows an OSPF environment that consists of three areas. Routers R1 and R2, R4 and R5, and R8 and R9 are intra-area routers for areas 1, 2, and 3, respectively. Furthermore, R1 is an area border router for Area 1,

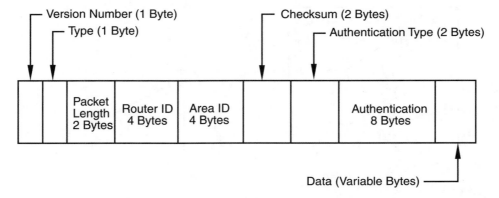

Figure 7-8. Contents of an OSPF packet header. The Version Number field contains the version of OSPF that is being implemented. The Type field specifies the type of OSPF packet that is being transmitted. Several types are possible: Hello messages, database descriptions, request and response messages, and acknowledgments. The Packet Length field specifies the length of the packet. The Router ID field identifies the packet source. The Area ID field indicates the OSPF "area" associated with the packet. The Checksum field is a standard CRC checksum. The Authentication Type field specifies the type of authentication required. The Authentication field contains the authentication. (Adapted from RFC 2328.)

R4 acts as an area border router for Area 2, and R7 is the area border router for Area 3. Each area is a separate autonomous system, and the intra-area routers only carry information about the networks within their areas. For example, packets originating on network N1 and destined for N3 are routed internally via R1 and R2. Packets originating on N1 and destined for N7, though, must be directed to area border router R1. These packets are then forwarded to R3 and R7.

Note that with areas in place, OSPF routing occurs at two different levels. The lower level is intra-area routing. The higher level is inter-area routing, which consists of traffic that traverses the backbone. The backbone in Figure 7-9 is comprised of routers R3, R4, R6, and R7. To minimize the amount of routing updates on the backbone, each area has a *designated router* and a *backup designated router*. Within an area, each router exchanges link state information with the designated router. This router, or its backup if the designated router fails, is then responsible for generating link state advertisements (LSAs) on behalf of that network.

When a new router is first added to a network, it sends a "hello" message to each of its neighbors. Hello messages are also sent periodically by all routers to inform their neighbors that they are still alive. Using a link-state algorithm like Dijkstra's shortest path algorithm (see Box 7-2), OSPF routers build a topological database consisting of their view of the network. This information is then transmitted via link state advertisements (LSAs) to neighbor routers. For intra-domain routers, LSAs are exchanged only with routers within their area. Area border routers exchange LSAs with other area border routers.

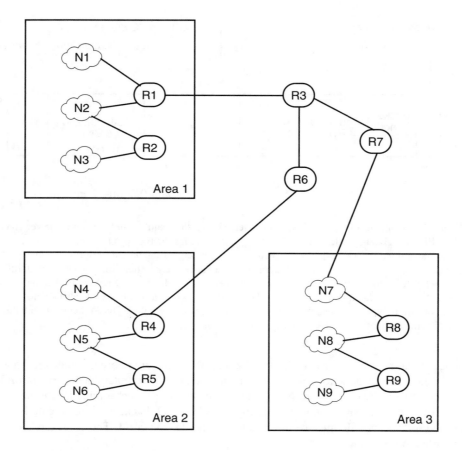

Figure 7-9. A sample OSPF routing environment. (Adapted from Moy, 1990.)

28. Are there any other routing protocols that I should know about?

Three in particular are IGRP, EIGRP, and IS-IS. All three are interior gateway protocols, and like OSPF are alternatives to RIP. IGRP and EIGRP are proprietary Cisco Systems protocols, and hence appropriate for Cisco environments. IS-IS is an OSI routing protocol. A brief description of each follows.

IGRP. The Interior Gateway Routing Protocol was developed by Cisco to address some of the problems associated with routing in large, heterogeneous networks. The key difference between IGRP and RIP is the routing metric. A mathematical formula that takes into consideration factors such as bandwidth and delay is used to calculate a metric value. The path with the smallest calculated metric is determined as the least-cost (i.e., "best") path. Another difference between the two protocols is IGRP employs the concept of "trusted neighbor," which is a neighbor router from whom a router will only accept routing updates. Trusted neighbors are defined as part of the configuration process. IGRP addresses issues related to routing loops by implementing the concepts of split-horizon and hold-downs similar to RIP's implementations.

EIGRP. Enhanced IGRP is another routing protocol designed by Cisco. It combines the best features of distance-vector and link-state routing protocols. For example, EIGRP uses "hello" messages to learn of neighbor routers. It also uses a specially designed protocol, the Reliable Transport Protocol, to transmit routing updates instead of using broadcasts. Subnet masking is also supported by EIGRP. Routing metrics are distance-vector based and are calculated via Cisco's diffusing-update algorithm (DUAL).

IS-IS. The formal title of this protocol is "Intermediate System to Intermediate System Intra-Domain Routing Exchange Protocol. It is an OSI protocol designed to run within an AS, which is called a "routing domain" in the OSI world. IS-IS uses a link-state routing algorithm to calculate least-cost paths. Overall, its operation is similar to OSPF.

29. I have heard the term "cider" used when discussing routing. Is this a protocol invented by Apple Computer? You know, like Apple Cider?

Cute. You are referring to *Classless Inter-Domain Routing (CIDR)*, which allows sites to advertise multiple Class C networks by using a single prefix. CIDR was developed as a solution to the routing table explosion caused by the rapid growth of the Internet. As the Internet grew, the folks in charge of assigning Internet address began issuing multiple class C addresses to organizations. This meant that more individual networks needed to be announced for routing purposes and maintained by routers. With more networks needing to be announced, coupled with RIP's "feature" of updating routing tables every 30 seconds, most of the available Internet bandwidth was being used for routing table updates rather than user data. CIDR alleviated this problem by summarizing Class C network prefixes and using them as routing entries instead of the actual network addresses. For example, in a CIDR-less environment, an organization that is issued 96 Class C network addresses must have an entry for each address in its router's routing table. With CIDR, though, a special prefix is assigned to these 96 networks that indicates they all belong to the organization's routing domain. Thus, only one routing entry is needed instead of 96. OSPF, BGP, and RIP support CIDR.

30. Now that I have some understanding of routing and routing protocols, could you tell me the difference between a router and a brouter?

Brouter, huh? There's a term we haven't heard in a while. As indicated earlier, routers operate at the network layer. Their job is to interconnect physically different networks and route packets from one network to another. They determine a path to a destination node and then start the packet on its way. Many routers support more than one network-layer protocol (e.g., IP, IPX, AppleTalk). Thus, if a packet originating from an IP network is passed to an AppleTalk network, a router rebuilds the packet to the proper form so it can be interpreted by a node on the AppleTalk network. Since routers operate at the third layer of the OSI model, they do not forward broadcast packets unless they are configured to do so. Routers also employ routing protocols that determine the least cost path a packet is to travel from source to destination nodes.

A *brouter* combines the features of a bridge and router. Its name comes from "bridging router." It has the forwarding capabilities of a router and the network protocol independence of a bridge. Brouters can process packets at either the data link or network layers. When used as a bridge, brouters forward frames and can be used to filter local traffic. When used as a router, brouters transfer packets across networks. Brouters had their 15 minutes of fame in the early 1990s. They have since been replaced by switches.

31. Speaking of switches, what's the difference between a switch and a router?

Before we examine the differences between switches and routers, let's briefly review the history of switches and switching. The concept of switching in the telecommunications industry has its roots in circuit switching. Recall from Chapter 2 that a circuit-switched network employs connection-oriented links. In a circuit-switched network, a dedicated hardware switch first establishes a physical circuit between the source and destination nodes before communication takes place. The switch also keeps this circuit in place for the duration of the transmission. Furthermore, the switch is responsible for managing the link and addressing all related end-to-end connection issues (e.g., flow control, circuit path).

In a packet switched network, instead of using a dedicated physical circuit for every node-to-node communication, nodes share a communications channel via a virtual circuit. Bandwidth in a packet-switched network is dynamically established and released on an as-needed basis. Thus, a packet switched network uses bandwidth more efficiently than a circuit-switched network. Furthermore, if the link is connectionless, then messages are partitioned into packets and sent to the destination one at a time and not necessarily in the correct order. By doing so, the switch does have to concern itself with end-to-end communication issues.

One of the key differences between a connection-oriented and a connectionless link is that the former requires knowledge of the *state* of the network, whereas the latter does not. Prior to the development of local and wide area data networks, switching was always connection-oriented. In the data network world, however, switching became connectionless. For example, when a router routes a packet through a network, no advance path is established, there is no concern about flow control, and heck, the router doesn't even care if the packets are arriving in the correct order. All of these issues are left for the upper layers. Thus, a router acts like a connectionless switch. So, the primary difference between a switch and a router is really one of semantics. Switches historically infer connection-oriented links; routers use connectionless links.

32. OK. But you answered my question from a conceptual perspective. What I want to know is what distinguishes a LAN switch at layer 2 from a router at layer 3?

Ahh! Sorry about that. Sometimes we get carried away. *In the strictest sense,* LAN switches are layer 2 devices that examine and use layer 2 data (e.g., MAC addresses) to forward or filter traffic. Since they operate at the data link layer, these devices are supposed to be transparent to protocols operating at higher layers. This implies that regardless of the network protocol being used, switches pass or discard frames independent of network protocols and cannot filter broadcasts. Similarly, and again *in the strictest sense,* routers are layer 3 devices that use layer 3 data (e.g., network addresses) to forward or filter traffic. Routers filter packets based on network protocols, and they can filter broadcasts. Most routers also incorporate some sort of bridging capability. Hence, they can operate at either layer 2 or layer 3.

In the real world, though, LAN switches have encroached on the router's territory. Many LAN switch vendors now incorporate traditional router functionality into their products. For example, some Ethernet switches are capable of examining layer 3 header information, which is then used to filter network protocols or broadcasts. Some switches also are capable of creating VLANs using either MAC sublayer addresses (layer 2) or network addresses (layer 3) as the basis for forwarding/filtering frames or packets. As a result, switches have begun replacing routers at the local area network level.

The replacement of routers with switches in LAN configurations did not go unnoticed by router manufacturers. Cognizant of the LAN switch's encroachment, router manufacturers began modifying their products to incorporate a switch's primary feature—wire speed operations. To provide routers with this capability, router manufacturers designed and implemented *application specific integrated circuit* (ASIC) chips that perform traditional router table lookups and packet forwarding at hardware speeds. ASIC-based routers still examine every packet and calculate network routes as traditional routers do; they just do it much faster. Thus, physically, this new breed of routers provides switch-like performance. Logically, however, they perform the same operations. Furthermore, unlike layer 2 switches, which establish connection-oriented links between source and destination nodes, routers still route packets on a connectionless basis. Nevertheless, ASIC-based routers are referred to as layer 3 switches or routing switches. Along this same line, because LAN switches have layer 3 functionality, they are referred to as layer 3 devices. Regardless of what you call them (is a router a switch, or is a switch a layer 3 device), the bottom line is this: Layers 2 and 3 of the OSI model are merging and it is becoming difficult to distinguish between switches and routers.

33. While we're on this topic, what is layer 4 switching all about?

The concept of layer 4 switching is based on using information from the upper layers (layers 4, 5, 6, or 7) to make routing decisions. For example, web-based packets might be routed in one direction and e-mail packets in another even if both packets have the same destination address. The web-based packets might take a route that has higher bandwidth capability; the e-mail packets' route might have more delays. Another illustration is web-browsing traffic might take a different path than an electronic commerce-based packet.

The idea behind layer 4 switching is to examine each packet and use its upper layer information to make routing decisions. Routers that have this capability are being touted as layer 4 switches. This terminology, however, is a malapropism. Recall our conceptual response to a previous question that asked to explain the difference between a switch and a router (question 31): Switches are connection-oriented; routers are connectionless. Switching implies establishing a connection between source and destination ports, which does not occur at layer 4. Regardless of the type of information being used to determine a path, or the layer that is providing this information, packets are still being forwarded on a connectionless basis. It is more appropriate to refer to layer 4 switches as either layer 2 or layer 3 *application switches* because application information from upper layers is being used for routing decisions.

34. At the risk of belaboring this topic, what is IP switching?

IP Switching initially was the name a network vendor (Ipsilon Networks) coined to describe its proprietary layer 3 switching strategy. Ipsilon has since been acquired by Nokia, and the term now refers to different strategies for speeding up the processing of IP traffic. The focus of each of these strategies is to apply layer 2 switching technology to layer 3 routing. The primary reason for doing this is to improve the packet forwarding performance of routers and to enable routers to provide sufficient network guarantees to support a specific quality of service (QoS) level. Several strategies are given below without explanation. (See the references for additional information about these strategies. See also Chapters 8 and 14 for additional information about QoS and Class of Service, CoS.)

One strategy is to run IP over ATM. (See Chapter 14 for more information about ATM.) This strategy itself has several approaches. These include ATM LAN Emulation (LANE), Classical IP Over ATM (IPOA), Next Hop Resolution Protocol (NHRP), and Multiprotocol Over ATM (MPOA), which is an extension of LANE and uses NHRP. Of these approaches, MPOA is receiving considerable attention. A second strategy is Ipsilon's IP Switching technology, which employs a specially designed IP switch that can distinguish between "flow-oriented" traffic (e.g., ftp, http, multimedia) and "short-lived" traffic (e.g., e-mail, name server lookups). The IP switch processes all short-lived packets just like traditional routers. Flow-oriented packets, however, get switched to their destinations at hardware speeds. A third IP switching strategy is the IETF's Multiprotocol Label Switching (MPLS) standard, which combines Cisco Systems' Tag Switching approach with IBM's ARIS (Aggregate Route-based IP Switching) strategy. Other strategies include extremely fast routers that process several million IP packets per second, and layer 3 switches as discussed earlier

35. Can you give me some more information about RSVP?

Sure. The Resource Reservation Protocol (RSVP), developed by the Internet Engineering Task Force (IETF), operates at layer 3 of the OSI model. RSVP can be thought of as an IP-based Quality of Service (QoS) protocol that provides a mechanism to control network latency for specific applications. This is done by prioritizing data and allocating sufficient bandwidth for data transmission. QoS is inherent in technologies such as token ring and ATM, but is absent in Ethernet/802.3 and IP. With RSVP, though, Ethernet/802.3 or IP end nodes can reserve a specific amount of bandwidth from the network for a particular transmission. This feature is critical for transmitting data from time-sensitive applications such as real time voice and video. For example, a video conferencing application might receive a high priority tag that requires a certain amount of bandwidth, a specific transmission rate, and maximum latency.

In order for RSVP to be effected across a WAN, every router that is along the path an RSVP data packet traverses must support RSVP. If not, then the application fails. Furthermore, if the WAN cannot support an RSVP request (e.g., there is insufficient bandwidth available), then the application will not run. These two issues pose serious challenges to running an RSVP application across the Internet. The IETF, however, is working diligently to address these issues. For example, IETF working groups have been established to integrate RSVP into the OSPF and BGP routing protocols. On another front, the IETF's

Integrated Services Working Group is considering modifying the type of information contained in an IP packet header's Type of Service field to identify the level of service a packet should receive. Finally, IPv6, the next generation of IP, has provisions for QoS.

ATM's QoS offers a more elegant approach to transmitting time-sensitive data across a WAN than RSVP. However, the current level of work and attention IETF is giving to the issue of QoS makes the concept of IP QoS more of a reality than a contradiction in terms.

36. OK. Let's move on. My company is considering using the Internet as its WAN for connecting satellite offices. Can you tell me something about this?

What you are referring to is a *virtual private network*, also known as a *VPN*. A VPN is an IP connection between two sites over a public IP network. Data packets transported across a VPN are encrypted so that only the source and destination can decrypt them. (*Note:* See Chapter 16 for additional information about encryption and decryption.) In this manner, a publicly accessible network can be used for moving highly confidential information in a secure manner. The VPN exploitation of the last couple of years is mostly centered on IP-based networks such as the Internet. One of the major problems of VPN technologies is the great variety of implementation styles and methods, which causes much confusion when trying to develop a strategy for their use in a company.

37. What kinds of VPNs are there, anyway?

Lots of them. A brief description of several VPN implementations follows:

Router-to-router VPN-on-demand tunnel connections between sites. In this implementation, a VPN-capable router is set up to know that when a connection is made to a specific IP address on the connected network, it should set up an encrypted linkage for all traffic between the two routers. This is often also called an encrypted "tunnel" facility, as the connection does not individually encipher the sessions as much as it creates a master session between the two routers and channels all user traffic inside the master session (like moving cars through a tunnel). The tunnels are created with the first user connection between the site(s) and are persistent until the last user disconnects from the site pair, which causes the routers to stop the tunnel session. This type of VPN relies on router compatibility. Among others, routers must have compatible VPN capabilities, key exchange, and cryptographic support. This method is also highly vendor specific—usually, two different vendors of routers will not interoperate in a tunneled manner. VPNs via a tunnel implementation may or may not be encrypted, depending upon vendor offering. A good example of this is Cisco's Layer Two Forwarding (L2F) protocol.

Router-to-router VPN-on-demand multiprotocol tunnel connections between sites over an IP network. Similar to the previous definition, this type of VPN implementation allows the customer to use an IP network between two sites to carry tunneled packets for other protocols besides IP. An IP-based VPN is established between two sites over the public IP network. The routers know that when another protocol, such as Netware's IPX or Apple's AppleTalk, issues a connection request to a specific node on the other side of the IP network that a "transparent" connection needs to be established and the non-IP protocol tunneled to the remote site. This type of connectivity is extremely useful where companies have small to medium sized remote sites who want the benefits and cost savings of connectivity to a shared IP network, but are not running IP as the only protocol between sites. It's also a big cost savings method for international network connections. The cost of a public IP network with multiprotocol VPN tunneling is considerably less than a 56 kbps private network connection.

Router-to-router VPN-on-demand encrypted session connections between sites. Like a tunnel, specific routers are defined with each other as to whether they support VPN, encryption, or other security. Unlike a tunnel, each session is encrypted and match-paired with its partner on the other side of the public network. While this is simpler to manage session-wise than a tunnel, it can have a greater amount of overhead for highly connected applications between the same two site pairs in a network.

Firewall-to-firewall VPN-on-demand tunnel connections between sites. (See Chapter 16 for more information about firewalls.) Like the equivalent router facilities, this provides an equivalent service. The major difference is the ability to impose security rule restrictions and traffic management, auditing, authentication, data encryption, and other security features that firewalls offer but routers do not. This provides additional security and accounting information useful for management of the facilities. An example of an emerging standard for this is *IP Security* (IPSec) from the Internet Engineering Task Force (IETF). IPSec is a suite of protocols that includes an Authentication Header (AH) and an Encapsulating Security Payload (ESP). AH provides address authentication for IP traffic, and ESP defines IP data encryption. (See Chapter 16 for additional information about IPSec.) IPSec enables the same or dissimilar firewall vendors to negotiate a protocol methodology that provides the described VPN facilities or subsets thereof. Be careful: Some vendors' offering of IPSec do not interoperate with other vendors and only support their own firewall implementations.

Firewall-to-firewall VPN-on-demand multiprotocol tunnel connections between sites over an IP network. Again, similar in nature to the router approach but with all the firewall facilities as well. For this type of VPN to work with multiple protocol tunneling, the firewall must be capable of handling multiple protocol filtering and security.

Client-to-firewall IP tunnel VPN facilities. In some recent implementations, a client VPN tunnel manager and encryptor software package is installed on a client system, such as a laptop. The firewall implements a proxy facility that knows how to deal with the client. The client, upon connecting to the site via the IP network, negotiates a VPN tunnel with the site firewall via the client VPN software. Once the session tunnel is activated, the firewall and client system provide a secure connection over the public IP network. In this approach, VPN client facilities are usually required for a variety of operating system environments to satisfy the remote connectivity facilities. This type of service, although it is becoming more common, is usually not seen implemented on a router-based VPN solution. This is jointly due to the need to maintain database information on the client side and the complexity of key distribution and management, which usually require a disk-based system to deal with the items involved (most routers are diskless). An example of this is the V-One implementation called *SmartGate*, which implements a proxy on the firewall side of the connection and either a soft-token or hard-token software package on the client side to connect to the proxy on the firewall for the VPN facility. Another is the proxy suite from Aventail that provides many equivalent services for NT.

Client-to-server IP tunnel VPN facilities. Companies such as Microsoft are implementing a VPN tunneling facility that allows the software on a client to initiate and connect a VPN tunnel between itself and either a local or remote server on a network. This provides the ability for end-to-end VPN services and with encryption, the opportunity to provide secure VPN facilities from the source of information to the destination of information. Microsoft provides this capability with their Point-to-Point Tunneling Protocol (PPTP) currently available in Windows NT and very soon for other operating system offerings (e.g. Windows 98). PPTP works hand-in-hand with IP.

Client and server firewall implementation with full VPN capabilities. This approach provides the greatest level of complexity and the greatest level of security by implementing a full firewall facility on every system on the network. This provides the VPN facilities previously described but also the ability to support full network security policy management and control on both sides of the connection (client-only VPN facilities do not provide client network access control services). An example of this type of approach is the server and client versions of Network-1 Security Solutions' *FireWall/Plus*, where the server and desktop machines have full firewall facilities to provide full network access control between the systems and network in addition to VPN facilities.

Dedicated VPN box. Some vendors have come up with dedicated systems that can connect either in front of or behind a router facility to implement VPN facilities between a company and a public IP network such as the Internet. These boxes are simple to implement and usually provide much higher performance than software-based solutions implemented in firewalls or via other schemes. Normally, however, they do not provide an adequate client-level security facility for VPNs and are mostly dedicated for site-to-site access. They also can be expensive for highly connected sites.

As you can see, there is a bewildering array of VPN choices and solutions, depending upon need and fiscal resources.

38. Can you give me an illustration of how a company might benefit from a VPN?

Sure. Following is a case study of an organization with more than 60 sites located in the United States, Europe, and Asia. This should give you an idea of the costs and benefits associated with VPNs. (*Note:* All costs are given in U.S. dollars.)

The current network, used to interconnect the sites, is an extensive network composed of frame relay, leased line, dial-up, and X.25 packet switching. In this network, the average connection speed is 56 kbps with an average per-month connection cost of approximately $176,000. This amount is for communications costs only and does not include any provision for the required modem pools and other types of interconnection hardware. By using frame relay and upgrading only 20 of the 60 sites to T1 circuits (1.544 Mbps), the monthly communications costs are expected to exceed $510,000 per month, $360,000 of which is for the 20 T1 sites alone because of their overseas locations. The other 40 sites require the same services, but not necessarily the entire range of connection speeds required at other, larger sites. In the major sites, the need to upgrade from 56 kbps to T1, and in a couple of cases, T3 (45 Mbps), is forthcoming due to a major change in corporate use of network resources to move large amounts of data. Other needs include:

- allowing customers to access specific applications on in-house systems (there may be up to 20,000 customers doing this daily in the future);
- providing extranet connectivity to customer sites using the SNA, AppleTalk, and IPX protocols in addition to IP;
- enabling remote, secure, corporate user access via modems (there could be as many as 2,000 users accessing internal resources daily);
- expanding small business sites and office presence worldwide so that a small office in a remote city consisting of two to four users and associated equipment can rapidly interconnect newly acquired companies;
- enabling rapid implementation of high-speed connections due to seasonal changes or promotional issues at offices worldwide;
- managing network resources with minimal or no human utilization from internal resources;
- adding modem, ISDN and other remote low-speed connections without affecting specific in-place network resources from a configuration perspective;
- adding customer and vendor connections quickly for multiple protocol suites with minimal or no internal resource expenditure to add connection capability;
- providing intranet server capabilities to all employees domestically and internationally regardless of network protocol access type used in a user's local area;
- developing consistent configuration rules and conformance criteria;
- implementing internationalized method of standards and performance criteria for all sites so that consistent performance and access reliability are achieved;
- allowing network performance to scale from very small (single system) to millions of session accesses per day at a given site with the same connection methodology for simplicity;
- implementing expandable network architecture that can handle not only multiple protocols and interconnection of same, but multiple versions of the protocols at the same time;
- supporting audited and logged network access via secured facilities at each site;
- implementing very stringent security controls for highly critical systems and network interconnects to ensure that only properly authorized users gain access to critical components; and
- providing a redundant and resilient network environment in the case of performance adversity or network outage by one or more vendors to critical locations.

To solve these problems, a network was designed with the following components:

(1) The same public IP provider at all sites will be used whenever possible. For this implementation, UUNET and CompuServe were selected as network vendors for interconnection of sites since they possess high-speed access facilities at all the customers site locations. Further, both vendors have substantial dial-up and ISDN facilities that allow remote location interconnection at very low or fixed price configurations. Selecting two vendors also allows for diversity and support of user sites that may not have connection facilities to the preferred vendor of the two but do have access to the other.

(2) A multiprotocol firewall was selected to provide site-to-site multiprotocol VPN for all protocols, five-layer network security (frame, packet, application, stateful, and proxy in the same product at the same time), scaling (Intel 80486 through Alpha SMP systems), client VPN proxy facilities for remote single system and laptop users, strong authentication for specific systems personnel, remote management of the firewall, and many other facilities that are essential in providing secure networking connectivity. An additional reason for selection is the ability for the product to be used on Internet connections, intranet (there is a server and desktop version) and extranets when connecting to customer or known third party sites.

(3) Common network vendor for all interconnection WAN routers and hubs to ensure proper network interconnectivity, management and minimization of manpower and technical expertise requirements.

With this approach, the 20 main sites—which had an average upgrade fee of $18,000 per site per month, and required specific routing topologies to one or two centralized sites—can be upgraded for an average per-site cost of $7,000 per month. (This figure is higher in some countries, but substantially lower in others, for a T1 connection.) This per month communications fee is normal for a public IP connection. This means that flat-rate costs per month for the 20 sites are approximately $140,000. This is 39 percent of the original cost estimate for the upgrade at the same speed, but also includes all the other ancillary network connectivity requirements.

Additional costs for this implementation include 20 full-functionality firewall facilities (an average of $20,000 per site for an Alpha-based Windows NT system including firewall software and support). Since the new connectivity method provides a $13,000 per month savings, the firewall and all facilities for its interconnection is paid for in less than two months per site. Additional expected per-user costs for Client VPN is approximately $250 per system, which will grow slowly. Costs for modem and ISDN pools are eliminated as are the maintenance, operations, and network management costs and efforts.

For completeness, the customer examined the potential use of a router-only solution with VPN capabilities, but the solution could not solve the remote laptop and small site VPN problem nor the filtering and security management issues that only a firewall can solve. While a router is required for this type of connection to be feasible, so is the right type of firewall so that all the ancillary controls, audit trail, logging, security services and multiple protocol session control and management are available regardless of how the customer needs to connect to the facility. While this solution is still implemented at this writing, initial results are very positive and the cost savings described in this example are real.

End-of-Chapter Commentary

In this chapter we examined many aspects related to layer 3 of the OSI model. Several of the topics or concepts developed here are further explored in other chapters. For example, telephone circuits are revisited in Chapter 15 as part of a discussion on modems, and VPNs are examined from a network security perspective in Chapter 16. Several WAN technologies and services are also discussed in subsequent chapters. These include ISDN (see Chapter 11), frame relay (see Chapter 12), SMDS, (see Chapter 13), and ATM (see Chapter 14).

Chapter 8

Ethernet, Ethernet, and More Ethernet

In this chapter we focus our attention on Ethernet. In previous chapters, we informally mentioned Ethernet in order to illustrate various network concepts. For example, at the data link layer Ethernet was used as an example to demonstrate frame formats, MAC hardware addresses, and network switches. In this chapter the subject of Ethernet is presented in a more formal and comprehensive manner, including its history and its latest evolution, Gigabit Ethernet. An outline of the topics discussed follows:

- History of Ethernet (Questions 1–3)
- Ethernet vs. IEEE 802.3 (Questions 4–13)
- The IEEE 802.3 Protocol and 10 Mbps Ethernet (Questions 14–27)
- Partitioning/Segmentation (Questions 28–32)
- Switched Ethernet (Questions 33–37)
- Virtual LANs (VLANs) (Questions 38–41)
- Fast Ethernet (Questions 42–50)
- 100VG-AnyLAN (Questions 51–56)
- Gigabit Ethernet (Questions 57–68)
- Data Prioritization—IEEE 802.1p and 802.1q (Questions 69–73)
- IsoEthernet (Question 74)

1. What exactly is Ethernet and what is its origin?

Ethernet is a local area network protocol developed jointly by Xerox, Intel, and Digital Equipment Corporation (DEC) at the Xerox Palo Alto Research Center (PARC) in the mid-1970s. It was designed as a technology that would allow for the interconnection of office devices. Although the concept of Ethernet was originally developed at PARC, Ethernet's genesis is with Norman Abramson of the University of Hawaii in the late 1960s to early 1970s. Abramson developed a network called ALOHA, which was used to connect the main campus site in Oahu to seven other campuses on four of the Hawaiian islands. Using a technique called *contention*, Abramson demonstrated that multiple nodes on a network could use the same channel for communications and they could send data whenever they had data to send. The primary difference between the ALOHA network and Ethernet is that ALOHA permitted any node to transmit data at any time, made no provision to allow a node to detect if another node was sending data, and there was no procedure for dealing with what would come to be known as *collisions*. Collisions occur when two or more nodes attempt to transmit data simultaneously. Without a mechanism for dealing with the eventuality of simultaneous transmissions, ALOHA required many retransmissions. Ethernet, on the other hand, was designed with both carrier sense capability (CSMA) and collision detection (CD). (See Chapter 5.)

2. How did Ethernet get its name?

The name Ethernet was derived from the old electromagnetic theoretical substance called *luminiferous ether*, which was formerly believed to be the invisible universal element that bound together the entire universe and all its associated parts. Thus, an "ether" net is a network that connects all components attached to the "net."

3. Is Ethernet a standard?

Yes. Through a consortium organized in the early 1980s, Xerox, Intel, and DEC published a vendor standard now known as the *Ethernet Blue Book*. This book described the methods in which Ethernet would be developed and implemented. It also described how Ethernet hardware and data link services would function. Work on this standard continued to evolve, culminating in the 1982 publication of a cooperative standard titled *Ethernet Version 2.0*.

4. So what happened? Why is there Ethernet and IEEE 802.3?

Although the Xerox-Intel-DEC consortium developed and produced an Ethernet standard (V2.0), it was not an acceptable domestic or international standard for LAN technology. Consequently, the IEEE formed subcommittee 802.3 and produced an IEEE standard for a technology very similar to the Ethernet V2.0 specification. Rumor has it that the IEEE wanted to make Ethernet V2.0 its standard but the Xerox-Intel-DEC consortium wanted to maintain the patent. To avoid any type of patent infringement, the IEEE modified Ethernet V2.0 and produced the IEEE 802.3 specification. These patents have since been given to the IEEE and anyone can now license Ethernet from IEEE for a flat fee of $1,000. Due to its influence with U.S. and international standardization authorities, IEEE 802.3 eventually became ISO standard IS88023.

5. How different is IEEE 802.3 from Ethernet V2.0?

The two specifications are similar since IEEE used the technological details of Ethernet V2.0 as a basis for the 802.3 standard. However, several serious technical differences were introduced in the IEEE version that make the two standards incompatible. First, the physical characteristics of the prescribed cable differ. In the V2.0 standard, the Ethernet cable (thick coax) is prescribed with a 0.395-inch diameter. In the IEEE specification, the cable's diameter was increased to 0.405-inch.

6. Why did IEEE do this? Why not just use the same cable?

The IEEE's rationale for increasing the cable diameter was that the larger diameter provided better electrical characteristics. The only problem a larger diameter cable presented was that V2.0 compliant transceivers could not be used on IEEE 802.3 compliant cable. This presently is not a serious issue because a "thick" Ethernet network is something you are more apt to inherit than install. Vendors manufacture transceivers capable of connecting to both V2.0 and IEEE 802.3 cables.

7. What are the other differences?

A second modification to the V2.0 standard is the manner in which transceivers function. Recall from Chapter 6 that a transceiver enables a node to communicate with the cable. Specifically, it transmits and receives simultaneously, and it notifies a node if a collision occurred. When a transceiver is connected to the cable there is usually no way to determine if the transceiver is working unless there is a data transmission. In the V2.0 specification, a signal known as *Signal Quality Error (SQE)* is periodically generated by the transceiver and read by the controller of the host to which it is connected. Historically, this is called *heartbeat* and effectively informs the host's controller that the transceiver is "alive." In the IEEE 802.3 standard, transceivers do not generate a heartbeat unless a real signal quality error occurs. Thus, SQE effectively is used for network management. Given this difference in the operation of V2.0 and 802.3 transceivers, if a V2.0 controller (a NIC) is mated with an IEEE 802.3 transceiver, the controller interprets the absence of a heartbeat from the transceiver as a "dead" transceiver. To accommodate both standards vendors incorporated a switch into their transceivers that can enable or disable SQE.

8. Aha! So that's what that switch means. I've often wondered about that. Tell me about some other differences.

Unfortunately, this next difference, which entails how data frames are formatted at the data link layer, does not have a similar workaround. Although V2.0 and IEEE 802.3 frames range from a minimum of 64 bytes to a maximum of 1,518 bytes (see Chapter 5), they do have one major difference: V2.0 frames contain a two-byte "type" field, which is used to identify the different higher-level protocol types used by DEC, Intel, and Xerox (e.g., IP, IPX). The IEEE 802.3 specification does not support a protocol type field. Instead, the V2.0 "type" field is replaced with a "length" field, which specifies the length in bytes of the bit string that represents user data. (See Figure 5-3.) The exclusion of a "type" field in the 802.3 standard means that compatibility cannot be maintained between 802.3 and V2.0. Furthermore, unlike the previous two differences of cable diameter and SQE function, nothing can be done to compensate for the different frame formats.

9. If an 802.3 frame does not have a protocol type field, how does the network layer know what protocol is being used for the frame?

This information is provided by the Logical Link Control (LLC). Recall from Chapter 5 that the IEEE partitions the OSI data link layer into the MAC and LLC sublayers. In an 802.3 frame, an LLC header containing higher-level protocol information is provided at the beginning of the frame's data field. The combination of LLC header and data field is known as the LLC Protocol Data Unit (LLCPDU). Ethernet V2.0 frames do not have an LLC component. Thus, once again, V2.0 and 802.3 frames are incompatible at the data link layer. (*Note:* For completeness sake, the LLC sublayer also contains a source service access point, SSAP, and a destination service access point, DSAP. These SAPs provide the mechanism for source and destination nodes to communicate, and are needed for protocol-type identification. See the Internet's Request for Comment, RFC 1340, for additional information.)

10. Are there any other differences?

Yes. They include topology and cable type. IEEE 802.3 supports both bus and star topologies, but Ethernet V2.0 supports only a bus topology. Finally, 802.3 compliant networks can be either baseband or broadband, but in V2.0 only baseband Ethernet networks are supported.

11. Is IEEE 802.3 considered superior to Ethernet V2.0?

It depends on what you mean by superior. Rather than comment on whether one standard is better than another, we will say this: There is nothing intrinsically wrong with V2.0 other than it is a proprietary standard that does not comply with the prescribed ISO standard for Ethernet-like networks. Furthermore, although the two standards are similar—802.3 was designed after V2.0—they are different enough to be considered incompatible. This incompatibility resulted from political as well as technical issues and is best left to historians and analysts.

12. So what's the bottom line? Do I have to be concerned with V2.0?

The bottom line is that vendor support for IEEE 802.3 overshadows that for Ethernet V2.0; any new "Ethernet" network you install probably will be based on the IEEE 802.3 protocol. Nevertheless, there are still many "old" Ethernets in existence and it is possible that you might inherit one that incorporates both V2.0 and 802.3 compliant products.

13. How important is it to distinguish between V2.0 and 802.3 when discussing Ethernet networks?

In casual usage, IEEE 802.3 is commonly referred to as Ethernet. What you should realize, though, is that technically it is *not* Ethernet—only V2.0 is considered Ethernet. Consequently, in this book, to play it safe, we use the notation "Ethernet/802.3" when referring to Ethernet networks.

14. Let's move on to the 802.3 protocol.

OK. At the physical layer (Chapters 4 and 6), the IEEE 802.3 standard addresses issues such as cable type, cable length, and connector types. Ethernet/802.3's physical layer also encodes data prior to transmission using a technique called *Manchester encoding*, whose purpose is to ensure that the end of a transmission (carrier-sense failure) is properly detected. Manchester encoding differs from standard digital transmission in two ways. First, instead of "high" equaling "1" and "low" equaling "0," a timing interval is used to measure high-to-low transitions. Second, instead of the timed transmission period being "all high" or "all low" for either 1 or 0, a state transition is encoded into the transformation. Specifically, a 1 is sent as a half-time-period low followed by a half-time-period high, and a 0 is sent as a half-time-period high followed by a half-time-period low. (See Figure 8-1.) Consequently, the end of the last bit transmitted is easily determined immediately following the transmission of the last bit.

At the data link layer (Chapters 5 and 6), the standard is based on 1-persistent CSMA/CD and uses a binary exponential backoff algorithm to calculate the wait time. The average wait time for a new packet is set to an arbitrary initial value. This value is then doubled each time a collision results when a transmission is attempted with the same packet. The Ethernet/802.3 data link layer also specifies a minimum frame size of 64 bytes and a maximum frame size of 1,518 bytes. The frame format consists of a 7-byte preamble, a 1-byte start frame delimiter, a 6-byte destination address, a 6-byte source address, a 2-byte length

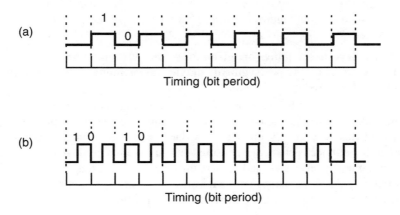

Figure 8-1. Part (a) shows a typical digital transmission. When an electrical pulse is "on," the line is at a "high" level; when there is no pulse during a transmission ("off" state), the line is at a low state. For each bit-period, there is either a pulse or no pulse. Part (b) shows a Manchester encoded digital transmission. Here, each bit period has two intervals. A 1 is sent as a half-time-period "low" followed by a half-time-period "high," (i.e., a low-to-high transition), and a 0 is sent as a half-time-period "high" followed by a half-time-period "low" (i.e., a high-to-low transition). Instances where no transition occurs at the midpoint of a bit interval are used for control purposes.

count, a data field that ranges between 46 and 1,500 bytes, a pad field that ranges from 0 to as many bytes is necessary to get the data field to a minimum 46 bytes, and a 4-byte CRC checksum field. (See Figure 5-3 and Chapter 5.)

An Ethernet/802.3 address consists of 48 bits, represented as 12 hexadecimal digits (0-9, A-F), and partitioned into six groups of two. The higher-order three bytes (the left-most six hexadecimal digits) represent the manufacturer of the Ethernet device; the lower-order three bytes represent the serial number of the device. For example, the address 08:00:20:01:D6:2A corresponds to an Ethernet/802.3 device manufactured by Sun Micro-systems (as indicated by Sun's code 08:00:20) that has the serial number 01:D6:2A. The IEEE is responsible for assigning Ethernet addresses. (A list of Ethernet address prefixes assigned to specific vendors is given in Appendix A. See also Box 5-2 in Chapter 5 for additional information about Ethernet/802.3 addresses.)

15. What do Ethernet designations like 10BASE-T mean?

IEEE 802.3 LANs are designated using the following general format:

Signaling Rate (Mbps)—Band (Base or Broad)—Length (meters) or Cable Type

Thus, a 10 Mbps baseband LAN that uses UTP cable is designated as *10BASE-T* (the T is for twisted-pair), and a 10 Mbps ThickWire baseband LAN is designated as *10BASE5* (the 5 is for 500 meter segment length). A brief description of the various IEEE 802.3 10 Mbps LAN specifications is given in Table 8-1. Examples of the various types are also provided in Figures 8-2 (ThickWire), 8-3 (ThinWire), 8-4 (UTP), and 8-5 (UTP). We suggest you study Table 8-1 and Figures 8-2 through 8-5 before proceeding further.

16. In Table 8-1, several attributes are given for each LAN type. For example, you list maximum number of nodes per segment, maximum segment length, and so forth. How significant are these?

Very significant. The IEEE 802.3 specifications for the maximum number of nodes per segment and maximum segment length, coupled with minimum and maximum frame sizes of 64 and 1518 bytes, respectively, are necessary due to Ethernet's contentious nature. The maximum number of nodes per segment ensures that an Ethernet network does not get saturated; the minimum packet size and maximum cable-segment length enable Ethernet nodes to accurately detect collisions on the network; and the maximum frame size allows nodes to detect the completion of a transmission, which facilitates error detection.

17. In Table 8-1, you use the term "max diameter" as part of a network's description. For example, you indicate that 10BASE5 has a maximum diameter of 2,500 m, and 10BASE-T has a maximum diameter of 500 m. What is a network "diameter?"

Diameter in this context is a term that emanates from the branch of mathematics called *graph theory*, which is frequently employed by theoretical and applied computer scientists in the study of network design. The diameter of a 10 Mbps Ethernet/802.3 network is the overall length between the network's two most remote nodes. For example, consider the 10BASE-T LANs shown in Figures 8-6 and 8-7. The first one has a network diameter of 200 m; the second LAN's diameter is 300 m.

Table 8-1. Summary of IEEE 802.3 Specifications for 10 Mbps Ethernet

Type	Description[1]
10BASE5 ThickWire	**Cable:** Thick Coax (RG-8); **Topology:** Bus; **Connectors:** Transceivers, transceiver cable, 15-pin AUI; uses "vampire" tap; **Max Segment Length:** 500 m; **Max Nodes per Segment:** 100—spaced in 2.5 m increments; **Max Diameter:** 2,500 m; **Misc:** 50-ohm termination at each end of cable; one end grounded to building ground
10BASE2 ThinWire	**Cable:** Thin Coax (RG-58); **Topology:** Bus; **Connectors:** BNC; **Max Segment Length:** 185 m; **Max Nodes per Segment:** 30—minimum 0.5 m between nodes; **Max Diameter:** 925 m; **Misc:** 50-ohm termination at each end of cable; one end grounded to building ground
10BASE-T UTP Ethernet	**Cable:** Cat 3, 4, or 5 UTP; **Topology:** Star; **Connectors:** RJ-45, patch panels, repeaters; **Max Segment Length:** 100 m; **Max Nodes per Segment:** 2; **Max Diameter:** 500 m; **Misc:** Each node is connected directly or indirectly to a hub; indirect connections are via wallplates or patch panels
10BASE-FB[2] Fiber Backbone	**Cable:** Fiber; **Topology:** Point-to-Point; **Connectors:** Fiber-optic transceivers, ST; **Max Segment Length:** 2,000 m; **Max Nodes per Segment:** 2; **Max Diameter:** 2,500 m; **Misc:** Backbone-only technology used to interconnect Ethernet repeaters; maximum of 15 repeaters permitted; uses synchronous signaling to re-time the optical signals for data transmissions
10BASE-FL[2] Fiber Link	**Cable:** Fiber; **Topology:** Point-to-Point or star; **Connectors:** Fiber-optic transceivers, ST; **Max Segment Length:** 2,000 m; **Max Nodes per Segment:** 2; **Max Diameter:** 2,500 m; **Misc:** Can be used to interconnect workstations or repeaters; maximum of five repeaters permitted; replaces Fiber Optic Inter-Repeater Link (FOIRL); if 10BASE-FL is mixed with FOIRL, max segment length is 1,000 m
10BASE-FP[2] Fiber Passive	**Cable:** Fiber; **Topology:** Star; **Connectors:** Fiber-optic transceivers, ST; **Max Segment Length:** 500 m; **Max Nodes per Segment:** 33; **Max Diameter:** 2,500 m; **Misc:** Used for small installations such as workgroup LANs; specifies a passive hub, which means it uses no electronics (including power) and hence is immune to external noise

[1] All types subscribe to the 5-4-3 repeater placement rule.

[2] Part of the 10BASE-F Standard for Fiber-optic Ethernet.

18. Why are the maximum diameters different for the various LAN types?

The maximum diameter of a 10 Mbps Ethernet/802.3 is the maximum distance possible for a *single* Ethernet/802.3 LAN. By *single* we mean an Ethernet/802.3 LAN that consists of either one segment or multiple segments connected by repeaters. Maximum diameters vary among LAN types because they use different cable. For example, the network diameter of a 10BASE5 LAN, which uses RG-8 coaxial cable, ranges from a minimum of 500 meters (for one segment) to a maximum of 2,500 meters (five segments connected by four repeaters). Similarly, a 10BASE-T LAN uses unshielded twisted-pair cable and has a network diameter that ranges from 200 m to 500 m. (See Figure 8-8.)

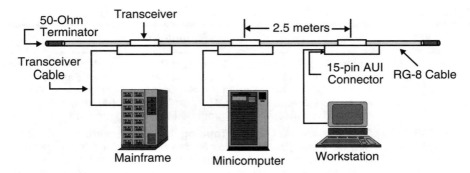

Figure 8-2. Example of a 10BASE5 (ThickWire Ethernet) LAN. The topology is a bus configuration, the maximum length of a single segment is 500 meters, and a single segment supports up to 100 nodes. Nodes are connected to the cable via transceivers and transceiver cable; transceivers are spaced 2.5 meters apart to prevent signal interference. The actual physical connection of a transceiver involves drilling into the cable using a "vampire tap." Each end of the cable is terminated with a 50-ohm resistor, and one end of the cable must be grounded.

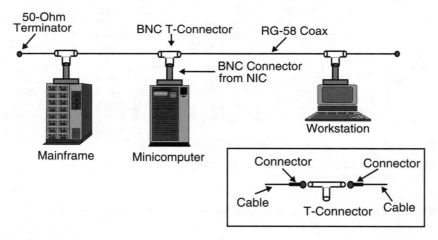

Figure 8-3. Example of a 10BASE2 (ThinWire Ethernet) LAN. The topology is a bus configuration, the maximum length of a single segment is 185 meters, and a single segment supports up to 30 nodes. Nodes are connected to the cable via BNC T-connectors, which must be spaced at least 0.5 meter apart to prevent signal interference. Each end of the cable is terminated with a 50-ohm resistor, and one end of the cable must be grounded. A segment is composed of several pieces of cable with each piece being connected via a T-connector (see inset).

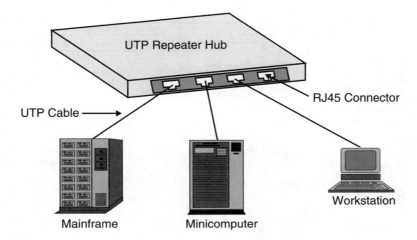

Figure 8-4. Example of a typical 10BASE-T (Twisted Pair Ethernet) LAN. The topology is a star configuration, and the maximum length of a segment is 100 m. Note that only two nodes can be connected per segment—a workstation and a repeater. Both the hub and a device's network interface card (NIC) contain 8-pin modular (RJ45) connectors. Cable can be Category 3, 4, or 5; higher grade cables provide better performance.

19. In Figure 8-8, you mention the 5-4-3 repeater placement rule. What is this rule?

In order for a network to function properly, it must comply with its design rules. The *5-4-3 repeater placement rule* is a general rule of thumb to follow when configuring an Ethernet/802.3 LAN to ensure that it follows IEEE specifications. Ethernet/802.3 LANs are based on CSMA/CD (see Chapter 5). Thus, collisions are an inherent part of an Ethernet/802.3 LAN. If a LAN consists of a single segment (Figures 8-1 and 8-2), or a single UTP repeater hub (Figures 8-4, 8-5, and 8-6), then the 5-4-3 repeater placement rule is of no practical concern. However, if a LAN's diameter is going to be extended using repeaters, then the 5-4-3 repeater replacement rule becomes extremely critical. You see, every Ethernet/802.3 LAN has what is known as a *collision domain*. A collision domain consists of a single network where two nodes can cause a collision. In the case of a single-segmented Ethernet/802.3 LAN, the independent segment represents the collision domain; in a multisegmented Ethernet/802.3 LAN, however, the collective segments comprise the collision domain. For example, in Figures 8-2 and 8-3, the collision domain comprises the single ThickWire or ThinWire segment. In Figures 8-4, 8-5, and 8-6, the collision domain comprises the segments connected to the single repeater. In Figures 8-7 and 8-8, though, multiple segments are interconnected via multiple repeaters. This extends the network's diameter, which increases the distance between the two most remote nodes. Physically, the networks in Figures 8-7 and 8-8 appear to be separate. Electrically, though, these physically separate networks belong to one collision domain. The bottom line is a single collision domain contains a maximum of 1,024 end nodes, and its diameter cannot be more than 2,500 m.

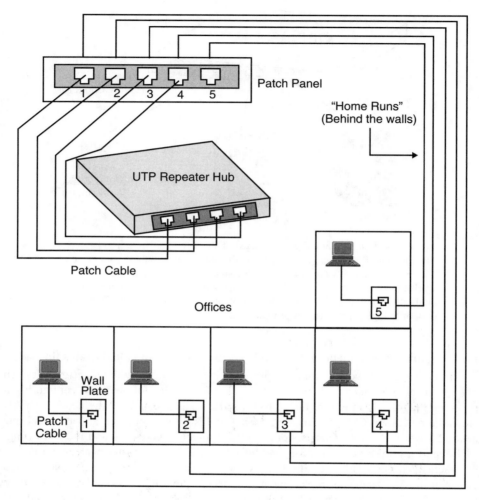

Figure 8-5. A typical 10BASE-T wiring scheme involves a centralized hub located in a wiring closet and cable installed between a patch panel and a wall plate located in an office or room. This length of cable is referred to as a "home run." Each end of these home runs is then "punched down" behind the patch panel and wall plates. Patch cable is used to connect ports on the patch panel to the hub, and workstations to wall plates.The total length of all cable for one workstation (hub to patch panel, home run, and patch cable from wall plate to NIC) must be no more 100 m.

Although patch panels provide a certain level of convenience, they also represent a potential source of additional noise. Nevertheless, patch panels are useful in many situations. For example, note that patch panel port 5 is wired to office 5, but the workstation in office 5 does not have a connection to the LAN because patch panel port 5 does not have a connection to the hub. Connectivity can be provided to office 5, though, by simply disconnecting a patch cable from one of the patch panel ports and reconnecting it to port 5.

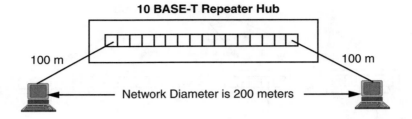

Figure 8-6. A network diameter is the distance between the two most remote nodes of a network. In this illustration we have a 10BASE-T LAN that can connect up to 16 nodes via a UTP repeater hub. If each node is connected to the hub with the maximum segment length permitted (100 m), then the network diameter is 200 m—100 m from sending node to repeater port plus 100 m from repeater port to receiving node.

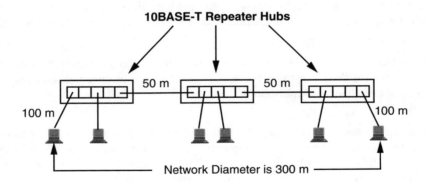

Figure 8-7. In this illustration, a 10BASE-T LAN consists of four segments interconnected by three repeaters. If the links between nodes and their respective ports are 100 m each, then the network diameter is 300 m—100 m from sending node to port, plus two 50 m hub links, plus 100 m from port to receiving node. Remember: The network diameter is always the distance between the farthest two nodes.

20. What does all of this have to do with the 5-4-3 repeater placement rule?

We're getting there. We want to first set the stage by extending our discussion about collision domains. CSMA/CD design rules specify that if a node's transmission results in a collision, the node must be able to detect the collision before it stops transmitting. If not,

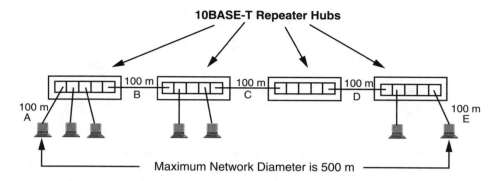

10BASE-T Repeater Hubs

Maximum Network Diameter is 500 m

Figure 8-8. The maximum diameter of a 10BASE-T LAN is 500 m. Note how this configuration complies with the 5-4-3 repeater placement rule. There are 5 segments (labeled A through E), 4 repeaters, and at most only 3 segments are populated with end nodes.

the node will never know that the frame it transmitted was corrupted. For example, look at Figure 8-8 and consider the following scenario involving the nodes at the opposite ends of the collision domain (i.e., the workstations attached to segments *A* and *E*, respectively):

• Node *A* transmits a frame.

• Around the same time, node *E* wants to transmit a frame. It senses the channel but does not "hear" anything because *A*'s transmission has not reached *E*. Sensing an idle channel, *E* transmits a frame.

• The two frames collide.

• *E* must now send a jamming signal to all the nodes connected to the network, including *A*. Furthermore, the jamming signal must reach *A* before *A* stops transmitting. If the collision occurred at *E*'s "front door," that is, just before *A*'s frame reached *E*, the jamming signal must travel a considerable distance.

On an Ethernet/802.3 LAN, timing is everything. Although electrical signals on Ethernet media travel at nearly the speed of light, it still requires a specific amount of time for a signal to travel from one node to another across the network. In Ethernet/802.3 jargon, time is measured using the unit *bit-time*, which is equal to 0.1 μs. Thus, a one bit transmission requires 0.1 μs. Recall that the smallest Ethernet/802.3 frame is 64 bytes long, which is 512 bits. This implies that to transmit a 64-byte frame requires 512 bit-times or 51.2 μs. This means that a 64-byte frame has a collision domain of 512 bit-times or 51.2 μs. Thus, any delay cannot be greater than 51.2 μs. Returning to our scenario above, in order to maintain a roundtrip delay of no more than 512 bit-times, node *E* has to send a jamming signal before *A* transmits more than 256 bits (i.e., 256 bit-times). This will then give *E* 256 bit-times for its jamming signal to reach *A*. If the LAN is up to spec, then the roundtrip delay will not exceed 512 bit-times.

21. Oh! I get it. And because repeaters introduce delay, we have to limit how many are connected to the network so we can maintain that 512 bit-time upper limit.

That's right. Repeaters—like other electronic devices such as cables, NICs, bridges, and switches—add to the overall delay of a network. This delay, which is also called *latency*, is measured by how long it takes the repeater to transmit a regenerated signal after receiving it (i.e., the amount of time the signal remains inside the box). Since the amount of delay introduced by repeaters varies from one vendor to another, the 5-4-3 repeater placement rule gives us a general rule of thumb to follow if you do not want to calculate the total delay yourself. The 5-4-3 rule requires: no more than 5 segments of up to 500 m each; no more than 4 repeaters; and no more than 3 segments can have end nodes connected to them. This rule is also known as the 4-repeater rule, or the 5-4-3-2-1 rule. In the latter, the "2" implies that two of the five segments are used as interrepeater links, and the "1" implies that a configuration using the maximum parameters permitted results into one collision domain.

22. I am curious as to how would you calculate the total delay?

Easy: (1) get the vendor latency specifications for all the repeaters, NICs and cable used on your network; (2) add the delays; (3) multiply the sum by two (you want roundtrip values); and (4) see if the product is less than or equal to 51.2 μs. If it isn't, then your network is not Ethernet/802.3 compliant and could have problems.

23. What kind of problems?

Some problems manifest themselves as bad or invalid frames. These include oversized frames, runt frames, jabbers, alignment or frame errors, and CRC errors; all were discussed in Chapter 5. Timing errors can also lead to retransmissions. For example, a sending node that does not receive an acknowledgment from the receiving node within a prescribed time period, assumes the frame was lost and retransmits the frame. Continual retransmissions can ultimately lead to degradation of network performance. Probably the biggest problem with Ethernet networks is collisions. Box 8-1 contains a description of some common causes of collisions, and Box 8-2 addresses Ethernet performance issues.

24. Is there any way to get around the 5-4-3 repeater placement rule?

Yes. One way to increase the number of Ethernet ports and still comply with the 5-4-3 repeater placement rule is to use chassis-based repeater hubs. (See Figure 6-7.) These hubs have individual slots in which multiport Ethernet interface boards (also called *blades, cards,* or *modules*) are installed. The primary feature of a chassis hub is that each board is connected to the same backplane to which the repeater unit is connected. Since all boards share the same backplane with the repeater, all of the devices connected to the hub use only one repeater.

Another workaround is stackable repeater hubs. (See Figure 6-8.) These devices consist of individual hubs "stacked" one on top of another. Instead of a common chassis backplane, stackable hubs use a "pseudo-backplane" based on a common connector interface.

BOX 8-1: Common Causes of Collisions

Common causes of collisions in Ethernet/802.3 include the following:

Propagation Delay. Different types of media have different propagation delays, as do repeaters and bridges. If nodes are far apart on long segments, there is a greater chance of collisions due to propagation delay, especially in high traffic environments. Add repeaters or bridges to the configuration and the probability increases. Thus, the length of certain types of Ethernet/802.3 media can have dramatic effect on whether collisions occur.

Nodes Not Following The Rules. The IEEE specifications establish specific rules for collision detection and retransmission. Unfortunately, not all vendors follow these rules. When a vendor violates the rules on collision detection, it can affect the performance of the network. The 802.3 standard specifies that after a collision, retransmission of a packet should occur after generation of a random amount of timer delay not to exceed 1024 slot-times, which occurs on the tenth to fifteenth consecutive collision. (One slot-time is defined as 51.2 μs for 10 Mbps cable plants.) This means that if a collision occurs, a jamming signal is sent, a random number is generated, and the controller waits that long before retransmission. The controller then seizes the cable (after sensing it) and sends the packet again (if the cable is idle). Although the wait interval is supposed to be between 1 and 1024, some vendors violate this rule and set a ceiling lower than 1024; doing so does not allow random numbers higher than a predetermined value, thus allowing a system to acquire the network quicker than those that generate a higher random number in accordance with the IEEE standard.

Noise. Noise is a pretty obvious source of collisions. Recall that noise is any type of undesirable signal. Noise can come from a variety of locations including external sources or harmonic distortion. Various everyday office equipment such as copiers, laser printers, ballast transformers on fluorescent tube lighting, and HVAC motors also causes noise problems. Noise is also more problematic with UTP cable.

Improper Segmentation of Cable. This reason is restricted to coaxial cables. Thick-Wire cable should be cut in accordance with the standard and at specific lengths (e.g., 23.4 m, 70.2 m, etc.); ThinWire networks should have at least 0.5 m distance between nodes. Improper segmentation can cause noise and harmonic distortion problems, thus increasing the likelihood of collisions.

Babbling Transceivers. When a transceiver fails it begins to spew all kinds of trash on a cable; collisions inevitably occur.

An external cable interconnects the individual hubs in a daisy-chain. Once interconnected, the entire chain of hubs becomes a single logical unit that counts as only one repeater hub on the network. Stackable hubs are less expensive than chassis-based devices, and permit additional hubs to be added to the stack without any need for worrying about repeater hop counts. There is an upper limit, though, to the number of hubs that can be stacked. Known as the *stacking height*, this number is between 6 and 12, depending on the manufacturer.

BOX 8-2: Ethernet/802.3 Performance Issues

Many Ethernet/802.3 performance-related problems stem from poorly designed and installed Ethernets, systems that are configured incorrectly, and standards violations (e.g., incorrect cable length, too many devices connected to a segment, etc.). Following are some additional problems that can adversely affect an Ethernet/802.3 LAN's performance:

Frame Deferrals. When a host is ready to transmit a frame but the network is busy, a frame deferral occurs. Thus, the transmitting node must defer or wait until the network is idle. If the average load is high (over 30%), then deferrals might be normal. If, on the other hand, network load is light, there are few errors, and frame deferrals are present, then a high burst rate contention most likely exists on the network. As a general rule, frame deferrals, should never exceed 10% of the transmitted frames of a given system.

Collisions. High traffic loads for short bursts of time on nodes that are close (electrically speaking for propagation delay) do not necessarily translate into collisions. However, high traffic loads from bursty nodes that are electrically distant do tend to cause serious collision problems on the network.

Session Disconnects. Nodes that cannot communicate effectively with each other eventually time-out. Such a disconnect might be due to network congestion (due to bursty traffic), or the inability of the network to send traffic back to the node in a prescribed time-frame.

Congestion. Hardware controllers for Ethernet/802.3 devices have a finite amount of CPU power and a finite amount of memory on the cards. When a burst of traffic arrives, the controller must collect all data frames—regardless if the node is the correct recipient—before the controller logic can determine if the frames are valid for the node. A high burst rate of traffic can cause all buffers on a node to fill quickly, and can cause the controller to lose data destined for that node while collecting data destined for other systems. When a node cannot receive data because its buffers are full, the frames are lost. Eventually, data retransmission occurs resulting in increases in both traffic load and bursting rates.

Retransmissions. As nodes lose data destined for them, the data must be retransmitted. This causes additional bursts of traffic and an artificially inflated traffic level on the network. The single most common problem that results in retransmissions is due to controller congestion—the Ethernet controller on the receiving host is not capable of reading the frames on the cable fast enough to capture all the frames offered by the sending node the first time.

25. Is there a similar rule for bridges, switches, and routers?

No. Repeaters are layer 1 devices that regenerate all incoming signals, including collisions, and propagate these regenerated signals to all the segments connected to its ports. Repeaters extend the diameter of a network, but are considered to be part of the same collision domain of networks designed using only repeaters. Bridges, switches, and routers, however, are layer 2 or 3 devices. They perform filtering and frame translations (e.g., from an 802.3 format to an 802.5 format). They do not propagate collision signals from one segment to another. Hence, these devices effectively partition a network into multiple collision domains. For example, in Figure 8-8, if the third repeater from the left were a bridge, then there would be two separate collision domains. The first contains the first two repeaters, and the second contains the last repeater. (The network diameter remains the same.)

26. It would seem that as more nodes are added to an Ethernet/802.3 LAN, the more likely collisions will increase, which in turn degrades overall network performance. How can you tell when an Ethernet/802.3 LAN is overloaded and what can you do about it?

You are correct in your observation. Given its design Ethernet/802.3 LAN performance could indeed degrade considerably as more nodes are connected. As for assessing whether an Ethernet/802.3 LAN is overloaded, two strategies are available. The first one follows a basic management principle: delegate it to someone—in this case, the users. If user complaints become persistent, frequent, and loud enough, then the network probably is overloaded. The second strategy is to approach the task of analysis scientifically—get the proper tools and training, and then systematically measure the LAN's performance.

27. If I were to use the scientific approach, what do I need to consider?

First, you need to understand that it is very difficult to measure the true performance of any Ethernet/802.3 LAN because it does not use fixed frame sizes. For example, an Ethernet/802.3 LAN that transmits only maximum-sized frames (1,518 bytes) has a theoretical maximum efficiency rate of more than 95 percent. This means 95 percent of the LAN's transmission time is being used to transmit real user data. At the other end of the scale, a LAN that transmits only minimum-sized frames (64 bytes), where user data is only one byte plus 45 bytes of padding, has a theoretical maximum efficiency rate of less than two percent. So, the efficiency of an Ethernet/802.3 LAN is a function of the frame sizes transmitted.

A second concept of performance is *utilization*, which is the amount of time the LAN spends successfully transmitting data. Many performance monitoring tools will provide a user with average and peak utilization times, which are reported as a percentage. Both have different meanings. For example, an average utilization of 20 percent means that over some period of time (e.g., a 10-hour period), on average, 20 percent of the LAN's capacity is used for successfully transmitting data. On the other hand, a 20 percent peak utilization means that at a specific moment in time, 20 percent of the LAN's capacity was utilized. Associated with the concept of utilization is *throughput*, which is a measure of the amount of data transmitted between two nodes in a given time period (see Chapter 4). Throughput and utilization are the same except they use different units of measure. For example, if the average utilization of a 10 Mbps Ethernet/802.3 LAN is 20 percent, then this implies that 20 percent of the possible 10 Mbps bandwidth, 2 Mbps, is being used on average to successfully transmit data.

28. What are some acceptable parameters?

Now you are asking us to address an often debated topic—the subject of "acceptable" Ethernet/LAN performance parameters. Rather than commit to specific parameters, we will give you some guidelines so you can decide what is acceptable. First, every LAN is different. For example, a 50-percent average utilization rate might be acceptable in one context but unacceptable in another. Some network managers believe that when average utilization exceeds 30 percent of a 10 Mbps Ethernet/802.3 LAN (3 Mbps), access times to the channel become unacceptable and overall network performance degrades. Hence, they set their thresholds accordingly and take action when they are reached. Second, don't get alarmed at high peak utilization rates. It is not uncommon, particularly during large downloads from a server, for an Ethernet/802.3 LAN to experience a peak utilization of 95 percent or higher. If this rate is sustained for a prolonged period of time (e.g., five or ten minutes), then there probably is a problem. Third, be sensitive to response times. Increased response times could imply that the network is becoming *saturated*, which implies a sustained utilization rate of more than 80 percent. Note that the way CSMA/CD is designed, nodes even on a saturated LAN will eventually be serviced. However, the response time might not be acceptable. The bottom line is this: Although a 10 Mbps Ethernet/802.3 LAN has a theoretical capacity of 10 Mbps, actual utilization will always be less than this theoretical value. Furthermore, it is up to you to decide what parameters are acceptable for your LAN.

29. What strategies can I use to increase the efficiency of my Ethernet/802.3 LAN?

Partition it.

30. What does that mean?

Partitioning, which is also called *segmentation*, involves configuring a network so that it consists of several separate (but still interconnected) segments. Partitioning improves overall network performance, enhanced security, and increased reliability.

31. How is this done?

One way to partition a network is to create separate segments with fewer users. This is illustrated in Figure 8-9. In part (a) a typical Ethernet LAN consisting of nine hosts is shown. In part (b) this network is partitioned into three separate segments, each consisting of three hosts and a bridge. Segments are interconnected by a common backbone and isolated from each other using the bridges. An alternative to the configuration of (b) is shown in part (c). Once again the original Ethernet LAN of (a) is partitioned into three isolated segments, each consisting of three hosts. In this illustration, though, the segments are interconnected via a multiport bridge rather than a common backbone. Thus, the backbone of (b) has been "collapsed" into the multiport bridge. Comparing the configurations of (b) and (c) to that of (a) in Figure 8-9, it can be seen that segmentation helps reduce network traffic loads by reducing the number of nodes having to contend for the same shared medium. In part (a) nine hosts are in contention, but in (b) and (c) only three hosts each

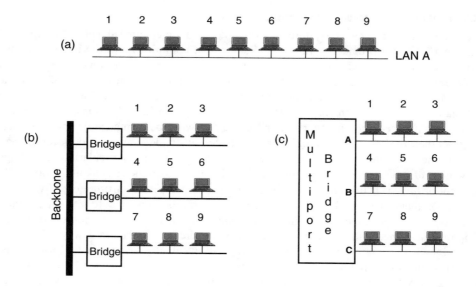

Figure 8-9. In (a) an unsegmented Ethernet LAN is shown. In (b) this LAN is partitioned into three separate segments using individual bridges connected to a backbone, and alternatively, in (c) a multiport bridge is used in which the backbone of (b) is "collapsed" into the multiport bridge. In a properly segmented network, at least 80% of the network traffic generated by the nodes on a LAN remains local to that LAN. Keeping remote access to a minimum (no more than 20%) minimizes backbone congestion and increases network performance.

contend for the same medium. This strategy works well as long as it follows the 80/20 rule—80 percent of the traffic between nodes remains on the same physical cable segment; the remaining 20 percent of traffic traverses a layer 2 or 3 device. If not, then this configuration can actually degrade a network.

Another strategy is to partition a network by physically connecting all workstations and servers that need to communicate with each other to the same segment. One way in which this can be implemented is to place all servers at partition boundaries. This is illustrated in Figure 8-10. You can also partition a network in a similar manner using switches, firewalls, or routers.

32. The concept is simple enough to understand, but how difficult is it to partition a network?

Partitioning requires proper network analysis prior to implementation. If not properly configured, you can actually increase traffic loads rather than reduce them. For example, suppose in Figure 8-10, a node on the "C" segment needs to communicate with the server on the "A" segment on a frequent basis. Now, instead of keeping this node's transmissions local to the "C" group, traffic must cross the backbone. This increases backbone traffic,

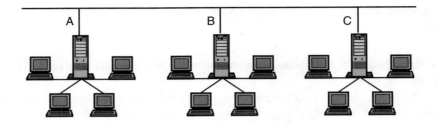

Figure 8-10. Another way to partition a network is to physically connect all nodes with their server, and placing all servers at partition boundaries. In this illustration, there are three separate partitions—A, B, and C. Note that network traffic is reduced since the majority of communication occurs within a separate segment. At the same time, by having the servers on the partition boundaries, nodes from one segment are not locked out from communicating with a server located on another segment.

which increases overall network congestion. Partitioning a network into separate, physical segments is easy to do and maintain when dealing with static workgroups. However, in dynamic workgroup settings where employees are assigned to work on different projects for different periods of time, partitioning is difficult to implement. For example, suppose 50 people located in three different buildings are assigned to a project that uses applications installed on a centrally located server. It is quite impractical to move these people and their workstations to the same physical location and segment that supports the server. Consequently, 100 percent of this workgroup's network traffic will traverse the backbone.

33. Can anything be done to rectify this situation?

Yes. You can establish *virtual local area networks*, or *VLANs*. VLANs are created using Ethernet switches, which are part of a switched Ethernet environment.

34. Hold it. Before you get into VLANs, brief me on Ethernet switches and the concept of switched Ethernet.

OK, but you should also review Chapter 6, which contains a general discussion about Ethernet switches and switch architecture. The concept of *switched Ethernet* is based on the following principle: If the traffic a node receives is restricted to only the traffic destined for it, then network loads are reduced because every host would not need to examine every frame placed on the network. Thus, switched Ethernet transforms traditional Ethernet/802.3 from a broadcast technology to a point-to-point technology—it isolates network traffic between sending and receiving nodes from all other connected nodes. This is done using Ethernet switches, which are improved bridges that were first introduced in 1990. Today, Ethernet switches are a key element in Ethernet/802.3 LANs, and the switch concept is now a part of ATM, token ring, FDDI, and 100 Mbps and 1000 Mbps Ethernet networks. Ethernet switches are available in various varieties including workgroup, private, and backbone.

35. Are these different from the store-and-forward and cut-through switches discussed in Chapter 6?

The terms *store-and-forward* and *cut-through* are used to describe a switch's architecture, that is, how it operates. The terms *workgroup, private,* and *backbone* are used to describe a switch's application. For example, *workgroup switches* (also called *segment switches*) might support 1,024 MAC addresses per port. (Recall that 1,024 is the maximum number of nodes permitted on an Ethernet/802.3 LAN.) These switches are really fast multiport bridges because each port supports a shared medium. A workgroup switch partitions a single, shared medium into multiple, shared media. For example, in Figure 8-11 (a) each node is contending for a piece of a 10 Mbps channel. In part (b), though, only 10 nodes per segment now content for the shared medium. Thus, each node in part (b) effectively receives 1/10 of the channel rather than 1/100th as in (a), which improves overall network performance tenfold.

Unlike workgroup switches, *private switches* support only one MAC address per port providing each node with its own dedicated 10 Mbps segment. This eliminates contention for the cable, thereby liberating the end nodes from performing collision detection. Private switches are appropriate for workstations running applications requiring high-bandwidth. An illustration of a private Ethernet switch is given in Figure 8-12.

Switches supporting 100 Mbps and 1000 Mbps are available. These switches are particularly appropriate for client-server applications. For example, if, in Figure 8-12, node 8 were a server and nodes 1-7 were clients, all traffic would be to or from the server. Since each port supports a dedicated 10 Mbps link, a bottleneck could conceivably exist at the server port. This situation is resolved by using a 10/100 switch, which includes dedicated 10 Mbps and 100 Mbps ports. Clients are connected to the 10 Mbps ports, and servers are connected to the 100 Mbps ports. This is shown in Figure 8-13. Some switches accommodate both shared and dedicated segments. Thus, dedicated ports are assigned to users who require greater bandwidth (e.g., those who frequently transfer large graphical images to or from a server), and shared LAN segments are used for low bandwidth users (e.g., those whose applications include only e-mail). An illustration is provided in Figure 8-14.

A third and final application of Ethernet switches involves incorporating them into the network backbone. Within this context, switches are referred to as *backbone switches*, and the network topology is described as a *collapsed backbone*. Backbone switches can be employed either at the building level or for the entire enterprise. They usually are chassis-based devices and accommodate different media types. Backbone switches also are available with fault-tolerance (e.g., multiple power supplies) and redundancy features. Deploying a building backbone switch can contribute to a gradual reduction of overall backbone traffic, and collapsing the entire backbone into a single hub centralizes the backbone, which can enable better management control over the network elements. An example of a backbone switch is given in Figure 8-15.

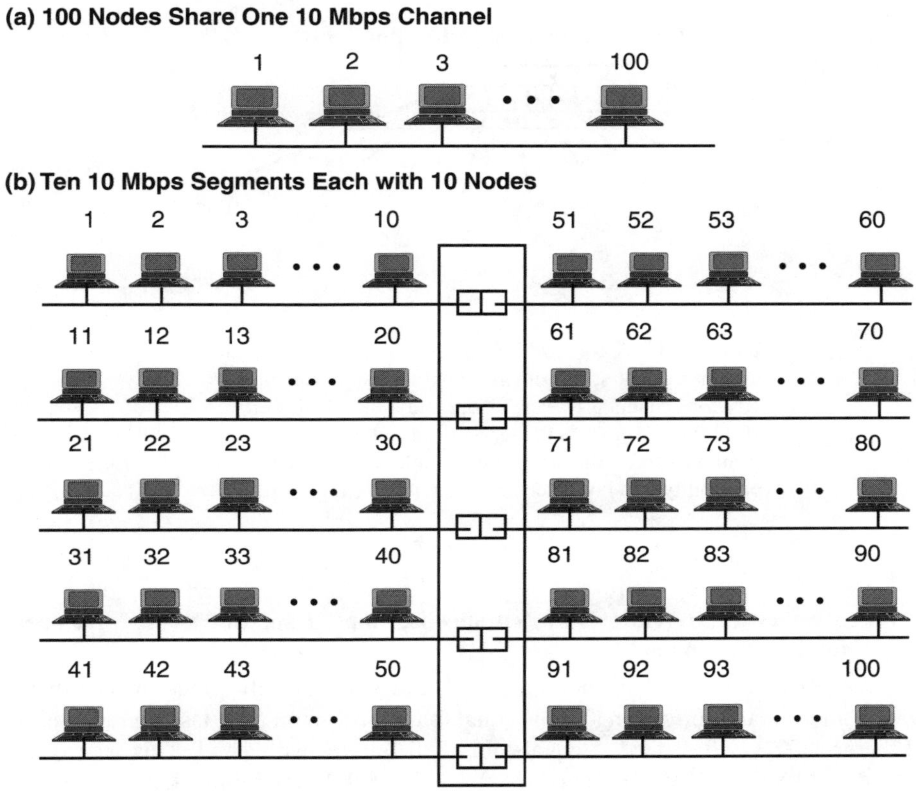

(a) 100 Nodes Share One 10 Mbps Channel

1   2   3   100

(b) Ten 10 Mbps Segments Each with 10 Nodes

1   2   3   10   51   52   53   60

11   12   13   20   61   62   63   70

21   22   23   30   71   72   73   80

31   32   33   40   81   82   83   90

41   42   43   50   91   92   93   100

Figure 8-11. The 100-node unsegmented 10 Mbps Ethernet network in (a) implies each node occupies 1/100 of the shared medium. In (b) a workgroup Ethernet switch is used to partition this network into multiple LAN segments with 10 nodes each. Each node now receives 1/10 of a 10 Mbps channel, and overall network performance for all nodes increases by a factor of 10.

Private 10 Mbps Ethernet Switch

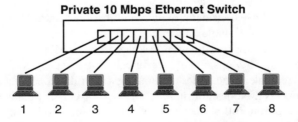

1   2   3   4   5   6   7   8

Figure 8-12. A private 10 Mbps Ethernet switch resembles a UTP repeater hub. Unlike a repeater hub, a private switch dedicates a full 10 Mbps channel to each port, which supports only one node (i.e., one MAC address). Since each node has its own dedicated segment, there is no need for a node to perform collision detection.

Private 10/100 Mbps Ethernet Switch

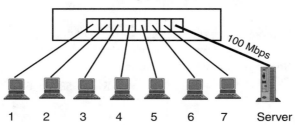

Figure 8-13. A 10/100 Mbps private Ethernet switch can be used in a client-server environment to assign dedicated 10 Mbps channels to each client, and a full, dedicated 100 Mbps channel to the server. Since all traffic is to and from the server, the higher bandwidth segment reduces the possibility of a bottleneck existing at the server port.

36. When reviewing a vendor's switch specifications, I see the term "wire speed" used. What does this mean?

Wire speed, when used in the context of a switch's specifications, means that the device's filtering and forwarding rate is equal to the maximum (i.e., fastest) rate possible. In Ethernet/802.3, wire speed is equal to 14,880 frames per second. This is frequently reported as 14,880 packets per second (pps). (See Box 8-3 for additional information.)

37. If a private Ethernet switch eliminates contention, is it possible for nodes to transmit and receive data simultaneously?

What you are referring to is *full-duplex Ethernet*, and the answer is yes. Full-duplex Ethernet requires a private Ethernet switch that supports full-duplex ports, and hosts require full-duplex NICs. Full-duplex Ethernet cards are best suited for servers rather than clients because servers have considerably more bidirectional traffic than clients. With collision detection disabled, full-duplex nodes can transmit and receive data at the same time. Thus, aggregate throughput per segment is doubled from 10 Mbps to 20 Mbps—10 Mbps on the transmit pair and 10 Mbps on the receive pair. The advantages of full-duplex Ethernet cannot be realized unless end nodes are running a multithreaded operating system such as UNIX or Windows NT. Nodes not running this type of OS will realize only a marginal performance increase from full-duplex hardware. Compared to other high-speed networking initiatives such as 100/1000 Mbps Ethernet or FDDI, full-duplex Ethernet is relatively inexpensive, easy to implement, and has no real price penalty. As with all networking initiatives, the issue of interoperability needs to be considered and addressed before a decision is made to upgrade a 10 Mbps Ethernet to full-duplex Ethernet.

BOX 8-3: Understanding Ethernet "Wire Speed" and Capacity

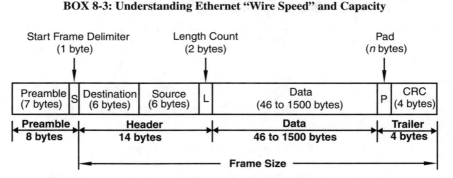

In an IEEE 802.3 frame (pictured above), observe that the data field, also referred to as the frame's *payload,* is accompanied by the fields containing addressing, length, and error control information. These header and trailer fields require 18 bytes. Ignoring the 8-byte preamble, which is not considered part of the frame because it contains no interpretable data, the size of an IEEE 802.3 frame varies from 64 bytes to 1,518 bytes. Clearly, as the size of the data field increases, the ratio of fixed overhead to data increases. Thus, 64 bytes is not only the smallest, but also the most inefficient IEEE 802.3 frame size. A worst-case scenario for network devices such as bridges, switches, and routers is constantly having to process 64-byte frames. Thus, various performance tests of networking devices are usually conducted using 64-byte frames.

Let us calculate the frame rate for these minimum-sized IEEE 802.3 frames. At 10 Mbps, a 64-byte Ethernet frame requires 51.2 µs. (Sixty-four bytes equal 512 bits; ten megabits per second equal ten bits per microsecond. It follows that 64 bytes are transferred in 51.2 microseconds.) The 8-byte Preamble requires another 6.4 µs, and between each two frames is an *interframe gap* requiring 9.6 µs. Summing all these times, we obtain a total of 67.2 µs per frame. If we divide one second by this sum, we get 0.0148809 µs. Thus, one frame occupies 0.0148809 µs. Since there are one million microseconds in one second, if we multiply 0.0148809 by 1,000,000, we get 14,880. Therefore, a 10 Mbps Ethernet transmits a maximum of 14,880 64-byte frames in one second. This frame rate, 14,880 frames per second, is referred to as *wire speed* in the literature. Cut-through switches have wire speed filtering and forwarding rates. (*Note:* Since the frame format for Fast Ethernet is the same as 10 Mbps Ethernet, the time parameters given above for 10 Mbps hold except for the interframe gap, which is one-tenth as long or 0.96 µs. Doing similar calculations, the wire speed for Fast Ethernet is 148,809 frames per second.) We further calculate that a 1,518-byte frame plus all its associated overhead is transmitted in 1230.4 µs, yielding a frame rate of 812.

Using these calculations, we can now estimate the amount of payload that can be transferred each second on a 10 Mbps Ethernet/802.3 LAN. We multiply the frame rate by the size of the data field. As noted above, this ranges from 46 to 1,500 bytes, which, at frame rates of 14,880 and 812 per second, respectively, yields 5.476 Mbps and 9.861 Mbps, respectively. Clearly, a network dealing with only the largest possible frames would come closest to delivering the promise of 10 Mbps Ethernet; however, in reality, we can expect a transmission rate closer to the middle of the range we just calculated.

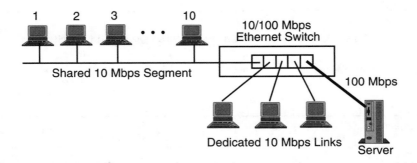

Figure 8-14. Some Ethernet switches are capable of supporting a mix of different segments. Here, ten nodes are connected to a shared 10 Mbps segment, three nodes have their own dedicated 10 Mbps segments, and a file server is connected to a dedicated 100 Mbps segment.

38. Remind me again why standard Ethernet cannot operate in full-duplex mode.

Ethernet was initially designed as a broadcast network based on a physical bus topology. Its operation is limited to half-duplex because nodes have to use the receive pair to listen for collisions while transmitting.

39. OK. Let's get back to VLANs. What are they?

A VLAN is a virtual local area network. Unlike nodes connected to a physical LAN, nodes that comprise a VLAN are not physically connected to the same medium. They are connected in a virtual sense using specially designed software that groups several ports in a switch into a single workgroup. Nodes connected to these ports are considered to be part of a workgroup, and network traffic from any node/port is (usually) limited to only those nodes or ports assigned to the workgroup. Depending on the switch, traffic filtering is performed using either MAC addresses (layer 2) or network addresses (layer 3). In the case of the latter, a switch must operate at layer 3 (the network layer), and the switch must support the routing protocol used in the network. In an IP-based network, if the switch supports the Internet Protocol, then workgroups are created by using a node's IP address. The advantage of using layer 3 protocols on which to base a VLAN is that an individual node can be assigned to more than one virtual subnetwork at the same time. A server, for example, can be shared on a virtual basis by more than one workgroup. VLANs based on MAC addresses enable any node to be assigned transparently to a workgroup, but virtual subnets cannot share nodes. An illustration of a VLAN is shown in Figure 8-16.

40. How do VLANs fit into the partition schema?

In a dynamic work environment, various workgroups are formed for short-lived projects. Personnel selection criteria for these projects are usually based on employee strengths and expertise, not employee location. Consequently, a workgroup might involve

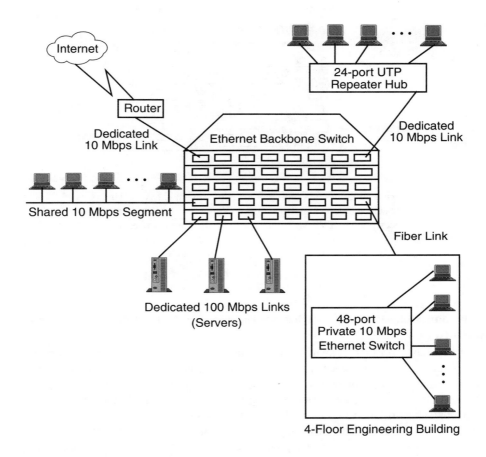

Figure 8-15. A backbone Ethernet switch enables an organization's entire network to be collapsed into the switch. These switches are chassis-based and have gigabit per second backplanes. They also support multiple media types, shared or dedicated segments, and both 10 Mbps and 100 Mbps segments. To compensate for a single source of failure, backbone switches have provisions for fault tolerance and redundancy.

25 people who are dispersed throughout an organization and who require access to equally dispersed servers. VLANs can resolve this problem because they permit users who are connected to different physical segments to be organized into logical workgroups, independent of users' physical location. As users relocate within an organization by changing job assignments, offices, or computers, their node addresses (MAC or network) are deleted from one workgroup table and added to another. VLAN also can reduce congestion, problems of isolation, and improve network security.

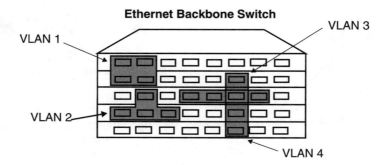

Figure 8-16. Some Ethernet switches support virtual LANs, which group selected ports together to form independent subnets. Traffic between ports of a VLAN is restricted to only those members of a "port group." Some switches also support routing protocols so that ports can belong to more than one VLAN as is illustrated in VLANs 3 and 4.

41. It sounds like Ethernet switches are the cure for the limitations of the common Ethernet.

It depends. An Ethernet switch certainly helps improve the overall performance of a heavily loaded LAN. However, if a network's architecture is poor to begin with, a switch will only mask the problems by increasing throughput without really identifying and resolving the true problems. Consequently, prior to installing a switch it is prudent to first study how a network is being used. This includes performing a network analysis to determine traffic loads and patterns, user applications, location of users and servers, and type of data transmissions. In some cases, giving attention to specific network administration tasks might prove sufficient. For example, Ethernet/802.3 performance and efficiency can be improved through collision management, standards adherence, proper system configurations, software upgrades, and segmentation using bridges. Nevertheless, there are certain situations that lend themselves to switching. These include dynamic workgroup settings, frequent data transmissions involving large data files such as graphical images, distributed network environments that employ several servers, and LANs that must support video or multimedia applications. If a decision to "switch" is made, remember that all switches are not alike. Switches have different architectures, are designed for different types of applications, and some switches also have routing capabilities (called layer 3 switches). Once again it is important to understand how a network is being used before modifying it.

42. What's next?

100 Mbps, also known as Fast Ethernet, and 1000 Mbps Ethernet, also known as Gigabit Ethernet.

43. Why are these needed when switched and full-duplex Ethernet are available?

Although switched and full-duplex Ethernet—and segmentation—improve overall network performance, these implementation strategies for enhancing 10 Mbps Ethernet performance do not actually increase data transmission rates, that is, they do not speed up the network. To address this issue of speeding up the network, IEEE increased Ethernet/802.3's 10 Mbps data transmission rate, first to 100 Mbps, and then to 1000 Mbps. This strategy is different from the 10 Mbps Ethernet strategies discussed earlier and can be best understood by viewing a network as a crowded highway. A strategy that employs segmentation, switched Ethernet or full-duplex Ethernet adds more lanes to the highway. A 100 Mbps or 1000 Mbps technology, however, actually increases the speed limit of the highway by orders of magnitude, from 10 Mbps to 100 Mbps to 1000 Mbps.

44. Why do we need to increase the speed of the LAN?

There are several reasons. First, the introduction of more sophisticated operating systems and applications, faster processors, and greater disk and memory capacities, has led to a pronounced degradation in overall network and application performance. Second, many companies now use Internet technologies to build private, corporate intranets that rely on standard web browsers such as Netscape's *Communicator* and Microsoft's *Internet Explorer* to provide employees with access to critical corporate data. These web browsers are capable of supporting bandwidth-intensive rich media data types, including high-resolution graphics, 3D imaging, audio, video, and voice. Third, the introduction of multimedia client/server applications, the deployment of network computers and *Java*-based servers, and an increasing number of network users, are taxing first-generation Ethernet.

45. What's the history of Fast Ethernet?

The concept of 100 Mbps Ethernet was first introduced in 1992. By August 1993, the Fast Ethernet Alliance (FEA) was formed. Within two years, membership grew to more than 80 vendors, including 3Com, Cabletron, Intel, DEC, and Sun Microsystems. The primary purpose of FEA was to entice the IEEE to adopt Fast Ethernet technology as a standard. In June 1995, this new technology became the IEEE 802.3u standard and was given the specification 100BASE-T. With its goals accomplished, the FEA concluded its activities in September 1996.

46. Presumably, 100BASE-T was derived from 10BASE-T. How does Fast Ethernet compare to 10BASE-T and conventional Ethernet?

Your presumption is correct; 100BASE-T did indeed evolve from 10BASE-T, specifically, and conventional Ethernet, generally. At the physical layer, 100BASE-T employs a star topology and supports twisted-pair and fiber-optic cable. Unlike 10BASE-T, though, Fast Ethernet has three different media specifications: 100BASE-TX, 100BASE-T4, and 100BASE-FX. (See Table 8-2.) The first two use twisted-pair cable; the third one uses fiber-optic cable. (Note the absence of coaxial cable, which was the mainstay of the original Ethernet specification.) All three components of the standard are designed to interoperate with one another. Fast Ethernet also uses the same connector types as 10BASE-T,

Table 8-2. Summary of IEEE 802.3u (Fast Ethernet—100 Mbps) Specifications

Type	Description
100BASE-TX	**Medium:** 2-pair Category 5 UTP or IBM Type 1 STP; **Topology:** Star; **Maximum Segment Length:** 100 m; **Connectors:** Category 5 compliant 8-pin modular (RJ-45), patch panels, patch cables, punch-down blocks; **Media Access Control:** CSMA/CD; **Network Diameter:** 200 m when used with one Class I or one Class II repeater; 205 m when used with two Class II repeaters; 261 m when used with mix of UTP/Fiber cable and one Class I repeater; 289 m when used with mix of UTP Fiber cable and one Class II repeater; 216 m when used with mix of UTP/Fiber cable and two Class II repeaters; **Miscellaneous:** Full-duplex operation.
100BASE-T4	**Medium:** 4-pair Category 3, 4, or 5 UTP or IBM Type 1 STP; **Topology:** Star; **Maximum Segment Length:** 100m; **Connectors:** 8-pin modular (RJ-45), patch panels, patch cables, punch-down blocks; **Media Access Control:** CSMA/CD; **Network Diameter:** 200 m when used with one Class I or one Class II repeater; 205 m when used with two Class II repeaters; 231 m when used with mix of UTP/Fiber cable and one Class I repeater; 304 m when used with mix of UTP/Fiber cable and one Class II repeater; 236 m when used with mix of UTP/Fiber cable and two Class II repeaters; **Miscellaneous:** Half-duplex operation
100BASE-FX	**Medium:** 2-strand 62.5/125 multimode fiber-optic; **Topology:** Star; **Maximum Segment Length:** 412 m (half-duplex) or 2 km (full-duplex); **Connectors:** ST, SC, or FDDI's Media Interface Connector; **Media Access Control:** CSMA/CD; **Network Diameter:** 272 m when used with Class I repeaters; 320 m when used with one Class II repeater; 228 m when used with two Class II repeaters; **Miscellaneous:** Designed primarily to interconnect Fast Ethernet repeaters.

encodes data using Manchester encoding, and maintains a 512 bit-time collision domain. There is one obvious difference, though—speed. Fast Ethernet is ten times faster than conventional Ethernet—100 Mbps vs. 10 Mbps. This ten-fold increase in speed has two direct implications. First, it reduces the amount of time it takes to transmit one bit by a factor of ten. In Fast Ethernet, 512 bit-times is equal to 5.12 µs instead of 51.2 µs. Second, the network diameter is reduced by a factor of ten. These diameters are summarized in Table 8-2.

At the data link layer, Fast Ethernet is unchanged from its 10 Mbps counterpart. The frame format, the minimum and maximum frame sizes (including the amount of user data a frame can transmit), and the MAC address format are all identical to conventional Ethernet. Perhaps most important, though, Fast Ethernet uses exactly the same media access method, namely, CSMA/CD as conventional Ethernet. This provides an easy, simple, and seamless migration path for current users of 10 Mbps Ethernet/802.3, particularly shared or switched 10BASE-T users. (*Note:* Many network fundamentalists equate Ethernet with CSMA/CD. It is their belief that if the MAC sublayer protocol of a LAN technology is not CSMA/CD-based, then the word "Ethernet" should not be used to either reference or describe the technology.)

47. Could you expand on the information provided in Table 8-2.? What would be helpful is a comparison among the three specifications.

OK. We'll take them in their order of appearance.

100BASE-TX transmits and receives data over two pairs of EIA/TIA 568-compliant Category 5 UTP cable, or two pairs of IBM Type 1 STP cable. It uses a full-duplex signaling system based on FDDI's Twisted Pair Physical Medium Dependent (TP-PMD) sublayer, which is an ANSI standard that defines the manner in which data are encoded/decoded and transmitted. (*Note:* TP-PMD was once called CDDI—Copper Distributed Data Interface—which applied to running FDDI over UTP. FDDI is discussed in Chapter 10.) Networks based on the 100BASE-TX standard must be Category 5-compliant throughout, including wire, connectors, patch panels, and punch down blocks. Since many new network installations employ four-pair Category 5 UTP cable, a 100BASE-TX installation leaves managers with an "extra" two-pairs of wires that can be used for voice communication or be reserved for future network enhancements. Presently, these "extra" two-pairs cannot be used to support another high-speed LAN.

100BASE-T4 uses a half-duplex signaling system to transmit and receive data over four pairs of Category 3, 4, or 5 UTP cable, or four pairs of IBM Type 1 STP cable. One pair of wires is used exclusively for transmitting data, one pair is used exclusively for receiving data and collision detection, and the remaining two pairs are used either for transmitting or receiving. As a result, three pairs of wires can be used for data transmission or three pairs can be used for data reception. This scheme of using three wire pairs for transmitting or receiving of data reduces overall cable frequency because the signal can be divided among these wires. A direct effect of this design is that lower quality cable such as voice-grade Category 3 can be used to support a higher speed technology like Fast Ethernet. 100BASE-T4's advantage over 100BASE-TX is that the former can be used in Category 3 or 4 wiring installations. Thus, organizations can scale-up their 10 Mbps Ethernet networks to 100 Mbps without modifying their existing cable plants, or they can opt to install Category 3 wire—which is less expensive than the superior grade Category 5 wire—and still benefit from 100 Mbps Ethernet. Although 100BASE-T4 supports inferior cable such as Category 3, it does not support 25-pair Category 3 wire for horizontal runs, which is what is commonly installed for voice transmission. 100BASE-T4 is not without its drawbacks, however. Unlike 100BASE-TX, which uses only two pairs of wire, 100BASE-T4 must use all four wire pairs. It also does not support full-duplex operation.

100BASE-FX supports 100 Mbps Ethernet operation over two strands of 62.5/125 micron multimode fiber-optic cable (one strand for transmitting data and one pair for receiving data). It shares the same signaling system as that of 100BASE-TX except it uses FDDI's Fiber physical media dependent sublayer. Unlike 100BASE-TX or 100BASE-T4, 100BASE-FX segments are known formally as *link segments*, which are designed to connect only two nodes in a point-to-point topology. Consequently, 100BASE-FX's primary application is at the backbone and is used to connect Fast Ethernet hubs.

48. Does Fast Ethernet also follow the 5-4-3 repeater placement rule?

No. The repeater rules for Fast Ethernet are different than for conventional Ethernet. First, IEEE 802.3u defines two classes of repeaters. *Class I* repeaters support both of Fast

Ethernet's signaling schemes (100BASE-T4 and 100BASE-TX/FX), and *Class II* repeaters support only one signaling scheme (100BASE-T4 or 100BASE-TX/FX, but not both). Class I repeaters have a latency of no more than 0.7 µs; the latency of Class II repeaters is less than or equal to 0.46 µs. The two signaling types are interoperable at both node and hub levels. When maximum cable lengths are used, only one Class I repeater, or a maximum of two Class II repeaters—with a maximum interrepeater link of 5 m—can exist within any single collision domain. Furthermore, since Class II repeaters can only be used to connect segments that have the same signaling schemes, 100BASE-T4 segments cannot be connected to 100BASE-TX/FX segments using a Class II repeater. A direct consequence of these new classes of repeaters is that the 5-4-3 repeater placement rule for 10 Mbps Ethernet does not apply to Fast Ethernet. The network diameters for 100BASE-T also have different ranges depending on which repeater is used, the number of repeaters used, and the cable type. (See Table 8-2.)

49. How difficult is it to convert or migrate from 10 Mbps Ethernet to Fast Ethernet?

Assuming the physical layer satisfies Fast Ethernet specifications, all that is required to convert from 10 Mbps Ethernet/802.3 to Fast Ethernet is to swap out a node's network interface card. New 10BASE-T nodes also can be accommodated for 100BASE-T migration by installing 10/100 Mbps NICs, which employ an autosensing/negotiation feature that enables them to operate at data rates of either 10 Mbps or 100 Mbps. Many Ethernet switches also incorporate both 10 Mbps and 100 Mbps ports. This makes it possible for 10BASE-T and 100BASE-T segments to be connected to the same switch. From a technological perspective, the designers of 100BASE-T made it easy for network managers to deploy Fast Ethernet at their sites in a relatively seamless fashion.

50. How easy or difficult is the conversion to Fast Ethernet?

From a practical perspective, *any* network migration or upgrade endeavor is usually problematic. Given this basic tenet, converting to Fast Ethernet is not necessarily easily accomplished. Consider the cable plant. Although 100BASE-T supports UTP, it requires four pairs of Category 3, 4, or 5 UTP cable (100BASE-T4). Four pairs of Category 3 cable means that all eight wires of a standard Category 3 UTP bundle must be used to achieve a data rate of 100 Mbps. This is not feasible for sites using two pairs of Category 3 UTP for their 10BASE-T networks if the other two pairs of wire are being used for telephone connections (or for additional Ethernet connections). For 10BASE-T LANs using 2-pairs of Category 5 UTP, all is not well either. Cable installation requirements for 100BASE-TX are extremely stringent requiring all components (from connectors to patch panels to number of twists per inch) to be certified Category 5 compliant. Many so-called Category 5 10BASE-T LANs do not meet these specifications and hence will have to be modified. Finally, coaxial cable-based LANs (ThinWire or ThickWire) also will require major changes to their cable plants since 100BASE-T does not support coaxial cable. In fact, none of the newer higher-speed LAN technologies supports coaxial cable, which is viewed by some as a diminishing technology without a future.

In addition to the cable plant, incorporating Fast Ethernet into an existing LAN or as a new LAN installation also has an impact on several network design issues. There are shorter cable lengths, and Fast Ethernet only permits two types of repeaters. This translates to pronounced limitations on network diameters and collision domains. These restrictions can have a dramatic effect on how a network is designed. For example, more wiring closets might be necessary for a 100BASE-T than for a 10BASE-T installation, and additional hardware (e.g., bridges or switches) will be required to extend a 100BASE-T LAN.

Finally, attention should be given to both topology and network nodes. Fast Ethernet must be configured as a star, not as a bus. Furthermore, Fast Ethernet was designed with switches in mind, not bridges. Deployment of 100BASE-T also presupposes the use of nodes capable of supporting the increase in speed. Hence, LANs consisting of ISA bus-based nodes will not benefit from Fast Ethernet, and workstations using anything less than a 32-bit operating system will not realize an increase in throughput either.

Here's the bottom line: Networks are nontrivial and Fast Ethernet is no exception. Network managers considering implementing Fast Ethernet as part of a new LAN installation, or integrating it into an existing 10 Mbps Ethernet LAN, need to give serious attention to the various physical limitations, restrictions, and design issues related to 100BASE-T. It is also prudent for managers to understand the IEEE specifications and their ramifications before getting involved with Fast Ethernet. (See Box 8-4 for additional information.)

51. While we are on the subject of 100 Mbps Ethernet, what is 100VG-AnyLAN?

100VG-AnyLAN is a competing technology to Fast Ethernet. Formally specified as IEEE 802.12, 100VG-AnyLAN was approved as an IEEE standard in June 1995; it was designed to serve as an upgrade path for 10 Mbps Ethernet/802.3 and 4/16 Mbps token ring. There are relatively few 100VG-AnyLAN installations today compared to Fast Ethernet installations. The primary reason for this dearth is that 100VG-AnyLAN is not compatible with conventional Ethernet. Specifically, its MAC sublayer is not CSMA/CD; it is a technology called *demand priority*, which is similar to that of token ring.

52. Besides the MAC sublayer, how does 100VG-AnyLAN compare to Fast Ethernet?

Rather than provide a lengthy dialogue, Table 8-3 contains a summary of the standard, and Table 8-4 compares it to Fast Ethernet.

53. OK. Fair enough. Can you at least explain demand priority for me?

Sure. 100VG-AnyLAN uses cascaded repeater hubs in a hierarchical star topology. The demand priority protocol specifies the manner hubs poll their ports to identify nodes with data to transmit and the order of these transmissions. The protocol works in the following general manner (an example of this polling strategy is given in Figure 8-17):

A 100VG-AnyLAN repeater hub polls each node connected to it for a transmission request. The hub performs this query by continuously scanning its ports sequentially, from lowest connected port to highest connected port. If a node needs to transmit data, a transmission request is conveyed to the hub at the time the node is polled. Only one data frame per node per polling cycle is transmitted, and data frames are identified by the hub as either normal- or high-priority. Frames designated high-priority (e.g., real-time video and audio) are processed (i.e., given access to the network) before normal-priority-designated frames (e.g., data files).

BOX 8-4: Migrating or Upgrading to 100BASE-T

Following are several strategies to consider if you are planning to migrate or upgrade an existing 10 Mbps Ethernet/802.3 LAN to Fast Ethernet:

1. For organizations that are not yet ready to implement 100BASE-T, but are still adding new users to their 10BASE-T LAN, the simplest and most cost-effective 10BASE-T to 100BASE-T migration strategy is to install 10/100 Mbps network interface cards in new nodes. These cards can automatically sense the correct data transmission rate based on the hub port to which they are connected. This strategy will also preserve an organization's current investment in its 10BASE-T LAN.

2. For organizations that want a "blended" 10 Mbps/100 Mbps network, of paramount concern is how to interconnect the two networks. Several strategies are possible. One method is to use a bridge. This is probably the least expensive and easiest installation. A second method is to use a router. This can be cost-prohibitive, though, and usually increases the complexity of a network. A third strategy is to use a switch that can support both 10 Mbps and 100 Mbps connections. Some switches permit shared 10 Mbps segments to be mixed with dedicated 10 Mbps and dedicated 100 Mbps segments. Although more costly than bridges, switches do provide a nice migration strategy for a mixed environment.

   In a mixed or blended environment, be careful with network diameters and collision domains. It is possible to maintain a 500 m network diameter in this type of environment. One configuration involves 100 m segments to a Fast Ethernet Class II repeater. This repeater is then interconnected to a 10/100 Mbps switch that contains 10BASE-T connections. The switch interconnects to an unpopulated 10/100 Mbps switch, which then connects to a second Class II repeater. This second Class II repeater can support end nodes such as servers.

3. For organizations planning to upgrade to 100BASE-T:
   a. Confirm that you really need to upgrade. "Tuning" a network through network analysis, re-engineering, segmentation, software upgrades, and collision management can provide tremendous improvements in network performance.
   b. Confirm that your cable plant meets the proper specifications.
   c. Confirm that all nodes have sufficient horsepower (e.g., PCI bus-based, 32-bit OS), and that all servers have sufficient buffering capacity.
   d. Confirm that all users require 100 Mbps. If not, item (2) above might be more appropriate; consider installing full-duplex 10 Mbps switches.
   e. Know, understand, and follow the various specifications related to 100BASE-T.
   f. Plan on installing only one repeater hub per collision domain.
   g. Use bridges or switches to connect to secondary wiring closets.
   h. Use two-port switches to extend network diameter.
   i. Invest in 100BASE-T compliant diagnostic equipment.

Table 8-3. Summary of IEEE 802.12 (100VG-AnyLAN) Specifications

Category	Description
Media	4-pair Cat 3 UTP (100 m); 4-pair Cat 4 UTP (100 m); 4-pair Cat 5 UTP (200 m); 2-pair Category 5 UTP (under investigation); 2-pair Type 1 STP (200 m); 25-pair UTP cable using 50-pin telco connectors; 2 strands 62.5/125 multimode fiber (2,000 m)
Media Components	8-pin modular (RJ-45) connectors; patch panels; patch cables; punch-down blocks
Network Cards	100VG-AnyLAN compliant NICs
Hubs	100VG-AnyLAN compliant repeater hubs—all hubs have an uplink port to connect to another VG hub; all ports can be used as downlink ports to connect to end nodes or another VG hub; all ports can be configured in normal mode (only receives data destined for it) or monitor mode (receives all data)
Maximum Nodes	1,024 on a single-shared (unbridged) LAN; no more than 250 is recommended, however
Collision Domain	N/A; However, the term priority domain, is used to describe a 100VG-AnyLAN network that consists of a root hub and all of its connected nodes, including lower-level hubs and nodes
Network Diameter	8,000 m
Topology	Hierarchical star with up to five levels of cascaded repeater hubs
MAC Sublayer	Demand Priority—uses a priority-based round-robin arbitration scheme to determine network access; supports both Ethernet/ 802.3 and IEEE 802.5 frame formats
Transmission Mode	Half-duplex hubs cannot transmit and receive simultaneously because of crosstalk; this is due primarily to Category 3's lower electromagnetic characteristics)
Future Enhancements	The following are currently under consideration as of this writing: (1) Data transmission rates of 1.063 Gbps and 1.25 Gbps for fiber-optic links and 500 Mbps for 4-pair Category 5 links; (2) Single mode fiber permitted; (3) Fiber-optic links based on Fibre channel 8B10B link protocol; (4) Use of VG switches and full-duplex operation for dedicated links; (5) 8 km maximum network diameter with up to five levels of cascaded repeaters

Each hub has at least one uplink port, which connects to a higher-level hub; every port can be used as a downlink port to connect to an end node or a lower-level hub. Hub ports can be configured to operate in either *normal* or *monitor mode*. Ports operating in normal mode receive only those data frames destined for it as determined by a frame's destination address. Monitor mode on the other hand is similar to Ethernet's *promiscuous mode*—every data frame received by the hub is directed to all ports configured to operate in monitor mode. (*Note:* An Ethernet NIC set in promiscuous mode collects all messages placed on the medium regardless of their destination address.) Using a round-robin scheme, repeaters continuously poll all their connected ports in sequence to determine which nodes

Table 8-4. A Comparison Between 100BASE-T and 100VG-AnyLAN

	100BASE-T (IEEE 802.3u)	100VG-AnyLAN (IEEE 802.12)
Media		
Category 3 UTP	4-pair (100 m)—100BASE-T4	4-pair (100 m)
Category 4 UTP	4-pair (100 m)—100BASE-T4	4-pair (100 m)
Category 5 UTP	2-pair (100 m)—100BASE-TX	2-pair (N/A)
	4-pair (100 m)—100BASE-T4	4-pair (200 m)
25-pair UTP	Not supported	Supported
IBM Type 1 STP	Yes (100m)—100BASE-T4/TX	Yes (100 m)
Fiber-optic (62.5/125)	412 m half-duplex—100BASE-FX	Yes (2,000 m)
	2 km full-duplex—100BASE-FX	
Topology		
Network diameter	Varies from 200 m to 320 m depending on cable type and repeaters used	8 km
Cascading repeaters	Two levels	Five levels
MAC Sublayer		
Media Access	CSMA/CD	Demand Priority
IEEE 802.3 Frames	Yes	Yes
IEEE 802.5 Frames	No	Yes
Application Support		
Time-sensitive data	No	Yes
Performance		
100 m throughput	80%	95%
2,500 m throughput	Not supported	80%

have data transmission requests pending. A polling cycle begins when a hub polls the lowest numbered port connected to it and ends when the highest-numbered connected port is polled. A polling cycle is repeated continuously in port-order. Nodes are permitted to transmit only one frame of data per polling cycle. The process of polling and determining data transmission order is called *prioritized, round-robin arbitration* and is the heart of the demand priority protocol. Theoretically, a maximum of five levels of cascading are permitted in a 100VG-AnyLAN network. However, in practice, a maximum of three is the general rule.

The type of priority assigned to a data frame is not part of the demand priority protocol and hence does not occur at the MAC sublayer. Instead, data priority assignment is performed by the upper layer application software and passed to the MAC sublayer as part of a data frame. It is the demand priority protocol's design that enables it to identify the type of data transmission request and process high-priority data before normal-priority data. As a result, this media access method is highly suited for transmitting isochronous data, that is, time-sensitive data such as multimedia applications and real-time video and audio for video conferencing. To guard against high-priority data transmissions from

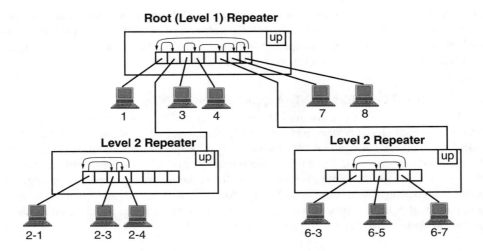

Figure 8-17. An example of a two-level 100VG-AnyLAN network. The hub's polling order in this illustration is 1, 2-1, 2-3, 2-4, 3, 4, 6-3, 6-5, 6-7, 7, 8. If during a polling cycle nodes 3, 2-4, 6-5, and 7 have high-priority requests pending, then the data transmission order is 2-4, 3, 6-5, 7, 1, 2-1, 2-3, 4, 6-3, 6-7, 8 for that cycle. If priority requests are the same (all normal or all high), then the data transmission order is the port order. However, if the priority requests are not the same, then the transmission order is determined by considering the priority of the node's pending request and the physical port order of the node. For example, if nodes 3 and 7 have normal- priority requests, but node 4 has a high-priority request, then the transmission order is 4, 3, 7. (Adapted from Schnaidt, 1994a.)

monopolizing a network, VG hubs are designed with a *watchdog protocol* that monitors the "wait time" of pending normal-priority request. All normal-priority requests that have been waiting between 200 ms and 300 ms have their priority label changed automatically from normal to high. They are then placed on the hub's high-priority list and processed in port-order fashion. Thus, all normal-priority data are guaranteed access to the network.

54. Demand priority is interesting. It must be much more efficient than Ethernet.

You are correct in your observation. 100VG-AnyLAN's demand priority protocol is a very robust technology. It is deterministic, collision-free, supports a priority scheduling scheme, exhibits stable behavior during high load times, and uses bandwidth efficiently (demonstrated 95 percent throughput at 100 m). Demand priority also improves some of the shortcomings of Token Ring, including eliminating token rotation delays.

55. Why does 100VG-AnyLAN have an IEEE 802.12 designation instead of an IEEE 802.3 designation like Fast Ethernet? Aren't they both 100 Mbps Ethernets?

Many Ethernet purists do not consider 100VG-AnyLAN "Ethernet" because of its access method. They contend that Ethernet implies a contention-based MAC sublayer protocol and since demand priority eliminates collisions and the concept of collision domains, 100VG-AnyLAN is therefore not Ethernet. The absence of CSMA/CD led the IEEE to prohibit the 100VG-AnyLAN working group from using the Ethernet designation. IEEE also believes that Ethernet is not Ethernet without CSMA/CD.

56. I see. Should I consider 100VG-AnyLAN for my LAN?

That is up to you. If you compare the market share of the two technologies, you will find that the battle for 100 Mbps turf has already been won by Fast Ethernet. Regardless of IEEE's (and others') view about 100VG-AnyLAN not being "Ethernet," 100VG-AnyLAN supports both Ethernet/802.3 and token ring frame formats. It is also a compelling alternative to Fast Ethernet as an upgrade path for 10 Mbps Ethernet, and can serve as an upgrade path for 4/16 Mbps token ring LANs as well. Any decisions about LAN upgrades or new installations should be driven by an organization's networking needs and the best technology available that satisfies those needs.

57. Let's move on to Gigabit Ethernet. So far I've learned that the IEEE has gone from 10 Mbps Ethernet to two different 100 Mbps Ethernet specifications. Now there is 1000 Mbps Ethernet. That's 1 billion bits per second. When did this get started?

Just as the dust was beginning to settle on the Fast Ethernet standard, the IEEE, in March 1996, commissioned the Higher Speed Study Group (HSSG) to investigate increasing Fast Ethernet's data transmission rate tenfold to 1000 Mbps. In July 1996, the IEEE 802.3z Task Force was approved to define standards for the next evolution of Ethernet— *Gigabit Ethernet*. To support the IEEE's standards efforts in this endeavor, and to educate customers and the networking industry on this new technology, the Gigabit Ethernet Alliance (GEA) was formed in May 1996. Using the Fast Ethernet Alliance as its model, the Gigabit Ethernet Alliance sought to rally the same combination of suppliers and consumers of FEA to (1) support the extension of Fast Ethernet standards and (2) address customers' needs for interoperability among 10/100/1000 Mbps Ethernet products. GEA quickly grew in size to more than 100 vendor-members within six months of its creation.

58. Talk about working fast. Do we really need Gigabit Ethernet, though? When will we ever use that much capacity?

In the world of networking, fast is never fast enough. The deployment of bandwidth hungry multimedia applications, the integration of faster computer systems, and the migration of Fast Ethernet from the backbone to the desktop are creating bottlenecks at the server level or at inter-switch connections. Gigabit Ethernet alleviates this congestion by providing a faster backbone technology. Remember, when Ethernet was first developed, the majority of the applications and computer systems of that era could not saturate a 10 Mbps channel. Today, though, we have 64-bit servers, improved bus speeds, 100 Mbps desktop units, and applications such as real-time two-way video conferencing. So yes, Gigabit Ethernet really is necessary.

59. So the bigger and faster the pipe, the better the network. Right?

No. Bigger is not necessarily always better. It is not prudent to increase bandwidth for the sake of increasing bandwidth. Bigger and faster backbones are no panacea for network congestion. Deploying Gigabit Ethernet undoubtedly will reduce overall network congestion, but without conducting an a priori network analysis to determine the source of the congestion, the deployment of Gigabit Ethernet will do nothing more than mask the problem. Some people call this strategy "bandwidth bandaid." Before deploying any new high-speed backbone technology, including Gigabit Ethernet, network managers should examine all areas of potential bottleneck (e.g., desktop, servers, and backbone). This will help them assess exactly where increased bandwidth is to be deployed, when it needs to be deployed, and provide a sound rationale for deploying it.

60. OK. Tell me about Gigabit Ethernet.

Gigabit Ethernet has two separate standards: IEEE 802.3z and IEEE 802.3ab. At the physical layer, IEEE 802.3z supports three specifications: 1000BASE-SX (short wavelength fiber), 1000BASE-LX (long wavelength fiber), and 1000BASE-CX (short-haul copper). The IEEE 802.3ab standard has one physical layer specification: 1000BASE-T (Category 5 UTP). Table 8-5 compares Gigabit Ethernet with conventional and Fast Ethernet, and Table 8-6 contains specific media and distance information for each Gigabit Ethernet specification. See also Figure 8-18, which summarizes the various IEEE 802.3 Ethernet specifications.

At the data link layer, Gigabit Ethernet uses the same 802.3 frame format, supports full-duplex and switched connections, maintains the same 96-bit interframe gap (see Box 8-3), and has a 64-byte minimum frame size. Gigabit Ethernet also supports the same CSMA/CD access method in full-duplex mode, but uses a slightly modified version of CSMA/CD in half-duplex mode—the minimum CSMA/CD carrier and slot-times are 512 bytes instead of 64 bytes. Thus, the minimum sized frame of Gigabit Ethernet is 512 bytes, not 64 bytes. This modification was necessary to maintain a 200 m collision diameter in half-duplex. If this hadn't been done, then the maximum diameter would have been one-tenth the size of a Fast Ethernet LAN (25 m) because when you increase the bit rate, the collision domain and overall network diameter decreases. A maximum network diameter of 25 m is not very practical.

Table 8-5. Conventional Ethernet vs. Fast Ethernet vs. Gigabit Ethernet

	Conventional Ethernet	Fast Ethernet	Gigabit Ethernet
Data Rate	10 Mbps	100 Mbps	1000 Mbps
Max Segment Lengths:			
Cat 5 UTP	100 m	100 m	100 m
IBM Type 1 (STP)	500 m	100 m	25 m
Multimode Fiber	2 km	412 m (half-duplex) 2 km (full duplex)	260-550 m
Single Mode Fiber	25 km	20 km	3 km

Source: 3Com (Adapted from Tolley, 1997a.)

Table 8-6. Media and Distance Comparisons of Gigabit Ethernet

	Media	Max Distance
1000BASE-SX	62.5-µm Multimode Fiber	220 m to 275 m[1]
	50-µm Multimode Fiber	500 m to 550 m[2]
1000BASE-LX	62.5-µm Multimode Fiber	550 m
	50-µm Multimode Fiber	550 m
	9-µm Single-Mode Fiber	5,000 m (5 km)
1000BASE-CX	Twinax or Quad	25 m
1000BASE-T	Category 5 UTP	100 m

[1]200 m for TIA 568 fiber optic wiring standard; 275 m for ISO/IEC 11801 building wiring standard
[2]550 m based on ANSI Fibre Channel specifications

(Adapted from Conover, 1998; Henderson, 1998; and Tolley, 1997a.)

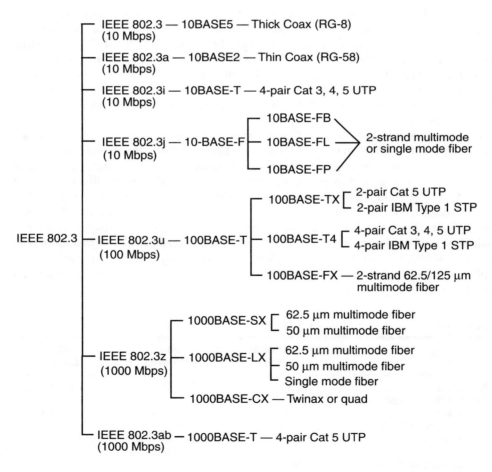

Figure 8-18. Various IEEE 802.3 specifications for 10/100/1000 Mbps baseband Ethernet and their respective media.

61. Why are there separate fiber and twisted-pair specifications?

To provide a 1000 Mbps Ethernet standard expeditiously, the IEEE adopted the ANSI Fibre Channel signaling protocol and modified it for IEEE 802.3z. Since there was no similar existing protocol to run gigabit speeds over Category 5 UTP, IEEE created a separate task force (IEEE 802.3ab) to address this endeavor. By doing this, the IEEE 802.3z task force was able to maintain a dedicated focus to establishing a fiber-based gigabit Ethernet standard. IEEE 802.3z was approved as a standard in June 1998; IEEE 802.3ab is expected to become an approved standard sometime in 1999.

62. Wait a minute. I've got two questions here. First, I know there were Gigabit Ethernet products available in 1997, almost a year before the standard was approved. How is this so? And second, what's a Fibre Channel?

You are right. There were indeed Gigabit Ethernet products available well before the standard was approved. In January 1997, the 802.3z task force closed the specification to new features, thus enabling leading network vendors to develop Gigabit Ethernet products. By agreeing on a stable first draft of the specification, vendors were able to get a jump on product development. They also were able to demonstrate their products' interoperability at the October 1997 Networld+Interop show. Remember, the Gigabit Ethernet Alliance, which was comprised of network vendors, was formed for the express purpose of designing a Gigabit Ethernet specification. So it was in their best interest to resolve any issues related to the specification as quickly as possible. In the end, Gigabit Ethernet was one of the fastest standards to be approved among the second generation, high-speed LAN standards. GEA was a quick study of the Fast Ethernet Alliance.

63. What about Fibre Channel?

Fibre Channel (FC) is a family of ANSI (American National Standards Institute) standards that defines a specific communications interface for high-speed data transfers between different hardware systems. FC's applications include the medical profession, where large images (e.g., 100 MB+ X-rays) are transferred from a scanner to a computer to a screen, and the electronic publishing industry, where large files are transferred from an designer/creator's machine to a publisher's computer. It has also become the "backbone" of high-speed data storage systems.

FC is organized into a five-level hierarchy (FC-0 through FC-4). IEEE 802.3z signaling is based on FC-0 and FC-1. FC-0 supports a variety of physical media and data rates; FC-1 defines the signaling encoding technique used for transmission and synchronization across a point-to-point link (8B/10B—8 bits of data are encoded into 10-bit characters and transmitted serially). IEEE 802.3z modified the link frequency from the 1.062 GHz ANSI standard to 1.25 GHz so that a full 1000 Mbps data rate is supported. That's all we are going to say about FC. The references listed in the appendix provide additional sources of information about FC. You can also check out the Fiber Channel Association (FCA) website at http://www.amdahl.com/ext/carp/fca/fca.htm, or call FCA at 1-800-272-4618.

64. In what ways can Gigabit Ethernet be deployed?

There are several scenarios. Gigabit Ethernet's primary application will be to provide a faster backbone. As Fast Ethernet becomes more widespread and deployed at the desktop, the need for a higher speed backbone becomes paramount. Thus, one scenario is to connect all interconnected Fast Ethernet switches directly into a Gigabit Ethernet switch. This effectively upgrades the 100 Mbps links between the Fast Ethernet switches to a Gigabit link. Along this same line, Gigabit Ethernet switches can be used to replace any Fast Ethernet switch that functions as a collapsed backbone. Another method is to swap out all the Fast Ethernet switches that provide connectivity to servers and replace them with Gigabit Ethernet switches. You will also need to upgrade the server NICs to Gigabit Ethernet NICs if you opt to do this. Remember, all of these connections are fiber-based.

65. Will Gigabit Ethernet really work over Category 5 UTP?

That's a good question. Although it is theoretically possible to transmit data over Category 5 UTP at gigabit speed, success depends on a clear signal path. What this means is that if anything obstructs the signal as it travels from source to destination, then reflections can occur and reduce the reliability of network performance. What objects can cause reflections, you might ask? Oh, little things like eight-pin modular (RJ-45) connectors or punch-down blocks. It is important to note that this is not unique to Gigabit Ethernet. Reflections are always present in copper cable when used for radio frequency transmission in both 10 Mbps and 100 Mbps Ethernet links. (See Chapter 4.) The difference is that at these relatively lower speeds reflections and related interference are not as serious. Nevertheless, the official balloting for a Gigabit Ethernet over copper standard (1000BASE-T) has started and ratification is expected March, 1999.

66. What about some of the newer copper cable specifications like Category 6 or 7?

New high-speed copper cable designed specifically for gigabit speed is indeed available from various vendors. Called "gigabit copper," these new offerings include Category 6 UTP, Category 6 STP, and Category 7 UTP. (See Table 4-1.) Although gigabit copper has higher frequencies, this does not necessarily translate to higher speeds. Contrary to what some network managers might believe, there is not a 1:1 ratio between megahertz and megabits. From a design perspective, though, gigabit copper supports gigabit encoding schemes. For example, 100BASE-TX (Fast Ethernet over Category 5 UTP) uses only two pairs of wire—one pair to transmit and one pair to receive. On the other hand, 1000BASE-T (Gigabit Ethernet over Category 5 UTP) requires four-pairs and transmits signals bidirectionally on all four of them, that is, 250 Mbps per pair.

One drawback to gigabit copper is a lack of standards. This means that parameter specs provided by vendors are subject to different interpretations. Case in point: One cable manufacturer uses the number 350 in the name of one of its products, giving the impression that the cable is rated at 350 MHz. Upon further investigation, the cable's spec sheet reveals that the cable cannot support data transfers beyond 200 MHz. It is so named, though, because it provides "stable electrical performance" up to 350 MHz. Another potential problem with gigabit copper is that standards committees like EIA/TIA are vendor-based consortia and therefore politically charged. Trying to assess what a final gigabit copper standard will look like is difficult enough without being influenced by politics. The bottom line is wait—wait until gigabit copper standards are ratified; wait until IEEE 802.3ab is ratified, deployed and tested; wait for others to find out what works and what doesn't, that is, adopt a "state of the practice" and not a "state of the art" mindset.

67. How does Gigabit Ethernet compare to ATM?

First, Gigabit Ethernet is a connectionless technology that transmits variable-length frames; ATM is a connection-oriented technology that transmits fixed-sized cells. Second, Gigabit Ethernet (any Ethernet for that matter) as originally specified, is designed specifically as a local area network technology—it is optimized for transmitting data from one node to another on a LAN. It was never designed to support multimedia-type applications such as real time voice and video. ATM, on the other hand, is designed specifically to transmit any type of data, including voice and video traffic. ATM also supports different *Class of Service (CoS)* for data prioritization, and can guarantee a *Quality of Service (QoS)* needed for real-time voice and video traffic. ATM also has been deployed successfully as a WAN technology, and has been modified to support the LAN environment as well. (See Chapter 14.)

Although many people view Gigabit Ethernet and local ATM as competing LAN backbone technologies, the reality is both have their pros and cons, both can fill specific LAN needs, and both can co-exist. For example, if network traffic is primarily data-based and cost is a consideration, Gigabit Ethernet is the logical choice. If explicit QoS is paramount for voice and video traffic support, or if a seamless LAN-to-WAN or WAN-to-LAN connection is desired, then ATM is the more appropriate technology. A third illustration has Gigabit Ethernet being deployed within buildings to provide a gigabit-speed building backbone, and ATM being deployed as the enterprise-wide backbone. In this example, both ATM and Gigabit Ethernet are used as complementary technologies instead of competing technologies. See Chapter 2 for information about connection-oriented vs. connectionless services, and Chapter 14 for additional information about ATM.

68. I want to know more about Class of Service and Quality of Service. Prior to pursuing this, though, let me ask two more questions about Gigabit Ethernet: What's the bottom line on it and will Ethernet max out at 1000 Mbps?

On the positive side: It's a tenfold increase in raw performance over Fast Ethernet; it provides familiar technology so that existing investments in hardware, software, and personnel are maintained (and protected); it represents a relatively small learning curve; it offers tremendous scalability; it is a natural extension to 10/100 Mbps Ethernet networks; it supports all existing networking protocols; it is complementary to ATM; it is intended to run over Category 5 UTP; it's an IEEE standard (fiber-based) or will soon be (copper-based); and it might support acceptable levels of CoS and QoS for real-time video and voice transmissions. On the negative side: It requires new switches and NICs; workstations might have to be upgraded to take advantage of the increase in speed; overall maximum distance restrictions are considerably less than for Fast Ethernet; until all standards are approved, it is expensive; and there is not inherent CoS and QoS support.

As for Ethernet maxing out at 1000 Mbps, well, probably not. There already is considerable talk of multigigabit Ethernet. Some think the next evolution of Ethernet should support transmission rates of 10 Gbps. Other, more prudent approaches, call for Ethernet to achieve multigigabit rates gradually, increasing first to 2 Gbps, then to 4 Gbps, 8 Gbps, and maybe 10 Gbps. Whatever strategy is taken, though, the development of multigigabit Ethernet most likely will not happen as quickly as the development of either Fast or Gigabit Ethernet because there are no current physical layer technologies from which multigigabit can borrow. (Recall that Fast Ethernet is based on FDDI technology, and Gigabit Ethernet is based on Fibre Channel technology.) Although SONET (see Chapter 7) might appear as a likely candidate, this is mere speculation. Finally, any multigigabit Ethernet strategy will undoubtedly be fiber-based, not UTP-based.

69. OK. Now let's deal with CoS and QoS. What do they mean?

CoS and QoS are considered by many to be physical layer concepts. CoS refers to data prioritization; QoS refers to the parameters associated with a specific transmission. Both are required in order to deliver real-time voice and video traffic. CoS is needed so data can be tagged with a specific priority level. This is important because during periods of congestion you do not want voice or video data sets to be dropped by switches or routers. A high priority assignment to these data sets ensures their delivery. Data prioritization is only part of the equation, though. The delivery of time-sensitive data also requires that sufficient bandwidth be available, and that transmission delays (i.e., latency) be predictable and guaranteed. This is the essence of QoS. ATM brings to the table both CoS and QoS. Thus, ATM guarantees that all transmissions, regardless of their type (data, voice, or video), receive the necessary bandwidth and appropriate priority based on the importance of their delivery.

In contrast, Gigabit Ethernet does not directly support CoS or QoS. However, the IEEE developed IEEE 802.1p, which specifies how data prioritization is handled within a MAC-layer device. Another protocol related to this concept is IEEE 802.3x Full-Duplex/Flow Control, which enables full-duplex switch ports to send flow control commands to workstations that are connected to them. Both are deployed in silicon at the port-level of Gigabit Ethernet switches. The IEEE also has introduced 802.1q, which adds prioritization to Ethernet/802.3 in general. Extending this concept to the upper layers, the Internet Engineering Task Force (IETF) has developed the Resource Reservation Protocol (RSVP), which operates at layer 3 and enables end nodes to reserve a specific amount of bandwidth throughout an IP network for a particular transmission. (See Chapter 7 for more information about RSVP.) ATM's CoS and QoS undoubtedly offer a more elegant approach to transmitting time-sensitive data than the combination of 802.1p, 802.3x, 802.1q, and RSVP. Nevertheless, many people believe that this combination provides Gigabit Ethernet with an acceptable level of CoS and QoS for the short-term.

70. What does data prioritization give me that increased bandwidth doesn't?

Let's try to put the concept of data prioritization into perspective. Ethernet/802.3 is a shared-media standard based on contention. Thus, congestion is an inherent feature of

Ethernet/802.3 networks, and it is normal for frames to be dropped. Two questions emerge from this: How much congestion is acceptable? and Does it matter which frames are being dropped? If congestion levels are too excessive and unacceptable, or if you do not want to lose any frames, then increasing bandwidth will help resolve these problems; data prioritization will not. An Ethernet/802.3 network will continue to experience congestion and lose frames regardless if a data prioritization scheme is implemented. The function data prioritization adds is control over which frames get lost. For example, if e-mail is the highest priority application on your network, then e-mail frames will be tagged as such and their transmission will take precedence over all other traffic. If web-based applications are the highest priority, then they can be tagged as such using a data prioritization scheme.

71. Do I need to be concerned with prioritization? After all, I am running Fast Ethernet with a Gigabit Ethernet backbone.

Once again, bandwidth is not the answer to everything. If your network is transmitting only data and you do not care about what frames are being discarded, then you probably do not need to be concerned with data prioritization. However, if your network is currently supporting, or if you are planning to implement on your network, bandwidth intensive applications such as videoconferencing, distance education applications, or those electronic whiteboards that enable people to collaborate on-line, then you might want to consider a data prioritization scheme. If you are unsure whether you need a prioritization scheme, then play it safe. Ensure that the Ethernet NICs and switches you purchase support IEEE 802.1p and 802.1q. Also confirm that your layer 3 devices (routers, switching routers) support multiple levels of queuing so that if data prioritization is implemented, queues will not get overloaded.

72. OK. So tell me about 802.1p and 802.1q.

IEEE 802.1p is an extension to IEEE 802.1d, which specifies how MAC-level bridges are to interoperate regardless of the IEEE LAN standard being used. What 802.1p adds to the 802.1d standard is a specification for implementing prioritization in 802.1d compliant bridges. IEEE 802.1p defines a 3-bit priority scheme, which provides eight different levels of priority. This new standard can be used on LANs that support prioritization, including 802.4 (token bus), 802.5 (token ring), 802.6 (DQDB), and 802.12 (100VG-AnyLAN). It can also be incorporated into an FDDI network. However, it cannot be used with current Ethernet/802.3 networks because Ethernet has never had a prioritization scheme.

To resolve this, the IEEE developed 802.1q, which provides a data prioritization scheme to Ethernet/802.3. There is one small problem, though—in order to do so, the 802.3 frame had to be altered. Specifically, a 4-byte 802.1q header is inserted between the source address and length fields. (See Figure 8-19.) Thus, an 802.3 frame that includes an 802.1q header is incompatible with a standard 802.3 frame. This also makes an 802.1q-compliant device incompatible with an 802.3 device. Instead of seeing the length field, an 802.3 device will be greeted with 802.1q header information. One workaround to this device incompatibility issue is for vendors to manufacture 802.1q devices with a switch that disables 802.1q, similar to the way NICs have a switch that disables SQE. Although

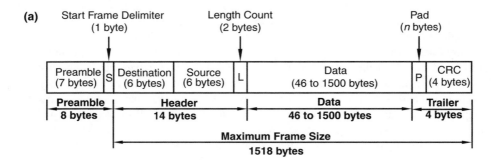

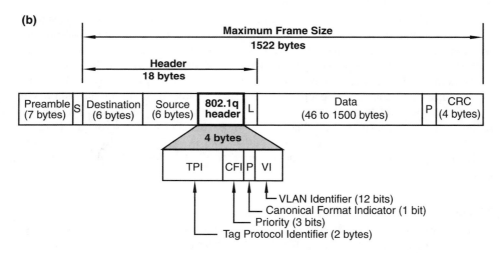

Figure 8-19. An IEEE 802.3 frame (a) with an IEEE 802.1q header (b) adds four bytes to the 802.3 frame. This changes the size of the frame's header from 14 bytes to 18 bytes, which increases the maximum frame size from 1518 bytes to 1522 bytes. The 802.1q header consists of a 2-byte Tag Protocol Identifier (TPI), a 3-bit Priority (P), a 1-bit Canonical Format Indicator (CNI), and a 12-bit VLAN Identifier (VI). The TPI field identifies the frame as an 802.3 frame that contains 802.1q data; the P field specifies user priority values; the CFI field specifies whether the MAC addresses are in canonical format; and the VI field identifies the frame's VLAN.

disabling 802.1q also disables data prioritization, it enables 802.1q-compliant products to be purchased and installed in anticipation of migrating to a data prioritization scheme.

The frame-length difference, however, is not as easily addressed. At issue is the frame size. Ignoring the preamble, the maximum size of a standard 802.3 frame is 1,518 bytes. The maximum size of an 802.3 frame that includes the 802.1q header is 1,522 bytes. Two possible solutions abound: (1) Increase the size of 802.3 frames by four bytes, or (2) reduce the length of the payload of 802.3 frames by four bytes so they can accommodate

8021q header information. Rather than making a decision, the IEEE instead put the onus on the vendors. That is, the IEEE 802.1q specification allows for either solution to be incorporated. This means that it is up to the vendors to decide which method they want to implement. It also raises the question of interoperability.

73. What other Ethernet-related projects are there?

Besides those discussed, there are two noteworthy enhancements to the original IEEE 802.3 standard that have either been made or are being reviewed by the IEEE 802.3 working group. They are: (1) IEEE 802.3y 100BASE-T2, which provides full-duplex 100 Mbps operation over two pairs of Category 3 UTP or better cable; and (2) IEEE 802.3w Binary Logarithmic Access Method (BLAM), which serves as a fully compatible and interoperable alternative to Ethernet's current Binary Exponential Backoff algorithm. Finally, IEEE 802.12 (100VG-AnyLAN) is being modified to support both Ethernet and token ring frame formats at 531 Mbps and 850 Mbps. See the IEEE web site (http://www.ieee.org) for additional information about these and other IEEE standards.

74. One last question. I have heard of another technology that bears the Ethernet name—IsoEthernet. What is this?

IsoEthernet is short for Isochronous Ethernet, and is an IEEE standard—IEEE 802.9a. The term isochronous means time-sensitive. Hence, in the context of networking, IsoEthernet is designed to support time-sensitive applications such as videoconferencing and telephony. It is also inextricably linked to ISDN technology (see Chapter 12)—it runs both Ethernet and ISDN B channels over the same network. The Ethernet channel is used for normal data networking needs; the ISDN B channels are used for time-sensitive applications. Thus, IsoEthernet is really two networks in one. It contains a 10 Mbps Ethernet channel for 10BASE-T traffic, and a separate 6.144 Mbps channel for isochronous traffic. IsoEthernet requires IsoEthernet network adapters at all end nodes requiring isochronous capability, and IsoEthernet hubs at wiring closets.

IsoEthernet has been overshadowed by Gigabit Ethernet and local ATM technologies, and therefore has found little vendor support. Nevertheless, it is anticipated that the 802.9a standard will be modified to include support for 100BASE-T, switched 10BASE-T, and 16 Mbps ATM.

End-of-Chapter Commentary

In this chapter we presented a formal discussion of Ethernet and the various IEEE "Ethernet" protocols. Several concepts discussed in this chapter are also presented in other chapters in an informal manner. These include network topologies and architectures (see Chapter 2), physical layer concepts (see Chapter 4), the concepts of framing, flow control, and MAC and LLC sublayer issues (see Chapter 5), Ethernet switches (see Chapter 6), CoS/QoS (see Chapter 7), and ATM issues (see Chapter 14). In the next chapter, we present some of these same concepts but apply them to token ring networks.

Chapter 9

Token Ring

In this chapter we present an overview of token ring networks, IEEE 802.5. Unlike Ethernet/802.3 LANs in which nodes contend for media access, token ring LANs use a token-passing scheme; that is, media access in token ring LANs is controlled by the possession of a token. We discussed general issues relating to token passing, including a comparison of random-access and token-passing protocols, in Chapter 5, which you might want to review before proceeding. In addition to token ring, the IEEE standards include a second token-passing protocol called token bus. Although token bus use is uncommon, we present a brief comparison of the two token-passing schemes for completeness. The major topics covered in this chapter include:

- Definition and Operation (Questions 1–2)
- Frame Formats (Question 3)
- Priority Scheduling (Question 4)
- Monitor Stations (Questions 5–6)
- Physical Layer Issues (Questions 7–8)
- Token Ring vs. Token Bus (Question 9)
- Advantages and Disadvantages of Token Ring Networks (Question 10)
- Switched, Dedicated, and Full-Duplex Token Ring (Questions 11–14)
- High-Speed Token Ring (Question 15)
- Token Ring's Future (Question 16)

1. What is a token ring network?

A *token ring* network is a local area network technology based on a token-passing protocol for media access control. Data frames on a token ring network are transmitted from node to node, in either a clockwise or counter-clockwise direction, over a point-to-point link. A token ring LAN is implemented either as a logical ring using a physical ring topology (see Figure 9-1), or as a logical ring structure arranged in a physical star configuration (see Figure 9-2). It is also possible to extend the configuration in Figure 9-2 to include a

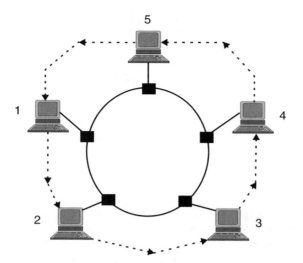

Figure 9-1. A token ring network consists of a logical ring implemented in a physical ring topology. A token, which is a special frame, and data are transmitted in a point-to-point manner from one node (called a lobe) to the next. The direction of circulation is fixed and either clockwise or counterclockwise (but not both). For example, on a counterclockwise rotating ring, if node 3 has a "free" token and wants to send data to node 2, data frames must circulate the ring in the order 3-4-5-1-2. On a clockwise rotating ring, though, the transmission order is 3-2.

ring consisting of several interconnected hubs. This is shown in Figure 9-3, which describes the arrangement in the special language of token rings.

Token ring networks are defined by IEEE 802.5. However, IBM, which is the primary vendor associated with token ring LANs, has its own set of token ring specifications. Although they differ from the official IEEE specs, most people usually speak about the IBM specs when discussing token ring LANs.

2. How does a token ring network work?

Access to the network is controlled by a special "token" frame, which circulates around the ring when all nodes are idle. A token frame comprises a one-byte Start Frame Delimiter, a one-byte Access Control, and a one-byte End Frame Delimiter. (See Figure 9-4.) If the token bit of the Access Control field is set to 0, the token is considered "free" or idle. Only one free token is permitted on the ring, and the node that has the free token controls the ring and is permitted to transmit data. Thus, only one node at a time can transmit data on a token ring network.

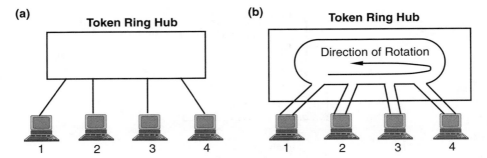

Figure 9-2. A typical token ring network consists of nodes connected to a hub in a physical star configuration (a). Internally, nodes are actually interconnected via a logical ring (b).

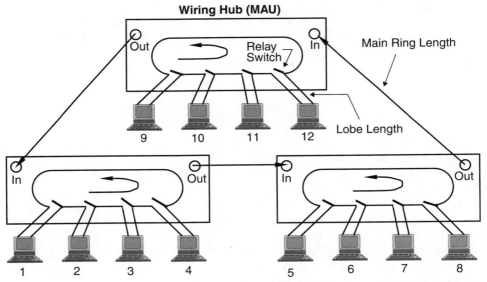

Figure 9-3. This is an example of a typical token ring network configuration. Token ring hubs are called Multistation Access Units (MAUs), and nodes are called lobes. The main ring length is the distance between MAUs, and the lobe length is the distance between an MAU and its lobes. Physically, lobes are connected to an MAU in a star configuration. Within an MAU, however, a logical ring topology exists. Lobes are connected to the ring using an IBM Data Connector, which enables lobes to be removed without disrupting the ring. MAUs also can be interconnected using special "Ring In/Ring Out" ports, which preserve the ring structure. Note the presence of relay switches within each hub. Relay switches (also called bypass switches) are used to maintain the integrity of the ring in the event of lobe failure. For example, if lobe 12 stops working, or if there is a break in the cable connecting lobe 12 to the ring, the ring is broken. In such instances, the relay switch closes, thus preserving the ring.

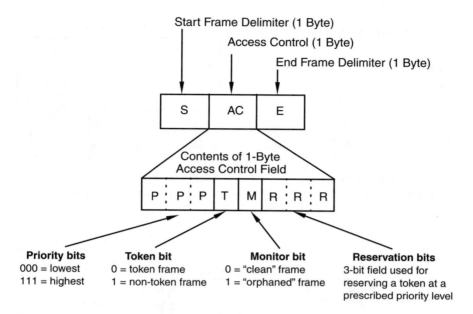

Figure 9-4. Format and contents of an IEEE 802.5 token frame.

A node (called a *lobe* in the IBM world) that possesses the free token and has data to transmit, changes the Access Control field's token bit to 1 and then augments the token frame by including a Frame Control field, Destination and Source addresses, user data, a CRC checksum, and a Frame Status field. In other words, the token frame is transformed into a data frame (see Figure 9-5), which is then transmitted around the ring from node-to-node. When a node receives this frame, it will identify the frame as data (not a token) and check the destination address. If the node is not the intended recipient, it then places the frame back on the ring. When the intended destination node receives the frame, it copies the frame into memory. The node then sets the A and C bits of the Frame Status field to 1 and places the entire frame back on the ring where it will continue to be transmitted from node-to-node. When the sending node receives the frame after the frame's complete pass around the ring, it examines the Frame Status field. If the A and C bits are set to 1, then data transmission was successful. If not, then the frame is retransmitted. In the case of a successful transmission, the node removes the data from the frame and changes the token bit to 0. Thus, the data frame is transformed back to a token frame. This free token is then placed on the ring and sent to the next node in line. The node that has possession of the token is permitted to continue transmitting data until it has no more data to send or its time limit expires, whichever comes first. In IEEE 802.5, the length of time a node can possess a token—called the token-holding time—is 10 ms.

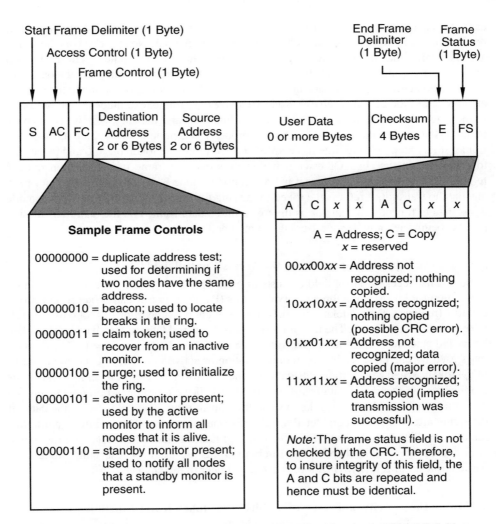

Figure 9-5. Format and contents of an IEEE 802.5 frame. Note that the S, AC, and E fields comprise the token frame. Thus, an IEEE 802.5 data frame is really a modified token frame that includes the frame control, destination and source addresses, user data, checksum, and frame status fields.

To illustrate this operation, consider the sample LAN in Figure 9-1. Let's assume that node 2 has data to transmit to node 5, and node 4 has data to transmit to node 1. Let's further assume that node 2 has the free token. Node 2 modifies the free token to "busy," inserts its data, and sends the frame to node 3. Node 3 examines the frame, determines it is not the intended recipient, and returns the frame to the ring where it is transmitted to node 4. Node 4 grabs the frame off the ring and sees that it is data and not a token. Hence, it cannot transmit its data. Node 4 also determines that it is not the intended recipient so it returns the frame to the ring where it is transmitted to node 5. Node 5 receives the frame and ascertains that its destination address matches that of the frame's. The node then makes a copy of the frame and stores it in memory. If the frame is valid and the data successfully copied, node 5 then sets the A and C bits to 1 and returns the frame to the ring. (It also processes the data it receives.) Node 1 receives the frame, examines it, and returns it to the ring. The frame, having completed a full pass around the ring, is now received by node 2. Seeing that the A and C bits were properly set, node 2 strips the data from the frame. If its token-holding time has elapsed, it then resets the token bit to 0 and places the token frame on the ring. Otherwise, it transmits another frame of data. When node 2 returns the free token to the ring, it is transmitted to node 3. Since node 3 does not have any data to transmit, it returns the token to the ring for transmission to node 4. Since node 4 has data to transmit, it transforms the token into a data frame and the data transmission process begins again with node 1 being the intended recipient.

3. Could you explain the contents of the Access Control field?

Sure. The Access Control field consists of eight bits: three priority bits (P), a token bit (T), a monitor bit (M), and three reservation bits (R). Priority bits can be set from 0 (lowest) to 7 (highest). Thus, a token ring network has eight possible priorities (000 to 111) relative to data transmission. The use of these bits is discussed later in the chapter. The token bit, as indicated above, identifies the frame as a token (T = 0) or data (T = 1). The monitor bit is used by one node, called the monitor station or active monitor, to oversee the status of the token. When a node transmits data, or when the token is idle, M is set to 0. When the monitor station receives a data frame, it sets M to 1. If the monitor station now receives a data frame that has M set to 1, it knows that the transmitting node did not strip the data off the frame after the frame completed a full pass around the ring. The monitor station then removes this "orphaned" frame from the ring and issues a new token. The monitor station is discussed later in the chapter. The reservation bits are used for reserving a token at a particular level of priority. This, too, is discussed later in the chapter.

4. How do the priority and reservation bits in the token frame function?

As indicated above, a token can have several different priority levels, ranging from 0 (lowest) to 7 (highest). When a node receives a free token, it must first compare the priority value contained within the token to the priority of the data it has to transmit. If a node's data has a priority level equal to or greater than that of the token's, then the node may transmit its data. If the token's priority is higher than the node's data, then the node cannot transmit its data and must pass the token to its neighbor node. During a particular transmission, a node may reserve the token at a higher level than the token's current level. By doing so, it pre-empts the node that is currently transmitting data. To illustrate this, consider the token ring LAN in Figure 9-2(b). Let us make the following eight assumptions: (a) the ring rotates counterclockwise; (b) node 2 has data to transmit to node 1; (c) the priority level of node 2's data is 0 (e.g., an e-mail message); (d) node 2 has just received a free token with a priority level of 0; (e) node 3 has data to transmit to node 4; (f) node 3's data priority is 1; (g) node 4 needs to transmit a video frame to node 3; and (h) the priority level of node 4's data is 5. Given these assumptions, the operation of the ring is as follows:

1. Node 2 transforms the token frame into a data frame.
2. Node 2 transmits the data frame to node 3.
3. Node 3 examines the frame, but takes no action because it is not the recipient. It also cannot transmit its data because the token is busy. Node 3 passes the frame to node 4.
4. Node 4 receives the frame. Because it has data with a priority of 5, node 4 makes a reservation at priority 5 by setting the three reservation bits of the token's access control field from binary 000 to 101 (i.e., 5). Node 4 passes the frame to node 1.
5. Node 1 receives the frame. Since it is the recipient, it saves the source address (node 2), computes the 32-bit checksum, changes the frame's Frame Status field to reflect that it received the data, and then transmits the frame to node 2.
6. Node 2, seeing that the transmission was successful, strips the data from the frame. Normally, node 2 would continue transmitting data until it has no more data to transmit or until its time limit expired. It would then issue a free token with a priority level of 0 to node 3. However, because the frame that was returned has a reservation priority of 5, node 2 cannot transmit anymore data frames because their priority level is 0, which is less than the reserved priority of 5. As a result, node 2 must issue a new free token with a priority level of 5 and transmit it to node 3.
7. Node 3 receives the free token but is not permitted to transmit its data because the data's priority level is less than 5. It passes the token to node 4.
8. Node 4 receives the token, changes it to "busy," and transmits its data to node 1.
9. After the frame is returned to node 4, if there are no additional frames to transmit, or if the time limit expired, node 4 transmits a free token to node 1; the priority level remains at 5, though.
10. Node 1 passes the token to node 2.
11. Node 2 receives the token and notes that the token is "free" and the priority level is the same one it used when it last issued a new token. Node 2 re-issues a new token at its previous priority level of 0. (The node that upgraded the priority level of the token is also responsible for re-establishing the previous level after all higher-priority data frames are transmitted.)

IEEE 802.5's priority scheduling is excellent for transmitting time-sensitive data such as real-time video or voice. Any node which has data frames with a higher priority than that of the frame currently being transmitted, can reserve the next token at this higher level when the current token and frame are passed to it. As demonstrated in the illustration above, when the next token is issued it will be at this higher level. Furthermore, no other node is permitted to transmit data unless its data frames have a priority level equal to or greater than the newly issued one. As beneficial as this scheme is, though, token ring priority makes it possible for nodes with high priority data to prevent nodes with low priority data from ever accessing the medium.

5. What do you mean by an "active monitor"?

A token ring network employs a monitor station to oversee the ring and ensure that it is functioning properly. This monitoring node is called the *active monitor*, which is usually a high-priority node. All other nodes are known as *standby monitors*, which monitor the active monitor. If the active monitor becomes disabled, a contention protocol is invoked among the standby monitors to elect a new active monitor.

6. What does an active monitor do?

When a token ring network is first started, the active monitor generates the first token and begins the process that enables each node to learn the address of its neighbor that is next in line (called the "downstream" node). During the operation of the ring, the active monitor performs several tasks, including monitoring the ring for valid frame transmissions, maintaining the ring's master clock, and ensuring there are proper delays in the ring. The active monitor also is sensitive to two possible error conditions. The first is a lost token. If no token is detected after a predetermined amount of time expires, the active monitor assumes the token is lost and issues a new one. The second possible error is a persistently busy token. To check for this condition, a special bit within the token is set. If this bit is still set when the token is returned to the active monitor, it assumes the source station did not remove the data from the network. It then changes the token to "free" and passes it to the next node. One task an active monitor cannot do is detect breaks in the ring, which can occur if a node fails or the cable connecting the node to the ring is broken. To recover from either of these cases, special relay switches (also called bypass switches) are used. In case of a host failure, a bypass switch can be closed either manually or automatically, effectively removing the dead node from the ring. This is illustrated in Figure 9-3.

7. So far we have discussed the data link layer of token ring networks. Tell me about the physical layer.

At the physical layer, IEEE 802.5 supports STP, UTP, coaxial, and fiber-optic cable. STP cable has a 150 ohm impedance; UTP cable has a 100 ohm impedance. The topology is usually star-based using token ring hubs (called wiring concentrators or *Multistation Access Units*—MAUs), with hubs being interconnected to form a main ring path. (See Figure 9-3.) Data rates include 4 and 16 Mbps, although some variations can include 20 and 40 Mbps. In a 4 Mbps token ring, nodes can transmit only one frame at a time during a single transmission. Nodes connected to token rings with higher data transmission rates, however, can transmit multiple frames during a single transmission.

Maximum cable lengths for node connections (called *lobe lengths*) are 100 meters if IBM Type 1 or 2 cable is used, 66 meters for Types 6 and 9, and 45 meters for UTP. (See Chapter 4 for an explanation of IBM Type cables.) Maximum cable lengths for hub interconnections depend on several factors, including the number of repeaters used, the number of hubs, and so forth. Some general guidelines are as follows: 200 meters if using Type 1 or 2 cable; 120 meters if using Type 3 cable; 45 meters if using Type 6 cable; and 1 kilometer if using fiber-optic cable. Type 1 and Type 3 networks can operate at 4 or 16 Mbps. Also, with STP cable, 260 devices can be connected to a single token ring network; with UTP cable (Category 3, 4, or 5), only 72 devices can be connected to the ring.

8. Does token ring also use Manchester encoding as in Ethernet/802.3?

No, but it does use a form of Manchester encoding called *differential Manchester encoding*. Manchester and differential Manchester encoding are similar in that each bit-period is partitioned into two intervals and a transition between "high" and "low" occurs during each bit-period. The difference between the two techniques is the interpretation of this transition. In Manchester encoding (see Chapter 8 and Figure 8-1), a 1 bit represents a low-to-high transition, and a 0 bit represents a high-to-low transition. In differential Manchester encoding, the interpretation of these low-to-high and high-to-low transitions is not as simple—they are a function of the previous bit-period. A low-to-high transition could be a 0 or a 1, depending on the value of the previous bit-period. More specifically, the presence of a transition at the beginning of a bit period is coded 0, and the absence of a transition at the beginning of a bit period is coded 1. The implication of these different interpretations is that Manchester encoding is used for signaling purposes and data; differential Manchester encoding is used for clocking purposes only. Note also that in order for a token ring network to achieve its maximum bandwidth, its clock speed must be twice the transmission rate. Thus, a 16 Mbps token ring must have a clock speed of 32 MHz.

9. You mentioned token bus in the introduction as another token-passing LAN. How does it compare to token ring?

Token bus is defined in IEEE 802.4. A token bus network is characterized as a logical ring on a physical bus—physically, the network resembles a bus topology, but logically, the network is arranged as a ring with respect to passing the token from node to node. An illustration of a token bus network is shown in Figure 9-6. Although token passing is point-to-point (i.e., from node-to-node), data transmission is based on broadcasting. For example, in Figure 9-6, if node 44 has the token and wants to send data to node 70, it simply places data frames on the bus. The broadcast nature of the bus topology causes all nodes to hear the transmission, but only node 70 reads and processes the data. After node 40 has completed its transmission it then passes the token to node 32. Thus, from the perspective of actual data transmission, IEEE 802.4 is similar to that of IEEE 802.3—it is based on broadcasting. However, medium access control is similar to IEEE 802.5.

At the physical layer, IEEE 802.4 uses 75 ohm coaxial cable or fiber-optic cable. If coax is used, data rates include 1, 5, and 10 Mbps. If fiber-optic cable is used, data rates are 5, 10, and 20 Mbps. IEEE 802.4 also supports priority scheduling and can be configured to operate in one of four priority modes, 0 (lowest), 2, 4, and 6 (highest). As is the case with IEEE 802.5, this priority scheme makes it possible to allocate network bandwidth to high priority (level 6) data such as video, digitized voice, and multimedia applications. Lower priority data get transmitted if sufficient bandwidth is available.

IEEE 802.4 is not a popular LAN protocol; it is primarily used for control of industrial and factory automation processes. It also is the basis of the General Motors Manufacturing Automation Protocol (MAP), which supports real-time applications.

10. What are some of the advantages and disadvantages of token ring networks?

Some of IEEE 802.5 advantages include its ability to run on many different media types, its efficient use of bandwidth (e.g., if packet size is 1,000 bits, efficiency is 99 per-

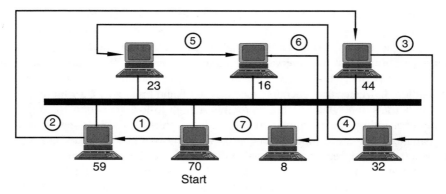

Figure 9-6. A token bus network physically resembles a bus topology; logically, however, it is a ring. A token is transmitted from node to node using network addresses and occurs in descending order. The node that possesses the token is permitted to transmit data. The node-order in the figure is 70-59-44-32-23-16-8.

cent), its stable behavior during high load times, and its deterministic nature (it has a known upper bound on channel access). Disadvantages include the need for special recovery procedures when the network fails, the difficulty with adding new hosts, and in the case of priority scheduling, the susceptibility of low priority hosts to increased delays in acquiring the free token.

11. I realize that token ring is not as popular as Ethernet. However, is there a "second generation" token ring as there is with Ethernet?

Yes. Token ring has benefited from some of the technological advances made for Ethernet/802.3. These include switched token ring, dedicated token ring, full-duplex token ring, and 100 Mbps token ring. A gigabit token ring specification is also in development.

12. Let's start with switched token ring. I can understand how switches benefit traditional Ethernet/802.3 LANs. But how do token ring LANs benefit from switching technology? They don't have collisions.

You are right. Ethernet/802.3's MAC layer protocol (CSMA/CD) is contention-based and highly susceptible to performance problems during periods of high activity. Token ring's token-passing protocol, however, is inherently deterministic and quite stable during peak load times. Token ring networks do not experience the same type of performance problems as those found in Ethernet/802.3 networks. A token ring network's performance, for example, does not begin to degrade until its utilization rate approaches 90 percent, and in many cases can achieve a bandwidth utilization rate as high as 95 percent. So, yes, Ethernet/802.3 networks are a better candidate for switching technology than token ring networks since the former can benefit more from the type of performance boosts available from switches. With the introduction of client-server applications, imaging, multimedia, and the consolidation of servers, however, token ring networks—including 16 Mbps token ring, which has higher bandwidth than 10 Mbps Ethernet—are experiencing congestion and performance problems similar to those of Ethernet/802.3 networks. To help alleviate these problems, several vendors have ported the switched technology originally developed for Ethernet/802.3 to token ring.

13. Are the switches like those found on Ethernet networks?

Yes. Token ring switches are similar to Ethernet switches in that they are capable of supporting workgroups, desktop, or backbone connections, and they use either store-and-forward or cut-through technology to forward frames from one network to another. In a workgroup environment, individual token ring networks are interconnected via the switch. In this capacity, the token ring switch acts like a multiport source routing bridge that is connected to multiple ring numbers. (See Chapter 6 for information about the concept of source routing and source routing bridges.) With private connections, individual stations have a full, dedicated 16 Mbps link to the switch. Nodes do not share a 16 Mbps channel with other nodes. Finally, as a backbone switch, an organization's entire network backbone is incorporated into the switch, which resembles the collapsed backbone concept discussed earlier for Ethernet/802.3 networks.

In large token ring networks, workgroups usually feed into the backbone. This configuration promotes congestion, particularly if the workgroups are 16 Mbps networks and the backbone also is operating at 16 Mbps. Although source routing bridges or routers are used to segment the network into smaller components, this introduces additional delay into the network. Consequently, one of the primary applications of token ring switches is at the backbone where they replace source routing bridges. This application enables organizations to consolidate local servers into centrally located "super" servers since the backbone is now the switch itself. An illustration is shown in Figure 9-7.

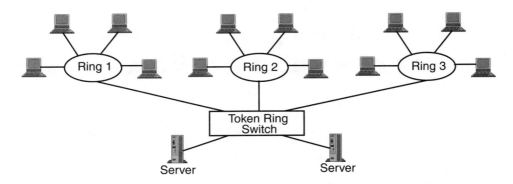

Figure 9-7. Incorporated within the backbone, a token ring switch acts as a multiport source routing bridge and enables large networks to be partitioned into smaller segments. The net effect is a collapsed backbone, which reduces both overall network traffic and traffic at the server ports. (Compare this configuration to the one shown in Figure 6-14 in Chapter 6.)

Some token ring switches also provide support for *virtual rings* and source route transparent bridging. With virtual rings, several individual token ring networks are collectively viewed as a single (virtual) ring. Although these individual networks are indeed separate and connected to different switch ports, source routing between nodes connected to two separate networks is now transparent since the networks appear to be on the same (virtual) ring. Virtual Rings support also eliminates the need to configure new ring numbers when connecting new token ring networks to a switch since the new rings appear to the network as part of the original ring. An illustration of the virtual rings concept is given in Figure 9-8.

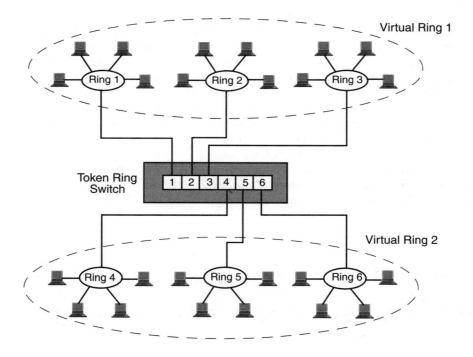

Figure 9-8. Token ring switches that support virtual rings enable multiple, independent rings to be viewed as a single ring. For example, rings 1, 2, and 3 are viewed by the switch as a single ring, namely, virtual ring 1. Support for virtual rings eliminates the need to configure new ring numbers when a new ring is added to the switch. Additionally, since the networks comprising a virtual ring are considered a single ring, transparent bridging is in effect. Thus, transparent bridging exists for the rings connected to switch ports 1, 2, and 3, and for the rings connected to switch ports 4, 5, and 6. Source routing bridging, however, is necessary for exchanging data between virtual rings 1 and 2.

14. I see. And with private switches in the configuration, token ring LANs can have nodes connected to dedicated segments and operate in full-duplex mode just like Ethernet. Is this correct?

Yes. As is the case with switched Ethernet, a token ring switching environment advances the concept of dedicated token ring, which enables nodes to have access to a full 16 Mbps channel instead of sharing the segment with other nodes. Dedicated token ring does not require any new hardware or software either—all you do is connect a node (via its NIC) to a port on the switch. In a dedicated switched environment, only two nodes are involved in the transmission and receipt of data. Consequently, dedicated nodes can transmit data whenever they have data to send. A new method for dedicated token ring, called Transmit Immediate (TXI), also is defined by IEEE 802.5. In TXI, dedicated nodes are not permitted to begin transmitting data until they possess a token. Assigning nodes, especially those that transmit and receive a high volume of traffic, to dedicated links can improve overall network performance since this further segments a network.

Although dedicated switched ports enable nodes to have their own private network segments, they are still operating in half-duplex. By installing additional software drivers or upgrading the firmware of NICs, nodes can support full-duplex token ring, which provides 16 Mbps of bandwidth in both directions. This enables stations to transmit and receive data at the same time. Stations such as "super" servers, which are the source of high volume traffic, are excellent candidates for full-duplex token ring. The combination of full-duplex token ring with a dedicated switched environment can dramatically boost the performance of a token ring network. (See Figure 9-9.)

15. You mentioned that 100 Mbps and gigabit token rings are in development. What is their status?

The IEEE 802.5 working group has created three separate initiatives for high-speed token ring (HSTR): IEEE 802.5t, which is HSTR over Category 5 UTP cable; IEEE 802.5u, which is HSTR over fiber-optic cable; and IEEE 802.5v, which is gigabit token ring. The first two specifications are expected to be completed in 1998 with products available in 1998 as well. The third specifications is expected to be ratified in 1999. HSTR is a switched-only 100 Mbps technology. Deployment is restricted to the backbone, interswitch links, and server connections. There are no shared links as with classic token ring. HSTR uses the same MAC sublayer as 4/16 Mbps token ring, and incorporates auto-negotiation into its NICs for 4/16/100 Mbps auto-sensing.

16. Why all this fuss about a technology whose market share pales in comparison with that of Ethernet? Does token ring really have a future?

These are tough questions. Compared with Ethernet, the installed base of token ring networks and the market for token ring products are indeed relatively insignificant. Nevertheless, the vendors that comprise the High-Speed Token Ring Alliance (HSTRA) feel an obligation to protect the existing market and established users by advancing token ring technology to be on par with that of Ethernet. At the very least, HSTR gives users and managers of token ring technology hope that token ring is not being ignored.

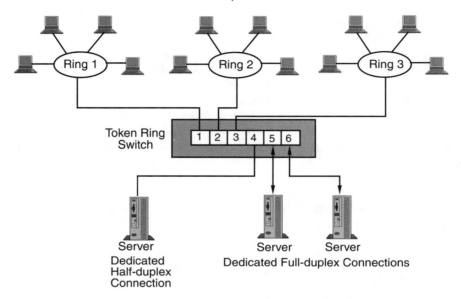

Figure 9-9. Dedicated token ring connections provide nodes with private network segments instead of shared segments. Incorporating support for full-duplex token ring into a dedicated node's NIC, bandwidth to the node is doubled to 32 Mbps since the node can simultaneously transmit and receive data. A token ring switch, in combination with dedicated and full-duplex support, dramatically increases overall network performance.

Unfortunately, all is not well with the political and marketing sides of HSTR. Cisco, Cabletron, and Texas Instruments—all charter members of HSTRA—withdrew from the organization. Furthermore, Cisco reported that it will not develop any products that are IEEE 802.5 compliant, but instead will develop and market its own proprietary HSTR products. Many token ring managers also have indicated via surveys that they intend to migrate to Fast Ethernet or ATM and hence will not purchase HSTR products. So, although HSTR appears to be a promising IEEE technology standard that will serve as a smooth migration from 4/16 Mbps token ring, vendor support is problematic at best. Additional information about HSTR can be found at the High-Speed Token Ring Alliance's home page at http://www.hstra.com.

End-of-Chapter Commentary

This chapter presented an overview of token ring networks. Two related chapters are Chapter 10, FDDI, which uses a token ring technique similar to the IEEE 802.5 specification, and Chapter 14, ATM, which is viewed by various token ring managers as the logical migration path for classic token ring LANs. In addition to these chapters, you also might want to review Chapter 5, which contains a general discussion and comparison between random accessing protocols and token-passing protocols.

Chapter 10

Fiber Distributed Data Interface (FDDI)

In this chapter we present an overview of a network technology called Fiber Distributed Data Interface or FDDI. FDDI employs a ring topology, with fiber-optic cabling as its physical layer medium. We also discuss a "sister" standard called Copper Distributed Data Interface (CDDI), which uses copper instead of fiber. An outline of the terms and concepts we will define and discuss follows:

- General Information (Questions 1–6)
- Physical Layer Issues (Questions 7–10)
- Data Link Layer Issues (Questions 11–13)
- Operation and Configuration Issues (Questions 14–22)
- FDDI and Ethernet/802.3 (Questions 23–24)
- FDDI and ATM (Question 25)
- CDDI (Questions 26 through 28)
- Future of FDDI (Question 29)

1. What is FDDI?

FDDI stands for *Fiber Distributed Data Interface*. FDDI networks are described by ANSI standard X3T9.5 created in 1986 for interconnecting computer systems and network devices typically via a fiber ring topology at 100 Mbps. Figure 10-1 shows where FDDI networks fits in the hierarchy of network architectures. (*Note:* For information about the other network architectures listed in this figure, see the appropriately named chapters.)

2. In what capacity are FDDI networks used?

FDDI's bandwidth gives it considerable flexibility in how an organization allocates its resources. Its applications include directly connecting workstations and servers in workgroups, and serving as a high-speed backbone to connect other networks in a building, in a campus environment, or in a city. An example of the first application is the interconnection of high-speed servers to other high-speed servers. For instance, a very large video server

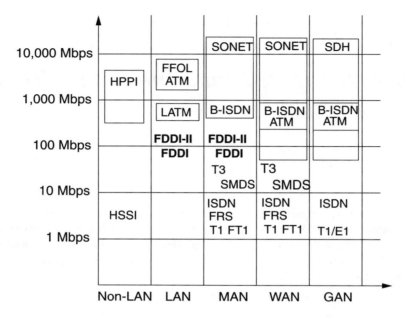

Figure 10-1. Schematic that shows how the various networking technologies compare against each other in terms of bandwidth.

system cannot be effectively connected to a broadcast video server at 10 Mbps Ethernet/ 802.3 or token ring speeds, but at FDDI's data rate of 100 Mbps, the connection is adequate for server transmission. As a backbone network, FDDI interconnects network devices such as routers, bridges, switches, and concentrators to create a large network environment consisting of smaller networks. FDDI networks are not used for wide area networks where network radii typically exceed 100 km. FDDI was very popular in networks that required 100 Mbps capability prior to 1996.

3. You say FDDI *was* popular prior to 1996. What happened?

At the outset, FDDI's data transmission rate of 100 Mbps was ten times faster than 10 Mbps Ethernet/802.3 systems. Since 1996, however, 100 Mbps Ethernet/802.3 (Fast Ethernet) and 1000 Mbps Ethernet/802.3 (Gigabit Ethernet) technologies have become widely available and have begun to displace new FDDI installations.

4. So why should I bother studying about FDDI networks?

Simple. You are going to encounter FDDI networks in just about any larger company. Additionally, many telecommunications companies operate metropolitan area networks (MANs), which consist largely of FDDI or FDDI emulations over faster networks such as the synchronous optical networks, SONET. (See Chapter 7.)

5. What makes FDDI special compared to other 100 Mbps networks?

First, FDDI can be configured as two independent, counter-rotating ring networks, called a Class A configuration. (See Figure 10-2.) This greatly increases reliability of the network. If the physical topology of the network is designed such that both fiber paths for both networks are physically "diverse" (geekspeak for putting the two fiber paths for the two networks in completely different physical locations so that one backhoe does not kill both networks at the same time while trenching up the lawn), then it is very difficult to kill the network with a single or even multiple fiber cuts to the network cable plant. Second, FDDI has the ability to "self heal" if the ring topology is cut in a single spot. This is called *auto-wrapping*. The break in the active ring is corrected by establishing a loopback connection to the inactive ring. This creates a single virtual ring and allows the FDDI network to continue to function at full speed. (See Figure 10-3.) The auto-wrapping feature makes FDDI much less susceptible to a network disruption. Third, FDDI transmits information in frames up to 4500 octets (bytes), which increases network efficiency and lowers protocol overhead. Finally, FDDI encodes data quite a bit differently from other types of networks to increase transmission efficiency.

6. What does "self-healing" (auto-wrapping) really mean?

Self-healing resembles the expression "Physician, heal thyself." The network hardware is capable of detecting a fiber path failure between connection points on the rings. Since there are two fibers (one transmitting clockwise, the other counterclockwise) in the configuration, the stations that detect the failure join the two rings together and effectively "wrap" together to make a single fiber network twice as long as the original two-fiber network (hence the term *auto-wrapping*). If the network fiber path is destroyed in two different spots, the result is two *healed* network rings. So, self-healing is very beneficial for a single location failure—the network continues to function (see Figure 10-3). If there are two failures, which network components work and which do not is determined by which need to talk to which and how the network was designed. Self-healing is not for all situations in which the network could be disrupted.

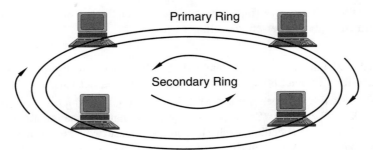

Figure 10-2. Example of FDDI's counter-rotating ring architecture. The primary ring is active in normal operation; the secondary ring provides redundancy. All devices on the ring are dual attachment stations (Class A nodes) or dual attachment hubs.

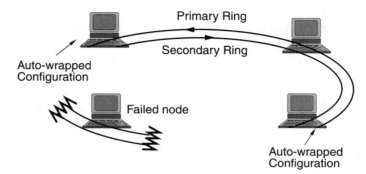

Figure 10-3. Example of FDDI's "self-healing capability. In the event of a fiber cut or an inoperative node, an FDDI network automatically "heals" itself by wrapping the ring at the point of failure. This is done by interconnecting the primary and secondary rings into a single, functional ring. (Adapted from Daniels, 1990.)

7. Obviously, FDDI's physical layer is based on fiber-optic cable. What kinds of fiber are allowed and what are the rules?

FDDI uses either 62.5/125 μm or 85/125 μm multimode fiber, or 8.7/125 μm single mode fiber. Alternatives of 50/125 μm and 100/140 μm are also specified. Smaller fibers allow higher speeds, but also cause higher connector loss. Further, the fiber must be specified for light transmission at the 1300 nm wavelength. Since most fiber plants transmit at 850 nm, 1300 nm, or 1550 nm, finding compliant fiber is usually not a problem for a network manager. Usually, in networks less than 1 km in length, 850 nm is adequate; however, as the need for performance of the medium increases, the 850 nm light source becomes inadequate. Light transmission above 1550 nm usually requires a sophisticated and expensive light source, such as a laser system. Fiber runs cannot be longer than 2 km between connections for multimode fiber (up to 60 km with single mode fiber) and there is a total allowable distance of 100 km per FDDI ring (two rings are allowed). Each ring consists of two fibers. Thus, two rings, obviously, use four fibers. (See Chapter 4 for additional information about fiber-optic cable.)

8. How is FDDI data encoded? I heard that FDDI uses a technique different from what is used for Ethernet/802.3 or IEEE 802.5 token ring networks.

FDDI's physical layer does not use Manchester encoding, which is used in Ethernet/ 802.3 and 802.5 token rings. (See Chapter 8 for additional information about Manchester coding.) In Manchester encoding, each bit requires at least two signal transitions or baud. This means that a 16 Mbps token ring network requires a signaling rate of 32 MHz. Ethernet/802.3 running at 10 Mbps requires 20 MHz. If we were to use Manchester encoding on an FDDI network, more than 200 MHz would be required to provide the FDDI rated speed of 100 Mbps. Instead, FDDI uses a "group" encoding scheme known as the 4B/5B method, which stands for four bits in five baud, or four-bit to five-bit.

9. Could you please expand on this?

Certainly, but we will have to get a little technical.

10. Go for it. If it's over my head I can always ignore it or seek additional information for further clarification.

OK. The 4B/5B encoding method takes data in four-bit codes and maps them to corresponding five-bit codes. These five-bit codes are then transmitted using a technique called *NRZI*, which stands for *non-return to zero, invert on ones*. By transmitting five-bit codes using NRZI, a logic 1-bit is transmitted at least once every five sequential data bits resulting in a signal transition. The 4B/5B-NRZI scheme makes it possible for FDDI to operate at a rate of 125 MHz and provides a data rate of 100 Mbps. The use of one extra bit for every five bits translates to only 20 percent overhead for every clock encoding. In contrast, Manchester coding requires 50 percent bandwidth overhead for clock encoding because it guarantees at least one signal transition for every bit transmitted. The 4B/5B-NRZI scheme allows FDDI networks to provide high-speed capability over less optimal media and data symmetry that allows for simpler implementation of analog capture circuitry for receiving nodes. (See Table 10-1.)

Table 10-1. FDDI Symbols and Codes

FDDI Code	Bit Encoding
0	1 1 1 1 0
1	0 1 0 0 1
2	1 0 1 0 0
3	1 0 1 0 1
4	0 1 0 1 0
5	0 1 0 1 1
6	0 1 1 1 0
7	0 1 1 1 1
8	1 0 0 1 0
9	1 0 0 1 1
A	1 0 1 1 0
B	1 0 1 1 1
C	1 1 0 1 0
D	1 1 0 1 1
E	1 1 1 0 0
F	1 1 1 0 1
S (Set)	1 1 0 0 1
R (Reset)	0 0 1 1 1
Q (Quiet)	0 0 0 0 0
I (Idle)	1 1 1 1 1
H (Halt)	0 0 1 0 0
T (Terminate)	0 1 1 0 1
J (Start 1)	1 1 0 0 0
K (Start 2)	1 0 0 0 1

11. I think that's enough for the physical layer. What about FDDI's data link layer? Is it equivalent to the data link layer of a Token Ring network since FDDI is a ring topology?

Not quite. FDDI uses a token passing scheme as its MAC sublayer protocol similar to that of IEEE 802.5 token ring type networks. However, FDDI does not operate like a "classic" token ring network.

12. In which way or ways is FDDI different from token ring?

We mentioned a few differences earlier in Question 5. We'll summarize them here and include some additional ones. You should also review Chapter 9's discussion on token ring networks.

- FDDI networks can have two counter-rotating fiber-optic rings. This allows configurations of redundant topologies for highly reliable networks. IEEE 802.5 networks operate on a single ring topology. (See Figure 10-2.)

- On IEEE 802.5 token ring type networks, it is possible for stations to implement a priority scheme whereby token ring nodes can "reserve" a token for access to the medium. This scheme does not exist on FDDI networks because it would not work properly in the FDDI environment. FDDI nodes usually send a token at the end of a data transfer, which means that reservation techniques do not work. This is referred to as "new token after send" which is different than IEEE 802.5's "new token after receive."

- FDDI networks have an explicit maximum data size of 4500 octets per frame. There is no such explicit data frame size for IEEE 802.5 networks. Specification of an explicit frame size precludes a node from "hogging" the cable.

- FDDI networks have the capacity to support a distributed recovery capability in case of ring failure. This means that if the ring is cut, nodes on the FDDI network automatically isolate the fault and actively reconfigure the network to provide maximum availability.

Other differences between FDDI and IEEE 802.5 token ring networks include:

- FDDI does not use bit definitions for various fields. All FDDI fields are defined by at least four bits and may be defined by a byte of information so that the various fields can easily be modified or replaced by the nodes on the network as the frames and token travel through the ring(s). (See Question 8.)

- An optional technique in token ring networks, but implemented as a feature in FDDI, is the concept of *early token release* (ETR). ETR places a token on the network *before* the generated frame has had the opportunity to circulate throughout the entire network.

- FDDI tokens are not modified to a Start of Frame (SOF) like on other token ring networks. Tokens are absorbed and regenerated after a message has been sent. Tokens in an FDDI network also react differently from those of other token ring networks in that there are more accommodations for statistical network interconnections than on classic token ring architectures.

- On token ring networks, one clock on the network is responsible for providing clocking signals for all nodes on the cable. The main clock node also provides an "elastic" buffer capability that slides to compensate for speed differentials that appear on the network; this is referred to as *jitter*. In a 100 Mbps FDDI environment, this type of clocking mechanism is impractical and difficult to maintain. At 4 Mbps, the bit time is 250 ns as compared to 10 ns per bit time at 100 Mbps. Consequently, FDDI nodes provide their own clock (hence a "distributed" clocking scheme) and correct for timing jitter via each node's own internal elastic buffer.

13. What about the format of an FDDI frame? How different is it from the format of a token ring frame?

FDDI networks employ two types of "frames." The first is the token, which is a special frame that enables a node to access the ring; the second is the frame itself. FDDI token and frame formats are quite different from a token ring frame format (Chapter 9). Instead of bit definitions, FDDI networks use "symbols," which are defined by at least four bits. (See Table 10-1.) Following is a summary of the token and frame formats:

Token. An FDDI token consists of a Preamble (PA) of 16 or more I symbols, a Starting Delimiter (SD) of a JK symbol pair, a Frame Control (FC) consisting of two symbols, and an Ending Delimiter (ED) field of two T symbols. The FDDI token format is shown in Figure 10-4. There also are two classes of tokens. A *restricted* token enables two specified nodes to use all of the unused or unreserved bandwidth of the network for the duration of their data transmission. An *nonrestricted* token is used for normal operation. Only one token is permitted on the ring. Thus, only one node is permitted to transmit data.

Frame. An FDDI frame consists of a Preamble (PA) of 16 or more I symbols, a Starting Delimiter (SD) field consisting of a JK symbol pair, a Frame Control (FC) field of two symbols, Destination and Source Addresses (DA and SA) each consisting of four or 12 symbols, an Info field of zero or more symbol pairs for user data, a Frame Check Sequence (FCS) of eight symbols, an Ending Delimiter (ED) of one T symbol, and a Frame Status of three or more R or S symbols. The format of an FDDI frame is shown in Figure 10-5.

Note that the first two fields (PA and SD) are collectively called the *Start of Frame Sequence*; the next five fields (FC, DA, SA, Info, and FCS) are collectively known as the *Frame Check Sequence Coverage*; and the last two fields are collectively referred to as the

Figure 10-4. FDDI token format. The Preamble consists of 16 or more I symbols; the Start Delimiter consists of one JK symbol pair; the Frame Control consists of two symbols; and the End Delimiter consists of two T symbols.

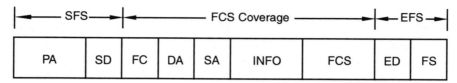

Figure 10-5. FDDI frame format. The Preamble (PA), Start Delimiter (SD), Frame Control (FC), and End Delimiter (ED) are the same as for a token (Figure 10-4). The Destination Address (DA) and Source Address (SA) are 4 or 8 symbols. The INFO field is user data and consists of 0 or more symbols. The Frame Check Sequence (FCS) consists of 8 symbols and uses a 32-bit CRC checksum. The Frame Status (FS) consists of 3 or more R or S symbols. The status can be "E" for error detected in frame, "A" for destination address recognized, or "C" for frame copied. The entire frame can be grouped into three primary fields: Start of Frame Sequence (SFS), Frame Check Sequence (FCS) Coverage, and End of Frame Sequence (EFS).

End of Frame Sequence. Also note that addresses can be either 16 or 48 bits in length. Finally, the FCS uses a 32-bit CRC checksum for error control.

14. How does an FDDI network operate?

In order to access the ring, a node must first gain possession of the token. Once it has the token, the node is permitted to transmit multiple frames until a timer expires. When its time is up, the node retransmits the token on the ring. Only one token is permitted, thus only one node can access the ring at any time.

As frames circulate around the ring, if the bits do not match a specific pattern then the receiving station is aware that the token is used and that this frame should be examined to see if it is to continue being passed along the ring. If the node examining the frame is not the intended recipient, then the frame is re-generated to the next station in the path. If the current station is the intended recipient, then the station "snapshots" the data, passes it to the host system, and marks the bit pattern at the beginning of the frame to signify that it was received and read into the receiving node. The frame is then passed along to the next node, continuing until it eventually reaches the sending node, which "strips" the frame by not retransmitting it. This scheme is really critical in view of the potential size of FDDI networks—1000 or more systems. It would take a very long time for frames in a classic token ring network to traverse such a large network (most token ring networks have less than 250 stations on them).

15. One *thousand* or more systems? That sounds like a large network!

It can be. It's not uncommon to find FDDI networks with over 400 connections in a single campus environment, although most FDDI networks have fewer than 100 connections to ensure good performance. (See Figure 10-6.) Having such a large number of nodes on a single network implies that if it is not carefully designed to avert network outages, a very large number of people who rely on the network will find themselves unable to accomplish anything.

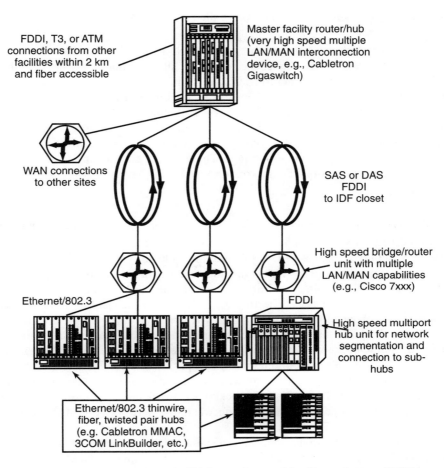

Figure 10-6. An example of a typical high-speed network backbone that uses FDDI to interconnect several different types of LANs and WANs.

16. What are the rules in configuring an FDDI network?

Pretty simple, really. A few specific fiber types are supported and specific lengths are required between optical interconnections, depending upon the vendor hardware selected. The two individual fiber rings' total length must not exceed 200 km when autowrapped.

17. How many systems are allowed on a single FDDI network?

The ANSI standard specifies that a maximum of 500 nodes is permitted on an FDDI network with a maximum ring circumference of 100 km and a maximum distance of 2 km between hardware devices. Some vendors allow a greater number of nodes depending upon their hardware and configuration rules. Some allow fewer. FDDI networks of over 1000 nodes are not uncommon.

18. Earlier you mentioned something called a Class A configuration. Could you please elaborate?

You betcha. Within FDDI, there are two types of network connections (nodes): Class A and Class B. Class A nodes are connected to two full, dual-fiber rings and have the ability to reconfigure the network to form a valid network from components of the two rings in case of a failure. Class B nodes only connect to the primary pair of fibers and can be isolated from the network in the case of some types of failure. Class A nodes are called *dual-attachment stations (DAS)*; Class B nodes are called *single-attachment stations (SAS)*. Some Class B nodes are equipped with bypass connections, which allow light source continuation even if the node connection fails. These bypass connections serve to maximize uptime of the network. An FDDI network designed with Class A nodes is called a Class A configuration.

19. How would an FDDI network be configured as the main or backbone network?

In most FDDI wiring configurations, the network designer configures a main backbone to be set up as a series of Class A nodes for reliability purposes. The length of the backbone is a function of how widely distributed a network is in a building, in a campus, or in a metropolitan area. In a building environment, the backbone may be located in a single room with all segments connecting to it. The backbone may be located vertically throughout telephone closets in the building. There may be other variations as well. In all these cases, the FDDI backbone network is contained within the building. In a campus environment, the backbone could also be in a single room in a single building, but most likely runs from building to building in the campus. In this configuration, each building has a main network control closet, so there is only one tap on the network backbone at each building location. In any case, the backbone network may vary in size and number of connection points, depending heavily upon where the network is located and how it is used.

An FDDI network also may appear as a subsidiary backbone within a building that is connected to the main FDDI backbone. In this example, there are two FDDI network levels: the main backbone and a separate FDDI network per building. This may be expanded further to an FDDI network on a floor connected to the building hub, which is, in turn, connected to the main backbone in a campus building environment. In this configuration, we run the fiber to the actual machine(s) on the network; other networks may or may not be bridged onto the FDDI.

20. How is a system connected to the FDDI fiber?

For a node to be connected to a fiber-optic network, the network must have a fiber coupler (tap) attached to it. These couplers require that the cable be cut and terminated properly with approved connectors. These are typically the SC or Media Interface Connector (MIC) variety of fiber connectors. (MICs are designed to be used by untrained personnel.) Splices in fiber may be done via a "score and break" technique where the fiber is scored, broken with special tools, and the ends of the two fibers connected with epoxy. A second method is to use a fusion splicer, which may employ an electrical arc to connect the ends of two fibers together. Splices are reasonably straightforward. Termination of cable, however, requires that the ends be cut and polished before they are inserted into terminating hoods. Polishing is typically done in a coarse way with a hand tool and completed with a polishing machine. This allows a smooth, flawless end that will properly pass the light from the source to the destination transceiver or repeater. This polishing effort may take up to 40 minutes per fiber strand (imagine this on a 48-fiber run!), which accounts for the high cost of fiber installation. Improper polishing and connection of the termination points on a fiber will at most render the fiber useless or will, at the very least, result in poor network performance. After it is terminated, the fiber must be tested to ensure proper installation. This normally involves using an optical time domain reflectometer (OTDR), an expensive testing device. In summary, properly installing fiber for FDDI is painful, time-consuming, and expensive.

21. So now I know how FDDI networks generally work. How would I use one in a "real" environment?

Glad you asked. Typically, FDDI networks implement backbone configurations for buildings and campus environments. In this design, a master FDDI "switch" connects separate FDDI networks on each floor in the building. This configuration is called a *collapsed backbone* design, where the master backbone is the switch and all major connections have been connected to the network switch (thus "collapsed" into a single box). This enables expansion and traffic isolation between the networks and reduces network failure potential. If the switch is "intelligent," it further isolates traffic and may include redundant facilities to keep the switch operational in adverse conditions such as motherboard failure or power supply failure.

The master "hub" switch of the building would be a very high speed, multinetwork concentration facility. Some hubs can support up to 36 FDDI networks (in the extended configuration) and can support T3 and Asynchronous Transfer Mode (ATM) technologies in the same box. (See Chapter 7 for information about T3 circuits and Chapter 14 for information about ATM.) This tiered interconnection scheme using a very high-speed concentrating device is essential in developing high-speed, high-reliability networks.

22. What is an FDDI "switch?"

An FDDI "switch" interconnects many FDDIs through a common "box." This "box" or switch manages and sorts traffic between switches so that it is sent only to where it needs to go. On an FDDI, all connected systems "see" all frames on the network. On a switch, the only traffic viewed by a specific FDDI is that which originates on it or is destined to it. All traffic on all other FDDI segments is isolated to each individual segment by the switch. This reduces overall traffic between the segments, reduces unnecessary traffic between networks, and improves performance overall network performance. (See Chapter 6 for additional information about switches.)

23. I have an Ethernet/802.3 LAN. How do I interconnect it to FDDI?

It's easier than ever to do that, especially given the communications hub technologies in the market today. What is normally required is an Ethernet/802.3 to FDDI bridge unit.

Such bridge units are available in many varieties—for example, a card in a hub or a dedicated box that does nothing but interconnect the two networks. Most manufacturers of hub units produce Ethernet/802.3 and FDDI cards that allow interconnecting the two types of networks.

One thing to be careful about is the issue of frame size conversion. Frames headed from Ethernet/802.3 networks to the FDDI are no biggie—the frame formats have nearly identical addressing and data containers. However, machines on the FDDI network that use the maximum frame size of 4500 bytes will cause the Ethernet/802.3network to be very unhappy. Therefore, the bridge must segment the network frame when moving it from the FDDI network to the Ethernet/802.3 network. This segmenting can cause all sorts of problems. If this situation exists, we recommend that you restrict the maximum frame size generated by a FDDI system to 1500 octets of data, which will reduce the magnitude of the problem. While this decreases the efficiency of the FDDI network, the hassle of large-frame-to-small-frame conversion would otherwise offset any potential performance benefits.

Another option is to use a router to interconnect the two network types. The benefit here is that the router can also handle frame conversions for specific protocols and automatically segment the traffic for routable protocols such as TCP/IP, AppleTalk, Novell's IPX, DECnet, SNA and others. The downside is that routers are usually substantially slower than switching bridges and can be pricey.

24. I've heard that the Boeing 777 jetliner has an FDDI network that serves as its backbone, with Ethernet/802.3 connections at the passenger seats. Could you give me a little more information?

We'll give you a high-level case study. The Boeing 777 is one of the most technologically advanced commercial airplanes in the world, so it is fitting that it is delivered with advanced networks installed. Its designers implemented an MLAN (mobile local area network) consisting of two complete FDDI rings, one in the cabin and one in the cockpit. The FDDI network in the cabin is connected to Ethernet/802.3 LANs in the three compartments (economy, business class, and first class) by "brouters" (see Chapter 7). The purpose of these LANs is to transmit information to the multimedia units at each of the seats. The FDDI ring in the cockpit conveys data from two redundant servers to multimedia instrumentation units and navigation displays while it collects and stores maintenance information.

The Litton FiberCom Avionics Bridge/Router (Brouter) is the main internetworking device on the Boeing 777 aircraft. The Brouter is a networking bridge which supports FDDI and Ethernet/802.3 network interfaces. The Brouter has the built-in capacity to internetwork between three dual FDDI networks, a 10BASE2 Ethernet, and two 10BASE-T Ethernet hubs with eight ports each. The Brouter is designed to be the boundary device for the two main aircraft FDDI networks on the 777 aircraft: the Optical LAN (OLAN, formerly called PlaneNet) and the Cabin LAN (CABLAN). The Brouter design also provides a Gatelink connection via the third FDDI interface.

The Brouter allows the aircraft maintainer easy access to the aircraft's on-board maintenance system via multiple Ethernet ports. These Ethernet ports are tapped by portable maintenance access terminals via connectors located at various points around the aircraft (wheel well ports, tail port, electronic equipment bay port, etc.). The Brouter can support both software and hardware upgrades for additional capabilities (e.g., OSI, TCP/IP, IPX protocols). The Brouter is data-loadable onboard the aircraft via the FDDI interface to support future Brouter software upgrades.

If you would like to play with network configuration and deployment on a Boeing 777 jetliner, you can purchase one from Boeing for about $150 million. At that price, the networks are included.

25. We're thinking about implementing ATM networking in the future. Will FDDI connect to that as well?

Of course. In fact, high-speed technologies such as Cabletron's *Gigaswitch* and the Cisco *Catalyst* series of switches support not only FDDI networks but also ATM networks in the same box at the same time. The only "gotcha" with these technologies is that any time large data frames, such as those of FDDI, must traverse an ATM network, the frames must be pared to the payload size of ATM cells, which is 44 octets. (The overall cell is 53 octets, with the remainder keeping track of such things as where the cell is going.) Taking a full 4500-octet FDDI network connection frame and chopping it up into 53 octet cells is time-consuming and demanding of the networking hardware. Therefore, even if the ATM network is faster than the FDDI (such as an OC-12 622 Mbps ATM connection), the effective throughput may actually be lower due to the additional processing required to "cellify" the FDDI frames to ATM and then deliver the cells to their destination. If the connection is an ATM network interconnecting two or more FDDI networks, then the workload is even greater on the link path between the two locations.

26. You mentioned CDDI in the introduction to this chapter. I'm guessing it's the same as FDDI with copper instead of fiber at the physical layer. Am I right?

Right you are. However, the use of copper wire in CDDI is restricted to connections between concentrators on the ring and single attachment devices, not for the ring itself. (*Note:* FDDI concentrators are DAS devices that can be used to connect multiple SAS devices.) Copper is, at present, somewhat cheaper for use in short runs (up to 100 m).

27. What type of cabling does CDDI use?

CDDI supports both unshielded twisted-pair (UTP) and shielded twisted-pair (STP). As for which type of UTP, the familiar and popular EIA/TIA-568 Category 5 cabling, already installed in many buildings' wiring closets, may be used for CDDI. Similarly, IBM Type 1 STP is acceptable for CDDI use; occasionally you may encounter the abbreviation SDDI, which is sometimes used in reference to CDDI networks employing shielded cabling. At one time there was also a proprietary CDDI product that supported ThinWire coaxial.

28. Are CDDI and SDDI real standards, like FDDI?

They started out as de facto standards created by a group of five vendors. In 1995, ANSI issued a standard for CDDI, X3.263-1995, entitled *Fibre Distributed Data Interface (FDDI)—Token Ring Twisted Pair Physical Layer Medium Dependent (TP-PMD)*.

29. What about the future of FDDI? Is there a bigger-better-faster version to look forward to?

There was at one time, but the introduction of other, faster network technologies such as Gigabit Ethernet and ATM have caused a halt to any development efforts on FDDI follow-ons. For example, a technology called FDDI-II was intended to handle not only traditional FDDI network traffic, but also synchronous, circuit-switched PCM data for voice or ISDN systems. Development has all but ceased and no commercial systems have been deployed in the FDDI-II environment, especially given the growth of other, more popular technologies such as ATM and SONET. As we mentioned earlier in this chapter, FDDI is now rarely used as a direct-system connection network platform, being primarily relegated to backbone deployments. Other network types, such as Ethernet/802.3, have impinged upon the applicability of FDDI, displacing it because of less expensive implementation, interconnection, and upgrade paths. Therefore, any implementation of an FDDI network needs an upgrade strategy in order to provide for the day when it will be too slow for its applications. Current network designers looking toward FDDI for expansion may find cheaper methods to provide 100 Mbps connectivity with greater longevity and expansion capabilities than FDDI.

Summarizing, although FDDI is still a viable and ubiquitous network technology, its days are numbered as less expensive Ethernet/802.3 100 Mbps and 1000 Mbps systems supplant what were traditionally FDDI network environments. ATM also is encroaching on FDDI deployments with its scalability and support of isochronous transmission (used for video). FDDI still has its fans, however, and will not be leaving anytime soon—especially given its ability to provide very high bandwidth and redundancy failover capabilities, while remaining stable for all types of networking applications.

End-of-Chapter Commentary

FDDI was one of the first "second-generation" LAN technologies designed specifically to meet the needs of users with high bandwidth requirements. Other second-generation LAN technologies discussed in this book are the various evolutions of Ethernet, including full-duplex Ethernet, switched Ethernet, Fast Ethernet, and Gigabit Ethernet. (See Chapter 8.) We also look at a revolutionary "Ethernet" technology called 100VG-AnyLAN, which at one time competed against Fast Ethernet for the 100 Mbps marketplace. (See Chapter 8.) In Chapter 9, we examine some evolutionary changes to traditional 4/16 Mbps Token Ring networks, including dedicated token ring, switched token ring, full-duplex token ring, and 100 Mbps token ring. Finally, in Chapter 14, Asynchronous Transfer Mode (ATM) networks are discussed from both LAN and WAN perspectives.

Chapter 11

Integrated Services Data Network (ISDN)

The Integrated Services Digital Network (ISDN) represents the overhaul and redesign of our conventional telephone network from an analog system to an end-to-end digital network. This new, completely digital-based network is capable of transmitting voice and data communications over a single telephone line using inexpensive and conventional twisted-pair cable (i.e., standard copper telephone wire). A brief overview of various fundamental ISDN concepts was provided in Chapter 7 as part of our discussion of WAN technologies and services. In this chapter, we extend this discussion and provide more detailed information about ISDN. The major topics presented in this chapter are

- History of ISDN (Questions 1–3)
- General Overview and Components (Questions 4–6)
- Channel Types (Question 7)
- BRIs, PRIs, and SPIDs (Questions 8–9)
- Line Sets and Feature Sets (Questions 10–12)
- ISDN Protocols (Questions 16–18)
- AO/DI and B-ISDN (Questions 19–20)
- Implementation Strategies (Questions 21)

1. What is ISDN?

The Integrated Services Digital Network is a carrier service that is offered by telephone companies (telcos) and designed to transmit voice and nonvoice (e.g., computer data, fax, video) communications on the same network. The advantage ISDN offers over other services is that separate connections are not needed for these different transmissions. Thus, instead of having a telephone line for voice communications, a second telephone line for fax or computer dialup connections, and a coaxial cable link for video communications, a single ISDN connection will support all of these transmissions. That is, ISDN *integrates* all of these services into a single system. ISDN service (and hence, an ISDN connection) is completely digital from end-to-end. This represents both a departure from and an improvement in today's conventional telecommunication services, which use a hybrid of

(a)

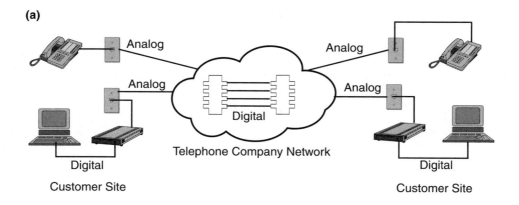

(b)

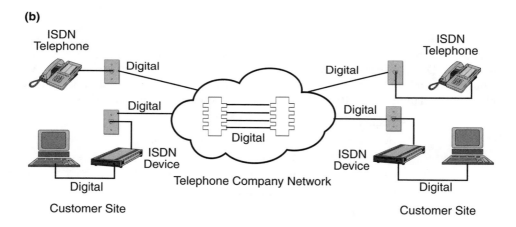

Figure 11-1. Today's conventional telephone network (a) is a hybrid of analog and digital technologies. Note that a computer connection requires four conversions: Digital-to-analog from the PC, which is digital, to the customers phone system, which is analog; analog-to-digital from the customer's site to the telephone company's site, which is all digital; digital-to-analog from the telephone company's site to the customer site; and analog-to-digital from the customer's phone system to the PC. An ISDN connection (b), however, which uses special ISDN-compatible devices, is all digital from end-to-end. In the case of the computer connections, no digital-to-analog or analog-to-digital conversions are necessary, which result in faster connections.

analog and digital technologies. (See Figure 11-1.) Furthermore, ISDN's technology permits standard twisted-pair wiring to carry circuit- or packet-switched digital data. ISDN also provides a cost-effective strategy for internetworking. Instead of paying for dedicated leased lines, remote sites (i.e., user workstations or LANs) can interconnect with other sites via dialup links.

2. How did ISDN get started?

The advent of digital technology in the telephone industry marks the roots of ISDN in the 1970s. During this time, telcos modernized their central offices (COs) with digital switching equipment, replacing the analog-based public switched telephone network (PSTN) that was originally designed for voice transmission with one predicated on digital signaling and circuitry. What emerged was an Integrated Digital Network (IDN), which engendered a vision of a network capable of transmitting any information source—voice, video, graphics, images, and text—directly to customers regardless of their location. In today's jargon, this vision was to treat all of these information sources as data, market them as services needed by businesses and consumers (e.g., video conferencing), and then deliver these services directly to the desktop or home. There was one problem, though: Delivery of these services required end-to-end digital connectivity. Although IDN was digitally-based and capable of voice, data, and video transmissions, it was not end-to-end. Delivery of these services was restricted because the local loop (the circuit between a user and the telco's nearest point of presence) was still analog. In the 1980s, standards for digital end-to-end connectivity and transmission of both voice and nonvoice services to the user were approved. This new network was named the Integrated Services Digital Network, or ISDN.

The development, approval, and acceptance of ISDN standards spurred widespread deployment of ISDN services throughout Europe where the telcos were, at the time, mostly government-owned. (More on this later.) In the United States, though, ISDN essentially became a product looking for a market and laid dormant for nearly ten years. It wasn't until the Internet achieved critical mass in the mid-1990s before ISDN came to life in the United States. Given this ten-year period, from the approval of ISDN standards to its widespread availability and ultimate implementation in the United States, alternative interpretations of the ISDN acronym emerged. These included, among others, I Still Don't Need it, Innovative Services users Don't Need, I Still Don't kNow, and It's Still Doing Nothing. Today, ISDN has emerged as a viable, cost-effective solution for remote and WAN applications and its acronym for some now represents Innovations Subscribers Do Need.

3. Who is responsible for ISDN standards?

ISDN standards development is conducted under the auspices of the International Telecommunications Union (ITU), which is the former Consultative Committee for International Telephony and Telegraphy (CCITT). A subgroup of ITU, Telecommunications Standardization Section (ITU-TSS), is responsible for communications, interfaces, and other standards related to telecommunications. ITU also works in cooperation with other accredited standards committees such as the American National Standards Institute (ANSI).

The initial set of ISDN recommendations, formally called the I-series Recommendations, was published by CCITT in 1984. These recommendations were published in CCITT's "Red Books," which comprises all CCITT standards. Additional work on the I-series Recommendations continued after 1984, and in 1988 an updated and more complete set of ISDN standards were incorporated into CCITT's "Blue Books." Although subse-

Table 11-1. Summary of ISDN I-Series Recommendations

Series Number	Description
I.100	Describes the general concepts of ISDN. It addresses fundamental ISDN principles, objectives, and vocabulary.
I.200	Specifies the various services ISDN provides.
I.300	Discusses ISDN network requirements—including its architecture and addressing scheme—and specifies the manner in which an ISDN network is to provide the services described in I.200.
I.400	Addresses issues related to the user interface from the perspective of the first three layers of the OSI model. Examples include data transmission rates, hardware configurations, and data link and network layer protocols.
I.500	Discusses interconnectivity issues (e.g., interconnecting ISDN networks with non-ISDN networks).
I.600	Devoted to ISDN maintenance issues.

quent updates have been made, the 1988 publication still adequately describes the basic principals and reference model of ISDN. A summary of the I-series Recommendations is given in Table 11-1, and a copy of the ISDN reference model is shown in Figure 11-2.

Speaking of standards, in the United States the regional Bell operating companies (RBOCs)—which are now called incumbent local exchange carriers (ILECs)—established a National ISDN initiative to foster end-user equipment interoperability. A presumption of this initiative is that any ISDN end-equipment that is National ISDN compliant should be able to connect to any telco switch. The initiative's first protocol, National ISDN-1 (NI-1), was ratified in November, 1992 with a better than 80 percent compatibility rate. (Some RBOCs opted not to upgrade to NI-1.) The goal of subsequent protocols (e.g., NI-2) is 100 percent compatibility.

4. Figure 11-2 is a bit confusing. Can you please explain it to me?

We can understand your confusion. Figure 11-2 shows the basic components of an ISDN connection from the perspective of a reference or block diagram. These components, which do not necessarily correspond to actual pieces of equipment, include two types of network termination modules (NT1 and NT2), two types of terminal equipment (TE1 and TE2), and terminal adapters (TA).

The *NT1* module provides the interface between the customer's premise equipment and the telco's equipment. It consists of a two-wire U interface at one end and up to seven T interfaces at the other end. Its purpose is to convert the two-wire ISDN link provided by the telco into 4-wire ports that connect ISDN devices. From an OSI model perspective, an NT1 is a layer 1 device since it deals with the physical and electrical termination of the circuit at the customer's site. An NT1 also performs synchronous time division multiplexing (TDM—see Chapter 4) to combine more than one channel. (More on this later.)

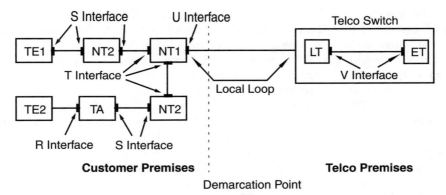

Customer Premises   **Telco Premises**

Demarcation Point

NT1   Network Termination 1—provides connectivity between a customer's site and the telco's site. It converts the two-wire U Interface into a four-wire S/T Interface. NT1 modules can support up to eight connections (TEs, TAs, or NT2s).

NT2   Network Termination 2—converts the T interface into the S interface. NT2 provides data link and network layer functions. Connectivity to ISDN devices (TE1 or TE2) is via an S interface, and connectivity to an NT1 unit is via the T interface. An example of an NT2 device is a PBX system.

TE1   Terminal Equipment 1—an ISDN compatible device. TE1s have built-in ISDN network interfaces and can connect directly to NT1 units via an S/T interface. Examples of TE1 devices include ISDN telephones and ISDN fax machines.

TE2   Terminal Equipment 2—a non-ISDN compatible device. TE2s can be connected to an ISDN network via a terminal adapter (TA) through an R interface. TAs are then connected to NT2 units via an S/T interface. Examples of TE2 devices include analog telephone or fax machines, and computers without an ISDN connection.

TA   Terminal Adapter—provides ISDN connectivity to non-ISDN devices (TE2s).

LT   Line Termination—represents the local loop connection; that is, it is where a circuit from a customer's NT1 module terminates at the telco's switch.

ET   Exchange Termination—connects a telco's ISDN switch to other ISDN switches within the telco's network.

Figure 11-2. An ISDN reference diagram showing the relationship between ISDN equipment and interfaces. The local loop (also called the subscriber loop) is the access line between the telco's central office (CO) and the customer's site. This link is terminated at the customer site via an NT1 device. In the United States, NT1 devices are purchased by the customer. This makes the demarcation point (the point that separates customer premise equipment from the telco equipment), the U interface. In Europe, the telcos own NT1 devices and install them on the customers' premises. In this setting, NT1 devices are considered telco equipment and the demarcation point is now the T interface. (Adapted from Frank, 1995, and Leeds, 1996.)

    The second network termination unit, *NT2*, is a secondary termination module that converts the T interface from the NT1 module into S interfaces that connect terminal equipment or adapters (TE or TA). An example of an NT2 unit is a PBX (Private Branch Exchange), which is a telephone switching system that provides telecommunication services throughout an organization's private network. If an organization's PBX is a digital switch, which implies that the telephones connected to it are digital, then ISDN connectivity can be provided throughout the enterprise by connecting the PBX to an NT1 module. Another example of an NT2 unit is a LAN device such as a router. An NT2 performs functions that operate up to the third layer of the OSI model.

The terminal equipment (TE) represent specific communication devices that connect to the network. Two TEs are referenced, *TE1* and *TE2*, to distinguish between compatible and incompatible ISDN equipment. TE1 examples include digital telephones and computers with built-in ISDN ports (e.g., a Sun SparcStation 10 was one of the first computers to have built-in ISDN capability). TE2 examples include analog telephones (i.e., those with RJ-11 jacks) and computers without built-in ISDN ports (e.g., RS-232C or equivalent serial ports). Most ISDN compatible devices have built-in NT2 modules and connect directly to an NT1. (*Note:* From a technical perspective, all ISDN devices must go through an NT2 unit.) Some ISDN TE1 devices also have built-in NT1 and NT2 modules (sometimes referred to as NT12), with U-interfaces that enable them to connect directly to the local loop. Such devices eliminate the need to purchase a separate NT1 unit. They also eliminate the capability of connecting more than one device to the network.

Finally, a terminal adapter, *TA*, is a device that connects incompatible ISDN devices to an ISDN network. If a TA is used for an ISDN dialup connection, then it can be thought of as a modem (see Chapter 15); if a TA is used to connect a device to a LAN, then it can be thought of as a network interface card (see Chapter 6). It should be noted that although a TA is frequently referred to as an ISDN modem or digital modem in the context of an ISDN dialup connection, this reference is incorrect. By definition, a modem performs analog-to-digital and digital-to-analog conversions. Since ISDN is completely digital, no such conversions are necessary, which makes the expressions, ISDN modem or digital modem, incongruous. Nevertheless, both expressions are frequently used because the general public can better relate to them than the term *terminal adapter*.

To help clear up any residual confusion, perhaps a more conceptual illustration of these units will help. Figure 11-3 provides examples of two typical home-based ISDN connections. In this figure, various home-based telecommunication devices are connected to an ISDN network. The devices at Home 1 are ISDN terminal equipment (TE1). They have built-in NT2 modules and ISDN ports with the proper S/T-interfaces that enable them to connect directly into an NT1 module. The devices at Home 2 in Figure 11-3 are not ISDN-capable. Thus, they require terminal adapters in order to connect to an ISDN network. These devices connect to their respective TAs via an R interface. TAs can be external units (as shown in Figure 11-3), or internal adapter cards that plug into a device's motherboard.

5. Thanks. That helped. I still have one more question about this, though. What's with all of those interfaces?

ISDN defines three primary interfaces to foster global interoperability of ISDN equipment—R, S, and T. (See Figure 11-2.) The U and V interfaces are U.S.-specific. The R interface provides a mechanism for non-ISDN devices to connect to an ISDN network. The ISDN device that supports the R interface is the ISDN terminal adapter (TA), which is similar to and functions like a network interface card (NIC) (see Chapter 6) or an analog modem (see Chapter 15). For example, to connect a computer to the Internet via a conventional (i.e., analog) dialup line, requires either an internal or external modem. An internal

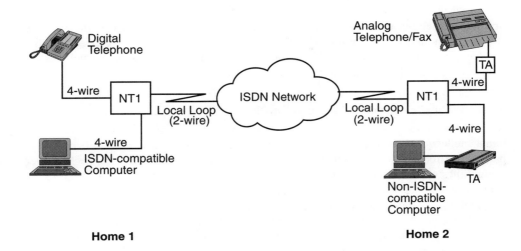

Figure 11-3. A home-based ISDN connection consists of a 4-wire circuit that connects the home to the telco's ISDN network. This circuit physically and electrically terminates at each house's demarcation point, which is an NT1 module. All of the communication devices at the left have built-in NT2 modules with ISDN connector ports that provide an S/T interface to connect directly to the NT1 module. The devices at the right, however, are not ISDN-compatible. They do not comply with ISDN interface requirements, and hence require terminal adapters (TA) in order to connect to the NT1 module. The devices on the left side of the figure are TE1 devices; those on the right side are TE2 devices. (*Note:* The TA connected to the computer at Home 2 is commonly, although incorrectly, called an ISDN modem.)

modem is connected directly to the computer's logic board and provides an RJ-11 port for the telephone line, and an external modem provides two interfaces—a serial port (e.g., RS232-C or equivalent) and an RJ-11 port. To connect this same computer to an ISDN network via a dialup line, a TA is used to provide the necessary interfaces (e.g., serial and R) to connect the non-ISDN compatible computer (or other device) to an ISDN network. In this capacity, a TA is often referred to as an ISDN modem or digital modem.

The S and T interfaces are standard ISDN digital interfaces that are electronically equivalent. They are four-wire connections that partition the two-wire access line provided by the telco into separate transmit and receive lines. All ISDN-compatible equipment have S interfaces and plug directly into an NT1 module via a T interface. A distinction between these two interfaces is made because in Europe, the T interface serves as the point of demarcation that separates the customer premise equipment (CPE) and the telco provider's equipment. In the United States, the demarcation point is the U interface. The reason for these two points of demarcation has to do with the way providers in the United States and Europe deliver ISDN service. U.S. customers are expected to purchase their own NT1 modules, which makes them CPE, while in Europe, NT1 modules reside at the customer's site, but are owned by the telcos making them part of the telco's premise equipment. NT units usually label their interfaces as S/T.

As indicated earlier, the U and V interfaces are U.S.-specific. The U interface, in addition to representing the point of demarcation, is where the telco's access line from its switch is terminated at the customer's site. This access line is commonly referred to as the *local loop* or *subscriber loop*. The V interface is used to connect the exchange and line terminations (ET and LT) within an ISDN switch.

6. OK. What else can you tell me about ISDN?

Well, for starters, as a completely digital service, ISDN eliminates the need for traditional modems, which perform analog-to-digital and digital-to-analog conversions. This provides extremely fast connections. For example, a traditional modem connection over analog lines requires anywhere from 30 to 60 seconds to establish a connection; an ISDN connection takes approximately two seconds.

ISDN also maintains a logical separation of user data (voice and non-voice) from signaling and control information. ISDN uses *Bearer* or *B* channels for transmitting data, and a *signaling* or *D* (Delta) channel for transmitting signaling and control information. Since there is a separate channel for signaling information, 100 percent of the bandwidth allocated for an ISDN *B* channel is used for data transmission. This offers an advantage over traditional T1 service where control information is in-band. For example, a 128 kbps fractional T1 line (two DS-0 circuits) provides only 112 kbps for data because 8 kbps per DS-0 channel is used for control. A 128 kbps ISDN circuit (two *B* channels), however, provides a clear 128 kbps because both *B* channels are free of any signaling overhead. (See Chapter 7 for additional information about T1 circuits.)

ISDN is also a connection-oriented service, which implies that fixed virtual circuits are established between source and destination nodes. A virtual connection is first established between sender and receiver prior to transmission, the circuit remains in effect and dedicated exclusively to this session for the duration of the transmission, and the circuit is then disconnected after the transmission ends. (See Chapter 2.)

Although call setups between source and destination nodes are nailed up and torn down by the ISDN provider, the customer's access line (the connection between a customer's site and provider) is fixed and physical. To reduce call charges between a customer site and provider, most ISDN hardware devices support automatic dial-on-demand connections. Instead of continuously keeping the customer-provider circuit up, dial-on-demand establishes a connection only when data frames have to be transmitted. After a certain period of time (which is user-configurable) in which no traffic is being transmitted from the customer's site to the provider's network, the device automatically terminates the call (hangs up). This is analogous to the way we use our telephone—whenever we need to talk to someone we place the call; in all other situations the phone is kept on-hook.

ISDN also supports both circuit- and packet-switched connections and is an international standard based on the concepts and principles of the OSI model (see Chapter 2).

7. Tell me more about these separate channels.

ISDN defines several different channel types. These include *B, D,* and *H* channels. The *B* channel is a 64 kbps clear channel used to transmit computer data (text and graphics), digitized voice, and digitized video. (*Note:* A clear channel means no signaling information is sent on the channel.) *B* channel transmissions are either circuit- or packet-switched. Data also can be exchanged via frame relay (Chapter 12) or through a dedicated leased line arrangement. In a leased line configuration, no call-control information needs to be transmitted on the *D* channel. Most basic ISDN services are based on multiple *B* channels.

The *D* channel is either a 16 kbps or 64 kbps channel, depending on the specific service level provided. (More on this later.) The *D* channel is used to carry signal and control information for circuit-switched user data. It is the *D* channel on which information related to call initiation (call-setup) and termination (call tear-down) between an ISDN device and the telco's central office for each B channel is transmitted. Thus, when a telephone call is made between two sites, the *D* channel handles all of the call-related information for the *B* channels. This is why the *B* channels are clear 64 kbps channels. The *D* channel also can be used to transmit packet-switched user data (provided that no signal or control information is needed), data from security alarm signals of remote sensing devices that detect fire or intruders, and low speed information acquired from telemetry services such as meter reading. (*Note:* Telemetry applications involve obtaining measurements remotely and relaying them to another site for recording or display purposes.)

The *H* channel is used for transmitting user data (not signal or control information) at higher transmission rates than the *B* channel provides. Four *H* channels are defined: *H0*, *H10*, *H11*, and *H12*. *H0* comprises six *B* channels for a total capacity of 384 kbps. The *H10* channel is U.S.-specific and aggregates 23 *B* channels for a total capacity of 1.472 Mbps. The *H11* channel is the equivalent of the North American DS-1 (see Chapter 7) and consists of 24 *B* channels for an aggregate bandwidth of 1.536 Mbps. The *H12* channel, which is European-specific, comprises 30 *B* channels and has an aggregate bandwidth of 1.920 Mbps. Examples of applications that might use an *H* channel include video conferencing high-speed fax, or high-speed packet switched data, and high-quality audio.

B and *D* channels are generally combined (i.e., multiplexed using TDM) by ISDN service providers and offered to customers in different bundled configurations. The most common package is the $2B + D$ arrangement, which consists of two *B* channels and one *D* channel. This channel structure is known as *Basic Rate Interface (BRI)*. Two other common basic interface structures are $B + D$, and *D* only. In the BRI structure, the *D* channel is 16 kbps. A second type of channel structure is called *Primary Rate Interface (PRI)*, which has a general configuration of $nB + D$. The two most common PRIs are $23B + D$, which is equivalent to the North American DS-1 rate of 1.544 Mbps, and $30B + D$, which is equivalent to the European E-1 rate of 2.048 Mbps. In the PRI structure, the *D* channel is 64 kbps.

8. Please elaborate on BRI and PRI.

OK. We will treat these one at a time.

BRI. The ISDN Basic Rate Interface (also known as *basic access*) is a 192-bit channel that consists of two 64 kbps *B* channels, one 16 kbps *D* channel, and 48 bits of overhead used for framing and other functions. (See Figure 11-4. See also Chapter 5 for more information about framing.) The two *B* channels and the *D* channel are combined into a single pair of standard copper telephone wires. Both *B* channels can support any combination of

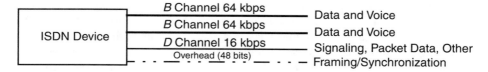

Figure 11-4. ISDN's Basic Rate Interface (BRI) is a 2*B* + *D* package provided by the telcos. BRI consists of two 64 kbps *B* channels used for transmitting data or voice (or both), and one 16 kbps *D* channel used for transmitting signaling and control information. If no signal or control information is present, then the *D* channel can be used for transmitting data as well. BRI also consists of an additional 48 bits used for framing and synchronization.

voice or data transmissions (e.g., both voice, both data, one voice and the other data). BRI provides a full-duplex data rate of 128 kbps. If call or signal information is not being carried by the *D* channel (e.g., transmitting data via packet-switching), then the rate increases to 144 kbps if the *D* channel is carrying data. Data rates also can be increased anywhere from four to eight times more through data compression (Chapter 15). (*Note:* Some telcos might still use older signaling software that requires ISDN signaling to be done in-band. In such instances, 8 kbps per *B* channel must be reserved for signaling resulting in a BRI service that provides 112 kbps instead of 128 kbps.)

ISDN BRI has two telephone numbers assigned to it—one for each *B* channel—and hence effectively provides consumers with two telephone lines via a single connection. Thus, at home, one *B* channel can be used for standard voice service (except here it is digital and not analog), and the other *B* channel for a fax machine. Alternatively, one *B* channel can be for standard voice and the other *B* channel for an Internet connection. Also at home, the *D* channel can be used for telemetry services. For example, utility companies could use this channel to obtain readings from the electric, gas, or water meter.

ISDN BRI *B* channels, through inverse multiplexing (Chapter 4), also can be combined to form a single channel with an effective bandwidth of 128 kbps. This process is called *BONDING*, a protocol named *Bandwidth ON Demand Interoperability Network Group*. An inverse multiplexer (imux), enables the two *B* channels to be used simultaneously. When a standard BRI connection is first established, the receiving device negotiates various communications parameters with the sending device for the current session. In a BRI BONDING scenario, these parameters include two connections and a 128 kbps transmission rate. Once the receiving device receives and accepts these parameters, it instructs the sending device to establish a second connection by calling its second telephone number. An alignment process then occurs that effectively combines the two lines into a single channel. An alternative to BONDING is the *Multilink Point-to-Point Protocol (MPPP)*, which aggregates two or more *B* channels and runs PPP across these multiple *B* channels.

PRI. As noted earlier, the Primary Rate Interface (also know as *primary access*) has two standard configurations. The first is based on the North American DS-1 (1.544 Mbps) format and the second is based on the European E-1 (2.048 Mbps) format (see Chapter 7). PRI service is essentially the same as BRI except PRI has 23 (or 30) *B* channels instead of two, and PRI's *D* channel operates at 64 kbps instead of 16 kbps. (See Figure 11-5.)

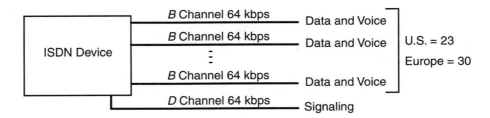

Figure 11-5. ISDN's Primary Rate Interface (PRI) is packaged in two forms. The first is a 23*B* + *D* configuration, which is based on the North American DS-1 format and rated at 1.544 Mbps. The second is a 30*B* + *D* configuration, which is based on the European E-1 format and rated at 2.048 Mbps.

Unlike BRI, which is appropriate for the home or small office, PRI is more appropriate for organizations that have to provide telecommunication services to a large number of sites. For example, large corporations with various satellite offices or remote sites, corporations with PBXs, and Internet Service Providers are more likely to subscribe to PRI service than BRI. With PRI, it is possible to have up to 23 (or 30) separate, independent, simultaneous ISDN connections.

9. A friend of mine has an ISDN connection and said that his phone numbers are called SPIDs. Is this true?

Not really. The telephone numbers assigned to ISDN *B* channels have associated with them something called *Service Profile Identification (SPID)* numbers. SPIDs are provided by the telcos and are usually defined by adding a prefix or suffix, or both, (it depends on the telco's switch) to an assigned telephone number. For example, assume the number assigned to a *B* channel is 4075551469. If the telco uses a prefix of 05 then the SPID is 054075551469. SPIDs are used to identify the various processes of an ISDN device. By assigning a SPID to a device, the telco's ISDN switch can identify the processes associated with each device. This prevents contention among the processes. Thus, each device connected to an ISDN line must be assigned a unique SPID. Normally, if only one ISDN device is connected, a SPID is not needed. However, if more than one ISDN device is connected, then SPIDs are required. Some ISDN equipment manufacturers support an auto-SPID function that acquires the telco's assigned SPID to a particular connection and configure the end equipment automatically. (*Note:* SPIDs are used only in North America.)

10. I have also seen the term "line set" used with ISDN. What is this?

The term *line set* is used by the National ISDN Users' Forum (NIUF), which is an organization that provides users with a voice in the implementation of ISDN applications. (See http://www.ocn.com/ocn/niuf/niuf_top.html.) Line Set describes two specific characteristics of ISDN service: The number of multiplexed *B* and *D* channels, and the type of service supported. For example, Line Set 1 specifies a *D* configuration that supports packet switched data transmissions on a single *D* channel. Line Set 4 specifies a 1*B* configuration that supports alternate voice and data transmissions on a single *B* channel. Line Set 27 specifies a 2*B* + *D* configuration that supports alternate voice and data on two *B* channels and packet switched data transmissions on the *D* channel. Associated with each line set is a *feature set*, which identifies specific ISDN features that can be ordered as part of the service. Feature set examples include Call Forwarding and Calling Number Identification (i.e., Caller ID). Additional information about line and feature sets can be acquired via http://www.ocn.com/ocn/niuf/capable/attach1.txt.

11. Wait a minute here. I didn't know that ISDN had features like Call Forwarding and Caller ID. I thought people got an ISDN connection for the Internet. What other features does ISDN offer?

This is a common misconception. Remember, ISDN is an integrated services network. In addition to fast Internet connections, ISDN supports various telephone-related services including Call Forwarding, Calling Number Identification (CNI), Call Transfer, Call Waiting, and Call Hold. These services are similar to their non-ISDN counterparts that are offered through the telcos. There is one exception, though. With Call Waiting, when a second call comes in, you do not get interrupted as is the case with non-ISDN Call Waiting. This is because the *D* channel handles all the call control information, keeping it separate from the *B* channels.

ISDN also supports several teleservices including capability for 64 kbps Group IV fax, teletex, and videotext. *Teletext* and *videotex* are electronic information utilities that use computers or standard television sets equipped with adapters to display information. Teletext is a one-way communication system; videotext is a two-way (i.e., interactive) system. Teletext broadcasts data as part of a television signal; videotext uses cable television or telephone lines to transmit data. Typical applications available from these services include information retrieval (news weather, sports access to medical databases), electronic transactions (airline reservations, electronic funds transfer, shop-at-home services), interpersonal messaging (e-mail), computing, and telemonitoring (remote sensing, telemetry services). Clearly, many of these applications are now available via the Internet's World Wide Web. However, teletext and videotext services have been available in countries such as France, Canada, and Great Britain since the early 1980s. Furthermore, trials of these two services were conducted in the United States during the 1983-84 time period. Examples include Videotron by Knight-Ridder Newspapers in Southeast Florida, Keyfax by Keycom Electronic Publishing in Chicago, and Gateway, by Times Mirror Videotex Services in Southern California in 1984.

12. Is an ISDN phone similar to a regular phone? For example, can I use one to call someone who doesn't have an ISDN phone or ISDN connection?

Yes. You can use your ISDN phone to call someone whose phone service is provided by the analog-based Plain Old Telephone System (POTS). The reverse is also true. However, you will not be able to achieve high-quality connect sessions because only one part of the connection is digital; the other is analog. As such, there will not be any improvement in line performance.

As for any differences in telephones, ISDN telephone sets have many more built-in functions and capabilities than conventional analog phones. Aside from that, both types of phones function similarly, with one exception. The analog-based POTS provides power to its telephones. (This is why the telephone system is still able to operate during power outages.) This is not the case with ISDN—ISDN does not provide power to its telephones (or to any ISDN terminal equipment). Thus, unless the ISDN TE is protected by an uninterruptable power supply (UPS) or equivalent, a power outage will also bring down your telephone connection.

13. Did the Internet and the World Wide Web make ISDN obsolete?

In some ways, yes. In other ways, no. For example, the services and capabilities available via the Internet today make ISDN less attractive. There is no need to subscribe to ISDN simply to have information retrieval, electronic transaction, or interpersonal messaging capabilities. All of these applications, and more, are available via the web. Even ISDN's telephone-related services are now available for analog telephones via the telcos. However, given the restrictions of the analog modem service, ISDN dialup Internet connections have become very popular. Many people are subscribing to ISDN, not for its applications, but because it provides a faster gateway to the Internet. For example, an ISDN BRI service, with BONDING, provides 128 kbps connection. With compression, this connection increases to over 500 kbps. Compared to a 56 kbps modem, which provides a data transmission rate of over 200 kbps with compression, an ISDN connection wins out.

14. Speaking of the Internet, what does a typical dialup ISDN Internet connection look like?

A dialup ISDN Internet connection requires ISDN service for both the user and the Internet Service Provider. This is usually BRI for the home and PRI for the ISP. At home, an ISDN terminal adapter is needed for any computer that does not have a built-in ISDN port. At the ISP side, an ISDN communications server (or equivalent) is needed to support remote ISDN connections. The ISP link to the Internet is generally a T1 circuit, inverse multiplexed T1 circuits, or T3 or fractional T3 circuits. This is illustrated in Figure 11-6. The Point-to-Point Protocol (PPP) is the primary protocol used for data transmission. Furthermore, if the end user equipment supports Multilink PPP (MP), both B channels can be combined into a single 128 kbps channel.

15. This is the second time you mentioned Multilink PPP. Please explain what this is.

Multilink PPP (MP) is an IP protocol that combines multiple physical links (i.e., telephone lines) into a single, high capacity channel. The development of this protocol was precipitated by the desire to aggregate multiple ISDN B channels. Unlike BONDING, which is implemented in hardware, MP is achieved via software. MP is also applicable to analog dialup connections. For example, if each of three separate phone lines is connected to 33.6 kbps modems, then MP can aggregate these lines into a single 100.8 kbps channel. Both ISDN and analog MP solutions are supported by various Internet service providers.

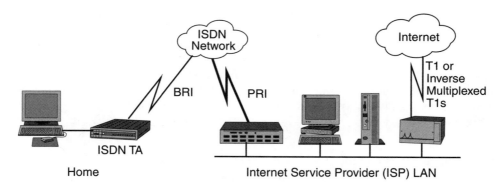

Figure 11-6. A typical home-based ISDN Internet connection consists of a BRI connection from the home to the telco's ISDN network, and a PRI connection between the ISP and the telco's ISDN network. The entire connection, from home to ISP is completely digital. Home-based ISDN Internet connections are an alternative to conventional analog dialup connections using 28.8 kbps or 56 kbps modems.

Thus, if your ISP offers MP dialup service, then you too can achieve higher capacity connections to the Internet. For more information about MP, see RFC 1990. (*Note:* Although PPP is normally associated with IP, it nevertheless is a general purpose link layer protocol that supports several upper layer protocols.)

16. While we are on the subject of protocols, on what protocols is ISDN based?

ISDN relies on many different protocols, all of which conform to the layers of the OSI model. These protocols are defined in the ISDN I-series (see Table 11-1)—specifically the I.400 series—and are applicable to the first three layers of the OSI model. At the physical layer, the physical interfaces for both BRI and PRI are specified in I.430 and I.431. These specifications are applicable to *B, D,* and *H* channels. At the data link layer, the *D* channel is based on the ITU-T standard, Q.921, known as the *Link Access Protocol-D channel (LAP-D)*. The *B* and *H* channels rely on frame relay protocols (see Chapter 12) for circuit switched connections and an X.25 protocol called *Link Access Protocol- Balanced (LAP-B)* for packet switched connections. At the network layer, the *D* channel relies on the ITU-T standard, Q.931, for call control, and X.25 protocols for packet data. The *B* and *H* channels also use X.25 protocols for packet switched connections. No layer 3 protocols are necessary for circuit switched connections. A summary is given in Table 11-2.

17. Why does the *D* channel use different protocols at layers 2 and 3 than *B* and *H* channels?

As noted earlier, the *D* channel is a multipurpose channel. It is used for call-setup and call tear-down when the *B* channel is used to transmit circuit switched user data. If no signaling or control information is needed—for example, a dedicated leased line connection is used or the *B* channel is transmitting packet switched user data—then the *D* channel can

Table 11-2. Summary of ISDN Protocols

OSI Layer	D Channel			B and H Channels	
	Call-control	**Packet Data**	**Telemetry**	**Circuit-switched**	**Packet-switched**
3	ITU-T Q.931 / I.451	X.25 Protocols	——	N/A	X.25 Protocols
2	ITU-T Q.921 (LAP-D) / I.441			Frame Relay Protocols	LAP-B
1	ISDN I-series: I.430 (BRI) and I.431 (PRI)			ISDN I-series: I.430 (BRI) and I.431 (PRI)	

(Adapted from Stallings, 1997.)

be used to transmit packet switched user data as well. Finally, the *D* channel can be used to transmit information from telemetry services. These applications require different protocols at the data link and network layers than the *D* and *H* channels, which simply transmit circuit or packet switched data.

18. Could you expand on LAP-D? I've seen this before and I am interested in it.

Sure. The frame format for the Link Access Protocol for *D* channel is shown in Figure 11-7. Note that the frame carries encapsulated layer 3 data (Information field). Following is a brief explanation of the various fields:

Flag—Signals the beginning or ending of the frame

Address—Provides addressing information. The service access point identifier (SAPI) identifies where the layer 2 protocol provides service to layer 3. Specific addresses identify specific services. For example SAPI = 16 is for X.25 packet data transmissions. The command/response (C/R) bit specifies whether the frame is a command or response. The extended address (EA) bits specify the beginning and ending of the address field. If EA is 0, then another byte of address information follows. An EA of 1 implies that the current byte is the last byte of the address. Thus, given a two-byte address, EA = 0 in the higher-order byte and EA = 1 in the lower-order byte. The terminal endpoint identifier (TEI) represents the specific address or ID assigned to each ISDN terminal equipment connected to an ISDN network via an S/T interface.

Control—Provides layer 2 control information (e.g., specifies the type of frame being transmitted, maintains frame sequence numbers).

Information—Provides layer 3 protocol information and user data. The protocol discriminator (PD) identifies the specific layer 3 protocol. The length (L) byte specifies the length of the CRV field, which is either one or two bytes. The call reference value (CRV) is the number assigned to each call. Once a call is completed, this number can be reassigned to a new call. Message type (MT) identifies specific messages related to circuit-switched connections. For example, during call-setup, the message, CONNECT, indicates that the receiving terminal equipment end node has accepted a call by the initiating TE. When a call has been completed, the message, RELEASE COMPLETE, is sent to indicate that the channel has been torn down (call tear-down). The mandatory and optional information elements (MOIE) field carries additional information specific to the message type being transmitted.

CRC—Provides for data integrity (error control) via CRC checksums (see Chapter 5).

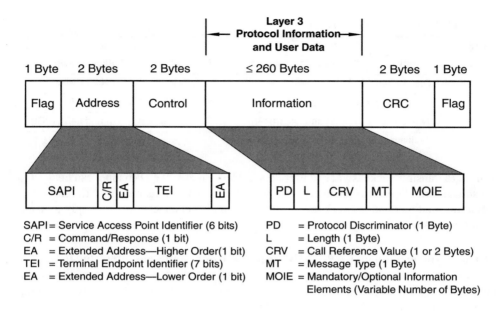

SAPI = Service Access Point Identifier (6 bits)   PD   = Protocol Discriminator (1 Byte)
C/R = Command/Response (1 bit)   L   = Length (1 Byte)
EA   = Extended Address—Higher Order(1 bit)   CRV = Call Reference Value (1 or 2 Bytes)
TEI = Terminal Endpoint Identifier (7 bits)   MT   = Message Type (1 Byte)
EA   = Extended Address—Lower Order (1 bit)   MOIE = Mandatory/Optional Information
                                                               Elements (Variable Number of Bytes)

Figure 11-7. Frame format of ISDN's Link Access Protocol-D channel (LAP-D). Note that the information field contains encapsulated layer 3 data.

19. Are there any current ISDN initiatives that I should be aware of?

Yes. Two key ones are *Always On/Dynamic ISDN (AO/DI)* and *Broadband ISDN (B-ISDN)*. We will discuss these separately.

AO/DI. Always On/Dynamic ISDN is an initiative from the Vendor's ISDN Association (VIA). The concept of AO/DI is to use a portion of the D channel, which is always active and constantly connected to the provider's switch, to transmit user packet data. Given that most ISDN implementations assess a charge whenever a B channel is active—usually so much per minute for every minute the link is up—keeping a channel up can be quite expensive. For example, a five-cent per minute charge translates to $3 per hour, which is $72 per day. With AO/DI, transmitting user data across the D channel is free.

AO/DI uses 9600 bps of the D channel's 16 kbps capacity; the remaining bandwidth (6400 bps) is used for control and signaling information. If user data transmission rates exceed the 9600 bps reserved for AO/DI, then one of the B channels is automatically activated (i.e., a circuit-switched connection is established) to carry the load, and the D channel assumes its normal role of providing control and signaling information. If additional capacity is required, then Multilink PPP is used to automatically activate and combine the second B channel with the first to get an aggregate bandwidth of 128 kbps. Once bandwidth requirements drop to the point where neither B channel is needed, then the channels automatically become inactive and the D channel resumes its low-capacity packet data transmission function. Thus, you can receive data without paying for any B channel usage until one of the B channels becomes active.

The primary application of AO/DI is transmitting IP packets. This offers several advantages to end users. For example, AO/DI provides users with a free, permanent connection to the Internet. As long as the IP packet transmissions can be carried satisfactorily via a 9600 bps link, then the connection is free. (*Note:* The telcos might assess a nominal monthly charge for AO/DI service, though, since it will be considered part of ISDN's feature set.) Examples of such transmissions include e-mail, small text files, stock quotes, and sports and headline news information. Furthermore, since the connection is permanent, users do not have to manually make a connection to the Internet every time they want to check for e-mail or stock quotes. AO/DI is also appealing to telcos because it reduces the number of B channels they have to nail up.

In short, AO/DI represents a technology that satisfies users and telcos. Users, at best, get free service, and at worst, reduce the cost of their service. Telcos, on the other hand, still get to provide the service, but their switches become less saturated because the amount of B channel transmissions is reduced. AO/DI is a win-win solution for everyone.

B-ISDN. Broadband ISDN is an extension of ISDN, which is sometimes called Narrowband ISDN (N-ISDN). B-ISDN provides full-duplex data transmission at OC-12 rates (622.08 Mbps) and is designed for delivery of two primary types of services: interactive services (e.g., videoconferencing and video surveillance), and distribution services (e.g., cable TV and high definition TV). B-ISDN is also the basis for ATM (see Chapter 14).

20. I am interested in AO/DI. Is this something my ISP offers?

We can't say. You need to ask your ISP representative. AO/DI was deployed in early 1998, and AO/DI products are available from major Internet equipment manufacturers like Ascend, Bay Networks, and Cisco. Implementing AO/DI requires that both your telco and ISP support it. Your ISP also must have a connection to the telco's X.25 network because D channel packet data transmissions are carried via the telco's X.25 network. (See Table 11-2.) Packets are first transmitted from the end user to the telco via the *D* channel where they are placed on the telco's X.25 network and transmitted to the ISP. The ISP then transmits these packets to their destination via the Internet. Similarly, packets arriving from the Internet are transmitted to the telco via the ISP's X.25 network connection. From there, the telco transmits the packets to the end user across the *D* channel. (See Figure 11-8.)

21. One last question. Besides serving as an alternative to traditional Internet dialup connections, what other uses does ISDN have?

ISDN is ideal for the small office/home office (SOHO). With an NT1 module, you can connect a fax machine, a computer, and your telephone directly to an ISDN network via a single connection. Furthermore, if two *B* channels are inadequate, ISDN's flexible packaging scheme enables you to purchase additional *B* channels. ISDN also provides LAN-to-LAN connectivity, enabling an organization's remote LANs to be connected to each other or to its corporate LAN. (See Figure 11-9.) This implementation of ISDN is a cost-effective solution if remote sites do not have to be in continuous communication with one another. If this is not the situation, then frame relay is a better alternative because ISDN phone charges can become exorbitant. Even in situations where frame relay is used for

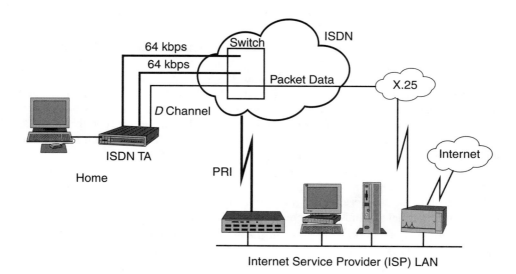

Figure 11-8. Always On/Dynamic ISDN (AO/DI) is ideal for Internet applications. Implementing AO/DI at home requires AO/DI support from both the telco and ISP. Furthermore, the ISP must have a connection to the telco's X.25 network because this is the network that handles *D* channel packet data transmissions.

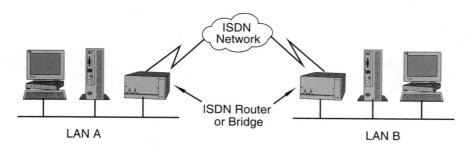

Figure 11-9. ISDN can be used for LAN-to-LAN connectivity. To reduce call charges, a dial-on-demand feature available in most ISDN routers and bridges will automatically call the telco's ISDN switch only when data need to be transmitted. When no traffic is seen on the port, the router or bridge will then hang up the call. This setup is exactly the same that is used for connecting a LAN to the Internet. The only difference is one of the LANs would have a link to the Internet as shown in Figure 11-6.

LAN-to-LAN communication, though, ISDN still can play a role. ISDN has proven to be an effective backup strategy to frame relay (see Chapter 12). ISDN can also be integrated with frame relay using fallback switches. If the frame relay network fails, the ISDN network automatically takes over. Although the transmission rate is less than what is available via frame relay, it nevertheless keeps the data flowing. Finally, ISDN provides affordable desktop-to-desktop videoconferencing. So you see, there are several niche applications that can be filled quite nicely by ISDN.

End-of-Chapter Commentary

In this chapter, we presented an overview of ISDN. Many of the concepts discussed can be found in other chapters throughout this book. For example, a discussion of circuit- and packet-switching, as well as information about standards organizations, are given in Chapter 1. The concepts of bandwidth and channel capacity are discussed in Chapters 2 and 4. Chapter 3 contains information about the Internet, and issues related to the data link layer are discussed in Chapter 5. ISDN also serves as the basis for other WAN technologies and services, including frame relay, which is the subject of the next chapter (Chapter 12), SMDS (see Chapter 13), and ATM (see Chapter 14). Finally, Chapter 15 presents information about home networking and examines various networking strategies (e.g., 56K modems, cable modems) to ISDN.

Chapter 12

Frame Relay

Frame relay is a WAN packet-switching protocol that provides LAN-to-LAN connectivity. It relies on higher-level protocols to do error correction and to request retransmissions if packets are lost or discarded. Frame relay has two strong features: It is economical and efficient. It also provides a single point of network access for multiple LAN-to-LAN connections, which is not true in networks using private links. This feature offers considerable savings on local loop charges. Frame relay also can be implemented using existing bridges or routers. In this chapter we examine the various concepts related to frame relay from both conceptual and technical perspectives. The main topics we address include:

- History of Frame Relay (Questions 1–3)
- Basic Concepts—PVCs and CIRs (Questions 4–16)
- PVCs vs. SVCs (Questions 17–20)
- Technical Overview and Frame Relay Frames (Questions 18–28)
- Voice Over Frame Relay (Question 29)
- Frame Relay vs. ATM and SMDS (Question 30)
- AT&T's Frame Relay Network Crash (Question 31)

1. What is frame relay?

Frame relay, which was originally part of the ISDN standard, is a public WAN packet-switching protocol that provides LAN-to-LAN connectivity. Its name implies what it does, namely, relays frames across a network between two sites.

2. What do you mean it was originally part of the ISDN standard?

As we noted in Chapter 11, ISDN was developed in the 1970s to eventually replace the public switched telephone network (PSTN). As part of its development, ISDN was designed to provide both voice and data service. Although ISDN was considered a significant improvement to the PSTN, it was still an evolution of the PSTN and hence was circuit-switched. This did not bode well for providing data applications efficiently. If data applications were going to be supported in an efficient manner, then a packet-switching component needed to be included with the ISDN standard. (See Chapter 1 for additional information about circuit- and packet-switching.) The only packet-switching technology available at the time was X.25. This technology, however, did not support the ISDN model of keeping user data separate from control data. Consequently, frame relay was developed specifically as a packet-switching technology component of ISDN for data applications. (*Note:* X.25 is not discussed in this book.)

3. So what happened? How did frame relay separate itself from ISDN?

Prior to frame relay's development, LANs were primarily interconnected by dedicated (i.e., private) leased lines using point-to-point protocols or X.25. This design was acceptable if only one or two LANs required interconnectivity. However, as internetworking became more prevalent, multiport routers were needed to provide multi-LAN connectivity, and additional dedicated leased lines had to be installed. (See Figure 12-1(a).) LAN-to-LAN connectivity became a more expensive endeavor with the addition of each dedicated circuit. These costs were further escalated, and the network design became more complex, when a partially- or fully-meshed network design was needed. (See Figures 12-1(b) and 12-1(c).) (*Note:* In a fully-connected network, the number of links is always one less than the number of interconnected nodes or LANs. Thus, if five LANs are fully interconnected, then each LAN requires four links.)

Since frame relay's role in ISDN was to provide connectivity between routers, ISDN developers realized that traditional LAN-to-LAN connectivity costs could be reduced substantially if frame relay is used in place of dedicated leased lines. What frame relay provides is a single connection into a public network instead of multiple interconnections. (See Figure 12-2.) This reduces both the cost and complexity of the network, especially in a fully-meshed design. For example, in the frame relay configuration shown in Figure 12-3, each LAN only needs one link into the cloud for full interconnectivity among the five LANs. In a comparable, fully-meshed private leased line network, each LAN would require four links. (See Figure 12-1(c).) Furthermore, unlike traditional private leased line service, frame relay's circuit costs are not distance-based and the circuits themselves do not necessarily have to be permanent. This led to frame relay being offered and further developed as a separate protocol.

4. At the end of your answer you stated, "the circuits themselves do not necessarily have to be permanent." What do you mean by this?

In a black and white networking world, there are only two types of telecommunications links—private and virtual. Private links (also commonly referred to as standard leased lines) provide dedicated connectivity between two sites. Virtual links, on the other hand, are shared among several sites. Frame relay is a connection-oriented protocol that employs virtual links. (See Chapter 2 for additional information about virtual circuits.) As a connection-oriented protocol, frame relay must first establish a connection before two nodes can communicate. Instead of establishing and maintaining a permanent, dedicated link between a source and destination, frame relay relies on Permanent Virtual Circuits (PVCs) to interconnect two sites. Thus, PVCs establish a logical connection between two sites instead of a physical one. This is what distinguishes a frame relay network from one that

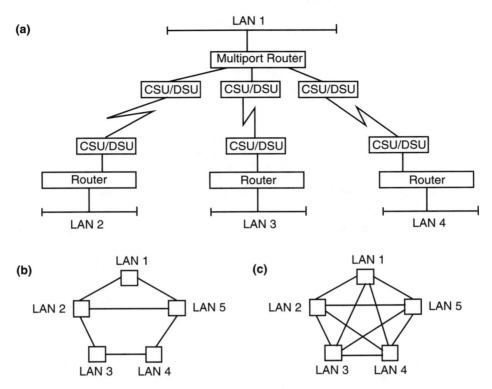

Figure 12-1. In a standard private line network, at least one circuit is required for LAN-to-LAN connectivity. Several topologies are possible including (a) a star configuration, (b) a partially-meshed configuration, and (c) a fully-meshed configuration. Note that the star configuration is the least expensive because only one LAN requires a multiport router and multiple circuits. All other LANs require a single-port router and one circuit. This configuration is also the least reliable because it has a single source of failure. An improvement in reliability calls for partially-meshed or fully-meshed designs. These topologies significantly increase the cost and complexity of the overall network design, though, because more than one LAN requires multiport routers and multiple circuits for LAN interconnectivity. (Adapted from Fitzgerald & Kraft, 1993.)

uses standard leased lines. Through the use of virtual circuits, data from multiple sites can be transmitted over the same link concurrently. (*Note:* Frame relay also supports Switched Virtual Circuits or SVCs. These circuits are discussed later in the chapter.)

5. I'm confused. How is a PVC different from a private leased line? Aren't you still using a permanent circuit with a PVC?

Sort of. PVCs do indeed have a predetermined link between a source and destination just as private leased lines. In fact, PVCs appear as private circuits because frame relay, as a connection-oriented protocol, must first establish circuits (i.e., "nail them up") between end nodes prior to data communications. The difference is PVCs are virtual circuits, not

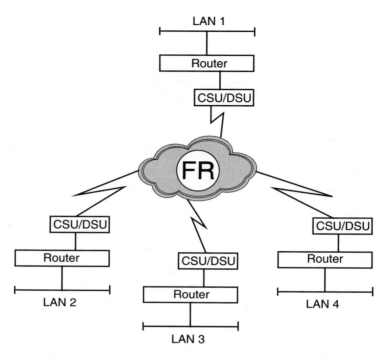

Figure 12-2. In a frame relay network, a single access into a frame relay "cloud" is all that is required. This simplifies the network design and makes it a less expensive endeavor.

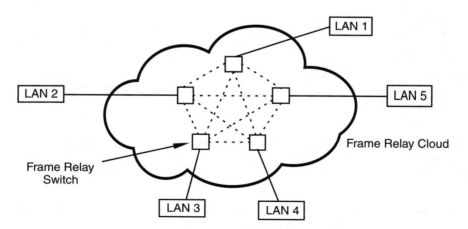

Figure 12-3. Frame relay provides a single connection into a public network instead of multiple connections. This translates into considerable savings in connectivity cost as well as complexity in network design, maintenance, and analysis.

dedicated ones. This means that the bandwidth is shared among multiple sites instead of being dedicated between two sites. Thus, PVCs provide nondedicated connections through a shared medium. This is done by multiplexing a physical link so that it can be shared by multiple data transmissions. (See Chapter 2.)

6. Can you give me an example?

Sure. When you subscribe to frame relay service from your telecommunications carrier, a PVC is assigned between your LAN and all of your organization's other LANs that require interconnectivity. For example, in the network shown in Figure 12-4(a), four PVCs are used to provide connectivity respectively from LANs 2, 3, 4, and 5 to LAN 1. These PVCs are shown as one-way arrows, which imply that the PVCs are simplex links (i.e., data transmissions are unidirectional). Note that the links that connect a LAN to the frame relay network are not PVCs. Only the links within the cloud are PVCs. If two-way connectivity is needed, then duplex PVCs are used. A fully-meshed design is also possible. This is shown in Figure 12-4(b). A fully-meshed design involving five LANs is accomplished using either 10 duplex PVCs or 20 simplex PVCs. (*Note:* The use of duplex or simplex PVCs for meshed designs is a function of the local exchange carrier, LEC, providing the frame relay service.) Regardless of the assignment, though (simplex or duplex), a fully-meshed design still only requires a single network connection from each LAN.

7. Are simple and fully-meshed designs the only two choices one has in configuring a frame relay network?

No. You can also have a partially-meshed design in which some nodes are fully-interconnected and others are not. Configuration decisions are based on customer needs and network traffic requirements.

8. I can see the advantage frame relay has over private links, but aren't you still paying for all that bandwidth to interconnect the LANs?

Yes, but the cost is substantially less because PVCs have associated with them a *committed information rate* (CIR). A CIR is the amount of throughput a frame relay provider guarantees to support under normal network loads. A CIR, which can range from 16 kbps to T3 (44.8 Mbps), is assigned to a PVC as part of network configuration. It is the minimum guaranteed throughput of a PVC.

9. Does a CIR represent a fixed amount of bandwidth?

No. Instead of committing a fixed amount of bandwidth, a frame relay provider calculates the average amount of traffic that has been transmitted across a PVC over a specified period of time (e.g., one second). Using this information, the provider then determines the average amount of bandwidth that has been used. This serves as the basis of the CIR on the provider's part. If a PVC's assigned CIR (which, again, was set when the network was first configured) is greater than or equal to this average, then data transmissions are guaranteed. If the assigned CIR is less than this average, (i.e., the "pipe" is not big enough), then data transmissions are not guaranteed. Thus, the assignment of a CIR to a PVC is extremely

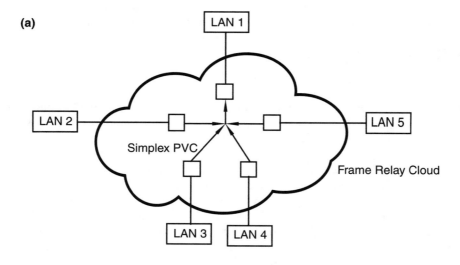

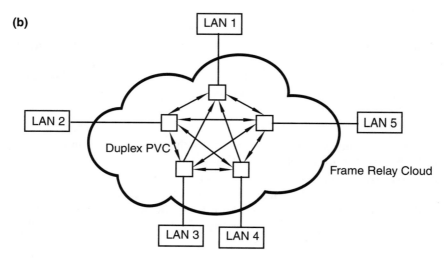

Figure 12-4. A frame relay network consisting of five LANs requires at least four simplex PVCs for LAN interconnectivity. In (a), simplex PVCs are used to connect LANS 2, 3, 4, and 5 to LAN 1. In this illustration, LANS 2, 3, 4, and 5 might be remote sites and LAN 1 might be corporate headquarters. In (b), a fully-meshed design using duplex PVCs is shown. Here, every LAN can communicate with every other LAN using only a single connection to the frame relay network. (*Note:* A fully-meshed design requires $\frac{n(n-1)}{2}$ full-duplex PVCs, where n is the total number of LANs to interconnect.) (Adapted from Fitzgerald, 1993.)

critical to both network cost and performance. If a PVC's CIR is too little, then when the network becomes congested, frames may be dropped. On the other hand, if the CIR is too high, then you are paying for excessive bandwidth. This is analogous to the way banks calculate the monthly maintenance fee of a checking account. If the monthly average of the funds in the account is less than a prescribed minimum, then a fee is assessed. If, however, the monthly average grossly exceeds the minimum average, then you probably have too much money in the account. The penalty for having too much money in a checking account is usually lost interest, since many checking accounts pay no or little interest.

10. Is the CIR of a duplex PVC the same in both directions?

Not necessarily. A CIR can be assigned to a PVC either symmetrically or asymmetrically. A symmetric CIR guarantees the same amount of bandwidth in each direction of a duplex PVC; an asymmetric CIR permits different bandwidth guarantees to be committed in each direction. This flexibility in CIR assignments is one of frame relay's greatest features. The support of asymmetric PVCs makes frame relay an ideal service for client-server applications. For example, Internet or intranet based web servers could be configured to have inbound CIRs two or three times (or more) greater than their outbound CIRs. This accommodation of different data transmission rates for inbound and outbound traffic can result in considerable savings for an organization. (See Figure 12-5.)

11. What happens if a data transmission exceeds the CIR?

Data transmissions that exceed the CIR will be transmitted by the frame relay service provider on a "best effort" basis. What this means is the service provider will attempt to deliver the data but will not guarantee delivery. At best, data frames that require more bandwidth for delivery than what is called for by the CIR will be transmitted without any problem. At worst, the frames will be discarded and will have to be retransmitted.

12. Could you expand on this concept of transmitting frames that require more bandwidth than what the CIR provides?

Certainly. When a data transmission exceeds the CIR, it is referred to as a *burst*. Two types of bursts are defined in frame relay. The first, called the *committed burst* (B_c), is the maximum amount of data the provider guarantees to deliver within a specified time period, T. Note that $CIR = B_c/T$. Given that most providers use a one-second time interval to calculate the average amount of bandwidth utilization, CIR is usually equal to B_c. The difference between these two parameters is their units. CIR is measured in bps; B_c is measured in bits. The second type of burst, called the *excessive burst* (B_e), is the maximum amount of *uncommitted* data a provider will attempt to deliver within a specified time period. In other words, a provider will guarantee a committed burst of B_c bits and will attempt to deliver (but not guarantee) a maximum of $B_c + B_e$ bits. For example, a PVC assigned a 128 kbps CIR might have associated with it an excessive burst rate of 64 kbps. This means that the provider will attempt to support data transmissions requiring a capacity of up to 192 kbps. (See Figure 12-6.)

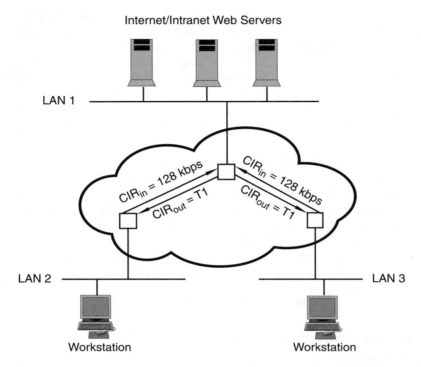

Internet/Intranet Web Servers

LAN 1

CIR$_{in}$ = 128 kbps

CIR$_{out}$ = T1

CIR$_{in}$ = 128 kbps

CIR$_{out}$ = T1

LAN 2

LAN 3

Workstation

Workstation

Figure 12-5. A frame relay network can be configured with asymmetric PVCs to accommodate different traffic flows. In this figure, LAN 1 consists of a configuration of web servers and LANs 2 and 3 consist of workstations that access these servers. Client web requests usually consist of small URLs, but web server responses are usually large graphic files. Thus, LAN 1's outbound link is configured to have greater bandwidth than its inbound links. (Adapted from Wu, 1997.)

13. I understand the concepts of B_c and B_e. What I don't understand is how you can burst to a higher rate than the CIR. Isn't the CIR the maximum link capacity?

Good question, and we can understand your confusion. We forgot to mention one other parameter—*port speed*. In addition to defining logical connections (PVCs) and bandwidth requirements (CIRs), you must also determine the appropriate port speed of the physical link that connects your LAN to your provider's frame relay network. This link, called the *port connection* or *access line*, is the local loop connection between your LAN's frame relay end node (usually a router) and the provider's frame relay switch. At the customer's site, the access line is connected to the end node's interface and is called the User-to-Network interface (UNI). Depending on the carrier's policy, port speeds can be less than, equal to, or greater than the sum of the CIRs for a particular port. For example, in Figure 12-7, LAN 1 consists of Internet/Intranet web servers, which must serve up web pages to the clients on LANs 2 and 3. Note that the sum of LAN 1's originating CIRs is 256 kbps + 256 kbps = 512 kbps. Further note that LAN 1's port speed is T1, which is more than twice the capacity of the sum of its CIRs. LAN 2, however, demonstrates a con-

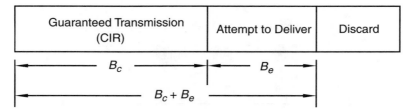

Figure 12-6. Data frames that fall within an agreed-upon committed information rate (CIR) are guaranteed transmission. This is called the *committed burst (B_c)*, and represents the maximum amount of data the frame relay service provider guarantees to deliver within a specified time. Under normal conditions, the provider will also attempt to deliver (but not guarantee) an additional amount of data beyond the CIR. This extra amount is called the *excessive burst (B_e)*. Thus, a provider will guarantee delivery of B_c bits, but will attempt to deliver a maximum of $B_c + B_e$ bits. Anything greater than this sum will be discarded.

dition known as *oversubscription*. Its port speed (128 kbps) is less than its aggregate CIRs (192 kbps). LAN 2 has oversubscribed its connection—the capacity of its connection into the frame relay network is less than the total bandwidth guaranteed by the provider. Finally, LAN 3's port speed is equal to the aggregate of its originating CIRs.

Frame relay service providers will attempt to deliver frames that exceed a CIR if two conditions are met. First, the data bursts cannot be greater than the port speed, and second, the provider must have sufficient bandwidth available within its own network to accommodate the burst. Burst rates are only supported by a carrier for a limited time period (e.g., 2 seconds). The actual time period in which burst rates are supported varies among carriers. Thus, given the configuration of Figure 12-7, the provider will attempt to support data transmissions from LAN 1 up to T1 capacity.

In a private leased line network, the issues of port speed and CIR are irrelevant—if a T1 line is provisioned, the port speed is 1.544 Mbps and it is a fixed rate. With frame relay, though, we now have considerably more flexibility in configuring the bandwidth requirements of our LAN-to-LAN connections. The trade-off for this flexibility is more detailed knowledge and understanding of the traffic patterns and flows of these connections. Given the typical bursty nature of LAN traffic, it is usually prudent to set the CIR below the port speed to accommodate for data bursts. One rule of thumb is to ensure that the total CIR of a connection does not exceed 70% of the port speed. Thus, if the total CIR is 256 kbps, then the port speed should be no less than 384 kbps. It is also important to note that some providers place a restriction on the maximum burst rate permitted. The bottom line is to discuss these issues with your provider.

14. I am fascinated by the concept of oversubscription. How can a provider guarantee a certain amount of bandwidth but provision a link between a LAN and the frame relay network that contains less capacity than what is guaranteed?

It has to do with multiplexing and buffers. Frame relay uses statistical multiplexing (see Chapter 4) for channel allocation, and providers' frame relay switches have large

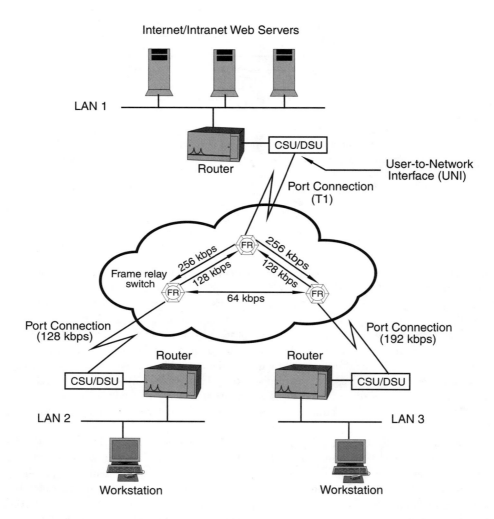

Figure 12-7. In a frame relay network, the port connection is the local loop circuit that connects a LAN's frame relay node (usually a router) to the service provider's switch. The capacity of this connection, called the *port speed*, can be less than, equal to, or greater than the sum of the CIRs. In this illustration, LAN 1's port speed is 1.544 Mbps, which is more than twice as great as the sum of its originating CIRs. Thus, LAN 1 can support data bursts of up to T1 speeds. In LAN 2, however, the sum of the originating CIRs (192 kbps) exceeds the port speed (128 kbps). This is a situation known as *oversubscription*. LAN 2 has oversubscribed its service since its aggregate guaranteed bandwidth is greater that its port speed. LAN 3's port speed is equal to the sum of its originating CIRs. (Adapted from Wu, 1997.)

buffers. Given a sufficiently large buffer size, coupled with a low probability that not every user will need the channel at the same time, it is possible for a provider to deliver data frames successfully to a LAN that has oversubscribed its service. Not all frame relay providers permit oversubscription though. Some mandate that the port speed be at least equal to the aggregate CIRs.

15. Given the concept of oversubscription, what's to stop a customer from establishing a CIR of zero and effectively steal bandwidth from the provider?

Nothing. Some service providers offer a CIR of zero and even encourage customers to subscribe to this service to get an accurate assessment of bandwidth needs. In some cases, this might be a little more expensive than establishing nonzero CIRs, but it also can be beneficial if traffic rates between sites are unknown. After a few months, specific traffic usage patterns will emerge and appropriate CIRs and ports speeds can then be set.

Be careful though. Remember that a CIR is *contractual* bandwidth. It represents the maximum data transmission rate a service provider guarantees to provide. A CIR of zero implies that every date frame transmitted on the network is considered a burst and hence delivery is not guaranteed. If the provider has surplus bandwidth (e.g., unused capacity from customers who are paying for a certain CIR but are not using all of it) available within its network, then you might not experience any network transmission problems with a CIR of zero. However, as this surplus diminishes, expect to see pronounced degradation in the performance of your LAN-to-LAN connections.

16. What happens if you need to increase or decrease the CIR of a PVC?

You contact your provider and request the change. Because the circuits are virtual, no new circuits need to be provisioned; only the PVC's assigned CIR needs to be changed in a database.

17. What other concepts or issues do I need to know about frame relay besides PVCs and CIRs?

There are several, including switched virtual circuits (SVCs), voice over frame relay, video over frame relay, ATM vs. frame relay, and the technical aspects of frame relay.

18. Let's start with SVCs. What are they and how are they different than PVCs?

Switched Virtual Circuits are sort of like cousins of Permanent Virtual Circuits—they share certain similarities (e.g., they are both virtual circuits), but have enough dissimilarities to make them different. As we discussed earlier, frame relay is a connection-oriented protocol and hence a circuit must first be established (i.e., "nailed up") between end nodes prior to data communications. With PVCs, two sites are permanently interconnected with a circuit similar to the way two sites are interconnected using private leased lines. The difference is PVCs are shared by other subscribers within a provider's frame relay network. With SVCs, however, circuits between source and destination nodes are established on the fly and then removed after data communications have ended. This makes SVCs logical *dynamic* connections instead of logical permanent connections as with PVCs. Thus, SVCs provide switched, on-demand connectivity.

An SVC-based frame relay network is analogous to the Public Switched Telephone Network. When a node on LAN *A* needs to send data to a node on LAN *B*, the frame relay switches within the frame relay network automatically nail-up a circuit from source to destination prior to data communications. This circuit remains in effect only for the duration of a transmission. When the transmission is over, the switches then tear down the circuit. Thus, the path of every communication between source and destination nodes is not necessarily the same with SVCs as it is with PVCs. Furthermore, frame relay switches that support SVCs can automatically configure a path on-demand between two sites, and then remove this path from their tables at the end of a transmission. With SVCs, any frame relay subscriber can communicate with any other frame relay subscriber provided both have SVC capabilities.

19. Are SVCs assigned CIRs like PVCs?

Yes. Everything we discussed earlier about CIRs applies to SVCs as well.

20. Are there any advantages or disadvantages to using PVCs or SVCs?

Each type of circuit has its own set of advantages and disadvantages. PVC advantages include widespread availability (every frame relay provider supports PVCs), less complex network designs (any two sites that want to communicate must have a permanent connection between then), and less expensive equipment (switches do not have to automatically configure and remove paths dynamically). On the other side of the coin, PVCs are permanent. This implies that regardless of use, you are always paying for a specific amount of bandwidth. A second disadvantage is that every time a new connection is required, a new permanent circuit must be established. Thus, the number of PVCs a customer might need may increase dramatically, making the PVCs difficult to manage. This is especially true if a fully-meshed design is required. For example, an organization with 50 sites will require $(50)(49)/2 = 1,225$ PVCs for a fully-meshed network. If full connectivity is required among 100 sites, the number of PVCs needed increases dramatically to 4,950.

Compared to PVCs, SVCs are more versatile. Customers do not have to establish permanent circuits between any two sites because connectivity is provided on an as-needed basis, and as a usage-based service, bandwidth is only used when needed. This can translate to considerable savings for customers. On the other hand, PVCs' advantages are currently SVCs' primary disadvantages. First, widespread SVC availability among frame relay service providers is lacking (although MCI WorldCom and Sprint have announced plans to deploy SVCs). SVC-based frame relay networks are also more complex in design, and switches are more sophisticated and hence expensive.

21. I think I am ready to learn about some of the technical aspects of frame relay. Can you begin with a brief technical overview of frame relay and how it works?

You bet. Frame relay is a data link layer protocol. It is synchronous in nature and is based on the concept of packet switching. Thus, every frame relay frame carries source and destination addresses. As indicated earlier, frame relay also uses statistical multiplexing. This enables multiple subscribers to share the same backbone.

Although frame relay operates at the data link layer, it does not provide flow control, error detection, frame sequencing, or acknowledgments. These tasks, which represent overhead, are performed by frame relay end nodes (usually a router) at the customer's site and not by the frame relay switches. If the network becomes congested and a frame relay switch's buffers get filled, the switch will discard any subsequent frames it receives until its buffers are free. Recovery from these lost frames is left to the frame relay end nodes. Transmission errors are also ignored by the switches. All frame integrity checks are, once again, performed by the customer's end nodes. Freeing the protocol from these tasks makes frame relay a very fast and highly efficient LAN-to-LAN connection.

The physical components of a frame relay network include end nodes, frame relay switches, and communication links. End nodes serve as the interface between a customer's site (LAN) and the service provider's network; switches are responsible for transmitting data from the source LAN's end node to the destination LAN's end node. End nodes are then connected to switches via an access line (i.e., a port connection), and switches are interconnected via PVCs or SVCs.

Frame relay end nodes include bridges (see Chapter 6), routers (see Chapter 7), special concentrators, and workstations or personal computers. Of these devices, the most common implementations use frame-relay capable routers or conventional routers with frame relay-capable CSUs/DSUs. Collectively, end nodes are known as frame relay access devices (FRADs). (*Note:* The term FRAD once meant special frame relay devices that were used for simple implementations. Today, however, the term is all-encompassing and implies any frame relay end node.) Regardless of the type of device used, end nodes assemble or disassemble frame relay frames between two LANs. FRADs accept data frames from the local network (e.g., an Ethernet/802.3 frame) and assemble them into frame relay frames (see Figure 12-8) by encapsulating the data contained in layers 3 through 7. This new frame is then placed on the access line for transmission across the network. When a FRAD receives a frame relay frame, it disassembles it by stripping off the frame relay headers and trailers, does any necessary reassembly of the LAN frame, performs an integrity check on the frame, and (assuming the frame is valid) places it on the local backbone for delivery to the destination node. Frame relay is also protocol independent. Thus, different LAN protocols such as Ethernet/802.3 and token ring, and different network protocols such as TCP/IP, SNA, and IPX, can run over frame relay.

22. Could you review the contents of the frame relay frame shown in Figure 12-8?

Sure. The frame relay frame is of variable length. (The standard does not specify a frame size limitation.) The maximum size is set by (and is different among) providers and is generally a function of hardware limitations. Typical implementations range from 1,600 to 4,096 bytes. This implies that frame relay can fully support Ethernet/802.3 and token ring frames without having to segment (and reassemble) LAN frames for transmission across the frame relay network. Although this variable size feature makes the protocol compatible with the type of bursty traffic inherent in LANs, it also makes it susceptible to data processing delays across the network.

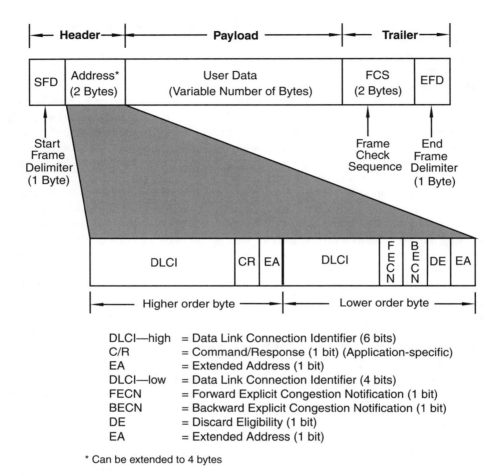

Figure 12-8. The contents and format of a frame relay frame. (Adapted from Parsons & Beach, 1996.)

As shown in Figure 12-8, a frame relay frame consists of the following fields: start and end frame delimiters (SFD and EFD), address, user data, and frame check sequence (FCS). The SFD and EFD fields are one byte each and consist of the bit pattern 01111110 to indicate the beginning and ending of a frame. The address field is two bytes and can be extended to either three or four bytes. The components of a two-byte address are shown in Figure 12-8. These components include a 10-bit *Data Link Connection Identifier* (DLCI) that is split between the two bytes, two 1-bit *Extended Address* (EA) fields (one per byte), and 1-bit each for *Command/Response* (C/R), *Forward and Backward Explicit Congestion Notification* (FECN and BECN), and *Discard Eligibility* (DE). The user data field is of variable length. This field contains encapsulated data from the sending node. The FCS field is used to check the integrity of the frame.

Focusing on the two-byte address field, the DLCI represents the network address of the frame and includes the virtual circuit number that corresponds to the destination port of the destination LAN's end node (more on this later). The C/R bit is application-specific and not used by the protocol. It is passed transparently from switch to switch. The EA bits specify whether the address is extended to three or four bytes. If EA is 0, then another byte of address information follows; an EA of 1 implies that the current byte is the last byte of the address. Thus, a two-byte address has EA = 0 in the higher-order byte and EA = 1 in the lower-order byte. The FECN and BECN bits are used to convey congestion information to end nodes in either direction. These bits are set by frame relay switches as the frame is being transmitted across the network from source to destination. If FECN or BECN is set to 1, then a sending or receiving end node, upon receipt of a frame, will know that the frame encountered congestion and can take whatever action is necessary to enact flow control. The DE bit specifies whether or not a frame should be discarded when the network gets congested. Frames with the DE bit 1 are considered low priority. When the network becomes congested, if a customer's capacity exceeds its CIR, frames with DE = 1 are the first to be dropped by frame relay switches. A more detailed explanation of DLCI, FECN, BECN, and DE is given in answers to subsequent questions.

23. Please explain DLCIs a little more and give me an example of how they work.

OK. Data Link Connection Identifiers are virtual circuit addresses assigned to PVCs or SVCs. DLCIs enable multiple virtual circuits, which represent logical connections, to be multiplexed using a single network link. For a two-byte address, DLCIs are 10 bits in length. (See Figure 12-8.) This implies there are $2^{10} = 1,024$ possible circuit numbers. Of these, however, only 992 are available for use. The remaining 32 are reserved. For example DLCI #0 is reserved for call control, which establishes and releases a logical connection, and DLCI #1023 is reserved for exchanging information about the virtual circuits that have been established. To accommodate larger networks, the frame's address field can be extended to three or four bytes. A three-byte address field supports a 17-bit DLCI, and a four-byte address field supports a 24-bit DLCI. Outside of the frame relay cloud, DLCIs represent the destination network's end node's port number. End nodes maintain a cross-connect table that maps its port's DLCI to a specific network address. For example, in a TCP/IP-based network, the end node (e.g., a router) is configured so that each IP address assigned to WAN interface corresponds to the correct DLCI. An illustration is shown in Figure 12-9.

DLCIs are assigned at call set-up time, or they are premapped to a destination node when PVCs are initially established with a service provider. This latter approach is used in the majority of frame relay networks. Although DLCIs must be unique within the cloud, end nodes may use the same DLCIs. For example, in Figure 12-9, the UNIs of LANs 2 and 3 are assigned the same DLCI (83). In this context, DLCIs have only local significance and care must be exercised to ensure that the DLCI is not announced outside the local arena. In contrast to local addressing, global addressing is also available. In this context, a DLCI is assigned on a universal basis throughout the entire network. Thus, a globally-assigned DLCI would identify the same destination regardless of where the originating end node is located in the network. Although global addressing simplifies the management

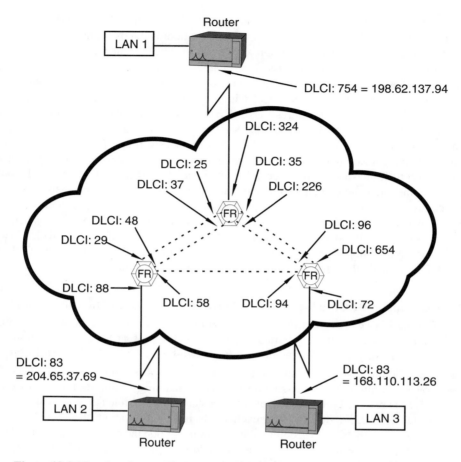

Figure 12-9. The virtual ports (PVCs and SVCs) of a frame relay network are uniquely identified by the Data Link Connection Identifier. Cross connect tables within the frame relay switches map incoming DLCIs to corresponding outgoing DLCIs. For example, the virtual connection between the switches connecting LANs 2 and 3 map DLCI #58 to DLCI #94. End nodes (routers) also must maintain tables that map port addresses (i.e., the user network interfaces) to the correct DLCIs. Although DLCIs must be unique within the cloud, end nodes can use the same DLCIs. For example, the UNIs of LANs 2 and 3 are assigned the same DLCI (83). Thus, DLCIs have only local, not global, significance. (Adapted from Parsons & Bahr, 1996.)

of DLCIs, it also reduces further the number of DLCI numbers available for use since no DLCIs can be reused by different networks.

Data transfer in a frame relay network involves first establishing (i.e., "nailing up") a logical connection between the source and destination nodes and assigning a unique DLCI to the connection. Data frames are then transferred across the network with each frame containing the assigned DLCI. The same circuit is used for the duration of the transmission. At the conclusion of the transmission, the circuit is released. Logical connections are established and released in frame relay by using frames with DLCI = 0. These frames, called *call control* frames, are exchanged between the sending and receiving nodes and include information related to the proposed connection. Among this information is the DLCI that will be assigned to the connection. Either the sending node includes this DLCI in its connection request, or it can be assigned by the receiving node at the time it accepts the sender's connection request.

To understand the process of frame relaying, let's assume that a frame of data is transmitted from LAN 2 to LAN 3 in Figure 12-9. When LAN 2's router constructs the frame for transmission, it will assign a DLCI of 83. The router places the frame on its access line and the frame is transmitted to the switch connected at the other end of the link. When the switch receives the frame, it checks the frame's integrity via the two-byte FCS contained in the frame's trailer. If any errors are found, the switch discards the frame. If the frame is valid, the switch then checks its routing table to determine the channel on which the frame should be placed. (We will assume the frame is valid throughout this illustration.) Let's agree that the switch's routing table shows frames arriving via circuit 88 must go out the port assigned DLCI = 48. The switch then rebuilds the frame to include this new DLCI and ships it out the appropriate port. The next switch (1) receives the frame on the port assigned DLCI = 37, (2) does its integrity check, (3) consults its routing table and discovers that frames arriving on circuit 37 get transmitted to the port assigned DLCI = 35, (4) rebuilds the frame to include a DLCI of 35, and then transmits the frame via circuit 35. This process continues until the destination LAN's end node (in this case, LAN 3's router) receives the frame.

24. If switches discard invalid frames, who notifies the end nodes?

No one. If acknowledgments are not received within a certain time interval, the source end node assumes that the frame was discarded. It will then retransmit the frame. One thing you can count on frame relay to do is discard frames. It is a no-nonsense protocol. Frame relay also does not operate too well in a noisy environment. If there is any line noise during a transmission, bit errors will occur and you can bet your house frame relay will drop those frames.

25. Yes, but if transmission errors occur frequently and frame relay starts discarding frames, which causes retransmissions, don't we get into a vicious circle? You know: Discarded frames lead to retransmission, which leads to more network traffic, which leads to network congestion, which causes more frames to be discarded.

Yes. Your observation is correct.

26. Well, if this is the case, and frame relay doesn't provide flow control, how, then, is congestion addressed in frame relay?

Congestion is addressed in frame relay from two perspectives. The first perspective is grounded in management and design issues. Frame relay service providers should always strive to provide an agreed upon quality of service. To do so, though, and to do it consistently, service providers should: (1) design their networks so that sufficient bandwidth is provisioned; (2) ensure that all links are clean; (3) keep customers from establishing connections where the aggregate CIRs exceed 70 percent of the port speed; (4) ensure that any one end node is kept from monopolizing the network at the expense of other end nodes; and (5) distribute resources across the network in a fair and equitable manner. Unfortunately, these considerations are carrier-dependent and vary from one provider to another.

The second perspective is standards-based. The frame relay protocol provides a mechanism for addressing congestion. This is done via the forward and backward explicit congestion notification bits. (See Figure 12-8.) FECN and BECN are designed to inform (i.e., notify) end nodes that a frame has experienced network congestion. If congestion emerges along a virtual circuit, these bits are set to 1 by the frame relay switch connected to that circuit as the frame passes through the switch. The FECN bit is set in frames going toward the destination node; the BECN bit is set in frames going toward the sending node.

Of the two bits, congestion notification via BECN produces the most direct action. If the sending end node receives a frame with BECN = 1, it can simply reduce (or temporarily suspend) its transmission rate. This action is direct and effective. A different strategy needs to be employed by the destination end node if it receives frames with FECN = 1. Since the destination node cannot directly slow down the sender's data transmission rate, it must rely on indirect methods. One method is to increase the length of time receipt-of-frame acknowledgments take when sent to the sender. This will slow down acknowledgment transmissions. After the sending node's acknowledgment timers have expired several times, it will eventually increase the timer interval to accommodate the new rate being used by destination node. This action indirectly causes the sender to reduce its transmission rate. A second method is to effect flow control in the higher layers. For example, if a TCP-based application such as FTP is running over TCP, and IP is being used as the network layer protocol (layer 3), then the destination node can reset its transmission window value to 0. (*Note:* In TCP/IP, the transmission window represents the maximum number of bytes a remote node can accept.) Doing so informs the sender that the maximum number of bytes the receiver can accept is zero. Thus, a zero window informs the sender to stop transmitting data to the receiver until a non-zero window size is received from the receiver.

Incorporating the FECN and BECN bits in the frame relay frame produces shared responsibility between the network and the end nodes for congestion control: The network's role is to monitor itself for congestion and then notify the end nodes that congestion exists. Upon notification, the end nodes then take the necessary action to reduce the flow of frames onto the network.

27. Where does the discard eligibility bit fit into all of this?

Ah! The discard eligibility bit . . . we forgot all about it. Thanks for reminding us. Besides FECN and BECN, the DE bit can be used as another strategy for congestion control. Its role is to give the network guidance in determining which frames should be discarded. This is important because setting FECN and BECN bits does not guarantee that end nodes will respond to this notification, or if they do, that the response will be in a timely manner. Furthermore, the implementation of FECN and BECN in frame relay is not mandatory. Without any guidance, the network (i.e., frame relay switches) will discard frames arbitrarily at the onset of congestion. Although discarding frames randomly produces the desired effect—it helps reduce congestion—it does not give any consideration to frames that have a "contractual right" to remain. For example, frames transmitted within the parameters of a contracted CIR are just as likely to be dropped as frames transmitted at a burst rate above the CIR. This situation can be resolved by configuring end nodes to set the DE bit to 1 for all frames transmitted at a rate higher than the CIR. Now, in the presence of congestion, network switches will discard frames with DE = 1 before they discard frames that do not have their DE bit set. Discarded frames will then be retransmitted at a later time when congestion has subsided. (*Note:* Retransmission occurs after the sending node has detected that the packet was dropped, that is, after it failed to receive an acknowledgment.) The DE bit also can be used to distinguish between high and low priority frames. For example, if e-mail data is considered more important than web data, then the end node can be configured to set the DE bit of all web-based frames. This gives e-mail frames a higher transmission priority than web frames because if congestion occurs, switches will drop web frames first.

The DE bit enables frame relay customers to adopt a frame-discard strategy that is predicated on their preferences. Although this provides a more fair and equitable approach to discarding frames than arbitrary selection, it does not guarantee that only DE-flagged frames will be dropped. The topics of congestion and congestion management strategies are part of a bigger picture called network performance, which includes metrics such as network uptime, delays, and frame or packet loss. These metrics vary from one provider to another. For example, network uptime guarantees can range from 99 percent, to 99.95 percent, to 99.99 percent among different providers. Although these rates are relatively close to one another, the difference in the number of minutes (or hours) of downtime is staggering. For example, uptimes of 99 percent, 99.5 percent, and 99.99 percent translate to downtimes of 1 percent, 0.5 percent, and 0.01 percent, respectively. Table 12-1 shows the differences in these rates measured daily, monthly, and yearly. Thus, a network provider that guarantees a 99 percent uptime measured on a monthly basis means that the guarantee does not become effective until the network has been down for more than 432 minutes (7.2 hours) over a 30-day period. If the guarantee is on an annual basis, then it does not take effect unless downtime exceeds 5,256 minutes (87.6 hours) over the 365-day period. These same downtimes for a 99.99 percent guarantee are 4.32 minutes per month and 52.56 minutes per year. As you can see, there is quite a difference. The bottom line is customers who are subscribing to frame relay service need to investigate, probe, and negotiate network performance issues with their provider.

28. As a data link layer protocol, what provisions does frame relay have for link management, which is a layer 2 function?

The frame relay protocol specifies a *link management interface* (LMI) for link control. LMI provides an interface for link status information to be exchanged between an end node (e.g., router or switch) and the network. LMI's functions are quite basic, though, and limited to activities such as PVC notification (end nodes are notified whenever PVCs are added to or removed from the network), PVC monitoring (circuits are monitored so end nodes know which ones are available), and link establishment between an end node and the network. Given frame relay's ISDN roots, link management is provided out-of-band, thus a separate virtual circuit is used for transmitting link status information messages.

Table 12-1. Network Downtime Comparisons at Different Levels of Uptime Guarantees

	99% Uptime	99.5% Uptime	99.99% Uptime
Measured Daily 24 hr/day × 60 min/hr = 1,440 minutes/day	1440 x .01 = 14.4 minutes downtime/day	1440 x .005 = 7.2 minutes downtime/day	1440 x .0001 = 0.144 minute downtime/day
Measured Monthly 1,440 min/day × 30 days/month = 43,200 minutes/month	43200 x .01 = 432 minutes = 7.2 hours downtime/month	43200 x .005 = 216 minutes = 3.6 hours downtime/month	43200 x .0001 = 4.32 minutes downtime/month
Measured Yearly 1,440 min/day × 365 days/year = 525,600 minutes/year	525600 x .01 = 5256 minutes = 87.6 hours downtime/year	525600 x .005 = 2628 minutes = 43.8 hours downtime/year	525600 x .0001 = 52.56 minutes downtime/year

29. OK. Thanks for the information. Let's change gears and get back to some of the other aspects of frame relay. For example, you mentioned voice over frame relay. What is that all about?

Frame relay has evolved from a data only service to one that can support voice, fax, and video transmissions. *Voice over frame relay* (VOFR) has benefited from the development of voice-capable FRADs, which have been designed with advanced technologies to accommodate the nuances associated with transmitting voice traffic. These technologies include voice compression, echo cancellation, and delay control techniques. Voice compression eliminates pauses and redundant information typical of human communication. This reduces the amount of bandwidth required to transmit voice signals. Voice compression also permits voice transmissions over lower-speed channels. Voice compression methods include two international standards, ITU G.729 and ITU G.728, as well as proprietary solutions. Echo cancellation eliminates voice echoing, which occurs when propagation delays reflect voice traffic back to its point of transmission. In addition to echoing, delays can also cause voice distortion. For example, if jitter is high, then the receiving-end equipment will not be able to satisfactorily regenerate the voice signal. Delay control techniques that have been developed to eliminate problems related to delay include traffic prioritization and fragmentation. With prioritization, voice transmissions are assigned a higher priority than data frames, which are buffered until voice traffic has been transmitted. Fragmentation minimizes delay by segmenting large data frames into smaller-sized frames so that voice transmissions are not impeded by the transmission of large data frames. In a typical VOFR application, a customer's PBX is connected to a FRAD just as the data network. In most cases, additional PVCs are needed, and CIRs will have to be increased to accommodate voice traffic. Frame relay service provider switches also must be capable of transmitting voice traffic. A typical implementation is shown in Figure 12-10. In addition to voice, several vendors have also produced FRADs that are capable of supporting real-time video. Once again, attention needs to be paid to adequate bandwidth and CIRs.

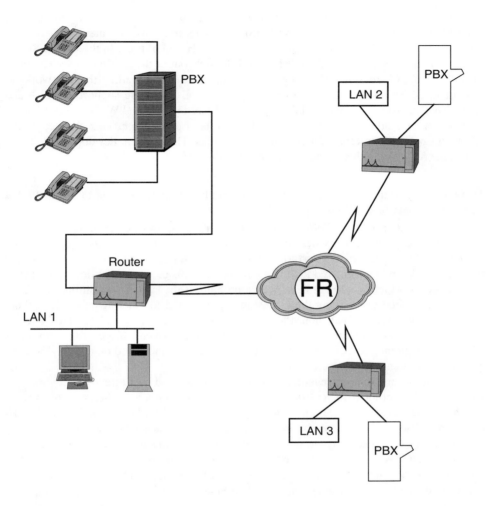

Figure 12-10. A typical implementation of *voice over frame relay* (VOFR) involves a PBX system connected to a voice-capable FRAD, which also links a LAN.

30. How does frame relay stack up against SMDS or ATM?

During the late 1980s to early-to-mid-1990s, frame relay, SMDS, ATM, and broadband ISDN (B-ISDN) were all in the spotlight as new fast packet switching technologies or services. Frame relay, which originally was a subset of ISDN, was defined initially to transmit data at rates ranging from 56 kbps to T1/E-1. These rates dovetailed nicely with the local loop—the link between a customer's site and the telco's nearest point of presence (POP). SMDS and B-ISDN were initially designed to transmit data, fax, graphics, video, and voice at speeds from 45 Mbps to 155 Mbps. ATM was designed initially to offer the same kinds of services as SMDS and B-ISDN, but its transmission rates were from 45 Mbps to 2.4 Gbps. Much has changed in such a short period of time. In the United States, frame relay has essentially pushed SMDS and B-ISDN out of the spotlight. (See Chapters 11 and 13.) Frame relay now operates at T3, and telcos are upgrading their networks to support rates greater than DS-3. Frame relay is now also capable supporting voice and video. This makes frame relay a viable option for LAN-to-LAN and WAN connections, as well as a broadband service. Furthermore, frame relay frames can be encapsulated within ATM's 53-byte cell and transmitted across ATM links. These recent developments ensure that frame relay will either compete or coexist with ATM.

31. One last question. Wasn't that AT&T network that crashed back in April, 1998 a frame relay network? What happened?

Yes it was. On April 13, 1998, AT&T's frame relay network crashed as a result of a firmware upgrade to a core switch. According to a report in the June 1998 issue of *Data Communications*, a technician performed the upgrade on a live switch that was connected to the network, and then entered incorrect commands. This generated spurious administrative messages, which would not have been a problem if the switch was offline. However, because the switch was online, these messages propagated to other switches throughout the network and within a half-hour the entire network was down. This left AT&T's frame relay customers without connectivity for more than a day. (*Note:* If a customer's service uptime was guaranteed at either 99 percent to 99.5 percent and based on a yearly rate, the guarantee would not have applied. See Table 12-1.)

Although frame relay is regarded as a highly reliable and cost-effective network, it is still nonetheless prudent for customers to give serious attention to the issue of disaster recovery. The AT&T crash demonstrated this quite effectively. For example, AT&T customers who had secondary (i.e., backup) ISDN circuits in place, or redundant frame relay circuits from a different provider, were able to maintain connectivity. Given the additional cost of these measures, one might be tempted to ask, "Why bother?" The answer to this question can be given by paraphrasing the edict used to explain why George Bush lost his bid for a second term as president of the United States in 1992: "It's technology, stupid."

End-of-Chapter Commentary

In this chapter several concepts and technologies related to frame relay were discussed, including circuit- and packet-switching, virtual circuits (PVCs and SVCs), bandwidth (CIRs), design and topology issues, and ISDN. Additional information about these concepts can be found in earlier chapters within this book. For example: Circuit- and packet-switching are discussed in Chapter 1; network design and topology issues, as well as virtual circuits, are discussed in Chapter 2; bandwidth is discussed in Chapters 2 and 4; and ISDN is discussed in Chapter 11. Other technologies and services that were also discussed are addressed in subsequent chapters. These are SMDS, which is the topic of the next chapter (see Chapter 13), and ATM (see Chapter 14), which follows our discussion of SMDS.

Chapter 13

Switched Multimegabit Data Service (SMDS)

In Chapter 7, we gave an overview of Switched Multimegabit Data Service (SMDS) as part of our discussion of various WAN technologies and services. In this chapter we present more specific information about SMDS. The main topics we address follows:

- Overview of SMDS (Questions 1–2, 6)
- SMDS and Local and Inter-Exchange Carriers (Questions 3–5)
- The DQDB and SMDS Protocols (Questions 7–9)
- SMDS Addressing (Question 10–11)
- SMDS Applications (Question 12)
- SMDS vs. Frame Relay and ATM (Questions 13–14)
- Current Status and Future of SMDS (Question 15)

1. What is SMDS?

Switched Multimegabit Data Service is a cell-based, connectionless, high-speed, public, packet-switched, broadband, metropolitan area data network.

2. That's a mouthful. Can you break it down for me?

Sure. SMDS is a wide area network service designed for LAN-to-LAN connectivity. It is not a technology like Ethernet or ATM. SMDS is also a data service, which means that it can only transmit data (although it is capable of transmitting voice and video). SMDS uses fixed-length cells as its basic unit for transmitting data. These cells are similar to ATM cells, namely, they contain 53 bytes—a 44-byte payload plus a 7-byte header and a 2-byte trailer. (See Chapter 14 for more information about ATM.) As a connectionless data service, SMDS does not establish a connection between sending and receiving hosts prior to data transmission. Instead, an SMDS switch establishes a virtual circuit between sending and receiving machines. Cells are placed on the medium when they are ready for transmission and then transmitted independently of each another. Thus, data cells are transmitted without delay and in no particular order. This provides bandwidth on demand for the kind of bursty traffic inherent in LAN applications. (In contrast, ATM and frame relay are connection-oriented.) SMDS is available from telco providers as a shared, public network that uses an international standards-based addressing plan known as E.164. Operating like a shared LAN (e.g., Ethernet/802.3), each SMDS cell contains a destination address enabling any SMDS subscriber to exchange data with any other SMDS subscriber—only those nodes with the correct destination address respond to the transmission. SMDS can support several data rates including DS-1, DS-3, and SONET OC-3. Low-speed SMDS (56 kbps/64 kbps) is also available from some telcos. Since SMDS is a technology-independent service, customers can subscribe to SMDS at a specific data rate for guaranteed throughput. The broadband aspect of SMDS comes from its compatibility with broadband ISDN (B-ISDN) and its potential for supporting voice and video. (See Chapter 11 for additional information about B-ISDN.) SMDS also is based on and compatible with the IEEE 802.6 metropolitan area network (MAN) standard.

3. Who developed SMDS?

SMDS was developed by Bellcore and the Regional Bell Operating Companies (RBOCs) to address customer demand for interconnected multimegabit LANs within a major metropolitan area. It was designed to be a high performance, reasonably priced, switched service to provide connectivity and extend LAN-like performance. SMDS is implemented by local exchange carriers (LECs), which are companies that provide local telephone and telecommunications services within the same Local Access and Transport Area (LATA). (*Note:* In contrast to a LEC, an inter-exchange carrier, IEC or IXC, is any company that provides long distance telephone and telecommunications services. Examples include AT&T, Sprint, British Telecom (BT), and MCI WorldCom.)

4. Hold the phone. What's a LATA?

The concept of a local access and transport area was introduced in 1984 when the U.S. Justice Department broke up AT&T. An area of concern that emerged from the breakup regarded the issue of revenue from the long distance calling market. AT&T did not want the LECs to have control over both the local and long distance calling markets. This problem was resolved by establishing 195 geographical and administrative areas (LATAs) that are controlled by the LECs. Calls that cross a LATA are handled by IECs. Thus, a LEC provides intra-LATA services and an IEC provides inter-LATA services. Calls originating in one LATA and destined for another LATA are initially handled by the first LATA's LEC, which then hands it over to an IEC for inter-LATA transport. The IEC, in turn, hands it over to the LEC that has control over the destination LATA. Tariffs related to long distance calls are based on which networks the calls are carried (the LEC's or the IEC's). It is thus not uncommon for a long distance call from New York City to Los Angeles to be less expensive than one placed between two cities within the same state and only 50 miles from each other. The New York–LA call might be carried exclusively by an IEC, but the intrastate call might have to cross one or more LATA boundaries.

Much of this is changing, though, as a result of the U.S. Telecommunications Act of 1996. This act permits LECs to provide long distance service and IECs to provide local calling service, thereby blurring the distinction between an LEC and IEC. The act also introduced new terminology. The LECs that existed prior to the Telecommunications Act are now referred to as *incumbent LECs* (ILECs), and new telecommunication service providers formed after the Telecommunications Act are known as *competitive LECs* (CLECs).

5. If SMDS is offered through LECs, what happens if the LANs that are to be connected are in different LATAs?

Good question. Prior to the Telecommunications Act of 1996, this was a problem because LECs were prohibited by law from carrying any type of traffic across LATA boundaries. To address this issue, a service called *Exchange Access SMDS* (XA-SMDS) was deployed in 1993. Through XA-SMDS, LECs offered SMDS service to IECs for delivery across LATAs. Connectivity was usually established via a private link where standard SMDS routers transferred traffic from one network to another. XA-SMDS also specified a standard Inter-Carrier Interface (ICI) for the LEC–IEC connection.

Today, as a result of the Telecommunications Act of 1996, LECs and IECs can compete in each other's business so this is no longer an issue. The only restriction is that LECs are regulated separately by each state's public utilities commissions. Thus, if the LEC providing SMDS service operates in two different states, then the types, cost, and rules of the service might vary considerably. MCI WorldCom also has established a national SMDS network that provides connectivity among SMDS networks located in different parts of the country. In this context, SMDS is considered both a MAN and WAN service.

6. OK. Thanks. Why was SMDS developed?

Prior to SMDS' development in the late 1980s and early 1990s, the only method network administrators had for interconnecting their LANs within a metropolitan area was via leased lines at either 56 kbps or T1 rates. Given the LAN data rates of the time (4 Mbps/16 Mbps for token ring and 10 Mbps for Ethernet/802.3), the leased line approach was insufficient from three perspectives. First, the leased lines represented a bottleneck for LAN-to-LAN transmissions. Data frames being transferred between two Ethernet/802.3 nodes residing on separate LANs interconnected by a 56 kbps or T1 line resulted in congestion and transmission delays. The LAN data rates simply overwhelmed the capacity of the leased circuit. Second, leased line costs were nontrivial. If an organization wanted to interconnect multiple LANs located at different locations across a metropolitan area (e.g., within a local county), it would need multiple leased lines. Depending on the topology used, the cost of multiple T1 service can be exorbitant. Although 56 kbps service would be more affordable, the inherent delays and congestion would make it unacceptable. Finally, private leased lines did not scale up well economically. If congestion and delays of T1 service were unacceptable, the next step up was T3 service, which was too expensive for many organizations. Figures 13-1 and 13-2 compare traditionally designed MANs to an SMDS network. With SMDS, however, an organization can create a corporate LAN internet (i.e., a corporate network of LANs) across a metropolitan area cost-effectively.

7. You said SMDS is a service, not a technology. On what technology is SMDS based?

SMDS is based on a subset of the IEEE 802.6 physical layer and MAC sublayer standard, which specifies a high-speed network protocol similar to token ring. At the physical layer, IEEE 802.6 specifies a dual bus design using fiber-optic cable. (See Figure 13-3.)

(a)

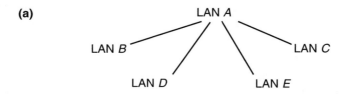

(b)

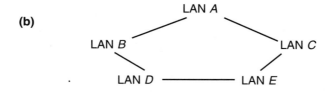

(c)

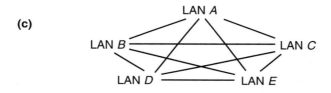

Figure 13-1. The traditional method of establishing metropolitan area networks (MANs) is to interconnect LANs within a metropolitan area using dedicated leased circuits. Several methods are possible, and each has its own advantages and disadvantages. In (a) LANs *B, C, D,* and *E* are indirectly connected via LAN *A*. One problem with this design is that if LAN *A* fails, then the remaining LANs cannot communicate with one another. In (b), the single source of failure of design (a) is removed and all neighboring LANs are directly interconnected. However, non-neighboring LANs are still indirectly connected. The design in (c) represents a fully-meshed MAN in which every LAN is directly connected to every other LAN. Although more robust, this design is extremely expensive.

The buses, which are labeled *A* and *B*, transmit in only one, but opposite, direction. This is similar to FDDI's counter-rotating ring. (See Chapter 10.) Together, the buses provide full-duplex operation. IEEE 802.6 networks can be designed as either an open or looped bus. The difference between the two topologies is where each bus begins and ends. In the open design, the buses begin and end at different nodes; in the loop design, the buses begin and end at the same node. Both designs are illustrated in Figures 13-4(a) and 13-4(b), respectively. SMDS uses the open bus topology.

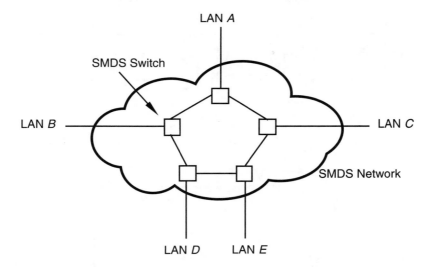

Figure 13-2. In contrast to traditionally designed MANs (Figure 13-1), an SMDS network provides direct connectivity among LANs within a geographical region using only a single link for each LAN.

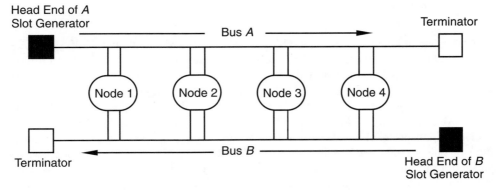

Figure 13-3. The physical layer of an SMDS network consists of two fiber-optic buses, *A* and *B,* which transmit data in opposite directions. The direction of data flow is from the head of the bus, which acts as a slot generator, to the terminator. Nodes are connected to both buses in a logically adjacent manner and read all transmitted data. (Adapted from Bates & Gregory, 1998.)

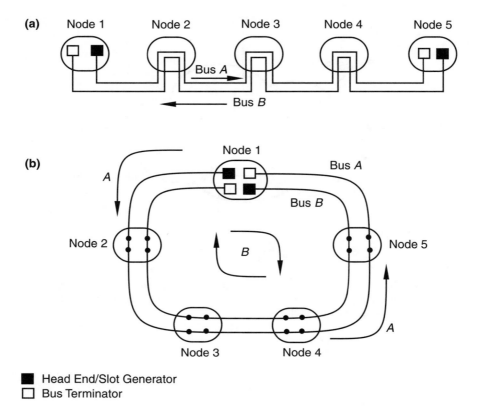

Figure 13-4. In an open bus design (a), the head end of the buses is located in two different nodes. In the closed loop design (b), the head of both buses is located in the same node. (Adapted from Bates & Gregory, 1998.)

At the data link layer, access to the SMDS network is governed by the IEEE 802.6 *Distributed Queue Dual Bus (DQDB)* protocol. This protocol partitions each bus into time slots, which are used to transmit data. Each slot contains a Busy bit and a Request bit. If the slot contains data, then the Busy bit is set to 1. A slot with its Request bit set implies that a node is requesting to send data. If the Busy bit is not set (i.e., busy bit = 0), then the slot is considered empty. Nodes can only transmit data using empty slots.

The DQDB protocol works as follows: Prior to sending data, a node must first reserve slots on one bus to be used on the second bus. For example, in Figure 13-3, if node 1 wants to send data to node 3, it must use bus *A* because *A* transmits in the direction of node 3. This implies that node 1 must reserve a slot on bus *B*. Similarly, if node 3 wants to send data to node 1, it must use bus *B*, which implies it must reserve a slot on bus *A*. As mentioned above, slots are reserved by setting the Request bit of an empty slot.

Reserving slots on one bus to be used on the second bus enable nodes to notify their neighbors that they have data to transmit. The process of reserving slots also prevents nodes from monopolizing the bus. Without a reservation system, upstream nodes can continuously fill empty slots with data and hence deny downstream slots from ever seeing an empty slot. For example, in Figure 13-3, slots are generated at the head end of bus *A* and flow from left-to-right. Thus, node 1 will always see an empty slot first, followed by node 2, then node 3, and finally node 4. Similarly, on bus *B*, slots are generated and flow from right-to-left. Thus, node 4 will always see an empty slot on this bus before any of the other nodes.

Once a node has requested a slot, it then monitors both buses and maintains a request counter. The purpose of the counter is to maintain an accurate count of the number of unfilled data transmission requests made by downstream nodes. (Unfilled requests are identified whenever a slot has its Request bit set.) This counter specifies the number of empty slots a requesting node must let pass before it can access an empty slot itself. Each time a slot that has its Request bit set passes by, the counter is increased by one; each time an empty slot passes on the second bus, the counter is decreased by one. When the counter reaches zero, the node is permitted to transmit data—that is, it can access the next empty slot on the other bus. This procedure permits nodes to essentially transmit data on a first-come-first-served basis, and enables nodes to know the state of queued requests throughout the entire network. This process also represents a form of CSMA/CA—*carrier sense multiple access with collision avoidance* (see Chapter 5), which prevents nodes from sending data at the same time.

Time slots are sampled by connected nodes at a rate of 8,000 per second. This makes the timing of an SMDS network consistent with the T1/E-1 hierarchies as well as SONET/ SDH. (See Chapter 7.) The number of slots on a network is also a function of bus speed. For example, if the transmission rate is 34 Mbps, then there are eight slots available per frame. DQDB supports both connectionless and connection-oriented service, and is capable of transmitting data, voice and video. As a subset of IEEE 802.6, though, SMDS is connectionless based and transmits only data.

8. OK. So SMDS is based on a subset of IEEE 802.6. Isn't there a specific SMDS protocol, though?

Yes there is. The *SMDS Interface Protocol* (SIP) was defined by Bellcore, which is the research branch of the RBOCs. SIP consists of three protocol levels, formally called SIP Level 3, SIP Level 2, and SIP Level 1. As we describe these protocol levels you will note a similarity between their functions and the first three layers of the OSI model. It is important to note that although these protocol levels are based on the first three OSI layers, they do not directly correspond to these layers. Instead, the three protocol levels represent SMDS's MAC sublayer and hence operate at the data link layer.

Before we get into any detail about SIP, it might help to first identify the components of an SMDS network. A simplified diagram is provided for this purpose in Figure 13-5. LANs are interconnected via SMDS using three components: SMDS routers, SMDS DSUs (SDSUs), and SMDS switches. Collectively, these three components form the basis of an SMDS network and support the DQDB protocol. Router, DSU, and switch connections are established as in any LAN–WAN configuration, and the major router manufacturers (e.g., Cisco, Bay Networks) support SMDS routing. The point of demarcation, called the *subscriber network interface (SNI)*, separates the router and SDSU, which are

CUSTOMER'S PREMISE   **SMDS NETWORK**

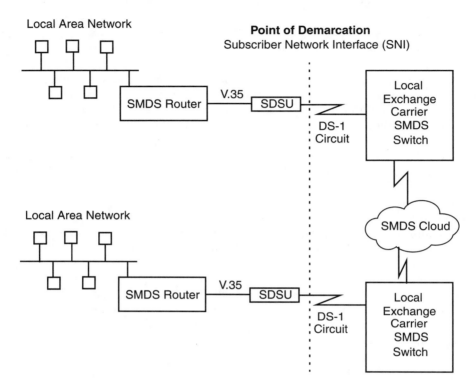

Figure 13-5. The components of a SMDS network consist of a router that supports the SMDS Interface Protocol, an SMDS CSU/DSU, a circuit, and a SMDS switch. The point that separates the customer's equipment from the SMDS network is called the point of demarcation and is the interface between the circuit and the SDSU. This is usually a punchdown block located at the customer's telecommunications office. This interface is formally called the subscriber network interface (SNI). (Adapted from Sharer, 1993.)

called the *customer premise equipment (CPE)*, from the telco's SMDS network equipment. A SMDS switch represents the head end of one of the buses (e.g., bus *A*), and all other nodes are CPE nodes. Thus, in Figure 13-4(a), node 1 is the SMDS switch, and nodes 2 through 5 are CPE nodes. The end CPE node (node 5 in Figure 13-4(a)) serves as the head end of the second bus (i.e., bus *B*).

When data frames destined for a remote LAN are received by the SMDS router from the local LAN, the router encapsulates these frames into special SMDS frames via SIP Level 3. Called SIP Level 3 PDUs (short for *Protocol Data Units*), these frames are then transmitted across the V.35 interface between the router and SDSU. SIP Level 3 PDUs provide the connectionless service of SMDS and contain up to 9,188 bytes of user information, plus related header and trailer information. (See Figure 13-6.) At the SDSU, SIP

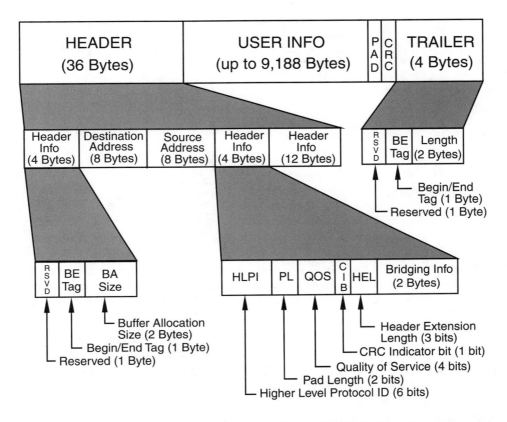

Figure 13-6. Contents of an SMDS Interface Protocol Level 3 PDU. This frame is partitioned into a 53-byte fixed-length cell by SIP Level 2. (See also Figures 13-7 and 13-8.) The PAD and CRC fields vary from 0 to 3 bytes and 0 to 4 bytes, respectively. (Adapted from Bates & Gregory, 1998.)

Level 2 accepts the Level 3 PDUs and partitions them into fixed-length segments of 53-bytes each. (See Figure 13-7.) The various length and tag fields contained in the Level 3 PDUs provide the necessary information for this partitioning (and eventual reassembly). These 53-byte cells, called SIP Level 2 PDUs, consist of 44 bytes of user information (called the payload or segmentation unit), a 7-byte header, and a 2-byte trailer. (See Figure 13-8.) SIP Level 2 PDUs represent the basic data unit on an SMDS network. These data units are then processed by SIP Level 1, which provides the physical interface to the SMDS network. This last level of SIP consists of two sublayers: the *transmission system* and the *physical layer convergence protocol*. The transmission system specifies how cells are to be placed on the medium; the physical layer convergence protocol formats the 53-byte cells for actual delivery across the network. The cells are then reassembled into Level 3 PDUs at the receiving end. Thus, an SMDS router provides SIP-3, and the SMDS DSU provides SIP-2 and SIP-1.

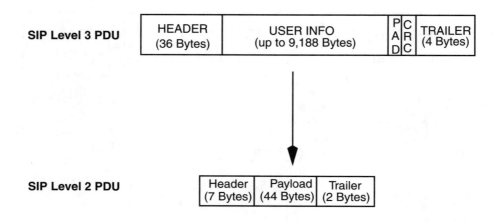

Figure 13-7. SIP Level 3 PDUs are fragmented into 53-byte cells by SIP Level 2. These Level 2 PDUs are the slots that are placed on the medium. SMDS nodes read all slots placed on the bus, and write to empty slots. The number of slots placed on the bus is a function of the bus's data rate. The expanded version of a SIP Level 2 PDU is shown in Figure 13-8.

When SMDS was initially deployed, the LECs required their customers' SMDS interface equipment to deliver Level 2 PDUs to the LECs' SMDS switches. This meant that customers could not use standard CSU/DSUs; they had to purchase special SMDS DSUs. This made SMDS an expensive service because SDSUs, in some cases, cost three times more than conventional CSU/DSUs. Today, however, the Level 3-to-Level 2 conversion is performed within the LEC's SMDS switch, enabling subscribers to use conventional CSU/DSUs.

9. I see in Figure 13-8 that the Access Control field of the header contains the Request and Busy bits. I also notice that there are three different Request bits. What's that all about?

SMDS supports three Request bits, Req0, Req1, and Req2. Each one corresponds to a different level of priority. Priority levels are similar to that of Token Ring. Regardless of which priority is used, request bits indicate that a node has data to transmit.

10. What do SMDS addresses look like?

SMDS addresses are based on the standard ISDN global numbering addressing format specified by ITU-T standard E.164. These addresses are just like telephone numbers. They are 15 decimal digits long and include a country code, area or city code, and a local number. Country codes are two or three digits long and consist of a zone code followed by a one- or two-digit national identifier. Area or city codes are up to 4 digits long. If an address contains less than 15 digits, then it is padded with hexadecimal Fs. For example, country

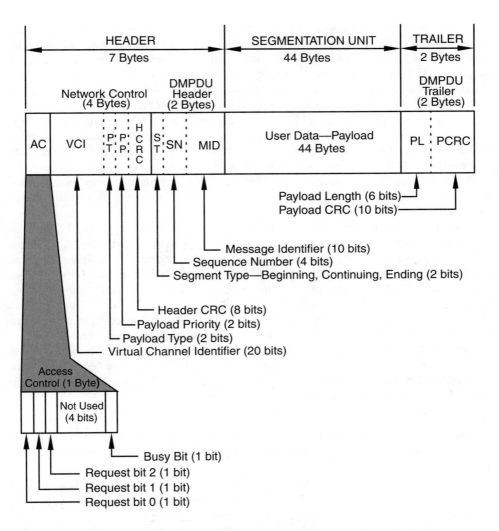

Figure 13-8. The basic data unit on a SMDS network is a 53-byte cell. This cell, which consists of a 7-byte header, a 44-byte payload, and a 2-byte trailer, is the result of a fragmentation process that is performed by the SMDS Interface Protocol Level 2. (See Figure 13-7.) SIP Level 2 receives from a router (via SIP Level 3) an initial MAC frame that contains up to 9,188 bytes of user data, plus related header and trailer information. This frame, called the *initial MAC protocol data unit* (IMPDU), is then partitioned into 53-byte cells for transmission over the network via SIP Level 1. At the receiving end, cells are then reassembled into their original form. Key to this reassembly process is the header and trailer information of the IMPDU. This information is also partitioned as part of the fragmentation process and carried via the 2-byte derived MAC protocol data units (DMPDU), which are included as part of the 53-byte cell. (See also Figure 13-6.) (Adapted from Bates & Gregory, 1998.)

codes for the United Kingdom (UK), Australia, and Taiwan are 44, 61, and 886, respectively. Sample city codes within the UK include 171 and 181 for London, 141 for Glasgow, 151 for Liverpool, and 1232 for Belfast. Sample city codes in Taiwan include 2 for Taipei and 37 for Chunan. There are no city codes for Australia. In the United States and Canada, country codes are not used. Instead, these countries use the zone code 1, which is followed by a three-digit area code and a seven digit local number.

There are also two types of SMDS addresses. *Individual addresses* are used for unicast transmissions; *group addresses* are used for multicast traffic. To distinguish between the two, individual addresses begin with a hexadecimal C and group addresses begin with a hexadecimal E. If an address contains less than 15 digits, then it is padded with hexadecimal Fs. Thus, the SMDS address, C14075557235FFFF, identifies an individual location in the 407 area code within the United States, and E160462284422961 is a group address in British Columbia, Canada.

The SMDS service provider (i.e., the LEC) assigns a block of up to 16 individual addresses to each subscriber network interface (SNI), which can exchange data among 128 individual or group addresses. More than one SMDS node can be assigned the same group address in addition to an individual address. There are restrictions, though. For example, an individual address cannot belong to more than 32 groups, and a group address cannot represent more than 128 individual addresses.

Group addressing also can be used as a filtering mechanism. For example, assume five LANs (*A, B, C, D,* and *E*) within a local county are interconnected via SMDS. Further assume that all five LANs are running IP; *A, B,* and *C* are also running IPX; and *D* and *E* are also running AppleTalk. Using group addressing, IPX traffic can be isolated from LANs *D* and *E,* and AppleTalk traffic can be isolated from LANs *A, B,* and *C.* Group addressing also can be used to create virtual ports over SMDS.

11. Since data transmission in an SMDS network occurs via the subscriber network interface, who configures what addresses get to exchange data, the customer or the LEC?

The service provider does this configuration based on customer specifications. Thus, the customer simply informs the LEC which addresses are to communicate with each other, and at what rate, and the LEC does all the configurations.

12. How do companies know if SMDS is an appropriate service for them?

Companies that can benefit from SMDS include organizations that have at least four remote sites across a metropolitan area that need to be interconnected in a seamless, cost-effective manner; require high-speed, bulk data transfers at a reasonable cost; need to transfer quickly large files including video and high-resolution images such as blueprint schematics, MRIs, CAT scans, and X-rays. In short, SMDS is appropriate for any enterprise with distributed sites that uses bandwidth-intensive applications. Prime candidates include hospitals, publishing companies, graphic design houses, insurance companies, police departments, automobile manufacturers, colleges and universities, and municipal governments. Applications include CAD/CAM, LAN-to-LAN connectivity, telemedicine and teleradiology, collaborative printing and publishing, image and multimedia file transfers, distance education, video conferencing, and high-speed access to the Internet.

13. How does SMDS compare to frame relay and ATM?

First, SMDS is a service, not a technology; frame relay and ATM are technologies. Since it is technology-independent, SMDS can operate over frame relay or ATM. Technology independence also implies protocol independence. Thus, SMDS can support any LAN protocol such as token ring and Ethernet/802.3, as well as various network protocols including TCP/IP, OSI, IPX, and AppleTalk. Second, SMDS is a packet switching, connectionless service; frame relay and ATM are connection-oriented. This means that it is not necessary to establish a connection through the network prior to data transmission. Instead, packets are transmitted without any delay for setting up or tearing down a circuit. There also is no need to define private virtual circuits (PVCs) or committed interface rates (CIRs) as is the case with frame relay. Thus, an SMDS network is simpler to design than frame relay. Third, SMDS's bandwidth range (56 kbps to SONET rates) provides a better range at the low end than ATM and a better range at the high end than frame relay. Furthermore, unlike frame relay, an SMDS circuit is fully committed to its specified rate, and you only pay for the bandwidth used. Fourth, SMDS provides several network management features including usage-based billing and users' usage statistics. The SMDS's addressing scheme also provides a sort of built-in security measure by restricting data transfers to nodes assigned a specific group address. Many of these features are not available from SMDS's competition. Table 13-1 summarizes many of the features and benefits of SMDS; Table 13-2 lists some of SMDS's disadvantages.

14. I must be missing something here. If SMDS has all of these features and benefits, how come it doesn't receive the kind of attention and hype frame relay and ATM receive?

You are right in your observation that SMDS seems to have been overshadowed by frame relay and ATM. However, this is only true in the United States. In Europe, SMDS is popular. (See the next question.) Many reasons have been cited in the trade publications explaining why SMDS got off to a slow start in the United States and then never did materialize into a universally compelling and accepted service. We will summarize them here for you.

First, as is the case in trying to sell any new technology or service, success depends on proper prior planning and marketing. It has been speculated that the LECs failed in both of these areas when it came to SMDS. Poor planning on the LECs' part resulted in expensive equipment, which gave SMDS the reputation of being an expensive service. Contributing to this reputation was SMDS's initial lack of support for low data rates (less than DS-1). Many organizations that could have benefited from SMDS service were locked out because they could not afford (or justify) the high cost associated with high speeds and the potential wasted bandwidth. Although some LECs now offer low-speed SMDS, which makes the service more attractive to companies with limited resources and bandwidth requirements, it's a matter of too little too late since these companies are opting instead for frame relay.

Table 13-1. SMDS Features and Related Benefits

Feature	Related Benefit
1. Service, not a technology	1. Can operate over frame relay or ATM
2. Protocol-independent	2. Supports multiple LAN or network protocols
3. 56/64 kbps to SONET speeds	3. Complete range of speeds for all applications
4. Connectionless	4. Obviates need to define PVCs as w/frame relay
5. Packet switched	5. Packets transmitted without delay
6. Logical, fully meshed connectivity	6. Reliable and robust LAN-to-LAN connectivity
7. Shared, public network	7. Subscribers can exchange data with each other
8. Uses 53-byte cells similar to ATM	8. Smooth migration to ATM
9. No CIRs as with frame relay	9. Guaranteed bandwidth; pay only for usage
10. Built-in management	10. Provides usage-based billing and statistics

Table 13-2. SMDS Disadvantages

SMDS Disadvantages
1. Restricted availability—the number of LECs offering SMDS is very limited.
2. Limited nationwide/global service—MCI is the only IEC to offer inter-LATA SMDS.
3. Perceived as an expensive service.
4. Overshadowed by frame relay and ATM.
5. Although capable, SMDS does not provide voice or video support.
6. Need for private networks via public backbone is provided by the Internet and VPNs.

From a technology perspective, insufficient attention also was given to how neighboring LECs would interconnect their SMDS networks. This led to incompatible methods that made customers with LANs that crossed LATA boundaries hesitant to subscribe to SMDS. Although this issue also has been addressed, it is once again a matter of too little too late. Since the SMDS market never materialized, commitment to SMDS among the LECs has been spotty at best. LECs have been opting instead to concentrate on frame relay and ATM. For example, in the United States, among the various LECs, NYNEX does not offer SMDS service, whereas Bell Atlantic does. Furthermore, among the major IXCs (AT&T, MCI WorldCom, and Sprint), only MCI WorldCom offers nationwide SMDS service. This lack of support makes customers wary of the service and less likely to subscribe to it. In fact, the final nail in SMDS's coffin was AT&T's decision to provide frame relay and ATM instead of SMDS.

Another reason for SMDS's lack of market share in the broadband community is it was never designed to support isochronous data, which is needed to transmit real time digital voice and video applications. SMDS was to eventually support voice and video in addition to data. Its DQDB access method provides the necessary technology for this support. However, it doesn't appear that SMDS will be further developed to incorporate support for isochronous services.

Finally, although SMDS has built-in security that enables it to use a shared, public network as the backbone for a private network, this concept has been overshadowed by the Internet and virtual private networks (VPNs).

15. What is the current status and future of SMDS?

From all accounts, SMDS is probably "dead" in the United States. Consider, for example, the following:

(a) The SMDS Interest Group, which was the biggest promoter of SMDS, folded in 1997.

(b) In *Data Communications'* 25th anniversary issue (October 21, 1997), SMDS was identified as one of the top 25 flops. "Switched multimegabit data services were designed to deliver LAN-like performances over the wide area. And it's just what they did, to the dismay of users who got high bandwidth, lots of flexibility—and the variable delays associated with Ethernet. Now the SMDS Interest Group has folded, presumably for lack of interest" (p. 143).

(c) MCI WorldCom is the only inter-exchange carrier that offers SMDS.

(d) Some local exchange carriers have discontinued offering SMDS service. US West, for example, cited a dearth of customer demand as its reason for canceling SMDS.

On the other hand, since it is a service, SMDS can coexist with ATM and frame relay. That is, SMDS subscribers can migrate to ATM or use ATM or frame relay as the underlying technology for their SMDS service. It is uncertain, though, whether this will ever come to fruition on a large-scale basis in the United States. From all accounts it is unlikely that SMDS will grow in market share or be developed further. It might, however, survive as a niche market.

Although SMDS is not in widespread use in the United States, it is still popular in Europe. Providers include British Telecommunications (London), Telecom Eireann (Irish Republic), France Telecom (Paris), Belgacom (Brussels), and Deutsche Telekom (Bonn). Other countries in which SMDS deployment is high include Denmark, Switzerland, Austria, Italy, Sweden, and Australia.

End-of-Chapter Commentary

This concludes our brief discussion on SMDS. For additional information about this service, you are encouraged to consult the references listed in the appendix. You also might want to review Chapter 12 (Frame Relay) and Chapter 14 (ATM) to compare SMDS to these two technologies.

Chapter 14

Asynchronous Transfer Mode (ATM)

Asynchronous Transfer Mode (ATM) is a high-speed switching network architecture that was created in the late 1980s/early 1990s to apply circuit switching concepts to data networks. ATM is also known as *cell relay* to distinguish it from frame relay (see Chapter 12). In many regards ATM is considered a "universal" network because it can combine the delivery of a wide range of services (data, voice, and video) over a single network, has a robust quality of service (QoS) facility, can provide seamless interconnectivity between local and wide area networks, and supports a wide range of data rates—from 25 Mbps to 155 Mbps over copper, and from 100 Mbps to 622 Mbps (OC-12) and higher over fiber (multimode or single mode). A common implementation is 155 Mbps ATM over SONET (see Chapter 7). ATM has been briefly presented from various perspectives in nearly every chapter of this book. In this chapter we provide a more detailed examination of this technology. The major topics we discuss include

- Definition and History of ATM (Questions 1–3)
- General Concepts and Operation of ATM (Questions 4-–7)
- ATM Interfaces and the Anchorage Accord (Questions 8–10)
- ATM Components and Addressing (Questions 11–13, 22)
- ATM Cells, Switches, and Virtual Connections (Questions 14–22)
- ATM Adaptation Layer (AAL) (Questions 23–26)
- Data Types Insights (Questions 27–29)
- ATM vs. Gigabit Ethernet (Questions 30–32)
- ATM and LANs (Question 33–34)
- ATM, Frame Relay, and SONET (Question 35–36)
- ATM Forum (Question 37)

1. What is ATM?

Asynchronous Transfer Mode (ATM) is a sophisticated, multispeed network environment that provides a variety of complex network services for applications requiring various types of network solutions. It can be used to carry data, voice and video—separately or simultaneously—over the same network path, and is one of the most complex communications technologies available today for public or private network infrastructures. ATM can be used in LANs, MANs, and WANs, all at the same time if needed. Using terminology developed in previous chapters, ATM might also be considered a "hyphenated" protocol—it is connection-oriented, full-duplex, point-to-point, and cell-switched.

2. I know about connection-oriented, full-duplex, and point-to-point. What is "cell-switched"?

The concept of cell-switched is very similar to frame relay (Chapter 12), which uses switches to transfer variable-length frames within the frame relay cloud from source to destination. Instead of using frames, ATM uses fixed-length *cells*, which contain exactly 53-bytes—48 bytes for user data and 5 bytes for overhead. As a result, ATM is sometimes referred to as *cell relay*, which dates back to the late 1960s. The concept of cell relay is predicated on time domain multiplexing (TDM, see Chapter 4) and packet switching. The term "asynchronous TDM" (ATDM) was used to describe cell relay by a Bell Labs researcher in 1968. We will discuss ATM cells in more detail later in the chapter.

3. How did ATM get started?

ATM has its roots in broadband ISDN (B-ISDN), which some people refer to as second-generation ISDN. (*Note:* In the presence of B-ISDN, "standard" or "first-generation" ISDN is called *narrowband ISDN*. See Chapter 11.) In 1986, the standards organization, CCITT (now part of ITU), decided to make cell relay the transfer mode of B-ISDN. The CCITT also decided to change the name of this cell-based technology from ATDM to ATM. CCITT's decision meant that broadband networks throughout the world would be based on ATM. Two years later, in 1988, a three-layered referenced model for ATM was defined by CCITT. These layers, which represent the first three layers of the B-ISDN reference model, include the physical layer, the ATM layer, and the ATM adaptation layer. It is important to note that the ATM layers do not necessarily correspond to the layers of the OSI model. The ATM layers are summarized in Figure 14-1. (*Note:* Much of the information presented in Figure 14-1 is discussed later in this chapter.) After much discussion, the CCITT also defined ATM's cell format to consist of 53-bytes—48 bytes for user data and 5 bytes for overhead. Finally, in 1990, the CCITT issued its first set of recommendations that specified the details of ATM for B-ISDN. For a good overview of ATM's history, see Gould (1994).

4. What else can you tell me about ATM?

ATM operates as a "network within a network" concept. It has its own internal handshaking and management protocols, quality of service (QoS) facilities, performance and flow control facilities, and many other components that are usually separated on network technologies such as frame relay. ATM is very much like building a subway system that can support other transportation systems on top of it. The "upper" transportation systems do not know that ATM is acting as an independent freeway and are oblivious of the complex nature of ATM networking.

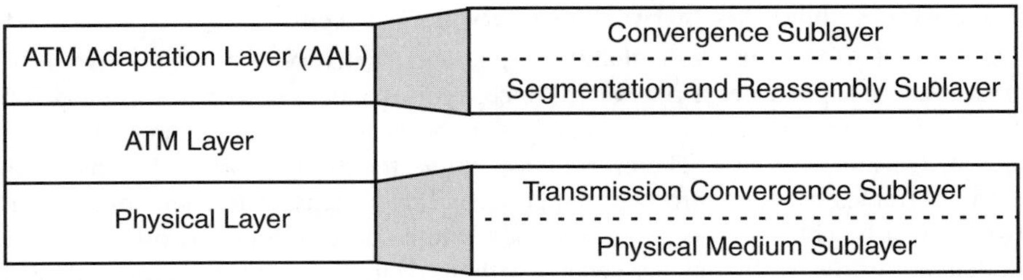

ATM Adaptation Layer (AAL)	Convergence Sublayer
	- -
	Segmentation and Reassembly Sublayer
ATM Layer	
Physical Layer	Transmission Convergence Sublayer
	- -
	Physical Medium Sublayer

Physical Layer

- Transports cells from one interface to another via a communications channel.
- Supports both optical and electrical communications channels.
- LAN support ranges from 25 Mbps to 155 Mbps for copper and fiber.
- WAN support includes SONET/SDH rates over fiber.
- Contains two sublayers: The *Physical Medium Sublayer* function is restricted to only medium dependent functions such as bit transfer, bit alignment, and electrical-to-optical conversions. The *Transmission Convergence Sublayer* performs functions related to converting cells from the ATM layer into bits on the sending node, and converting bits into cells on the receiving node.

ATM Layer

- Performs cell multiplexing/demultiplexing and switching.
- Provides virtual connections between end points.
- Generates appropriate cell headers on a sending node based on information received from higher layers; extracts cell header on a receiving node and passes cell payload to higher layers.

ATM Adaptation Layer (AAL)

- Partitions higher level user data into 48-byte cells plus necessary overhead.
- Defines five different adaptation types to support different service classes:
  — *AAL1:* Supports Class A services, which are connection-oriented, constant-bit rate (CBR) (e.g., voice transmissions).
  — *AAL2:* Supports Class B services, which are connection-oriented, variable-bit rate (VBR) (e.g., synchronized data, packet-based video).
  — *AAL3 / AAL4:* Supports Class C and Class D services, which are, respectively, connection-oriented VBR (e.g., bursty data used for file transfers) and connectionless VBR (e.g., LAN data).
  — *AAL5:* Supports Class C and Class D services; known as the *Simple and Efficient Adaptation Layer* (SEAL) and used for bursty data transfers in which higher-layer protocols perform error control. AAL5 is a modification of connection-oriented VBR.
- Consists of two sublayers. The *Convergence Sublayer* (CS) provides a specific AAL service at an AAL network service access point (NSAP). The *Segmentation And Reassembly Sublayer* (SAR) segments higher-level messages into an ATM's cell's 48-byte information field on the sending node, and reassembles this information for delivery to the higher layers on the receiving node.

Figure 14-1. The ATM layers. The physical layer corresponds to OSI's physical layer; the ATM layer generally corresponds to OSI's data link and network layers; the AAL generally corresponds to OSI's higher-level layers (transport, session, and application). (Adapted from Atkins & Norris, 1995; and Bates & Gregory, 1998.)

5. Tell me more about this "network in a network" concept.

OK. One of ATM's features is that it can guarantee delivery of time-sensitive information over the designed network. For instance, typical video as seen on a television set transmits 30 frames of video per second over the airwaves. Not 29, not 31—30 only. That's it. No more, no less. Therefore, it is critical for the network to be able to move exactly 30 frames of video information per second over the network. This means that the network must be able to properly reserve bandwidth space on the network to accommodate delivery of the 30 frames per second without degrading the throughput between the source and destination locations. To do this, all intermediary locations (typically ATM switch devices) between the source and the destination must allocate network "space" to move the information efficiently in the required timeframe. (This is called *isochronous* communications.) This requires various handshaking between systems, bandwidth allocation and management facilities, QoS delivery facilities, and a host of other technologies, algorithms, and techniques to ensure the path between source and destination is clean, fast, and efficient. All this adds up to the need to have a "network in a network" so that ATM devices can properly manage the path of activity between the source and destination systems on the network.

6. Does this mean that communication protocols such as TCP/IP and SNA do not know all of this work is taking place in the ATM hardware?

Yes, Grasshopper. You have searched for enlightenment and found a little.

7. So, is ATM like Ethernet or any other network we have discussed?

Yes and no, unfortunately. It can provide many services that are somewhat equivalent to Ethernet/802.3. It can also be used in a LAN for desktop connectivity instead of Ethernet/802.3. Networking software "thinks" that the ATM environment reacts like OSI Layer 2 hardware, just like Ethernet/802.3, token ring, or FDDI. In terms of functionality, ATM can "be" like Ethernet/802.3 or, more specifically, can be used where Ethernet/802.3 might be used. How it works, however, is a completely different story and is not at all similar in function to other standard LAN technologies.

8. Before we get into some of the technical details of how ATM works, can you give a simple example of an ATM network?

Sure. An ATM network fundamentally resembles a frame relay network. Cells are transmitted from source to destination via an ATM switched subnet. End nodes communicate with an ATM device via a user-to-network interface (UNI), and ATM switches communicate with each other via a network-to-network interface (NNI). The UNI and NNI components are just two of a wide variety of ATM component standards. A typical configuration is shown in Figure 14-2. Also, a simplified example of how ATM facilitates multiservice networking is shown in Figure 14-3.

9. What other component standards are there besides UNI and NNI?

In ATM, there is a hierarchy of standardized interfaces called the *Anchorage Accord*. The basic hierarchy, as defined by the accord, is shown in Figure 14-4. Separate standards

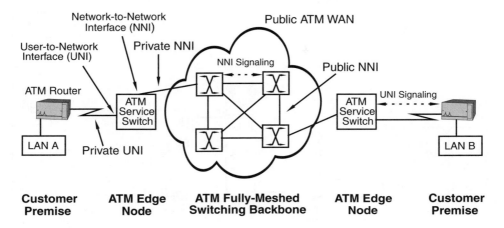

Figure 14-2. In an ATM connection, end nodes communicate with an ATM device via a user-to-network interface (UNI), and ATM devices communicate with each other via a network-to-network interface (NNI). (Adapted from Mehta, 1996.)

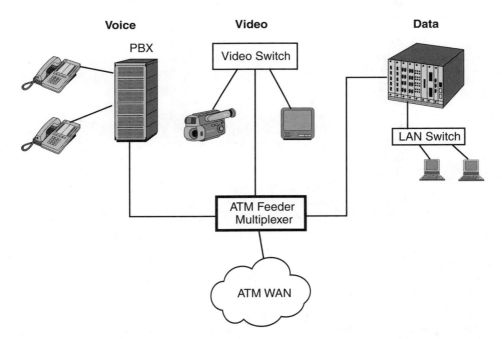

Figure 14-3. A simplified example of how ATM facilitates multiservice networking. ATM is the only network that was built from the ground up to support data, voice and video at the same time. Therefore, an ATM network can be used for almost any type of network environment in use today and in the future.

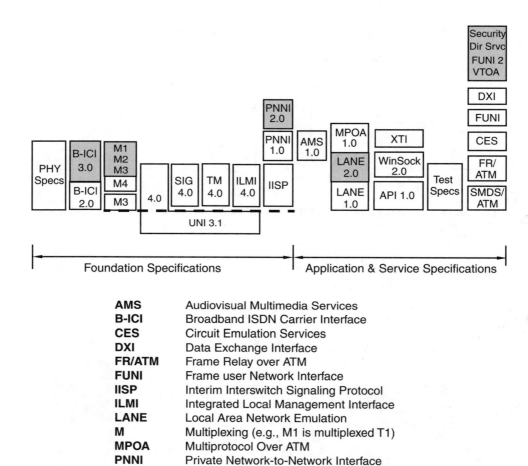

Figure 14-4. The Anchorage Accord hierarchy of standardized ATM interfaces. (*Note:* Shaded components are presently under development; all others are complete.)

define the manner in which network components are interconnected and how they interact with each other. Working from left to right in Figure 14-4, the various components of the ATM environment are defined by the functional specifications listed. At this writing, the various numbers indicate current versions of the specifications. These version numbers, however, will be ever increasing over time as the standards mature and change. Components that are shaded are presently under development; all others are complete.

Note that the standards are divided into two basic groups: Foundation Specifications, and Application and Service Specifications. The former define ATM base function sets; the latter define how other networks and applications interoperate with ATM network components. It is outside the scope of this book to get into the massive details of each functional component due to their complexity and also the amount of time it takes to properly define and illustrate every item. However, we do need to spend a little time on some of the components to understand how ATM works and why the functional layers are necessary.

10. Is this how ATM is able to provide for the various types of services?

In a general sense, yes. In an ATM network, the type of computer being used is irrelevant to the network transportation capabilities. This means that PBXs and data networks from computer-to-computer or video-to-display facilities can all share the same network infrastructure simultaneously. This is done by using all the functional standards shown in Figure 14-4 to provide exact interfaces for different data types to the network infrastructure. In this manner, the network supports all the different types of interconnection services required as well as all the different types of transmission requirements.

11. How does an ATM network keep all the traffic sorted out so that the right messages get to the right places?

Just like any other type of network, ATM uses addresses for each connection point. Two types of addresses are used. For private networks, ATM uses OSI's (see Chapter 2) network service access points (NSAPs) for its addressing mechanism. NSAPs are 20-byte addresses and include a 13-byte prefix that can be used to identify a specific location including a country, region, or end system. Public ATM networks, however, use E.164, the standard ISDN global numbering addressing format specified by ITU-T (see Chapter 13). There is a move underfoot to standardize on NSAP-based addresses for all devices, public or private.

12. Could you expand on the components of an ATM network and explain how they interconnect with each other?

Certainly. Let's start with the source node. In order for a device to be connected to an ATM network, it must first have an ATM-based network interface card (NIC) installed. (See Chapter 6 for more information about NICs.) These NICs, which are layer 2 devices and contain on-board ATM circuitry, are then connected to a local switch that is usually provided by the corporate networking people. The physical connection between the workstation and the local switch (also called a "private switch") can be copper (typically UTP category 5 running at 25 Mbps or 155 Mbps), fiber (at various speeds from 155 Mbps to terabit ranges), or wireless (10 Mbps or greater). The specification for a NIC to "talk" to a switch is the user-to-network interface (UNI) functional specification, which was mentioned earlier. The purpose of the UNI specification is to define exactly how an end station communicates to the next level of network interface, which is a private switch at a site. This specification is quite large and complex. Among others, it specifies the handshaking between the NIC and switch, the quality of service requirements for traffic between the

NIC and switch, and all the other connection-oriented facilities ATM requires to ensure that the NIC and switch are content with each other when connected on the network. Furthermore, UNI also specifies sections of the hardware physical attributes like copper interface issues, fiber interface issues and wireless component functionalities. These collective specifications and functions are generally referred to as UNI signaling. (See Figure 14-2.) Thus, UNI is specifically intended for end-point communication to the ATM switch environment.

13. So does this mean that switches and other components communicate to each other differently?

Yes. Switch-to-switch communication in a private (premises) network is called *Private Network-to-Network Interface (PNNI)*. PNNI provides some specific functionality that switches need between each other but that end stations could not care less about. Other specifications exist: the Broadband ISDN Inter-Carrier Interface (B-ICI), which is used for connecting two public ATM networks between different network service providers, and LAN User-to-Network Interface (LUNI), which specifies how an emulated LAN user connects to an ATM environment. For example, if you have an existing Ethernet/802.3 or other LAN, then there is a specification called LANE (Local Area Network Emulation) to help you connect to an ATM network. Similarly, if you have an existing frame relay WAN facility that needs to interoperate with ATM, there is the Frame User Network Interface (FUNI). There are many others. Thus, wherever there is a network connection point on an ATM network that connects to a dissimilar connection point, a functional specification (and related abbreviation, of course) associated with the connection method is defined. (See Figure 14-4.)

14. Tell me more about ATM switches.

An ATM switch implements a routing method called a switch fabric. Switch fabric algorithms come in a wide variety of implementations, but the most common types are called *Batcher-Banyan* and *Delta* switching environments. The algorithms in the switch exchange information with other interconnected switches to learn where source and destination SAP locations are in the overall network. By using these high-speed methods, a very large network of components can quickly be mapped and discovered when traffic hits the physical network and needs to be forwarded to the proper location. When first powered-up, switches configure themselves by going into an autodiscovery mode, which enables them to automatically learn about other connected switches. They also provide temporary NSAP addresses to ATM connection points that may need one to interoperate and help manage the overall network environment from a configuration and traffic management perspective.

15. How does ATM transport data across the network via switches from source to destination?

To answer this question, we need to discuss, from a more technical perspective, the three main parts of an ATM network: ATM cells, virtual connections, and switches. These three components represent the essential building blocks of all ATM networks and are highly interrelated. Let's begin with cells. Feel free to interrupt us at any time.

As we stated earlier in the chapter, ATM uses 53-byte (octet) cells comprising a 5-byte header and a 48-byte payload (user data). ATM cells are the basic unit of data that cross the UNI, and they are fixed length. Thus, cells are *always* the same size—never larger, never smaller. It is set up this way for throughput and buffer management reasons (video gets real unhappy when the network is slow). The structure of a cell is shown in Figure 14-5. The cell's header carries the information needed to transport a cell across an ATM network.

16. Time out. I need a point of clarification. Why is the word "octet" suddenly being used instead of "byte?"

The term "octet" means eight bits. The term "byte," however, does not necessarily mean eight bits to some people. During the early days of computing, "byte" was used to represent a unit of information composed of some number of consecutive bits. Thus, depending on the system, you could have four-bit bytes, eight-bit bytes, 16-bit bytes, 32-bit bytes, and so forth. As the computer industry matured, most people accepted a byte to have exactly eight bits. The use of octet in ATM instead of byte can be viewed from two perspectives. The first perspective is one of definition: Octet is the better term since it is well-defined—it has always represented exactly eight bits of information. The second perspective is one of snobbishness: Some people use the word "octet" to remind others that they have been around systems a long time and that some systems used bytes of varying sizes.

17. OK. Thanks. Let's get back to the ATM cell. Given its size, how can a cell carry routing information? For example, LAN addresses used for Ethernet or token ring are six bytes. Thus, source and destination addresses must occupy 12 bytes. How does this fit into a cell?

This is true *if* ATM were using LAN-type addressing schemes. Remember: ATM networks are based on a "network within a network" concept and, therefore, can do some clever things that don't require each cell to carry complete source and destination addresses in them like a LAN frame does.

18. Please explain.

OK. In fact, this is probably a good time to introduce the second of ATM's basic building blocks, namely, virtual connections. In ATM, two types of virtual connections are defined: *virtual channel connection (VCC)*, and *virtual path connection (VPC)*. A virtual channel connection is a virtual circuit that provides a logical connection between a source and destination. These virtual circuits can be either permanent (PVC) or switched (SVC). (*Note:* PVCs and SVCs are discussed in detail in Chapter 12, Frame Relay.) A *virtual channel identifier (VCI)*, which is contained within the header of a cell (Figure 14-5), is used to identify the channel. VCIs are similar to frame relay's data link connection identifiers (DCLIs), which were discussed in Chapter 12.

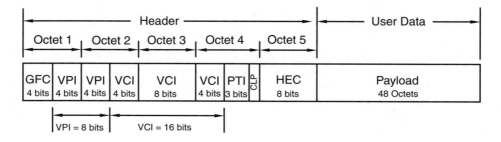

GFC   Generic Flow Control—controls the flow of data across the user-to-network interface (UNI) permitting multiple ATM devices to be attached to the same network interface. GFC bits are reassigned and become VPI bits at the network-to-network interface (NNI) thus providing additional support for more virtual paths.

VPI   Virtual Path Identifier—part of the network address used to identify a grouping of channels between network entities. The first 4 bits of the VPI are in the first octet, the remaining bits are in the second octet.

VCI   Virtual Channel Identifier—a pointer that identifies the virtual channel the system is using on a particular path. The VPI/VCI combination make up the data link running between two network nodes. The VCI is 16 bits long and uses the second 4 bits of octet 2, all 8 bits of octet 3, and first 4 bits of octet 4.

PT   Payload Type—indicates the type of information contained in the cell. Because cells are used for transporting different types of information, several types of payload type indicators have been defined:

— A 0 in the most significant bit (000, 001, 010, and 011) denotes that the cell is carrying *user information*. User information cells with a middle bit of 1 (010 and 011) indicate that the cell has experienced congestion.

— A 1 in the most significant bit (100, 101, 110, and 111) denotes that the cell is carrying *control* or *resource management information*.

• 100 and 101 represent network maintenance and control.

• 110 is for resource management.

• 111 is reserved for future definition.

CLP   Cell Loss Payload—specifies whether or not to discard the cell in the presence of congestion. If set to 1, the network can discard the cell; If set to 0, then the cell might not be discarded. (Similar to BECN and FECN in frame relay.)

HEC   Header Error Control—provides error correction for single-bit errors, and error detection for multiple-bit errors in the cell header.

Figure 14-5. Structure and contents of an ATM UNI cell. Note that a NNI cell is nearly identical to the UNI cell. The only difference is there is no need for the GFC field. In the NNI cell, GFC is subsumed by VPI, which totals 12 bits instead of 8. (Adapted from Atkins & Norris, 1995.)

A virtual path connection is a semi-permanent connection that provides a logical collection of virtual channels that have the same end points. In other words, a VPC carries a group of virtual channels all with the same end points. For example, a multimedia application between two physicians' workstations might consist of a single path that supports two virtual channels: one channel for computer conferencing and a second channel for transferring large image files such as X-rays. Thus, in this illustration, a single virtual path supports two virtual channels. For another application, consider the common situation of an organization providing connectivity to a remote site. In a non-ATM environment, separate links are needed for voice, data, and video support. With ATM, though, a single virtual path can be established that supports several virtual connections. For example, one VCC could be for telephone service, a second VCC could be used for a frame relay connection, and a third VCC could be used for video conferencing. Thus, virtual paths enable any connection that uses the same network path from source to destination to be bundled into a single unit. A virtual path identifier (VPI) is used denote a virtual path and is included in a cell's header (Figure 14-5). A virtual channel can only be established after a virtual path connection is in place.

An illustration of VCCs, VPCs, VPIs, and VCIs is given in Figure 14-6. Note that on each physical link a VPI specifies a virtual path and a VCI specifies a specific virtual channel. Further note that VCIs only have local significance. Thus, different virtual paths may reuse VCIs. However, VCIs on the same virtual path must be different. Finally, virtual paths can be used to establish a logical network topology independent of the physical topology.

19. Reference your last statement: Does this mean that there doesn't have to be a physical link between switches?

That's correct. Two switches can be interconnected via a VPC without having a direct physical link between them. Remember: ATM is connection-oriented, which means that a circuit is first established prior to data transmissions. Thus, as part of a call setup, two non-adjacent switches without a physical link can be included as part of a virtual path for a particular session. Note further that virtual paths can also provide a form of traffic control by logically (not physically) partitioning network traffic based on the type of data being carried and associated quality of service.

20. How do VPIs and VCIs help with addressing?

By using virtual path information to move data between connection points on the network, a full addressing scheme is not necessary. This means that much smaller "addresses" can be used to move information between connecting points on the network. By using such a scheme, full addressing information for the source and destination is not required in each cell and this reduces overall overhead in the cell formats. The process (albeit simplified) is as follows: An ATM switch receives a cell at an incoming port. The switch examines the cell's header to identify the values contained in the VPI/VCI fields and then consults its translation table to determine the appropriate outgoing port based on the VPI/VCI values. Once the correct port is identified, the switch transmits the cell out the port.

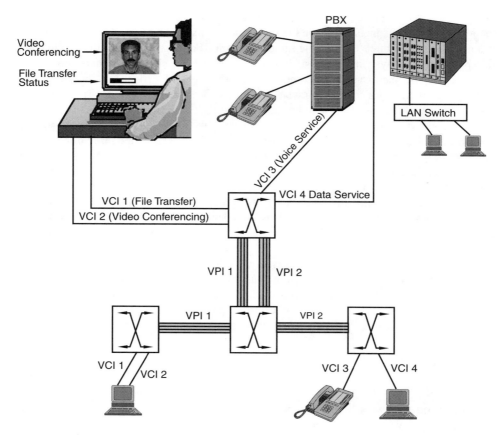

Figure 14-6. In an ATM network, a virtual path connection is a logical collection of virtual channels that have the same end points. Virtual paths indicators (VPIs) and virtual connection identifiers (VCIs) are used to label these respective connections. In this illustration, virtual channels 1 and 2 are carried by the same virtual path (VPI 1), and virtual channels 3 and 4 are carried by the same virtual path (VPI 2). (*Note:* VPI 1 and VPI 2 between the two central ATM switches *could* be combined into a single path and still carry all four virtual circuits and their corresponding VCIs). (Adapted from Minoli, 1992.)

21. So instead of carrying source and destination addresses like TCP/IP packets do, ATM relies on VPIs and VCIs to transport cells across the network. Is this correct?

Yes it is. In a nutshell, ATM switches switch based on information contained in the cell header. In other words, ATM transports data via fixed-length cells based on the VPI/VCI values contained within a cell's header. During call setup, a route from source to destination is established by ATM end nodes and switches. As this path is being established, VPIs and VCIs are assigned. Thus, the determination of a route is made only once. Furthermore, unlike TCP/IP internetworking devices (routers or layer 3 switches), ATM switches do not have to decode large and relatively complicated headers in order to determine the appropriate output port. A direct consequence of this simplification is forwarding decisions are implemented in silicon, thus enabling them to be implemented at wire speed. (*Note:* At one time this was considered an ATM advantage. However, ASIC technology has since enabled routers to perform traditional table lookups and packet forwarding at hardware speeds, thus providing them with switch-like performance. See Chapter 7 for more information about ASIC-based routers.) ATM also avoids collisions by having users negotiate throughput and quality of service in advance. Using these parameters, ATM can multiplex several users, each on a separate virtual channel, onto a single virtual path. Additional virtual paths can then be added by increasing the size of the switch.

22. Can you summarize the various concepts related to ATM addressing for me?

Sure. Each ATM station has a unique hardware address—called a *station identifier*—that is part of its network interface card. A station identifier is similar to a MAC sublayer address used in Ethernet/802.3 and token ring LANs. In addition, an ATM station also has a network-layer address (or equivalent) that provides the station with a global address. The addressing method used for these network-layer address equivalents is either NSAP (for private ATMs) or E.164 (for public ATMs). These two addresses are the only addresses that actually bind an ATM station to a physical link. Finally, when a connection is established from source to destination, VPIs and VCIs assignments are made that specify the virtual connection path. It is these VPI/VCI assignments that get incorporated into a cell's header and are used for route determination. (*Note:* This is a rather simplified summary of ATM addressing concepts and does not include issues such as looping, multicasting, or routing protocols.)

23. OK. I think I have a fairly good grasp of some of the basic ATM concepts. What I still do not understand, though, is how ATM can support different types of data simultaneously.

ATM accommodates different types of traffic via the ATM Adaptation Layer (AAL) protocol (see Figure 14-1), which consists of two sublayers: convergence; and segmentation and reassembly (SAR). On the sending side, the convergence sublayer accepts data messages from higher-layer application protocols, interprets the type and format of the messages, and then prepares them for processing by the SAR sublayer. The SAR sublayer then translates the messages into ATM format by packaging them into the 48-byte payload portion of an ATM cell. The reverse is done on the receiving side. (*Note:* The AAL protocol actually does more than what is described here. For example, the AAL also resolves transmission errors, takes care of lost or misinserted cells, and provides flow and timing control. We will not discuss these services.)

The convergence sublayer's interpretation of data type and format is based on the specific *class of service (CoS)* assigned to the data by the application. The AAL provides support for four different service classes. These are summarized in Table 14-1. When the SAR sublayer receives data from the convergence sublayer, it processes the data so they are consistent (i.e., meets the transmission needs) with the specified type and format. Depending on the data type, the AAL protocol provides five different AAL types to accommodate

Table 14-1. ATM Service Classes and Descriptions

Service Class	Description
Class A	Constant-bit rate (CBR), connection-oriented transmissions that require a strict timing relationship between source and destination nodes (e.g., circuit emulation and voice transmissions).
Class B	Variable-bit rate (VBR), connection-oriented transmissions that require a strict timing relationship between source and destination nodes (e.g., synchronized data transmissions, or packet-mode video for video conferencing).
Class C	Connection-oriented VBR transmissions that do not require a strict timing relationship between source and destination nodes (e.g., LAN data transfer applications such as frame relay).
Class D	Connectionless VBR transmissions that do not require a strict timing relationship between source and destination nodes (e.g., LAN data transfer applications such as SMDS).

Table 14-2. ATM Adaptation Layers (AAL) Types and Corresponding Service Classes

AAL Type	Service Class
AAL1	Class A
AAL2	Class B
AAL3	Class C and D
AAL4	Class C and D
AAL5	Class C and D

a particular service class. For example, AAL1 is used for data that require connection-oriented, constant-bit rate transmissions. An example of this data type is traditional voice service. AAL2 is used for data types that require connection-oriented variable-bit rate data transmissions. An example of this data type is packet video, which might be used in a videoconferencing application. AAL3 and AAL4 are used for connection-oriented or connectionless variable-bit rate transmissions. Examples of these data types include bursty data typical of LAN applications such as those found on frame relay (connection-oriented) and SMDS (connectionless) networks. Lastly, AAL5, which initially was labeled the Simple and Efficient Adaptation Layer (SEAL), is used for transmissions in which higher layer protocols provide error recovery. AAL5 is an improvement to AAL3. As a result, through the AAL protocol and its adaptation layers, an ATM transmission is able to accommodate different types of transmissions simultaneously on the same network. The correspondence between AAL types and service classes is summarized in Table 14-2.

24. There almost seems to be a one-to-one correspondence between service class and AAL type. Is this the way it was designed?

The initial design was to have a different AAL type for each service class. Specifically, AAL1 through AAL4 were designed, respectively, to support service classes A through D. As in most cases, though, reality got in the way. As AAL3 and AAL4 were being developed, it was observed that there was considerable overlap between the two specifications. Consequently, they were combined into a single type, which is now referred to as AAL Type 3/4.

25. So how did AAL5 get created?

AAL5 was developed to provide a less complex Type 3/4 AAL. Many of the services supported in classes C and D did not warrant the level of sophistication that was incorporated into Type 3/4. As a result, a more simple and efficient adaptation layer (hence AAL5's original name, SEAL) emerged.

In reality, only AAL5 is widely implemented and used. The reason for this is that one of the ATM standards bodies, the ATM Forum, originally defined AAL5 for efficient transmission of TCP/IP. Because AAL5 uses a very small amount of the cell for its overhead, it is very popular in its use by vendors and ATM technology implementors. Whether AAL is used or not in a connection is up to the vendor of the protocol stack that uses the ATM hardware in a network topology.

Given the popularity of the AAL5 protocol, the format of its protocol data unit (PDU) at the segmentation and reassembly (SAR) level is shown in Figure 14-7. (*Note:* Recall that a block of higher-level data is encapsulated in a PDU at the convergence sublayer. This PDU is then passed to the SAR sublayer where it is segmented into a 48-byte "chunks" so that it can be transported in the payload area of an ATM cell. What is shown in Figure 14-7 is the format of AAL5's SAR PDU.) As can be seen, a cell can have many additional fields in it besides the general ATM format.

26. So all the other AAL layers really are not used?

That's correct. There will probably be some of them implemented over time, new ones invented and older ones discarded. It's the Zen of Networking at work.

27. OK. Now that I have a basic understanding of ATM, why do I care about it?

As with any network environment, there is change. If you look at the direction of overall network trends, you'll see a strong movement toward the convergence of data, voice, and video applications. To satisfy all three network types, some basic functions must be created to allow all three types of network technologies to coexist.

28. What kinds of technologies are required for data, voice, and video that are so different from each other?

Data networking allows traffic characteristics that can be bursty in nature, and data can have variable-length packets or frames. Data traffic also can tolerate a certain amount of

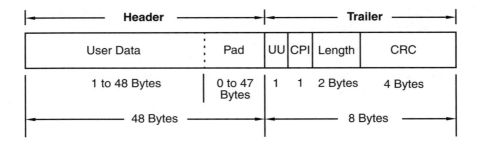

User Data This is the actual user information being transported across the network. Although it can range in length from 1 byte to 65,535 bytes, it is segmented into 48-byte chunks.

Pad This field is used to pad the data unit to 48 bytes. Its length varies from 0 to 47 bytes.

UU This one-byte *User-to-User* field allows one byte of information to be conveyed transparently between users.

CPI This one-byte *Common Part Indicator* is intended to identify subsequent fields but it is not currently being used.

Length This two-byte field stores the length of the transmitted data. This field is necessary to distinguish between user data and padding.

CRC The *Cyclic Redundancy Check* field uses a 32-bit checksum to provide data integrity of the entire PDU.

Figure 14-7. Format and contents of the AAL5 segmentation and reassembly (SAR) protocol data unit (PDU). (Adapted from Atkins & Norris, 1995.)

transmission delay, especially for non-real-time traffic. This implies that data arrival rates can be variable in nature, which suggests that variable-bit rate (VBR) transmissions are acceptable to data applications.

Voice traffic, on the other hand, is more sensitive to the arrival time of traffic. It's a good idea for packets carrying part of a conversation to arrive quickly enough to avoid blank spots of time ("dead air") in the conversation. This suggests a constant-bit rate (CBR) transmission be used for voice. There also is a problem with full duplex speech, where two or more people speak at exactly the same time and can be heard simultaneously. Networks don't necessarily agree with this concept very well. Voice, however, is not a big bandwidth hog, as a rule, so fast data networks with VBR can support voice communications as long as the network is swift and does not suffer congestion or loss delays.

Video is even more sensitive to timing. Such transmissions expect the number of frames transmitted from one site to another to arrive in order and in a very specific time-frame (usually measured in milliseconds). Technologies such as constant-bit rate, where the number of arrival bits in a transmission are constant and consistent, are essential to making a standard traffic arrival rate possible. However, CBR is not enough. The frames must be transmitted in the proper order and must arrive at the correct speed within a specific timeframe. To do this, the network must pre-reserve bandwidth in the path from the source to the destination to ensure that all the bits arrive in order and on time. This general method of providing CBR with a guaranteed delivery sequence in a specific timeframe while pre-reserving path "space" is called *isochronous communications* and is common to all ATM networks. (*Note:* There was a brief push for something called "isochronous Ethernet," which is discussed in Chapter 8. IsoEthernet never gained widespread support in the industry.) When you add to the discussion that different network applications will ultimately require more and more bandwidth in the future to satisfy consumer needs, ATM is the only network presently on the drawing board that provides the transmission technologies, transmission rates, and quality of service (QoS) required to address user needs . . . at least for now.

29. What you are saying, then, is that the merging together of network functions, which seems to be the "wave of the future," requires technologies only ATM can currently deliver?

That is correct. Furthermore, these are issues of which the industry is aware. There will be plenty of applications in the future where ATM as we know it will probably not be sufficient to provide all the capabilities required and a new "super ATM" will be needed to solve those problems. That is some time off from now, though.

30. What about Gigabit Ethernet? Isn't it fast enough for all of this?

For data and voice, probably so. However, it is still a VBR technology, which has great problems with video equipment. This becomes acutely evident in the presence of network congestion, or when a specific delivery timeframe is required. A good example of this is High Definition Television (HDTV), which will eventually appear on global networks as a standard transmission method. Furthermore, Gigabit Ethernet, while nice and quick, cannot serve as a global WAN; it is designed for local or metropolitan network environments.

31. Even so, I thought new protocols like RSVP and RTP were supposed to remedy Gigabit Ethernet's QoS shortcomings.

It looks like you have been doing some additional reading. The Resource Reservation Protocol (RSVP) and the Realtime Transport Protocol (RTP) are indeed designed to address the Ethernet-QoS issue. Both protocols permit applications to reserve a specific amount of bandwidth for data transmission. When you consider what the incorporation of these protocols with Gigabit Ethernet brings to the table, and then compare their functions to ATM, several problems emerge. First, Ethernet/802.3 frames are of variable length ranging from 64 bytes to 1,518 bytes. This alone suggests that the delivery rate will not be consistent. ATM uses fixed-size cells, which does guarantee a constant delivery rate. Second, in an Ethernet/802.3 transmission, frames are queued in a switch on a first-in first-out basis. (See Chapters 6 and 8 for information about Ethernet switches.) Furthermore, before a switch transmits queued frame, n, the entire contents of queued frame, $n - 1$, must be transmitted. Thus, a switch transmits queued frames sequentially and in the order in which they were buffered. The problem with this scheme is that if two frames, both of which are reserving bandwidth, arrive at a switch port simultaneously (within a few microseconds of each other), the frame arriving first gets transmitted first, and the frame arriving second gets buffered. ATM switches, on the other hand, can simultaneously create and service multiple, independent queues having different priorities (class of service) and different transmission needs based on data type (i.e., quality of service). Moreover, these simultaneous and multiple transmissions are performed with a constant delivery rate. (*Note:* Additional information about the Gigabit Ethernet-ATM debate is provided in Chapter 8.)

32. So, just making the network faster will not solve the convergence problems?

Ja. Das ist richtig. Even the work on Terabit Ethernet, currently underway at this writing, will yield a network faster than the currently fastest commercially available ATM network (today). However, it is not slated to have the proper traffic controls and network reliability factors that are inherent in an ATM environment. It is also not expected to provide a network larger than that used in a campus environment or possibly around a city (in a metropolitan network environment).

33. Well, what about the campus environment? Isn't ATM a bit pricey? Doesn't its data rate of 25 Mbps fall short when compared to Fast Ethernet or Gigabit Ethernet LANs?

Good question. ATM was initially designed as a WAN technology for use in B-ISDN. This has not stopped its encroachment, however, as a technology for MANs and LANs. ATM's infiltration on the LAN front was designed to serve as a 155 Mbps backbone technology and deliver 25 Mbps (called "low-speed" ATM) to the desktop. This grand scheme of a unified ATM WAN, MAN, and LAN, however got hijacked by Ethernet, specifically, Fast Ethernet, which delivers 100 Mbps to the desktop, and Gigabit Ethernet, which provides a 1,000 Mbps backbone. So, yes, compared to Fast and Gigabit Ethernet, ATM data rates are low and the deployment of ATM is quite expensive. However, the ATM Forum is working on a 2.5 Gbps ATM specification for the LAN backbone. So just when you thought Gigabit Ethernet has emerged victorious as the only logical choice for the high-speed LAN backbone, it appears as if another ATM contender is among us.

34. What else does ATM have available for LAN support?

For starters, there's ATM's local area network emulation (LANE) interface (see Figure 14-4), which provides a technology that enables ATM to emulate Ethernet/802.3 or token ring. LANs that incorporate LANE are called *emulated local area networks (ELANs)*. In ATM's protocol hierarchy, LANE is above AAL5 in the ATM Adaptation Layer. The LANE protocol defines a service interface for the network layer that functions identically to the one used by Ethernet/802.3 and token ring LANs. Data that cross this interface are encapsulated in the appropriate MAC sublayer format. In an ELAN environment, LAN end nodes are connected to a special LAN emulation device that runs a LAN emulation client (LEC) process. The LEC functions as a proxy ATM end node. In addition, a native ATM end node runs a LAN emulation server (LES) process, which is responsible for resolving MAC hardware addresses to ATM addresses.

As an example of this process consider the situation where an Ethernet/802.3 source node wants to transmit a data frame to an Ethernet/802.3 destination node across an ATM switch fabric. To do this, the source node transmits a frame of data to the LEC process that resides on a LAN emulation device. The LEC then issues an ARP (address resolution protocol) broadcast requesting a MAC-to-ATM address resolution. (See Chapters 3 and 7 for more information about ARP.) The MAC address is the hardware address of the transmitting Ethernet/802.3 end node. An LES process, which resides on a native ATM device, responds to the ARP broadcast and returns to the LEC the ATM address of the remote LAN emulation device (and residing LEC) to which the destination node is connected. The source LEC then establishes a virtual circuit to the destination LEC. The LAN emulation device then translates the Etherent/802.3 frame into an ATM cell via the SAR sublayer. (See Figure 14-8.) Note that implementing this scheme does not involve modifying any higher layer protocols. Note further that in this implementation, the ATM network is effectively operating as a fast data link layer for the Ethernet/802.3 network.

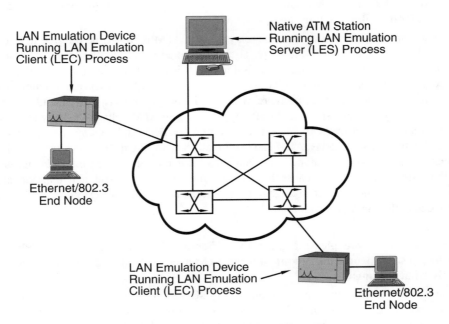

Figure 14-8. A typical ATM Local Area Network Emulation (LANE) configuration in an Ethernet/802.3 environment. (Adapted from King, 1994.)

In addition to resolving MAC-ATM address issues, another issue that needs attention is connection-type. LAN protocols are connectionless; ATM is connection-oriented. Thus, if ATM is going to emulate an Ethernet/802.3 or token ring LAN, then it must be able to carry full source and destination addresses in every frame transmitted. This poses quite a challenge given ATM's five-byte header. Furthermore, a connection-oriented technology does not adequately support bi-directional broadcast or multicast transmissions, which are inherent in Ethernet/802.3 and token ring LANs. To address these issues, a special UNI (user-to-network interface) was developed for LANs. This LAN UNI (called LUNI) enables ATM to emulate the connectionless nature of LANs across the ATM switch fabric.

A second strategy ATM provides for desktop support is a technology called *cells in frames (CIF)*, which defines a method for transporting ATM protocols over Ethernet and token ring LANs. CIF is a LAN technology that provides LANs with ATM features including QoS and the seamless integration of data, voice, and video. CIF extends ATM's virtual connections to the desktop via a special CIF attachment device, which provides an interface similar to ATM's Frame User-to-Network Interface (FUNI). This device performs most of the segmentation and reassembly (SAR), but the Ethernet/802.3 or token ring node still must build the ATM Layer's PDU. More information about CIF is available from the CIF Alliance website at http://cif.cornell.edu. A second resource for CIF is the document http://www.ziplink.net/~lroberts/Atmf-961104.html.

35. OK. I think I have had my fill of LUNI and FUNI to the point where I'm going loony now. Let's wrap things up with a few more "clean-up"–type questions. First, how does frame relay stack up against ATM?

Recall that ATM is similar to frame relay. In fact, ATM is sometime referred to as cell relay to distinguish it from frame relay. The key difference here is that frame relay uses variable-length frames as its main transmission unit, whereas ATM uses fixed-length packets (exactly 53 bytes) known as cells. Although ATM's use of smaller, fixed-length cells results in higher overhead than frame relay incurs, it also provides two critical advantages over frame relay, namely, speed and traffic type. Since all ATM cells are exactly the same size, they are much easier (and hence, faster) to process. Second, by using short cells with predictable transmission delay, ATM can combine cells carrying delay-sensitive traffic like interactive video and voice along with data cells. This concept, called *interleaving*, isn't possible with frame relay because longer data frames create longer and unpredictable delays when processing voice and video traffic. Thus, frame relay is less suitable for real-time videoconferencing for example.

36. Next is, could you please explain the difference between ATM and SONET? I have heard some people talk about running ATM over SONET and I am a bit unclear exactly what this means.

First, it is important to realize two things: (1) SONET is nothing more than a transport mechanism (see Chapter 7), and (2) ATM does not require the use of any specific physical layer protocol. As a high bandwidth carrier service, SONET can serve as the transport facility for any network technology or service, including ATM, FDDI, SMDS, and ISDN. SONET also can support various topologies including point-to-point, star, and ring.

Frequently, though, SONET is used to carry ATM traffic. The two are kind of linked to each other to the point where they can be considered as "words that come in pairs" (e.g., hue and cry, or table and chair)—ATM and SONET. There is a reason for this. Instead of developing a new physical layer, the designers of ATM borrowed SONET's link-level technology and used it for ATM switching. Furthermore, the ATM Forum has defined 622 Mbps ATM (OC-12) (and higher) to run over only SONET. This does not mean though, that OC-12 is ATM. As we discussed in Chapter 7, OC-12 is simply the label given to denote the concatenation of 12 DS-3 channels, which provides an aggregate bandwidth of 622.08 Mbps. So, in a nutshell, SONET is a carrier service that transports bits from a source to destination, and ATM is a technology and protocol that was designed to use SONET as its carrier service.

37. Finally, what new ATM-related technologies are there?

This is a difficult question to answer. ATM, as is the case with many technologies, continues to evolve. Instead of providing a list of various ATM-related protocols or technologies being considered, we direct you to the ATM Forum web site at (http://www.atm-forum.com). The ATM Forum is an international nonprofit consortium of equipment manufacturers, service providers, researchers, and users. Quoting from its web site, Forum was "formed with the objective of accelerating the use of ATM (Asynchronous Transfer Mode) products and services through a rapid convergence of interoperability specifications."

There is one evolving technology that has caught the eye of WAN operators. It's CIF, which was mentioned earlier as a technology for transporting ATM protocols over Ethernet and token ring LANs. The CIF Alliance is actively modifying CIF to work over SONET and PPP links. Furthermore, the ATM Forum is working with the CIF Alliance to bring the concept of using CIF to carry ATM protocols to fruition. This proposed WAN version of CIF presumably maintains all of native ATM's key features, but requires less overhead.

End-of-Chapter Commentary

This concludes our discussion of ATM. The information contained in this chapter provides only a working overview of the technology. For detailed technical information, you are encouraged to visit the ATM Forum web site, or consult some of the references given for this chapter. You might also want to revisit other chapters within this book that included ATM as part of the discussion, most notably: Chapter 7, which includes a discussion of SONET; Chapter 8, which examines Gigabit Ethernet and its relationship to ATM; and Chapters 12 and 13, which provide a comparison among frame relay, SMDS, and ATM. Finally, the glossary at the back of this book provides definitions of additional ATM terms, and the website http://www.techfest.com/networking/atm.htm is a terrific resource for ATM information.

Chapter 15

Dialup and Home Networking

In this chapter we discuss the concepts and methods of extending networking to the home or small office/home office (SOHO) environment. The major topics we address include

- Dialup Networking Concepts and Issues (Questions 1–3)
- Analog Modem Concepts (Questions 4–10)
- 56K Modems (Questions 11–14)
- *x*DSL (Questions 15–19)
- Cable Modems (Questions 20-24)
- Home Networking Concepts and Issues (Questions 25–38)

1. What is dialup networking?

Dialup networking refers to a network connection that is established by "dialing" into the network through the public telephone system. Dialup connections can be analog or digital. Analog connections involve the use of a modem; digital connections require end-to-end digital connectivity. (See Chapter 11 on ISDN for more information about end-to-end digital connections.) Dialup connections can also be terminal-based or network-based. In a dialup *terminal* connection, special terminal emulation software is used to make the local system a terminal of the remote machine. In a dialup *network* connection, special networking software makes the local machine become a true networked host.

2. Could you please expand on the concept of a dialup *terminal* connection?

Certainly. As stated above, a dialup terminal connection involves the use of special terminal emulation software. This type of connection is sometimes called a *tty* connection, which is an acronym for *teletype*, a term used in the early days of computing to denote a terminal connection between a device and a centralized host. In a tty dialup connection, terminal emulation software is used to make the local system (the one dialing in) appear as a terminal to a centralized host. There are many different kinds of terminal emulation software available, each with its own capabilities. Two in particular are *Kermit* and *ProComm*. Windows 3.1, Windows 95, and Windows 98 also come bundled with terminal emulation software, and modem manufacturers usually include a version of their own emulation software with their modems. Common emulations are vt100 and vt102. In a dialup tty environment, control of the local machine is transferred to that of the remote system. The emulation software converts the local node into a terminal of the centralized host. A direct consequence of this conversion is some keyboard functions or mouse capabilities do not work correctly if they are not mapped properly and supported by the remote system.

In a tty dialup connection, the remote system (the one being dialed into) can be another computer as shown in Figure 15-1(a), or it can be a specialized device called a *terminal server* or communications server that is connected to a LAN. (See Figure 15-1(b).) When a terminal/communications server is used, the server acts as an intermediary node that establishes a terminal connection between the local system and a networked machine. For example, in Figure 15-1(b), the PC client dials into the terminal server, which then enables the PC to connect to any machine on the local network, or (assuming proper authorizations are in place) any machine connected to the Internet. (*Note:* This is the basis of what is referred to as a Unix "shell account" available from some Internet service providers.)

Although it is possible to dial into a computer that is connected to a network and gain access to the network via this system, a dialup tty connection is not a network connection. This is because the local machine is considered nothing more than a terminal of the remote system. Anything you do through this connection (e.g., read e-mail, transfer files) is all done relative to the remote system, not the local host. For example, let's assume that in Figure 15-1(b) a terminal connection is established from the local PC to one of the networked hosts via the terminal server. If you read e-mail on this host and save it, it will be saved on the host, not the PC. Similarly, if you transfer a file from the Internet and save it, it will be saved on the host, not the PC.

3. OK. But I use a PPP account from home to connect to the Internet. Is this considered a networked connection or a terminal connection?

A Point-to-Point Protocol (PPP) link is an example of the second type of dialup connection, namely, a dialup *network* connection. A dialup network connection transforms the local machine into a true networked node and enables it to behave exactly as if it were directly connected to a LAN. This enables a local machine to become a directly connected Internet host via a telephone line. Thus, in Figure 15-1(b), a dialup networked connection effectively makes the local PC appear as if it were directly connected to the LAN. Furthermore, all actions performed on the local machine are now done relative to the local machine and not to some remote node, as is the case with a tty connection. Dialup networked connections are established using special networking software such as PPP or SLIP (Serial Line Internet Protocol). On the local side, the client version of PPP or SLIP makes a connection to a remote machine running the server version of PPP or SLIP. The remote machine can be another computer or it can be a terminal server. Once the connection is established, the local machine is assigned a network address. Depending on the configuration, the server either selects from a pool of available addresses and dynamically assigns the remote machine a network address, or the server issues a pre-assigned address. Regardless of the type of assignment, the network address remains in effect for the duration of the session.

(a)

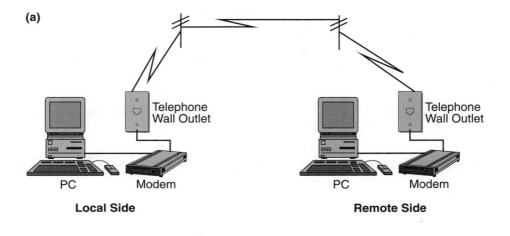

(b)

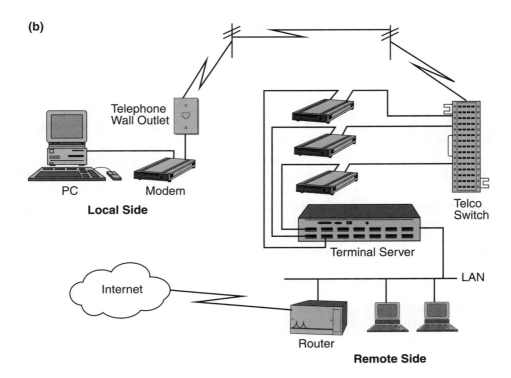

Figure 15-1. A typical dialup connection uses a standard telephone line as the medium for providing a computer-to-computer connection (a) or a computer-to-network connection (b) via a terminal server.

4. Regardless of the type of dialup connection, though, it looks like a modem is required. Could you review the concept of a modem?

You bet. A modem, which stands for modulator/demodulator, transmits and receives data through a telephone line. (*Note:* Wireless modems are used for wireless dialup connections.) A modem transforms a computer's digital signal into analog form at the sending side so the signal can be carried across a standard telephone line. On the receiving side, the modem demodulates the signal. That is, it reconverts the transmitted analog signal from the phone line to digital form before it is passed to the computer.

5. Are there any standards for modems as there are for other networking equipment?

Yes. There are many industry standards for modems. Some are defined by international committees, others by modem manufacturers. For universal interoperability, though, modems should be compliant with standards formalized by the telecommunications sector of the International Telecommunications (ITU-T), which establishes worldwide communications standards. ITU-T is the former Consultative Committee for International Telephony and Telegraphy (CCITT). Modem standards defined by ITU-T are known as the V-series (ITU-T prefaces these standards with the letter "V"), and specify techniques for modulation, error control, and compression. A brief description of some of these standards is given in Table 15-1. Note that a second or revised version is denoted by *bis*, and a third version is denoted by *ter*.

6. Tell me more about modulation, error control, and compression as they relate to modems. Start with modulation first. What does it refer to?

When a dialup connection is first initialized, the two modems at each end of the connection begin screaming at each other—a negotiation process (called handshaking) that the modems engage in so they can come to some agreement on certain communication parameters. One parameter is the data transmission rate, which is formally known as the DCE rate, and informally referred to as "speed." The modulation technique determines this speed. (*Note:* DCE stands for data communications equipment. Also, you might want to reference the first part of Chapter 7 for specific information about the analog-to-digital conversion process.)

7. Wait a minute. Explain this DCE rate please.

OK. As we stated above, DCE stands for data communications equipment. In a dialup connection, the modem is a DCE device, and the telephone line connects the DCE device to the phone jack. Furthermore, the DCE-to-DCE rate is the data transmission rate between the two end modems. That is, it is the speed at which the two modems will exchange data. The ITU-T protocols specify modulation standards for modem speeds. The most widely used speeds (and their corresponding protocols) today are 14,400 bps (V.32 *bis*), 28,800 bps (V.34), 33,600 bps (V.34 with software enhancement), and 57,600 bps (V.90). (See Table 15-1.) Note that the DCE-to-DCE rate is fixed because modems must agree on a specific modulation technique.

Table 15-1. Selected V.x Modem Protocols

Protocol	Description
V.21	Standard for 300 bps modems using full-duplex transmission over a dialup line.
V.22	Standard for 600 bps and 1200 bps full-duplex modems over dialup and 2-wire leased lines. Compatible with the Bell 212A standard used in the U.S.
V.22 *bis*	Standard for 2400 bps full-duplex modems over dialup and 2-wire leased lines; cycles to 1200 and 600 bps operation.
V.23	Standard for 600 bps or 1200 bps synchronous or asynchronous half-duplex modems used on dialup lines. Used in the United Kingdom.
V.29	Standard for 9600 bps facsimile service.
V.32	Standard for 9600 bps modems, cycles to 4800 bps when line quality degrades, and cycles forward when line quality improves.
V.32 *bis*	Standard that extends V.32 to 7200, 12,000, and 14,400 bps; cycles to lower rate when line quality degrades; cycles forward when line quality improves.
V.32 *ter*	Pseudo-standard that extends v.32 *bis* to 19,200 bps and 21,600 bps.
V.34	Standard for 28,800 bps modems. (*Note:* Some V.34 modems were enhanced with new software that provided them with the capability to achieve data rates of 31,200 bps or 33,600 bps.)
V.FAST	Proprietary, pseudo-standard from Hayes and Rockwell for modems transmitting at data rates up to 28,800 bps; served as a migration path for V.34.
V.42	Standard for error correction instead of for a modem. Uses LAPM as the primary error-correcting protocol, with MNP classes 1 through 4 as an alternative. (See Table 15-2.)
V.42 *bis*	Standard that enhances V.42 by incorporating the British Telecom Lempel Ziv data compression technique to V.42 error correction. Most V.32, V.32bis, and V.34 compliant modems come with V.42 or V.42 *bis* or MNP.
V.90	Standard for 57,600 bps modems (commonly called "56K modems") in which asymmetric data rates apply (i.e., the send and receive rates are different). Depending on telephone line conditions, upstream rates (send) are restricted to 33,600 bps, and downstream rates (receive) are restricted to 57,600 bps. V.90 modems are designed for connections that are digital at one end and have one digital-to-analog conversion.

Although modems will always try to negotiate the fastest link possible, speeds are dependent on line quality. For example, if two V.34 compliant modems are trying to communicate with each other, they will try to negotiate a 33,600 bps connection. If this is not possible, the modems will then try to connect at the next highest rate the line can support. If the line quality deteriorates during an established connection, then the modems will cycle down ("fallback") to a lower speed. When line quality improves, the modems will fall forward to a higher speed. Modem speed is also limited by the slowest modem in the connection. Thus, if a V.34 modem is trying to establish a connection with a V.32 *bis* modem, the fastest link possible is 14,400 bps regardless of line quality.

8. I have heard that if you have a 28,800 bps modem, then you can attain transfer rates as high as 115,200 bps. Is this true, and if so, how is it accomplished?

Yes, this is true. It is accomplished with compression, which is another one of those parameters modems negotiate when a dialup connection is first initialized. Compression is a process that codes repetitive patterns within a data set. For example, if a text message contains the string "XXXXXX," then instead of using six bytes to represent the data (one for each character), a compression technique might code the string so that only two bytes are used to represent it—one byte to identify the repetitive character, and one byte to specify the number of times it is repeated. Compressed files can be sent at a faster rate than uncompressed files. For example, a 1 Mbyte uncompressed file transferred at 28,800 bps takes nearly 5 minutes, depending on the file transfer protocol used. (*Note:* This is calculated as follows: Assuming 8 bits per byte, 28,800 bits per second = 28800/8 = 3,600 bytes per second. Since 1 Kilobyte = 1024 bytes, then 1 Megabyte = 1024 × 1024 = 1,048,576 bytes. Thus, to transfer 1 Megabyte at 28,800 bps requires 1048576/3600 = 291 seconds, which is approximately 5 minutes.) If this same file is compressed by a 4 to 1 ratio, then the time it takes to transmit the compressed file is one-quarter of the original time, which effectively quadruples the data transfer rate to 115,200 bps. Remember, though, compression is only achieved if there is redundancy in the data set.

The two primary standards used for data compression involving modems is V.42 *bis* and the Microcom Networking Protocol (MNP) Level 5. V.42 *bis* defines a technique that can generate a 4 to 1 data compression ratio, depending on the type of file being transmitted. MNP 5 uses a data compression algorithm that compresses data by a factor of 2 to 1. MNP was initially a proprietary protocol developed by Microcom Incorporated that became an industry standard for data compression and error control in the 1980s. A brief summary of the various MNP levels are given in Table 15-2.

To benefit from compression and the potentially higher effective throughput rates, the computer must be able to transmit with its connected modem at a rate that is equal to the possible speed that can be achieved by the compression ratio. This speed is called the DTE-to-DCE rate and is commonly referred to as the computer's "port speed" or "serial

Table 15-2. The MNP Protocols

Protocol	Description
MNP 1–4	Used for hardware error control. All four levels are incorporated into V.42.
MNP 5	Incorporates the first four levels of MNP. Also uses a data compression algorithm that compresses data by a factor of 2 to 1.
MNP 6	Supports both V.22 *bis* and V.29.
MNP 7	Same as MNP 5 except it employs a data compression algorithm that compresses data by a factor of 3 to 1.
MNP 8	Extension of MNP 7; lets half-duplex devices operate in full-duplex mode.
MNP 9	Used for a variety of different circuits.
MNP 10	Used in cellular modems and poor line quality settings.

port rate." DTE stands for data terminating equipment. In a dialup connection, the computer is the DTE device. (*Note:* DCE was defined earlier as data communicating equipment, which is the modem in a dialup connection.) Thus, the DTE-to-DCE rate is how fast the computer can talk to its modem, and the DCE-to-DCE rate is how fast the two modems can talk to each other. The DCE-to-DCE rate is a function of the modem standard and cannot be changed. However, the DTE-to-DCE rate is user configurable through the modem's communications software. Thus, a computer that is connected to a V.34 modem, should maintain a port speed of 115,200 bps in order to benefit from a 4 to 1 compression ratio. Similarly, a computer using a V.90 modem should maintain a port speed of 230,400 bps. (*Note:* On PCs, serial ports are more commonly known as the *universal asynchronous receiver/transmitter*, or *UART*.)

9. Where does error control come into play?

Error control (see Chapter 5) refers to error detection and correction. Modem standards for error control are specified by V.42 and MNP levels 1 through 4. Note that V.42 includes MNP 1–4. V.42 also includes something called link access procedure for modems (LAPM), which uses cyclic redundancy check (CRC) and automatic repeat request (ARQ) for error control. CRC is used for error detection, and ARQ prevents the modem from accepting any more data until the defective frame has been retransmitted successfully. V.42's default is LAPM. Thus, if a connection is being initialized between two V.42 compliant modems, they will use LAPM for error control. If one of the modems is not V.42 compliant, then the modems will negotiate to use MNP 1–4.

10. Would you summarize all of this modem information for me?

Be glad to. Modems are DCE devices that convert between analog and digital signals. Modem standards, as defined by ITU-T, specify modem speeds (called the DCE-to-DCE rate), the type of error correction methods they will use (V.42), and the data compression technique (V.42 *bis*). Given redundancy in the data set, the effective throughput of a modem connection can be doubled, tripled, or even quadrupled, depending on the compression technique used. To take advantage of this increase in effective throughput, though, the speed at which the PC talks to the modem (called the DTE-to-DCE rate) must match the potential compression ratio. Thus, if the DCE-to-DCE rate is 28,800 bps, then the DTE-to-DCE rate must be 115,200 bps to benefit from a 4 to 1 compression rate. How's that?

11. Terrific. You really cleared up a lot of things for me. Let's talk about 56K modems for a moment. How different are they from other modems like V.34 and V.32 *bis*?

A 56K modem is a hybrid modem that involves a path consisting of both analog and digital connections. To understand this, let's consider a standard analog modem. According to Shannon's Limit (see Chapter 4), the highest possible speed a modem can achieve over an analog line is somewhere between 33,600 bps and 38,400 bps, depending on line conditions. Analog modems also require four analog-digital conversions in each direction. At the sending side, a digital-to-analog conversion converts digital data from the PC to

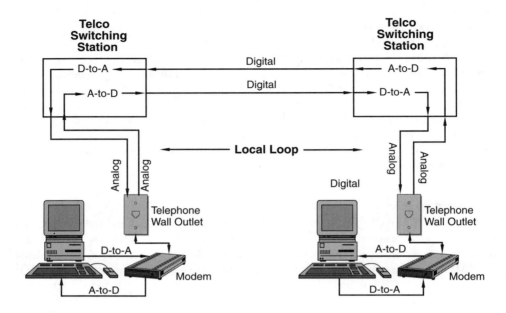

Figure 15-2. A typical analog dialup connection between two nodes involves four analog-digital conversions in each direction. (*Note:* A-to-D = Analog-to-Digital conversion; D-to-A = Digital-to-Analog conversion.)

analog form for transmission over the phone line to the telephone company's nearest switching station. Once there, the signal is then converted back to digital form where it is transmitted across the telephone company's digital network. When the signal reaches the switching station that serves the destination site, it is reconverted back to analog form and carried to the destination site. Finally, the modem at the destination site demodulates the signal from analog to digital form before it is passed to the receiving computer. This conversion process is shown in Figure 15-2.

12. Time out. Why are there so many conversions? I thought the telephone company's network is completely digital.

It is. However, unless a digital circuit has been installed (as is the case with ISDN), the circuit between a home and the telephone company's nearest switching station is analog. This circuit is called the *local loop*, or more formally, the digital subscriber loop. It is also commonly referred to as "the last mile." The local loop is predominately copper-based and represents the bottleneck to high-speed, home-based dialup networking. As such, it has become the focus of a tremendous amount of attention, ranging from cable modem service by cable operators to *x*DSL modem service by telephone carriers.

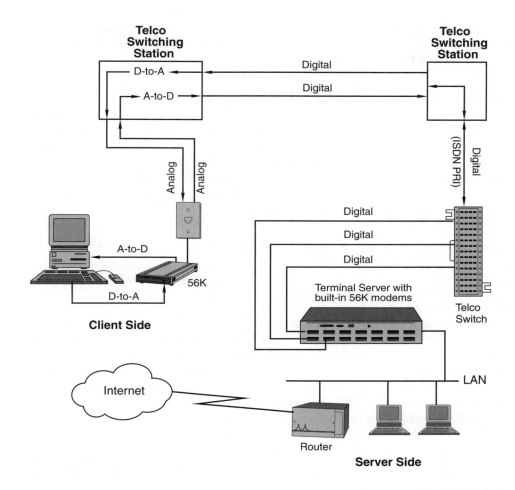

Figure 15-3. A 56K modem connection involves a hybrid analog-digital path. Unlike traditional analog modems, a 56K modem requires only two analog-digital conversions in each direction.

13. I want to know more about *x*DSL and cable modems. For now, though, please continue with 56K modems. How many conversions are needed with a 56K modem?

A 56K modem only requires two analog-digital conversions in each direction. The two conversions required occur at the local site. A digital-to-analog conversion converts digital data from the PC to analog form for local loop transmission. Once the signal arrives at the telephone company's switch the signal is converted from analog to digital form. The remaining part of the journey, however, is digital. Thus, a 56K modem involves a hybrid analog-digital path. The path is analog from the client site to the central office switching station, but the path from the switching station to the server site is completely digital. This is depicted in Figure 15-3. The highest "upstream" transmission rate (from client to server) is 33,600 bps. However, "downstream" rates (from server to client) can be as high as 57,600 bps, depending on line conditions. (*Note:* In the United States, an FCC regulation limits the highest data rate to a little less than 56 kbps.) Users of 56K modems should set their DTE-to-DCE rate to 230,400 bps.

14. I have heard people talk about x2 and K56flex. What are these?

x2 and K56flex are two early, competing, and incompatible proprietary standards for 56K modems. x2 was developed by USRobotics (3Com), and K56flex by Lucent Technologies. Both technologies have since been absorbed by the ITU-T standard, V.90. Thus, as long as your 56K modem is V.90 compliant, you should be able to connect to another V.90 compliant modem without having to be concerned with x2 or 56Kflex. However, do note that 56K modems cannot be used for global connectivity. The signaling schemes used on international connections reduce speeds to a maximum of 33.6 kbps.

15. Let's move on to *x*DSL service. What is this all about?

DSL stands for *digital subscriber line*, which is a technology that enables data, voice, and video to be mixed and carried over standard analog, (copper) telephone lines. This is accomplished by using the unused frequencies that are available on a telephone line. Thus, DSL can deliver data services without interfering with voice transmissions.

The leading *x* in *x*DSL is a variable that represents a descriptor, which, when combined with DSL, defines different DSL variants. Presently, there are nine variants. These are summarized in Table 15-3. DSL was first developed in 1987 by Bell Communications Research (Bellcore) to deliver video on demand and interactive TV over copper wires. Many regard the technology as the telephone companies' answer to cable modems in competing for "the last mile." DSL network topology is a star; thus, each subscriber has its own dedicated connection.

16. Reviewing the information in Table 15-3, I notice that some of those data rates are pretty impressive. I also notice that there are local loop distance restrictions. Could you please explain all of this?

Sure. DSL transmission rates are a function of line quality and the distance a customer's site is from the local switching station. The longer the local loop distance, the lower the rate; likewise, the poorer the quality of the local loop circuit, the lower the rate. DSL should be implemented with quality copper circuits at the local loop because of possible line attenuation and EMI problems (see Chapter 4), both of which can degrade data transmission. Also keep in mind that DSL rates represent the speed at which data are delivered across the local loop. If there is congestion at the switching station, or if there is congestion at some point within the network cloud, it doesn't matter how fast your connection is because a bottleneck exists somewhere beyond your loop. Something else to be cognizant of is the DTE-to-DCE rate, which we discussed earlier. Most current model PCs or Macintoshes are not equipped with serial ports that have the capacity to keep up with a DSL connection. The bottom line is, DSL data rates are certainly impressive. However, these are the *theoretical maximum rates possible*, which do not reflect real world constraints.

Table 15-3. The Digital Subscriber Line (DSL) Variants

Type	Name	Description
ADSL	Asymmetric DSL	Traffic transmitted at different rates in different directions. Downstream rates range from 1.5 Mbps to 9 Mbps; Upstream rates range from 16 kbps to 1 Mbps. Rates depend on line quality and local loop distance. Maximum local loop distance is 18,000 ft. (5.4 km). Suitable for Internet or intranet access, video-on-demand, database access, remote LAN access.
ADSL lite	ADSL lite	Slower ADSL; also called G.lite. Downstream = 1 Mbps; Upstream = 128 kbps. Intended primarily for homes.
HDSL	High-bit-rate DSL	Symmetrical service that delivers T1 rates over 2 pairs of UTP, and E1 rates over 3 pairs of UTP. Maximum local loop distance is 15,000 ft. (4.5 km). Telephone service not supported. Applications include connecting PBXs, serving as an alternative to T1/E1, suitable for campus networks and ISPs.
HDSL 2	High-bit-rate DSL 2	Modified HDSL designed/packaged for corporate clients.
IDSL	ISDN-like DSL	Symmetrical service that delivers maximum of 144 kbps each way. Uses ISDN hardware. Maximum local loop distance is 18,000 ft. (5.4 km).
RADSL	Rate-adaptive DSL	Transmission rates similar to ADSL; transmission rates can be adjusted based on distance and line quality. Up to 7 Mbps downstream rate.
SDSL	Symmetric DSL	Traffic transmitted at same rate in each direction. Maximum transmission rate is 768 kbps. Maximum local loop distance is 22,000 ft. (6.6 km). Uses single-wire pair. Telephone service not supported. Suitable for videoconferencing.
UDSL	Universal DSL	Symmetrical service that delivers 2 Mbps each way.
VDSL	Very High-speed DSL	Asymmetric service that runs over fiber. Maximum distances range from 1,000 ft. (0.3 km) to 4,000 ft. (1.2 km). Downstream rates range from 13 Mbps to 52 Mbps; Upstream rates range from 1.5 Mbps to 2.3 Mbps. Suitable for Internet or intranet access, video-on-demand, database access, remote LAN access, and high-definition television.

17. Are there specific standards for the DSL variants?

Presently, ADSL is the only standard DSL variant. It has been standardized by ANSI and European Telecom Standards Institute (ETSI). Standards for others are forthcoming, however. For example, ITU is expected to approve an ADSL lite (also called G.lite) standard by the end of 1998. The G.lite standard will be based on ADSL's ANSI standard. Nevertheless, standards aside, many of the DSL variants have been deployed in various stages throughout the United States, and end-user equipment has been developed. The most popular DSL variant is ADSL, which is expected to be deployed throughout the United States by several telcos in 1999.

18. What does an ADSL connection require and what are some of its advantages?

An ADSL connection requires an ADSL modem at the local end and at the telco switching office. (*Note:* The term, "modem," used in this context is really misapplied because ADSL is a digital technology. Hence, there is no modulation or demodulation of analog and digital signals. Nevertheless, "modem" is accepted and understood by the general public as any device that provides a dialup connection.) You will also need to purchase an ADSL service from your local phone service provider. Service might be available directly from an Internet service provider as well. Since ADSL operates over the same copper wire you currently use for phone service, you do not have to install a second line or new termination unit (which is required for ISDN). To use the service, you essentially connect the ADSL modem to your computer (or network) and telephone line. (See Figure 15-4.) It is quite similar to using an analog modem except you can now transmit different types of data (voice, data, and video) simultaneously over the same circuit. ADSL is also powered like conventional telephone service so during a power outage voice service will still be available. Other ADSL-connected devices such as a computer, however, still require power to run.

One of ADSL's advantages is that an ADSL connection is always "up." In fact, an ADSL link essentially apes a leased line connection—the service is always available for transmitting or receiving data. Thus, unlike ISDN or analog modem service, you do not have to dial a number to connect to a service provider for Internet access. An ADSL connection, as are all DSL variants, is point-to-point. Thus, unlike cable modem service, the local loop bandwidth is not shared. This offers better security and dedicated bandwidth between the telco's switching station and your link.

Another of ADSL's biggest advantages is that it keeps data traffic off the voice network. With an analog modem service, dialup users use the public switched telephone network (PSTN) to call up their Internet service provider to gain access to the Internet. This ties up a port on the telco's voice switch, which reduces the number of voice ports available for voice calls. With ADSL, voice calls (i.e., signals) are segregated from data traffic via a line splitter and directed to the telco's voice switch for transmission across the PSTN. Data signals, however, are aggregated via an ADSL access multiplexer (ADSLAM), which feeds directly into a data switch for transmission across the telco's data network backbone. Thus, data signals bypass the voice switch thereby freeing up ports for voice calls. (See Figure 15-4.)

19. What kind of problems can one expect with an ADSL connection?

The biggest problem will be local loop distance restrictions. In order to get an idea of what kind of data rate you can expect, you need to have an accurate measurement of your local loop distance. A second potential issue is the quality of cooper on which your local loop circuit is based. Both were discussed earlier. A third potential problem is interoperability of ADSL equipment from different manufacturers. Standards are just now being ratified and equipment manufacturers will need time to make their proprietary-based

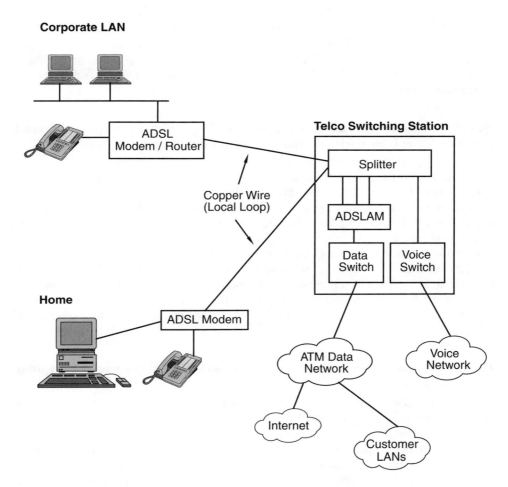

Figure 15-4. An ADSL connection involves ADSL modems at the local site, and a "splitter" and ADSL access multiplexer (ADSLAM), which incorporates an ADSL modem, at the telco switching station. (The splitter can also be incorporated within the ADSLAM device along with the ADSL modem.) The splitter is used to separate voice and data signals. Voice signals are directed to the telco's voice switch for transmission through the public switched telephone network (PSTN). Data signals are aggregated by the ADSL multiplexer and directed to the telco's data switch for transmission through the telco's data network. (Adapted from Aber, 1997.)

equipment DSL standards-compliant. A fourth potential issue is service availability. Deployment of ADSL service is not widespread yet. Consequently, many telco carriers might not offer it, or might not have knowledgeable and skilled people onboard yet to help design or implement an ADSL-based connection. One final potential problem is relieving the headache you are sure to get trying to sort through all the rhetoric and hyperbole about DSL-service, cable modem service, ISDN, and 56K modem service. For more information about ADSL go to the ADSL Forum web site at http://www.adsl.com. Information about G.lite is available from the Universal ADSL Working Group (the authors of the G.lite standard) at http://www.uawg.org. To keep abreast of *x*DSL developments, go to http://www.xdsl.com. Finally, the DSL Sourcebook is available from http://www.paradyne.com/sourcebook_offer/index.html.

20. Let's see. We have discussed analog modems, 56K modems, and *x*DSL modems. I guess that leaves cable modems. What can you tell me about them?

Don't forget that we also discussed ISDN "modems" in Chapter 11.

Cable modems represent the cable companies' infiltration into the telecommunications business. Cable modems use cable television lines for data communications. These lines use broadband coaxial cable (see Chapter 4), which has a multitude of frequencies available and significantly higher bandwidth than the UTP cable used by the telcos. Cable operators specify a frequency range within the cable and run data over it. Cable modems provide the interface (i.e., connection point) between a computer and the cable. Specifically, this interface is an Ethernet/802.3 network interface card. Thus, a PC must have an Ethernet/802.3 NIC installed in order to be connected to a cable modem. Once connected, it is as if the PC were connected to an Ethernet/802.3 LAN. The connection is always "up," and multimegabit data rates are possible. (See Chapter 8 for more information about Ethernet/802.3.)

21. How are cable operators able to provide two-way data communications using their cable plant?

To answer this question, we first need to examine a typical cable TV network. Cable networks were specifically designed for downstream transmission only—they serve as a one-way broadcast facility for transmitting television signals. They were never designed for two-way transmissions. (*Note:* CATV originally stood for Community Antenna Television, which was designed to provide television broadcasts in areas where broadcast reception was poor.) The network design is a tree topology that consists of a signal source (called the head end), a local neighborhood distribution site, and a bunch of amplifiers. The head end aggregates signals from different locations and modulates them to the frequencies that are assigned to the destination sites. (The head end usually receives a master signal from a satellite dish or a fiber backbone.) These modulated signals are then piped along the cable to a neighborhood distribution site, where they are delivered directly to a customer's home. En route from the head end to the neighborhood distribution facility, and then again to the customer's site, the signal is regenerated via one-way amplifiers. (This is similar to the use of repeaters in an Ethernet/802.3 network.) This is necessary to maintain signal quality while increasing cable distances. A simple diagram illustrating this design is shown in Figure 15-5.

In order to provide for two-way transmission, cable networks have to be upgraded. Current upgrade plans include replacing the one-way amplifiers with two-way amplifiers, and replacing the coaxial cable with fiber-optic cable. The cable plant upgrade is occurring in two phases. The first phase involves replacing the coaxial cable with fiber at the head

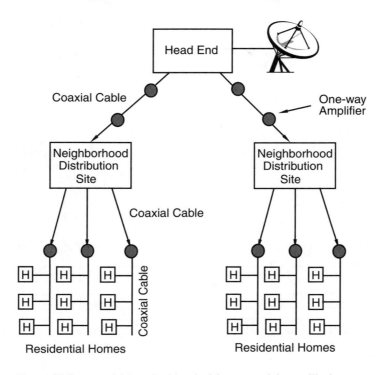

Figure 15-5. A coaxial-based cable television network is tree-like in nature and designed for one-way transmission. Amplifiers are used to maintain signal quality while increasing distances. (Adapted from Fitzgerald, 1996.)

end. This eliminates the need for amplifiers but yet still allows the network diameter to increase without signal degradation. The fiber-optic cable also will carry more data. This resulting network is called a hybrid fiber-coaxial (HFC) network. Work on this phase in the United States is expected to be completed before the year 2000. The second phase involves replacing the coaxial cable at the neighborhood distribution site. Once fiber is deployed to the neighborhood, optical-to-electrical converters can replace the amplifiers, resulting in less amplification and a more robust cable plant. (See Figures 15-6 and 15-7.)

22. What is being done presently?

Presently, the HFC-based cable plant has its limitations. Until two-way amplifiers are installed, cable operators can only offer high-speed downstream (from head end to customer site) data transmissions. Upstream transmissions (from customer site to head end) are restricted to 33.6 kbps via an analog modem dialup connection through the telephone network. Even those areas where two-way amplifiers are in place, because coax is still deployed to the neighborhood, upstream transmission rates are considerably less than their downstream counterparts. Depending on the cable operator and service, current upstream

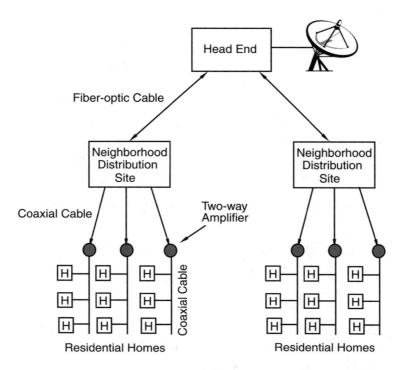

Figure 15-6. A hybrid fiber-coaxial (HFC) cable network consists of fiber-optic cable between the head end and neighborhood distribution sites. Coaxial cable is still deployed to the neighborhood, however. (Adapted from Fitzgerald, 1996.)

rates are somewhere between 500 kbps to 3 Mbps; downstream rates range between 10 Mbps to 30 Mbps.

23. What's wrong with those numbers? It's a lot better than 56K modem service.

True. However, remember that the cable network is still a shared system. It is very similar to 10 Mbps Ethernet/802.3, which is a broadcast technology. Thus, as more subscribers come online, there will be more contention for the available bandwidth. (Contrast this with ADSL, which is a point-to-point topology. See also, Chapter 8 for more information about Ethernet/802.3 LANs.) Most cable systems today support around 5,000 users from the head end, and serve somewhere between 500 and 2,500 homes on a single line.

24. Where can I get information about cable modem service?

The service in the United States receiving the most attention today is the @Home network by Tele-Communications, Incorporated (TCI), which was acquired by AT&T. For more information, we suggest you start at TCI's web site: http://www.tci.com.

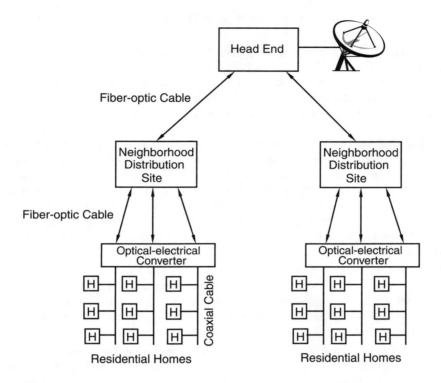

Figure 15-7. When completed, the upgraded cable network will be able to provide high-speed two-way transmissions for data, voice, and video service. (Adapted from Fitzgerald, 1996.)

25. OK. Let's talk about home networking for a moment. A network at home?

Why not? Both of your favorite authors have computers and small networks at home. We use them to connect our multiple computers together, to access common printers, share files and a rash of other requirements. One of your author's (Hancock) network is fairly comprehensive. It has switched 100 Mbps capability to all systems at home, a Windows-NT cluster, some fiber-optic cabling, and a high-speed cable modem connection to the Internet. Albeit, this home network is more advanced than most, but it does show where things are going rather quickly.

26. So a network at home is really no different than a network at the office or at school, right?

Correct. In fact, many times the same technologies are used for both. To set up a network at home, however, some advanced planning on what you want the network to do and how flexible it needs to be is useful. We'll get to that later.

27. Well, all I really want to do is connect my PC to the Internet. That's not too hard, is it?

Not really, but how do you plan to connect it to the Internet? In this chapter alone, we presented several options, including traditional analog modem connections, 56K modem connections, *x*DSL connections, and cable modem connections. Other strategies were also discussed in previous chapters including ISDN and frame relay. Following is a brief summary of some of the most common methods used to connect a PC to Internet from the home:

Analog Modem. This is by far the most common and most popular method. A modem is connected via a phone line to the ISP and you can get access to the Internet at whatever speeds the modem and ISP support. At this writing, the most popular modem for sale is the ITU-TSS standardized V.90 56 kbps modem or the dual-56 kbps load-balanced modem. This second type of modem provides a dialup via two phone lines and load balances between them, yielding a throughout of about 112 kbps if everything goes as planned. In any case, a modem, phone line, access software (like PPP protocol), and ISP account are required for connectivity.

ISDN. This can provide a little faster connection to an ISP and, of course, you pay more for it. There are two modes: dialup and a permanent ISDN. To make an ISDN connection work, an ISDN-compatible phone line and an ISDN terminating device (commonly, but incorrectly, called an ISDN modem) is required with software and an ISP connection account.

Cable Modem. In this scenario, the local cable company installs a cable set-top box that has the ability to connect to your PC. Your PC will "think" it's connected to an Ethernet/802.e LAN. An Ethernet/802.3 NIC is required. The set-top box provides a broadband access capability to the cable company and they in turn have a router connection somewhere to the Internet. With this type of Internet connection, you will be "live" on the Internet 24 hours a day, 7 days a week, just like a corporate Internet connection. Your cable vendor will usually provide everything you will need to connect except the PC (cable modem, software, Ethernet/802.3 card, cables, etc.).

Asymmetric Digital Subscriber Loop (ADSL). In this method, the phone company provides all the hardware and software and a high speed connection capability. "Asymmetric" means that the connection speed from your house to the network is a different speed than the network to your house. In many cases, the uplink speed (home-to-network path) is about 1 to 2 Mbps. The downlink speed (network-to-home) is anywhere from 4 Mbps to as much as 12 Mbps, depending on the system implemented by the phone company. You will need an ADSL adapter (commonly, but incorrectly, called an ADSL modem), software, cabling, and an ISP account. Normally, all of these are provided by the vendor of the ADSL service.

High-Speed Wireless. In this method, neighborhood wireless relay stations are installed in your local neighborhood. These stations have a wireless relay to a small dish or flat data collector unit attached to your home. A wire from the dish goes to a relay system in your home and your system is connected to the network in a manner similar to an Ethernet (a NIC in the PC is required). Some commercial systems provide up to 10 Mbps symmetric connectivity to your home and do not depend on wire from the telephone company or a cable provider. Again, the vendor will provide the connection hardware and software. What is needed includes service in the area, a dish on the home, a decoder system, cables, an Ethernet NIC in the PC, software, and an ISP account.

28. So which one is best?

Often, it's not so much a problem of "which is best" as much as "what is available." Telephone lines and modems are ubiquitous, and thus easy to install and configure. The other four described methods vary in availability depending on where you go. Thus, some research will need to be done. We have used all five methods and find that they work OK once they are mature (the technology, not the authors—we never claimed to be mature). The biggest differentials are the cost per month for service, reliability issues, and one-time capital equipment costs to implement the service. You will need to shop around for what works best for you.

29. OK. I think I now understand the ways I can get connected to the Internet. What if I have more than one computer at home and want to hook them all up to the same connection?

Ah. Now you need to think about a network at home to connect the systems together and then connect that network to your Internet provider. This is true home networking and is rapidly becoming a popular solution due to the growth of multicomputer households worldwide. In the United States, for example, studies claim that over 64 percent of all households have a personal computer. A recent study also said that 39 percent of all households have two or more computers. It's rapidly becoming the norm to be a networked house with more than one computer.

30. That's all really great, but I need to hook my systems up at home "on the cheap." Any suggestions?

Plenty. Hooking up computers very cheaply has never been easier. The cost of network hardware has dropped dramatically in the past few years to the point where network hardware is very inexpensive. For instance, to connect two PCs to each other via Ethernet in a home you need two 10 Mbps Ethernet cards ($20 each), two 15- feet long Category 5 UTP cables ($11.00 each), and one 5-port 10BASE-T "hublet" and power supply ($40). Thus, the total expenditure $102. Even better, some companies offer what is called a "starter kit," which contains all the above for about $20.00 less.

31. Great! But that's only hardware. What about software?

This depends largely on the operating system you are using. If you are using Windows 95, Windows 98, Windows NT, Windows 2000, or MacOS, then you already have the software needed on your system as part of the operating system. The same applies to many UNIX environments, including freeware versions such as Linux and FreeBSD. To make the two systems talk to each other, you must set up a peer-to-peer connection (see Chapter 1). This is when one system connects directly to the other with no intermediate router or server. On most systems, you must configure a protocol that is not dependent upon a router or naming service to discover route paths or name translation of addresses to get things to work. For instance, on a PC running Windows, you enable the NetBEUI protocol and adapter services in the network control panel in the Windows operating system version you are using. You must also select File and Print Sharing and allow the system to install the software (have your system CD-ROM nearby). Once you do this and re-boot the systems, all you have to do is enable disk sharing on your systems. This is usually via the disk's Properties facilities; select the Sharing tab at the top. You will also need to decide on what security features you want to implement. By enabling "sharing" mode, you can now access the hard disks of the remote system. In Windows, you can double click on Network Neighborhood to find out what is on the network. Connectivity to a particular system is effected by simply clicking on the system icon. You are now sharing disks from your systems over your little Ethernet in your home just like you would at the office.

32. OK. What about sharing printers at home? I don't want to buy two of them if I don't have to.

Print sharing is even easier to implement than disk sharing. In Windows, just select the printer you want to share from the Printers folder on the system disk, select the target printer's icon to highlight it, and then select Sharing from the File menu. Once you enable sharing, the other system can "see" your printer on the network and access it. Don't forget to install the printer software and drivers on the remote system so it prints correctly!

33. OK. Now the big question: How do I share my Internet connection from one system with another on my little home-based Ethernet?

This takes a bit more work, but nothing major. There are several ways to do it If you are using Windows 95, you can use a variety of packages such as WinGate. These act as routers and allow multiple systems to be connected to a single dial-out over a network. If you are using Windows NT or UNIX, these operating systems are equipped with routing kernels that can be configured to allow your Internet-attached node to route packets from the Internet connection to your other systems on the mini-Ethernet. If you read the system manager's documentation, there are instructions on how to configure the routing kernel on both operating system environments. If you are using Windows 98, Microsoft includes the RIP routing protocol for IP on the distribution kit CD-ROM. By installing RIP, you can configure the system as a router for other IP nodes on your network and share your connection with them. Other operating systems will or will not have similar capabilities. Of course, another option is to purchase a small dial-up router. This will cost between $200 and $1,000, depending upon connection type, speed, and router configuration required. So, as you can see, getting your systems configured to route to and from your Internet connection is not very hard or expensive.

34. What about security? Will my system be exposed just like the office connection without a firewall?

Most certainly. It is a fantasy to think that small-site connections are not vulnerable to attack. A home-based Internet connection is just as vulnerable to attack as a corporate connection. This is especially the case with Internet connections that are always "on," such as cable modem connections, residential regional wireless links, ISDN permanent connections, and most ADSL connections. All the protocols work the same whether you are a large company or a one-bedroom apartment location, and all locations can be compromised by an unauthorized user.

35. What can I do to keep from being attacked?

Nothing can stop an attack from happening. The best you can do is put in safeguards to keep someone from getting to your systems and their files. Tools like personal firewalls on your system, encryption software for files and disk drives, and virtual private network (VPN) software to safely connect to corporate resources all help keep prying eyes away from your systems.

36. Do attacks on home networks happen that often?

Not really, but when they do, they can get ugly. One of the authors had a friend who was fortunate enough to be one of the first in his neighborhood to get a cable modem connection. He installed the proper hardware and software on the system, and life was good. In the first week of operation, he left the PC on at all times and was, effectively, hooked into the Internet 24 hours a day. In that timeframe, an unauthorized user got onto his system and set up an IRC chat redirection program that allowed the hacker to get on to chat groups, be as rude and obnoxious as desired, and seriously disturb the chat groups that the hacker was attacking. In the process of this, the various larger chat bulletin board systems traced the IP address back to the friend's PC; then a lawyer got involved. The friend first found out that something was amiss when he and his ISP received a "cease and desist" letter that threatened a lawsuit. Since the friend had been out of town that whole time, and since no one else had touched the system, it was investigation time. Examination of the system showed that the hacker really had been there and how he gained access. The software was deleted, the ISP helped explain things to the lawyer, and all went back to normal. So, in a home networking environment, you have to take security seriously and use the proper precautions just like the company environment unless you want to lose your data, allow someone to set up camp on your system, or possibly have your privacy compromised in an ugly way.

37. What kinds of problems can I expect when setting up my home network?

There are several things that seem to trip people up when they configure a home network. Most are pretty straightforward to solve if you think ahead. The most common ones we have seen are summarized here.

Phone Line. In this situation, the phone company does not properly install a phone line in the residence to the proper noise level allowances as posted by the FCC in the United States and other organizations that set phone standards in other countries. When the line voltages, attenuation, crosstalk, and other settings are out of whack on the line, you get noise, signal degradation, and a myriad of other problems. Sometimes, especially when there is a lack of phone lines in a community, the phone company will put an electronic box on a single pair of lines called an "active multiplexer," which allows the phone company to put the equivalent of more phone signals on the same pair of lines. These boxes are notorious for introducing serious noise and reduced signal strength on telephone connections, which degrades a modem's capabilities and the speed of the link. Phone line noise is a very common problem with home networks and can be very irritating.

Cable. This is a problem area even for seasoned network professionals. Because there are so many ways to hook up devices and so many standards for different devices, there are a plethora of cable connectors, pinouts, pair-matches, and so forth that plague the well-connected network. It is therefore extremely easy to get the wrong cable in the wrong configuration between two systems when trying to configure a network. Other cable problems include trying to get the right connector type for a connection port, proper cable length, proper cable type (e.g., shielded, unshielded, coaxial), and connector types. Cables can be a real hassle when configuring home networks. (See Chapter 4 for additional information about cables.)

NIC Settings. In some NICs there are various jumpers (small wire pins on the board) or dual in-line package (DIP) switch blocks. You must configure the jumpers or DIP switches to match the type of network connectivity options required for the network type you are using. You might also have to specify DIPs or jumpers for bus speeds, memory utilization, and other parameters. Many network cards now are software configurable, so more and more equivalent DIP switch settings are now done in software, but the aggravation factor is about the same. If you get DIPs, jumpers, or internal software settings wrong, the card will not work as planned or desired.

Network Protocols. Problems involving network protocols will always emerge when setting up any network connection. Although recent versions of popular operating systems are making it easier to identify and correctly configure the required protocols, the problems that emerge can still be related to complex issues that will need to be resolved before things can work correctly. The bottom line is: If you are not comfortable working with network protocols, then get help from someone who is.

Power. In most homes, the circuit where the PC is plugged into has all kinds of other stuff connected to it as well. Most homes are not configured for "clean" power. Furthermore, the circuit breaker serving a set of outlets is usually not of sufficient capacity to support all the computer-related devices (e.g., PC, monitor, scanner, printer, hublet) plus all the other electrical appliances. If the power output of the circuit drops below what a device requires, a "brown out" occurs and the system will re-boot as if a power failure had happened. It's usually a good idea to invest about $75.00 and purchase a battery backup power conditioning unit (sometimes called an Uninterruptible Power Supply or UPS) to ensure that the system and components will continue to function properly during power "hiccups."

38. Is there anything else I need to know about dialup or home networking?

There is always something else. That's one of the curses of networking—you can never know enough, and trying to keep current is almost a fulltime job in itself. The material presented here should give you a good understanding of the concepts and issues related to dialup and home networking.

End-of-Chapter Commentary

On this note, we conclude our discussion of dialup and home networking. Additional information about some of the material presented here is available in other chapters. For example, Chapter 1 provides a discussion of network standards that is quite relevant to the discussion of modem and *x*DSL standards. Chapter 4 contains detailed information about hardware and cables. It also provides a discussion of Shannon's Limit and how it is applied in determining the maximum speed of analog modems. The concept of error control is explained in Chapter 5, and Chapter 7 has specific information about the analog-to-digital conversion process. The discussion on Ethernet/802.3 networks might also be beneficial in further understanding some of the inherent restrictions of cable modem service. Chapter 11 provides information about ISDN, which is considered one of the solutions to the local loop bottleneck problem. Finally, the next chapter, Chapter 16, presents a discussion on network security issues that you might find enlightening relative to home network security.

Chapter 16

Network Security Issues

In this chapter we discuss various concepts of network security, including techniques, issues and problems involved in implementing a safe and secure network environment. The material in this chapter represents an overview of network security, not a detailed treatise. An outline of the terms and concepts we define and discuss follows:

- Definition of Network Security (Question 1)
- Threat Assessment (Questions 2–12)
- Network Attacks (Questions 13–22)
- Firewalls (Questions 23–30)
- Cryptography and Encryption Techniques (Questions 31–34)
- Digital Certificates and Other Authentication Techniques (39–43)
- Virtual Private Networks (VPNs) and IP Security (IPSec) (Questions 44–47)
- Future of Network Security (Question 48)

1. What is network security?

Network security refers to the proper safeguarding of everything associated with a network. This includes data, media, and equipment. It involves administrative functions, such as threat assessment, and technical tools and facilities such as cryptographic products, and network access control products such as *firewalls*. It also involves making certain that network resources are used in accordance with a prescribed policy and only by people who are authorized to use these resources.

Network security is one of the most controversial subjects these days. Everyone wants it, but few even approach solving the problem. Most people usually view "networking" and "security" as two mutually exclusive words. Sure, there are ways to achieve security, but these usually involve serious cash expenditures as well as threats of violence and death to all users of the network. Proper implementation of network security is neither trivial nor cheap, and it requires expertise that encompasses most areas of network science. Box 16-1 provides information about network security and network *ethics*, which is frequently absent from most discussions involving network security.

BOX 16-1: Network Security and Ethics

Network security involves the various measures to protect a network's components and resources from various threats including physical (e.g., fire, natural disasters, environmental, and sabotage), and illegitimate uses by personnel. There are no simple solutions to the issue of network security. It is prudent, however, for organizations to have established policies in place to protect themselves from security threats. Examples of such policies include: a disaster-recovery plan, a data back-up policy, giving users access to only those areas or levels of a system warranted by their job requirements, setting file permissions to reflect authorized access, using personnel to monitor or test a network's security, and encrypting data. Of all these measures however, none compares to making users cognizant of their role in security. It is critical that employees be made aware of security policies and the reason for these policies.

Network ethics refers to specific standards of moral conduct by network users for the responsible use of network devices and resources. Access to these devices and resources is a privilege and should be treated as such by all users. Responsible, ethical behavior should be the rule rather than the exception and is perhaps the ultimate security measure that an organization can establish. The issue of ethics is important because people are usually the weakest link in any network security scheme. People are susceptible to threats or bribes, they can make mistakes (e.g., writing down a password and leaving it on top of a desk), and they can suddenly subscribe to some new ideology that contradicts their company's policies. When placed in a questionable situation, users must be cognizant of what constitutes right or wrong behavior if they are to be held account-able for their actions. The Division Advisory Panel (DAP) of the National Science Foundation (NSF) Division of Networking and Communications Research and Information (DNCRI), defines as unethical "any activity which purposefully or through negligence: disrupts the intended use of the networks; wastes resources through such actions (people, bandwidth or computer); destroys the integrity of computer-based information; compromises the privacy of users, [or] consumes unplanned resources for control and eradication" (*Communications of the ACM*, June, 1989, p. 688).

---

2. OK, I'll agree that security is important. Where do I start?

One of the problems of network security is determining how much security is necessary for proper control of system and network assets. This gets down to the concept of *threat assessment* or, more specifically, what do you have and who would want it? While it sounds relatively simple to state, it's not that easy to assess corporate network threats unless you approach things in a structured manner. For example, there are threats to hardware (e.g., theft of computers or related equipment, destruction of computer equipment), threats to software (e.g., viruses or software bugs, software deletions from a hard disk, theft of CD-ROMs), threats to information (e.g., database data corruption or deletion, theft of key database files), threats to system or network operations (e.g., network congestion, electrical interference, power outages), and threats to security measures (e.g., thefts of passwords or IDs). See Box 16-2 for information about creating strong passwords.

3. So what do I do first?

The initial problem of threat assessment is to identify what is really a critical asset and what is not. Of course, we all consider everything we have to be a critical asset, but really identifying what is critical to business and what is not is the most important factor. For instance, pharmaceutical companies have an enormous amount of information they keep around for a variety of reasons—sales figures, customer order information, R&D efforts, clinical trial information, FDA filing and documentation, agreements with partners and suppliers and just about any other standard office information system facilities common among any other company. In the case of pharmaceutical companies, the single source of maximum aggravation in the long term is comprised of technologies such as the compound database, which stores information about products and research efforts underway. This is the technology that eventually generates deliverables and thus, profits. Compromise it and the business is critically injured.

In the airline industry, key to its operations are scheduling and load management and that means computing. Scheduling is an enormously complex task involving the management of crews, equipment, supplies, cargo, passengers, and many other tasks. While scheduling is extremely important and essential to business, a very critical problem for an airline is the computation of weights and balances. Pilots need to know their aircraft's take-off weight based upon its load (e.g., fuel, passengers, cargo) so they can set the aircraft's flight systems for the calculated takeoff speed in specific weather conditions. Miscalculations can lead to disaster.

In many companies, people are most sensitized to the leak or theft of sales figures and cash flow information. Sure, it's important, but does it really matter more than a business quarter, especially for public companies? Or is it more important to safeguard strategic product plans, exposure of the company that might generate a lawsuit, customer records that are subject to privacy laws and the like? What if something happens to your web server that is so embarrassing that you spend a great deal of money managing public relations to explain what happened? High visibility companies have a lot of business to lose through simple PR problems. Imagine that it becomes public knowledge that a bank got hacked. Who wants to save their money at or do business with a bank that cannot safeguard its own information? Every business has items that are crucial to safeguard from external parties. Identifying what they are and how damaging they could be to the company is the first step to threat assessment.

4. Fine. I think I understand why threat assessment is important. Are there other steps to it?

Now that you have an idea of which resources are crucial to a company, the next problem is determining who would want them and how they might use these resources against you. In the case of the pharmaceutical company, it is obvious that gaining access to corporate product information of a long-term nature can cause competitors to change their rollout plans for competing products. For patent or patent-worthy research, the long-term

BOX 16-2: Creating Strong Passwords [1]

The single most important component of any network security scheme is the password assigned to networked devices. It is important that strong passwords (i.e., difficult to guess) be created and maintained. Failure to do so can compromise the security of the entire network.

When selecting a password avoid using: (1) Any type of name, including yours or any family members or relatives (spouse, children, parents, aunts, uncles, cousins, in-laws, pets); the name of your company or colleagues; the name of an operating system such as "windows," "unix," or "macintosh"; the host name of your computer or your e-mail address; (2) Anyone's home, work, cell, or fax telephone number; (3) Any part of a social security or student number; (4) Anybody's birthdate; (5) Any dictionary word (English or foreign); (6) A geographical area (e.g., city, state, county, park); (7) Any string of characters comprising the same letters, numbers, or pattern of numbers or letters (e.g., xxxxx, 12345, wysiwyg); (8) Any of the above that begins or ends with a digit (e.g., unix1 or 5xxxxx).

Passwords that are difficult to guess include a mix of uppercase and lowercase letters, digits, punctuation symbols, and special characters (e.g., =, *, ^, @), and are usually seven or eight characters in length. Three suggestions for creating strong passwords are as follows:

- Intermix the first letters of an easy to remember (short) phrase with digits, punctuation symbols, or special characters. For example, *It was twenty years ago today* is represented as Iw$ty^aT.
- Combine two relatively short words with a special character, digit, or punctuation symbol. For example, *buzz* and *off* combined with the tilde character produces the password: BuzZ~OfF.
- Use letters, special characters, and punctuation symbols to represent an English (or foreign) sentence. For example, *You are so lazy!* is represented as UrSoLaz!

Also refrain from writing down passwords. A password committed to memory is more secure than one that is written down. If it is necessary to write down a password then: (1) do not label the written text as a password; (2) keep the corresponding username separate from the password; (3) never tape the paper on which the password is written to any part of a computer or its peripheral units; (4) do not maintain an electronic version of the password; and (5) make the written version different, yet still discernible to you, from the real password. For example, if your real password is *IMover4T* (I am over 40), then you might write down *IM>4T!!* (I am greater than 40), or vice versa.

Remember: *A single user with a weak password can compromise the security of an entire network.*

[1] Adapted from Garfinkel & Spafford, 1991.

effect of information compromise might result in millions of dollars of lost revenue. Determining who can use what you have identifies potential threat locations and helps identify who would attempt to take what a company deems vital to operations.

Sometimes the threat to a company is not the competition but those who believe that a company's actions make it deserving of some sort of retribution. Companies that do animal testing for product safety verification (e.g., cosmetics companies, defense contractors) come under attack by activist groups. Some of these groups have a paramilitary faction that actually breaks into labs and destroys equipment and data. Some have even attacked networks and computing infrastructure with specific viruses designed to work their way into a company's systems and subsequently attack research data. In short, the threat to your data may come from places you least expect.

5. What do you mean by that? Who would threaten my network more than my competition?

In 1991, an FBI study revealed that over 80 percent of network crimes were caused by insiders at a company. In 1997, the number was adjusted to about 75 percent (direct internal and "known" dial-in users) through a joint study by the FBI and the Computer Security Institute, mostly due to the fact that Internet and external break-ins were better documented. This means that, still, the greatest threat to corporate security are the company's employees.

In reviewing your security needs, look at what is available on the network that an employee would want to: (a) threaten the company, (b) cause asset loss, (c) abuse fiscal fidelity, (d) sell to a competitor, (e) cause public relations problems, (f) hurt customer relations or compromise customer information integrity, or (g) cause internal outage of resources that would hurt corporate operations. Indeed, look for anything that, if compromised, would hurt a company's ability to do business and generate revenue.

Most companies assume total trust of internal network assets. This is a big mistake. Specific security arrangements are made to protect corporate networks from external attack but virtually nothing is done to prevent internal attacks—where the bulk of the threat exists. Make certain you understand what your threats are internally so that you keep the honest folks honest and catch the criminals in the act before they cause problems.

6. OK, so now I can't trust anyone, right?

Not exactly, but you do have to be very careful about who has access to what and why. That includes internal personnel.

7. Now that I am good and paranoid, what else do I have to worry about to properly implement network security?

To properly understand the threat to a company, you have to assess how much a loss is going to cost a company. This concept is called *risk analysis* and can be quite involved in larger companies with many assets. In most cases, performing some simple arithmetic on what it will cost to replace, upgrade, repair, or manage a threat situation will yield some startling numbers. You should compare the costs to managing a threat situation to defending the situation. To assist you in this endeavor, specially designed risk analysis software is available. Prices range from $100 to as much as $20,000 per license. The National Institute of Standards and Technology (NIST, formerly the National Bureau of Standards) publishes a risk-analysis software guide, "Guide for Selecting Automatic Risk Analysis Tools," Publication Number 500-174.

8. Give me an example of the impact poor risk analysis can have on an organization.

OK. A large public company we know got its web pages changed with some obscenities. Company personnel did not think it was a big deal and felt that the web pages were not a threat to the company, so they placed the web server outside of a firewall system. While no corporate assets were lost, the security breach caused two major problems and major expenditures for the company. First, a large amount of publicity arose in the local and national news about this that caused a great deal of embarrassment. A professional "crisis management" PR agency was hired for over $300K to do nothing but manage media attention. Then, the repairs to the web server and addition of the security technologies had to be done very quickly at great expense. Haste makes waste. This all cost substantially more than necessary had things been properly set up at the outset.

The second problem was that the web pages were used as a buyer's catalog, hurting business in two ways. First, web crawlers that used blocking software based on URLs placed the company's web pages in a blocking state in their databases. This effectively locked out potential customers who use these web crawlers because they were denied access to the company's web site. Second, confidence in the integrity of the web site was compromised badly. Many companies that were considering using the web site for e-commerce backed out of the deal for over six months until they could be satisfied that the company cleaned up their act. In short, something as simple as an unauthorized web change caused a ripple effect that resulted in several million dollars loss of revenue and a serious public relations problem that took several months to cure. It doesn't take much to cause a major problem that costs a bundle to correct if the problem was never properly planned for in the first place.

9. What else can I do to better understand the threats to my network environment?

War games.

10. Really? War Games? Like the 1980's movie?

Sort of. The Pentagon does it. Large companies do it. Kids play them on the weekends and in school. Role playing games or "war games" in security terms are essential to truly understanding the threat environment and making decisions on what can and cannot be protected.

11. Sounds interesting. What kinds of things am I trying to simulate?

In a network attack, the idea is to examine all the potential points of attack and then try some out to see if they work, how they can be detected and defeated and how to handle the repercussions (e.g., business, politics, PR, technology) of the attack. War games, simulations, role playing or whatever you wish to call it are extremely useful in properly identifying threats and counter-threats. It also allows proper identification of actions in the areas of information warfare which any warrior understands must happen for a proper defense. These include (a) set up information defenses, (b) monitor for information attack, (c) delay the attack until assessment can be made and reinforcements are available, (d) counterattack and capture or destroy, and (e) clean up and fix any problems found. By taking on role facilities and exercising with the above concepts, all threats can be identified and proper defenses planned.

12. So far, so good. Any final items to think about for the threat assessment part of network security?

Documentation and updates. All of the previous items are for naught if documentation does not follow-up the work. The legacy for others is what is written down and updated as the threats change. This can take a substantial amount of time and effort and should be part of any well thought-out plan for threat management and countermeasures.

13. What is the most common method to attack a network resource?

"Social engineering."

14. Really? What is that?

Social engineering, is, basically, lying your way into a facility. It takes a certain amount of self-confidence and the ability to talk your way out of situations where you might get caught. It also takes a certain amount of "on your feet" thinking so that you do not get into a situation where you are discovered too soon. The idea is to test the facilities in your purview without getting caught too soon, if at all, so that improvements can be made.

The main idea of social engineering is to put the human element in the network breaching loop and use it as a tool. For instance, showing up at the computer room with network hardware in hand and with an appropriate vendor ID usually results in someone helping you into the communications closet and even to the point of helping to install the hardware on the network. By appealing to the victim's natural effort to help users and other folk involved in the communications environment, it can be fairly easy to breach the physical perimeter of a company and gain access to the network and all its treasures.

15. Any ideas on how someone might socially engineer themselves into my company?

One favored technique is to walk into a branch office or main office of a customer and tell a story of woe to those around that you work for the corporate office and have to kill a few hours before a flight. "Do you think that there might be an empty cubicle around where I can work for a while? I don't need anything except a place to park and work." Usually, someone finds an empty space for the "corporate visitor" to work and almost invariably, there is a live network connection in that space. Most laptops have either a built-in Ethernet/802.3 controller chip or PC Card—perhaps also a token ring PC Card. With such a network-capable laptop loaded with various network analysis and protocol analysis tools, this intruder can collect data from the network and gain valuable network attack information (e.g., passwords or user IDs). A further enhancement to the deception tactic is to use a business card of someone else in the company from another state or office to impose the illusion that (a) the intruder is indeed that person, (b) the intruder does indeed work for the company, and (c) the position on the card is of enough importance that whoever is helping provide access to a work area knows that the intruder is high enough up the food chain that helping get access to the network might be career-enhancing.

16. That sounds like you have to have some technical skills. Are there easier ways?

Yes. One customer site developed a rather elaborate method of users gaining access to its network resources. Confederates, posing as vendors, called up network personnel and offered to demonstrate software on their systems. This resulted in the company's established security procedures for creating user accounts to be completely circumvented. A set of accounts with unrestricted access was acquired with very little effort and with no permission from upper management, as was required by procedure. There are many ways to divert security procedures because people basically want to be helpful.

17. What are the principle obstacles to implementing network security?

The greatest obstacles are lack of personnel, money, and tools—and the apathy of top management. In a recent survey about network security, nearly 60 percent of respondents blame weak security on a lack of staff to handle the issue. Another 55 percent say their budgets are insufficient to the task. More than 40 percent attribute the problem to nonexistent software tools, and 45 percent blame the problem on top management. Management claims security is extremely important because of the myriad potential threats including current and former employees, suppliers, customers, and competitors. Complicating matters is there usually is no management support or funding to protect a company. Absent from most network budgets are line items for personnel support and security.

18. How hard is it to find information about how to breach or hack a site?

On the Internet, there are, quite literally, thousands of locations with network hacking information on them that include very specific instructions on how to attack almost any type of protocol, operating system, or hardware environment that exists. Doing a web search using the search string "Hacker + Phreak + Anarchy" yields several sites dedicated to these activities. The titles of some the documents that are available are quite revealing: "The Hacker's Handbook," "Novell Hacking Tools," "A Beginner's Guide to Hacking UNIX," "Hacking Answering Machines," and "Hacking CompuServe Information Services." The really sad commentary is that there are over 30,000 locations on the Internet where hacking or security breaching information, tools, and experiences can easily be obtained. It's big and it's serious.

19. What kinds of system or application attacks can happen through the network?

Good network security begins with the systems on the network. In many cases, the network itself can increase a company's risk to data manipulation and destruction of information repositories. In a research site, jealous co-workers might taint extensive research data, causing scientists to reach improper conclusions. Financial analysts might find that their carefully crafted spreadsheets produce improper computations on critical budgeting line items due to static, dynamic, or formulaic information being changed. Word processing documents containing standard contracts and procedures might be modified to weaken the document's meaning and undermine the intent of a contract. Database demographic information may be erased or modified to produce false market data that is critical to a roll-out of service or business offerings, causing much time and money to be wasted in the creation of market products and services. The list of opportunities for malicious manipulation goes on and on. Without good system security, the network expands the opportunity for security breaches.

20. Are there companies or special targets for security breaches?

Yes. The nature of some businesses makes them prime targets for security breaches. For example, companies that engage in animal testing might be the targets of groups that engage in the willful destruction and infiltration of corporate assets to bring attention to the issue of animal testing and to disrupt corporate entities involved in such testing. Medical practices, such as family planning centers and abortion services facilities, are often the targets of groups formed for the express purpose of putting such operations out of business. Other companies may contain technologies of particular interests to industrial espionage specialists who wish to sell information about the technologies to competitive companies. Companies with extensive telecommunications systems are often the subject of PBX attacks that allow the intruder access to free long-distance services for their use without the corporate entity knowing about the attack for a long time—if at all.

21. How do I implement network security properly, then, if it is so complex?

Network security, properly implemented, consists of a series of security barriers, not merely a single network security control point. Any single control point could be breached by an expert. However, by placing multiple security barriers in the path of a critical asset or resource, the chances of someone getting through without detection is diminished greatly.

The concept is much like that of the strong castle protected by a series of moats. As the storming hoard nears the castle, they must traverse the moats. It is possible to traverse some moats by pole-vaulting, but eventually the invader is bound to fall into one of the moats and be caught. If there is only one moat and the invader is a good jumper, there is not much protection. If there are moats, concertina wire, razor wire, tall fences with broken glass on them, land mines, cans full of pennies suspended by trip wires, Doberman Pinschers, and other such traps in the path from the intruder to the "jewels," one or more of the obstacles is going to alert the keepers of the castle that someone is trying to infiltrate the castle and that something must be done to protect the assets and destroy the intruder.

The notion that a singular perimeter is an effective defensive mechanism for network asset protection is long gone. Since many network assets are attacked by internal personnel, the need to protect the assets from external and internal attack is rapidly becoming the norm. This notion is similar to the plan advanced by the Great Wall of Texas Society in the United States. The Society's intent is to build a 30 foot-high wall around the northern sections of the state of Texas border with New Mexico, Oklahoma, Arkansas, and Louisiana. Their whole premise is that the concern over the border with Mexico is outdated; they assert that the real enemy is to the north, not the south, and that "we have been watching the wrong border for too long." Considering that the bulk of all network break-ins happen from inside the company, the assertion that others in the same organization (in this example, the United States) are the real enemy may be true. Therefore, intrusion protection for a network should never be limited to outside network connections and should always start directly with the information repository itself as the first line of defense. Box 16-3 provides some basic network security measures.

BOX 16-3: Network Security Measures

Following are several measures that can enhance the security of a network:

1. Use dual power supply modules for network critical devices.
2. Connect devices to uninterruptible power supplies (UPS).
3. Ensure that all network devices are connected to "clean" power.
4. Install surge protection directly to the main circuit panels that feed the electrical outlets to which devices are connected.
5. Ensure all rooms with network devices are properly ventilated or air conditioned.
6. Do not place devices in combustible areas, and restrict the use of volatile materials (e.g., cleaning supplies) in these areas.
7. Install smoke detectors and adequate fire-extinguishing equipment in all rooms with network critical devices.
8. Do no place network devices in areas that are susceptible to flooding or exposed to water (e.g., a utility closet with a sink).
9. Do not place network devices near windows.
10. Place critical devices such as servers in locked rooms with an alarm system, and restrict access to these rooms to authorized personnel only.
11. Create and maintain strong passwords to all systems, and educate users to do the same.
12. Educate users to the potential consequences of providing their access privileges to unauthorized users.
13. Enable, maintain, and review system accounting and log information regularly.
14. Install virus protection software and update virus definitions files regularly.
15. Enforce idle time-outs for dial-up connections.
16. Prevent users from uploading data to a system's hard disk. If this is not feasible, then restrict uploads to an area that is automatically virus-checked.
17. Maintain proper file permissions.
18. If possible, place all critical data on a centralized server and protect the server.
19. Edit configuration files carefully and always save a copy of the current file prior to making modifications.

Continued on next page

BOX 16-3: Network Security Measures (Continued)

20. Minimize the physical exposure of copper-based cable by enclosing it in conduit; any taps that penetrate the conduit will be noticeable.

21. Maintain a physical map of your network that includes a wiring diagram so you know if any cable has been tampered.

22. Identify the location of any buried media before the ground is dug up.

23. Use a cable scanner to scan the cable and record values. Do this periodically and compare readings.

24. Maintain a secure wiring closet. This includes using a separate, enclosed space with a locked door for the wiring closet.

25. Enclose all cable buried underground in metal pipe and document its location.

26. Do not use copper cable to interconnect buildings. If you must use copper, enclose it in metal conduit and place it high enough so that it is not easily accessible.

27. Use fiber-optic cable when possible, particularly in high-security locations.

28. Always encrypt data prior to transmission.

29. Use line-of-sight transmissions instead of broadcast transmissions.

30. Use optical-based links instead of RF-based links.

31. Use wired-based media instead of wireless media.

32. To minimize the effect of unauthorized packet-sniffing programs, design your network using switches so that each workstation has its own dedicated network segment. This reduces the overall amount of network traffic, and it limits the type of data that can be collected to broadcast or multicast messages. Alternatively, encrypt all messages prior to placing them on the network.

33. Educate all users about the potential security risks related to connecting their workstations to the Internet via a dial-up line.

34. Train users on the differences between client and server processes and the security implications related to enabling server versions of Internet utilities.

35. Require users to virus-check all software downloaded from the Internet.

36. Ensure that users disable TCP/IP routing if their workstation is connected to a LAN and if they intend to use it for Internet access.

37. Do regular and frequent backups of all data onto tape or disk and store backups in a different location than the original data.

38. Establish and enforce acceptable use policies for all users.

39. Develop, implement, and review on a regular basis a disaster recovery plan.

40. Keep current with Computer Emergency Response Team (CERT) publications.

41. Subscribe to various network security listservs.

42. Attain network security tools and learn how to use them and interpret their output.

---

22. What kinds of technology can be implemented to help me make my network more secure?

There are a lot of them. Three in particular are firewalls, encryption, and digital certificates. (There are many others.)

23. What's a firewall?

Traditionally, a firewall is a "wall" placed between the car floorboard and the engine to keep an engine fire or explosion from entering the passenger compartment. In the context of network security, a firewall performs a similar function between network connections on a network. Specifically, firewalls are devices or products that allow the systems or network manager to restrict access to components on the network. Various types of products claim to be firewalls but clearly are not. One sad part about firewalls is that the terminology is much like the word "virus": What is a firewall and what is not a firewall is subject to much interpretation by the vendor and the consumer.

At the simplest level, a firewall is a packet filter facility that can restrict the flow of packets to and from a network via a set of rules implemented in an interconnection device. Examples of this might be a filtering router unit that is capable of restricting which packets can be transmitted and which ones can be received from an Internet connection based upon packet addresses (source and destination), or specific IP transport protocol type. Other types of firewalls might include intelligent port and socket (application) filters, session-level (user) filters, and a variety of other types of filtering tools that restrict traffic flow. From these definitions, it is plain that a firewall is frequently a sum of many different components that work together to block transmission and reception of traffic.

24. What types of firewalls are there?

There are five generally accepted types of firewalls used on Internet connections: frame-filtering, packet-filtering, circuit gateways, stateful and application gateways, and proxy servers. Other lesser-known proxy firewall implementations and variants all function somewhat the same, with varying degrees of performance and difficulty in configuration. Following is a brief description of each type:

Frame-Filtering Firewalls. A frame-filtering firewall can filter to the bit level the layout and contents of a LAN frame (such as Ethernet/802.3, token ring/802.5, FDDI and others). By providing filtering at this level, frames that do not belong on the trusted network are rejected before they even reach anything valuable, even on the firewall itself.

Packet-Filter Firewalls. A packet-filtering firewall is either a router with packet-filtering capabilities (see previous section) or a dedicated device that does packet-filtering. A packet-filtering firewall is best used as a dedicated unit in conjunction with a router. This way the router does not have to perform a dual (and contradictory) function—it can facilitate communication as it is designed to do, and the packet-filtering firewall can provide the network security. The performance of packet-filtering firewall will degrade greatly as more filters and conditional filter handling are set up. Packet filtering also does not handle certain types of transactions on a network that are context-sensitive (i.e., many packets are required to do something, which, taken as a whole, means a certain condition has occurred that may not be a happy situation).

Circuit Gateway Firewalls. A circuit gateway firewall typically involves monitoring the session set-up between a system and the user security options relative to that system for a particular user. For instance, a circuit gateway might check user IDs and passwords for a connection request. Other types of circuit firewalls might implement proxy connection authorization or other types of authentication services. Circuit firewalls are also responsible for logging who came from where and went to what, which is not trivial.

"Stateful" Firewalls. Following the establishment of proxy firewalls (described next), the need to examine the transaction condition between two interoperating applications became essential to defeating certain sophisticated types of network attacks. IP address spoofing, session hijacking, piggyback session acquisition, and many other technical attacks were allowing hackers access to applications and eventually entire systems. To stop this type of attack profile, the firewall must be intelligent enough to watch all transactions between two systems and understand enough of the details of how a protocol works to identify a specific condition in the transaction between two applications, be able to predict what should transpire next in the transaction, and be able to detect when normal operational "states" of the connection are being violated. This type of firewall is called a *stateful inspection facility* and allows the network security manager to specify rules and filters for specific technical transactions between the systems and applications and what to do if they are violated by anyone.

Many vendors of stateful firewall facilities also include detailed filtering capabilities similar in many respects to proxy filtering. In some cases, however, proxies do a better security job (depending on the application being secured) so stateful firewalls, for the most part, are capable of providing a full security rule-base range of services but sometimes not as complete for specific applications as a proxy might be.

Application Gateways or Proxies Firewalls. An application gateway firewall provides protection at the application level. If viewed from the perspective of functionality, an application gateway firewall is the opposite of a packet-filtering firewall—the former is application- or program-specific and the latter is general-purpose. For example, consider a typical file transfer session. Suppose you want users to be able to download files from the Internet using the file transfer protocol (FTP) but you do not want anyone from outside your organization placing files on any of your networked hosts. More specifically, you want to permit "get" FTP sessions but reject "put" FTP sessions. With a packet-filtering firewall you have an all or none case—either it allows file transfers (get and put) to occur or it does not. An application gateway firewall, however, can be configured to permit "get" sessions and reject "put" sessions because they can examine the details of the application. Another example might be a Telnet firewall facility that provides security facilities, full packet content scanning, session management, session capturing, and other facilities. This type of firewall is specific to a particular IP application, Telnet, and is usually much more secure than packet and address filtering in a router as it might not only worry about user IDs, passwords and proxies, but it also might consider application-specific access methods and security issues.

An application gateway firewall uses custom programs for each protected application. If a new application that requires protection is added to the network, a new program has to be written and added to the set of other programs that reside on the firewall. These custom-written application programs act as both a client and server and effectively serve as proxies to the actual applications. For example, if e-mail is to be protected, a custom e-mail application is written that includes specific security rules (e.g., what type of e-mail is permitted). When users want to use e-mail, they must either log into the application gateway and use this special application, or use a client application on a host that supports this secured e-mail service. Since these specially written applications act as proxies to their "real" counterparts, the collective set of these programs is referred to as *proxy services,* and application gateway firewalls are often called *proxy server* or *proxy gateways.*

There are two type of proxy gateways. In the first type, an incoming connection for a destination would be intercepted by the proxy and a "new" connection from the proxy to the destination would be created. In this manner, a connection originating from outside the firewall is not able to directly "touch" the destination, and full filtering of the application is accomplished. The second variant of the proxy gateway allows the firewall to appear as the only destination for all applications to a trusted network from an untrusted network. Through this facility, the internal network is completely "hidden" from network view to any outside connections. This has the by-product of allowing an internal network to use unregistered address ranges for IP users to access Internet and other external networks expecting valid address ranges. It also increases security by not allowing an external network direct access to an internal address or even know what the internal address is for a specific node on a trusted network.

25. Is there any simple way to select a firewall? Isn't there one vendor that does all the types of firewalls in one package?

Since firewall requirements vary dramatically from company to company, there are many situations in which more than one product from more than one vendor is required to properly provide firewall facilities. A router with packet filters would be almost a necessity for each site. A user terminal security facility for Telnet users is also necessary, but no router can provide *all* the sophisticated security facilities for terminal traffic as well as provide swift routing facilities. As a result, these two functions alone result in different systems for control and access.

26. How hard is it to set up a firewall, anyway?

One of the problems of firewall implementation is the need for some technical expertise to configure a firewall. If one does not understand TCP/IP to a reasonable level, there is little hope of properly setting up a packet filter facility. How much technical knowledge is required varies from firewall to firewall, but none is exactly straightforward and clear to set up. In almost all situations, no matter how mature and well written the firewall software is, there are a myriad of administrative tasks involved.

27. Can a firewall be defeated by an attacker?

Even with fairly decent firewalls for Internet access, there are situations that, left to their own, will defeat the firewalls. For instance, tunneling a protocol within a protocol from site to site can be difficult, if not impossible, to filter and control. Some sites, for purely political reasons, will not permit restrictions on certain applications that allow remote Internet users to gain access to critical data about a site that may be used to exploit the network. There are plenty of other situations, but it is important to note that firewalls are not forever and may be defeated from time to time even in the best of environments.

28. So far it looks like a firewall is for TCP/IP only. Is that true?

Unfortunately, for the most part, yes. There is one firewall on the market that covers TCP/IP and all other protocols. Multiple protocols are the norm on an intranet and extranet network—not just TCP/IP.

With "real" networks on corporate facilities, the existence and use of protocol suites besides the IP facilities found on Internet provide the bulk of networking protocol use. In most corporate networks, especially those established in the 1980s and early 1990s, Novell's IPX, Digital Equipment Corporation's Pathworks environment (DECnet, LAT, LAST), IBM's System Network Architecture (SNA), Apple Computer's AppleTalk, and Banyan's VINES environment (StreetTalk) are still very active and very much a part of the corporate culture at many companies. Other corporate environments such as airlines have developed specialized protocols (such as ALC) for terminal applications that are very popular in a particular vertical industry segment but not seen in mainstream computing. Still other network types, such as industrial networks, warehouse networks, process control networks, and many other types of specialized networks utilize custom protocols for maximum efficiency or for specialized applications where commercially accepted protocol suites are much too large or too general to solve a network problem.

In 1995 and 1996, the blossoming of the concept of generally accepted Internet applications (e.g., web servers, POP- and IMAP-based e-mail) being deployed on internal networks for employee access began a steady and dramatic increase in both scope and size. Mission-critical applications have begun to be deployed on these "Intranets" while existing network technologies continue to co-exist on the same network environment.

To protect only one protocol, such as IP, is ludicrous in a standard corporate network environment where it is the norm to deploy between 3 and 18 protocol suites to satisfy legacy and current computational requirements. Popular operating systems, such as Windows NT, come configurable with multiple protocols to satisfy corporate clients (NT V4.x comes with IP, IPX, NetBEUI, and AppleTalk standard on each system) and provide connectivity to the variety of systems on a corporate network. Protection of an IP application environment is fine if that is all a system is using, but many systems utilize other popular protocols.

Protection of a single protocol on intranet or extranet environments without consideration for the other operating protocol's security needs is much like locking the front door of a house and thinking the whole house is secure. Proper network security requires all entities to receive equal protective treatment to truly address the network security threat.

29. Yeah, but we decided to only use TCP/IP for our protocols. We aren't multiprotocol, right?

This is a common misconception. Even in locations where IP is the predominant protocol, there is the upcoming problem of a new version of the IP protocol stack referred to as IPv6. (*Note:* See Chapter 3 for additional information about IPv6.) Sometimes referred to as IPng (for "next generation"), IPv6 is not only different in addressing structure (it uses a 16-octet address as compared to IPv4's 4-octet address) but also in the mechanics of how a system receives its address (it is done dynamically) and what the remainder of the protocol does to address routing issues, security layer issues, and other new features of the protocol. To say that the current IPv4 is "compatible" with IPv6 is a gross mistake, as evidenced by the published RFCs on the protocols that call for "coexistence" and not "compatibility." Coexistence, in technospeak, means that a machine may run both protocols at the same time to achieve the ability to use both at the same time (coexistence), not run the new one and continue to converse with the old one (compatibility). Therefore, for environments running only IPv4 at this time, they are about to become multiprotocol, like it or not, even if all that is running is the current version of IP and the upcoming upgrade to the protocol. No network manager who is cautious about the network environment will totally cut over to IPv6 without a parallel phase in which both protocol suites are running. In some cases, this will be a lengthy time period for sites where applications may require IPv4 to remain for application "survival" indefinitely. Therefore, to protect the internal network from attack by internal personnel and to support multiple versions of protocols, such as IP, with external networks, such as the Internet, networks are either multiprotocol now or will be in very short order (e.g., IPv4 and IPv6 on the same network). The need to protect the internal network is as great or greater than the need to protect the external network.

30. So which type of firewall is better than the others?

Each firewall architecture has its strengths and weaknesses. Router screening is fast and allows rejection of common errors, hack attacks, and user strangeness that is part of any network connection. Application filtering firewalls provide extensive application control and monitoring of application behavior. Proxy facilities provide application control and session control between sources and destinations as well as address translation facilities. Stateful firewalls prevent technical attacks from breaching a network and provide sophisticated filtering techniques that rival almost any proxy or application gateway.

What is best for the customer is security for the right reasons, implemented in the most productive manner depending on what is being secured and how. This means that the optimal firewall configuration is one that can do all the various types of rule-based filtering we've discussed, depending on the type of application being used and the best security methodology approach to solve the security problem for the application environment. No one security rule-base approach previously described can properly solve all security issues in a networked environment. Most network security professionals will tell you that it is impractical to expect a single approach to be useful in all environments.

31. OK, I think I understand firewalls. You also mentioned encryption. What is that?

Encryption is a process that converts sensitive data into a coded form. When retrieved by authorized users, this coded form is then reconverted (i.e., decoded) into meaningful text. Encryption essentially hides or disguises information from unintended recipients, but enables authorized users retrieve it. The study of secret communication is called *cryptology,* and the practice or art of encoding messages is called *cryptography.* Unencrypted data is referred to as *plaintext* and its encrypted output is called *ciphertext.*

A simple encryption technique is a letter-substitution cipher. For example, let's agree that we will use the following "key" for coding and decoding messages:

A—O	H—P	O—E	V—Q
B—D	I—Y	P—B	W—U
C—C	J—M	Q—G	X—J
D—I	K—F	R—N	Y—T
E—S	L—R	S—K	Z—L
F—V	M—Z	T—W	,— #
G—A	N—X	U—H	

Now, the message,

DEAR JANE, NOT GETTING ANY BETTER, HURRY HOME

is coded by substituting the plaintext characters with those of our cipher. Thus, the encrypted message is,

ISON MOXS# XEW ASWWYXA OXT DSWWSN# PHNNT PEZS

This message can now be sent via public channels and decoded by an authorized person who knows the key. If the message is intercepted or finds its way into the hands of an unauthorized person, it will most likely appear as meaningless gibberish. Of course, it is always possible that an unintended recipient could crack the code.

32. Does this have anything to do with DES?

Yes. Developed by IBM and NIST in the 1970s, the Data Encryption Standard (DES) is a mathematical model or algorithm that is used as a coding device. It is also the most widely used commercial encryption algorithm. As with letter-substitution cipher, a key is used to determine the transformation from plaintext to ciphertext. The key for a DES user consists of any one of 2^{56} possible keys, each one of which is a list of 56 zeros and ones (plus eight parity bits). This translates to approximately 10^{17} or 100,000,000,000,000,000 possible arrangements of 56 zeros and ones.

DES, which can be implemented in hardware or software, has been the single, most thoroughly tested encryption algorithm. In over 20 years of testing, DES was never cracked. However, in 1998, John Gilmore and Paul Kocher broke the code in 56 hours using a homemade supercomputer they built for $220,000. Funding for the supercomputer, which is a configuration of hundreds of Intel processors, was provided by the Electronic Freedom Foundation (EFF). The project was sponsored by the U.S. government and carried a $10,000 prize.

The DES standard was scheduled to be renewed in 1998. To enhance its cryptographic capabilities, additional safeguards have been suggested. One is to increase the number of keys from 56 zeros and ones, to 1024 zeros and ones. This increased key size makes the algorithm more complex and hence more difficult to crack. A second suggestion is to replace DES with a completely different algorithm called *Skipjack*, which uses an 80-bit key space. A third suggestion is to replace DES with the "public-key" method of cryptography (described below). A fourth suggestion is to use a variant of DES called *Triple DES*, which uses three DES operations instead of one. Even these strategies, however, might prove useless. Scientists at Oxford University claim that within a few years they will have a quantum computer that can crack any-length encryption within seconds.

33. Hold it. I think I know about public-key cryptography. Isn't this what PGP uses?

You are correct. *Pretty Good Privacy (PGP)* is indeed a public-key application. It is an e-mail encryption package written by Philip Zimmerman that combines three separate algorithms: RSA, which stands for the first initials of the last names of the designers—Ronald Rivest, Adi Shamir, and Len Adleman; IDEA, which stands for International Data Encryption Algorithm; and the message-digest algorithm, version 5 (MD5). RSA is a public-key encryption algorithm, which is discussed later in this chapter. IDEA is a conventional encryption algorithm similar to DES that uses a 64-bit block cipher with a 128-bit key space. MD5 is a hashing algorithm—developed in 1991 by Ron Rivest and described in RFC 1321—that takes a message of arbitrary length and generates a 128-bit message digest. (A message digest is used for digital signature applications.)

PGP provides both encryption and digital signature services. Encryption enables a user to encode files; a digital signatures enables a user to "sign" a document so that the document's authenticity can be confirmed by checking the signature. Thus, encryption provides confidentiality; a digital signature proves a message was not modified. Encryption service is provided via RSA and IDEA. PGP first encrypts messages with IDEA, and then uses RSA to encrypt the IDEA key that was used to encrypt message initially. Intended recipients then use RSA to retrieve the IDEA key, which is used to decode the message. PGP also uses MD5 to create digital signatures, which are encrypted via RSA.

PGP has been the source of much attention by U.S. legislatures. First, encryption algorithms with key sizes of greater than 40 bits in length cannot be exported outside the Unites States. Since PGP incorporates IDEA, which uses a 64-bit block cipher with a 128-bit key space, its exportation outside the U.S. is prohibited. Unfortunately, someone made PGP available on the Internet without Phil Zimmerman's knowledge and Zimmerman was indicted for exporting PGP outside the United States. (*Note:* There is no limit on key sizes within the United States.) Another incident involved patent infringement. Earlier versions of PGP (v2.3 or earlier) contained the RSA algorithm, which is patented in the United States. Consequently, users of these versions risked patent infringement if they used PGP in the United States without a license. In May 1994, however, an agreement with the RSA patent holder was reached and subsequent versions (v2.6 or later) of PGP can now be used legally, for noncommercial purposes, in the United States without a license. However, PGP is also subject to the rules of the International Traffic in Arms Regulations and cannot be exported without an export license. Additional information about PGP can be found at http://www.pgp.com.

34. What if I put a cryptographic product like PGP on my notebook computer so that I can communicate with the office securely? What legal trouble will I get into?

Most likely, you can probably use the products without trouble. Nevertheless, it is prudent to consult your government's regulations relative to this issue. If information is to leave your country of origin, there are usually export laws regarding the use of cryptography either in or out of your country. In the United States, the cryptotechnologies that can and cannot be used is regulated by the Department of Commerce. DOC also regulates which countries can do business with U.S. companies using cryptography. The Department of Trade and Industry (DTI) helps regulate security issues in the United Kingdom and determines what can and cannot be exported or used outside the country. In France, rules on cryptographic use in communications are extremely strict and in many cases cryptography is not allowed at all unless your company is an approved financial institution. It gets pretty complex country-to-country.

35. Can you give me an example of a public-key encryption method?

Sure. Let's consider RSA, which is a widely accepted and implemented method of public-key encryption. RSA requires two keys for each user, one public and the other private. Each user's public key is available to anyone, whereas the private key is secret and known only to the user. A message coded with the public key is decoded with the private key and vice versa. This system provides three distinct methods of sending coded messages. The first method involves sending a coded message to a receiver from a sender whose identify is verifiable. To illustrate:

> *If we wish to send you a coded message, we code our message using your public key. This way you can decode it using your private key.*

The problem with this method is that the receiver of the message can never be absolutely certain who the sender is because it is the receiver's public key that is being used to code the message. The second method involves sending a coded message from a sender whose identity is verifiable, but the message can be decoded by anyone. To illustrate:

> *If we wish to send you a coded message and we want you to be absolutely certain that it is from us, then we will code our message using our private key. You in turn decode our message using our public key. Since it is our public key that actually decodes our message, you are certain that the message came from us.*

Authentication of a sender's identity, as demonstrated by this second method, is very important in certain transactions such as in electronic funds transfers. Now, to be absolutely clandestine, if we want to send you a coded message and we want you to know it is from us, a third method is used:

> *We first code our message using your public key. (This makes the message secret.) We then encode this code once more using our private key. (This guarantees that the message is from us.) Upon receiving the message, you must decode it twice, first using our public key and then using your private key. Now, only you can read the message and it could only have been sent by us.*

36. I've always heard that if something is encrypted, it's secure. Right?

Nope. Nothing is forever and that includes cryptography. There is always a way to exploit a weakness in an algorithm or key structure in cryptography, but it may be very difficult to do so. The real issue with the use of cryptography is economics: Do you have something valuable enough that warrants the compute power and people power to try to decrypt whatever you are transmitting over a network? If so, then you may be a target anyway. If not, then less complex cryptography facilities may be more than sufficient for your security requirements.

37. Wait a minute. You mean that cryptographic security comes in different strengths?

Absolutely. There are a lot of components to cryptography done correctly. The algorithm and key lengths are two of the more important components that help determine how hard it is to break the cryptographic facilities being used. But there are issues such as key exchange methods (this is the same idea as how to get new passwords in a secure way to the users—the key exchange is basically a computerized method to exchange cryptographic keys), standardized implementation of the cryptographic methods, export laws in various countries, and many other issues. How "strong" a cryptographic facility you really need is a function of how sensitive the information is that you are trying to protect. For instance, sales figures are really only good for a quarter of the calendar year and in a public company, will be reported next quarter. Therefore, the cryptographic "strength" required is really only something that is going to safeguard the information from general viewing for a short period of time (assuming, of course, that the information cannot be viewed by some other method on the systems on the network or easily compromised by people who know about the information). If you are dealing with patent information or something that has a longer economic life, more care needs to be exercised in safeguarding the information and more care must be taken in the selection of the cryptographic methods used to safeguard the information.

38. Which algorithm is best to use for encrypting network traffic?

Tough question. There are really two aspects to encrypting network traffic that have to be addressed to determine which algorithm(s) and key length(s) you will need. They are (1) identifying what you are trying to protect and assessing its value, and (2) any plans you might have for encrypting traffic destined for outside the borders of your country and the laws governing this.

As we said before, the algorithm and key length are important for safeguarding the information. In the United States, the ANSI Data Encryption Standard implements a 56-bit key length and contains variants that implement 40-bit keys and 128-bit keys. The keys themselves may be protected by a variant of DES called Triple DES which is, essentially, the key being encrypted three times. So, 40-bit DES may be plenty strong enough for the bulk of the traffic you are going to pass around, whereas 56-bit or 128-bit may be necessary for the really sensitive data like five-year plans and the like. Triple DES may be essential for safeguarding the keys of the cryptographic method, which is critical. If someone knows the keys for the method, then it does not matter how secure the method is—it's broken! Which is best depends on what you are trying to protect and where.

Speed may also be an issue. Some algorithms are much slower than others and this may factor into the decision as to which one to use. For example, DES is faster than RSA in real-time applications. RSA, as is all public-key encryption schemes, is time-consuming. Time is needed to "sign" a message and verify it at the receiving end. DES, on the other hand, requires more keys than RSA. Public-key systems can do authentication and encryption, but DES can only do encryption. As you can see, there are trade-offs. One alternative is to use a combination of conventional encryption and public-key methods, ala PGP.

39. You mentioned something called "digital certificates." What are they?

Digital certificates are kind of an electronic passport. People use a variety of techniques to identify each other: looks, sounds, smell, feel. Fingerprints, retinal scans, facial thermography, and other biometrics also help identify someone as being who they claim to be. In most cases, though, implementation of biometric security devices is in its infancy at this writing and expensive to boot. So, a simpler method is to have someone identify certain things about themselves to a separate entity in which a sender and receiver both have a level of trust. This third party issues the user a numerical value, pattern or key called a digital certificate. The certificate, in conjunction with cryptographic tools, identifies a specific user on the network, regardless of where the user is located or what application the user is using, in a reliable method. Digital certificates are available from a wide variety of trusted parties such as *VeriSign*. Unfortunately, there are as many ways to provide digital certificate authentication as there are vendors and this means that use of them tends to be spotty and somewhat chaotic at this writing.

40. So a digital certificate allows me to be authenticated to a remote node?

Yes. However, authentication means that the remote node believes you are who you say you are. That is, it proves the sender of a message knows the "key." There is also the access control problem, though.

41. Access Control?

Yep. Just because you have a key to the front door of the house does not mean that you have permission to go through every dresser drawer in the house. Network security involves authentication (digital certificates) and access control (like a firewall proxy facility) to ensure that you are who you say you are and then allow you access to only what you are supposed to access. All of this activity might also be encrypted. There are many pieces to making sure network security works well.

42. Is a digital certificate anything like a smart card?

Smart cards are similar to digital certificates in that they represent another form of authentication. A smart card is like a credit card with integrated circuits embedded in them that stores information in electronic form; the card controls this information. Smart cards use personal identification numbers, biometrics (e.g., fingerprints, voice, signature), and encryption methods to authenticate a user. Smart cards communicate with an external "reader," which can be a computer system, a cash register, or any other type of input device. The method of communication is either by direct contact or by radio signals. In either case, once contact is established, the "reader" provides the required voltage to power the card.

Smart cards have several applications besides providing authentication service for network security. For example, the medical profession uses smart cards to store patients' personal medical histories. This technology provides privacy and protection of patient records, enables the tracking of medication and medical information, and makes it possible for a patient's insurance coverage to be verified almost immediately. Smart cards can also store patient's X-rays and other graphics data. Another application is in education. Many universities provide students with smart cards for meal plan authorization. These cards also can be used as credit or debit cards for purchasing campus products, as a library card for checking out books, as a "vending" card for vending or copy machines, and for accessing secured buildings or dormitories.

43. I have also heard of something called Kerberos. Could you shed some light on this for me?

Cerberus was the three-headed dog in Greek mythology that guarded the gates to Hades. Its namesake is used to describe a client-server network security authentication system. Originally developed at MIT, *Kerberos,* which is based on DES encryption, is an Internet standard that uses a three-pronged approach for authentication: a database that contains users' rights, an authentication server, and a ticket-granting server.

To illustrate how Kerberos works, let's assume you want to access a data file stored on one of your company's primary servers. When you first log on to your workstation and request access to this file, an authentication server searches its database for your access rights. Once the server confirms that these rights include the requested service (i.e., you have permission to access the file), it generates an encrypted "ticket," which enables your workstation to access the ticket-granting server. The authentication server also returns the "key" that was used to encrypt something called an "authenticator," which contains your name, network address, and current time. Your workstation then sends the ticket and authenticator to the ticket-granting server, which decrypts both pieces of data. If they match, the ticket-granting server generates a ticket for the requested service to be used only by you. This ticket is then returned to your workstation, which you then present to the company's server on which the file is stored. Once this server receives your ticket, it gives you access to the file.

A Kerberos-generated ticket is programmed to have a short life cycle (e.g., one hour or one day). This way if an unauthorized person acquires a session ticket, it will only be valid for that time period. In order to use Kerberos, every network application has to be rewritten to support it. Kerberos is available in Windows NT 5.0. The Internet RFC that describes Kerberos is RFC 1510, which is available from http://info.internet.isi.edu:80/in-notes/rfc/files/rfc1510.txt. Additional information about Kerberos and other network security information can be obtained from http://www.securityserver.com. (*Note:* See also http://www.rfc-editor.org/rfc.html for information about RFCs.)

44. What about Virtual Private Networks? What are they?

A *Virtual Private Network* (VPN) is an IP connection between two sites over a public IP network that has its payload traffic encrypted so that only the source and destination can decrypt the traffic packets. A VPN enables a publicly accessible network to be used for highly confidential, dynamic, and secure data transmissions. Of course, this type of security can be mostly implemented by pre-encrypting files and other user data before transmission, but it is not quite as secure as a VPN. VPNs provide further security as they are capable of encrypting not only the actual user data, but many of the protocol stack informational items which may be used to compromise a customer site in a technical session attack profile.

The current VPN exploitation that has emerged in the industry in the last couple of years is mostly centered on IP-based networks such as the Internet. One of the major problems of VPN technologies is that there are a great variety of implementation styles and methods, which causes much confusion when trying to develop a strategy for their use in a company. Chapter 7 contains a summary of many current VPN implementations.

45. I was always under the impression that the Internet is not really secure. What security mechanisms other than firewall are there to secure transmissions across the Internet via a VPN?

You're right. IP, which is the underlying technology of the Internet (see Chapter 3), was never designed with security in mind. Aside from firewalls, several VPN protocols have been developed to help secure VPNs. These include the *Point-to-Point Tunneling Protocol (PPTP), Layer 2 Forwarding (L2F), Layer 2 Tunneling Protocol (L2TP),* and *IP Security (IPSec).* Following is a brief description of these protocols.

PPTP. The Point-to-Point Tunneling Protocol was developed by several organizations including the Internet Engineering Task Force (IETF), Microsoft, and U.S. Robotics. PPTP, which is integrated in Windows NT, uses Microsoft's proprietary Point-to-Point Encryption algorithm, which provides encryption and authentication for remote dial-up and LAN-to-LAN connections. For dial-up users, PPTP can be provided either directly by a PPTP-enabled client, or indirectly via a PPTP-enabled server through an Internet Service Provider (ISP). Regardless of who provides the service, two connections are established. A control session is responsible for establishing and maintaining a secure tunnel from sender to receiver, and a data session provides data transmission. In LAN-to-LAN applications, a tunnel is established between NT servers. PPTP supports several network protocols including IP, IPX, NetBEUI, and NetBIOS. It is anticipated that PPTP will eventually be incorporated into IPSec.

L2F. The Layer 2 Forward protocol provides tunneling between an ISP's dial-up server and the network. In this application, a user establishes a dial-up Point-to-Point Protocol (PPP) connection to the ISP's server. This server then wraps the PPP frames inside an L2F frame, which is then forward it to a layer 3 device (a router) for network transmission. The router is responsible for users authentication and network addressing. L2F does not provide any data encryption, and its user authentication capability is weak.

L2TP. The Layer 2 Tunneling Protocol defines a method for tunneling PPP sessions across a network. It combines PPTP and L2F. This protocol is still being developed as a standard and as of this writing has not been fully implemented.

IPSec. IP Security is a suite of protocols developed by IETF. The suite includes an Authentication Header (AH), an Encapsulating Security Payload (ESP), and the Internet Key Exchange (IKE). (*Note:* IKE was originally known as the Internet Security Association and Key Management Protocol with the Oakley key exchange protocol—ISAKMP/Oakley Resolution.) Operating at layer 3, IPSec provides address authentication via AH, data encryption via ESP, and automated key exchanges between sender and receiver nodes using IKE. Although PPTP, L2F, and L2TP support multiprotocol routing and provide some VPN security services, they are more applicable to remote access connections (i.e., dial-up). IPSec, on the other hand, provides end-to-end data encryption and authentication for VPNs. IPSec-complaint products are quickly becoming available, and the International Computer Security Association (ICSA) has developed an IPSec certification program to ensure products are indeed compliant and interoperable. Many people believe that VPNs will grow rapidly once IPSec compliant products are deployed on a full-scale basis.

46. Tell me more about IPSec.

As indicated above, IPSec is really a suite of protocols that contains an Authentication Header, Encapsulating Security Payload protocol, and Internet Key Exchange. The Authentication Header contains six fields. (See Figure 16-1.) The *Next Header* field is one byte long and identifies the higher-level protocol that follows the AH. The *Payload Length* field is also one byte long and specifies the length of the Authentication Data field. The *Reserved* field is just that—it is a two-byte field reserved for future use and always set to zero. The *Security Parameters Index (SPI)* field is four bytes long and identifies the security protocols (called the "security association") being used in the packet. This is followed by the four-byte *Sequence Number* field, which serves as a counter that identifies the number of IP AH packets it has received that bear the same destination address and SPI data. Although the sending node must include this information in outgoing packets, the receiving node does not have to process this field. The Sequence Number also protects against the receipt of duplicate packets. The last field is the *Authentication Data*. This is a variable-length filed that contains the Integrity Check Value (ICV), which is a digital signature of a packet. Authentication algorithms used to generate this signature include DES, MD5, the Secure Hash Algorithm (SHA-1), and others. The AH immediately follows the IP header in a standard IPv4 packet, but after the hop-by-hop, routing, and fragmentation extension in an IPv6 packet. (The destination options extension header of an IPv6 packet can precede or follow the AH.)

The Encapsulating Security Payload header contains seven fields. (See Figure 16-2.) The first two fields, the *Security Parameters Index* and *Sequence Number*, are the same as those in the Authentication Header. Collectively, these two fields are referred to as the Control Header. The next field, *Payload Data,* contains the encrypted version of the user's original data. It also contains optional Initialization Vector (IV) information if the encryption algorithm used to encrypt user data requires any type of synchronization (e.g., DES control information). The fourth field, *Padding,* provides for any necessary padding requirements of the encryption algorithm or for byte-boundary alignments. This ensures that the payload data has the correct length. The *Pad Length* field specifies the number of pad bytes used in the Padding field. The *Next Header* field references the payload data by identifying the type of data contained in the Payload Data field. These last three fields— Padding, Pad Length, and Next Header—are called the ESP trailer. The last field, *Authentication Data,* is optional and similar to the Authentication Data field of the Authentication Header—it is a digital signature applied to the entire ESP (sans this field). The ESP header, like the AH, immediately follows the IP header in a standard IPv4 packet, but after the hop-by-hop, routing, and fragmentation extension in an IPv6 packet. (The destination

IPv4 Packet without AH

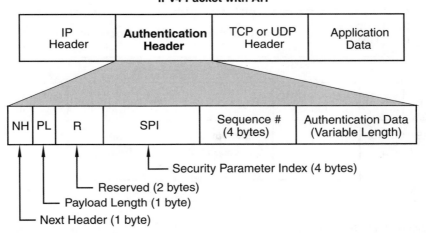

Figure 16-1. The Authentication Header, which is part of the IPSec protocol suite, provides authentication service to IP. AH safeguards data from being altered during transmission. The AH immediately follows the IP header in a standard IPv4 packet, but after the hop-by-hop, routing, and fragmentation extension in an IPv6 packet. NH identifies the higher-level protocol that follows the AH. PL specifies the length of the Authentication Data. R is reserved for future use and is set to zero. SPI identifies the security protocols (called the "security association") being used in the packet. The Sequence Number serves as a counter that identifies the number of IP AH packets it has received that bear the same destination address and SPI data. The Sequence Number also protects against the receipt of duplicate packets. The Authentication Data field contains the Integrity Check Value (ICV), which is a digital signature of the packet. Authentication algorithms used to generate this signature include DES, MD5, the Secure Hash Algorithm (SHA-1), and others. (Adapted from Thayer, 1997.)

options extension header of an IPv6 packet can precede or follow the ESP header.) If ESP and AH are to be used together, then ESP follows AH.

The Internet Key Exchange provides a mechanism for automating key exchanges between sending and receiving nodes when authentication (AH) and encryption (ESP) are used together. In such instances, both sender and receiver have to know their respective keys. Furthermore, in order to ensure secure communications across the network, these keys must be known only to the parties communicating. The IKE protocol delivers this

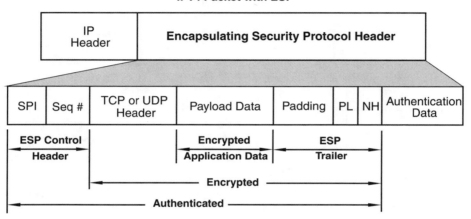

Figure 16-2. The Encapsulating Security Protocol Header, which is part of the IPSec protocol suite, provides encryption service to IP. The ESP header immediately follows the IP header in a standard IPv4 packet, but after the hop-by-hop, routing, and fragmentation extension in an IPv6 packet. The Security Parameter Index (SPI) and Sequence Number (Seq #) are the same as in the Authentication Header. (See Figure 16-1.) The Payload Data contains the encrypted version of the user's original data as well as optional Initialization Vector (IV) information if the encryption algorithm used to encrypt user data requires any type of synchronization (e.g., DES control information). The ESP Trailer consists of Padding, Pad Length (PL), and the Next Header (NH) fields. Padding provides for any necessary padding to ensure that the payload data has the correct length; PL specifies the number of pad bytes used in the Padding field; and NH identifies the type of data contained in the Payload Data. The Authentication Data field is optional and contains a digital signature applied to the entire ESP (sans this field). (Adapted from Thayer, 1997.)

service by using the Diffie-Hellman algorithm for key generation, and provides three different methods of key exchange. *Main Mode, Aggressive Mode,* and *Quick Mode.* In Main Mode, six messages (i.e., three back and forth exchanges) are sent between a sender and receiver. The first two messages establish a specific security policy, the next two messages contain key information, and the two last messages provide authentication information. Aggressive Mode is similar to Main Mode and achieve the same result. The difference is that there are only two exchanges (four messages sent between sender and receiver) instead of three. Quick Mode is used to generate new keys after all necessary information has been exchanged between the communicating nodes via Main or Aggressive Modes.

IPSec essentially operates in one of two modes. In *tunnel-mode,* the entire IP packet is encrypted and wrapped within a new IPSec packet. (This is shown in Figure 16-2.) In *transport-mode,* only the data payload is encrypted. For more information about IPSec, see http://www.ietf.org/html.charters/ipsec-charter.html.

47. How do I protect my connection from home to the office with VPNs?

Multimegabit technologies such as cable modems, *x*DSL, and others enable high-speed access from home, small office, hotel and other remote locations. As such, the need for VPNs is greater than ever to allow remote computing and distributed connectivity. Attendant to this is the need to provide VPN and full firewall security. (Remember that the greatest security threat is still from within.) With "push" technologies, personal computers at the residence and on the road will be connected more hours of the day and, in many cases, continuously connected to access information from providers around the world. This also means that while the system that occasionally dials in to a public IP network is hard to hack, this will not always be the case. In the very near future, working with corporate documents at home will entail being continuously connected to public IP networks and VPNs. Desktop firewall products will be instrumental in securing these environments.

48. Do I need cryptography for VPNs to work?

Not really. In fact, many implementations do not implement cryptography facilities because they slow down the connection between the systems using the VPN. Obviously, an encrypted link is more secure than one that is not encrypted. However, VPN, especially the tunneling varieties, don't need cryptography to provide the needed connectivity. Cryptography helps make the link more secure.

49. So, if network security is this complex already, what's that mean about the future of network security?

It's going to get even more complex, just like network protocols must do and operating systems must do. New technologies and new techniques to provide authentication and access control will be coming out over the next few years and this will cause methods of implementation of network security to change. Firewall facilities will be available on desktop, workstation, and server systems just like they are provided on network-to-network connections today. More electronic access to financial facilities will be forthcoming and this means that the entire area of electronic commerce (e-commerce) is exploding and will continue to grow. Hackers and the threats they provide will increase as technology becomes more available to everyone—this means that the methods to provide network security must change to adapt to new threats. Consequently, the network security business will be a growing segment of the industry for a long time.

End-of-Chapter Commentary

This completes this chapter. Please note that there is much more to network security than what is presented here. We do not have the space to address every aspect of network security in this book. This is best left for books specifically dedicated to this topic. You are encouraged to consult the chapter references for additional information.

Appendix A

Vendor Ethernet Prefixes

Ethernet/802.3 vendor prefixes are the first six (leftmost) hexadecimal digits of an Ethernet/802.3 address. Vendor prefixes, officially called *Organizationally Unique Identifiers (OUIs)*, are assigned by IEEE, which maintains a web site of all publicly released OUI assignments. (Not all organizations make their assigned prefixes public.) This web site, located at http://standards.ieee.org/regauth/oui/index.html, is updated quarterly. Note that OUI assignments do not always match the original equipment manufacturer (OEM) of a network interface. Some organizations elect to license their vendor codes to other manufacturers. In such cases, the prefix will reflect the OEM and not the IEEE assignment. For example, the Ethernet prefix 00400B is officially assigned to Cisco Systems, but field reports show that it appears on Crescendo devices. As a result, a second, unofficial list of prefixes has been published that contains reports of prefixes observed in the field. This second list, which is subject to errors, is available at http://map-ne.com/Ethernet/Ethernet.txt.

Page constraints prevent us from listing a complete table that merges the official and unofficial lists in this appendix. However, this table is available for download in either PostScript or PDF form at http://www.network-1.com.

Appendix B

Using Parity for Single-Bit Error Correction

Let us define a *codeword* to have the following structure (each X_i is a bit in the data set):

$$X_1 X_2 X_3 X_4 X_5 X_6 X_7 X_8 X_9 X_{10} X_{11} X_{12} \ldots$$

Also, let every bit with a subscript that is a power of two be a *check bit*, denoted by r_j, which will contain redundant information for error-correction. Thus, X_1, X_2, X_4, and X_8 are check bits and we replace them with r_1, r_2, r_4, and r_8, respectively.

$$r_1 r_2 X_3 r_4 X_5 X_6 X_7 r_8 X_9 X_{10} X_{11} X_{12} \ldots$$

Since the X_i bits are predetermined (they represent user data), we need a rule for forming check bits. This rule is based on parity and is defined as follows:

Each check bit, r_j, is formed by collecting all corresponding X_i bits. These are determined by expressing the subscript of each X_i as the sum of a power of 2. For example, X_3 corresponds to r_1 and r_2 because its subscript, 3, is equal to the sum of check bits r_1 and r_2's subscripts (i.e., $3 = 1 + 2$). Once the set of X_i bits is identified for each r_j, the check bit then forces the parity of each set to be even or odd, depending on the parity selected.

This rule is implemented by first expressing the subscript of each X_i bit as a power of 2:

- X_3 corresponds to r_1 and r_2 ($3 = 1 + 2$)
- X_5 corresponds to r_1 and r_4 ($5 = 1 + 4$)
- X_6 corresponds to r_2 and r_4 ($6 = 2 + 4$)
- X_7 corresponds to r_1, r_2, and r_4 ($7 = 1 + 2 + 4$)
- X_9 corresponds to r_1 and r_8 ($9 = 1 + 8$)
- X_{10} corresponds to r_2 and r_8 ($10 = 2 + 8$)
- X_{11} corresponds to r_1, r_2, and r_8 ($11 = 1 + 2 + 8$)
- X_{12} corresponds to r_4 and r_8 ($12 = 4 + 8$)

Using the list generated above, we now identify all X_i bits that correspond to each r_j:

- r_1 corresponds to $\{X_3, X_5, X_7, X_9, X_{11}\}$
- r_4 corresponds to $\{X_5, X_6, X_7, X_{12}\}$
- r_2 corresponds to $\{X_3, X_6, X_7, X_{10}, X_{11}\}$
- r_8 corresponds to $\{X_9, X_{10}, X_{11}, X_{12}\}$

Given the preceding information, we now construct a codeword for a specific data set. Let's assume the data string to be transmitted consists of the bit pattern 10001100. Let's further assume even parity. Our goal is to generate a single-bit error correction code for the given eight data bits. This codeword will be of the form:

		b_1		b_2	b_3	b_4		b_5	b_6	b_7	b_8
r_1	r_2	X_3	r_4	X_5	X_6	X_7	r_8	X_9	X_{10}	X_{11}	X_{12}

Substituting the data bits into this structure we have:

		b_1		b_2	b_3	b_4		b_5	b_6	b_7	b_8
r_1	r_2	1	r_4	0	0	0	r_8	1	1	0	0

We now determine the check bits (assuming even parity).

- Since r_1 corresponds to $\{X_3, X_5, X_7, X_9, X_{11}\}$, r_1 is based on the parity of bits 10010. Thus, r_1's parity is 0.
- Since r_2 corresponds to $\{X_3, X_6, X_7, X_{10}, X_{11}\}$, r_2 is based on the parity of bits 10010. Thus, r_2's parity is 0.
- Since r_4 corresponds to $\{X_5, X_6, X_7, X_{12}\}$, r_4 is based on the parity of bits 0000. Thus, r_4's parity is 0.
- Since r_8 corresponds to $\{X_9, X_{10}, X_{11}, X_{12}\}$, r_8 is based on the parity of bits 1100. Thus, r_8's parity is 0.

As a result, the codeword is:

		b_1		b_2	b_3	b_4		b_5	b_6	b_7	b_8
0	0	1	0	0	0	0	0	1	1	0	0

This is the data string that's transmitted. Let's now assume the receiving node receives the string 001001001100. A visual inspection clearly reveals that the sixth bit (from the left) is incorrect; it's 1 when it should be 0. Unfortunately, the receiving node cannot see this. It must rely on an algorithm to both detect and then correct the error. This is done as follows:

(1) Check the parity of each check bit using the data string that was received.

- r_1 = 10010. Given even parity, r_1 = 0 = Correct (C)
- r_2 = 11010. Given even parity, r_2 = 1 = Error (E)
- r_4 = 0100. Given even parity, r_4 = 1 = Error (E)
- r_8 = 1100. Given even parity, r_8 = 0 = Correct (C)

(2) Based on the check bits, which are based on parity, r_1 = C, r_2 = E, r_4 = E, and r_8 = C. Let C = 0 and E = 1. If we multiply the subscript of each checkbit by its corresponding C or E value we get the following:

$$C(1) + E(2) + E(4) + C(8)$$
$$= 0(1) + 1(2) + 1(4) + 0(8)$$
$$= 0 + 2 + 4 + 0$$
$$= 6$$

Thus, the sixth bit is in error and should be complemented.

Appendix C

Guidelines for Installing UTP Cable

1. Know and understand the related premise wiring standards. First and foremost it is important that you are knowledgeable of the published standards related to UTP premise wiring. Network cable installation is governed by a standard known as EIA/TIA-568. This standard was jointly developed by the Electronic Industries Association (EIA) and the Telecommunications Industry (TIA). EIA/TIA-568 is a North American standard that specifies the type of cable that is permitted for a given speed, the type of connectors that can be used for a given cable, and the network topology that is permitted when installing cables. The standard also defines the performance specifications cables and connectors must meet. In short, EIA/TIA-568 represents a comprehensive standard for premises wiring that addresses network design and performance characteristics for physical media. Familiarize yourself with this standard as well as EIA/TIA-569 (*Commercial Building Standard for Telecommunications Pathways and Spaces*) standards. Although a nonstandard cabling system might work, this is something you should not chance. Also, do not let the issue of cost take precedence over standards. It is better to spend a little more money for something that is consistent with published standards than not. Standards were written for a purpose and should not be ignored.

2. Check local building codes. Prior to any wiring installation, contact the facilities people of your company to ensure that the planned cable plant is consistent with electrical and fire codes. Also consult the following: Section 800 of the National Electrical Code for telecommunications cable installations; EIA/TIA-607, the standard on the grounding and bonding of a building premises cabling plant; and IEEE 1100-1992, *Recommended Practice for Powering and Grounding Sensitive Electronic Equipment* (known as the *Emerald Book*).

3. Think globally and locally. If your cable installation is parochial, you are encouraged to think about how it might impact the entire organization. At the very least, and as a courtesy, contact your organization's designated network administrator and share your plans with this individual.

4. Plan and document. Not enough can be said about these two activities. Planning is extremely important to ensure that all factors have been considered including: who is responsible for installation, termination, and certification of the installation; who will manage the cable plant; whether existing cable should be used; what minimum specifications the cable plant must meet; what interruptions there will be to company business prior to, during, and after the installation; what facilities modifications are needed in order to facilitate to support the installation; what future needs might be and how the current installation lends itself to meeting these needs; and so forth. As for documentation, it is extremely important that network maps be constructed and maintained. There should be a general topology map, and a wire map that identifies cable lengths, termination points, grounding information, etc. In our experiences we found it easier to maintain handwritten maps than to use a software program. Copies of these maps should be in a centralized location and at key sites throughout an organization. Modifications to the cable plant should be documented at the time they are made.

5. Be sensitive to physical security and the physical environment. Include security issues as part of the planning process. Try to acquire dedicated space with a locked door to serve as wiring closets. Also make certain these areas are clean, air-conditioned, and free of corrosive material. (See Box 16-3 in Chapter 16.)

6. Test the cable on the spool and after installation. This is important. If you only test the cable after installing it, you cannot be certain if any detected post-installation problems were the result of the installation process or bad cable.

7. Label the cables. Regardless of how diligent you are in documenting the cable plant, there will be instances when your map is not readily available when examining the cable plant. By labeling both ends of a cable—use Avery stickers or their equivalent—you will have a built-in map that (among others) identifies each cable, its termination point and length, and electrical characteristics.

8. Inspect the installation, ensure the cable has been tested properly and accurately, and get a warranty from the cable installer. Check for the following: Make certain cables have been installed neatly and securely; look for cinch marks and worn insulation (there should be none); be sure cables are not resting directly on ceiling tiles, have been pulled near anything that radiates heat, are near electrical fixtures, and have not been placed where people can step on them or roll over them in a chair; make sure that the minimum bend radius has not been exceeded; and ensure that cable runs do not exceed maximum recommended lengths. Also, make sure the cable plant is certified, that is, it meets all published certification standards such as those found in the EIA/TIA Technical Service Bulletin (TSB)-67. Finally, since a certified installation does not guarantee quality of work, obtain a warranty (at least 10 years) on the installed cable.

9. Consider STP rather than UTP. Before committing to UTP, you might want to consider installing STP. This would be prudent especially if the installation site is a source of high electromagnetic interference (EMI).

10. Install a sufficient number of pairs. Consider installing 16 pairs to each location—four pairs for a LAN, four pairs for voice, and eight pairs (four each) for alternate LANs. Although using fewer pairs might be functional, it is much more difficult to manage in a live network. Most networks will be upgraded in the future and this will mean parallel network connectivity for a period of time while the new network is tested and the old one is running.

Appendix D

Network Design and Analysis Guidelines and Network Politics

Network design and analysis refers to the essential methods required to properly design a network. A properly generated network design provides the following benefits:

- Proper analysis of existing equipment for network installation.
- List of requirements for network installation.
- Proper configuration of network components for optimum cost savings.
- A flexible and adaptable network topology.
- Correct selection of network hardware and software.
- Documentation of the network for future enhancements and modifications.
- Migration path into future network technologies without redesign.
- A long network life-cycle.
- Interconnect paths and methods for multiple network architectures.
- User analysis and configuration of network resources for optimal use.
- Network management plan and methodology to reduce downtime and allow for maximum use of available resources.
- Expectations for performance, reliability, and usability.
- Optimal programming environment for network applications.
- Training needs for programmers, users, and network managers.
- Recurring expense forecasting and budgeting methods.
- Network support needs (programming, management, user support).
- Use of mathematical modeling tools to help insure the success of the network design and topology.
- Optimal design to prevent network congestion, queuing delay, and proper placement of routing and management resources on the network.

Unfortunately, many network administrators do not take the time to perform a network design and analysis. Instead, they rely exclusively on vendor recommendations. Network design and analysis involves much more than ordering hardware and software from a vendor. If you want to trust a vendor, that is your choice. However, few vendors are qualified network designers, and those who are do not offer this service free of charge. Be forewarned: You get what you pay for, and in the end, you will be the person who will be blamed for poor network performance or problems, not the vendor. (See Figure D-1.) *Networks are neither trivial nor cheap.* If implemented incorrectly, expect to spend more time correcting problems, increased network downtime, and increased stress in your life.

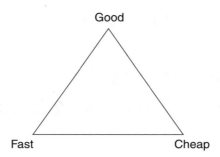

Figure D-1. This triangle is called Truman's Triangle," named after its inventor, Truman Reynolds. Truman's Triangle serves as a good guide for anything that is network related. Pick any two vertices of the triangle, and then apply the word "not" to the remaining description (vertex). For example, if you want a network that is Fast and Good, it will *not* be Cheap.

The Steps of Network Design and Analysis

1. *Identify the Need.* Today, networks are an integral part of nearly every organization and network managers are constantly faced with decisions to upgrade an existing network or install a new network. Before any action is taken, make sure you really need to upgrade or install a network. Don't be pressured into a new installation or an upgrade. Thus, before you swap out your Token Ring network for Ethernet/802.3, or before you decide to replace your 10 Mbps Ethernet hubs with switches, or before you decide to upgrade your backbone from Fast Ethernet to Gigabit Ethernet, justify the need for doing so.

2. *Identify Function and Cost.* What is the network supposed to do and how much is it going to cost? The first part of this question can be answered by defining what functionality the network is to offer. If it is e-mail, file transfer, task-to-task communications, great, but write it down. In addition to functionality there is the issue of cost. Networks are just like systems—they have a life-cycle. Networks require periodic upgrading and expansion; have recurring costs such as software and hardware maintenance, training, telco service, and replacement equipment purchases; require personnel to manage and maintain the network components; and might require custom software development, which implies costs for software engineering or application programming. Networks are expensive to install and operate over a period of time because they are service-intensive.

3. *Site Survey.* A site survey involves the careful examination of company facilities, building architecture, phone facilities, existing computer hardware and software components, examination of existing contracts, power facilities, HVAC facilities, wireways and wire centers, electromagnetic interference possibilities, radio frequency interference possibilities, safety issues, security issues, building wiring and fire codes, electrical codes, reception and shipping facilities, building maintenance capabilities, onsite or vendor maintenance capabilities, and other related items. As a result, a thorough inspection of the network site is necessary. Furthermore, this inspection should not be done alone. You should include the director of management facilities or equivalent, as well as managers of departments that might be affected.

4. *Basic Design, Data Collection/Reduction, and Data Analysis.* This step involves the use of mathematical modeling tools (manual and computer-based) to address issues such as data flow ratios, probabilities of error, queuing delays, interconnect problems, least-cost network topological layout, routing paths, and redundancy paths. Following the modeling of the network, a financial analysis is done to determine how much the network is going to cost to implement, start up, maintain, and expand. An assessment analysis is also performed to identify networks that are most useful (closest to desired functionality) and least useful (on the right track, but not closest to desired combination of price, performance, and ease of use). Finally, an analysis of personnel needs and operational considerations is performed. This analysis describes the type of personnel necessary to get the job done, what kind of personnel will be needed for the day-to-day support of the network and its related components, and the costs associated for such personnel.

5. *Formal Design Document.* The last step in the design and analysis of a network is the formal design document. This document is a summary of all the previous steps. It documents the rationale for the network design, a description of the components, a network topology, a wiring diagram, expansion capabilities, expected life-cycle, applications support environment, network management environment, potential problems, data throughput analysis, testing and verifications procedures, identification of network installation resources, an implementation timetable, personnel and training needs, cost analysis, and risks. This document is the backbone of the network design and serves as a guideline for implementation and expansion.

Why go through all of this? The answer is simple and complex (sort of the yin and yang of networks): it's proper business procedure and it reduces potential risk. Many people approach network design and analysis in the same manner as buying stocks—they use the "gut feeling" approach; they rely on emotion instead of reading a prospectus, doing some research, or hiring a financial planner or stock broker. They say that network design and analysis activities are not necessary to install wire, hardware, and software. They also "prove" this by identifying other installed networks, which did not undergo a design and analysis, but are working without any problems. This might indeed be the case. Sometimes it works, sometimes it doesn't. However, just as you might get lucky at the stock market using a gut feeling approach, chances are you will be less fortunate. In fact, studies have been done that indicate a gut-feeling approach works only about 25% of the time. When looking at network design and analysis, the main mistake many companies make is they approach a network in the same manner that they approach the "self-broker" methodology. This is not prudent since networks have some fairly serious restrictions on them that require both formal training and experience before someone is in a position to design a network properly.

Components of Good Network Design

Good network design is characterized by the following main points:

1. *It meets or exceeds the needs defined in the specification.* (This is self-explanatory.)

2. *It is cost effective and cost predictable.* Cost effective is obvious; cost predictable, however is not. Over the period of life of any network, there is a need to predict the costs the network will incur upon corporate finances. Some obvious costs include component upgrades, software maintenance, hardware maintenance, and operational management tools and personnel. Some of the less obvious costs that need to be predictable are documentation, training, code maintenance, system downtime due to network component failure, productivity delays due to congestion or network failure, and consulting assistance. These costs should be part of the design so no surprises surface after the fact.

3. *Its capabilities are obvious and beneficial.* If a network is obviously useful and beneficial, the life of the network can be more easily justified and the corporation will utilize the network and its capabilities in all appropriate areas. Thus, the capabilities of a network should be demonstrable upon demand so that its merits are recognized by management. If this can be done, then the needs of a network can be addressed properly and funding for the network assured.

4. *It is capable of being managed by both system-manager-level and network-manager-level personnel.* This is necessary to protect a company from the eventual exit of trained network personnel. Both network and systems people should be capable of managing an organization's network.

5. *It is user-transparent.* Users should not have to know the intricacies associated with the network. They should be able to use it in as easy and efficient manner as possible.

6. *It is easily expanded.* A network should be capable of being expanded without redesigning it. Management structures change, corporate directions change, people change. There is no reason that the network should not be able to change as well.

7. *It is well documented.* Proper documentation of how a network was configured, why, and the politics behind it is critical to future support, expansion, and interpretation of the original goals of the network. Furthermore, any network-related activities (e.g., errors detected and how they were resolved, changes made to configuration files, breaches of security) should be logged for future reference and network history.

8. *The technology is state of the practice, not state of the art.* State of the practice means that the network architecture reflects proven, useful, current technology that is not leading edge. Why not leading edge? The reason is simple. Leading edge technology is good for daredevils, but it has no place in a business or engineering environment unless it is the only reasonable method to do a job. Leading edge technology is usually bug- and problem-laden, few people understand it, it imposes unnecessary risk upon the functionality of a network, and it might not receive wide acceptance upon review by the industry and other vendors. State of the practice technology reflects what is in use. It might not be the latest on the market, but it is proven, reliable, manageable, cost predictable, and there is plenty of talent to manage the technology that is available. When working with and configuring networks, it is essential that cost and risk constantly be kept in mind.

9. *It is supportable and maintainable at all node locations.* Regardless of where a network node is located, network managers should be able to have access to that location to provide necessary support or maintenance if needed.

10. *Network diagnostics and management are thought out and available.* If network diagnostic and management issues are not addressed a priori, then users suffer and network managers cannot be expected to manage the network properly. As a result, attention must be given to such issues as management strategies, type of diagnostic tools needed, appropriate training and support for network managers, and disaster-recovery procedures.

11. *The network provides future interconnectivity.* Do not configure a network for one type of computer. Although the battle for the desktop essentially has been won by the Intel platform and Microsoft Windows, this does not mean that you only need to consider this hardware-software platform. The network should provide for interconnectivity among different products and architectures that either currently exist or might emerge as a result of network and corporate expansion.

12. *The network has predictable performance as loading changes.* System performance will change over the life of any system. When a network is initially configured it is generally underutilized. As time passes, though, it becomes overutilized to the point where its performance is impacted negatively. This underutilization/overutilization syndrome causes problems in network design. As a result, when considering network performance, it is necessary to look at not only the network topology and components, but also the loading history of critical processor and applications to insure that there is a clear picture of how fast and how well things are going to perform.

13. *Its load on networked systems is predictable and reasonable.* Increased network use will eventually impact the performance of networked systems. For example, hub, switch, or router performance can degrade, and end user workstations can (particularly those running a single-task operating system) freeze up. A good network design will take these issues under consideration and provide some means for addressing them.

14. *It provides security adequate to the corporate or application needs.* Accept the following dictum: Networks are not secure. Although it is possible to make it quite difficult for someone to break into a network, you cannot keep out a professional. If someone wants to get into your network bad enough, there is very little you can do to stop it from happening. To insure the success of a network, a security audit is performed during the design phase to identify sources of network and component vulnerability and what can be gained through penetration. This information is then presented to management, which will decide the resources needed to address these deficiencies.

15. *It supports system upgrades and enhancements.* It is impractical to expect network software and hardware to be upgraded simultaneously within all systems as new hardware and software become available. As a rule, any systems upgrade will disrupt operations on an entire network if the upgrades are not carefully considered network-wide. A good network design will allow for network and systems upgrades and provide for a method to do both. Good network design requires that the future be considered as well as the present.

16. *It survives the politics of the company and provides for political needs.* Network designs must encompass not only the needs of the technical end, but also the needs of the practical end. That is, it must address the day-to-day needs of the corporation as well as the political needs of its management. For a network to survive the political environment, care must be taken to allow proper placement of the network in the political environment. If the network is not properly introduced, placed, and controlled by the appropriate level of management, the political machine can turn on the network and associated personnel, and proceed to squash everything in its path.

Network Politics

When designing and configuring networks, funny things creep in that make no logical sense, have no basis for reasonable reality, and are of questionable use. These things are called *politics*. In a networked environment, politics take on a whole new role. The more nodes of a network, the more likely politics will invade the design and operation of the network, especially when competition exists between the various departments networked together. Politics are further exacerbated if competing departments depend on each other for technical support, assistance, and worst of all, funding. Another problem is that of machine ownership. Although all machines are owned by the corporation, department managers get very possessive over the systems and resources they have a day-to-day interest in using, and adopt a "my machine syndrome." Avoiding network politics generally tends to increase the political problem as a whole. To help keep politics to a minimum, consider the following items:

1. Spend time describing and documenting to users what you do and why.
2. Always get the local management at each location involved.
3. Do not underestimate any network user.
4. Good rapport is all-important when dealing with personnel from different departments. Get to know the users and managers at all locations and keep everyone in the loop.
5. Do not take an attitude of "I'm technical and don't do politics." This will in the long run increase your political problems. In the networked environment, politics are part of the design and support. Get used to it.
6. If possible, get some sensitization training. There is nothing worse to a user than a surly answer from the support organization. Try to show some empathy toward a user, but keep the sympathy to a minimum.
7. If you do not write well, get some training. Written communication is very important to tracing problems in the political structure.

If a political situation arises, take action but do not react to the situation. Many political moves occur due to power plays, inconsideration, or just to instigate a situation. If one arises, do not let your emotions get in the way of solid, logical reasoning and fact. You also must learn to discern a political problem from a real nonpolitical problem. If there is a system down, that's a real problem; don't escalate it into a political one.

Glossary

AAL See *ATM adaptation layer.*

AAUI See *Apple Attachment Unit Interface.*

Access Line A term used in *frame relay* to denote the *local loop.* Also called *port connection.*

Active Monitor A station on a token ring network that oversee the ring and ensure that it is functioning properly. Also called a *monitor station.*

Address A unique number assigned to a device to identify its location within a network. An address also can uniquely identify a network application process.

Addressing A network concept that describes the process of assigning unique identification numbers (called *addresses*) to a networked device.

ADSL See *Asynchronous Digital Subscriber Line.*

ADSL Lite A slower *ADSL* in which downstream rates equal 1 Mbps and upstream rates equal 128 kbps. Intended primarily for homes. Also called *G.lite.*

Alignment Error An Ethernet/802.3 frame that does not end on a "byte-boundary."

Always On/Dynamic ISDN (AO/DI) An initiative from the Vendor's ISDN Association (VIA) in which a portion of the D channel, which is always active and constantly connected to the provider's switch, is used to transmit user packet data.

Ambient Noise Electrical *noise* that is always present and is generated primarily by transmission equipment like transmitters, receivers, and repeaters. Ambient noise also can be induced by external sources such as fluorescent light transformers, electrical facilities, and heat. Ambient noise makes it difficult for receiving equipment to distinguish between incoming signals. Also called *thermal noise.*

Analog Refers to any physical device or signal that varies continuously in strength or quantity over an infinite range of voltages or currents. An example is voltage in a circuit.

Analog Communication Refers to any communication method based on analog principles. In analog communications, signals flow across a wire in the form of electromagnetic waves. These waves resemble a sine curve and have the following three characteristics: *amplitude*, which is the level of voltage on a wire (or the intensity of a light beam when dealing with fiber-optic cable); *frequency*, which is the number of oscillations, or cycles, of a wave in a specified length of time; and *phase*, which is the point a wave has advanced within its cycle. Typically associated with voice transmission rather than data transmission because voice transmission facilities, such as the telephone, were initially analog-based.

AO/DI See *Always On/Dynamic ISDN*.

Apple Attachment Unit Interface (AAUI) Apple Computer Corporation's proprietary *AUI*.

Application Gateway Firewall See *Proxy Server*.

Application Program Software that performs a specific function such as e-mail.

Application Protocol Defines how an application is to be implemented on a network. Also includes specific user programs for interacting with an application.

ARP An acronym for *address resolution protocol*, which is an Internet protocol that binds a node's *IP address* to its corresponding *MAC* sublayer (hardware) address.

Asynchronous Communication A data transmission method that requires the sending node to encapsulate special start and stop bits within each unit of data being transmitted. Thus, data can be transferred at any time by the sending node without the receiving node having any advance notification of the transfer.

Asynchronous Digital Subscriber Line (ADSL) A *DSL* variant in which traffic is transmitted at different rates in different directions. Downstream rates range from 1.5 Mbps to 9 Mbps; upstream rates range from 16 kbps to 1 Mbps. Rates depend on line quality and local loop distance. Suitable for Internet or intranet access, video-on-demand, database access, remote LAN access.

Asynchronous Transfer Mode (ATM) A connection-oriented, full-duplex, and point-to-point high-speed cell-switched network architecture that was created in the late 1980s/early 1990s to apply circuit switching concepts to data networks. Designed to carry data in 53-octet cells, ATM can be used to transmit data, voice and video—separately or simultaneously—over the same network path. Although not based on any specific physical layer protocol, ATM is generally carried over *SONET*. Also known as *cell relay* to distinguish it from *frame relay*.

ATM See *Asynchronous Transfer Mode*.

ATM Adaptation Layer (AAL) An ATM layer that interprets the type and format of user data messages, and then translates these messages into ATM format by packaging them into the 48-byte payload portion of an ATM cell. The AAL's interpretation of data type and format is based on the specific class of service assigned to the data by the application. The AAL provides support for four different service classes and provides five different AAL types to accommodate a particular service class. *AAL1* is used for data that require connection-oriented, constant-bit rate transmissions (e.g., voice transmissions); *AAL2* is used for data that require connection-oriented variable-bit rate transmissions (e.g., a videoconferencing application); *AAL3* and *AAL4* are used for connection-oriented or connectionless variable-bit rate transmissions (e.g., bursty data typical of LAN applications such as those found on frame relay and SMDS networks); and AAL5, which is an improvement to AAL3, used for transmissions in which higher layer protocols provide error recovery.

Attachment Unit Interface (AUI) A 15-pin "universal" connector that allows a device to be connected to UTP, thick or thin coax, or fiber-optic cable via an external transceiver.

Attenuation The decrease in signal strength, which occurs as the signal travels through a circuit or along a cable. The longer the cable, the greater the attenuation. Also, the higher the frequency of the signal, the greater the attenuation.

AS   See *Autonomous System.*

AUI   See *Attachment Unit Interface.*

Autonomous System (AS)   A collection of networks controlled by a single administrative authority, and which share a common routing strategy. Routers connecting networks within an AS trust each other and exchange routing information using a mutually agreed upon routing protocol. Also known as a routing domain or protocol area.

Auto-wrapping   A term used to describe the "self healing" of a token or FDDI ring that has been cut in a single spot. The break in the active ring is corrected by establishing a loopback connection to the inactive ring. This creates a single virtual ring and allows the network to continue to function at full speed.

Backbone Switch   A term used to describe one application of an Ethernet switch in which the switch serves as the backbone for the entire LAN. In this application, the network topology is called a "collapsed backbone."

Backward Explicit Congestion Notification (BECN)   A one-bit field in a *frame relay* frame that is set to 1 by a frame relay switch to denote that a frame transmitted toward the sending node experienced congestion.

Bandwidth   In *analog communications*, bandwidth is the total capacity of a communications channel measured in Hertz (Hz). It is the difference between the highest and lowest frequencies capable of being carried over a channel. The greater the bandwidth, the more signals that can be carried over a given frequency range. In *digital communications* and networking, bandwidth is the theoretical capacity of a communications channel expressed in bits per second (bps), which is called *data rate*.

Bandwidth On Demand Interoperability Network Group (BONDING)   A protocol that aggregates two *ISDN B* channels into a single 128 Mbps circuit.

Baseband Cable   Uses the entire bandwidth of the cable to carry a single signal.

Basic Rate Interface (BRI)   An *ISDN* basic access channel that comprises two 64 kbps B channels, one 16 kbps D channel, and 48 bits of overhead used for framing and other functions. Commonly written as $2B + D$.

Baud   A unit of signaling speed, named after the French engineer Jean Maurice Emile Baudot (1845–1903). It is another term used to express the capacity of a channel, but is different from bits per second.

Baud Rate   A measure of the number of times line conditions (i.e., frequency, amplitude, voltage, or phase) change each second. At low speeds (under 300 bps) data rate (measured in bps) and baud rate are the same because signaling methods are relatively simple. As speed increases, signaling methods become more complex. Baud rate then differs from data rate because several bits are typically encoded per baud. That is, each signal can represent more than one bit of information.

B Channel   A 64 kbps ISDN clear channel (no signaling information is sent on the channel) used to transmit computer data (text and graphics), digitized voice, and digitized video. Most basic ISDN services are based on multiple B channels. Also called a *bearer channel.*

Bearer Channel   See *B Channel.*

BECN   See *Backward Explicit Congestion Notification.*

Bend Radius The radius in which cable (copper or fiber) can be curved or "bent" without breaking. Fiber is much more flexible than copper cable and can be bent in much smaller radii than equivalent copper.

B-ISDN See *Broadband ISDN*.

Bit-Time A unit of measure equal to 0.1 µs. Thus, a one-bit transmission requires 0.1 µs. Transmitting a 64-byte Ethernet/802.3 frame requires 512 bit-times or 51.2 µs.

BNC Connector A type of connector used with thin coaxial cable. There are several interpretations of BNC, including Bayonet Neill-Concelman (named after its developers), Bayonet Nut Connector, Barrel Nut Connector, and British National Connector.

BONDING See *Bandwidth On Demand Interoperability Network Group*.

BRI See *Basic Rate Interface*.

Bridge A layer 2 device that interconnects two or more individual LANs or LAN segments. A transparent bridge is used in Ethernet/802.3 and 802.5 (Token Ring) networks; a source routing bridge (introduced by IBM) is used exclusively in token ring networks. Bridges keep local traffic local, but forward traffic destined for a remote network. Forwarding/filtering decisions are based on MAC sublayer (i.e., hardware) addresses. Bridges partition Ethernet/802.3 networks into multiple collision domains.

Broadband Cable Shares the bandwidth of a coaxial cable among multiple signals.

Broadband ISDN (B-ISDN) An extension of ISDN that provides full-duplex data transmission at OC-12 rates (622.08 Mbps) and is designed for delivery of interactive services (e.g., videoconferencing and video surveillance) and distribution services (e.g., cable TV and high definition TV). B-ISDN is also the basis for *ATM*.

Broadcast A data transmission that is destined to all hosts connected to a network. A broadcast message is a special *multicast* message.

Broadcast Design A network configuration that consists of nodes sharing a single communications channel. Every node connected to this shared medium "hears" each other's transmissions.

Broadcast Storm A network phenomenon that occurs when several broadcast messages are transmitted at the same time. Broadcast storms can use up a substantial amount of network bandwidth, and in many cases can cause a network to crash or shut down.

Brouter A combination bridge-router; a bridge with routing capabilities.

Buffering Switch See *Store-and-Forward*.

Bus Design A specific design based on a broadcast topology. All nodes are directly connected to the same communications channel.

Cable See *Wire*.

Cable Modem A modem that uses cable television lines for data communications. These lines use broadband coaxial cable, which has a multitude of frequencies available and significantly higher bandwidth than the UTP cable used by the telcos. Cable modems provide an Ethernet/802.3 network interface that enables a computer to connect to the cable. Once connected, it is as if the PC were connected to an Ethernet/802.3 LAN. The connection is always "up," and multimegabit data rates are possible. Depending on the cable operator and service, current upstream rates for cable modems are somewhere between 500 Kbps to 3 Mbps; downstream rates range between 10 Mbps to 30 Mbps.

Capacitance   The property of a circuit that permits it to store an electrical charge. The capacitance of a cable determines its ability to carry a signal without distortion. The lower the capacitance, the longer the distance a signal can travel before signal distortion becomes unacceptable.

Carrier Sense Multiple Access (CSMA)   A protocol that serves as the basis for various *random access protocols*. CSMA-based protocols include *one-persistent CSMA, nonpersistent CSMA, CSMA with Collision Detection (CSMA/CD),* and *CSMA with Collision Avoidance (CSMA/CA)*.

Carrier Sense Protocol   A network protocol that requires nodes to first listen ("sense") for the "sound" of another node's transmission prior to accessing a shared channel.

CCITT   See *Consultative Committee for International Telephony and Telegraphy.*

CDDI   See *Copper Distributed Data Interface.*

Cell   A unit of data that is transmitted across a network. Similar to a data *frame*. When used in the context of *ATM*, a cell contains exactly 53-bytes—48 bytes for user data and 5 bytes for overhead.

Cells in Frames (CIF)   A method of transporting *ATM* protocols over *Ethernet* and *token ring LANs*. CIF is a LAN technology that provides LANs with ATM features including *QoS* and the seamless integration of data, voice, and video.

Centralized System   A single computer that provides all the computing resources for all offices and departments within an organization via computer *terminals* that are connected to the centralized system.

CERT   See *Computer Emergency Response Team.*

Channel Service Unit (CSU)   A device used for terminating T-carrier circuits. A CSU regenerates the signal, monitors the line for electrical anomalies, provides proper electrical termination, performs framing, and provides remote loopback testing for diagnosing line problems. Usually combined with a *DSU* to form a single unit called a *CSU/DSU* or DSU/CSU.

Channel Service Unit/Data Service Unit (CSU/DSU)   A device that combines the functions of a *CSU* and a *DSU*. A CSU/DSU works exclusively with digital signals; it provides an interface between a digital computing device and a digital transmission medium.

Check Bits   See *redundancy bits.*

Checksum   A parameter used to detect errors. Checksums are calculated using a predetermined *generator polynomial* and assigned to a specific checksum field of a data frame.

CIDR   See *Classless Inter-Domain Routing.*

CIF   See *Cells in Frames.*

Ciphertext   A coded message. See *Encryption.*

CIR   See *Committed Interface Rate.*

Circuit Gateway Firewall   A device or product that involves monitoring the session set-up between a system and the user security options relative to that system for a particular user. For instance, a circuit gateway might check user IDs and passwords, or it might implement proxy connection authorization or other types of authentication services. A circuit firewall is also responsible for logging who came from where and went to what.

Circuit-Switched Network A network design in which a dedicated physical circuit is established between the source and destination nodes before any data transmission can take place. Furthermore, this circuit must remain in place for the duration of a transmission.

CIX See *Commercial Internet Exchange*.

Class I Repeater A type of repeater used in *Fast Ethernet LANs*. Class I repeaters support both of Fast Ethernet's signaling schemes—100BASE-T4 and 100BASE TX/FX.

Class II Repeater A type of repeater used in *Fast Ethernet LANs*. Class II repeaters support only one of Fast Ethernet's signaling scheme—100BASE-T4 or 100BASE TX/FX.

Classless Inter-Domain Routing (CIDR) A routing mechanism that allows sites to advertise multiple *IPv4* Class C networks by using a single prefix.

Class of Service (CoS) A data prioritization scheme that tags data with a specific priority level. Higher priority data get delivered before lower priority data.

CLEC See *Competitive Local Exchange Carrier.*

Client A networked device that requests resources from a *server*.

Client-Server. A model or paradigm that describes network services and the programs used by end users to access these services. The client side (or front end) provides a user with an interface for requesting services from the network, and the server side (or back end) is responsible for accepting user requests for services and providing these services transparent to the user.

Coaxial Cable A type of cable that consists of a single-wire conductor, surrounded by a dielectric material and two types of shielding, a foil shield and a braided shield, arranged concentrically and encased in a PVC or Teflon outer jacket.

Collapsed Backbone A term used to describe a network topology in which all LAN segments are interconnected via a bridge or switch, which serves as the network backbone.

Collision The term used to describe what happens when two or more nodes attempt to transmit data simultaneously on an Ethernet/802.3 network.

Collision Domain A "field" within a single Ethernet/802.3 network where two nodes can cause a collision. In the case of a single-segmented Ethernet/802.3 LAN, the independent segment represents the collision domain; in a multisegmented Ethernet/802.3 LAN, the collective segments comprise the collision domain.

Commercial Internet Exchange (CIX) A subscription organization consisting of a consortium of commercial and nonprofit regional network providers that began offering Internet service independent of the NSFNET backbone and without NSF's restriction on traffic type. Today, CIX serves as an Internet interconnect site similar to a *NAP.*

Committed Burst (B_c) A term used in *frame relay* to denote the maximum amount of data a provider guarantees to deliver within a specified time period, T. $CIR = B_c/T$. Most providers use a one-second time interval to calculate the average amount of bandwidth utilization. Thus, CIR is usually equal to B_c. The difference between these two parameters is their units. CIR is measured in bps; B_c is measured in bits. See also *excessive burst.*

Committed Information Rate (CIR) The amount of throughput a *frame relay* provider guarantees to support under normal network loads. A CIR, which is assigned to a PVC when the network is initially configured, can range from 16 kbps to T3 (44.8 Mbps) and is the minimum guaranteed throughput of a PVC. If a PVC's assigned CIR is greater than or equal to the average amount of traffic transmitted across a PVC over a specified period of time (e.g., one second), then data transmissions are guaranteed. If the assigned CIR is less than this average, then data transmissions are not guaranteed.

Competitive Local Exchange Carrier (CLEC)   A new telecommunication service provider formed after the Telecommunications Act of 1996 in the United States.

Compression   A process that codes repetitive patterns within a data set. Compressed files can be sent at a faster rate than uncompressed files.

Computer Emergency Response Team (CERT)   A formal organization operated by the Software Engineering Institute at Carnegie Mellon University and dedicated to addressing computer and network security issues. CERT also serves as a clearinghouse for identifying and resolving security "holes" in network-related software or operating systems.

Computer Network   A collection of computers and other devices that use a common network protocol to share resources with each other over a network medium.

Conductor   That part of a wire which serves as the medium for the physical signal. It is composed of either copper wire, glass, or plastic fiber. In the case of copper, the wire can be stranded (composed of several thin wires) or solid (a single, "thick" strand). Furthermore, the thickness of a wire is given in terms of gauge, which represents the conductor's diameter. The lower the gauge, the thicker the wire. Most often, wire gauges are expressed in terms of AWG—American Wire Gauge—which is a classification system for copper wire based on a wire's cross-section diameter.

Congestion   A term used to describe a situation when a network is consumed with excessive network traffic (i.e., lots of packets) resulting in performance degradation. Congestion occurs when routers are too slow, causing queues to lengthen, or when routers are too fast, causing queues to build up whenever input traffic is greater than the capacity of output lines. The ultimate level of congestion is known as *deadlock*, which occurs when one router cannot proceed until a second router does something, and the second router cannot proceed because it is waiting for the first router to do something. Congestion control is provided by layer 3 of the *OSI* model.

Connectionless Service   A type of service in which messages are partitioned into *packets* and routed through the network. Each packet is independent of the other packets that carry parts of the message, and each packet carries a destination address. Unlike connection-oriented service, no physical link is established between sending and receiving nodes prior to data transmission.

Connection-Oriented Service   A type of service in which prior to the transfer of data a physical (and virtual) link is established between the sending and receiving nodes. This link remains in effect for the duration of the session. After the session is completed, the link is removed. Characteristics of a connection-oriented service include: wasted bandwidth (link must remain established even during idle periods of a transmission); a high potential for a hung network (there is always a possibility that a link will not be terminated); and guaranteed sequential arrival of packets at the destination node.

Connector   A layer 1 device that attaches network components together.

Consortia Standards   Network standards that are designed and agreed upon by a group of vendors who have formed a consortium for the express purpose of achieving a common goal. These vendors pledge their support for the standards being developed by the consortium and also develop and market products based on these mutually agreed upon sets of standards.

Consultative Committee for International Telephony and Telegraphy (CCITT) An international standards organization, which is now part of *ITU.*

Contention A phenomenon in which more than one node competes to access a shared medium simultaneously.

Contention Protocol A network protocol that specifies the procedures nodes are to follow when competing for access to the same communications channel at the same time. Also called *random access protocol.*

Copper Distributed Data Interface (CDDI) An interface that provides a 100 Mbps data transmission rate over copper. A CDDI network is similar to an FDDI network. CDDI also is restricted to connections between concentrators on the ring and single-attachment devices, not for the ring itself.

CoS See *Class of Service.*

CPE See *Customer Premise Equipment.*

CRC See *Cyclic Redundancy Check.*

CRC Checksum The result of a polynomial division that uses a predetermined *generator polynomial* as the divisor.

CRC Error An invalid *CRC* checksum.

Crosstalk Electrical interference (i.e., *noise*) that occurs when energy radiated from one wire-pair of a twisted pair wire "spills over" into another pair. In one type of crosstalk, called *near-end crosstalk* (abbreviated NEXT), a signal on the transmit pair is so strong that it radiates to the receive pair. A direct consequence of this spilled-over radiation is that the receiving device cannot decipher the real signal.

Cryptology The practice or art of encoding messages into secret code or cipher.

CSMA See *Carrier Sense Multiple Access.*

CSMA/CA See *Carrier Sense Multiple Access with Collision Avoidance.*

CSMA/CD See *Carrier Sense Multiple Access with Collision Detection.*

CSMA with Collision Avoidance (CSMA/CA) A variant of *CSMA/CD* except that it specifies a implementation scheme for *collision avoidance* instead of *collision detection.*

CSMA with Collision Detection (CSMA/CD) A variant of either *1-persistent* or *non-persistent CSMA* that specifies what a node is to do upon detecting a collision. One-persistent CSMA/CD is the MAC sublayer protocol used in Ethernet/802.3 LANs.

CSU See *Channel Service Unit.*

CSU/DSU See *Channel Service Unit/Data Service Unit.*

Customer Premise Equipment (CPE) Any telecommunication device that is owned and housed at a customer site.

Cut-Through A term used to describe a network switch architecture. Cut-through switches begin forwarding frames from one switch port to another as soon as the frame's destination address is read.

Cyclic Redundancy Check (CRC) An *error detection* method that constructs a polynomial whose terms' coefficients are the values of each of the bits of a data frame. This polynomial is divided by a predetermined *generator polynomial.* The remainder of this division, called the CRC *checksum*, is then assigned to a frame's checksum field. The most common CRC used in most LAN protocols is CRC-32, a 32-bit checksum.

DAM   See *Demand Access Multiplexing.*

DAS   See *Dual Attachment Station.*

Data Communications Equipment (DCE)   Generally used as a synonymous term for *modem.* A DCE device is placed between *DTEs* and is responsible for establishing, maintaining, and terminating the link connecting the two DTEs.

Data Encryption Standard (DES)   A specific coding technique developed by the National Institute of Standards and Technology (formerly the National Bureau of Standards) and IBM for protecting sensitive data during transmission.

Datagram   A grouping of bits organized as a logical unit of data at the network layer. *IP* datagrams serve as the Internet's primary unit of information. In the OSI model, a datagram is generically referred to as a *packet.*

Data Link Connection Identifier (DLCI)   A term used in *frame relay* to denote virtual circuit addresses assigned to *PVCs* or *SVCs.*

Data Link Layer   The second layer (layer 2) of the OSI Reference Model. The data link layer regulates and formats transmission of information from software on a node to the network cabling facilities. This layer is partitioned into two sublayers: The *logical link control* sublayer (LLC), which provides framing, flow control, and error control; and the *media access control* sublayer (MAC), which specifies the manner in which nodes access a shared medium.

Data Rate   A measure of the amount of data that can be transferred over a communications medium in a given period. Data rate is measured in bits per second (bps) and can vary considerably from one type of channel to another.

Data Service Unit (DSU)   A device used for terminating a T-carrier circuit. A DSU provides the interface (usually V.35, a type of serial interface) for connecting a remote bridge, router, or switch to a T-carrier circuit. The DSU also provides flow control between the network and the *CSU.* DSUs are usually combined with a CSU to form a single unit called a CSU/DSU.

Data Terminal Equipment (DTE)   End *devices* that communicate through their serial ports or expansion buses. Computers (PCs, workstations) are examples of DTEs. See also *DCE.*

DB Connector   Layer 1 device that serves as an interface between a computer and a peripheral device such as a printer or external modem. "DB" stands for "data bus."

DCE   See *Data Communications Equipment.*

DCE-to-DCE Rate   The speed at which two modems "talk" to each other. This rate is fixed and is a function of a modem's speed. Typical rates are 14,400 bps (*V.32*), 28,800 bps (*V.34*), and 57,600 bps (*V.90*).

D Channel   A 16 kbps or 64 kbps *ISDN* circuit that is used to carry signal and control information for circuit-switched user data. The D channel transmits call initiation (call-setup) and termination (call tear-down) information between an ISDN device and the telco's central office for each *B channel.* The D channel also can be used to transmit packet-switched user data (provided that no signal or control information is needed), data from security alarm signals of remote sensing devices that detect fire or intruders, and low speed information acquired from telemetry services such as meter reading. The "D" stands for "delta."

Deadlock   See *Congestion*.

Decentralized System   Computer systems that are independent of each other and maintain separate databases germane to specific activities.

Decryption   The process of taking an encrypted (coded) message and translating it into its original, meaningful form.

***De Facto* Standards**   Network standards, placed in the public domain, that have been met with widespread industry acceptance instead of formal approval from a standards organizations ("De facto" is Latin for "from the fact.")

***De Jure* Standards**   Network standards approved by a formal, accredited standards organization such as ANSI or ITU. ("De jure" is Latin for "by right, according to law.")

Demand Access Multiplexing (DAM)   A multiplexing technique in which a pool of frequencies is managed by a "traffic cop." Pairs of communications frequencies are assigned to a requesting station—one pair for transmission, a second pair for reception ("demand"). These two pairs of frequencies are connected to another set of frequencies ("access"). When one or both stations are finished communicating, the allocated frequencies are deallocated and returned to the frequency pool, where they are made available for other incoming requests ("multiplexing").

Demand Priority   A *MAC* sublayer protocol used in *100VG-AnyLAN* networks. Demand priority specifies the manner in which repeater hubs poll their ports to identify which nodes have data to transmit and the order of these transmissions.

DES   See *Data Encryption Standard*.

Desktop   Another name for a networked device. See *Workstation*.

Device   Any entity that is connected to a network. Examples include terminals, printers, computers, or special network-related hardware units such as communication servers, repeaters, bridges, switches, and routers. Local or sending devices originate communications; remote or receiving devices are the recipients of such communications.

Differential Manchester Encoding   A data transmission encoding scheme similar to *Manchester encoding*—each bit-period is partitioned into two intervals and a transition between "high" and "low" occurs during each bit-period. In differential Manchester coding, though, the interpretation of these low-to-high and high-to-low transitions is a function of the previous bit-period. The presence of a transition at the beginning of a bit period is coded 0, and the absence of a transition at the beginning of a bit period is coded 1. Differential Manchester encoding is used for clocking purposes only.

Diffused IR   A "broadcast" infrared transmission method in which a transmitter "floods" a specific area with a strong infrared signal that is spread over a wide angle. The IR signal is transmitted by reflecting off ceilings, walls, and other surfaces.

Digital   Refers to any device or signal that varies discreetly in strength or quantity between two values, usually zero and one. Zero implies "off"; one implies "on." Digital signals are represented as binary digits called "bits" and are *discrete*.

Digital Certificate   An electronic passport that consists of a numerical pattern, value, or key and used for personal identification. Creating a digital certificate involves a user identifying a specific personal trait to a trusted third party, which issues the certificate.

Digital Communication Refers to any type of communication in which data are represented in the form of binary digits.

Digital Signature A security authorization method in which a user "signs" a document so that the document's authenticity can be confirmed by checking the signature. A digital signature proves a message was not modified.

Digital Subscriber Line (DSL) A technology that enables data, voice, and video to be mixed and carried over standard analog, (copper) telephone lines. This is accomplished by using the unused frequencies that are available on a telephone line. Thus, DSL can deliver data services without interfering with voice transmissions. There are at least nine DSL variants: *ADSL, ADSL lite, HDSL, HDSL 2, IDSL, RADSL, SDSL, UDSL,* and *VDSL.*

DSL Access Multiplexer (DSLAM) A device that aggregates *DSL* signals so they can be transferred directly into a data switch for transmission across the telco's data network backbone.

Digital Subscriber Loop The formal term used to denote the *local loop*, which is the circuit between a *customer's premise equipment (CPE)* and the telco's equipment.

DIN Connector Similar to a *DB connector*, but is circular instead of rectangular and typically used to connect a keyboard to a computer. "DIN" stands for "Deutsche Industrie Norm," a German industrial standard.

Directed IR A "point-to-point" infrared transmission method that requires an unobstructed line-of-sight connection between transmitter and receiver. It is basically a "point and beam" medium.

Direct Sequence Spread Spectrum (DSSS) A physical layer technology used in wireless LANs (IEEE 802.11). DSSS operates by spreading a signal over a wide range of the 2.4 GHz band.

Discard Eligibility The name of a field in a *frame relay* frame, which, if set to 1 by an end node, denotes that the frame can be discarded in the presence of congestion. Discarded frames will then be retransmitted at a later time when congestion has subsided.

Distance-Vector Algorithm A routing algorithm that determines the distance between source and destination nodes by calculating the number of router hops a packet traverses en route from the source network to the destination network. An example of a distance-vector algorithm is the Bellman-Ford algorithm.

Distributed Queue Dual Bus (DQDB) A data link layer protocol (IEEE 802.6) that specifies the medium access method for *MANs*. Used in *SMDS*.

Distributed System Computers that are linked together to provide, in a transparent manner, the required computing resources and information processing needs of an entire organization. Distributed systems bear the greatest resemblance to computer networks.

DLCI See *Data Link Connection Identifier.*

DNS See *Domain Name Service.*

Domain Name A logical name assigned to an *IP address* and used as another type of addressing construct for identifying Internet nodes. The translation between logical name and IP address is called name resolution, which is provided by a *domain name service*.

Domain Name Service (DNS) An Internet translation service that resolves *domain names* to *IP addresses* and vice versa. Domain name service is provided by DNS servers.

DQDB   See *Distributed Queue Dual Bus*.

DS-0   A single, digital voice channel rated at 64 kbps. The notation *DS-0* stands for "digital signal at level 0," which refers to a voice channel multiplexed into a digital signal.

DS-1   A digital signal that carries 24 *DS-0* channels plus one 8 kbps channel reserved for framing for an aggregate bandwidth of 1.544 Mbps. A *T1* circuit carries a DS-1 signal.

DS-2   A digital signal that carries 4 *DS-1* channels for an aggregate bandwidth of 6.312 Mbps. A *T2* circuit carries a DS-2 signal.

DS-3   A digital signal that carries 28 *DS-1* channels for an aggregate bandwidth of 44.736 Mbps. A *T3* circuit carries a DS-3 signal.

DS-4   A digital signal that carries 168 *DS-1* channels for an aggregate bandwidth of 274.176 Mbps. A *T4* circuit carries a DS-4 signal.

DSL   See *Digital Subscriber Line*.

DSLAM   See *DSL Access Multiplexer*.

DSSS   See *Direct Sequence Spread Spectrum*.

DSU   See *Data Service Unit*.

DTE   See *Data Terminal Equipment*.

DTE-to-DCE Rate   The speed at which a computer "talks" to its modem. Typical rates include a 4:1 compression ratio between DTE and DCE speeds. Thus, for a *V.34* modem (28,800 bps), the DTE-DCE rate is 115,200 bps. This rate is user configurable.

Dual-Attachment Station (DAS)   An FDDI node that is connected to two full, dual-fiber rings and have the ability to reconfigure the network to form a valid network from components of the two rings in case of a failure. A DAS is also called a *Class A* node.

E-1   Describes the multiplexing of 30 separate 64 kbps voice channels, plus one 64 kbps control channel, into a single, wideband digital signal rated at 2.048 Mbps. E-1 is the basic telecommunications service used in Europe.

E-2   A multiplexed circuit that combines 4 *E-1* circuits and has an aggregate bandwidth of 8.448 Mbps.

E-3   A multiplexed circuit that combines 16 *E-1* circuits and has an aggregate bandwidth of 34.368 Mbps.

E-4   A multiplexed circuit that combines 64 *E-1* circuits and has an aggregate bandwidth of 139.264 Mbps.

E-5   A multiplexed circuit that combines 256 *E-1* circuits and has an aggregate bandwidth of 565.148 Mbps.

E.164   An ITU-T standard network addressing format that resemble telephone numbers. E.164 addresses are 15 decimal digits long and include a country code, area or city code, and a local number. Country codes are two or three digits long and consist of a zone code followed by a one- or two-digit national identifier. Area or city codes are up to four digits long. If an address contains less than 15 digits, then it is padded with hexadecimal Fs. Australia does not use city codes, and the United States and Canada use the zone code 1 followed by a three-digit area code and a seven digit local number in lieu of county codes.

E-commerce   Short for "electronic commerce," which involves using the Internet for credit card purchases of items such as automobiles, airline tickets, computer hardware and software, and books.

EGP   See *Exterior Gateway Protocol.*

EIGRP   See *Enhanced IGRP.*

Encapsulation   A process in which a *packet* or *frame* is enclosed or "wrapped" in a specific protocol header. For example, *routers* typically perform protocol encapsulation in which packets from one network protocol are wrapped into the header of another network protocol so the packet can be transmitted to a different network. Also called *tunneling.*

Encryption   The process of coding a message so that it is incomprehensible to unauthorized users. When retrieved by authorized users, encrypted messages are then reconverted (i.e., decoded) into meaningful text. Encrypted output is called *ciphertext.*

Enhanced IGRP (EIGRP)   A routing protocol designed by Cisco that combines the best features of distance-vector and link-state routing protocols.

Exterior Gateway Protocol (EGP)   Any Internet interdomain routing protocol used to exchange routing information with other autonomous systems. Also refers to a specific EGP defined in RFC 904. Another EGP is the Border Gateway Protocol (BGP), defined in RFC 1105 and RFC 1771. Both EGP and BGP are part of the *TCP/IP* protocol suite. Of the two, however, BGP has evolved into a robust Internet routing protocol and the term "Border Gateway Protocol" is used in favor of the term "Exterior Gateway Protocol."

Error Control   The process of guaranteeing reliable delivery of data. Error control can be provided through *error detection* or *error correction.*

Error Correction   The process in which a destination node, upon detecting a data transmission error, has sufficient information to correct the error autonomously. Error correction implies *error detection.*

Error Detection   The process in which a destination node detects a data transmission error and requests a retransmission from the sending node. Error detection is also called error correction through retransmission.

Ethernet   A local area network protocol developed jointly by Xerox, Intel, and Digital Equipment Corporation (DEC) at the Xerox Palo Alto Research Center (PARC) in the mid-1970s. The name "Ethernet" was derived from the old electromagnetic theoretical substance called luminiferous ether, which was formerly believed to be the invisible universal element that bound together the entire universe and all its associated parts. Thus, an "ether" net is a network that connects all components attached to the "net."

Excessive Burst (B_e)   A term used in *frame relay* to denote the maximum amount of uncommitted data a provider will attempt to deliver within a specified time period. A provider will guarantee a *committed burst* of B_c bits and will attempt to deliver (but not guarantee) a maximum of $B_c + B_e$ bits.

Exchange Access SMDS (XA-SMDS)   A special *SMDS* service through which *LECs* offered SMDS to *IECs* for delivery across *LATAs.*

Extranet   A popular networking term that describes an interconnection from an internal intranet to a customer or noncompany network that is not the Internet connection.

4B/5B   A data encoding method, which stands for *four bits in five baud*, or *four-bit to five-bit*, used in FDDI networks.

5-4-3 Repeater Rule   A general rule of thumb to follow when configuring an Ethernet/ 802.3 LAN to ensure that it follows IEEE specifications. The 5-4-3 rule requires: no more than 5 segments of up to 500 m each; no more than 4 repeaters; and no more than 3 segments can have end nodes connected to them. This rule is also known as the 4-repeater rule, or the 5-4-3-2-1 rule. In the latter, the "2" implies that two of the five segments are used as interrepeater links, and the "1" implies that a configuration using the maximum parameters permitted results into one collision domain.

568SC Connector   See *SC connector.*

Fast Ethernet   100 Mbps *Ethernet (IEEE 802.3u).* Three different media specifications are defined: 100BASE-TX, 100BASE-T4, and 100BASE-FX.

FDDI   See *Fiber Distributed Data Interface.*

FDDI-II   A now-defunct second generation *FDDI* technology that was intended to handle traditional FDDI network traffic as well as synchronous, circuit-switched *PCM* data for voice or *ISDN* systems.

FECN   See *Forward Explicit Congestion Notification.*

Federal Internet Exchange (FIX)   An Internet interconnect site similar to a *NAP.*

FHSS   See *Frequency Hopping Spread Spectrum.*

Fiber Distributed Data Interface (FDDI)   An ANSI standard, X3T9.5, created in 1986 for interconnecting computer systems and network devices typically via a fiber ring topology at 100 Mbps.

Fiber-optic Cable   A type of cable that carries data signals in the form of modulated light beams. The cable's conductor can be either glass or plastic. Fiber-optic cable is immune to electromagnetic interference (EMI) and other types of externally induced noise, including lightning; it is unaffected by most physical factors such as vibration; its size is smaller and its weight lighter than copper; it has much lower attenuation per unit of length than copper; and it can support very high bandwidth. Two general types are available: *single-mode fiber* and *multimode fiber.*

Fibre Channel   A family of ANSI standards that defines a specific communications interface for high-speed data transfers between different hardware systems. Applications include the medical profession, where large images (e.g., 100 MB+ X-rays) are transferred from a scanner to a computer to a screen, and the electronic publishing industry, where large files are transferred from an designer/creator's machine to a publisher's computer. It has also become the "backbone" of high-speed data storage systems.

Firewall   A device or product that allows systems or network manager to restrict access to components on a network. Five generally accepted types of firewalls are used on Internet connections: *frame-filtering, packet-filtering, circuit gateways, stateful* and *application gateways,* and *proxy servers.*

FIX   See *Federal Internet Exchange.*

Flow Control   A process that controls the rate at which data messages are exchanged between two nodes. Flow control provides a mechanism to ensure that a sending node does not overwhelm a receiving node during data transmission.

Forward Explicit Congestion Notification (FECN)   A one-bit field in a *frame relay* frame that is set to 1 by a frame relay switch to denote that a frame transmitted toward the receiving node experienced congestion.

Fractional T1   *T1* service that is sold in 64 kbps increments.

FRAD   See *Frame Relay Access Device.*

Fragmenting A process in which a *packet* is broken into smaller units to accommodate the maximum transmission unit a physical network is capable of supporting. Fragmented packets are sent to the destination separately and then reassembled at the destination node before it is passed to the higher levels. In *IP*, reassembly of a *datagram* occurs at the destination node and not at any of the intermediary nodes the packet traverses.

Frame A specially formatted sequence of bits that incorporates both data and control information.

Frame-Filtering Firewall A *firewall* device or product that filters (permits or denies access) at the *data link layer* by examining frames for both layout and content.

Frame Relay A public *WAN* packet-switching protocol that provides LAN-to-LAN connectivity. Its name implies what it does, namely, relays frames across a network between two sites. Frame relay was originally part of the *ISDN* standard.

Frame Relay Access Device (FRAD) Any *frame relay* end node.

Framing A *data link layer* process that partitions a bit stream into discrete units or blocks of data called *frames*.

Frequency Division Multiplexing (FDM) A multiplexing technique that partitions the available transmission frequency range into narrower bands (subfrequencies), each of which is a separate channel. FDM-based transmissions are parallel in nature.

Frequency Hopping Spread Spectrum (FHSS) A physical layer technology used in wireless LANs (*IEEE 802.11*). FHSS operates by transmitting short bursts of data on different frequencies. One burst is transmitted on one frequency, a second burst is transmitted on a second and different frequency, and so forth.

Full-Duplex Transmission A data transmission method that involves the simultaneous sending and receiving of data in both directions.

GAN See *Global Area Network*.

Gateway A software application that converts between different application protocols. The host on which this software resides is called a *gateway machine*. Historically, this term also refers to a *router* in the *IP* community.

Geostationary Earth Orbit (GEO) Satellite A satellite placed into orbit at an altitude of 22,000 miles (36,000 kilometers) above the equator. GEO satellites traverse their orbits at approximately the same rate as the Earth rotates. Thus, the satellite appears stationary with respect to the Earth's rotation. Also call *Geosynchronous Earth Orbit*. Only eight GEO satellites are needed to provide global communications coverage.

Gigabit Ethernet 1000 Mbps Ethernet (*IEEE 802.3z*).

G.lite See *ADSL lite*.

Global Area Network (GAN) A collection of *WANs* that span the globe.

Government OSI Profile (GOSIP) A U.S. government directive that mandated all government organizations purchase *OSI*-compliant networking products beginning in 1992. In 1995, however, GOSIP was modified to include *TCP/IP* as an acceptable protocol suite for GOSIP compliance.

GOSIP See *Government OSI Profile*.

Graded-index Multimode Fiber   A type of multimode fiber in which variations in the density of the core medium change its index of refraction such that light is refracted (i.e., bends) toward the center of the fiber.

Half-duplex Transmission   A data transmission method in which data may travel in either direction—from sender to receiver or receiver to sender—but only one unit can send at any one time. While one node is in send mode, the other is in receive mode.

Harmonic Motion   The basic model for vibratory or oscillatory motion. Examples include mechanical oscillators such as mass-spring systems and pendulums; periodic motion found in the earth sciences such as water waves, tides, and climatic cycles; and electromagnetic waves such as alternating electric currents, sound waves, light waves, radio waves, and television waves.

H Channel   An *ISDN* channel used for transmitting user data (not signal or control information) at higher transmission rates than a *B channel* provides. Four H channels are defined: *H0* (six B channels; 384 kbps); *H10* (United States-specific; aggregates 23 B channels; 1.472 Mbps); *H11*(equivalent of North American DS-1; 24 B channels; 1.536 Mbps); and *H12* (European-specific; comprises 30 B channels; 1.920 Mbps).

HDSL   See *High bit-rate Digital Subscriber Line*.

HDSL 2   A modified *HDSL* designed and packaged for corporate clients.

Hertz   A measure of frequency in cycles per second. A frequency rate of one cycle per second is defined as one hertz (abbreviated Hz). Named in honor of Heinrich Rudolf Hertz (1857–1894), a German physicist who in the late 1880s was the first to produce radio waves artificially.

HFC   See *Hybrid Fiber Cable*.

High bit-rate Digital Subscriber Line (HDSL)   A *DSL* variant that provides symmetrical service at *T1* rates over 2 pairs of *UTP*, and *E1* rates over 3 pairs of UTP. Telephone service is not supported. Applications include connecting PBXs, and serving as an alternative to T1/E1. HDSL is suitable for campus networks and *ISPs*.

Hold-down   A strategy used by *RIP* that requires routers to not update their routing tables with any new information they receive for a prescribed period of time, called the hold-down time. Designed to prevent routing loops. Hold-down is not standardized.

Hop   A term used to describe the passage of a *packet* through an intermediate gateway (*router*) en route to another network. For example, if a packet transverses through two routers in reaching its final destination, then we say the destination is two hops away.

Host   A networked computer system (see *workstation*). Also used to describe a computer system that provides service to users (see *server*).

Hub   Generically, any *device* that connects two or more network segments or supports several different media. Examples include repeaters, switches, and concentrators.

Hybrid Fiber Cable (HFC)   Describes a cable TV cable plant that has *fiber-optic cable* between the head end and neighborhood distribution sites, but coaxial cable between the neighborhood distribution and residential homes and businesses.

Hybrid Switching   A data transmission method that combines the principles of circuit and *packet-switching*. This technique first partitions a message into packets (packet-switching) and transmits each packet via a dedicated circuit (*circuit-switching*). As soon as a packet is ready for transmission, a circuit meeting appropriate bandwidth requirements is established between the sending and receiving nodes. When the packet reaches its destination, the circuit is broken down so that it can be used again.

IAB See *Internet Activities Board.*

IANA See *Internet Assigned Numbers Authority.*

IBM Cable System (ICS) A copper wire classification system established by IBM that specifies nine cable "types" (1 through 9). Of the nine "types" defined, specifications are available for only seven; types 4 and 7 are not defined.

ICANN See *Internet Corporation for Assigned Names and Numbers.*

ICMP See *Internet Control Message Protocol.*

ICS See *IBM Cable System.*

IDSL See *ISDN-like Digital Subscriber Line.*

IEC See *Inter-Exchange Carrier.*

IEEE See *Institute of Electrical and Electronics Engineers.*

IEEE 802 The primary *IEEE* standard for the 802.*x* series for *LANs* and *MANs.*

IEEE 802.1 *IEEE* standard that defines an architectural overview of *LANs.*

IEEE 802.2 *IEEE* standard that defines the Logical Link Control, which describes services for the transmission of data between two nodes.

IEEE 802.3 *IEEE* standard that defines the *Carrier Sense Multiple Access/Collision Detection (CSMA/CD)* access method commonly referred to as *Ethernet.* Supplements include **802.3c** (10 Mbps Ethernet); **802.3u** (100 Mbps Ethernet known as *Fast Ethernet*), and **802.3z** and **802.3ab** (1000 Mbps Ethernet known as *Gigabit Ethernet*).

IEEE 802.4 *IEEE* standard that defines the token bus network access method.

IEEE 802.5 *IEEE* standard that defines the logical ring *LAN* that uses a token-passing access method; known also as *token ring.*

IEEE 802.6 *IEEE* standard that defines metropolitan area networks (*MANs*).

IEEE 802.7 *IEEE* standard that defines broadband *LANs* (capable of delivering video, data, and voice traffic).

IEEE 802.9 *IEEE* standard that defines integrated digital and video networking—Integrated Services LANs (ISLANs).

IEEE 802.10 *IEEE* standard that defines standards for interoperable *LAN/MAN* security services.

IEEE 802.11 *IEEE* standard that defines standards for wireless media access control and physical layer specifications.

IEEE 802.12 *IEEE* standard that defines the "demand priority" access method for 100Mbps LANs; known also as 100 Base-VG or *100VG-AnyLAN.*

IEEE 802.13 (Defines nothing—IEEE was concerned about the superstitious overtones associated with "13.")

IEEE 802.14 *IEEE* standard that defines a standard for Cable-TV based broadband communication.

IETF See *Internet Engineering Task Force.*

IGP See *Interior Gateway Protocol.*

IGRP   See *Interior Gateway Routing Protocol.*

ILEC   See *Incumbent Local Exchange Carrier.*

Impedance   A measure of the opposition to the flow of electric current in an alternating current circuit. Measured in ohms (abbreviated by the Greek symbol, omega, Ω), impedance is a function of capacitance, resistance, and inductance. Impedance mismatches, caused by mixing cables of different types with different characteristic impedances, can result in signal distortion.

Impulse Noise   Electrical *noise* that consists of intermittent, undesirable signals induced by external sources such as lightning, switching equipment, and heavy electrically operated machinery such as elevator motors and copying machines. Impulse noise increases or decreases a circuit's signal level, which causes the receiving equipment to misinterpret the signal.

Incumbent Local Exchange Carrier (ILEC)   The contemporary name given to the seven *RBOCs* and GTE relative to the United States Telecommunications Act of 1996. With mergers, only four will remain: Ameritech, SBC, Bell Atlantic, and GTE.

Infrared (IR)   A line-of-sight transmission method that uses electromagnetic radiation of wavelengths between radio waves and visible light, operating between 100 GHz and 100 THz (Terahertz). IR transmission can occur in one of two ways: *directed* and *diffused.*

Institute of Electrical and Electronics Engineers (IEEE)   A professional society of engineers, scientists, and students. One of its many activities is to act as a coordinating body for computing and communication standards.

Insulation   Material surrounding the *conductor* of a wire. The insulation serves as a protective "barrier" to the conductor by preventing the signal from "escaping" and preventing electrical interference from "entering."

Integrated Services Digital Network (ISDN)   A carrier service that is offered by telephone companies (telcos) and designed to transmit voice and non-voice (e.g., computer data, fax, video) communications on the same network. In response to its long period of dormancy, "ISDN" is also known as, I Still Don't Need it, Innovative Services users Don't Need, I Still Don't kNow, and It's Still Doing Nothing.

Inter-Exchange Carrier (IEC)   Any company that provides long distance telephone and telecommunications services. Examples include AT&T, Sprint, British Telecom (BT), and MCI WorldCom.

Interior Gateway Protocol (IGP)   Any intradomain Internet protocol used to exchange routing information within an *autonomous system*. Examples include *RIP, RIP-2, OSPF, IGRP,* and *Enhanced IGRP (EIGRP).*

Interior Gateway Routing Protocol (IGRP)   A routing protocol developed by Cisco to address some of the problems associated with routing in large, heterogeneous networks.

Intermediate System to Intermediate System (IS-IS)   An intradomain routing protocol designed by *OSI* to run within an *AS* (called a "routing domain" in the OSI world). IS-IS uses a *link-state routing algorithm* to calculate least-cost paths, and is similar in operation *OSPF*. The formal title of this protocol is "Intermediate System to Intermediate System Intra-Domain Routing Exchange Protocol."

Intermodulation Noise   Electrical *noise* that occurs when two frequencies interact to produce a phantom signal at a different frequency. Occurs in *frequency-division multiplexed* channels.

International Organization for Standardization (ISO)   An international organization that develops and promotes networking standards worldwide.

International Telecommunications Union (ITU)   A global standards organization. ITU is the former *CCITT*.

Internet   When used as a noun and spelled with a lowercase *i*, "internet" is an abbreviation for *internetwork*, which refers to a collection of interconnected networks that functions as a single network. When used as a proper noun and spelled with a capital *I*, "Internet" refers to the world's largest internetwork, which consists of hundreds of thousands of interconnected networks worldwide and based on a specific set of network standards (*TCP/IP*).

Internet Architecture Board (IAB)   An organization that is part of the *Internet Society* responsible for the overall planning and designing of the Internet. Responsibilities include setting Internet standards, managing the publication of RFC documents, and resolving technical issues. Assigned to the IAB are the *Internet Engineering Task Force* and the *Internet Research Task Force*. Formerly known as the Internet Activities Board.

Internet Assigned Numbers Authority (IANA)   An organization that has authority over all number spaces used in the Internet including *IP addresses*. IANA control will soon be transferred to the *Internet Corporation for Assigned Names and Numbers (ICANN)*.

Internet Control Message Protocol (ICMP)   An *IP datagram* that carries messages about the communications environment of the *Internet*.

Internet Corporation for Assigned Names and Numbers (ICANN)   A private, nonprofit corporation with international representation expressly formed to assume the responsibilities currently being performed by IANA and other government organizations that provide domain name service.

Internet Engineering Task Force (IETF)   An organization that is part of the *Internet Architecture Board* and primarily concerned with addressing short- or medium-term Internet engineering issues. Relies on the Internet Engineering Steering Group (IESG) to prioritize and coordinate activities.

Internet Protocol (IP)   A layer 3 connectionless protocol. IP receives data bits from the lower layer, assembles these bits into packets, called IP *datagrams*, and selects the "best" route based on some metric to route the packets between nodes. This is the "IP" of *TCP/IP*.

Internet Registry (IR)   A formal hierarchical system used for assigning *IP addresses*. From top to bottom, this hierarchy consists of *IANA*, Regional Internet Registries (RIR), and Local Internet Registries (LIR), and works as follows: IANA allocates blocks of IP address space to RIRs; RIRs allocate blocks of IP address space to their LIRs; LIRs then assign addresses to either end users or ISPs.

Internet Research Task Force (IRTF)   An organization that is part of the *Internet Architecture Board* and primarily concerned with addressing long-term research projects. Relies on the *Internet Research Steering Group (IRSG)* to prioritize and coordinate activities.

Internet Service Provider (ISP)   An organization that provides its customers with access to the Internet.

Internet Society (ISOC)   An international organization comprised of volunteers who promote the Internet as a medium for global communication and collaboration. ISOC is considered the ultimate authoritative organization of the Internet.

Internet2   A collaborative project of the University Corporation for Advanced Internet Development (UCAID), which comprises over 100 U.S. universities, government organizations, and private sector firms. Internet2's mission is to develop advanced Internet technologies and applications that support the research endeavors of colleges and universities. Internet2 members use the *vBNS* to test and advance their research.

Interoperability   The degree in which products (software and hardware) developed by different vendors are able to communicate successfully (i.e., *interoperate*) with each other over a network.

Intranet   An internal network implementation of traditional Internet applications within a company or an institution.

Inverse Multiplexing   The reverse of *multiplexing*. Instead of partitioning a single communication medium into several channels, an inverse *multiplexer* combines several "smaller" channels (i.e., low-speed circuits) into a single high-speed circuit. This technique is also sometimes generically called *line aggregation*.

IP   See *Internet Protocol*.

IP Address   A network address assigned to a node's network interface and used to uniquely identify (locate) the node within the Internet. Two versions are currently implemented: *IPv4* and *IPv6*.

IPSec   See *IP security*.

IP Security (IPSec)   A suite of network security protocols that operates at layer 3 and provides address authentication, data encryption, and automated key exchanges between sender and receiver nodes.

IPv4   An acronym for *Internet protocol version 4*.

IPv4 Address   An *IP address* based on *IPv4*. These addresses consist of 32 bits (0 through 31) partitioned into four groups of eight bits each (called *octets*), and organized into five classes (A through E) based on the values of bits 0 through 3.

IPv6   An acronym for *Internet protocol version 6*, which is an evolutionary replacement to IPv4. IPv6 maintains most IPv4 functions, relegates certain functions that either were not working or were rarely used in IPv4 as optional, and adds new functionality that is missing from IPv4. Sometimes called IPng (for next generation).

IPv6 Address   An *IP address* based on *IPv6*. An IPv6 address consists of 128 bits and is 4 billion × 4 billion times the size of the IPv4 address space (2^{96} vs. 2^{32}). Unlike IPv4 addresses, IPv6 addresses use a colon as their delimiter (instead of a "dot" notation), and they are written as eight 16-bit integers expressed in hexadecimal form.

IR   See *Internet Registry* or *Infrared*.

IRTF   See *Internet Research Task Force*.

ISDN   See *Integrated Services Digital Network*.

ISDN-like Digital Subscriber Line (IDSL)   A *DSL* variant that provides symmetrical service at a maximum of 144 kbps each way. Uses *ISDN* hardware.

IS-IS   See *Intermediate System to Intermediate System*.

ISO   See *International Organization for Standardization*.

ISOC   See *Internet Society*.

Isochronous   A term used to describe the delivery of time sensitive data such as voice or video transmissions. Networks that are capable of delivering isochronous service (e.g., *ATM*) preallocate a specific amount of bandwidth over regular intervals to ensure that the transmission is not interrupted.

IsoEthernet   Short for *Isochronous Ethernet*, an IEEE standard (*IEEE 802.9a*), which is designed to support time-sensitive applications such as videoconferencing and telephony. IsoEthernet runs both conventional 10 Mbps *Ethernet* and *ISDN B channels* over the same network. The Ethernet channel is used for normal data networking needs; the ISDN B channels are used for time-sensitive applications.

ISP   See *Internet Service Provider.*

ITU   See *International Telecommunications Union.*

IXC   See *Inter-Exchange Carrier.*

Jabber   An *oversized* Ethernet/802.3 *frame* and an invalid *CRC checksum.*

Kerberos   A client-server network security authentication system, developed at MIT and based on *DES* encryption. It is an *Internet* standard that uses a three-pronged approach for authentication: a database that contains users' rights, an authentication server, and a ticket-granting server. Kerberos is named after *Cerberus*, the three-headed dog in Greek mythology that guarded the gates to Hades.

LAN   See *Local Area Network.*

LANE   See *LAN Emulation.*

LAN Emulation (LANE)   An *ATM* protocol that specifies a technology that enables ATM to emulate Ethernet/802.3 or *token ring* networks. In ATM's protocol hierarchy, LANE is above *AAL5* in the *ATM adaptation layer.* The LANE protocol defines a service interface for the *network layer* that functions identical to the one used by Ethernet/802.3 and token ring LANs. Data that cross this interface are encapsulated in the appropriate *MAC sublayer* format.

LAP-D   See *Link Access Protocol-D channel.*

LAPM   See *Link Access Procedure for Modems.*

LATA   See *Local Access and Transport Area.*

Latency   The amount of delay a network device introduces when data frames pass through it. It is the amount of time a frame spends "inside" a network device. For example, switch latency is usually measured from the instant the first bit of a frame enters the device to the time this bit leaves the outbound (i.e., destination) port.

Layer 2 Forward (L2F)   A protocol that provides tunneling between an *ISP's* dial-up server and the network.

Layer 2 Tunneling Protocol (L2TP)   A method for tunneling PPP sessions across a network. It combines *PPTP* and *L2F.*

Layer 3 Switch   A layer 2 switch that is capable of examining layer 3 header information, which is then used to filter network protocols or broadcasts. Also refers to a router that is capable of performing router table lookups and packet forwarding at hardware speeds via application specific integrated circuit (ASIC) chips.

Layer 4 Switch   A *router* that is capable of examining upper layer (layers 4 through 7) information to make routing decisions. It is more appropriate to refer to layer 4 switches as either layer 2 or layer 3 application switches because application information from upper layers is being used for routing decisions.

LEC See *local exchange carrier.*

Lightwave Wireless A line-of-sight laser-based connection facility that allows long-distance light-based wireless networking without the need to install cable.

Line-of-Sight A type of wireless transmission that requires the transmitter and receiver be able to "see" other, that is, they must be in each other's "line-of-sight."

Line Set A term used by the National ISDN Users' Forum to describe the number of multiplexed *B* and *D* channels, and the type of *ISDN* service supported.

Link Access Protocol-D Channel (LAP-D) An *ITU* standard on which the *ISDN D* channel is based.

Link Access Procedure for Modems (LAPM) A *modem* protocol that uses *CRC* and ARQ for *error control*. CRC is used for *error detection*; ARQ prevents the modem from accepting any more data until the defective frame has been retransmitted successfully. *V.42*'s default is LAPM. Thus, if a connection is being initialized between two V.42 compliant modems, they will use LAPM for error control. If one of the modems is not V.42 compliant, then the modems will negotiate to use *MNP 1–4.*

Link-state Algorithm A routing algorithm in which routers send each other information about the links they have established to other routers via a link state advertisement (LSA), which contains the names and various cost-metrics of a router's neighbors. LSAs are flooded throughout an entire router's domain. Thus, rather than storing actual paths (which is the case with *distance-vector algorithms*), link-state algorithms store the information needed to generate such paths. An example of a link-state algorithm is Dijkstra's shortest path algorithm, which iterates on length of path to determine a shortest route.

Lobe The name of a *token ring* node, as defined in the IBM world.

Lobe Length A term used to identify the cable length between *token ring* nodes.

Local Access and Transport Area (LATA) A specific geographical region in which a *LEC* provides local telephone and telecommunications services in the United States. There are 195 LATAs. Services that cross LATA boundaries are provided by *IECs.*

Local Area Network (LAN) A network that interconnects computing resources within a moderately sized geographical area. This can include a room, several rooms within a building, or several buildings of a campus. A LAN's range is usually is no more than 10 km in radius.

Local Exchange Carrier (LEC) A telecommunications provider that provides service within a prescribed geographical area. See also *CLEC* and *ILEC.*

Local Loop Refers to the circuit that connects the telephone central office or exchange (sometimes called *POP*) with a customer's location. In frame relay, this circuit is called the *port connection* or *access line*. Formally called *digital subscriber loop.*

Logical Link Control (LLC) Sublayer The top sublayer of the data link layer that provides framing, flow control, and error control. Defined in *IEEE 802.2.*

Loop A network configuration in which nodes are connected via dedicated wiring instead of through a centralized hub (as is the case of a *star* design). Loops can be either *simple* (only one connection between any two nodes), *partial* (some nodes are interconnected by more than one link), or *complete* (every node has a connection to every other node). A loop is also referred to as a *meshed* design.

Low-Earth Orbit (LEO) Satellite A satellite placed in orbit at an altitude of 300 miles to 1,200 miles above the Earth. Depending on their orbit, a constellation of up to 48 LEO satellites are needed for global coverage.

L2F See *Layer 2 Forward.*

L2TP See *Layer 2 Tunneling Protocol.*

Manchester Encoding A data transmission encoding scheme that differs from standard digital transmission schemes. Instead of "high" equaling "1" and "low" equaling "0," a timing interval is used to measure high-to-low transitions. Furthermore, instead of a timed transmission period being "all high" or "all low" for either 1 or 0, a 1 is sent as a half-time-period low followed by a half-time-period high, and a 0 is sent as a half-time-period high followed by a half-time-period low. Consequently, the end of the last bit transmitted is easily determined immediately following the transmission of the last bit.

MAE See *Metropolitan Area Exchange.*

MAN See *Metropolitan Area Network.*

MAU See *Media Attachment Unit* or *Multistation Access Unit.*

Media Access Control (MAC) Sublayer The bottom half of the *data link layer* that provides media access management protocols for accessing a shared medium. Example *MAC sublayer* protocols include IEEE 802.3 (*Ethernet*) and IEEE 802.5 (*token ring*).

Media Attachment Unit (MAU) Another term for a *transceiver.*

Medium The physical environment used to connect networked devices.

Medium-Earth Orbit (MEO) Satellite A satellite placed in orbit at an altitude of 6,000 miles to 12,000 miles above the Earth. A constellation of 20 MEO satellites are needed for global coverage.

Media The plural of *medium.*

Media Converter A layer 1 device that enables different network media to be connected to one another.

Meshed Design A term used to describe interconnectivity among multiple nodes or sites. In a fully-meshed design, every node or site is connected with every other node or site. In a partially-meshed design, only some nodes or sites are interconnected.

Metric A generic term used in *routing* to represent different quantities such as distance, number of router *hops*, and *bandwidth.*

Metro-Area Satellites A proposed satellite that consists of a specially equipped jets that fly 50,000 feet above cities.

Metropolitan Area Exchange (MAE) An *Internet* interconnect site similar to a *NAP.* A NAP is funded by the National Science Foundation; a MAE is not. There are currently two MAE points, one each on the east and west coasts of the United States and known as MAE East and MAE West.

Metropolitan Area Network (MAN) A network that interconnects computing resources that span a metropolitan area such as buildings located throughout a local county or city. MANs generally refer to networks that span a larger geographical area than *LANs* but a smaller geographical area than *WANs.*

Microcom Networking Protocol (MNP) Defines various levels of *error correction* and compression for *modems.*

Micron   One micrometer (one millionth of a meter) and abbreviated by the symbol *μm*. Used in specifying the size of fiber-optic cable.

Microwave   An *RF* transmission method that uses high frequency waves and operates at a higher frequency in the electromagnetic spectrum (usually above 900 MHz). Microwave transmissions are considered a *line-of-sight* medium.

MNP   See *Microcom Networking Protocol*.

MNP 1-4   The first four *MNP* levels used for hardware error control. All four levels are incorporated into *V.42*.

MNP 5   The fifth level of *MNP* that incorporates the *MNP 1-4*. Also uses a data compression algorithm that compresses data by a factor of 2 to 1.

MNP 6   The sixth level of *MNP* that supports V.22 *bis* and V.29.

MNP 7   The seventh level of *MNP* that improves *MNP 5*'s data compression algorithm to a 3 to 1 compression factor.

MNP 8   The eighth level of *MNP* that extends *MNP 7*; enables half-duplex devices to operate in full-duplex mode.

MNP 9   The ninth level of *MNP* that is used in a variety of circuits.

MNP 10   The tenth level of *MNP* that is used in cellular modems and in those situations where line quality is poor.

Modem   An acronym for *modulator/demodulator*. A modem transforms (modulates) a computer's digital signal into analog form at the sending side so the signal can be carried across a standard telephone line. On the receiving side, a modem demodulates the signal— it reconverts the transmitted analog signal from the phone line to digital form before it is passed to the computer.

Multicast   A data transmission that is destined to a group of recipients.

Multidrop Design   A network configuration in which each system node is connected to a common cable plant and assigned a specific number that is used to communicate with the system and also to establish priority of when a system will be communicated with from a master control system. Primarily used in factories.

Multilink PPP (MP)   An *IP* protocol that combines multiple physical links (i.e., telephone lines) into a single, high capacity channel. Unlike *BONDING*, which is implemented in hardware, MP is achieved via software. MP is also applicable to analog dialup connections.

Multimode Fiber   A type of fiber-optic cable with a core diameter ranging from 50 μm to 100 μm. In multimode fiber, different rays of light bounce along the fiber at different angles as they travel through the core. This results in some degree of signal distortion at the receiving end. Multimode fiber can be of two types: *graded-index* or *step-index*.

Multiplexer   A device that does *multiplexing*. Also called a *mux* for short.

Multiplexing   A technique used to place multiple signals on a single communications channel. Multiplexing partitions a channel into many separate channels, each capable of transmitting its own independent signal, thereby enabling many different transmissions over a single medium.

Multistation Access Unit (MAU)   A token ring hub.

Mux   Abbreviation for *multiplexer*.

NADH   See *North American Digital Hierarchy.*

NAP   See *Network Access Point.*

National Information Infrastructure (NII)   A Federal policy initiative to facilitate and accelerate the development and utilization of the nation's information infrastructure. The perception of the NII is one of a "seamless web" of telecommunications networks consisting of computers, specialized databases, radios, telephones, televisions, and satellites. The NII is expected to provide consumers with convenient and instantaneous access to nearly any kind of information ranging from research results, to medical and educational material, to entertainment.

NC   See *Network Computer.*

Near End Crosstalk (NEXT)   See *Crosstalk.*

NEXT   See *Near End Crosstalk.*

netstat   A UNIX program that generates a local host's routing table. Similar output can be generated on a Windows NT system using the command *route print.*

Network Access Point (NAP)   An *Internet* traffic exchange point that provides centralized Internet access to Internet service providers. A NAP serves as a critical, regional "switching station" where all different network backbone providers meet and exchange traffic on each other's backbone.

Network Architecture   A formal, logical structure that defines how network devices and software interact and function; defines communication protocols, message formats, and standards required for interoperability.

Network Computer (NC)   An inexpensive ($500 or less) network access device with functionality that allows some applications to be run, but not as complete as what would typically be found on a PC or a workstation of some sort. NCs are stripped-down systems that use the network to access their applications dynamically.

Network Diameter   The overall length between a network's two most remote nodes.

Network Ethics   Specific standards of moral conduct by network users for the responsible use of network devices and resources.

Network Interface Card (NIC)   A layer 2 device that performs standard *data link layer* functions, including organizing data into frames, transferring frames between the ends of a communication channel, and managing the link by providing error control, initialization, control termination, and flow control. A NIC is also known as a *LAN* adapter, network adapter, network card, and network board. When used in Ethernet/802.e networks, a NIC is called an Ethernet card or adapter.

Network Operating System (NOS)   Software that is installed on a system to make it network-capable. Examples include IBM's LAN Server, Banyan's VINES, and Novell's NetWare (also known as IntranetWare). A NOS is independent of a computer's native operating system—it is loaded "on top" of the computer's operating system and provides the computer with networking capability based on a particular protocol. If an operating system provides built-in network support (e.g., Microsoft's Windows NT and Sun's Solaris), then the OS is called a *networkable* operating system.

Network Protocol Suite   A set of related and interoperating network protocols. An example is the *TCP/IP* protocol suite, which consists of protocols for e-mail, web service, file transfers, and routing.

Network Security   Refers to the proper safeguarding of everything associated with a network, including data, media, and equipment. It involves administrative functions, such as *threat assessment*, and technical tools and facilities such as cryptographic products, and network access control products such as *firewalls*. It also involves making certain that network resources are used in accordance with a prescribed policy and only by people who are authorized to use these resources.

Network Service Access Point (NSAP)   An *OSI* addressing mechanism used by private *ATM* networks. NSAPs are 20-byte addresses and include a 13-byte prefix that can be used to identify a specific location including a country, region, or end system.

Network Standards   A formal set of rules, developed by and agreed upon by various organizations, defining hardware interfaces, communication protocols, and network architectures. Several standards exist, including *de jure, de facto, proprietary,* and *consortia.*

Network Termination Unit (NTU)   A device that terminates *E-1* circuits. An NTU provides broadly similar *CSU/DSU* functionality.

Network Topology   The basic design of a computer network that details how key network components such as nodes and links are interconnected.

Next Generation Internet (NGI)   An initiative to forge collaborative partnerships between the private and public sectors. Presumably, the *vBNS* will serve as the medium for NGI. Funding ($100 million for three years) has not been approved as of this writing.

NGI   See *Next Generation Internet.*

NIC   See *Network Interface Card.*

NII   See *National Information Infrastructure.*

Node   Another name for a *device*. Usually used to identify computers that are network hosts, workstations, or servers.

Noise   Any undesirable, extraneous signal in a transmission medium. There are generally two forms of noise—*ambient* and *impulse*. Noise degrades the quality and performance of a communications channel and is one of the most common causes of transmission errors in computer networks.

Nonpersistent CSMA   A *CSMA*-based protocol in which a node continually waits a random period of time whenever it detects a busy channel. Once it senses an idle channel, it may then transmit data.

North American Digital Hierarchy (NADH)   Describes a multiplexed *T1* structure used in North America that combines multiple T1 lines into higher rated T-carrier circuits. For example, a *T2* circuit consists of four multiplexed T1 circuits and has an aggregate bandwidth of 6.312 Mbps; a *T3* link consists of 28 multiplexed T1 circuits with an aggregate bandwidth of 44.736 Mbps; and a *T4* channel consists of 168 multiplexed T1 circuits and is rated at 274.176 Mbps.

NOS   See *Network Operating System.*

NSAP   See *Network Service Access Point.*

nslookup   A UNIX and Microsoft NT program used to acquire the *IP address* of a *domain name*. This program can also be used for IP address resolution, which translates a numerical IP address to its corresponding domain name.

NTU   See *Network Termination Unit.*

1-persistent CSMA   A CSMA-based protocol in which a node continuously monitors a shared channel until it is idle and then seizes the channel and begins transmitting data. The "one" in 1-persistent represents the probability that a single waiting node will be able to transmit data once it detects an idle channel ($p = 1$).

OC   See *Optical Carrier.*

Open Shortest Path First (OSPF)   An *interior gateway protocol* based on a *link-state algorithm.* Designed for large, heterogeneous *IP* networks.

Optical Carrier (OS)   A *fiber-optic* digital transmission hierarchy used for *SONET.* OC rates range from OC-1, which is the equivalent of 28 DS-1 channels (51.84 Mbps) to OC-192, which is the equivalent of 5,376 DS-1 channels (9.953 Gbps). OC rates are the optical equivalent of *STS* rates.

OSI   An abbreviation for Open Systems Interconnection. See *OSI Reference Model.*

OSI Reference Model   A network architecture for developing network protocol standards. The OSI Model formally defines and codifies the concept of *layered* network architecture. It uses well-defined operationally descriptive layers that describe what happens at each stage in the processing of data for transmission. The OSI Model consists of the following seven layers, which are numbered in descending order: Application (7), Presentation (6), Session (5), Transport (4), Network (3), Data Link (2), and Physical (1).

OSPF   See *Open Shortest Path First.*

Oversized Frame   An Ethernet/802.3 frame with more than 1,518 bytes but a valid *CRC checksum.*

Oversubscription   A term used in *frame relay* to denote when the capacity of a frame relay connection into the frame relay network is less than the total bandwidth guaranteed by the provider. More specifically, the *port speed* is less than the aggregate *CIR.*

Packet   The smallest unit of information that is transferred across a packet-switched network. In *TCP/IP* a packet is called a *datagram.*

Packet-Filter Firewall   A *router* or a dedicated device that filters network access at the network layer by examining packet addresses (source and destination), or specific network transport protocol type.

Packet-Switched Network   A network design that enables nodes to share a communications channel via a *virtual circuit.* Messages are partitioned into smaller messages called *packets*, which may contain only a few hundred bytes of data, accompanied by addressing information. Packets are sent to the destination node one at a time, at any time, and not necessarily in a specific order. The network hardware delivers the packets through the virtual circuit to the specified destination node, which is responsible for reassembling them in the correct order.

PAN   See *Personal Area Network.*

Parallel Communication   A data transmission method in which the bits representing a character of data are transmitted simultaneously on separate channels. (Also called *parallel transmission.*)

Parity   Refers to the use of an extra bit (called a *parity bit* or a *redundant bit*) to detect single-bit errors in data transmissions. Parity can be specified as even, odd, or none. Even parity means that there must be an even number of 1-bits in each bit string; odd parity means that there must be an odd number of 1-bits in each bit string; and no parity means that parity is ignored. The extra bit (i.e., the parity bit) is forced to either 0 or 1 to make the total number of bits either even or odd.

Partitioning A network configuration strategy that involves dividing a LAN into several separate (but still interconnected) network segments. Also called *segmentation*.

PBX See *Private Branch Exchange*.

PC Card A layer 2 plug-in adapter used in portable or laptop computers. Three different "types" are available. Type 1 cards are 3.3 millimeters thick and enhance the memory capabilities of a device; Type II cards are 5 mm thick and used for modems and network adapters for both Ethernet and token ring; Type III cards are 10.5 mm thick and generally either miniature hard disks or wireless *NICs*; and Type IV cards, when produced, will be approximately 16 mm thick and support hard disk drives that have a capacity greater than what is currently available from Type III cards. PC cards were formerly known as *PCM-CIA Cards*.

PCM See *Pulse Code Modulation*.

PCMCIA Card A layer 2 device that was originally designed to serve as memory cards for microcomputers. These cards are now known as *PC Cards*. "PCMCIA" stands for Personal Computer Memory Card International Association.

Peer-to-Peer A model or paradigm on which some network communications and applications are based. In a peer-to-peer environment, each networked host runs both the client and server parts of an application.

Period The reciprocal of the frequency. It is the amount of time it takes to complete a single cycle, that is, seconds per cycle.

Permanent Virtual Circuit (PVC) A communications channel that provides a logical connection between two sites instead of a physical one. In a *connection-oriented* protocol such as *frame relay*, PVCs appear as *private links* because a circuit must first be established between end nodes prior to data communications. The difference is PVCs are virtual circuits, not dedicated ones, and hence bandwidth is shared among multiple sites by *multiplexing* techniques. Thus, PVCs provide nondedicated connections through a shared medium, which enables data from multiple sites to be transmitted over the same link concurrently.

Personal Area Network (PAN) A home-based computer network.

PGP See *Pretty Good Privacy*.

Physical Layer The lowest layer (layer 1) of the *OSI Reference Model*. The *physical layer* translates *frames* received from the *data link layer* (layer 2) into electrical, optical, or electromagnetic signals representing 0 and 1 values, or bits. Abbreviated PHY in the documentation.

ping A UNIX and Microsoft NT program used to test the communication path between source and destination nodes. Ping is an *ICMP*-based application and is an acronym for "packet Internet groper."

Pinout The electrical signals associated with each pin and connector. Also called pin assignment.

Plaintext An uncoded message; a message in its original, meaningful (uncoded) form.

Plastic Fiber A type of fiber-optic cable in which the fibers (i.e., conductors) are constructed of plastic instead of glass.

Plenum Cable   Any type of cable that contains an outer sheath or "jacket" that is composed of a Teflon coating. Plenum cable is used for cable "runs" through a return air system. In the case the cable burns during a fire, both PVC and Teflon give off nasty toxic gases when burning. Teflon, however, is fire retardant and takes much longer to get to a burning point.

Point of Presence (POP)   In the context of telecommunications, a POP refers to a telco's central office or switching station.

Point-to-Point Network   A network design in which only adjacent nodes (nodes that are next to each other and only one hop away) can communicate with one another.

Point-to-Point Tunneling Protocol (PPTP)   A protocol that provides encryption and authentication for remote dial-up and LAN-to-LAN connections. PPTP establishes two types of connections: A control session for establishing and maintaining a secure tunnel from sender to receiver, and a data session for the actual data transmission.

POP   See *Point of Presence*. Usually refers to a telco's central office or switching station.

Port Connection   A term used in *frame relay* to denote the *local loop*. Also called *access line*.

Port Speed   A term commonly used in *frame relay* to denote the data transmission rate in bits per second of the *local loop*.

POTS   An abbreviation for *plain old telephone system*.

PPTP   See *Point-to-Point Tunneling Protocol*.

Pretty Good Privacy (PGP)   A *public key* application developed by Phil Zimmerman for e-mail security.

PRI   An acronym for *primary rate interface*, which is an *ISDN* primary access channel that comprises either 23 (United States) or 30 (Europe) 64 Mbps B channels and one 64 kbps D channel. Commonly written as $23B + D$, or $30B + D$.

Private Branch Exchange (PBX)   A telephone exchange used within an organization to provide internal telephone extensions and access to the public telephone network; it is the modern day equivalent of what used to be called a switchboard.

Private Link   A term used to describe a communications channel that provides a private, dedicated link between two sites. Also commonly referred to as standard leased line.

Private Switch   A term used to describe one application of an Ethernet switch. A private switch supports only one *MAC* address per port, which provides each node with its own dedicated 10 Mbps segment. This eliminates contention for the cable, thereby liberating the end nodes from performing collision detection.

Promiscuous Mode   A state in which an Ethernet interface can be placed so that it can capture every frame that is transmitted on the network. For example, an *Ethernet NIC* set in promiscuous mode collects all messages placed on the medium regardless of their destination address.

Propagation Delay   The amount of time a signal takes getting from one point in a circuit to another.

Proprietary Standards   Network standards that are developed in a manufacturer-specific manner. Their specifications are not in the public domain and are only used and accepted by a specific vendor.

Protocol An accepted or established set of procedures, rules, or formal specifications governing specific behavior or language. When applied to networks, a *network protocol* is a formal specification that defines the vocabulary and rules of data communication.

Proxy Server A device or product that provides network protection at the application level by using custom programs for each protected application. These custom-written application programs act as both a client and server and effectively serve as proxies to the actual applications. Also called application gateway firewall or proxy gateway.

PSTN See *Public Switched Telephone Network.*

Public Key A special code, available in the public domain, that can be used to code and decode messages.

Public Switched Telephone Network (PSTN) The traditional analog-based telephone system used in the United States that was originally designed for voice transmissions.

Pulse Code Modulation (PCM) A coding technique used to convert analog signals to digital signals and vice versa.

PVC See *Permanent Virtual Circuit.* Also and abbreviation for polyvinyl chloride.

PVC Cable Any type of cable that contains an outer sheath or "jacket" that is composed of polyvinyl chloride (PVC). Also called *non-plenum cable.*

QoS See *Quality of Service.*

Quality of Service (QoS) Parameters associated with data prioritization that specify such things as the amount of bandwidth a priority data transmission requires as well as the maximum amount of latency the transmission can tolerate in order for the transmission to be meaningful. QoS is needed for transmitting real-time voice and video traffic.

RA See *Routing Arbiter.*

Radio Frequencies (RF) A generic term used to describe a transmission method that uses electromagnetic waveforms.

Radio Transmission Refers to any wireless technique that uses *RF* to transmit information.

RADSL See *Rate-Adaptive Digital Subscriber Line.*

Random Access Protocol A network protocol that governs how nodes are to act in those instances where accessing a shared medium at will, on a first-come, first-served basis is permitted. Also called *contention protocol.*

Rate-Adaptive Digital Subscriber Line (RADSL) A *DSL* variant that provides transmission rates similar to *ADSL.* Transmission rates can be adjusted based on distance and line quality. Up to 7 Mbps downstream rate.

RBOC See *Regional Bell Operating Company.*

Redundancy Bits Extra bits incorporated into a data frame that provide error correction information. A data set composed of both user data and redundancy bits is called a *code-word.* Also called *check bits.*

Regional Bell Operating Company (RBOC) A regional telephone company in the United States formed after the AT&T breakup in 1984.

Reliable Service A type of service that requires a sending node to acknowledge receipt of data. This is called an acknowledged datagram service.

Repeater A layer 1 device that provides both physical and electrical connections. Their function is to regenerate and propagate signals—they receive signals from one cable segment, regenerate, re-time, and amplify them, and then transmit these "revitalized" signals to another cable segment. Repeaters extend the diameter of Ethernet/802.3 networks but are considered to be part of the same collision domain.

Request For Comments (RFC) The working notes of the Internet research and development community. RFCs provide network researchers and designers a medium for documenting and sharing new ideas, network protocol concepts, and other technically-related information. They contain meeting notes from Internet organizations, describe various Internet protocols and experiments, and detail standards specifications. All Internet standards are published as RFCs (not all RFCs are Internet standards, though).

Resource Reservation Protocol (RSVP) A layer 3 protocol developed by *IETF* to provide a mechanism to control network latency for specific applications. This is done by prioritizing data and allocating sufficient bandwidth for data transmission. RSVP can be thought of as an IP-based *QoS* protocol.

RF See *Radio Frequencies.*

RFC See *Request For Comments.*

Ring Design A network design that is based on a broadcast topology in which nodes are connected to a physical ring and data messages are transferred around the ring in either a clockwise or counterclockwise manner (or both).

RIP See *Routing Internet Protocol.* A distance-vector algorithm that determines the best route by using a *hops* metric. RIP was at one time the *de facto* standard for IP routing.

RIP-2 An updated version of *RIP*, formally known as "RIP version 2." New features include authentication, interpretation of *IGP* and *BGP* routes, *subnet mask* support, and multicasting support.

Risk Analysis The assessment of how much a loss is going to cost a company.

RJ A designation that refers to a specific series of connectors defined in the Universal Service Order Code (USOC) definitions of telephone circuits. "RJ" is telephone lingo for "registered jack."

RJ-11 A four-wire modular connector used for telephones.

RJ-45 An eight-wire modular connector used in 10BASE-T LANs.

Router A layer 3 device that is responsible for determining the appropriate path a packet takes to reach its destination. Commonly referred to as *gateway.*

Routing A layer 3 function that directs data packets from source to destination.

Routing Arbiter (RA) A project that facilitates the exchange of network traffic among various independent Internet backbones. Special servers that contain routing information databases of network routes are maintained so that the transfer of traffic among the various backbone providers meeting at a *NAP* is facilitated.

Routing Internet Protocol (RIP) A distance-vector algorithm that determines the best route by using a *hops* metric. RIP was at one time the *de facto* standard for IP routing.

Routing Protocol A specific *protocol* that determines the route a packet should take from source to destination. Routing protocols are a function of network protocols. For example, if your network protocol is *TCP/IP*, then several routing protocol options are available including *RIP*, *RIP-2*, and *OSPF*. If your network protocol is OSI's CNLP, then your routing protocol is IS-IS. Routing protocols determine the "best" path a packet should take when it travels through a network from source to destination, and maintain routing tables that contain information about the network's topology. Routing protocols rely on routing algorithms to calculate the least-cost path from source to destination.

Routing Table A data structure that contains, among others, the destination address of a node or network, known router addresses, and the network interface associated with a particular router address. When a router receives a packet it looks at the packet's destination address to identify the destination network, searches its routing table for an entry corresponding to this destination, and then forwards the packet to the next router via the appropriate interface.

RSA A *public key* encryption algorithm for encoding data. The abbreviation stands for Rivest, Shamir, and Adleman, the last names of the three individuals who designed it.

RSVP See *Resource Reservation Protocol*.

Runt Frame An Ethernet/802.3 frame that has at least 8 bytes but less than 64 bytes long and have a valid CRC checksum.

SAN See *Storage Area Network*.

SAS See *Single-Attachment Station*.

Satellite Communication System An *RF*-based broadcast network design involving Earth ground stations and orbiting communication satellites. Data transmissions from a land-based antenna to the satellite (called the uplink) are generally point-to-point, but all nodes that are part of the network are able to receive the satellite's transmissions (called the downlink).

SC Connector A TIA/EIA-568A standard connector for fiber-optic cable; also called a *568SC connector*.

SDH See *Synchronous Digital Hierarchy*.

SDSL See *Symmetric Digital Subscriber Line*.

Segmentation See *Partitioning*.

Serial Communication A data transmission method in which the bits representing a character of data are transmitted in sequence, one bit at a time, over a single communications channel. (Also referred to as *serial transmission*.)

Server A networked device that provides resources to *client* machines. Examples include print servers, mail servers, file servers, and web servers. Servers are shared by more than one user; clients have only a single user.

Service Profile Identification (SPID) Numbers assigned by the telcos and used to identify the various processes of an *ISDN* device. (Used only in North America.)

Shannon's Limit A mathematical theorem that describes a model for determining the maximum data rate of a noisy, analog communications channel. Shannon's Limit is given by the following formula, Maximum Data Rate *(MDR)* = $H \log_2(1 + \frac{S}{N})$, where *MDR* is given in bits per second, H = bandwidth in Hertz, and $\frac{S}{N}$ is a measure of the *signal-to-noise ratio*. Named for the mathematician who derived it, Claude Shannon.

Shielded Twisted Pair (STP) Twisted pair cable in which individual wire pairs are shielded (i.e., protected from *noise*).

Signal-to-Noise Ratio (SNR) A measure of signal quality expressed in decibels (dB). It is the ratio of signal strength to background noise on a cable. More specifically, SNR is the ratio between the desired signal and the unwanted noise in a communications medium.

Signal Quality Error (SQE) A signal generated by a transceiver and read by the controller of the host to which the transceiver is connected. In V2.0 Ethernet, SQE is called *heartbeat* and is generated periodically to inform the host's controller that the transceiver is "alive." In IEEE 802.3, SQE is only generated when a real signal quality error occurs.

Simplex Communication A data transmission method in which data may flow in only one direction; one device assumes the role of sender and the other assumes the role of receiver. These roles are fixed and cannot be reversed. An example of a simplex communication is a television transmission.

Single-Attachment Station (SAS) An FDDI node that is connected to only the primary pair of fibers and can be isolated from the network in the case of some types of failure. An SAS is also called a *Class B* node.

Single Mode Fiber A type of fiber-optic cable with a core diameter ranging from 7 μm to 9 μm. In single mode fiber, only a single ray of light, called the *axial ray*, can pass. Thus, a light wave entering the fiber exits with very little distortion, even at very long distances and very high data rates.

SIP See *SMDS Interface Protocol*.

SMA Connector A fiber-optic cable connector that meets military specifications.

Smart Card A type of "credit card" with embedded integrated circuits that store information in electronic form and used for authentication. Similar to a *digital certificate*.

SMDS An acronym for *switched multimegabit data service*, a cell-based, connectionless, high-speed, public, packet-switched, broadband, metropolitan area data network.

SMDS Interface Protocol (SIP) *SMDS* protocol that consists of three different levels: SIP Level 3, SIP Level 2, and SIP Level 1. These three protocol levels are similar in function to the first three layers of the *OSI* model but represent SMDS's MAC sublayer and hence operate at the data link layer.

SNR See *Signal-to-Noise Ratio*.

SOHO An abbreviation for *small office/home office*.

SONET See *Synchronous Optical Network*.

Spanning Tree A single path between source and destination nodes that does not include any loops. It is a loop-free subset of a network's topology. The spanning tree algorithm, specified in IEEE 802.1d, describes how bridges (and switches) can communicate to avoid network loops.

SPID See *Service Profile Identification*.

Split-Horizon A strategy employed by *RIP* to insure that a router never sends routing information back in the direction from which it came. Used to prevent routing loops.

Split-Horizon with Poisoned Reverse A modified *split-horizon* strategy in which routing information provided by a neighbor is included in updates sent back to that neighbor. Such routes are assigned a cost factor of infinity, which makes the network unreachable.

Spread Spectrum A radio technology that refers to a security technique. Spread spectrum transmission camouflages data by mixing signals with a pseudonoise (PN) pattern and transmitting the real signal with the PN pattern. The transmission signal is spread over a range of the frequencies in radio spectrum.

SQE See *Signal Quality Error.*

Statistical Multiplexing A *multiplexing* technique that allocates part of a channel's capacity only to those nodes that require it (i.e., have data to transmit). Based on the premise that, statistically, not all devices necessarily require a portion of the channel at exactly the same time.

Stackable Repeater Hub Individual repeater units "stacked" one on top of another. Instead of using a common shared backplane, stackable hubs use a "pseudo-backplane" based on a common connector interface. An external cable interconnects the individual hubs in a daisy-chained manner. Once interconnected, the entire chain of hubs becomes a single logical unit that functions as a single repeater.

Stacking Height The maximum number of stackable repeater hubs permitted.

Standby Monitor A station (i.e., node) on a token ring network that oversees the *active monitor.* Except for the active monitor, all token ring nodes are standby monitors.

Star A network configuration characterized by the presence of a central processing hub, which serves as a wire center for connecting nodes. All data must pass through the hub in order for nodes to communicate with each other.

Stateful Firewall A device or product that monitors all transactions between two systems and is capable of (1) identifying a specific condition in the transaction between two applications, (2) predicting what should transpire next in the transaction, and (3) detecting when normal operational "states" of the connection are being violated.

Static Route A fixed route that is entered into a router's *routing table* either manually or via a software configuration program.

ST Connector Similar to a *BNC connector* but used with *fiber-optic cable*.

Step-index Multimode Fiber A type of multimode fiber in which light pulses are guided along the cable from source to destination by reflecting off the cladding.

STM See *Synchronous Transport Module*.

Storage Area Network (SAN) A network dedicated exclusively for storing data. Usually involves *Fibre Channel* technology.

Store-and-Forward A method used by bridges and switches in which the contents of an entire frame are captured by the device before a decision is made to filter or forward the frame. A store-and-forward network switch is also called a *buffering switch*. A network that based on this principle is called a *store-and-forward network*.

STP (Shielded Twisted Pair) See *Twisted Pair Cable*.

STS See *Synchronous Transport Signal*.

Subnet Mask A special network address used to identify a specific subnetwork. Using a unique bit combination, a mask partitions an address into a network ID and a host ID.

Subnetting Refers to the partitioning of a network address space into separate, autonomous *subnetworks*. Key to subnetting is a network's *subnet mask*.

Subnetwork Refers to a network segment. Commonly abbreviated as *subnet*.

SVC See *Switched Virtual Circuit*.

Switch A network device that filters or forwards data based on specific information. A layer 2 switch (e.g., an Ethernet switch), filters or forwards frames from one node to another using Mac-level (i.e., hardware) addresses; a layer 3 switch filters or forwards packets based on network addresses; and layer 4 (or higher) switches filter or forward messages based on specific application protocols. Forwarding rates are usually done at wire speed and via "private" connections, i.e., no other node "sees" the traffic. Switches partition Ethernet/802.3 networks into multiple collision domains.

Switched Ethernet An Ethernet/802.3 LAN that is based on network switches instead of repeaters or bridges. A switched Ethernet LAN isolates network traffic between sending and receiving nodes from all other connected nodes. It also transforms traditional Ethernet/802.3 from a broadcast technology to a point-to-point technology.

Switched Virtual Circuit (SVC) A circuit between source and destination nodes that is established on the fly and then removed after data communications have ended. SVCs are logical, dynamic connections instead of logical permanent connections as with *PVCs*. Thus, SVCs provide switched, on-demand connectivity.

Symmetric Digital Subscriber Line (SDSL) A *DSL* variant in which traffic is transmitted at same rate in each direction. Maximum transmission rate is 768 kbps. Uses single-wire pair. Telephone service not supported. Suitable for videoconferencing.

Synchronous Communication A data communication method that requires sending and receiving nodes to monitor each other's transmissions so that the receiving node always knows when a new character is being sent. In this instance, the sending and receiving nodes are "in synch" with each other.

Synchronous Digital Hierarchy (SDH) An *ITU physical layer* standard that provides an international specification for high-speed digital transmission via optical fiber. SDH incorporates *SONET* and uses the *STM* signal hierarchy as its basic building block. SDH is essentially the same as SONET. At OC-3 rates and higher, the two are virtually identical.

Synchronous Optical Network (SONET) An ANSI *physical layer* standard that provides an international specification for high-speed digital transmission via optical fiber. At the source interface, signals are converted from electrical to optical form. They are then converted back to electrical form at the destination interface. The basic building block of the SONET signal hierarchy is *STS-1* (51.84 Mbps). See also *SDH*.

Synchronous Transport Module (STM) Represents a digital transmission carrier system used for *SDH*. STM rates range from STM-1, which is equivalent to OC-3 (155.52 Mbps) to STM-64, which is equivalent to OC-192 (9.953 Gbps).

Synchronous Transport Signal (STS) A digital transmission hierarchy used for *SONET*. STS rates range from STS-1, which is the equivalent of 28 DS-1 channels (51.84 Mbps) to STS-192, which is the equivalent of 5,376 DS-1 channels (9.953 Gbps). STS rates are the electrical equivalent of *OC* rates.

T-1 Describes the multiplexing of 24 separate voice channels, each rated at 64 kbps, plus one 8 kbps framing channel, into a single, wideband digital signal rated at 1.544 Mbps.

T-2 A multiplexed circuit that combines 4 *T1* circuits and has an aggregate bandwidth of 6.312 Mbps.

T-3 A multiplexed circuit that combines 28 *T1* circuits and has an aggregate bandwidth of 44.736 Mbps.

T-4   A multiplexed circuit that combines 168 *T1* circuits and has an aggregate bandwidth of 274.176 Mbps.

TCP   See *Transmission Control Protocol.*

TCP/IP   An abbreviation for *Transmission Control Protocol/Internet Protocol.* Refers to a formal network protocol suite based on its two namesake sub-protocols, *TCP* and *IP.*

TDM   See *Time Division Multiplexing.*

TE   See *Terminal Equipment.*

Telco   An acronym for *telephone company.*

Terminal Adapter (TA)   A device that connects noncompatible ISDN devices to an ISDN network. If a TA is used for an ISDN dialup connection, then it can be thought of as a modem. If a TA is used to connect a device to a LAN, then it can be thought of as a network interface card. It should be noted that although a TA is frequently referred to as an ISDN modem or digital modem in the context of an ISDN dialup connection, this reference is incorrect. By definition, a modem performs analog-to-digital and digital-to-analog conversions. Since ISDN is completely digital, no such conversions are necessary, so the expressions "ISDN modem" or "digital modem" are thus incongruous.

Terminal Equipment (TE)   Represents a specific communication device that connects to an *ISDN* network. Two TEs are referenced in the specification: *TE1* refers to an ISDN-compatible device (e.g., digital telephone or a computer with a built-in ISDN port), and *TE2* refers to a non-compatible ISDN device (e.g., an analog telephone or a computer without a built-in ISDN port).

Terminator   Layer 1 device that prevents signal reflections by providing electrical resistance at the end of a cable to "absorb" signals to keep them from bouncing back and being heard again by the devices connected to the cable.

Thick Ethernet   Describes IEEE 802.3 10BASE5, which uses "thick" coaxial cable (outer diameter between 0.375-inch and 0.405-inch) as its physical medium.

Thin Ethernet   Describes IEEE 802.3 10BASE2, which uses "thin" coaxial cable (outer diameter between 0.175-inch and 0.195-inch) as its physical medium.

Threat Assessment   An activity that involves determining how much security is necessary for proper control of system and network assets. Threat assessment is guided by answering the overriding question, "What assets are critical to the operation of my network and who do I think would want access to them?"

Throughput   A realistic measure of the amount of data transmitted between two nodes in a given time period. It is a function of hardware/software speed, CPU power, overhead, and many other items. Compared to *bandwidth*, throughput is what the channel really achieves, where bandwidth is what is theoretically possible.

Time Division Multiplexing (TDM)   A multiplexing technique that assigns to each node connected to a channel an identification number and a small amount of time in which to transmit. TDM-based transmissions are serially sequenced.

Token   A special frame on a token ring or token bus network. Possession of the token permits a node to transmit data.

Token Bus   A local area network technology based on a token-passing protocol for media access. Defined in IEEE 802.4. A token bus network is characterized as a logical ring on a physical bus—physically, the network resembles a bus topology, but logically, the network is arranged as a ring with respect to passing the token from node to node.

Token Passing Protocol A network protocol that requires nodes to first possess a special frame, called a *token*, prior to transmitting data. Token-passing schemes are both contention-free and collision-free.

Token Ring A local area network technology based on a token-passing protocol for media access control. Defined by IEEE 802.5. A token ring LAN is implemented either as a logical ring using a physical ring topology, or as a logical ring structure arranged in a physical star configuration.

traceroute A UNIX program that depicts the gateways a packet transverses. A corresponding Microsoft NT command is called *tracert*.

Transceiver A service used in Ethernet/802.3 networks to connect nodes to the physical medium. Transceivers serve as both the physical connection and the electrical interface between a node and the physical medium, enabling the node to communicate with the medium. Transceivers transmit and receive signals simultaneously.

Transmission Control Protocol (TCP) A layer 4 connection-oriented protocol that performs several functions, including: providing for reliable transmission of data by furnishing end-to-end error detection and correction; guaranteeing that data are transferred across a network accurately and in the proper sequence; retransmitting any data not received by the destination node; and guaranteeing against data duplication between sending and receiving nodes. It is the "TCP" of *TCP/IP*.

Tree A network configuration in which nodes are connected to one another in a hierarchical fashion. A root node or hub is connected to second level nodes or hubs; second-level devices are connected to third-level devices, which in turn are connected to fourth-level devices, and so forth.

Triple DES A variant of *DES* that uses three DES operations instead of one.

Tunneling See *encapsulation*.

Twisted Pair Cable A type of copper cable that uses at least two insulated copper wires that have been twisted together. There are two basic type: *unshielded twisted pair (UTP)* and *shielded twisted pair (STP)*.

UDP See *User Datagram Protocol*.

UDSL See *Universal Digital Subscriber Line*.

UNI See *User-to-Network Interface*. An end node's port where the *local loop* terminates at a customer's site.

Unicast A data transmission that is destined to a single recipient.

Universal Digital Subscriber Line (UDSL) A *DSL* variant that provides symmetrical service at 2 Mbps each way.

Unreliable Service A network service type that requires no acknowledgment of receipt of data from the receiving node to the sending node. This is called a *datagram service*.

Unshielded Twisted Pair (UTP) Twisted pair cable in which individual wire pairs are not shielded (i.e., protected from *noise*).

User Datagram Protocol (UDP)   A connectionless protocol providing an unreliable datagram service. UDP does not furnish any end-to-end error detection or correction, and it does not retransmit any data it did not receive.

User-to-Network Interface (UNI)   An end node's port where the *local loop* terminates at a customer's site.

Utilization   A network performance measure that specifies the amount of time a LAN spends successfully transmitting data. *Average utilization* means that over some period of time (e.g., a 10-hour period), on average, a certain percent of the LAN's capacity is used for successfully transmitting data. *Peak utilization* means that at a specific moment in time, a certain percent of the LAN's capacity was utilized.

UTP   See *Unshielded Twisted Pair.*

V.22 *bis*   ITU-T standard for 2400 bps full-duplex modems; cycles to 1200 bps/600 bps.

V.29   ITU-T standard for 9600 bps facsimile service.

V.32   ITU-T standard for 9600 bps modems; cycles to 4800 bps when line quality degrades, and cycles forward when line quality improves.

V.32 *bis*   ITU-T standard that extends *V.32* to 7200, 12,000, and 14,400 bps; cycles to lower rate when line quality degrades; cycles forward when line quality improves.

V.32 *ter*   Pseudo-standard that extends *V.32 bis* to 19,200 bps and 21,600 bps.

V.34   ITU-T standard for 28,800 bps modems. (*Note:* V.34 modems upgraded with special software can achieve data rates of 31,200 bps or 33,600 bps.)

V.FAST   Proprietary, pseudo-standard from Hayes and Rockwell for modems transmitting at data rates up to 28,800 bps; served as a migration path for *V.34*

V.42   ITU-T standard for modem *error correction*. Uses *LAPM* as the primary error-correcting protocol, with *MNP* classes 1 through 4 as an alternative.

V.42 *bis*   ITU-T standard that enhances *V.42* by incorporating the British Telecom Lempel Ziv data *compression* technique to V.42 *error correction*. Most *V.32, V.32 bis,* and *V.34* compliant modems come with V.42 or V.42 bis or MNP.

V.90   ITU-T standard for 57,600 bps modems (commonly called "56K modems") in which asymmetric data rates apply (i.e., the send and receive rates are different). Depending on telephone line conditions, upstream rates (send) are restricted to 33,600 bps, and downstream rates (receive) are restricted to 57,600 bps. V.90 modems are designed for connections that are digital at one end and have involve only two analog-digital conversions each way.

vBNS   See *Very High Speed Backbone Network Service.*

VCC   See *Virtual Channel Circuit.*

VCI   See *Virtual Channel Identifier.*

VDSL   See *Very High-speed Digital Subscriber Line.*

Very High-speed Backbone Network Service (vBNS)   A National Science Foundation-funded research and educational network. The vBNS is a nationwide backbone network that currently operates at 622 Mbps (OC-12) and is accessible to only those involved in high-bandwidth research activities. The backbone is expected to be upgraded to OC-48 (2.488 Gbps) in 1999.

Very high-speed Digital Subscriber Line (VDSL) A *DSL* variant that provide asymmetric service over fiber. Downstream rates range from 13 Mbps to 52 Mbps; upstream rates range from 1.5 Mbps to 2.3 Mbps. Suitable for Internet/intranet access, video-on-demand, database access, remote LAN access, and high-definition TV

Virtual Channel Connection (VCC) A virtual circuit that provides a logical connection between an *ATM* source and destination. Data can only be transmitted in one direction via a VCC. A VCC is denoted by a *virtual channel identifier (VCI)*, which is included as part of the ATM cell header. Multiple virtual channels that share the same connection can be packaged into a single *virtual path.*

Virtual Channel Identifier (VCI) A parameter used to identify *ATM virtual channels*. VCI information is carried within an ATM cell header.

Virtual Circuit A nondedicated connection through a shared medium that gives the high-level user the appearance of a dedicated, direct connection from the source node to the destination node.

Virtual Local Area Network (VLAN) A network consisting of nodes that are not physically connected to the same medium. Instead, they are connected in a virtual sense using specially designed software that groups several ports in a switch into a single workgroup. Nodes connected to these ports are considered to be part of a workgroup, and network traffic from any node/port is (usually) limited to only those nodes or ports assigned to the workgroup

Virtual Path Connection (VPC) A semi-permanent connection that provides a logical collection of *ATM virtual channels* that have the same end points. More specifically, a VPC carries a group of virtual channels all of which have the same end points. Virtual paths enable any connection that uses the same network path from source to destination to be bundled into a single unit. A *virtual path identifier (VPI)* denotes a virtual path and is included in a cell's header. A virtual path can also provide a form of traffic control by logically (not physically) partitioning network traffic based on the type of data being carried and associated *quality of service*.

Virtual Path Identifier (VPI) A parameter used to identify *ATM virtual path*. VPI information is carried within an ATM cell header.

Virtual Private Network (VPN) Refers to an *IP* connection between two sites over a public IP network that has its payload traffic encrypted so that only source and destination nodes can decrypt the traffic packets. A VPN enables a publicly accessible network to be used for highly confidential, dynamic, and secure data transmissions.

VLAN See *Virtual Local Area Network.*

VOFR See *Voice Over Frame Relay.*

VOIP See *Voice Over IP.*

Voice Over Frame Relay (VOFR) Refers to transmitting voice signals over a *frame relay* network.

Voice Over IP (VOIP) A technology that enables users to place telephone calls across the Internet.

VPC See *Virtual Path Connection.*

VPI See *Virtual Path Identifier.*

VPN See *Virtual Private Network.*

WAN   See *Wide Area Network*.

Wavelength   A measure of the length of a wave. It is the distance an electrical or light signal travels in one complete cycle.

Wavelength Division Multiplexing (WDM)   A *multiplexing* method used with fiber-optic cables. Involves the simultaneous transmission of light sources over a single fiber-optic channel. Light sources of different wavelengths are combined by a WDM multiplexer and transmitted over a single line. When the signals arrive, a WDM demultiplexer separates them and transmits them to their respective destination receivers.

WDM   See *Wavelength Division Multiplexing*.

Wide Area Network (WAN)   A network that interconnects computing resources that are widely separated geographically (usually over 100 km). This includes towns, cities, states, and countries. A WAN generally spans an area greater than five miles (eight kilometers). A WAN can be thought of as consisting of a collection of *LANs*.

Wire   A general term used to describe the physical layer of a network. The three main physical attributes of wire are *conductor, insulation,* and *outer jacket*. Wire also has three important electrical characteristics that can directly affect the quality of the signal transmitted across it: *capacitance, impedance,* and *attenuation*. Signal quality is affected most by the combination of attenuation and capacitance. The two primary forms of wire are copper and fiber. Also called *cable*.

Wireless Communications   A type of communications in which signals travel through space instead of through a physical cable. There are two general types of wireless communication: *radio transmission* and *infrared transmission*.

Wireless LAN (WLAN)   A *LAN* consisting of nodes that rely on *wireless communication* techniques for transmitting or receiving data. Specified by *IEEE 802.11*.

Wire Speed   A unit of measure used to describe a device's maximum (i.e., fastest) filtering and forwarding rates. In Ethernet/802.3, wire speed is equal to 14,880 frames per second. This is frequently reported as 14,880 packets per second. (See Box 8-3.)

WLAN   See *Wireless LAN*.

Workgroup Switch   A term used to describe one application of an Ethernet switch. A workgroup switch partitions a single, shared medium into multiple, shared media and supports more than MAC address per port. Also called *segment switches*.

Workstation   A computer system that has its own operating system and is connected to a network. A workstation can be a personal computer such as a Macintosh or Intel-based PC, a graphics workstation such as those manufactured by Sun Microsystems, a super-minicomputer such as IBM's AS/400, a super-microcomputer such as DEC's Alpha, or a mainframe such as an IBM ES-9000. Also called *host, server, desktop,* or *client*.

XA-SMDS   See *Exchange Access SMDS*.

Bibliography

Chapter 1: Elements of Computer Networking

Aiken, R. J., and J. S. Cavallini. 1994. Standards—When Is It Too Much of a Good Thing? *Connexions: The Interoperability Report* 8 (8): 18–33.

Comer, D. E. 1991. *Internetworking with TCP/IP Volume 1: Principles, Protocols, and Architecture.* Upper Saddle River, NJ: Prentice Hall.

Conrad, J. W. 1988. Communications Standards Organizations. In *Handbook of Communication Systems Management,* ed. J. W. Conrad, 227–36. Boston: Auerbach Publishers.

Gallo, M., and R. Nenno. 1985. *Computers and Society with Basic and Pascal.* Boston: PWS.

Hancock, B. 1989. *Network Concepts and Architectures.* Wellesley, MA: QED Information Sciences.

Kaufman, F. 1977. *Distributed Processing.* Newark: Coopers & Lybrand.

Martin, R. 1996. Intranets Taking over Communication Business. *Cisco World,* November, 12–13.

Milne, J. 1998. State of the NOS. *Network Computing,* 1 February, 50–77.

Molta, D. 1996. NC: Network Computer or No Contest. *Networking Computing,* 1 December, 153–54.

Schaeffer, H. 1987. *Data Center Operations: A Guide to Effective Planning, Processing, and Performance.* Upper Saddle River, NJ: Prentice Hall.

Stamper, D. A. 1991. *Business Data Communications.* Redwood City, CA: Benjamin/Cummings.

Stevens, W. R. 1990. *UNIX Network Programming.* Upper Saddle River, NJ: Prentice Hall.

Tanenbaum, A. S. 1988. *Computer Networks.* Upper Saddle River, NJ: Prentice Hall.

Vaughn-Nichols, S. J. 1996. The NC Follies: A Network Computer Is a Small Idea. *Internet World,* December, 72–73.

Wittmann, A. 1997. Pssst, Buddy! Wanna Buy a Network Computer. *Network Computing,* 15 January, 117.

Woods, L. D. 1988. Management Issues in Distributed Data Processing. In *Handbook of Communication Systems Management*, ed. J. W. Conrad, 47–57. Boston: Auerbach Publishers.

Chapter 2: Network Topologies, Architectures, and the OSI Model

Abrams, M. D. 1982a. *Computer Networking Tutorial*. Rockville, MD: Computer Network Associates.

———. 1982b. *Data Communications Tutorial*. Rockville, MD: Computer Network Associates.

Ambort, D. 1990. Standards from Where? *LANtimes*, July, 61–64.

Conrad, J. W. 1988a. Open Systems Interconnection. In *Handbook of Communication Systems Management*, ed. J. W. Conrad. 237–51. Boston: Auerbach Publishers.

———. 1988b. Application of Data Communications Protocol Standards. In *Handbook of Communication Systems Management*, ed. J. W. Conrad. 253–66. Boston: Auerbach Publishers.

———. 1988c. Standards and Architecture for Local Area Networks. In *Handbook of Communication Systems Management*, ed. J. W. Conrad. 291–97. Boston: Auerbach Publishers.

Fisher, S. 1990. OSI Across the Water. *LANtimes*, July, 70.

Hancock, B. 1989. *Network Concepts and Architectures*. Wellesley, MA: QED Information Sciences.

Higgins, K. J. 1994. How Evolution of TCP/IP Eclipsed OSI. *Open Systems Today*, 9 May, 54.

Malamud, C. 1991. TCP/IP—A Dependable Networking Infrastructure. *Networking Computing*, April, 84–86.

Martin, J., and K. Chapman. 1989. *Local Area Networks: Architectures and Implementations*. Upper Saddle River, NJ: Prentice Hall.

McCloghrie, K., and M. T. Rose. 1994. Back to Basics: The Internet Transport Layer. *Connexions: The Interoperability Report*, June, 2–9.

Miller, M. A., 1992. *Troubleshooting TCP/IP: Analyzing the Protocols of the Internet*. San Mateo, CA: M&T Books.

Noor, A. I. 1988. Comparisons of Internetworking Architectures. In *Handbook of Communication Systems Management*, ed. J. W. Conrad. 267–76. Boston: Auerbach Publishers.

Postel, J. 1981. Internet Protocol. *RFC-791*, September.

Quarterman, J. S., and J. C. Hoskins. 1986. Notable Computer Networks. *Communications of the* ACM, 10, 932–71.

Spencer, L. T. 1990. Defining the OSI Model. *LANtimes*, September, 59.

Tanenbaum, A. S. 1988. *Computer Networks*. Upper Saddle River, NJ: Prentice Hall.

Chapter 3: The Internet and TCP/IP

"The National Information Infrastructure: Agenda for Action." 1993. 58 Federal Regulation 49,025, 21 September.

Albitz, P., and C. Liu. 1992. *DNS and BIND*. Sebastopol, CA: O'Reilly & Associates.

Auerbach, K., and C. Wellens. 1995. Internet Evolution or Revolution? *LAN*, October, 60–65.

Baker, S. 1993a. The Evolving Internet Backbone. *UNIX Review*, September, 15–21.

———. 1993b. Joining the Internet Club. *UNIX Review*, October, 23–33.

Banta, G. 1996. Internet Pipe Schemes. *Internet World,* October, 62–70.

Bradner, S., and A. Mankin. 1995. The Recommendation for the IP Next Generation Protocol. *RFC 1752.*

Brown, R. 1993. TCP/IP: Reliable Glue for Enterprise Networks. *Networking Management,* June, 76–80.

Callon R. 1987. A Proposal for a Next Generation Internet Protocol. *Proposal to X3S3,* December.

Collinson, P. 1993. IP. *SunExpert Magazine,* October, 34–40.

Comer, D. E. 1991. *Internetworking with TCP/IP Volume 1: Principles, Protocols, and Architecture.* Upper Saddle River, NJ: Prentice Hall.

Cooper, L. F. 1996. Controlled Chaos at Work—The Commercialization of the Internet. *Communications Week,* 1 April, issue 603.

Cray, A. 1998. Voice over IP: Here's How. *Data Communications,* April, 44–58.

Dutcher, W. 1997. IP Addressing: Playing the Numbers. *Data Communications,* 21 March, 69–74.

Farrow, R., and R. Power. 1998. Internet Security: Trouble in the Stack. *Network Magazine,* May, 95–96.

Fenton, B. 1997. Death of the Internet. *Popular Mechanics,* January, 41–44.

Hall, E., and D. Willis. 1998. VOIP in the Enterprise. *Networking Computing,* 1 October, 41–62.

Held, G. 1997. IP for the Next Generation. *Network,* July, 65–70.

Hinden, R. M. 1996. IP Next Generation Overview. *Communications of the ACM,* 39 (6): 61–71.

Hudgins-Bonafield, C. 1995. How Will the Internet Grow? *Network Computing,* 1 March, 80–91.

———. 1996. The Prospect of IP Renumbering. *Network Computing,* 1 June, 84–92.

Huitema, C. 1994. The H Ratio for Address Assignment Efficiency. *RFC-1715,* November.

Hurley, H. 1998. Value-Added ISPs. *Network Magazine,* 35–38.

Karvé, A. 1997. IP Multicast Streams to Life. *Network Magazine,* October, 53–58.

———. 1998. IP Telephony Finds Its Voice. *Network Magazine,* January, 57–61.

Kleinrock, L. 1992. Technology Issues in the Design of the NREN. In *Building Information Infrastructure,* ed. Brian Kahin. 174–98. New York: McGraw-Hill Primis.

Krol, E. 1993. FYI on "What Is the Internet?" *RFC 1462,* May.

Lange, L. 1996a. Internet Inc.—Bandwidth Becomes Big Business. *CMP Media, Inc.,* 1 June, issue 48.

Mandelbaum, R., and P. Mandelbaum. 1992. The Strategic Future of the Mid-level Networks. In *Building Information Infrastructure,* ed. Brian Kahin. 59–118. New York: McGraw-Hill Primis.

McCloghrie, K., and M. T. Rose. 1994. Back to Basics: The Internet Transport Layer. *Connexions: The Interoperability Report,* August, 2–9.

Meehan, T. 1997. Six Great Myths of IPv6. *Data Communications,* November, 140.

Miller, M. A. 1992. *Troubleshooting TCP/IP: Analyzing the Protocols of the Internet.* San Mateo, CA: M&T.

Moskowitz, R. G. 1995. Plan Now for the New Internet Protocol. *Network Computing,* 1 May, 144–50.

Postel, J. 1981. Internet Protocol. *RFC-791*, September.

Shipley, G. 1997. Plumbing 101: Choosing the Right ISP. *Network Computing,* 1 March, 116–18.

Stevens, W. R. 1990. *UNIX Network Programming.* Upper Saddle River, NJ: Prentice Hall.

Stone, M. 1991. Guide to TCP/IP Network Addressing. *LAN Technology,* April, 41–45.

Tristram, C. 1995. The Trouble with TCP/IP. *Open Computing,* February, 52–54.

Willis, D. 1996. Interchange Carriers As ISPs: Long-Distance Runaround. *Network Computing,* 1 September, 104–15.

———, and J. Milne. 1996. Domestic Internet Service Providers: Adapt or Perish. *Network Computing,* 1 June, 100–8.

Chapter 4: Physical Layer Concepts

Breidenbach, S. 1990. Motorola Develops Wireless Network. *LANtimes,* 5 November, 15–16.

Chiquoine, W. A. 1997. Enterprise Cable Management. *Network Magazine,* July, 114–19.

Clark, E. 1997. WDM Expands Fiber's Horizons. *LAN Magazine,* March, 67–71.

———. 1998. Network Cabling's New High-wire Act. *Network Magazine,* March, 74–79.

Codenoll Technology Corporation. 1993. *The Fiber Optic LAN Handbook.* 5th ed. Yonkers, NY: Codenoll Technology Corporation.

Cray, A. 1997. Wiring for Speed, Playing for Time. *Data Communications,* April, 75–80.

Dyson, P. 1995. *The Network Press Dictionary of Networking.* 2d ed. San Francisco: Sybex.

Feibel, W. 1995. *The Network Press Encyclopedia of Networking.* 2d ed. San Francisco: Sybex.

Frank, A. 1994. Fiber Optics for Networks. *LAN Magazine,* November, 25–26.

Grier, J. 1995. The LAN Unleashed. *LAN Magazine,* September, 107–12.

Hancock, B. 1996. *Advanced Ethernet/802.3 Management and Performance.* Boston: Digital Press.

Henderson, T. 1995. Railroading the Category 5 Spec. *LAN Magazine,* October, 119–24.

Hudgins-Bonafield, C. 1998. Networking in the 21st Century: The Sky's the Limit. *Network Computing,* 15 March, 70–94.

Hume, B., and C. Ogden. 1993. Taming the Wire. *LAN Magazine,* September, 91–100.

Johnson, J. T. 1994. Wireless Data: Welcome to the Enterprise. *Data Communications,* 21 March, 42–55.

Jones, J. 1995. Cable Ready. *LAN Magazine,* September, 87–93.

Karvé, A. 1997a. Lesson 112: 802.11 and Spread Spectrum. *Network Magazine,* December, 25–26.

———. 1997. The Wide World of Wireless. *Network Magazine,* December, 42–48.

Keough, L. 1992. Premises Wiring: The Quiet Revolution. *Data Communications,* November, 103–15.

Kilarski, D. 1997. Satellite Networks: Data Takes to the Skies. *Network Magazine,* December, 52–58.

Kim, D. 1994. Cable Ready. *LAN Magazine,* January, 83–90.

LAN Technology. 1990. Wireless Networking Gains Momentum: Vendors Exploit Different Technologies. *LAN Technology,* December, 25–28.

Leeds, F., and J. Chorey. 1991. Cutting Cable Confusion: The Facts about Coax. *LAN Technology,* July, 31–49.

———. 1991. Round up Your Cable Woes. *LAN Technology,* October, 39–56.

———. 1991. Twisted-Pair Wiring Made Simple. *LAN Technology,* April, 49–61.

Mara, F. 1996. Rewiring the Workplace. *LAN,* May, 101–7.

———. 1997. Testing High-performance Copper Cabling. *Network Magazine,* July, 127–131.

Makris, J. 1998. The Copper Stopper? *Data Communications,* March, 63–71.

McMullen, M. 1995. Making Light of Data. *LAN Magazine,* September, 99–106.

Miller, K. 1994. Cellular Essentials for Wireless Data Transmission. *Data Communications,* 21 March, 61–67.

Molta, D. 1996. How Far Is It to 802.11 Wireless LANs? *Network Computing,* 1 June, 126–29.

———, and J. Linder. 1995. The High Wireless Act. *Network Computing,* 1 July, 82–100.

Morse, S. 1991. Sorting Out the Spaghetti: Ethernet Wiring Made Simple. *Network Computing,* October, 88–93.

Myers, T. 1997. Ensuring Proper Cable Installation. *Network Magazine,* July, 121–25.

Richardson, R. 1997. Home-style Wiring. *Network,* June, 95–99.

Sanders, R. 1992. Mapping the Wiring Maze. *LAN Technology,* 15 October, 27–36.

Saunders, S. 1992. Premises Wiring Gets the Standard Treatment. *Data Communications,* November, 105.

———. 1994. Bad Vibrations Beset Category 5 UTP Users. *Data Communications,* June, 49–53.

Schnaidt, P. 1994. Cellular Hero. *LAN Magazine,* April, 38–44.

Strizich, M. 1993. Networks Unplugged. *LAN Magazine,* December, 53–64.

Tolly, K., and D. Newman. 1993. Wireless Internetworking. *Data Communications,* 21 November, 60–72.

Wittman, A. 1994. Will Wireless Win the War? *Networking Computing,* 1 June, 58–70.

———. 1997. Earthquake or a New IEEE Standard? *Network Computing,* 15 August, 37.

Chapter 5: Data Link Layer Concepts and IEEE Standards

Campbell, R. 1994. The Last Word on Thick Ethernet. *LAN Technology,* January, 26–27.

Codenoll Technology Corporation. 1993. *The Fiber Optic LAN Handbook.* 5th ed. Yonkers, NY: Codenoll Technology Corporation.

Dyson, P. 1995. *The Network Press Dictionary of Networking.* 2d ed. San Francisco: Sybex.

Feibel, W. 1995. *The Network Press Encyclopedia of Networking.* 2d ed. San Francisco: Sybex.

Hancock, B. 1988. *Designing and Implementing Ethernet Networks.* Wellesley, MA: QED Information Sciences, Inc.

———. 1996. *Advanced Ethernet/802.3 Management and Performance.* Boston: Digital Press.

Hunt, C. 1995. *Networking Personal Computers.* Sebastopol, CA: O'Reilly & Associates.

Martin, J. 1989. *Local Area Networks: Architectures and Implementations.* Englewood Cliffs, NJ: Prentice Hall.

Metcalfe, R., and D. Boggs. 1976. Ethernet: Distributed Packet Switching for Local Computer Networks. *Communications of the ACM* 19 (7): 395–404.

Tanenbaum, A. 1988. *Computer Networks.* Englewood Cliffs, NJ: Prentice Hall.

The AG Group. 1993. Etherpeek Network Analysis Software User Manual Version 2.0. Walnut Creek, CA: The AG Group.

Chapter 6: Network Hardware Components (Layers 1 and 2)

Baker, F. 1995. Switching Gears. *LAN Interoperability: A Quarterly Supplement to LAN Magazine,* May, 45–52.

Bay Networks. 1996. *Fundamentals of Switching: A Guide to Workgroup Networking.* Santa Clara, CA: Bay Networks.

Boardman, B. 1996. Good Things Come in Small Packages: Combo PC Cards. *Network Computing,* 1 April, 108–16.

Breyer, R., and S. Riley. 1996. *Switched and Fast Ethernet.* 2d ed. Emeryville, CA: Ziff-Davis Press.

Chipcom. 1993. *Network Switching Solutions.* Southborough, MA: Chipcom.

Dyson, P. 1995. *The Network Press Dictionary of Networking.* 2d ed. San Francisco: Sybex.

Feibel, W. 1995. *The Network Press Encyclopedia of Networking.* 2d ed. San Francisco: Sybex.

Feltman, C. 1994. Sizzling Switches. *LAN Magazine,* February, 115–28.

Gerber, B. 1994. More PCMCIA Slots, Please. *Network Computing,* 1 August, 161–62.

Higgins, K. J. 1994. Switching Hubs: Rising Network Stars. *Open Systems Today,* 20 June, 50–58.

Krivda, C. 1995. Another Swipe at Switching. *LAN,* October, 129–134.

Kohlhepp, R. J. 1996. Stacking Managed Hubs in Your Favor. *Network Computing,* October, 112–15.

Magidson, S. 1994. PCMCIA: Finally, Standards Bring Compatible Products. *Network Computing,* 15 February, 124–27.

Majkiewicz, J. 1993. Switching—Everybody's Doing It. *SunExpert,* September, 48–63.

McMullen, M. 1993. Using PCMCIA Cards and Wireless Connectivity, PDAs May Become Handy. *LAN Magazine,* December, 40–48.

Schnaidt, P. 1994. Switch Hunt. *LAN Magazine,* June, 75–84.

Sharer, R. 1995. A Switch in Time. *LAN Magazine,* May, 109–14.

Steinke, S. 1995. Ethernet Switching. *LAN Magazine,* March, 25–26.

Tristram, C. 1994. PCMCIA on the Desktop. *Open Computing,* December, 81–82.

Ungermann-Bass Networks. 1995. *LAN Switching Buyer's Guide.* Santa Clara, CA: Ungermann-Bass Networks.

Wittman, A. 1994. The Switch. *Network Computing,* 1 September, 62–72.

Wobus, J. 1993. When to Avoid Adding Ethernet Hubs. *Network Computing,* January, 154–57.

Wong, H. H. 1996. Increase Ethernet Performance with Switched Technology. *Technical Support,* June, 37–43.

Chapter 7: WANs, Internetworking, and Network Layer Concepts and Components

Anderson, P., and G. James. 1998. Switching at Layer 4. *Network World,* 20 July.

Ascend Communications, Inc. 1998. *Virtual Private Networks for the Enterprise: A Resource Guide for Information Technology and Network Managers Worldwide.* Ascend Communications, Inc.

Baker, F. 1994. OSPF Fundamentals. *LAN Magazine,* December, 71–78.

Baker, S. 1994. Attaining Gigabit Speed. *UNIX Review,* 17–26.

Callon, R., V. Haimo, and M. Lepp. 1989. Routing in an Internetwork Environment. *Connexions: The Interoperability Report.* 3(8): 2–7.

Coluccio, F. A. 1996. Growing Beyond the T-1 Hierarchy. *LAN,* September, 117–24.

———. 1996a. The Going Rate. *LAN,* September, 10.

Coltun, R. 1989. OSPF: An Internet Routing Protocol. *Connexions: The Interoperability Report.* 3(8): 19–25.

Conover, J. 1998. Slicing through IP Switching. *Network Computing,* 15 March, 50–67.

Davie, B., P. Doolan, and Y. Rekhter. 1998. *Switching in IP Networks: IP Switching, Tag Switching, and Related Technologies.* San Francisco: Morgan Kaufman.

Dern, D. P. 1990. Standards for Interior Gateway Routing Protocols. *Connexions: The Interoperability Report.* 4 (7): 2–10.

Enger, B. 1989. Adopting a Gateway. *Connexions: The Interoperability Report.* 3(8): 32–37.

Fitzgerald, S., and L. Bicknell. 1998. Troubleshooting High-Speed WANs. *Network Magazine,* 15 January, 87–91.

———, and E. Greenberg. 1994. Ready for Takeoff. *LAN Magazine,* 97–104.

Garcia-Luna-Aceves, J. J. 1989. Loop-free Internet Routing and Related Issues. *Connexions: The Interoperability Report.* 3(8): 8–18.

Gaw, S. 1998. Building the Universal Backbone. *Network Magazine,* 15 January, 74–79.

Geier, J. 1996. Choose Your Own Route. *LAN,* September, 103–8.

Hagens, R. 1989. Components of OSI: ES-IS Routing. *Connexions: The Interoperability Report.* 3(8): 46–51.

Hall, E. 1998. Implementing Prioritization on IP Networks. *Network Computing,* 15 August, 76–79.

Held, G. 1996. Calculating WAN Operating Rates. *LAN,* September, 111–15.

———. 1998. The Price of High-Speed WANs. *Network Magazine,* 15 January, 80–85.

Henderson, T. 1996. I Shot the Tariff. *LAN, February,* 101–4.

Heywood, P. 1998. A Switch in Plans. *Data Communications,* July, 25–26.

Karvé, A. 1997. IP Switching Gets Focused. *Network Magazine,* June, 81–85.

———. 1997. Lesson 108: Synchronous Optical Network. *Network Magazine,* August, 23–24.

———. 1998. Lesson 119: IP Quality of Service. *Network Magazine,* June, 27–28.

Lepp, M. 1989. The IETF Open Routing Working Group. *Connexions: The Interoperability Report.* 3(8): 26–31.

Lewis, C. 1996a. Alternatives to RIP in a Large Internetwork. *Network Computing,* 1 October, 126–31.

———. 1996b. Should RIP Finally Rest in Peace? *Network Computing,* 1 September, 124–28.

Makris, J. 1998. The Bandwidth Barons. *Data Communications,* July, 44–56.

McQuillan, J. 1997. Routers and Switches Converge. *Data Communications,* 21 October, 120–24.

Moy, J. 1990. OSPF: Next Generation Routing Comes to TCP/IP Networks. *LAN Technology,* April, 71–79.

Newman, D., T. Giorgia, and F. Yavari-Issalou. 1998. VPNs: Safety First, but What about Speed? *Data Communications,* July, 59–67.

Roberts, E. 1997. IP on Speed. *Data Communications,* March, 84–96.

Scholl, F. 1997. Upgrading Your Backbone. *Network Magazine,* May, 95–99.

Stallings, W. 1996. Make Way for the Hot WANs. *LAN,* January, 48–54.

———. 1997. *Data and Computer Communications.* 5th ed. Upper Saddle River, NJ: Prentice Hall.

Steinke, S. 1996. Getting Data over the Telephone Line: Lesson 92: CSUs and DSUs. *LAN,* April, 27–28.

———. 1996. Lesson 89: Basic Phone Service and Circuits. *LAN,* 27–28.

———. 1996. The Internet as Your WAN. *LAN,* October, 47–52.

———. 1997. Lesson 105: Switching vs. Routing. *Network Magazine,* May, 27–28.

———. 1998. What Is a Switch Today? *Network Magazine,* January, 136.

Tanenbaum, A. S. 1988. *Computer Networks.* 2d ed. Englewood Cliffs, NJ: Prentice Hall.

Tsuchiya, P. 1989. Components of OSI: Routing (An Overview). *Connexions: The Interoperability Report.* 3(8): 38–45.

Weber, J. A. 1993. The Time Is Right for SONET. *Networking Management,* May, 19–24.

Willis, D. 1996. WAN! Cloud: Inadequate, Overpriced Bandwidth; Silver Lining: Choices Are Prevailing. *Network Computing,* 15 April, 50–67.

Chapter 8: Ethernet, Ethernet, and More Ethernet

Baldwin, C. 1994. *High Speed Networking Technologies: Options and Implications.* Southborough, MA: Chipcom Corporation.

Bolles, G. 1991. A Guided Tour of 10BASE-T. *Network Computing* (fall): 16–22.

Breyer, R., and S. Riley. 1996. *PC Week Switched and Fast Ethernet.* 2d ed. Emeryville, CA: Ziff-Davis.

Chae, L. 1995. Tutorial—Lesson 88: Fast Ethernet. *LAN Magazine,* December, 27–28.

Clark, E. 1998. Gigabit Ethernet Goes High Gear. *Network Magazine,* February, 61–65.

———. 1998. The Gigabit Gambit. *Network Magazine,* September, 48–53.

Cohen, R. 1996a. A Comparison of the Performance of 100BASE-TX and 100VG Networks. *Connexions: The Interoperability Report.* 10 (12): 16–24.

———. 1996b. 100VG and 100BASE-T Tutorial. *Connexions: The Interoperability Report.* 10 (11): 25–27.

Conover, J. 1997. The Road to Fast Ethernet Networks. *Network Computing,* 15 February, 146–49.

————. 1998. Building a Better Ethernet Infrastructure. *Network Computing,* 1 October, 88–94.

Costa, L. F. 1994. *Planning and Designing High Speed Networks Using 100VG-Any-LAN.* Englewood Cliffs, NJ: Prentice Hall.

Feltman, C. 1996a. Ethernet Earns Its Wings. *LAN Interoperability: Quarterly Supplement,* May, 14–20.

————. 1996b. Virtual LAN, Real Performance. *LAN,* January, 67–72.

Flynn, D., and T. Perkinson. 1994. Fast Ethernet vs. AnyLAN: Degrees of Separation. *Data Communications*, May, 158.

Frank, A. 1995. Flocking to a Faster Network. *LAN Magazine,* August, 67–77.

————. 1996. Multimedia LANs and WANs. *LAN Magazine,* July, 81–86.

————, and D. Fogle. 1996. 100VG-AnyLAN's High-speed Hopes. *LAN Magazine*, January, 128–33.

Fratto, M. 1997. Unlocking Virtual Private Networks. *Network Computing,* 1 November, 53–78.

Fogle, D. 1996. Tutorial—Lesson 90: Ethernet Frame Types. *LAN Magazine,* February, 27–28.

Geier, J. 1996. Up Close and Personal. *LAN Interoperability: Quarterly Supplement,* May, 39–45.

Gigabit Ethernet Alliance. 1996. *Gigabit Ethernet: White Paper,* August. Gigabit Ethernet Alliance.

Gohn, B. 1997a. Policy-based Services for Ethernet Networks. In Special Supplement by 3Com Corporation. *LAN,* January, 8–9.

————. 1997a. Switching and Routing—And Everything in Between. In Special Supplement by 3Com Corporation. *LAN,* January, 10–12.

Goralski, W., and G. Kessler. 1996. Changing Channels. *LAN Interoperability: Quarterly Supplement,* May, 6–12.

Greenstein, I. 1990. Fiber-optic LANs Improve in Price and Performance. *Network Management,* June, 84–89.

Hall, E. 1998. Bringing Prioritization Services to Ethernet. *Network Computing,* 1 August, 94–100.

Held, G. 1996. The LAN Guessing Game. *LAN Magazine,* May, 93–100.

Henderson, T. 1995. Flooring It with Ethernet. *LAN Magazine*, March, 55–62.

————. 1998. Gigabit Ethernet Blueprint. *Network Magazine,* September, 42–46.

Hindin, E. 1998. Say What? QoS in English. *Network World,* 17 August.

Johnson, J. 1995. The Need for Speed. *InformationWeek*, 23 October, 36–48.

Karvé, A. 1996. Multimedia Takes the Stage. *LAN Magazine,* May, 123–27.

————. 1997. Ethernet's Next Frontier. *LAN,* January, 40–47.

————. 1998. Pushing Beyond Gigabit Ethernet. *Network Magazine,* September, 54–58.

Kessler, G. 1993. Changing Channels. *LAN Magazine,* December, 69–84.

Krivda, C. 1995. Another Swipe at Switching. *LAN,* October, 129–34.

Lippis, N. 1996. Gigabit Ethernet Starts to Sizzle. *Data Communications,* November, 31–32.

Lounsbury, A. 1997. Gigabit Ethernet: The Difference Is in the Details. *Data Communications,* May, 75–80.

Makris, J. 1998. The Copper Stopper? *Data Communications,* March, 63–73.

Mandeville, R., and D. Newman. 1997. VLANs: Real Virtues. *Data Communications,* May, 83–91.

———, and D. Shah. 1998. Gigabit Ethernet Gets It Done. *Data Communications,* February, 66–81.

Metcalfe, R., and D. Boggs. 1976. Ethernet: Distributed Packet Switching for Local Computer Networks. *Communications of the ACM* 19 (7): 395–404.

Minoli, D. 1993. Isochronous Ethernet: Poised for Launch. *Network Computing,* August, 156–61.

Molta, D. 1996. The Ten Greatest Networking Myths. *Networking Computing,* 1 September, 121–22.

Pieper, K., and R. Fowler. 1997. The Next Step in the Ethernet Evolution. In Special Supplement by 3Com Corporation. *LAN,* January, 1–2.

Richardson, R. 1997. VPNs: Just between Us. *LAN,* February, 99–103.

Roberts, E. 1996. Weighed Down by Doubts: Is the Proposed High-Speed Spec Too Good to Be True? *Data Communications,* November, 55–58.

———. 1997. Gigabit Ethernet: Fat Pipe or Pipe Bomb? *Data Communications,* May, 58–72.

Saunders, S. 1994. Full-duplex Ethernet: More Niche Than Necessity? *Data Communications,* March, 87–92.

Schnaidt, P. 1994a Plug in at 100. *LAN Magazine,* March, 71–79.

———. 1994b. Tutorial—Lesson 73: Which Fast LAN? *LAN Magazine,* September, 25–26.

———. 1996. Is Gigabit Ethernet the Next Miracle Cure? *Network Computing,* 15 October, 33.

Scholl, F. 1993. 10BASE-F Stretches the Ethernet Backbone. *Data Communications,* October, 103–8.

Shimada, K. 1994. Fast Talk about Fast Ethernet. *Data Communications,* 21 March, 21–22.

Shipley, B. 1996. Ethernet's Endurance Contest. *LAN Magazine,* May, 67–72.

Skorupa, J., and G. Prodan. 1997. Battle of the Backbones: ATM vs. Gigabit Ethernet. *Data Communications,* April, 87–89.

Snyder, J. 1996. Ethernet in the Fast Lane. *MacWorld,* March, 128–33.

Stallings, W. 1997. *Data and Computer Communications.* 5th ed. Upper Saddle River, NJ: Prentice Hall.

Steinke, S. 1995a. Ethernet Switching. *LAN Magazine,* March, 25–26.

———. 1995b. The State of the Ethernet. *LAN Magazine,* March, 44–52.

Tolley, B. 1997a. Standards Emerging for Gigabit Ethernet. In Special Supplement by 3Com Corporation. *LAN,* January, 3–4.

———. 1997b. The Lowdown on High Speed: Gigabit Ethernet and ATM. In Special Supplement by 3Com Corporation. *LAN,* January, 5–7.

Tolly, K. 1994. Full Speed Ahead for Full-Duplex Ethernet. *Data Communications,* March, 39–40.

Ungermann-Bass Networks. 1995. *LAN Switching Buyer's Guide.* Santa Clara, CA: Ungermann-Bass Networks.

Wittmann, A. 1993. Fast Ethernet—The Curtain Rises on a New Debate. *Network Computing,* May, 18–22.

———. 1994. Faster Anyone? HP's 100VG-AnyLAN. *Network Computing,* 1 October, 47–49.

Wobus, J. 1993. When to Avoid Adding Ethernet Hubs. *Network Computing,* January, 154–57.

Wong, H. H. 1996. Increase Ethernet Performance with Switched Technology. *Technical Support,* June, 37–43.

Zeichick, A. 1997. Glossary: IEEE 802. *Network Magazine,* November, 28.

Chapter 9: Token Ring

Baldwin, C. 1994. *High Speed Networking Technologies: Options and Implications.* Southborough, MA: Chipcom Corporation.

Feibel, W. 1995. *The Network Press Encyclopedia of Networking.* 2d ed. San Francisco: Sybex.

Frank, A. 1995. Flocking to a Faster Network. *LAN Magazine,* August, 67–77.

———. 1996. Multimedia LANs and WANs. *LAN Magazine,* July, 81–86.

Gaw, S. 1996. Token Ring Flips the Switch. *LAN,* July, 67–72.

Goralski, W., and G. Kessler. 1996. Changing Channels. *LAN Interoperability: Quarterly Supplement,* May, 6–12.

Held, G. 1996. The LAN Guessing Game. *LAN Magazine,* May, 93–100.

Karvé, A. 1995. Lord of the Ring. *LAN Magazine,* August, 107–14.

———. 1996. Multimedia Takes the Stage. *LAN Magazine,* May, 123–27.

Krivda, C. 1995. Another Swipe at Switching. *LAN,* October, 129–34.

Lippis, N. 1997. The Token Ring Trap. *Data Communications,* February, 23–24.

Love, R. D. 1998. The Fast Track to High-Speed Token Ring. *Data Communications,* February, 95–100.

Martin, J. 1989. *Local Area Networks: Architectures and Implementations.* Englewood Cliffs, NJ: Prentice Hall.

Roberts, E. 1998. A Slow Start for High-speed Token Ring. *Data Communications,* February, 85–92.

Stallings, W. 1997. *Data and Computer Communications.* 5th ed. Upper Saddle River, NJ: Prentice Hall.

Tanenbaum, A. S. 1988. *Computer Networks.* 2d ed. Englewood Cliffs, NJ: Prentice Hall.

Ungermann-Bass Networks. 1995. *LAN Switching Buyer's Guide.* Santa Clara, CA: Ungermann-Bass Networks.

Chapter 10: Fiber Distributed Data Interface (FDDI)

American National Standard. 1986. FDDI Token Ring Physical Layer Medium Dependent PMD. *American National Standard,* ASC X3T9.5, February, rev. 7.

———. 1986. FDDI Token Ring Media Access Control MAC. *American National Standard,* ASC X3T9.5, July, rev. 10.

———. 1986. FDDI Token Ring Station Management SMT. *American National Standard,* ASC X3T9.5, September, rev. 2.1.

———. 1986. FDDI Token Ring Physical Layer Protocol PHY. *American National Standard,* ASC X3T9.5, October, rev. 14.

Burr, W. 1986. The FDDI Optical Data Link. *IEEE Communications Magazine,* May.

Cooper. S. 1989. Joining the Next LAN Generation. *Unix Review* 72:48–59.

Daniels, G. 1990. Implementing and Managing FDDI Networks. *Networking Management,* November, 56–61.

Hancock, B. 1989. *Network Concepts and Architectures.* Wellesley, MA: QED Information Sciences.

Joshi, S. 1986. High-performance Networks: A Focus on the Fiber Distributed Data Interface FDDI Standard. *IEEE Micro,* June.

Ross, F. 1986. FDDI—A Tutorial. *IEEE Communications Magazine,* May.

Sterling, D. 1987. *Technicians Guide to Fiber Optics.* Delmar Publishers, Inc.

The Institute of Electrical and Electronics Engineers. 1985. Logical Link Control. *American National Standard ANSI/IEEE Std. 802.2.* The Institute of Electrical and Electronics Engineers.

———. 1985. Token Ring Access Method and Physical Layer Specifications. *American National Standard ANSI/IEEE Std. 802.5.* The Institute of Electrical and Electronics Engineers.

Wolter, M. S. 1990. Fiber Distributed Data Interface FDDI—A Tutorial. *Connexions: The Interoperability Report* 4 (10): 16–26.

———. 1991. ANSI x3T9.5 Update: Future FDDI Standards. *Connexions: The Interoperability Report* 5 (10): 21–23.

Chapter 11: Integrated Services Data Network (ISDN)

Alvich-LoPinto, M. 1990. Piecing Together the ISDN Puzzle. *Today's Office,* October, 21–23.

Atkins, J., and M. Norris. 1995. *Total Area Networking: ATM, Frame Relay and SMDS Explained.* New York: John Wiley and Sons.

Bates, R. J., and D. Gregory. 1998. *Voice and Data Communications Handbook.* New York: McGraw-Hill.

Birenbaum, E. 1994. A Trio of Access Devices Aggregates ISDN. *Data Communications,* June, 147–48.

Brown, D. 1996. Blazing with Inverse Multiplexed ISDN. *Network Computing,* 1 December, 164–67.

Crane, E., and R. Raucci. 1995. Going Digital. *Open Computing,* February, 93–94.

Dortch, M. 1990. UNIX and ISDN: Partners on the Same Line. *UnixWorld,* 55–59.

Durr, M. 1994. ISDN Reemerges. *LAN Magazine,* January, 103–12.

Fitzgerald, S. 1994. Global Warming: ISDN Heats Up. *LAN Magazine,* June, 50–55.

Fogle, D., and A. Frank. 1996. The Ascent of ISDN. *LAN,* March, 120–25.

Frank, A. 1995. Lesson 82: The ISDN Connection. *LAN Magazine,* June, 21–22.

———. 1998. Lesson 117: Always On/Dynamic ISDN (AO/DI). *Network Magazine,* April, 23–24.

Hurwicz, M. 1996. On-line from a LAN. *LAN,* May, 85–90.

Johnston-Turner, M. 1991. Evaluating ISDN Options. *Network World,* 18 March, 40.

Leeds, F. 1996. Plugging in to ISDN. *LAN,* April, 93–96.

Levitt, J. 1993. Speed Is Only One Benefit of Installing an ISDN Link. *Open Systems Today,* 23 January, 1.

Miller, K. 1994. ISDN and Internetworking: Made for Each Other? *Data Communications,* February, 23–24.

Moskowitz, R. 1996. Bracing for the Last and Longest Mile Home. *Network Computing,* 1 April, 35–36.

Parnell, T. 1997. *LAN Times Guide to Wide Area Networks.* Berkeley, CA: Osborne McGraw-Hill.

Petrosky, M. 1992. Momentum Builds for ISDN as a Data Pipe. *LAN Technology,* August, 15–17.

Quiat, B. 1994. V.FAST, ISDN or Switched 56: Which Remote Solution is the Right One? *Network Computing,* 1 March, 70–87.

Robertson, B. 1993. Telecommuting via ISDN: Out of Sight, Not Out of Range. *Network Computing,* July, 134–38.

———, and J. Newman. 1995. ISDN Does It All! *Network Computing,* 1 May, 62–80.

———. 1994. Choose an ISDN Flavor: NIC or Digital Modem. *Network Computing,* 1 September, 174–76.

Schnaidt, P. 1993. Lesson 55: An ISDN Issue. *LAN Magazine,* March, 24–25.

Stallings, W. 1991. Broadband ISDN: A Standards Update. *Network World,* 18 March, 49–52.

———. 1997. *Data and Computer Communications.* 5th ed. Upper Saddle River, NJ: Prentice Hall.

Ubois, J. 1993. The Big Pipe. *SunWorld,* November, 86–91.

Willis, D., and J. Newman. (1996). ISDN: Prime for the Enterprise. *Network Computing,* 15 May, 45–65.

Wrobel, L. 1997a. ISDN: Innovations Subscribers Do Need—Part I. *Technical Support,* April, 41–44.

———. 1997b. ISDN: Innovations Subscribers Do Need—Part II. *Technical Support,* May, 34–38.

Chapter 12: Frame Relay

Atkins, J., and M. Norris. 1995. *Total Area Networking: ATM, Frame Relay and SMDS Explained.* New York: John Wiley & Sons.

Bates, R. J., and D. Gregory. 1998. *Voice and Data Communications Handbook.* New York: McGraw-Hill.

Brown, D., and D. Willis. 1998. Videoconferencing on Frame Relay Networks. *Network Computing,* 15 September, 47–62.

Clark, E. 1998. Frame Relay Goes Public. *Network Magazine,* April, 68–73.

Feibel, W. 1995. *The Network Press Encyclopedia of Networking.* 2d ed. San Francisco: Sybex.

Fitzgerald, S., and L. Kraft. 1993. A New Model for Frame Relay. *LAN Magazine,* August, 61–67.

———. 1993. Outfit Your WAN with Frame Relay. *LAN Magazine,* August, 52–59.

———. 1995. Designing Your Frame Relay Network. *Network Computing,* 15 January, 152–54.

Gareiss, R. 1996. Don't Take No for an Answer. *Data Communications,* November, 67–82.

————. 1997. Frame Relay vs. IP: It's Your Move. *Data Communications,* February, 89–96.

————. 1998. Frame Relay. *Data Communications,* June, 76, 78–86.

Harbison, R. W. 1992. Frame Relay: Technology for Our Time. *LAN Technology,* December, 67–78.

Held, G. 1997. Shopping for Frame Relay. *Network Magazine,* December, 83–87.

Krivda, C. 1996. Frame Relay Comes of Age. *LAN,* November, 117–24.

Merritt, J. 1992. Frame Relay Technology: The Right Link for Wide Area Backbones. *Network Computing,* 1 November, 75–76.

Newman, D., T. Giorgis, and F. Yavari-Issalou. 1998. FRADs: Halfway There. *Data Communications,* 21 September, 43–54.

Newman, J. 1997. Frame Relay Makes Its Voice Heard. *Network Computing,* 15 March, 134–38.

Parnell, T. 1997. *LAN Times Guide to Wide Area Networks.* Berkeley, CA: Osborne McGraw-Hill.

Parsons, T., and D. Bahr. 1996. Acing the Frame Relay Race. *LAN,* June, 95–104.

————, and T. Beach. 1996. Rapid Transit: Frame Relay to ATM. *LAN,* August, 115–20.

Reardon, M. 1998. Frame Relay. *Data Communications,* June, 77, 90–97.

Stallings, W. 1997. *Data and Computer Communications.* 5th ed. Upper Saddle River, NJ: Prentice Hall.

Willis, D. 1997. Make Room for Frame Relay. *Networking Computing,* 15 February, 73–86.

————. 1997. Framing the Perfect WAN Contract. *Network Computing,* 15 September, 136–40.

Wu, D. 1997. Client-Server over Frame Relay. *Network Magazine,* October, 105–9.

Chapter 13: Switched Multimegabit Data Service (SMDS)

Atkins, J., and M. Norris. 1995. *Total Area Networking: ATM, Frame Relay and SMDS Explained.* New York: John Wiley and Sons.

Bates, R. J., and D. Gregory. 1998. *Voice and Data Communications Handbook.* New York: McGraw-Hill.

Bellcore. 1990. Exchange Access SMDS Service Generic Requirements. *Bellcore Technical Advisory, TA-TSV-001060,* December.

————. 1991. Generic System Requirements in Support of Switched Multi-megabit Data Service. *Bellcore Technical Reference, TR-TSV-000772,* May.

Data Communications. 1994. SMDS Is Here: Where Are the Customers? *Data Communications,* October, 55–56.

————. 1997. The Top 25 Flops. *Data Communications,* 21 October, 142–43.

Fitzgerald, S. 1993. Packing Them In. *LAN Magazine,* September, 77–86.

Hughes, L., and S. Starliper. 1990. Switched Multimegabit Data Service (SMDS). *Connexions: The Interoperability Report* 4 (10): 34–37.

Krishnaswamy, P., and M. Ulema. 1991. Developments in SMDS. *Connexions: The Interoperability Report* 5 (10): 24–31.

Kumar, B. 1995. *Broadband Communications: A Professional's Guide to ATM, Frame Relay, SMDS, SONET, and BISDN.* New York: McGraw-Hill.

Mendes, G. 1996. SMDS: A WAN Alternative. *LAN Interoperability: A Quarterly Supplement to LAN Magazine,* August, 22–27.

Miller, M. 1994. *Analyzing Broadband Networks: Frame Relay, SMDS, and ATM.* San Mateo, CA: M&T.

Minoli, D. 1991. The New Wide Area Technologies: SMDS and BISDN. *Network Computing,* August, 88–92.

Parnell, T. 1997. *LAN Times Guide to Wide Area Networks.* Berkeley, CA: Osborne McGraw-Hill.

Sharer, R. 1993. The SMDS Express. *LAN Magazine,* July, 51–58.

———. 1994. Lighten Up. *LAN Magazine,* March, 109–12.

The Institute of Electrical and Electronics Engineers. 1990. Distributed Queue Dual Bus (DQDB) Subnetwork of a Metropolitan Area Network (MAN). *IEEE Standard 802.6-1990.* The Institute of Electrical and Electronics Engineers.

Chapter 14: Asynchronous Transfer Mode (ATM)

Askins, J. 1996. Migrating to ATM? Learn Before You Leap. *Data Communications,* December, 79–80.

Atkins, J., and M. Norris. 1995. *Total Area Networking: ATM, Frame Relay and SMDS Explained.* New York: John Wiley and Sons.

Bates, R. J., and D. Gregory. 1998. *Voice and Data Communications Handbook.* New York: McGraw-Hill.

Chipcom. 1993. *ATM: The Frontier of Networking.* Southborough, MA: Chipcom.

Cholewja, K. 1996. Affordable ATM. *Data Communications,* December, 94–102.

Clark, E. 1997. Real-World ATM. *Network,* July, 42–53.

Conover, J. 1996. ATM Access Is Ready, Willing and Able to Fly on Your Backbone. *Network Computing,* 15 November, 70–95.

Feltman, C. 1993. ATM Takes Off. *Interoperability,* 19–46.

———. 1993. ATM: The Grand Unifier. *LAN Magazine, November,* 52–70.

Fritz, J. N. 1998. ATM WAN Services: Picking a Winner. *Data Communications,* 21 April, 77–80.

Gould, J. 1994. ATM's Long, Strange Trip to the Mainstream. *Data Communications,* June, 120–30.

Gould, W. 1997. Fast Ethernet Pairs with ATM. *Network Magazine,* September, 74–77.

Hurwicz, M. 1997. ATM for the Rest of Us. *Network Magazine,* November, 75–79.

King, S. 1994. Switched Virtual Networks. *Data Communications,* September, 66–80.

Mehta, S. 1996. Telcos: Answering the Call for ATM. *LAN,* March, 46–52.

Minoli, D. 1992. ATM: The Future of Local and Wide Area Networks. *Network Computing,* 15 October, 128–34.

———. 1992. ATM Protocols: Let's Get Technical. *Network Computing,* 15 November, 156–63.

Newman, D. 1997. ATM: The Last Word. *Data Communications,* April, 105–33.

Parikh, A. 1993. The Challenge of Migrating to ATM. *Networking Management,* June, B11–B15.

Parnell, T. 1997. *LAN Times Guide to Wide Area Networks.* Berkeley, CA: Osborne McGraw-Hill.

Roberts, L. G. 1997. CIF: Affordable ATM, at Last. *Data Communications,* April, 96–102.

Ruiu, D. 1993. ATM at Your Service? *Data Communications,* November, 85–88.

Stallings, W. 1997. *Data and Computer Communications.* 5th ed. Upper Saddle River, NJ: Prentice Hall.

Taylor, M. 1996. Voice over ATM: A Sound Assessment. *Data Communications,* December, 86–92.

Taylor, S. 1994. ATM and Frame Relay: Back to the Basics. *Data Communications,* April, 23–24.

———. 1994. Making the Switch to High-Speed WAN Services. *Data Communications,* July, 87–94.

Wittman, A. 1993. Local ATM: Is ATM Ready for the Desktop? *Network Computing,* September, 160–66.

Zeichick, A. 1997. Glossary: Asynchronous Transfer Mode. *Network,* July, 28.

Chapter 15: Dialup and Home Networking

Aber, R. 1997. xDSL Supercharges Copper. *Data Communications,* March, 99–105.

Amati Communications Corporation. 1996. *ADSL Field Guide.* San Jose, CA: Amati Communications Corporation.

Angel, J. 1999. High-Speed Internet Access Comes Home. *Network Magazine,* February, 42–47.

Bolles, G. A. 1991. Modem Talk. *Network Computing,* August, 73–81.

———. 1992. Modem Talk: What's My Line. *Network Computing,* 1 October, 85–89.

Burkes, R. E. 1991. Making a Case for Dial-up LAN Links. *LAN Technology,* March, 49–54.

Cholewka, K. 1997. 56K Modems: The New Spin on Speed. *Data Communications,* May, 93–103.

Clark, E. 1996a. Data Meets the Dial Tone. *Interoperability: Supplement to LAN,* February, 20–33.

———. 1996b. PC, Phone Home! *LAN,* October, 125–32.

———. 1999. Pricing the Last Mile. *Network Magazine,* February, 36–41.

Fitzgerald, S. 1996. Reshaping the Digital Landscape. *LAN Interoperability: A Quarterly Supplement to LAN Magazine,* August, 14–20.

Frezza, B. 1996. Cable TV: Giving Us the Broadband Business. *Network Computing,* 15 May, 31–32.

Kalman, S. 1997. The Bright Future of CTI. *LAN,* January, 85–92.

Liebmann, L. 1996. Free Market Theory. *LAN,* July, 60–64.

Maclean, P. 1993. V.FAST and V.32TERBO: Faster Modems, Slower Standards. *Network Computing,* July, 110–30.

Makris. J. 1998. DSL: Don't Be Duped. *Data Communications,* 21 April, 39–52

Newman, D., M. Carter, and H. Holzbaur. 1998. DSL: Worth Its Wait. *Data Communications,* June, 101–12.

Newman, J. 1997. ADSL: Putting a Charge into Your Copper Cable. *Network Computing,* 1 May, 139–42.

Richardson, R. 1996. Tone Dialing, SOHO Style. *LAN,* October, 107–14.

———. 1997b. Betting WAN Access Technology. *Network Computing,* 1 July, 43–56.

Steinke, S. 1996. Competition Comes to the WAN. *LAN,* July, 52–58.

———. 1997. Rehab for Copper Wire. *LAN,* February, 57–62.

———. 1999. A Lineup of Local-Loop Contenders. *Network Magazine,* February, 30–35.

Tadjer, R. 1996. 56-kbps Modems Are in Search of a Home. *Network Computing,* 15 November, 24–26.

Zeichick, A. 1997. LAN Glossary: Computer Telephony. *LAN,* January, 138.

Zgodzinski, D. 1996. Enter ADSL. *Internet World,* October, 72–75.

———. 1996. The Cable Chase. *Internet World,* June, 63–66.

Chapter 16: Network Security Issues

Baum, M. 1994. *Federal Certification Authority Liability and Policy.* Cambridge, MA: Independent Monitoring.

Bird, T. 1998. Building VPNs: The 10-Point Plan. *Data Communications,* June, 123–32.

Bishop. M. 1992. Foiling Password Crackers. *UNIXWorld,* March, 85–91.

Bryant, B. 1988. Designing an Authentication System: A Dialogue in Four Scenes. *Massachusetts Institute of Technology,* 8 February.

Carl-Mitchell, S., and J. S. Quarterman. 1992. Building Internet Firewalls. *UNIXWorld,* February, 93–102.

Cheswick, W. R., and S. M. Bellovin. 1994. *Firewalls and Internet Security: Repelling the Wily Hacker.* Reading, MA: Addison-Wesley.

Dyson, P. 1995. *The Network Press Dictionary of Networking.* 2d ed. San Francisco: Sybex.

Ellis, J., B. Fraser, and L. Pesante. 1994. Keeping Internet Intruders Away. *UNIX Review,* September, 35–44.

Farrow, R., and R. Power. 1998. Is Someone Scanning Your Network? *Network Magazine,* September, 83–84.

Feibel, W. 1995. *The Network Press Encyclopedia of Networking.* 2d ed. San Francisco: Sybex.

Fratto, M. 1997. Unlocking Private Networks. *Networking Computing,* 1 November, 53–76.

———. 1998. IPSec—Compliant VPN Solutions: Virtualizing Your Network. *Network Computing,* 1 August, 72–80.

Gallo, M., and R. Nenno. 1985. *Computers and Society with Basic and Pascal.* Boston: PWS.

Garfinkel, S., and G. Spafford. 1991. Building a Network Firewall. *LAN Technology,* December, 59–68.

———. 1991. *Practical UNIX Security.* Sebastopol, CA: O'Reilly & Associates.

Hoover, A. 1995. Securing the Enterprise: Firewalls Can Keep You from Getting Burned. *Internet World,* February, 39–43.

Karvé, A. 1997. Lesson 104: Public Key Cryptography. *LAN,* April, 23–24.

———. 1997. Public Key Infrastructures. *Network Magazine,* November, 69–73.

———. 1998. Lesson 115: IP Security. *Network Magazine,* February, 27–28.

Morse, S. 1994. Network Security: How to Stay Ahead of Network Explosion. *Network Computing,* 15 February, 54–63.

Moskowitz, R. G. 1994. Firewalls: Building in That Peaceful, Easy Feeling. *Network Computing,* 1 June, 159–61.

Quarterman, J. S., and S. Carl-Mitchell. 1993. Tutorial: Local Protection for Networked Systems. *UNIXWorld,* July, 64–72.

Ranum, M. 1994. Internet Firewall Protection. *Open Computing,* September, 95–99.

Schwartau, W. 1995. Beyond the Firewall: New Systems Watch Intruders and Strike Back. *Internet World,* February, 44–48.

Simonds, F. 1996. *Network Security.* New York: McGraw-Hill.

Siyan, K., and C. Hare. 1995. *Internet Firewalls and Network Security.* Indianapolis: New Riders Publishing.

Stallings, W. 1993. Make It Real. *LAN Magazine,* September, 105–12.

———. 1995. Getting Cryptic: PGP for You and Me. *Internet World,* February, 34–39.

———. 1997. *Data and Computer Communications.* 5th ed. Upper Saddle River, NJ: Prentice Hall.

Steinke, S. 1998. Authentication and Cryptography. *Network Magazine,* January, 51–55.

Stephenson, P. 1995. Securing Remote Access. *Network Computing,* 1 February, 130–34.

Strebe, M., C. Perkins, and M. G. Moncur. 1998. *NT Network Security.* San Francisco: Sybex.

Thayer, R. 1997. Bulletproof IP. *Data Communications,* 21 November, 55–60.

Vaughn-Nichols, S. 1995. It's Alive: Clipper's Still Kicking. *Internet World,* February, 62–65.

Index